R 3106908H v.2
796.48 Atlanta Committee for
ATL the Olympic Games.
The official report
of the Centennial
Olympic Games

For Reference

Not to be taken from this room

SEQUOYAH REGIONAL LIBRARY

3 8749 0031 0690 8

W9-CKS-285

VOLUME II

THE CENTENNIAL OLYMPIC GAMES

THE OFFICIAL REPORT OF THE CENTENNIAL OLYMPIC GAMES

THE ATLANTA COMMITTEE FOR THE OLYMPIC GAMES

THE OFFICIAL REPORT OF THE CENTENNIAL OLYMPIC GAMES

VOLUME I ## PLANNING AND ORGANIZING

This volume is comprised of a prologue, which covers the history of the Bid process, and 28 chapters, organized by program and functional area, which address in detail the preparations for the 1996 Olympic Games. For the benefit of future organizing committees, each chapter contains conclusions and recommendations.

VOLUME II ## THE CENTENNIAL OLYMPIC GAMES

This volume is comprised of a prologue, three major sections, and an epilogue.

The prologue, entitled *Atlanta—Gateway for Dreams*, describes the city and its history.

Section I, *Spreading the Olympic Spirit*, begins with the arrival of the Olympic Torch in Los Angeles, California, on 27 April 1996, and progresses as the Torch Relay moves across the US, reaching Atlanta on 19 July, the day of the Opening Ceremony. This journey is juxtaposed with Atlanta's preparations for the Centennial Olympic Games during spring and summer 1996 and highlights of Cultural Olympiad exhibitions and events occurring prior to the official start of the Games.

Section II, *Celebrating the Games*, is a day-by-day account, 19 July–4 August, with highlights of Opening and Closing Ceremonies, athletic achievements, and descriptions of cultural events, as well as details of Games-time operations.

Section III, *Living the Dream*, gives information on the competition of each sport in the programme of the 1996 Olympic Games.

The epilogue, entitled *Nurturing the Memories*, describes some of the positive results of the Games on the city of Atlanta, including the status of the organizing committee's efforts to conclude the business of the Games and the use of some of the facilities built or given as part of the legacy of the Games.

VOLUME III ## THE COMPETITION RESULTS

This volume is comprised of the detailed results for all athletes in all events. Also included as a reference is a section on medal winners and record-setting performances arranged by sport and discipline, as well as a section of venue maps for the major locations used during the 1996 Olympic Games.

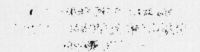

VOLUME II

THE CENTENNIAL OLYMPIC GAMES

THE OFFICIAL REPORT OF THE CENTENNIAL OLYMPIC GAMES

PEACHTREE
ATLANTA

THIS BOOK IS THE PROPERTY OF
SEQUOYAH REGIONAL LIBRARY
CANTON, GEORGIA

COLOPHON

The Official Report of the Centennial Olympic Games employs the typography and look developed for the 1996 Olympic Games by the Atlanta Committee for the Olympic Games (ACOG). The text type is Stone Serif. Univers is used for sidebar and tabular material. Display type is Copperplate Gothic. The Quilt of Leaves motif serves as a decorative element throughout the three volumes, in combination with the ACOG color palette in Volumes I and II.

Art direction by Loraine M. Balcsik. Design by Nicola Simmonds Carter and Loraine M. Balcsik. Typography by Loraine M. Balcsik and Robin Sherman. Four-color film was created by Bright Arts, Ltd., Hong Kong, with coordination by Imago, USA, Inc., New York.

Published by
PEACHTREE PUBLISHERS
494 Armour Circle NE
Atlanta, GA 30324

© 1997 by The Atlanta Committee for the Olympic Games
All Olympic marks protected by The United States Amateur Sports Act (36 USC 380).

All rights reserved. No part of this publication may be reproduced, stored in a retrieval system, or transmitted in any form or by any means—electronic, mechanical, photocopy, recording, or any other—except for brief quotations in printed reviews, without the prior permission of the publisher.

Manufactured in Singapore

First printing

Library of Congress Cataloguing-in-Publication Data

Atlanta Committee for the Olympic Games.
     The official report of the Centennial Olympic Games / the Atlanta
Committee for the Olympic Games.
          p. cm.
     Includes indexes.
     Contents: v. 1. Planning and organizing -- v. 2. The Centennial Olympic
games -- v. 3. the competition results.
     ISBN 1-56145-150-9 (set). -- ISBN 1-56145-168-1 (v. 1). -- ISBN 1-56145-151-7 (v. 2). -- ISBN
1-56145-169-X (v. 3)
     1. Olympic Games (26th : 1996 : Atlanta, Ga.) 2. Atlanta
Committee for the Olympic Games. I. Title.
GV722 1996.A86 1997
796.48--DC21   97-23578
                                                                           CIP

FOR SEVENTEEN DAYS in the summer of 1996 the world came together in peace and harmony in Atlanta for what became the largest gathering of athletes and nations in Olympic history. With arms linked and voices resounding, we celebrated the magnificence of our common humanity—the individual triumphs, the personal tragedies, the indomitable resilience of the human spirit.

With the conclusion of this XXVI Olympiad, we—the people of Atlanta—have realized our dream of hosting the Olympic Games, and our hearts are filled with gratitude to the Olympic Movement for the extraordinary opportunity. Our dream was achieved through the unwavering dedication and selfless participation of tens of thousands of individuals.

We thank each person; each smiling face and extended hand welcomed the world to our home and helped bridge the distances and differences that inevitably separate us, one person from another, one nation from another. These individual acts of goodwill exalted the Games and defined our place in Olympic history.

We understood Pierre de Coubertin's call to place sport at the service of humanity. The ideals of the Olympic Movement—joy in effort, the educational value of good example, and respect for universal ethical principles—deeply affected and inspired us. They united us in the initial Bid effort, and bound us together as our numbers swelled year after year.

We embraced the entire period of the Olympiad, just as we embraced Olympism as a way of life, and extended our programming across four years in the arts, education, and sport. We relied on our Olympic Spirit to accomplish our goals for the 1996 Games, and this served us well. We watched the Spirit ignite in our colleagues in schools, corporations, volunteer organizations, and government as together we worked cooperatively—always attempting to harmonize our efforts—to accomplish the tasks that lay before us.

This level of cooperation created Centennial Olympic Park, which symbolizes the grandeur of the Olympic Spirit and also its resilience. For it was here that the Olympic Spirit was tested and the people arose triumphantly to declare it would survive and flourish.

Just as the Olympic flame has guided us onward, each host city has contributed to the strength of the modern Olympic Games. Atlanta honored the traditions developed over the past century, and contributed new elements that reflect our place in the global community and our time at the close of the twentieth century. Our sophisticated competition venues were offered to the service of athletes. We endeavored in all ways to create playing conditions that were fair and that encouraged athletic excellence. Our broadcasting brought spectators around the world closer than ever to the competition.

We approached the Centennial Olympic Games with great idealism, with the belief that we could create a remarkable experience for all who participated. Our humanity will be the legacy of our conduct of these Games. We embraced the Olympic Movement, and it enriched and forever changed our lives.

This *Official Report of the Centennial Olympic Games* is our record of the staging of the event as well as a chronicle of its athletic achievements. We present these three volumes to our readers with pride, with faith in the future of the Olympic Movement, and with fulfillment for our place in its history.

William Porter Payne
President and CEO
The Atlanta Committee for the Olympic Games

TABLE OF CONTENTS

PREFACE

THE OFFICIAL REPORT *of the Centennial Olympic Games* was written by the professional staff of the Atlanta Committee for the Olympic Games. The content of the *Official Report* is strongly influenced by historical precedence and IOC requirements. The organizers and authors of this report have codified the experience and legacy of the Games for posterity and provided as much detail as possible to assist organizing committees in preparing for future Olympic Games.

This is the second of three volumes, entitled *The Centennial Olympic Games*. It covers the entire Games-time period beginning with the arrival of the Olympic torch in Los Angeles, California, on 27 April 1996. Section I, "Spreading the Olympic Spirit" provides highlights of the Torch Relay journey, which appear juxtaposed with Atlanta's activities as it prepares for the Games during the months just prior to the start of the Games.

The Opening Ceremony begins Section II, "Celebrating the Games." Each day of the Games is profiled with stories and pictures of ACOG operations, spectator experiences, athletes in competition, and cultural performances. This Games-time section concludes, like the Games themselves, with the Closing Ceremony, depicted in words and photographs.

A detailed summary of each sport, including venue information and medal-winning sport performances, are recapped in the final section of this volume, which is fittingly called "Living the Dream." The hopes and aspirations of the thousands of world-class athletes who participated in these Games cannot be chronicled here, but their performances are acknowledged.

These Centennial Olympic Games were for us, first and foremost, about people: the thousands who collaborated for years in developing the plans; the 53,540 volunteers who welcomed and assisted visitors to Atlanta and the southeastern United States during Games-time, many of whom worked with the organizing committee and in their communities for years preceding the Games; the citizens of Georgia who provided such enthusiasm and goodwill in support of our mission; and the 197 participating delegations and their dedicated athletes who gave 5 million spectators and the worldwide audience of 3.5 billion television viewers spectacular performances.

The details of these experiences—from planning through staging through dismantling—are documented in these pages. The three-volume *Official Report* provides an avenue for understanding the magnitude of the effort and the challenges integral to presenting the Games.

The success of the 1996 Centennial Olympic Games lies in the hearts of the people who made them a reality. The memories of the collaboration and the goodwill and fellowship generated will shape our futures and be recalled as the most enduring legacy of the Games.

Ginger T. Watkins
Editor
Atlanta, Georgia 1997

TO THE 53,540 VOLUNTEERS AND EMPLOYEES WHO COMPRISED THE ATLANTA COMMITTEE FOR THE OLYMPIC GAMES STAFF. YOUR ENTHUSIASM, DEDICATION, AND LOYALTY MADE THE 1996 OLYMPIC GAMES A PERSONAL, EXCITING, AND MEMORABLE EXPERIENCE FOR MILLIONS OF INTERNATIONAL VISITORS AND ATHLETES. AS SEEMS MOST FITTING, THE PAGES OF THESE THREE VOLUMES ARE ANCHORED WITH YOUR NAMES.

• BARBARA J FLORENCE • DEBORAH FLORENCE • DWAYNE D FLORENCE • JAMES FLORENCE • LACHANDA FLORENCE • MARTHAELLEN FLORENCE • MOSES N FLORENCE • SHARON FLORENCE • SHARONDA Y FLORENCE • ENRIQUE A FLORES • FRANCES FLORES • LUIS E FLORES • MARCELINA FLORES • MARIA JOSE FLORES • MICHAEL FLORES • SHARON F FLORES • EVELYN M FLORIN • DONNA M FLORIO • MELINDA B FLORIO • MICHAEL S FLORIO • STEVEN M FLORIO • TERRI FLORIO • JAMES N FLOURNOY • MARY K FLOWE • ALESIA FLOWERS • ALETHEA M FLOWERS • BARBARA B FLOWERS • BARBARA E FLOWERS • CHARLIE L FLOWERS • CLAUDIA D FLOWERS • CRYSTAL L FLOWERS • DEBORAH FLOWERS • DEBORAH K FLOWERS • KIMBERLY FLOWERS • KIMBERLY D FLOWERS • MARY W FLOWERS • NIKKI A FLOWERS • PAMELA D FLOWERS • PATRICIA W FLOWNORY • ANDREA FLOYD • BECKY L FLOYD • BILL FLOYD • CYNTHIA C FLOYD • DANIEL T FLOYD • DAVID H FLOYD • DIANA L FLOYD • FREDRICK C FLOYD • GARY L FLOYD • JUDY D FLOYD • KEVIN A FLOYD • LAUREL A FLOYD • LOUISE FLOYD • LYNNAE M FLOYD • MEREDITH L FLOYD • NAOMI E FLOYD • PATRICIA A FLOYD • PAUL D FLOYD • WILLIAM D FLOYD • WINIFRED S FLOYD • SHEILA FLUCKE • ALICIA S FLUELLEN • CALVIN L FLUELLEN • BARBARA I FLUGUM • ATOIA N FLUKER • DOROTHY I FLUKER • SLATE FLUKER • ANGELA J FLURRY • GREGORY A FLURRY • ANITA L FLY • CECILIA N FLY • JOHN M FLY • SHIRLEY A FLY • BETTY L FLYNN • ERIN N FLYNN • GRETCHEN A FLYNN • HELEN W FLYNN • JOHN F FLYNN • LEROY J FLYNN • NANCIE D FLYNN • PHYLLIS A FLYNN • SCOTT FLYNN • SUZANNE M FLYNN • AMY D FLYNT • MICHAEL S FLYNT • DALE K FLYTHE • JUDITH A FOCHT • MICHAEL E FOCHT • ROBERT P FOCHT JR. • VIRGINIA J FODERICK • JOAN A FODERINGHAM • MARY M FODOR • STEVE L FODOR • JOANA L FODOREAN • MICHAEL FOERSTNER • ELIZABETH V FOGARTIE • MATHEW FOGARTY • RICK P FOGARTY • PAUL D FOGLE • ERIC S FOILES • MARGARET A FOILES • ROLAND R FOISIA • ERIN M FOISIE • BRENDA B FOLDS • JERRY FOLDS • CAROLYN C FOLEY • DAVID J FOLEY • ETHEL W FOLEY • JAMES R FOLEY • JENNIFER D FOLEY • JOHN J FOLEY • JULIANNE FOLEY • MARK J FOLEY • MARLENE FOLEY • MAUREEN K FOLEY • MELVIN W FOLEY • PATRICIA M FOLEY • PETER A FOLEY • RICHARD G FOLEY • RICHARD HAMILTON FOLEY • STEVEN M FOLEY • SUSAN B FOLEY • THERRON A FOLEY • LAUREN L FOLEY ATC • CELESTINE E FOLGA • LOUIS M FOLINO • PATRICK FOLIO • ROGER T FOLLAS • MARCIA E FOLLENSBEE • AISHA FOLLETTE • KEVIN J FOLRATH • DONALD L FOLSOM • ELIZABETH J FOLSOM • JANICE L FOLSOM • MERRILL L FOLSOM • MICHELLE FOLSOM • OKSANA FOLTYN • HALE B FONDA • ANNE M FONTAINE • ROBERT B FONTANILLA • ANDRES F FONTAO • MARYLENE FONTEIX • MARTY W FONTENOT • SUSAN G FONTENOT • HELEN P FONTSERE • AMIE C FONVILLE • MARGARET E FOOKES • RUSSELL R FOOKES • JANICE R FOONG • JESSICA M FOOR • JENELLE E FOOTE • LUCINDA A FOOTE • SHIRLEY A FOOTE • ELFRIEDE A FOPPIANO • JUDITH W FOPPIANO • LESLIE E FOPPIANO JR • MICHAEL FORAKER • CYNTHIA F FORAN • BEVERLY B FORBES • DORIAN FORBES • HARRY FORBES • JESSICA M FORBES • LISA A FORBES • MARGARET M FORBES • MONICA L FORBES • RYAN A FORBES • JACKIE E FORBUS • ROBERT A FORBUSH • MICHAEL T FORCHETTE • ALICE S FORD • ALMA C FORD • ANGELA D FORD • ANTHONY L FORD • ARTHUR L FORD • BARBARA H FORD • BETTY J FORD • CRAIG A FORD • CYNTHIA L FORD • DEBRA B FORD • DIANA FORD • DOUG FORD • EDWIN W FORD • FREDERICK FORD • FREDERICK FORD • GENE C FORD • JEANNE C FORD • JOHN F FORD • JON M FORD • JULIANNE M FORD • LARRY FORD • LATISA M FORD • MARGARET N FORD • NICHOLETTE FORD • NORMA S FORD • PATRICK R FORD • PHILLIP J FORD • RICHARD D FORD • ROBERT L FORD • ROBERT L FORD • SHEILA R FORD • TRACEY D FORD • TRINA T FORD • UNDRAUS D FORD • VIRGINIA C FORD • WILLIAM F FORD • WILLIAM KENT FORD • JULIE T FORD-GUTKE • ANDREW M FORD ATC • R WAYNE FORD JR • CAMPBELL A FORDE • JENNIFER N FORDE • PAULINE FORDE • PAMELA E FORDHAM • CAROLYN W FORE • CONSTANCE FORE • KAY B FORE • THOMAS M FORE • DICK R FOREBACK • SARAH L FOREHAND • JONATHAN H FOREMAN • RAYMOND FOREMAN • JAMES C FORREST • NATALIESE D FOREST • REBECCA S FORGAY • VALMORE J FORGETT • GERI G FORKNER • KENNETH P FORLENZA • LINDA E FORLINI • DONNA M FORMAN • ARLENE FORMANSKI • BETH I FORMBY • CHARLES L FORMBY • PAULETA C FORMBY • HOLLY R FORNEL • JOSEPH P FORNASH • JENNIFER L FORNEK • GEORGE FORNERET • DAVID A FORNESS • BARBARA D FORNEY • DAVID L FORNEY • MARK A FORNWALT • ROBIN D FORNWALT • JUDY A FORRER • DAWN D FORREST • MARKY W FORREST • MICHAEL W FORREST • THOMAS FORREST • EDWARD J FORREST JR • AMY V FORRESTAL • J DANIEL FORRESTAL • JON D FORRESTER • PAMELA G FORRESTER • WILLIAM A FORRESTER JR • NATHAN W FORRISTER • ANDREA L FORS • MAUREEN R FORS • ASA M FORSGREN • MARTHA L FORSS • RICHARD ELLIOTT FORSTALL • GREGORY W FORSTER • KAREN L FORSTER • LISA FORSTER • MARGARET M FORSTER • MICHAEL R FORSTER • ROBIN F FORSTON • ALAN R FORSYTH • PATRICIA C FORSYTH • ROBERT A FORSYTH • HEATHER C FORT • MARTHA B FORT • PATRICIA B FORT • ELISABETH E FORTANIER • EDWARD J FORTAW • VALYNE B FORTAW • ANN E FORTE • FREDERICK F FORTE • JOSEPH P FORTE • KATHY FORTE • MICHAEL P FORTE • STEVEN F FORTENBERRY • CANDACE C FORTH • KARA FORTIN • KELLY FORTIN • TIMOTHY C FORTIN • CATHERINE P FORTNER • SUDIE A FORTNER • ELIZABETH ASHLEY FORTNEY • ELIZABETH C FORTNEY • ROBERT L FORTNEY • RICK FORTES • HELEN B FORTSON • JOE N FORTSON • MILTON S FORTSON • ROLAND C FORTSON • CAMILLA D FORTUNE • CARL E FORTUNE • JOHN W FORTUNE • JOSEPH F FORTUNE • NICOLE L FORTUNE • DENNIS H FOSDICK • MARILYN E FOSKEY • GLORIA J FOSS • JEANNE R FOSS • ADAM M FOSTER • ALLISON M FOSTER • ANGELA L FOSTER • AUDREY J FOSTER • BARBARA T FOSTER • BETTYE B FOSTER • BOOKECIA FOSTER • BRIGID K FOSTER • BRUCE H FOSTER • BURT B FOSTER • CATHERINE FOSTER • CHARLES B FOSTER • CHARLES W FOSTER • DIONE E FOSTER • ELIZABETH H FOSTER • EUPHANIA J FOSTER • GAIL FOSTER • GARY W. FOSTER • GEORGE J FOSTER • GRACE L FOSTER • GRADY W FOSTER • JAMES O FOSTER • JAMES T FOSTER • JEAN L FOSTER • JENNIFER FOSTER • JENNIFER L FOSTER • JOAN CRILE FOSTER • JOEL FOSTER • JOHN L FOSTER • JOYCE A FOSTER • JOYCE D FOSTER • JUDITH A FOSTER • KAREN L FOSTER • KASEY A FOSTER • KATHARINE S FOSTER • LESLEY A FOSTER • LYNNE C FOSTER • MARJORIE A FOSTER • MARK FOSTER • MARK A FOSTER • MARSHALL T FOSTER • MICHAEL D FOSTER • MICHAEL W FOSTER • NANCY C FOSTER • NANCY L FOSTER • NEIL R FOSTER • NIKKI M FOSTER • PATRICIA M FOSTER • PAUL B FOSTER • ROBERT B FOSTER • RON C FOSTER • ROSALYN FOSTER • RUTH A FOSTER • SARAH L FOSTER • SHANNON FOSTER • STEPHEN A FOSTER • SUSAN B FOSTER • VIRGINIA I FOSTER • WALTER P FOSTER • WHITNEY T FOSTER • YOLANDA FOSTER • ANDREW N FOSTER RN • GWENDOLYN M FOSTER • BOBBY L FOUCH • ANCA O FOUNTAIN • CURTIS A FOUNTAIN • ELIZABETH A FOUNTAIN • GAIL FOUNTAIN • JAMES A FOUNTAIN • JOHN T FOUNTAIN • KAY C FOUNTAIN • NANCY J FOUNTAIN • STANLEY R FOUNTAIN • CARINE FOUQUET • LAMIA FOURATI • LISA G FOURIEZOS • MIKHAIL FOURMAN • KAY E FOURNIE • BRUCE B FOUTS • JULIE A FOUTS • NANCY J FOUTY • MARGARET L FOWKE • AMY R FOWLER • ANTHONY W FOWLER • BRENDA M FOWLER • CAROL E FOWLER • CLEON R FOWLER • DAVID D FOWLER • DORIS B FOWLER • FRANCES R FOWLER • FRANKLIN DAVID FOWLER • GILLIAN M FOWLER • GLEN K FOWLER • HUGH D FOWLER • JAN E FOWLER • JOANNE E FOWLER • JOHN T FOWLER • JONATHAN A FOWLER • JOSEPH L FOWLER • JULILI S FOWLER • JULIUS F FOWLER • LAURA K FOWLER • LESLIE A FOWLER • M KATHERINE FOWLER • M PATTON BETHEA FOWLER • MARTHA H FOWLER • MARY A FOWLER • RUBY D FOWLER • RACHEL B FOWLER • RAYMOND L FOWLER • SANDRA M FOWLER • TILLIE FOWLER • TINA Y FOWLER • WANDA L FOWLER • DRAYTON D FOWLER JR • JOHN O FOWLER JR • HOWARD L FOWLER MD • GERALD S FOWLER SR • SAMUEL FOWLER SR • STEVE A FOWLKES • BRIAN A FOX • CHRISTIANE FOX • DANIEL J FOX • DIANE L FOX • DONNA W FOX • DRUCILLA S FOX • ELIZABETH M FOX • EUGENE A FOX • FRANCES N FOX • GABRIELLA M FOX • GARY A FOX • HAMPTON FOX • HOWARD B FOX • JAMES K FOX • KATHRYN A FOX • LENORE J FOX • PHILIP E FOX • ROBERT E FOX • TERESA M FOX • TOM G FOX • VIRGINIA FOX • WYNDELL B FOX • SHEILA R FOX TUCK • BRIAN K FOXCROFT • ELIZABETH D FOX • PAMVETTE D FRAGALE • JULIE M FRAHM • ARIANNE FRAIN • LEON FRALEY • PIPER K FRALEY •

CHARLES N FRAM • PATRICIA W FRAME • HEIDI R FRAMER • LAURA M FRANC • CAROLE G FRANCE • CATHERINE E FRANCE • ROBERT C FRANCE • CARLOS A FRANCESCHI • MARY R FRANCILLON • ALYSSA G FRANCINI • ANNA J FRANCIS • DONALD E FRANCIS • ERIKA A FRANCIS • JANET L FRANCIS • JANIS L FRANCIS • JENCY F FRANCIS • KAZUKO FRANCIS • KELLI A FRANCIS • RAYSHAWN S FRANCIS • SHEILA N FRANCIS • SHELLEY A FRANCIS • STEPHANIE J FRANCIS • ANNEMARIE C FRANCIS ATC • AIMEE C FRANCK • KATHRYN A FRANCK • WILLIAM R FRANCK • MELISSA M FRANCKOWIAK • JERI L FRANCOEUR ATC • DAVID A FRANCOIS • JEFFREY J FRANK • ANDREA C FRANK • DEBORAH R FRANK • FULKE G FRANK • GLENN S FRANK • GORDON B FRANK • JAMES M FRANK • KATHLEEN B FRANK • KIRBY FRANK • LISA A FRANK • MICHELLE P FRANK • SCOTT M FRANK • SHARI C FRANK • SHERRY FRANK • STEVEN J FRANK • TERRY FRANK • VICKY E FRANK • JOSHUA FRANK EMT • MILTON FRANK III • LORI A FRANKE • GARY FRANKEL • MARY ELBA FRANKEL • REBECCA FRANKEL • MARY E FRANKIEWICZ • RONALD J FRANKIEWICZ • BARBARA A FRANKLIN • GEOFFREROY-ALLEN S FRANKLIN • HAROLD E FRANKLIN • JAMES E FRANKLIN • JANIS R. FRANKLIN • JEANNE M FRANKLIN • JOHN C FRANKLIN • KEVIN L FRANKLIN • KIMBERLEY L FRANKLIN • LARRY A FRANKLIN • LAURENCE B FRANKLIN • LEONARD J FRANKLIN • LLOYD W FRANKLIN • L'TANYA M FRANKLIN • MALCOLM FRANKLIN • MARY ANN FRANKLIN • NANCY FRANKLIN • NELSON P FRANKLIN • NETTIE E FRANKLIN • RANDALL R FRANKLIN • RONALD FRANKLIN • SHARON M FRANKLIN • SHIRLEY C FRANKLIN • THOMAS FRANKLIN • THOMAS E FRANKLIN • VALENA R FRANKLIN • BRIAN M FRANKLIN ATC • JAMES M FRANKLIN JR • NICHOLAS FRANKLYN • DAVID L FRANKO • BELITA B FRANKS • BETH A FRANKS • CINDY J FRANKS • ERIC H FRANKS • SHIRLEY L FRANKS • DEBRA F FRANSEN • KARIN FRANSEN •

ANGELA M FREEMAN • APRIL M FREEMAN • BOBBY J FREEMAN • BRENDA S FREEMAN • BRIAN T FREEMAN • BRUCE E FREEMAN • CORNELIUS FREEMAN • CYNTHIA L FREEMAN • CYNTHIA S FREEMAN • DIANE C FREEMAN • DONNA KAY FREEMAN • GREG R FREEMAN • HARRY T FREEMAN • JACOB R FREEMAN • JAMES R FREEMAN • JOHN S FREEMAN • JOHN W FREEMAN • JOYCE FREEMAN • JULIA C FREEMAN • KAREN D FREEMAN • KAREN M FREEMAN • KEVIN B FREEMAN • KRISTEN F FREEMAN • LISA FREEMAN • LOUISE L FREEMAN • LURELIA M FREEMAN • MARIA J FREEMAN • NEISHA FREEMAN • PATRICIA D FREEMAN • PAUL B FREEMAN • RANDY L FREEMAN • SANFORD S FREEMAN • SYLVIA G FREEMAN • SYLVIA J FREEMAN • TERRELL FREEMAN • TERRY R FREEMAN • THEODORE C FREEMAN • WILLA FREEMAN • WILLIAM JR F FREEMAN • WILLIAM R FREEMAN • SARA A FREEMAN III • ERNEST J FREEMAN JR • TIMOTHY D FREETH • JEFFREY L FREHSE • JOELLE K FREIBERG • KIRSTEN A FREIBERG • DAYNA L FREUD • NANCY E FREUD • BARBARA H FREUND • JANICE E FREUND • PATRICIA V FREUND • RICHARD A FREUND • DEBRA L FREUND MT • RANDY FREW • ERICH FREY • PAUL J FREY • STEVEN L FREY • WILMA R FREY • PASCALE C FREYER • VALENTINO FRIAS • MARY E FRIBERG • J FRIBOURG • CHARLENE FRICK • ELIZABETH A FRICK • SANDRA G FRICK • KAYLA K FRICKS • LORRI E FRICKS • DEBORAH J FRIDAY • JENNIFER C FRIDAY • MARC FRIDAY • RONALD J FRIDAY • WILLIAM P FRIDAY • MANDY A FRIDGE • JENNIFER A FRIEDBERG •

MARK FUGEL • MARI C FUGERE • MARTHA L FUGITT • ANGELA J FUGO • DIANA M FUHRMAN • MIYUKI FUJIMA • ATSUKO FUJITA • MAKIKO FUKAYA • SHOKO FUKUDA • MAKI FUKUMOTO • DAVID A FULCHER • DOROTHY A FULCHER • RHONWYN A FULCHER • ROBERT A FULCHER • WALTER N FULCHER • ERIC S FULCOMER • FRANCIS A FULD • PETE P FULFORD • PEGGY L FULGHUM • ANGELA D FULKERSON • WAYNE L FULLENWIDER • ANDREW D FULLER • BERNARD CHRISTOPHER FULLER • CHARLES A FULLER • CHRIS D FULLER • CHRISTY D FULLER • DEBBIE A FULLER • EDWARD L FULLER • FREDDIE C FULLER • GEORGIA FULLER • GEORGIANA D FULLER • JOSEPH B FULLER • KELLY A FULLER • LINDA G FULLER • MILLICENT E FULLER • NAN ELLEN FULLER • PATRICIA A FULLER • RICK G FULLER • TODD B FULLER • TRACI M FULLER • TY S FULLER • VIVIAN L FULLER • JAMES M FULLER-II-PM • RUSSELL V FULLER JR • RICHARD L FULLER JR. • BRUCE WILLIAM FULLERTON • RICHARD N FULLERTON • JEANETTE FULLILOVE • KURT D FULMER • LEIGH A FULMER • PAUL W FULMER • TIMOTHY B FULMER • SVLIVA G FULTON • VERNON FULTON • EDWARD FULTON JR • TERRI L FULWOOD • SHARON B FUMAGALLI • SIDNEY FUMBANKS • MARY N FUNCHES • REGINA C FUNCK • EDNA J FUND • JOHN J FUNDERBURK • MICHAEL D FUNDERBURK • NELLE M FUNDERBURRY • ORSON M FUNDOM • DEBBIE FUNG-A-WING • JOSEPH P FUNK • LORA L FUNK • MARK R FUNK • JAMES F FUNK JR MD • BENNETT C FUQUA • CHRISTINE L FUQUA • KAREN A FUQUAY • BERTHA B FURCRON • CORLISS FURFURO • SUSAN L FURICK • BRIAN M FURIE EMT • MAUREEN FURLONG • ANTHONY B FURLOW • JOHN D FURMAN • MARGARET E FURNEY • LARRY R FURPHY • ANGELA L FURR • SHERRRY R FURR • CHRISTOPHER A FURR CATC • KRISNA FURROW • SHINKO FURUKAWA • FRANK F FUSARO • LAURIE A FUSARO • ROBERT J FUSILLO • RAY S FUSS • TA J FUSAWA • ROBERT J FUSILLO • SANDRA J FUSSEIL • LINDSAY M FUSSELL •

P.J. GALBRAITH • THOMAS H GALBRAITH • V GAIL GALBREATH • GARY O GALDI • JULIE A GALE • TARRAH D GALES • SCOTT R GALECIA • CARLOS GALIANO • JEANNETTE M GALINDO • ALICIA J GALLAGHER • AMY ANNE M GALLAGHER • BRIAN T GALLAGHER • COLLEEN C GALLAGHER • CYNTHIA L GALLAGHER • DAVID E GALLAGHER • DIANE S GALLAGHER • JERALD G GALLAGHER • JESSICA A GALLAGHER • JOFA A GALLAGHER • KATE N GALLAGHER • KIM E GALLAGHER • MARTINA M GALLAGHER • NANCY O GALLAGHER • COLLEEN GALLAHER • CATHERINE E GALLANT • JEFFREY A GALLANT • STACEY GALLANT • TONI GALLANT • ORLANDO GALLARDO • LEO M GALLARDY • MARK M GALLEGO • LYNDA I GALLER • DOREEN GALL • LARRY C GALLOWAY • ANY J GALLIPPI • ELAINE S GALLMAN • JAMES A GALLMANN • CAROLYN GALLMON • ANDREA M GALLO • JOHN C GALLO • MARGARET J GALLO • MICHAEL G GALLO • RICHARD L GALLO • PRISCILLA GALLOPS • L J. GALLOWAY • LARRY C GALLOWAY • LINDA A GALLOWAY • MARY GALLOWAY • MARY GALLOWAY • ANNE D GALLOWAY • TAMMY GALLOWAY • WILLIAM M GALLOWAY • LISA L GALLOWITZ • ARTHUR S GALLUP • PATRICIA J GALLUP • CATERINA GALPERINA • EILEEN E GALSHACK • JULIA 'CORIE' GALUSHA • BOB L GALVE • JEANNE F GALVIN • JOSEPH E GALVIN • MARC GALVIN • REBECCA R GALVIN • VIRGINIA G GALVIN • JULIAN J GALVIS • ROBIN D GALVEN • CURVOIS GALYON • HELEN M GALYON • ROBERT P GAMBARDELLA • TAMEKA GAMBARELL • PAUL S GAMBER • VICKY J GAMBER ATC • GRADY L GAMBLE • JAMES N GAMBLE • JANICE M GAMBLE • STEVE L GAMBLE • CYNTHIA A GAMBON • DENNIS G GAMBON • STEVE J GAMBON • DAVID P GAMBONE • ROBERT C GAMBRELL • DONALD L GAMBRIL • CHARLES F GAMEL • BETTY A GAMEZ • RAUL R GAMEZ • GRANT R GAMLEN • JOHN W GAMWELL • DOUGLAS P GANASSI ATC • JULIE S GANAWAY • GLORIA R GANDARA • CHARYLE F GANDEE • KINAL K GANDHI • ATUL A GANDRE • DANIEL L GANDY • DELBERT G GANDY • ROSS GANDY • NITHYA GANESAN • RAYMOND C GANGA • MELVIN M GANGLOFF • MELISSA GANLEY • BULA GANN • CAROLYN S GANN • CURTIS R GANN • EDGAR S GANN • LOUISE L GANN • M. FLAGG GANN • MARTHA A GANN • RICHARD D GANN • WHITNEY M GANN • MARCUS L GANN JR EMT • ERIN GANNON • REGINA M GANNON • STEPHEN P GANNON • PRABHA G GANPOLE • KATHLEEN H GANSEREIT • MATTHEW D GANSEREIT • WALT GANSSER • BRENDA D GANT • JOHN L GANT • CHERIE A GANTER • TAMMY M GANTNER • LILLIAN M GANTSOUDES • BRYANT K GANTT • KIMBERLY GANTT • LINDA S GANTT • STANLEY J GANTT • SUSAN P GANTT • WILLIAM D GANTT • AMY H GANTT ATC • GREG P GANTZERT • ADAM GANZ • JONATHAN GANZ • YI GAO • WILLIAM GAPAC • CARRIE GAPAE • RAYMOND GAPE • ROBERT HENRY GAPS • KATHLEEN C GARBE • RICHARD S GARBER • TERRY C GARBER • ANDREA GARBISCH • BARBORA GARBOVA • SUSAN H GARBOW • ABIGAIL GARCHEK • JEANNE M GARCHEK • CHANTEL C GARCHEK • ALLESSANDRA M GARCIA • BEATRIZ GARCIA • DAVID A GARCIA • DEANNA L GARCIA • FRANCIS J GARCIA • FRANK C GARCIA • FRANK R GARCIA • GABRIELA GARCIA • GALIA GARCIA • GRIZELLE GARCIA • JAIME GARCIA • JESUS ALBERTO GARCIA • JOANN L GARCIA • JOSE R GARCIA • JUANA C GARCIA • JULIE D GARCIA • LAURA M GARCIA • LORENZO GARCIA • MARIA M GARCIA • MIKKI GARCIA • NILA R GARCIA • PATRICIA GARCIA • RICHARD GARCIA • ROBERT S GARCIA • RUDY L GARCIA • SUE GARCIA • SUSETTE GARCIA • VICTOR GARCIA • VIVIAN M GARCIA • CARLOS G GARCIA-LOPEZ • HUMBERTO D GARCIA-SJOGRIM • ROY E GARCIA IV • OBDULIA GARCIALECKIE • BETSY GARD • DANIEL P GARDENER • MIKE B GARDENER • ALLISON L GARDINER • ANNE C GARDINER • GARY P GARDINER • LOLA GARDINER • ANITA M GARDNER • ANNE R GARDNER • BARBRA JILL GARDNER • CHRISTINA GARDNER • DAN J GARDNER • DANNY L GARDNER • DAVID R GARDNER • GAYLE GARDNER • GERALDINE A GARDNER • HOLLY GARDNER • JAMES A GARDNER • JEFFREY R GARDNER • JOLEE A GARDNER • JULIE E. GARDNER • KIMBERLEA J GARDNER • LANA J GARDNER • LLOYD D GARDNER • MICHAEL D GARDNER • MICHAEL S GARDNER • PAUL B GARDNER • ROBERT D GARDNER • SCOTT T GARDNER • TORVIS S GARDNER • WAYNE GARDNER • MARILYNN E GARDO • ROGER P GARDOCKI • VICKI GARDOCKI • WAYNE I GARFINKEL • AMIT GARG • VERA R GARGANO • TERRENCE L GARGIULO • TIFFANY A GARGIULO • MARGE S GARGOSH • BRANDA S GARLAND • CHRISTINA P GARLAND • MARY L GARLAND • KATHRYN A GARLICK • PAUL G GARLICK • ELLEN K GARLIN • DONIA A GARLINGTON • CHRIS E GARMAN • VIRGINIA A GARMON • JOYCE GARN • ADELE T GARNER • TAMEKA GAMBARELL • BRENDA H GARNER • DAVID C GARNER • DAVID G GARNER • DON E GARNER • DOUGLAS L GARNER • EDWARD B GARNER • GORDON GARNER • JENNIFER M GARNER • JIMMIE R GARNER • JULIA A GARNER • KENNETH E GARNER • MARCUS GARNER • MARIA H GARNER • NIKKI S GARNER • PEGGY L GARNER • SERENA A GARNER • SHANE GARNER • TERI G GARNER • VICKYLYNN T GARNER • VIRGINIA J GARNER • CAROLYN L GARNES • MARSHA B GARNETT • THOMAS H GARNETT • JOHN W GARNIER • JOHN T GARNJOST • GERALD L GARNTO • CHARLES M GAROFALO • IRA M GARONZIK • KRISTY A GARPNE • ELIZABETH J GARR • ANNIE F GARRARD • BILLY R GARREN • STEPHEN C GARRERY • DIANA R GARRET • ROGER W GARRET • ANNE M GARRETT • BESS M GARRETT • BETH T GARRETT • BETTY J GARRETT • BRETT A GARRETT • BRYAN K GARRETT • CAROL L GARRETT • CAROLINE K GARRETT • CHRISTOPHER L GARRETT • DANIELLE GARRETT • DEEANN GARRETT • DINA GARRETT • GAIL GARRETT • GREG GARRETT • JACQUELINE GARRETT • JACQUELINE P GARRETT • JOSHUA C GARRETT • KRISTI L GARRETT • KRISTY T GARRETT • LAURA A GARRETT • LAUREL L GARRETT • LINDA F GARRETT • LINDA H GARRETT • LINDSEY GARRETT • MATTY L GARRETT • MAYNARD L GARRETT • MELISSA GARRETT • NANCY S GARRETT • PATRICIA A GARRETT • PEGGY J GARRETT • REGINA GARRETT • ROBIN A GARRETT • SHARI A GARRETT • SHIRLEY GARRETT • TERI L GARRETT • TIMOTHY J GARRETT • BETH A GARRETT ATC • GENE E GARRETT III • THOMAS W GARRETT JR • HOLLY P GARRETT SAT • MARIA C GARRIGGO • CARL E GARRIGUS • JAMES J GARRIS • ALAN A GARRISON • ASHLEY GARRISON • CAROLYN S GARRISON • DEXTER GARRISON • HANNAH J GARRISON • HARRIET W GARRISON • KEVIN E GARRISON • MARK J GARRISON • R GLENN GARRISON • RYAN T GARRISON • SAMUEL G GARRISON • GINA M GARRO • DAVID R GARRON • MYRNA GARRON • BRIAN A GARRY • PHYLLIS J GARRY • BRANAN J GARSIDE • MICHAEL. W GARTEN • VANDELLA L GARTH • LISA E GARUTI • JAMES A GARVEY • SOLANGE GARVEY • J. DANNY GARVIN • LUCY S GARVIN • MARION H GARVIN • ROBERT J GARVIN • CHARLES E GARWOOD • BOBBIE L GARY • DARREN T GARY • DAPHNE D GARY • MONICA A GARY • ROBINEZ G GARY • ROD D GARY • TIFFANY V GARY • RHEA L GARY-TRICHE • CARLOS GARZA • JOSE G GARZA • REGGINA GARZA • GABRIELA GARZA-GRANDE • MAURICIO GARZA IV • MARGARET A GASIOR • PHILLIP E GASIOR • ANNE A GASKIN • BRUCE N GASKIN • CLAUDIA A GASKIN • GENEVA L GASKINS • BRENDA S GASKINS • KENNETH J GASKINS • STEVEN GASKINS • TONI D GASKINS • ROBERT EDGAR GASKINS JR • KERSTIN M GASKO • ROBERT C GASKO • CHARLES J GASPAR • DAVID C GASPARI • ALBERT M GASPARIAN • MICHAEL A GASPARINI • DELPHINE F GASPART • PAUL GASSEL • JOHN J GASSMAN • DOROTHY L GASTER • JAMES C GASTAUER • DONNA SUSANNE GASTON • FERNANDO E GASTON • JULIA P GASTON • ERIN M GASTON-DOAKES • PEARL E GASU • ANITA M GATCH • ALFRED D GATES • BRIAN J GATES • CHARLESSA GATES • FREDERICK A GATES • MARSHA A GATES • NATALIE A GATES • ROBERTA S GATES • SUSAN GATES • CLAUDIA A GATES • TAMIKO A GATES • CAMILLE M GATHERCOLE • JAMES M GATHERCOLE • LAURA M GATHERCOLE • TREVOR D GATHMAN • LISA A GATHRIGHT • LEE T GATINS • DONALD GATLEY • SHARON J GATLIN • DOUGLAS W GATLIN • LISA D GATLIN • JOHN GATTO • MICHAEL G GATTONE • NANCY A GATTONE • TERRI GATTONE • BRUCE W GAUDETTE • CHRISTOPHER L GAULDEN • DEBORAH S GAUNT • LISA M GAULDING • CHRIS D SAUN • TERRY J GAUNT • EFREM Z GAUSCH • SUSAN K GAUSE • TERESA GAUSE • WILLIAM H GAUTIER • JAMES B GAUVAIN • JAMES L GAVALIER • GERALD B GVEEDA • MARGARET D GAVENTA • MATTHEW S GAVZY MT • DONNA M GAWLAS • ANTHONY S GAY • BETH W GAY • CAROL R GAY • CYNTHIA A GAY • DEBRA L GAY • GEORGE E GAY • KAREN L GAY • RICHARD GAY • SANDRA V GAY • TERRA GAY • CURREY H GAYLE • CASSANDRA E GAYLE-PALMES • HAZEL M GAYLOR • LEILA C GAYLOR • SHARON S GAYNOR • MICHELLE L GAYTON • IRENE R GAZ • KITTIE N GAZAWAY • ROBERT A GAZAWAY • MARC GAZDIK • CATHERINE L GEARHART • PEGGY M GEARHART MT • CARLA GEARHEART • VAL GEARY • ROBERT GEARY • KENDRICK F GEARON • DONALD M GEDEON • SUSAN C GEDRICH • DANA M GEE • JACK F GEE • JEAN L GEE • KAREN A GEE • RODNEY GEE • NANCY P GEE • VICTOR E GEER • AG GEETER • ANGELA K GEHL • STEPHANIE GEHRING • JOSEPH J GEHRINGER •

SHERRI A FRANSEN • MARISE FRANSOLINO • KENT D FRANTZ • JOHN M FRANZ • MONICA RUTH FRANZ • GLORIA B FRANZEN • ZACHARY B FRANZEN • ROBERT T FRAPWELL • SHARON A FRAPWELL • KAREN L FRASCONA • ALEX FRASER • ALLAN W FRASER • ANDREW R FRASER • BARBARA P FRASER • CHARLIE B FRASER • DAVID S FRASER • HOWARD D FRASER • JAMES H FRASER • JANE E FRASER • LAURA H FRASER • LINCOLN THOMAS FRASER • LISA M FRASER • PETER FRASER • WILLIAM T FRASER • PAUL V FRASER JR • JESSE L FRASIER • LA DAWN FRASIER • FLORENCE S FRASURE • MARC A FRATELLO • MARIE E FRATONI • ROSANNE FRATTAROLI • RANDELL FRATTINI • ELLEN S FRAUENTHAL • LYNN S FRAWLEY • CANDICE C FRAWLEY • PATRICK M FRAWLEY • LIAM T FRAWLEY ATC • RICHARD E FRAZEE ATC • LESLIE R FRAZER • MEGAN FRAZER • VICKY L FRAZER • ARTHUR E FRAZIER • BONNIE S FRAZIER • CRYSTAL L FRAZIER • CRYSTAL L FRAZIER • DANA J FRAZIER • FRAN FRAZIER • GAIL Z FRAZIER • HARRIET K FRAZIER • LEROY FRAZIER • MARY S FRAZIER • MICHAEL A FRAZIER • PATRICIA L FRAZIER • RONALD A FRAZIER • TAMMY FRAZIER • TAMMY JOY FREAS • ANDREW C FRECKA • TIMOTHY R FRECKA • CHRISTOPHER J FREDERICK • CHRISTY E FREDERICK • DOUG J FREDERICK • ELEANOR F FREDERICK • JILL M FREDERICK • JOHN D FREDERICK • KENNETH W FREDERICK • LIAH L FREDERICK • LORETTE FREDERICK • METZ FREDERICK • TISHA L FREDERICK • MARGARET A FREDERICK ATC • ROBERT W FREDERICK • GRANT R FREDERICKS • DORTE S FREDERIKSEN • DENNIS J FREDETTE • ROLAND FREDETTE • PATRICIA L FREDRICKSON • SARAH E FREED • HARRIS J FREED MD • PAM FREELAND • DIANA JEAN-ETHEL FREEDMAN • LISA L FREEDMAN • MARCIA L FREEDMAN • PATRICIA FRIEDMAN • ROBERT I FREEDMAN • BE KAY FREEH • JENNA L FREEH • JENSIE L FREEH • SUSAN L FREEL • LARRY H FREELAND • LINDA J FREELAND • TILLIE L FREELAND • TREVOR K FREELAND • ADRIEN E FREEMAN • ALFREDA FAY FREEMAN • ANGELA D FREEMAN •

JUDITH A FRIEDBERG • NANCY R FRIEDBERG • LUCINDA FRIEDE • FRED J FRIEDEL • ALVIN FRIEDLANDER • JONATHAN A FRIEDLANDER • SCOTT FRIEDLANDER • ERIK M FRIEDLY • ADAM D FRIEDMAN • ROBERT FRIEDMAN • DONNA H FRIEDMAN • EVA FRIEDMAN • FRANCES R FRIEDMAN • IRA A FRIEDMAN • JEREMY F FRIEDMAN • JOEL BRIAN FRIEDMAN • JOHN D FRIEDMAN • LAURENCE FRIEDMAN • LEE E FRIEDMAN • MORRIS J FRIEDMAN • RUSSELL J FRIEDMAN • SUSAN M FRIEDMAN • ANJA FRIEDRICH • ILISA S FRIEDRICH • INGO J FRIEDRICH • JOSEPH G FRIEDRICH • MOSELLE M FRIEDRICH • RYAN M FRIEDRICH • MARGARET W FRIEL • MARY K FRIEND • CHARLES R FRIERSON • JOAN FRIERSON • MICHAEL F FRIERSON • LAURA B FRIESE • JOHN O FRIESE • STEVEN B FRIESE • DARRELL A FRIESEN • JANET E FRIESEN • MARTHA E FRIESEN • MELINDA J FRIESEN • SCOTT N FRIGARD • GEORGE FRILOT • WENDI R FRINDELL • CARLTON F FRIPP • BOB FRISBEE • GAYLE L FRISCH • KAREN J FRISCHMEYER • KELLIE B FRISCH • JO ANNE FRITH • ELICIA B FRITSCH • COURTNEY FRITTS • JOHN C FRITZ • JUDY A FRITZ • MICHAEL E FRITZ • SUZANNE W FRITZ • TRACEY FRITZINGER • ANNIE FROBOSE • CHARLES FROELICH JR • BRITTA N FROELICHER • FRANZ FROELICHER • MARGARET FROELICH-ER-GRUNDMANN • MELVIN R FROLI • KIMBERLY D FROMAN • GLENN D FROMER • JACK D FROMM • SCOTT W FROMME • MARIA H FRONCKOWIAK • MICHAEL A FRONTERA • RICHARD N FRONTERA • KENNY M FRONTIN • BRADLEY M FROST • CLIFTON D FROST • JOSEPH T FROST • KATHERINE L FROST • MICHAEL FROST • T SHEILA I FROST • STANFORD FROST • BARBARA A FRY • MARILYN D FRY • RAMONA J FRY • STEPHEN D FRY • NICOLE S FRYDMAN • JACQUELINE J FRYE • RANDALL FRYE • REA FRY • SARA A FRYE • ZOE FRYE • CONRAD FRYKMAN • KRISTEN FRYLING • AMANDA FRYMAN • BRIAN B FRYMAN • JOAN C FU • IRMA G. FUCHS • JASON W FUCHS • TRACEY M FUDGE • BERTHA M FUDGEN • ARTHUR W FUDGER • JOANNE FUDGER • BRENDA L FUENTES • ERIC M FUENTES • INGRID S FUGATE •

MICHAEL T FUSTERO • CRAIG G FUTCH • DELL R FUTCH • MARY E FUTCH • SHELLY R FUTCH • WILTON C FUTCH • LEONARDO J FUTRAL • DAVID M FUTRELL • KIMBERLY N FUTRELL • STEPHEN F FUTRELL • CATE C • AMELIA H FYE • EDWARD M FYE • HEDY M FYE • JUDI E FYOLA • DAVID FYRE • FLORENCIO HERNANDEZ • JANET D GAA • RICHARD K GAA • MICHAEL P GAAN • ROBIN E GAAN • DEBORAH A GAASCH • EARL E GABB JR • LYNDSAY J GABE • RICHARD GABE • CATHERINE R GABEL • GEOFFREY S GABERINO • DEBRA GABLE • RICKY R GABLE • SHARON B GABLE • SUZANNE L GABLE • KATHLEEN GABOARD • MOMO KATE GABORONE • SUSAN E GABRIELSON • VLADIMIR V GABRIJELCIC • SUZETTE GACONNIER • MONSTAFA I GAD • CEDRIC D GADDIS • STEVEN GADDIS • DENNIS GADDY • GARRETT N GADDY • GRACE M GADDY • PATRICIA L GADDY • PHYLLIS B GADDY • MAJOR GADDY II • SHARON K GADE • EDWARD M GADRIX • ELIZABETH D GADSBY • JAMES E CADSBY • BRIAN S GADSDEN • WANDA V GADSON • CONNIE J GADZIALA • DOROTHY G GAESS • LEONARD H GAFFGA • GREGORY C GAFFNEY • DIANA H GAFFORD • SANDRA L GAGE • JUDY M GAGLIANO • ANTHONY GAGLIARDI • CHRISTOPHER G GAGNE • ALAN GAGNON • EAMES C GAGNON • FRANK GAGNON • JESSICA R GAGNON • LUCILLE M GAGNON • PILAR GAIGE • JIM W GAILEY • KATHY J GAILEY • LAMAR M GAILEY • NICK J GAILEY • PATRICIA P GAILEY • TIMOTHY M GAILEY • VICKY D GAILEY • WARD H GAILEY • CINDY A GAILORD • WILLIAM E GAILLIARD • BRIGITTE R GAILLIS-DELEPINE • MARGARET GAINER • BENJAMIN H GAINES • BEVERLY J GAINES • BILLIE B GAINES • CAROLYN S GAINES • DORIS H GAINES • GAINES JR • DOROTHY M GAINES • GARY L GAINES • JANET L GAINES • KIT C GAINES • RICHARD L GAINES • WILLIAM B GAINES • ANNA GAINES • DANIEL P GAINES • ALLAN J GAINOK • SAMUEL M GAINOR • JULIE B GAINSLEY • DORIS H GAISER • JUARLYN S GAINES • DIVINE A GATHER • ROY J GAITHER • NADAV GAL • JAMES B GALARZA • CAROLYN S GALATAS • EDWARD A GALVIZ • VEIKKO GALAZKY • VINCE G GALBATO • DONALD

ATLANTA—GATEWAY FOR DREAMS

this page: Flowering dogwood trees bloom throughout Atlanta during the city's verdant springtime.

facing page: As the world's largest outcropping of granite, Stone Mountain has been a landmark since the Atlanta area was just a crossroads.

WELCOMING THE WORLD to the Centennial Olympic Games in 1996 was in keeping with Atlanta's long tradition as a crossroads. From its earliest history, the city was identified with change, diversity, and movement, welcoming all, whether they were just passing through or making a new home. Atlanta began, prospered, reemerged from destruction, and flourished as a center of business and commerce.

For centuries, trails and roads running north and south, as well as east and west, converged in the vicinity of a region that came to be known as Standing Peach Tree between the Chattahoochee River and a landmark called the "great stone mountain." In 1837, engineer Stephen Long drove a stake into the ground of the area to mark the terminus of a new railroad. Long chose the spot because of its proximity to a good river crossing and the strategic high ground of the area's seven ridges. By the time the first train left the settlement known as Terminus in 1842, enough workers and suppliers on the railroad project had decided to stay that they applied for a city charter the fol-

lowing year. In 1845, the city's name was changed to Atlanta.

By 1857, transport activity had increased so much that a national magazine *Harper's Weekly* featured an article calling Atlanta the "Gate City." This epithet would endure and expand

TAMARA GEHRIS • HESTER P GEHRM • JOHN A GEHRM II • PATRICIA E GEIER • CHRISTOPHER M GEIER ATC • ELAINE D GEIGER • GAYE R GEIGER • HARRY E GEIGER • LINDA F GEIGER • MARY T GEIGER • NITA GEIGER • REBECCA A GEIGER • DANA R GEIGLE • JEREMY S GEIGLE • DEBRA A GEISEL • KRISTY L GEISER • ADAM C GEISLER • ROBERT F GEISLER • TED GEISS • AMY L GEISSLER • GARY GEISSLER • KIMBERLY GEISSMAN • VERA GELBER • ERIC GELDART • JANICE CATHERINE GELFAND • ROBIN A GELFENBIEN • JANICE S GELHAUS • KENNETH R GELHAUS • JAMES ALEC GELIN • JOSE R GELL • JAMES S GELLAN •

JILL E GELLATLY • JEFFREY GELLER • CHRISTIAN GELLNER • GEORGE B GELLY • NICOLA L GELMETTI • JOSEPH L GELMINI • KATHLEEN R GELMINI • PATRICIA K GELMINI • PATTY L GELTZ • ELISABETH M GEMBECKI • JAMES H GEMMILL • YVONNE B GEMMILL • FRANK J GENCORELLI • MARIE GENDRON • HELEN C GENESCRITTI • JANICE W GENEST • DIANE E GENO • WADE B GENOVA • KATHRYN L GENRICH • RONELLE W GENSER • HOWARD GENSER JR • JANE F GENSKE • RALPH J GENSLER • ANGELA R GENTILE • JENNIFER L GENTLE • ALEXANDER G GENTLES • SCOTT E GENTLES • ALICE Y GENTRY • DON D GENTRY

from meaning a gateway to the South to meaning a gateway to the world.

In 1860, at the beginning of the US Civil War, Atlanta boasted several railroad lines, a bank, a newspaper, and 10,000 citizens. Because of its strategic importance as a transportation hub, it became a major target of Union forces during the war, and in 1864, the city was captured after a devastating siege. Most of what had not been destroyed was then burned to the ground. The inhabitants fled, and a detachment of US military forces guard-

left: **Even in 1895, when this picture was taken, the intersection of Marietta and Forsyth Streets in downtown Atlanta was bustling with activity.**

right: Phoenix Rising, **by sculptor Gamba Quirino, stands in the heart of Atlanta as a symbol of the city.**

ing the rubble was all that was left of the once-thriving community.

After the war—like the city's adopted symbol, the phoenix—Atlanta rose from its ashes to live again. This happened because of the vision, energy, and determination of men and women who were undaunted by apparent impossibility and saw opportunity in the ruins. People from all over the United States, including newly freed African Americans, as well as newly arriving immigrants set themselves a mutual task—to replace what was lost with everything that was new and better.

Within a decade, a rebuilt Atlanta became the capital of Georgia.

The World's Fair and International Exposition in 1881 attracted more than a quarter million visitors to the city. This event was Atlanta's first hosting of a major international gathering. Twelve years later, in 1893, Atlanta opened the Cotton States and International Exposition. A number of states contributed buildings and displays, as did a variety of European and South American countries. The hundred-day extravaganza—located in what would become Atlanta's Piedmont Park—drew more than 1.2 million visitors to the bustling

• JULIE A GENTRY • MILTON L GENTRY • MYNYOWN GENTRY • WILLIAM L GENTRY • RAYMOND J GEOR • ALLISON M GEORGE • ANDY GEORGE • DANA Y GEORGE • DEBBIE E GEORGE • DOUGLAS L GEORGE • FRANCES L GEORGE • GARY C GEORGE • GILES R GEORGE • HALVARD C GEORGE • KAMARIA S GEORGE • KIMBERLIE F GEORGE • KOMINOS GEORGE • L ANN GEORGE • LESLIE P GEORGE • LILLIAN R GEORGE • MARSHA W GEORGE • ROBERTA D GEORGE • SEAN C GEORGE • SHEREEN E GEORGE • SHERYL L GEORGE • VICKIE L GEORGE • VIRGLE E GEORGE • WANDA C GEORGE • LEONARD G GEORGE JR •

city of about 65,000 inhabitants. The world-renowned scientist and educator Booker T. Washington played a prominent role at the exposition by both promoting the South's agricultural products and urging racial reconciliation in the region.

Once again, roads and railroad lines stimulated growth and prosperity, and Atlanta's leaders kept their eyes open for opportunities emerging with the new century. The city embraced the fledgling flight industry, and the broadening spectrum of transportation facili-

ties generated a constant stream of people and goods through Atlanta, bringing an attendant flow of ideas and information. The nature of its commerce ensured that Atlanta, with a population of nearly 90,000 in 1900, would be more cosmopolitan than provincial, more outgoing than insular.

Enterprise continued to expand into many areas, and a vigorous business and professional population in both the black and white communities strengthened civic pride and public and private institutions in the burgeoning

This panoramic view, taken from the dome of the Capitol in 1903, shows the intersection of Washington and Hunter streets.

left: **In keeping with Atlanta's traditional interest in horticulture, flowers abound in public areas during the spring and summer.**

right: **Atlanta drew people from around the world in 1893, when the Cotton States and International Exposition was held in what is now Piedmont Park.**

metropolitan area. Numerous colleges and universities were founded, including some of the most respected historically black institutions of higher education.

Atlanta's tradition as an educational and cultural center expanded in the twentieth century under the watchful eyes of philanthropists like The Coca-Cola Company magnate Robert W. Woodruff. Known for many years as Mr. Anonymous, he worked behind the scenes to create a solid base to support Atlanta's important institutions, such as Emory University and the Woodruff Arts Center which comprises the High Museum of Art, the Atlanta Symphony Orchestra, The Alliance Theatre, and Atlanta College of Art.

Banks, insurance agencies, retail industry, and government facilities helped provide an ever-broadening financial base for the city. In the last 50 years, Atlanta and its surrounding metropolitan area have become home to many large corporations, service-based industries, and not-for-profit associations. A flourishing convention business—regional, national, and international—has not only acquainted millions of visitors with the city, but has also regularly introduced hospitable Atlantans to guests from near and far, to the latest products and technologies.

Its business focus helped to make Atlanta the "City Too Busy to Hate" during the civil rights movement. Its religious and educational institutions produced leaders such as Nobel Peace Prize Laureate, the Reverend Martin

• RICHARD L GERHARDT • RICHARD L GERHARDT • JENNIFER H GERHOLD • STACY A GERING • ROBERT J GERKER • BARBARA J GERLACH • DICK J GERLACH • DONNA D GERLACH • GREGORY E GERLACH • HUGH M GERLACH • PAULINE F GERLACH • MICHAEL R GERLACH ¬TC • GAY S GERLACK • AUBREY L GERLAUGH • FRED T GERLICH • KENNETH E GERLINGER • STUART R GERMAN • THOMAS L GERMAN • DAVID C GERMANESO • CAROL A GERMANN • JOHN W GERMANY • JUSTIN W GERMANY • SALLY M GERMANY • SAMUEL L GERMANY • JACK D GERMARY • ALICE GERMONDARI • LILLIAN M GERNAY • HENRY T GEROULD

Luther King Jr. The city is now home to the Center for Nonviolent Change founded to continue Dr. King's work, as well as to the Carter Presidential Center at Emory University, the location of former President Jimmy Carter's projects in conflict resolution, human rights concerns, and global health issues.

Another Atlanta sobriquet is the "City of Trees" because of the abundance of forest remaining in its urban landscape. Some trees in DeKalb County's Fernbank Forest that shaded Olympic visitors in 1996 were standing when

tion decreed not only the importance of transportation, but also an incredibly rich bounty of plants. Because of Atlanta's altitude—1,050 ft above sea level—and its temperate climate, both warm-weather and cool-weather plants flourish in the area. Given this variety of vegetation, the citizenry has naturally responded with a broad and energetic civic interest in gardening.

Atlanta was originally known as the "Gate City" because its land transportation facilities provided access to the entire southeastern

left: **Lake Clara Meer is the central feature of Piedmont Park, a peaceful area in the midst of Atlanta's busy midtown district.**

right: **Atlanta's skyline has changed dramatically in recent years with the construction of numerous skyscrapers.**

Stephen Long surveyed the area in the 1830s, nearly 60 years before the inauguration of the modern Olympic Games in 1896. The city's spring-flowering dogwood trees are legendary for their beauty.

Trees comprise only one part of Atlanta's botanical heritage. Geography has molded the city's destiny in two important ways. Its loca-

United States. In the latter part of this century, with its international and domestic air service, the city has been dubbed "Gateway to the World." In 1996, the current shifted dramatically, and Atlanta became a "Gateway for the World," greeting the millions of visitors from around the globe who attended the XXVIth

• ROBERT A GERRITZ • DOUGLAS S GERRY • TERRY THELMA G GERSHON • ANN S GERSNA • KIMBERLY B GERSON • MAURY I GERSON • SHELLEY L GERSON • STACI GERSON • MARSHALL S GERSTEL • SUSAN K GERSTEL • ERWIN L GERSTENBERGER • LINDA S GERSTENBERGER • ROSEMARIE M GERSTENBERGER • JULIE M GERTH • BRANDI M GERWICK • MELISSA I GESCHWIND • RACHEL S GESCHWIND • ANDREW GESKIE • HARRIETT M GESS • PETER L GESS • TIMOTHY R GESS • DEBRA F GETER • VICKYE W GETER • ARLENE M GETMAN • MARY A GETTER • MELISSA S GETTIS • LAURA K GETTLER • CYNTHIA P GETTY •

top: The Georgia State Capitol building is easy to find in Atlanta's crowded skyline because of its golden dome.

bottom: Atlanta's Botanical Garden showcases the beauty, variety, and design of Georgia gardens.

Olympiad. The world came to Atlanta—some people literally and billions more by television—for 17 days of pageantry, cultural celebration, and splendid athletic competition.

As host city for the Centennial Olympic Games, Atlanta once again welcomed all comers to its environs—its homes, schools and colleges, businesses, cultural and social institutions, parks and public spaces, highways and byways, and fields of play. Atlanta and Atlantans embraced with open arms and open hearts the dreams of the individual athletes, the aspirations of the 197 delegations they represented, and the hopes of all supporters of the Olympic Movement.

top: Woodruff Park in downtown Atlanta is named for the man whose contributions provided the foundation for many of Atlanta's cultural institutions.

bottom: The trees that line the streets of Atlanta's neighborhoods and fill its public spaces have earned the city the sobriquet, "City of Trees."

Atlanta 1996®

THOMAS A GIAMMATTEO • CATHERINE GIANARO • ELIZABETH A GIANNINI • DEBORAH A GIAQUINTO • CATHERINE M GIARRUSSO • KRISTEN L GIBB • KWABENA C GIBB • PAUL C GIBB • DONNA L GIBBAS • HENLEY F GIBBLE • ANNE M GIBBONS • BARBARA A GIBBONS • GRANT W GIBBONS • MELISSA M GIBBONS • DONALD J GIBBS • HEATHER J GIBBS • KATHLEEN L GIBBS • LINDA C GIBBS • LORI M GIBBS • MICHAEL A. GIBBS • MIRIAM J GIBBS • STEVEN G GIBBS • TRACY L GIBBS • TRACY T GIBBY • ADRIAN D GIBSON • ALICIA GIBSON • AMANDA K GIBSON • AMANDA M GIBSON • AMY L GIBSON • ANDY GIBSON •

SPREADING THE OLYMPIC SPIRIT

27 APRIL 1996

Los Angeles, California, to Huntington Beach, California

The fog is dense this morning as the *Centennial Spirit* MD-11 Delta Air Lines jet touches down at Los Angeles International Airport. When the plane taxies to a stop, the mayor of Athens and several Hellenic Olympic Committee officials disembark with ACOG CEO Billy Payne, who is carrying the Olympic flame in a ceremonial lantern. Waiting on the tarmac to greet them are members of ACOG's senior management group. A large audience watches on television screens at the Los Angeles Memorial Coliseum as the flame

stands beneath the site of the Olympic cauldrons of 1932 and 1984 with the container that holds the flame for the 1996 Games.

Payne touches a torch to the Olympic flame and then triumphantly turns to light the first ceremonial cauldron in the US. A round of welcoming speeches builds on the excitement of the moment, and then Nita Whitaker and a choir of Los Angeles youth rouse the audience with an emotional rendition of "Power of the Dream," while Rafer Johnson—the final torchbearer in 1984—lifts a torch to the cauldron. With his torch aflame, he runs through the ranks of 197 children, each

left: **Greek high priestess Maria Pambouki ignites the flame from the rays of the sun in Olympia, Greece.**

right: **Billy Payne disembarks from the *Centennial Spirit* carrying the Olympic flame in a ceremonial lantern.**

and its entourage board a helicopter for the short flight to the stadium.

The University of Southern California Band launches into a musical welcome, performing "Summon the Heroes," a new work by John Williams composed for the Centennial Olympic Games which will be played during the daily Torch Relay celebrations held en route to Atlanta. Maria Pambouki, the Greek high priestess who kindled the flame from the sun almost a month ago,

one proudly holding aloft the flag of the participating delegations of the Centennial Olympic Games.

When Johnson reaches the street outside the coliseum, he passes the flame to Gina Hemphill—the same person who passed the flame to him in 1984. From Hemphill, the flame is passed to Olympic gold medalist Janet Evans, who will also be one of the final torchbearers during the Opening Ceremony in Atlanta.

For the remainder of this first day of the Torch Relay, the Olympic flame is carried through the streets of Los Angeles, through neighborhoods and business districts, and past the Los Angeles Amateur Athletic Foundation, where Anita de Frantz, IOC Executive Board member,

KANGELA B GIBSON • ANNA M GIBSON • AURELIUS B GIBSON • BRIDGETT S GIBSON • CARA L GIBSON • CARLETON B GIBSON • CAROL GIBSON • CAROL A GIBSON • CHERYL A GIBSON • CHEVONNE L GIBSON • CLAUDE T GIBSON • COREY L GIBSON • DAVID S GIBSON • DENISE L GIBSON • DONN A GIBSON • DONNA W GIBSON • ELAINE W GIBSON • ELIZABETH A GIBSON • FAE M GIBSON • GERARD GIBSON • HERBERT J GIBSON • JACQUELINE A GIBSON • JAMES D GIBSON • JENNIE L GIBSON • JENNIFER A GIBSON • JESSE L GIBSON • JOHN E GIBSON • JOYA GIBSON • KAREN A GIBSON • KATHRYN H GIBSON •

Rafer Johnson, the first torchbearer in the 1996 Torch Relay, runs through a corridor of children holding flags representing the 197 participating delegations to the Olympic Games.

hosts a celebration. Wherever the torch goes, crowds gather along the roadside, cheering and waving flags and memorabilia from the 1984 Games.

As the sun sets on the Pacific Ocean, the Torch Relay reaches the sea and then moves onto the Santa Monica Pier for the first of hundreds of community celebrations that will mark its course through the US.

During the night, the Olympic flame winds its way along the dramatic California coastline. Flanking it on all sides is the caravan of support vehicles that will accompany the torch throughout its historic journey to Atlanta.

In Huntington Beach, California, well-wishers celebrate the flame's imminent arrival with a community breakfast, and as the torchbearer comes into view at 5:00 a.m., the cheering crowd forms an arch of surfboards to guide the runner onto a stage to light the ceremonial cauldron.

Atlanta, Georgia—83 days to the Games

Thousands of people in Atlanta pause this afternoon, putting their Olympic preparations on hold to turn their televisions to a special, nationwide broadcast of the arrival of the Olympic Torch in Los Angeles. When regular programming resumes, so does the myriad of activities and events aimed at getting Atlanta ready for the start of the 1996 Olympic Games.

Even today, a Saturday, construction crews are hard at work building facilities for the Games, as the 40 hour workweek has ceased to be the norm. While the Olympic Stadium, Georgia Tech Aquatic Center, Morehouse College Gymnasium, and Stone Mountain Park Tennis Center are nearly finished, other projects, including temporary installations for archery and track cycling and Centennial Olympic Park are little more than half complete.

Dozens of major improvements to the city's infrastructure are also moving toward completion. Pedestrian walkways, plazas, and parks are being created in the downtown area, and a $200 million expansion of Hartsfield Atlanta International Airport has been undertaken to provide more parking decks, baggage carousels, shops, and wayfinding systems.

Within the Olympic Ring, hundreds of citizens are taking part in weekend cleanup, beautification, and community service projects that will continue throughout the spring. Vacant lots are being cleaned and landscaped, and houses in neighborhoods around venues are being freshly painted. One especially ambitious project is the construction of 30 new homes near Olympic Stadium—built by volunteers over a series of weekends from March through June—that will be rented during the Games and subsequently sold to families who might not otherwise be able to afford a home.

At ACOG offices, the staff of the Ticket Sales Department is on duty 12 hours a day selling tickets to previously sold-out sessions and to the start and finish of the men's marathon. Some 250,000 newly available tickets went on sale this morning via phone and—in an Olympic first— on the World Wide Web. Additional tickets became available when review of final venue layouts revealed certain seats no longer had to be eliminated because of possible obstructed views.

Beautification takes place throughout the Centennial Olympic Park, as well as in public gathering places and walkways throughout Atlanta.

KENNETH B GIBSON • LORRAINE A GIBSON • LUKE R GIBSON • MARGURITE GIBSON • MYRNA S GIBSON • NICHOLAS S GIBSON • PHILIP K GIBSON • RACHEL C GIBSON • RONNIE GIBSON • SANDY Y GIBSON • SARAH M GIBSON • STEVEN P GIBSON • WALTER H GIBSON • WAYNE S GIBSON • JOSEPH A GIBSON JR • WILLIAM L GIBSON JR • HUEY D GIDDENS • JOEL E GIDDENS • MICHELE J GIDDENS • MARCIA Y GIDDINGS DEBARROS • DAWN M GIDNER • JAMIESON J GIEFER • CHRISTINA E GIELER • SOREN GIELOV • JENNIFER D GIENGER • WILLIAM E GIERS • LETHA A GIES • PATRICIA M GIESEKE • GEOFFREY W GIESEMANN •

1 MAY 1996

Las Vegas

top: **The Torch Relay caravan crosses Hoover Dam to enter the state of Nevada.**

bottom: **The Union Pacific train brings the flame across the US Southwest aboard a specially designed cauldron car.**

Kingman, Arizona, to Las Vegas, Nevada

The Olympic flame starts today's journey on famous Route 66 in the city of Kingman, Arizona. From there, the Torch Relay sweeps through the desert of northern Arizona, passing within just a few miles of the rim of the Grand Canyon.

The next stop is Hoover Dam—one of the nation's engineering marvels. At this enormous hydroelectric facility, the largest US flag in the world is unfurled against the face of the dam.

Four-time Olympic gold medalist Martha Watson carries the flame across the dam and into Nevada just before noon, as temperatures soar past 100°F (38°C). At the state line, representatives from both Arizona and Nevada await the arrival of the torch, which signals the start of a historic celebration.

Many miles and hours later, in Henderson, Nevada, the Torch Relay is greeted by the contestants in the Miss Universe Pageant. A late-afternoon ceremony at this international gathering celebrates the Olympic Spirit.

Tonight in Las Vegas, the arrival of the Olympic flame is the main attraction. Lights along the famous Las Vegas strip are turned off shortly after dusk, while a crowd of 300,000 witnesses one of the Torch Relay's most dramatic arrivals.

As the flame turns onto Fremont Street in the downtown area, still another crowd—this time some 250,000 strong—waits under a sparkling canopy of laser lights and fireworks.

After the ceremonial cauldron lighting and festivities, a torchbearer carries the flame onto a 19-car Union Pacific train, specially equipped with a cauldron car. This flatbed car displays the ceremonial cauldron, to allow this glowing symbol of the Olympic Games to remain in view at all times for the crowds who line sections of the tracks and stations along the way. This overnight, whistle-stop journey marks the first of many rail trips that will light up America's countryside from the southwest desert, through the Pacific Northwest, past the Great Salt Lake, and over the Rocky Mountains' Pikes Peak.

JERI M GIESLER • BRIAN K GIFFIN • KELLEY V GIFFIN • DAVID W GIFFORD • JOAN C GIFFORD • TONYA L GIFFORD • IVEY GIGLIO • MARTHA JEANE GIGLIO • PATRICIA L GIGLIOLI • MAUREEN GIGLIOTTI • ALEJANDRO GIL • ANA GIL • LESLIE GIL • MARC A GILBAR • DAPHNE M GILBERRY • ARMITTA E GILBERT • BONNIE J GILBERT • BRUCE M GILBERT • CAROL C GILBERT • CHARLES F GILBERT • CHARLOT GILBERT • CHERYL N GILBERT • DASHONZA GILBERT • DAVID J GILBERT • DEBBIE L GILBERT • HEATHER K GILBERT • JOYCE A GILBERT • KATHARINE T GILBERT • KATHRYN L GILBERT • MARLAND D GILBERT

Atlanta, Georgia—79 days to the Games

Most of the world will see the 1996 Olympic Games on television. To prepare for 17 days of almost continuous action, representatives of the more than 170 broadcast networks that will air the Games have begun arriving in Atlanta to preview the plans and facilities that will be critical to their coverage. Over the course of several days, the broadcasters will attend briefings by ACOG management and tour many of the sports venues to examine the broadcasting areas, camera positions, and lighting arrangements. They will also visit the Georgia World Congress Center, which will house the 500,000 sq ft (46,500 sq m) International Broadcast Center. This enormous maze of studios and editing facilities will be the largest broadcast center in the world when it begins operating in early July.

At every facility throughout Atlanta, finishing touches for the Games are being applied. Crews have begun to install the first of more than 24 mi (38.6 km) of temporary fencing to demarcate various venue areas. Entrances are being equipped with freestanding pillars and additional gates. Outside the venues, monumental banners displaying the sport pictograms are also being placed.

The plaza that has been created between Atlanta–Fulton County Stadium and the newly constructed Olympic Stadium is receiving its final coats of paint. The bright teals and blues used are taking the form of the distinctive Quilt of Leaves pattern that is the official Look of the 1996 Games.

Planning for the Opening and Closing Ceremonies is well under way, with hundreds of volunteers working daily in a huge warehouse near Olympic Stadium, painting props and sewing the more than 5,000 costumes that will be required. At the stadium, members of the ceremonies team are plotting the precise layout and movement of people and props for more than six hours of Opening Ceremony programming. Temporary structures are being built at the stadium and more than 4,000 additional lights are being installed. A rehearsal schedule with biweekly, four-hour sessions has been created and sent to the more than 9,000 individuals—from high school cheerleaders and band members to dance troupes and singing groups—who have been selected to participate after a series of auditions held during the past six months.

Students at almost every elementary and middle school in Georgia are also preparing for the Games. Their teachers have just received the fifth and final annual installment of ACOG's specially developed curriculum on the Olympic Games.

Earlier programs had presented various aspects of the history of the Games, sports, and participating countries. Now, with the 1996 Games just a short time away, this year's focus is on what the students will soon see: the ceremonial elements of the Games, competition formats and schedules, and the events of the Olympic Arts Festival.

Already open to the public—and drawing record crowds each day—is *Olympic Games Quilts: Georgia's Welcome to the World*, organized to showcase the 394 quilts made to present to the NOCs when they arrive at Olympic Village. These quilts, stitched by some 2,000 Georgia quilters, will be displayed at the Atlanta History Center until the end of May.

top: **Opening Ceremony cast members try out their butterfly costumes for the first time.**

bottom: **Crowds in the Atlanta History Center wait in line to see *Olympic Games Quilts: Georgia's Welcome to the World*.**

• MICHAEL D GILBERT • NATASHA GILBERT • ROBERT S GILBERT • RONALD S GILBERT • THELMA W GILBERT • WALTER O GILBERT • DAWNA L GILBERT ATC • DARYL M GILBERTSON • KATHERINE S GILBERTSON • EDWARD M GILCHRIST • JAMES E GILCHRIST • ROCHELLE GILDAR • ASHLEY A GILES • BLAKE GILES • CHARLES K GILES • CHERYL L GILES • DEBBIE F GILES • PAMELA K GILES • RAFER A GILES • RENEE E GILES • STEVEN A GILES • WALTER GILES • WENDI P GILES • GAIL P GILFILLAN • AMANDA S GILL • BALDIP S GILL • CAMILA A GILL • DEBRA S GILL • ELIZABETH GILL • KIRTAN K GILL

17 MAY 1996

Wichita

top left: The flame is carried on horseback across the Great Plains by riders from the National Pony Express Association.

top right: Bicyclists bring the flame through the rolling cornfields of Kansas.

bottom: Chief Eugene Stumbling Bear carries the flame toward a cauldron at the foot of the giant sculpture known as the Keeper of the Plains.

Topeka, Kansas, to Wichita, Kansas

In three weeks, the Torch Relay has traveled more than 4,000 mi (6,437 km) on its journey from Los Angeles to Olympic Stadium in Atlanta, and momentum and anticipation for the approaching Games are building with each new segment of the trip. Having traveled as far north as Seattle, Washington, and then across the Great Divide, the flame stopped in Colorado Springs, Colorado, home of the US Olympic Committee, where it received a rousing welcome from officials and Olympians training for the Games.

Since then, the flame has been carried by train, runner, cyclist, and on horseback across the Great Plains of the US. Riders from the National Pony Express Association rode for more than 56 continuous hours, carrying the flame as well as commemorative letters to deliver to patients in a children's hospital.

Today's trek begins with a celebration on the grounds of the state capitol in Topeka. The morning is still young when the Olympic flame leaves the city for a journey through the rolling cornfields of central Kansas, where high winds, gusting up to 40 mph (64 kmph), do not delay its steady progress.

At a brief stop in Eskridge, Kansas, a crowd of 3,000—more than three times the town's population—lines the main street. Dozens of schoolchildren clutch a colorful array of balloons that flutter back and forth in the still-gusting winds.

In Emporia, Kansas, the Torch Relay makes a longer stop at the Teachers Hall of Fame to celebrate educators and their contributions to the lives of children. Native American hero and Olympic great Billy Mills speaks to a cheering audience, encouraging all to strive to realize their dreams.

Later this afternoon, the Torch Relay makes another stop, this time in Newton, where the coming of the Olympic flame has inspired residents to refurbish a park and restore the historical locomotive at its center. Such remarkable displays of civic pride and enthusiasm will be seen again and again across the US, as cities prepare to salute the Olympic flame by creating or refurbishing public facilities, memorials, and other public works.

The Torch Relay reaches the city of Wichita at the end of the day and becomes part of Riverfest, an annual citywide celebration. With more than 100,000 people gathered along the banks of the Arkansas River, the

Olympic flame is passed to Chief Eugene Stumbling Bear. This well-known community figure paddles a traditional Native American canoe across the river as hundreds of loudspeakers resound with "Summon the Heroes."

After the canoe glides to a stop at a peninsula, the torch is passed to a torchbearer on shore who ignites a cauldron at the foot of a giant sculpture known as the Keeper of the Plains. As the day comes to an end, hundreds of performers demonstrate native dances and songs in a celebration that honors both the Olympic flame and Native American traditions.

• MICHAEL S GILL • MICHELLE M GILL • MONICA A GILL • PENNY W GILL • PHYDESIA GILL • ROGER F GILL • SANDRA E GILL • SUE H GILL • T J GILL • RUSSELL B GILL ATC • EMMETT L GILL JR • KATHY A GILLCRIST • EDWARD D GILLEN • RICHARD D GILLEN • WILLIAM B GILLEN • SHANNON L GILLEON • BONNIE A GILLESPIE • CAROL T GILLESPIE • CHRIS A GILLESPIE • CYNTHIA D GILLESPIE • DANIEL J GILLESPIE • ELIZABETH A GILLESPIE • JAMES C GILLESPIE • JAMES S GILLESPIE • JENNIFER L GILLESPIE • KENNETH M. GILLESPIE • KYLE V GILLESPIE • LARRY GILLESPIE • MARYANN F GILLESPIE •

Atlanta, Georgia—63 days to the Games

Olympic Stadium is now ready for its debut. The centerpiece of the 1996 Olympic Games will be put to the test as a premier athletics facility tomorrow, during the International Amateur Athletic Federation's Atlanta Grand Prix. This one-day event has drawn the world's top athletes, who are eager to try out the new facility before Olympic competition begins in July.

First, Olympic Stadium is put on display this evening during a celebration that includes IOC President Juan Antonio Samaranch and members of the IOC Coordination Commission for the 1996 Games who are in Atlanta for a final review of preparations. On cue, the huge banks of lights on the six towers that encircle the stadium blink on, casting a bright glow on its 85,000 blue spectator seats and 400 m of oval red track.

Tomorrow's competition will prove that the stadium is as good as it looks. Spectator seats are comfortable and well-positioned, providing splendid views of the field of play. Athletes praise the track for its hard surface, and predict record times on what is being called the fastest track in the world.

While the athletes are trying out the new track and other facilities, a convoy of 20 trucks loaded with the 228 tons (207 t) of steel that is the Olympic cauldron approaches Olympic Stadium. The trucks are on their way from Minnesota, where the 116 ft (35.4 m) tower and 21 ft (6.4 m) burner has been fully assembled and tested near the home of its designer, Siah Armajani.

Work on reconstructing the cauldron, which is to be located adjacent to Olympic Stadium, is scheduled to begin on Monday, 20 May, and will continue for four weeks until the massive structure is finally completed.

Across town, the 251 water jets installed in the Fountain of Rings at Centennial Olympic Park are being synchronized for the daily water and music shows that will become a crowd favorite. More than 10,000 sq ft (930 sq m) of grass has been installed for the park's center

lawn, and 30,000 of the 300,000 inscribed bricks that will be used for paths and walkways are already in place. The park buzzes with the sounds of bulldozers, heavy equipment trucks, and forklifts, 12–14 hours a day, seven days a week, as construction progresses on dozens of temporary food and entertainment pavilions and support facilities.

With the opening of *Rings: Five Passions in World Art* less than two months away, world masterpieces are arriving at the High Museum of Art. Exhibition teams carefully uncrate priceless works of art ranging from small paintings and bronzes to massive wall hangings and sculptures for placement throughout the museum's galleries.

top: Flags representing the delegations that will participate in the 1996 Games are carried as part of the celebration for the opening of Olympic Stadium.

bottom: Bricks, bearing the names and messages of the people who contributed to the park effort, are in place for the opening of Centennial Olympic Park.

NATHAN R GILLESPIE • PATRICK D GILLESPIE • SHARI A GILLESPIE • WILL GILLESPIE • ERIC D GILLET • DAVID E GILLETT • PAMELIA GILLETT • RICHARD C GILLETT • DONALD R. GILLETTE • JOHN J GILLETTE • ROBERT L GILLETTE • ELIZABETH A GILLEY • ELLA SUE J GILLEY • SEAN S GILLEY • TRAVIS L GILLEY • DARYL M GILLIAM • FREDDIE W GILLIAM • GWENDOLYN GILLIAM • JONIQUE N GILLIAM • KATRINA E GILLIAM • MARY A GILLIAM • STEVEN P GILLIAM • SUSAN L GILLIAM • CHAILA GILLIAMS • LOU GILLIARD • CHRISTOPHER T GILLIGAN • THOMAS G GILLIGAN • TARYN G GILLIKIN • WALTER R GILLIKIN •

3 JUNE 1996

Milwaukee, Wisconsin, to Gary, Indiana

After kindling the Olympic Spirit across the Great Plains, the Olympic flame moves on, traveling south to Oklahoma and the birthplace of Jim Thorpe, one of the world's greatest athletes and Olympians. From there, the Torch Relay traveled through Texas, Louisiana, Missouri, and Kentucky, in a journey that included a ride on a paddlewheel steamer.

On this early summer morning, the train that has traveled some 3,500 mi (5633 km) in the past 30 days departs Milwaukee, Wisconsin, on its way to Chicago, Illinois, with the Olympic flame clearly visible aboard

celebration. The Olympic flame is handed over to the first of 106 Greek youths who were selected by the Hellenic Olympic Committee to participate in a historic exchange program sponsored by ACOG. The young people, who have already toured Atlanta and Chicago with Greek-American hosts, have come to the US especially for this moment. In a symbolic tribute to the Greek origins of the Olympic Movement, they pass the Olympic torch from one to another around the perimeter of the amphitheater before the cauldron on the stage is lit.

Later, the flame makes its way to the University of Chicago campus, where Pierre de Coubertin attended

left: **ACOG staff members traveling with the Torch Relay greet crowds in Milwaukee from the platform of the cauldron car.**

right: **Crowds in Chicago's Grant Park hail the torch as it approaches Petrillo Bandstand for a special celebration.**

the cauldron car. Thousands of people wait along railroad tracks and at six whistle-stop stations. This final segment of train travel will be celebrated by more than half a million people.

Upon arrival in Chicago, the flame is taken by torchbearers into the city's Greektown and then along the section of Michigan Avenue known as the Magnificent Mile. On its route, the Torch Relay passes the Water Tower building, the only public structure to survive the Great Chicago Fire of 1871.

A crowd of more than 500,000 cheers the flame's passage through Chicago to Petrillo Bandstand in Grant Park, where the Torch Relay pauses for a special

the World's Fair of 1893 and found the site he would advocate for the 1904 Olympic Games.

The day ends in Gary, Indiana, where citizens join with state leaders to welcome the Olympic flame, which in this industrial town is also a symbol of rebirth and renewed growth.

Atlanta, Georgia—46 days to the Games

More than 311,000 packets of Olympic tickets are on their way to spectators around the country in what Olympic sponsor United Parcel Service is calling one of its largest-ever express delivery efforts for high-value shipments. A specially created computer tracking system and extra security measures have been designed to ensure that the tickets will be delivered promptly and safely.

Just a few weeks ago, another enormous delivery effort was made to get Olympic training materials into the hands of more than 35,000 volunteers. Now, the home study courses—complete with introductory videotape and notebooks providing detailed information on the 1996 Games—are being put to use in preparation for a series of venue orientations and job training sessions that are scheduled almost daily throughout June.

Thousands of telephone calls are being placed to volunteers from ACOG offices to confirm job assignments and schedules as each departmental area completes its staff rosters. The downtown accreditation center is operating 16 hours per day, seven days a week, so that as many volunteers and staff as possible can pick up their Games credentials before the arrival of athletes and officials.

Just outside downtown, ACOG has opened the uniform distribution center, where the majority of Games staff will come to receive their uniforms. Weeks of work have gone into stocking the 90,000 sq ft (8,370 sq m) warehouse with almost 1 million uniform pieces—including belts and hats, ties and scarves, shoes and socks, blouses and shirts, pants and skirts, and jackets and rain gear. A series of stations spread throughout the center allow about 200 people per hour to try on and pick up the uniforms assigned to them. In all, ACOG has created 67 different types of uniforms—based on different job descriptions—to clothe some 70,000 staff and officials.

Volunteers and visitors alike are flocking to the superstore in Centennial Olympic Park to get the latest Games merchandise. The huge store—covering more than 38,000 sq ft (3,534 sq m) and carrying the largest collection of Olympic products and memorabilia ever offered in one

location—has been attracting ever-growing crowds since it opened for business several weeks ago. Among the most popular items are T-shirts and caps, but no product is selling faster than Olympic pins.

Construction is still under way at the park, and installation of temporary facilities for the Games has moved into high gear now that the Georgia Dome and Georgia World Congress Center—where almost one-fourth of all competition events will take place—have been designated for ACOG's sole use.

In all, temporary facilities have required an investment of more than $30 million for items ranging from bleacher seats and tents to air-conditioning units and comfort stations. With little more than a month before the start of the Games, these items are being moved from ACOG's central warehouse to more than 30 different locations in the Atlanta area.

At the same time, thousands of pieces of sports equipment, furniture, and technology items—more than 1 million sq ft (93,000 sq m) of material—are arriving at the warehouse and being sorted by venue. They will later be loaded onto trucks destined for various Games locations.

Spring rains and warm temperatures have already done their job, ensuring that thousands of areas, along Atlanta streets and roadways and in office parks and residential neighborhoods, are sprouting plantings that are the official colors of the Games. Free brochures distributed earlier this year had provided information on creating the landscape plans of Quiltscape, an ACOG program to spread the Look of the Games across the city and beyond.

top: Games-time staff check out of the uniform distribution center.

bottom: ACOG's downtown accreditation center is busy as staff, volunteers, contractors, and media receive their badges.

7 JUNE 1996

Cincinnati, Ohio, to Columbus, Ohio

As a light rain falls at Fountain Square in downtown Cincinnati, the Olympic Torch Relay begins on this day that marks the halfway point of the 84-day journey to Atlanta. Running through rain for most of the morning, the torchbearers carry the flame into the open countryside of southern Ohio. In one small town after another, the flame is welcomed by families gathered along highways that cut through miles of farmland.

At day's end, the Torch Relay reaches Columbus, where more than 1 million people are gathered for

Atlanta, Georgia—42 days to the Games

The towering Olympic cauldron, now completed with the placement of the 8 ton (7.3 t) metal vessel that will hold the Olympic flame during the Games, has already become a popular backdrop for photographs by Atlanta residents and visitors alike. The cauldron is one of several pieces of public art commissioned by the Cultural Olympiad that are changing the city landscape. The work of the Cultural Olympiad can also be seen in the exhibitions and special programs of the Olympic Arts Festival. They offer

left: **Staff unloads luggage at a hotel that will serve as the operational headquarters for the next day.**

The Olympic cauldron and tower are assembled and connected to Olympic Stadium.

the annual Columbus Arts Festival. The Olympic flame is brought to the steps of City Hall, where a cauldron is lit and the evening sky over the Ohio River shimmers with a spectacular fireworks display.

Later tonight, many of the 320 people traveling with the Torch Relay hold their own special tribute to a successful first half of the journey to Atlanta. Drivers of the caravan of cars, trucks, buses, and motorcycles, together with advance managers, logistics staff, celebration crews, Georgia State Patrol staff, escorts, and others, gather for precious moments of relaxation, renewing their energies for the second half of this historic trip.

something for every taste, from the highly appropriate *Ways of Welcoming: Greeting Rituals from Around the World* to displays of the work of regional and international artists.

Most work will be available to visitors throughout the Games and beyond, but some are setting the stage for the Games—like the International Celebration of Southern Literature. Now in its second day, the four-day conference is being held in collaboration with Agnes Scott

CYNTHIA R GIPSON • ELLA M GIPSON • FRED M GIPSON • JEFFREY GIPSON • LEROY GIPSON • LOUISE S GIPSON • PHYLENE GIPSON • ALFONSO GIRALDO • GARY A GIRASOLE • MARIENE GIRDIS • DAVID C GIRLING • BERHANE A GIRMAY • LEISA B GIROUARD • HEATHER M GIRVIN • JULIO GISMERO • CHRISTINE M GISNESS • LEILA M GIST • RICHARD S GITOMER MD • MARGARET MARY GITTENS • WILLIAM P GITTINGS • LINDA F GIUDICE • GIANFRANCO FRANK J GIUSTA • CARLA A GIVAN • TOMMY A GIVAN • BARBARA GIVENS • LEIGH GIVENS • LETHA D GIVENS • STEUE M GIVENS • JAMES L GLADDEN • RICK W GLADIS

College. The conference has attracted hundreds of people who are on hand to hear the region's leading authors and distinguished international scholars explore new perspectives on the literature and culture of the American South.

Construction is the most apparent Olympic activity. With the focus having shifted to temporary installations, enormous tents are being put in place. ACOG has plans to install 1 million sq ft (93,000 sq m) of tent space. Estimates indicate that 3–4 times more than that amount will be assembled for corporations and international delegations that have rented parking lots and vacant land to set up hospitality areas.

Installation of the security fence that will encircle the Olympic Village has also begun—and with it has come the first street closings. Businesses and residents in the area around the Village have been prepared for the changes to their daily routines via a series of neighborhood meetings, and they have been given special passes for access.

The entrances of all the Games venues will be adorned with large containers of flowers. The hundreds of required planters are already being assembled at Atlanta Botanical Gardens and other places. Staff and volunteers are carefully tending the plants—Lantana "New Gold," Ipomoen batatas "Blackie" (sweet potato vine), Pennisetum setaceum "Rubrum" (red fountain grass), Alternanthera "White Cloud," Artemisia "Pow's Castle," Scaevola "Blue Wonder," and Solenostemon scutellarloides (red trailing coleus)—to ensure that brilliantly colored blooms will be ready in time for the move to venues about one week before the Games.

At ACOG headquarters, staff members work doggedly to coordinate the travel schedules for more than 125,000 members of the Olympic Family—including athletes, officials, dignitaries, press, and broadcasters—into a master plan. The plan is essential to the successful deployment of staff and vehicles needed to ensure that each individual and group will be met at their arrival point, taken to an accreditation site, and then driven to their accommodations.

ACOG's Ticket Sales Department is finalizing preparations for the opening of the first Games box offices. Three of what will eventually be 30 locations will open tomorrow morning, offering all remaining tickets to sports and Olympic Arts Festival events. Hours before these facilities open, people are already standing in line.

Staff and volunteers tend plants that will be used at the venues as part of the Look of the Games.

• HOWARD D GLADSTEIN • JAMES GLADULICH • DAVID J GLADWIN • JAMES GLADWIN • FRANCES E GLAESER • MARIE T GLANCY • CELINE GLANTENAY • JORDANA L GLANTZ • ELLEN K GLANTZBERG • ANDREW GLANTZMAN • AMY S GLASER • ANN KARRICK GLASER • LORI M GLASER • TAMMY D GLASER • CALUM M GLASGOW • JENNIE GLASGOW • SANDRA L GLASGOW • SHARI A GLASKIN RN • JEFFREY R GLASNAPP • OTTO R GLASNAPP • ALINA GLASS • DAN GLASS • DEBRA B GLASS • GARY C GLASS • GEORGE A GLASS • JURENA GLASS • MESHAWN L GLASS • PRISCILLA B GLASS • SUSAN J GLASS • GEORGE C GLASS MT •

12 JUNE 1996

Niagara Falls, New York, to Syracuse, New York

Even though the morning mist is heavy, rays of sunlight sparkle on the rushing waters of Niagara Falls. The fog breaks as a lone torchbearer holds the Olympic flame aloft and crosses Goat Island against a backdrop of cascading water. From this dramatic site, the Torch Relay moves on to quieter waters, as runners follow the path of the Erie Canal through the town of Lockport and across New York State.

A midday celebration in downtown Rochester concludes just as a tremendous thunderstorm begins.

The fog hanging over Niagara Falls breaks as a torchbearer crosses Goat Island holding the flame aloft.

Despite the driving rain, the flame continues on its eastward journey. Upon its arrival in the village of Camillus late this afternoon, the flame is taken aboard a newly constructed replica of a 19th-century mule-drawn packet boat. The torch, now waterborne, is pulled along a 2 mi (3.2 km) stretch of the old Erie Canal that has been restored especially for this brief but extraordinary journey.

As the Olympic flame travels on to historic Syracuse, the city and its citizens prepare to conclude another day of the Torch Relay with an evening of fireworks, music, and celebration.

Atlanta, Georgia—37 days to the Games

This morning, Atlanta drivers notice the sudden appearance of a long blue line amidst the white and yellow lane markers. The 26.2 mi (42.2 km) streak was painted yesterday—a Sunday—to demarcate the most direct course for participants in the Olympic marathon. A team of volunteers completed the work in just three hours, during which they spread 115 gal (435 l) of paint. A few gallons more are available for the last-minute retouches that will be done the night before each competition to fill in gaps caused by street repairs, repaving, and routine wear.

More symbols of the Games are evident at the Georgia World Congress Center, where workers are placing the Olympic Rings in each of five enormous windows. Standing 35 ft (10.7 m) high and spanning 170 ft (52 m) across, the rings are a highly visible statement that the facility will be one of the centers of Olympic activity during the Games.

Colors of green and gold are featured on the 4,000 yd (3,658 m) of specially created ribbon that has arrived at ACOG headquarters and must now be attached to the 2,600 gold, silver, and bronze medals that will be awarded during the Games. All the medals have been cast in the unique design created for the 1996 Games. The front—the obverse side—reflects the traditional elements for the Olympic Games that have been in use since 1928, with a partial border of delicate leaves added in honor of the Centennial Games. The reverse side, following tradition, is a unique design—this time featuring the torch logo and Quilt of Leaves and, in an Olympic first, the pictogram of the sport for which the medal is won. Because of the sport-specific design, ACOG has prepared protected packages for each venue based on the competitions being presented there.

Victory certificates will be given to athletes who place first through eighth in competition. Approximately 11,000 have been prepared and are being sorted prior to their delivery to the venues. Also ready for packaging and distribution are 50,000 commemorative medals that

JEFFRY L GLASSBURN • LARA GLASSCOCK • KAREN B GLASSER • ALISON GLASSMAN • JUDITH D GLASSMAN • KAY T GLATZER • MAURICE GLATZER • DONALD E GLAZE • JENNIFER J GLAZE • MARY KAY GLAZE • JAN K GLAZER • SIDNEY GLAZER • DAVID J GLAZNER • JAMES E GLEASON • KRISTI M GLEASON • RACHEL E GLEASON • EARL GLEATON • LAURA A GLEATON • WILLIAM F GLEBUS • CAROLINE GLEEKSMAN • DAVID H GLEESON • MARIA C GLEN • BEATRICE M GLENN • BRADLEY A GLENN • BRIAN A GLENN • CAROL L GLENN • JAMES GLENN • JEFFREY C GLENN • LIBBY M GLENN • LISA L GLENN • MARCIA W GLENN

will be given to all athletes and Olympic Family members.

ACOG's Youth and Education Department is planning the final graduation ceremony of the Dream Team Program. Each year since Atlanta was awarded the Bid for the Games, 100 youth ambassadors have been selected from high schools throughout Georgia. In addition to serving as ACOG representatives at various functions, the young people have led community service projects in their hometowns. Many of the Dream Team members are also planning

Deadline pressures are being felt in every ACOG department. But nowhere is the countdown clock ticking more loudly than at the headquarters for Opening Ceremony production. The number of Opening Ceremony rehearsals has just been increased to four times a week at Olympic Stadium and a half-dozen other locations around the city. Buses always seem to be lining the streets around the rehearsal sites, bringing groups of participants from as far as 50 mi (80.5 km) away to the 2–4 hour sessions.

top: The obverse of the victory medals is cast in a design that employs the traditional elements used since the 1928 Games.

bottom: Tailors sew together the ends of the ribbon that supports a victory medal.

to serve as Games volunteers, with a large number requesting assignments at the International Youth Camp.

This program, which is the final project of the Youth and Education Department, is in its final stage of preparations to convert the camp location—at Berry College north of Atlanta—and to complete the curriculum materials and program plans in time for the arrival of the first camp participants in less than a month.

• MELTON SAMUEL GLENN • MICHELLE M GLENN • VICKI J GLENN • WALLACE A GLENN • COLIN M GLENNAN • RICHARD S GLENZER • BARBARA B GLESSNER • JAMES T GLESSON • ERIC R GLICK • SHERI L GLICK • IVAN M GLICKMAN • KIA GLIMPS • DAVID P GLISSON • JANIE W GLISSON • LINDA L GLISSON • PATRICK C GLISSON • WILLIAM GLISSON • SIGRID GLITSCHER • RICHARD S GLOCK • NANCY L GLODOWSKI • DANIEL P GLON • NICHOLAS J GLON • JEFFREY T GLOR • BRADLEY J GLOSSINGER • BRIAN W GLOTZBACH MT • ALICE M GLOVER • AMY GLOVER • ANDREA A GLOVER • AZALINE GLOVER •

14 JUNE 1996

Albany, New York, to Nashua, New Hampshire

It is Flag Day, and the Torch Relay is leaving Albany, the capital of New York State, to travel along the Hudson River through towns that trace their roots to the days of the American Revolution. In the riverside community of Troy, US flags and banners of red, white, and blue are carried by many of the thousands of people there to greet the arrival of the Olympic flame.

From this celebration, the Torch Relay turns toward the state of Vermont to visit Bennington, hometown of an American icon, the artist Grandma Moses. The streets of this southern Vermont town are packed with welcoming spectators who stand shoulder-to-shoulder as the Olympic flame is carried onto the rural path that crosses the Appalachian Trail and the lower White Mountains.

In Brattleboro, the Torch Relay passes through a popular reminder of America's past, a 200-year-old covered bridge. A wheelchair athlete brings the flame to a stop for a midday celebration, where 2,000 schoolchildren gather for an up-close look at the most recognizable symbol of the Olympic Games.

Some of the largest crowds yet wait in Nashua, New Hampshire, where approximately 1 million people line

top: On Flag Day, patriots salute the torch by waving US flags as it passes through the riverside community of Troy.

bottom: A torchbearer carries the flag through a crowd standing shoulder-to-shoulder in Bennington, the hometown of American icon, artist Grandma Moses.

the streets for the 15 mi (24 km) stretch that leads to a celebration in the heart of downtown. With the sun setting, one torchbearer after another proudly holds the flame high for all to see, and fireworks illuminate the darkening sky.

After the celebration in Nashua ends, the flame is placed in a safety lantern and carried by helicopter to Kittery, the oldest town in the state of Maine. Here, a 5 km relay begins with 10 torchbearers passing the flame from one to another until it is handed to a local ice hockey star who was injured and later rehabilitated in Atlanta.

CAROLYN E GLOVER • CATHERINE A GLOVER • DANIEL L GLOVER • DARLEAN GLOVER • DEBORAH M GLOVER • DELORES S GLOVER • DEVELLUS L GLOVER • ELYSE A GLOVER • GILBERT L GLOVER • GIUSEPPINA F GLOVER • GWENDOLYN GLOVER • JEANIE L GLOVER • JUANITA B GLOVER • LISA M GLOVER • MARIE K GLOVER • MARK A GLOVER • MARVYN B GLOVER • MICHAEL C GLOVER • SCOTT H GLOVER • SHARRON GLOVER • STEPHANIE D GLOVER • TERRANCE A GLOVER • TODD GLOVER • FRANK GLOVER SR • JACK Z GLOVER SR • JOSEPH GLOYD • LAURIE F GLUCK • EDWARD M GLYNN • BARBARA A GNADT

Atlanta, Georgia—35 days to the Games

Atlanta is being transformed into a much more pedestrian-friendly city with the help of about two dozen downtown projects. Walkways, plazas, small public parks, and public art installations are the cornerstones of a $75 million improvement program directed by the Corporation for Olympic Development in Atlanta (CODA). Established by the city of Atlanta in 1992, CODA has collected both public and private funding for projects that include the revitalization of inner-city neighborhoods.

Among the most significant projects realized through these efforts is the newly opened 6.2 mi (10 km) pedestrian walkway through the Atlanta University Center—the complex of six historically black colleges that will be home to three competition venues and several Olympic Arts Festival events. Like CODA's other new walkways, this pedestrian corridor is lined with decorative plazas, bus shelters, wayfinding signs, and places to sit.

Pedestrians will also benefit from the large signs throughout the Olympic Ring that CODA is installing, which display maps on one side and the historical context of the location—conveyed through text and photographs—on the other. The text on the 9 ft (2.7 m) structures is displayed in English, French, Japanese, and Spanish.

On a pair of bridges over an interstate highway that passes through Atlanta, CODA is also installing the highly distinctive, eye-catching Folk Art Park. A metal canopy stands at the entrance, and all around is an array of whirligigs, animal sculptures, and mini-environments that will showcase the work of 20 local artists and also provide an entertaining respite for spectators and visitors during the 1996 Games and for years to come.

Olympic Stadium is being put to its second test with the start of the US Olympic trials for track and field. The nine-day event will provide a thorough review of the facility and the plans for athletes and spectators alike, as well as on-the-job experience for hundreds of staff and volunteers.

An enormously popular feature of the new stadium is a warm-up track underneath the field of play, only a short distance from the entrance to the competition arena. The surface of the warm-up track is a duplicate of the one on the competition track, offering athletes an ideal place to prepare for competition. A number of other practice sites are easily accessible, including the facility at nearby Cheney Stadium, where the identical track surface has been laid. Other tracks have been installed or upgraded at six Atlanta-area high schools and colleges.

Around the city, shops are filled with just-released publications that preview virtually every aspect of the Games. The official souvenir program is earning admiring glances—and undoubtedly greater sales—thanks to a holographic cover with an Olympic torch that appears to flicker with light and movement.

top: Public artwork, such as Cristóbal Gabarrón's *Olympic Forest*, is installed along many Atlanta walkways through the efforts of CODA.

bottom: Sports volunteers train to place the hurdles for athletic events.

• JOAN M GNAT • RAYMOND G GNAT • JUDITH M GNIECH • FRANCIS E GOALEN • STEVEN A GOARD • THERESA A GOARD • LAWRENCE D GOARE • GARY L GOBER • JARVIS L GOBER • MARCIA GOBER • RHONDA L GOBER • RICHARD S GOBIN • BONNIE R GOBLE • BRYAN M GOBLE • BRYAN M GOBLE • ELMER GOBLE • DOROTA GOCH • EDSEL T GODBEY • ALAN GODDARD • ANNE L GODDARD • KAREN GODDARD • VICTORIA AMANDA GODDARD • JILL GODEKE • ALICE M GODFREY • ANNIE M GODFREY • CAIT GODFREY • CASSANDRA B GODFREY • CHARLENE S GODFREY • DANA B GODFREY • GAEL S GODFREY • MARTHAC GODFREY

27

15 JUNE 1996

Nashua, New Hampshire, to Providence, Rhode Island

Having left Nashua this morning, the Olympic Torch Relay is on course for Hopkinton, Massachusetts, the starting point for the Boston Marathon. Just two months ago, the famous race celebrated its 100th anniversary and its roots in the 1896 Games in Athens, during which athletes from Harvard University competed and were inspired to bring the marathon home to Boston.

The Torch Relay follows the marathon route into downtown Boston. Past winners of the Boston com-

The Torch Relay follows the route of the Boston Marathon into downtown Boston.

petition and community heroes serve as torchbearers on this journey that leads to City Hall Plaza. There, the Olympic flame is met by thousands of children who are taking part in a series of events and games designed to spur their interest in sports.

The celebration in Boston continues as the Torch Relay travels south to Rhode Island on a course that will pass by a large, well-protected foundry where more than 2,000 gold, silver, and bronze medals for the Centennial Olympic Games have been cast.

As night falls, the Olympic flame arrives in Providence. The city and its residents greet the flame with a celebration at the state capitol. Under a clear, starlit sky, the Olympic flame takes an honored place in an event that lasts well into the night.

Atlanta, Georgia—34 days to the Games

Nowhere are the Games more visible than at a fabrication shop and warehouse south of downtown Atlanta. The entire facility is devoted to the production of banners, backdrops, signs, and all the other elements that will convey the Look of the Games.

A significant area of the shop is occupied by a crew of six who are completing construction, painting, and application of design features to the victory stands where Olympic medalists will be honored. ACOG's design staff had planned

Staff at ACOG's fabrication shop and warehouse prepare sponsor banners decorated with the Look of the Games and torch mark logo for hanging along the streets throughout Atlanta.

for the stands to be three-part modular units—a taller, cylindrical part in the center for gold medalists, and slightly lower parts on either side for silver and bronze winners. The project became more complex as the maximum number and size of units were calculated to ensure that the right combination of units would be readily available for the medal ceremonies.

Things were further complicated when a complex plan to move victory stands from one venue to another was changed, and it was decided to produce a greater number of stands. In all, fourteen 12 ft (3.7 m) podiums, seven 24 ft (7.3 m) podiums, and two 72 ft (21.9 m) podiums were made, as well as one podium in each of four other sizes—36 ft (10.9 m), 48 ft (14.6 m), 96 ft (29.2 m), and 108 ft (32.9 m).

With more than a month remaining before the first medals will be presented, target dates

• MARY K GODFREY • MICHAEL D GODFREY • ROBERT C GODFREY • VENITA GODFREY • WILLIAM R GODFREY • WELDON S GODFREY III • ROBERT S GODHIGH • CARYN S GODIN • LINDA T GODIN • CYNTHIA GODINE • ANDREINA D GODOY • SAM J GODSALL • KATRINA V GODSHALL • EVE H GODSTEIN • ALLISON E GODWIN • BARBARA J GODWIN • JAMES W GODWIN • MARGARET J GODWIN • PAMELA B GODWIN • SHEILA H GODWIN • VIRGINIA GODWIN • YVONNE A GODWIN • CANDACE R GODWIN ATC • ELDON L GOEBEL • JAMES V GOEBEL • ANN D GOEHE • ANUPAM GOEL • MARSHA A GOEN • RUDOLPH B GOENNEWICH

for delivery to each venue have already been set to allow time for logistics crews to determine and rehearse the most efficient plan for moving the units on and off the fields of play.

How many? and how soon? are questions that dominate the planning of thousands of aspects of Games preparations. For example, while plans for distribution of victory stands are being made at the fabrication shop, the staff of the Protocol Department is determining which country flags will be sent to each venue. Venues will fly only the flags of the countries of the athletes or teams that will compete there, and an identical set must be available for medal ceremonies. From Olympic Stadium—where flags representing all 197 participating delegations will fly—to Wolf Creek, where athletes from 22 countries are scheduled to participate—early calculations indicate that a total of 6,000 country flags will be needed. This calculation was done long ago so that a sufficient supply of flags could be produced in time for the Games. Now, the task is to assemble the sets for each venue based on more up-to-date information from athlete and team participation lists.

Also being calculated is the number of official maps of the Games that will be shipped to each venue for distribution to spectators at public information booths. Production of the publication—which provides walking and driving instructions, along with maps showing each Games venue—was finalized in April to allow time for printing and delivery to an ACOG warehouse of the 5 million copies that will be needed. The maps have been received—arriving aboard 20 trucks—and are now being apportioned for shipment to each venue on the basis of a plan that will continue throughout the Games, since storage space in public information booths and at the venues will not accommodate more than a two- to three-day supply.

ACOG staff members at the headquarters and at venues are now working well into the night every day, seven days a week. The same degree of intensity seems to be mirrored throughout Atlanta and the other cities where Games events will take place.

During this 30th day before Opening Ceremony, some people—including some ACOG staff members—take a much-needed break and participate in a tennis tournament at the newly completed Stone Mountain Park Tennis Center. The focus is on friendly competition, but behind the scenes, the staff that will work at the venue during the Games take the opportunity to observe and fine-tune its operating plans.

top: A set of flags at each competition venue represents every delegation with athletes competing there.

bottom: Venue preparation is complete for the Stone Mountain Park Tennis Center.

• WILLIAM A GOERING • ELIZABETH A GOERLITZ • RICHARD C GOERLITZ • MARSHA B GOERSS • LISE GOERTZ • NANCY J GOESSLING • JIM GOETTEL • KEITH A GOETZ CATC • ALLISON L GOFF • JAMES B GOFF • KELLY B GOFF • KIMBERLY P GOFF • MARVA I GOFF • STEVEN G GOFF • PATRICIA S GOFFE • ANNA D GOFORTH • ROBERT D GOGGANS • TERRI GOGGANS • MICHAEL P GOGGIN • HARRY E GOGGINS • TAMMY M GOGGINS • SUSANNA GOH • FAHAD M GOHAR • JAYANTI P GOHIL • KEN W GOHRING • DARLENE E GOINS • JOYCE GOINS • KENNETH S GOINS • PIERRE GOISQUE • RAVI R GOKARM • MAYA S GOKCE •

18 JUNE 1996

New York, New York, to Philadelphia, Pennsylvania

Yesterday, crowds 10–15 people deep cheered the Olympic Torch Relay through the boroughs of New York City, and now the Olympic flame rests at famed Rockefeller Center, ready for another day in the country's most populous city. With millions of people across the US watching a live broadcast on NBC's *Today Show*, the first torch that will carry the flame today is lit by a community hero and senior citizen from Brooklyn. *Today Show* anchor Katie Couric also takes a turn as torchbearer, and then the Olympic flame is passed from runner to runner along Broadway toward the tip of Manhattan. Thousands of workers in the city's financial district cheer as the Torch Relay turns onto Wall Street and journeys past Federal Hall, the first US capitol building.

Waiting in nearby New York Harbor is a ferry boat, and when the flame arrives, it is placed on the bow for a trip to Liberty Island and the Statue of Liberty. Universally recognized as an American symbol of welcome and freedom, the historic statue is also the world's largest torchbearer. This morning, Lady Liberty greets the three first-generation immigrants who pass the Olympic flame from one to another around the base of this grand statue.

After another journey by ferry, the Torch Relay begins its course through New Jersey. Every mile of road this afternoon is lined with some of the largest crowds to greet the Olympic flame since its arrival in Los Angeles.

Late this afternoon in Princeton, the Olympic flame is brought to the grave of William Milligan Sloane. A friend and confidant of Pierre de Coubertin, Sloane is considered the founder of the Olympic Movement in the US. His descendants are on hand for a memorial celebration for the man whom many historians credit with encouraging de Coubertin to turn his Olympic dream into reality.

After the Olympic flame leaves Princeton, it crosses the Delaware River in Trenton, and begins the trek through Pennsylvania. Even as darkness falls, thousands of people continue to arrive.

In Philadelphia—the nation's first capital city—crowds celebrate the arrival of the flame with a nighttime celebration at the Philadelphia Museum of Art. Early tomorrow morning, the flame will stop at the Liberty Bell at Independence Hall before leaving Philadelphia.

top: Torch Relay runners parade through New York City's financial district.

bottom: During its travels, the torch salutes Lady Liberty, the world's largest torchbearer.

TRICIA K GOKEN • SUSAN ROSSANNA GOKOOL • GARY M GOLD • ROBERT A GOLD • ROBERTA B GOLDBAUGH • GREG A GOLDBERG • JO ANNE GOLDBERG • JOANNE L GOLDBERG • STEVEN M GOLDBERG • THOMAS R GOLDCAMP • ALAN D GOLDEN • CARL J GOLDEN • CHE P GOLDEN • DALE A GOLDEN • DEBBIE E GOLDEN • JERMAINE GOLDEN • JUSTIN J GOLDEN • LINDA B GOLDEN • MATTHEW GOLDEN • PAMELA A GOLDEN • SHARON L GOLDEN • SHARON R GOLDEN • MICHAEL GOLDENBERG • ROY GOLDENBERG • VIVIEN M GOLDENSON • KURT M GOLDER • FELICIA A GOLDFARB • MICAH GOLDFARB

Atlanta, Georgia—31 days to the Games

Local drivers are beginning to witness significant changes in Atlanta's transportation infrastructure. A transportation demand management system—planned for several years and made possible largely through federal funding that came earlier than anticipated because of the 1996 Games—is moving into full operation.

Three traffic centers are now open in the metropolitan area, with operators at each in continuous communication through a network of fiber-optic cables. The system relies on nonstop information sent from sensors and video cameras along interstate highways and major thoroughfares. It has the ability to synchronize and quickly reprogram about 400 traffic signals and electronic signs that alert drivers to changing traffic conditions and can communicate directly with radio and television traffic monitoring services that convey accurate, up-to-date information to their audiences.

Less technologically sophisticated but equally essential are the thousands of traffic barricades which will be installed throughout the city. These will be critical not only to directing traffic, but also to reserving lanes for Olympic buses and other vehicles and maintaining zones around venues for loading and unloading passengers.

Buses will be the backbone of the huge fleet of vehicles that ACOG will use to provide transportation to spectators and the Olympic Family. More than 2,000 buses will be required—many of which are coming as loans from municipal transportation systems around the country. These buses arrive daily at an enormous holding yard outside downtown Atlanta where they are provided with new tires and given final overhauls for the many hours of operation that will be required during the Games.

ACOG's Transportation staff is also thoroughly cleaning each bus, stripping out interior signage, and then distinctively marking the outside—not only with the Look of the Games, applied with an enormous vinyl wrap, but also with pictograms and directional signage to inform passengers of routes and destinations.

In addition, dozens of Transportation staff are working at the Olympic park-and-ride lots around Atlanta where spectator buses will originate and return. These lots—which will hold more than 55,000 cars at any one time—are being lined with cones and markers. Signage that will lead spectators from major highways to the lots is also being placed.

At ACOG headquarters, exact routes and distances are being confirmed, schedules calculated, and thousands of maps produced for inclusion in the detailed instructional notebooks that will be given to the drivers of Olympic buses. Along with routes to Olympic venues, the drivers of the more than 6,000 cars and vans that will be deployed for Olympic Family transportation will also be given directions to Atlanta's sights, attractions, popular restaurants, and places of entertainment, as well as to the dozens of NOC headquarters and hospitality houses that will support the Games.

left: The MARTA rail, bus, and shuttle system, the backbone of Atlanta's Olympic Transportation System, prepares to expand its operations for the Games.

right: A bus decorated in the Look of the Games awaits the first Olympic arrivals at the Airport Welcome Center.

PHYLLIS GOLDFARB • JOAN GOLDING • ERIC GOLDKLANG • JOEL S GOLDMACHER • ALLISON D GOLDMAN • ANDREW GOLDMAN • BARBARA R GOLDMAN • BETH F GOLDMAN • DINAH L GOLDMAN • JAN A GOLDMAN • SANDRA G GOLDMAN • CYNTHIA GOLDNER • ANGELA GOLDSBY • BARBARA B GOLDSMITH • BETH G GOLDSMITH • GAIL F GOLDSMITH • HENI P GOLDSMITH • ROBERT H GOLDSMITH • ROBERT L GOLDSMITH • SUSAN K GOLDSMITH • ALISON A GOLDSTEIN • ALVIN H GOLDSTEIN • DAVID S GOLDSTEIN • LINDA H GOLDSTEIN • LORI JAN GOLDSTEIN • MARK G GOLDSTEIN • MELVYN GOLDSTEIN •

20 JUNE 1996

Baltimore, Maryland, to Washington, DC

Camden Yards, Baltimore's impressive baseball stadium in the heart of the city, is today's starting point for the Torch Relay. From this popular landmark, runners traverse the city and take to the road for historic Annapolis, Maryland.

Here, the Olympic flame travels through the grounds of the state capitol building, the former seat of the US government and the site upon which George Washington resigned his commission in the nation's army.

Later today, the Olympic flame enters Washington, DC, capital city of the United States of America, passing

The torch moves past numerous foreign embassies toward Mount Vernon College, which will serve as an Olympic Village for football competitors. Crossing into Virginia, runners pay tribute to the Iwo Jima Memorial and Arlington National Cemetery before crossing back over Memorial Bridge to reenter Washington, DC, by way of the Lincoln Memorial.

When the Olympic flame is brought onto the grounds of the White House, it is greeted by congressional and cabinet members. A lap around the South Lawn ends in front of the president and vice president of the United States. In a moment that testifies to the

left: In front of the US Capitol, the torch is greeted by the congressional delegation from Georgia.

right: US President Bill Clinton joins with the final torchbearer of the day to light a ceremonial cauldron in front of the White House.

Robert F. Kennedy Stadium, where in just a few weeks, the starting rounds of the Centennial Olympic Games' football competition will be played.

During a stop at the US Capitol, the Torch Relay is greeted by enthusiastic crowds who are joined by almost half the members of the US Congress, including the entire congressional delegation from Georgia.

The triumphal progression of the Torch Relay continues down Pennsylvania Avenue, following the route that US presidents take during inaugural parades. Crowds line both sides of the broad street, and the Olympic flame is the focal point of this citywide celebration led by the mayor and other dignitaries.

United State's commitment to the Olympic Movement, President Bill Clinton joins with the final torchbearer of the day to light a ceremonial cauldron.

Minutes later, torrential rain begins to fall, and the Olympic flame is transferred from the cauldron to a safety lantern and taken into the White House, where its light can be seen glowing throughout the night from the windows of the famous Blue Room.

RICK D GOLDSTEIN • STELLA J GOLDWASSER • DENNIS GOLDWATER • SUSAN GOLDWATER • JAY W GOLETZ • JULIANNA H GOLETZ • CECELIA K GOLIGHTLY • EWA M GOLISZEK-SWITKA • DORIS GOLITKO • TERESA K GOLLIHUGH • PAMELA E GOLLISH • AMY S GOLLNICK • SCOTT E GOLLNICK • THERESA G GOLSON • JANICE J GOLSTON • CARROLL F GOLUCKE • LAWRENCE L GOLUSINSKI • ELIZABETH B GOMES • JOSE R. GOMES • MARY ELLEN GOMES • RIGEL D GOMES • SIRI ANNE GOMES • DEBRA F GOMEZ • JOSE GOMEZ • LUIS GOMEZ • SORAYA N GOMEZ • VERA GOMEZ-CORDERO • MAGDA I GOMEZ-GARCIA

Atlanta, Georgia—29 days to the Games

Downtown Atlanta has just acquired eight new landmarks with the installation of the distinctive, 65 ft (19.8 m) light towers that mark the central plaza of Centennial Olympic Park. Throughout the park, work proceeds at a rapid pace. The more than 300,000 personally inscribed bricks are being laid along walkways, tents for exhibits and eating areas are being erected and equipped, and support facilities for more than 5,000 staff members are being put into place.

Construction has been complicated by the park's location between the Olympic Center—where the Georgia Dome, Georgia World Congress Center, and Omni Coliseum are being prepared to house a total of 11 sports competitions and the International Broadcast Center—and the Atlanta Market Center—where ACOG headquarters is located, the Main Press Center is being constructed, and an exhibition of Olympic stamps and memorabilia is being installed.

A complex delivery schedule is in place to prevent blockages and delays, but it demands that trucks be unloaded rapidly so that the next round of shipments can arrive. This work goes on around the clock, since many of the deliveries must be scheduled at night to minimize the impact on day-to-day operations in the area.

On the Georgia Institute of Technology campus, which is being prepared for its Games-time role as the Olympic Village, workers are erecting the largest tent to be installed for the Games. The massive 85,000 sq ft (7,905 sq m) structure will house the kitchens, where 30,000 athlete meals will be prepared daily, and the dining hall, which will be able to seat more than 3,500 people at one time.

Elsewhere on the campus, Olympic Village staff is just beginning to convert the college's dormitories into Games-time homes for 16,500 athletes, officials, and coaches. Trucks arrive almost hourly carrying furnishings for 126 buildings—including 16,500 beds in two different lengths, 150,000 clothes hangers, thousands of bars of soap, 110,200 towels, and other items that must be sorted and delivered in time for the Village to be ready to open in just 16 days.

At the same time, 85 additional tents are being constructed as entertainment and support facilities for the athletes and staff; 1,690 mi (2,720 km) of fiber-optic cable are being laid to

top: The athletes' dining hall, located in the largest single tent installed for the Games, will be able to seat more than 3,500 people at one time.

bottom: Downtown Atlanta acquires new landmarks with the installation of eight 65 ft (19.8 m) light towers in Centennial Olympic Park.

support a network of telephones, computers, and television monitors; and routes and times are being mapped and marked for the electric trams that will provide transportation within the 270 acre (109 ha) Village.

The most visibly international symbol of the Games is being installed at the Village's Transportation Mall—197 flags representing each of the participating delegations with athletes competing in the Centennial Olympic Games.

GREGG L GOMLINSKI • JOOST A GOMPELS • MARK GOMPELS • JOYCE E GOMPF • BECKY GONDEK • NICHOLAS G GONIS • EVELYN H GONSAHN • NANCY M GONSALVES • SAMIR D GONSALVES • BIRGIT D GONSER • RICHARD A GONTESKI • ABEL GONZALES • ALFRED M GONZALES • DAVID GONZALES • JUAN M GONZALES • KATHRYN A GONZALES • SAM C GONZALES • VENUS L GONZALES • CHERIE L GONZALES. • ANTONIO N GONZALEZ • BLANCA C GONZALEZ • CARLOS GONZALEZ • DIANE L GONZALEZ • DOLORES ANN M GONZALEZ • EDGAR GONZALEZ • EVANGELINA GONZALEZ • GINGER E GONZALEZ

21 JUNE 1996

Richmond

Washington, DC, to Richmond, Virginia

The skies are clear and the sun shines brightly this morning as the US president and vice president and ACOG CEO meet for a ceremony on the White House grounds that launches a crowd of schoolchildren on the first leg of today's Olympic Torch Relay.

Later, torchbearers cross the Potomac River into Virginia, the first of America's original 13 colonies, where the Olympic flame halts at the national headquarters of the United Way of America—an organization that has helped ACOG to identify some 5,500 torchbearers on the basis of their service to their com-

People gather along the banks of the James River to see the Olympic flame pass through Richmond, Virginia.

munities and fellow citizens. Employees and volunteers in the United Way offices cheer on this journey that they have helped make possible, not only by identifying torchbearers, but also by celebrating with the thousands of volunteers supporting the cross-country journey.

The next stop for the Torch Relay is Charlottesville, Virginia, hometown of the former US president and hero, Thomas Jefferson. On the great lawn of the University of Virginia, Jefferson's beloved alma mater, the arrival of the Olympic flame is celebrated in a ceremony that includes the daughter of a US athlete who participated in the 1896 Olympic Games in Athens.

The Torch Relay moves on toward Richmond, and the Olympic flame, now journeying through the geographical region known as the American South, is truly headed home. The Torch Relay is welcomed into Virginia's state capital with true southern hospitality, as 300,000 people gather along the banks of the James River for a celebration that continues into the night.

Atlanta, Georgia—28 days to the Games

Virtually every department at ACOG is focused on tomorrow, when the first of two volunteer orientation and training sessions are scheduled at 20 venues in what have been dubbed "Super Saturdays." At every location, hundreds—sometimes thousands—of volunteers will arrive at 9:00 am for both a general overview of the facility to which they are assigned and a meeting and discussion with the leaders of the area that they will support. In addition, many of the areas plan to extend the session into the afternoon to review job responsibilities and duties.

Copiers and printers are in continuous use to produce last-minute information and training materials, and schedules are being coordinated to ensure that representatives of each functional area are on hand at every location. ACOG CEO Billy Payne plans to visit as many of the venues as possible to welcome the volunteers and thank them for their support of the 1996 Games.

In all, more than 20,000 volunteers will participate in the Super Saturday.

The Community Relations and Youth and Education Departments are meeting another pressing deadline as they finalize packages that will be delivered to more than 250 not-for-profit youth organizations around the state. Through an application process handled independently by Special Audiences, Inc. a not-for-profit group specializing in ticket distribution, these organizations—and the youngsters they represent—have been selected to receive more than 17,000 tickets to Games events, food and beverage coupons, and souvenirs paid for with money raised by the Children's Olympic Ticket Fund. Once they receive their packages, the organizations will notify Community Relations about their travel plans so staff members can be scheduled to meet each group and guide them through their Olympic experience.

Final preparations are also under way for a major program of the Olympic Arts Festival,

• JOHN P GONZALEZ • JOHNNY GONZALEZ • JOSE G GONZALEZ • JOSE M GONZALEZ • JUANA C GONZALEZ • MAGGIE A GONZALEZ • MARI G GONZALEZ • MARIA A GONZALEZ • MATIAS F GONZALEZ • ROBERT J GONZALEZ • XAVIER GONZALEZ • YOLANDA I GONZALEZ-ALVAREZ • RAFAEL GONZALEZ DEMARTINO • KENNETH G GONZALEZ JR • ENRIQUE GONZALEZ LOPEZ • JUAN E GONZALEZ RODRIGUEZ • JOSEPH W GOOCH • JO-ANNE M GOOD • IRENE E GOODALE • PATRICIA S GOODALE • WENDY M GOODALE • APRIL S GOODE • CASEY L GOODE • JAMES W GOODE • KATRINA A GOODE • LARRY GOODE • MICHAEL S GOODE

the *Olympic Woman*, which will debut 23 June at Georgia State University's Alumni Hall. The Sunday afternoon opening will include a dedication ceremony with Olympic officials and dignitaries and a walk through the huge multimedia exhibition that chronicles the history of women in the modern Olympic Games.

The Olympic Arts Festival has already started, and its staff is also supporting a number of other programs, including *Picturing the South, 1860 to the Present* and *Mind and Body: The Revival of the Olympic Idea*, exhibits located in Atlanta venues,

top left: Village staff member gives an orientation tour to volunteers.

top right: More than 5,000 banners decorated in the Look of the Games are being hung along Atlanta's streets.

bottom: The *Olympic Woman* exhibition opens at Georgia State University.

and the *Vision of Ulysses Davis, American Folk Artist*, located in Savannah's Beach Institute African-American Cultural Center.

The Look of the Games is rapidly becoming familiar throughout Atlanta as ACOG workers hang more than 5,000 banners on streets leading to the venues and on the major highways coming into the city. Also being placed are 259 new street markers created under a city program aimed at making Atlanta more pedestrian-friendly.

Earlier this month, ACOG also shipped special street banners to the hundreds of Georgia communities through which the Olympic torch will travel. These banners are currently being installed throughout the state and in the Atlanta metropolitan areas as citizens anticipate this most formal herald of the Games.

• OSCAR GOODE • STACY L GOODE • BETTY J GOODE-WHITE • BARRY GOODEN • DENNIS N GOODENOUGH • KAREN I GOODENOUGH • DIANE A GOODERMOTE • NELDA F GOODGAMES • BRENDA M GOODGER • GLENN O GOODHAND • MARY A GOODISKI • LILLIAN H GOODLETT • ALAN H GOODMAN • ALICE M GOODMAN • ALISON C GOODMAN • CHARLES R GOODMAN • FRANCES K GOODMAN • HENRY L GOODMAN • JAMES D GOODMAN • JENNIE D GOODMAN • LOUISE A GOODMAN • LYNN R GOODMAN • MICHAEL M GOODMAN • NATOSHIA L GOODMAN • STEPHEN R GOODMAN • SYLVIA C GOODMAN • SYLVIA M GOODMAN

35

26 JUNE 1996

Knoxville

top: **After traveling through the Great Smoky Mountains, the torch arrives in Gatlinburg, Tennessee.**

bottom: **At a nighttime celebration in Knoxville, Tennessee, torchbearers celebrate with friends and family members.**

Greenville, South Carolina, to Knoxville, Tennessee

In the deep mist of a southern morning, the Torch Relay leaves the city of Greenville in South Carolina and heads for its sister state, North Carolina. The first stop of the day's journey is for a ceremony in Flat Rock at the home of American literary great Carl Sandburg.

The next stop is Hendersonville, where the arrival of the Olympic flame is heralded by thousands of children who are attending summer camps in the area. Runners then bear the flame up and down an arduous course along the North Carolina mountain roads that leads to

Asheville. There, thousands of people—both residents of and visitors to this summer resort town—participate in the midday celebration.

After leaving Asheville, the Torch Relay heads deep into the Smoky Mountains, passing through Cherokee, home of the Native American tribe of the same name, and crossing the Great Smoky Mountain National Park into Tennessee. In Sevierville, Tennessee, the flame emerges from the mountain range for a country music showcase that has drawn an unprecedented crowd of 100,000 people to this small town. As night falls, the final celebration of the day is held on the grounds that

hosted the 1982 World's Fair in downtown Knoxville. More than 50,000 people are gathered in the International Pavilion on the fairgrounds when the Olympic flame arrives to a fireworks display and an official welcome in Greek by the city's deputy mayor.

• YVETTE C GOODMAN • ALLISON A GOODRICH • JULIE K GOODRICH • LISA M GOODRICH • MARGARET J GOODRICH • RAYMOND M GOODRICH • LENNOX M GOODRIDGE • VERA H GOODRIDGE • NEQUILA N GOODS-GUIDRY • ARNOLD R GOODSON • EDWARD M GOODSON • JOSEPH A GOODSON • RITA E GOODSON • RONALD N GOODSON • ROY L GOODSON • JAMES L GOODSPEED • JAMIE M GOODSTEIN • AMY B GOODWIN • BETTY F GOODWIN • CLARK M GOODWIN • GAIL B GOODWIN • GAIL V GOODWIN • HOBBS GOODWIN • JOHN C GOODWIN • LYNDA F GOODWIN • MICHAEL J GOODWIN • NICOLE GOODWIN •

Atlanta, Georgia—23 days to the Games

The first international Olympic arrivals, elite horses, landed at Hartsfield Atlanta International Airport two days ago, and are now out of quarantine and on their way to the stables at Georgia International Horse Park. The 26 horses—which will soon be joined by many more—were transported from various locations in Europe aboard a cargo plane equipped with stalls that each featured padded walls, slide-proof flooring, and a seat for an attendant.

More and more equipment is arriving at the Olympic Village, where crews of 150 workers are assigned to around-the-clock shifts to meet the 6 July official opening of the facility. Already completed is the Olympic Plaza, which will become a permanent fixture of the Georgia Tech campus. The large outdoor space features a fountain, a 300-seat amphitheater, and a striking, 80 ft (24.4 m) stainless steel obelisk.

In the Village kitchens, staff members are preparing to meet the dietary requirements of Olympic athletes—usually 8,000–10,000 calories per day. Specially created boxed lunches have been shipped to the Olympic Village. Thousands of the sturdy cardboard containers with carry handles and Olympic logos will be packed each day, beginning well before the start of the Games, to provide meals for athletes who are training in locations too distant to have lunch in the Village. A fleet of refrigerated trucks will deliver the lunches to their destinations each day.

Supplying sufficient water and ice for spectators and visitors traveling to and from Olympic venues has been a key concern of the 16 public and private agencies that are coordinating their efforts to provide water stations throughout the Olympic Ring. Inside the venues, ACOG staff will supply free water to spectators.

Religious organizations throughout Atlanta are also planning to help meet the needs of visitors and spectators for refreshments and resting places. Most will keep their facilities open to the public throughout the Games, offering various forms of entertainment, as well as moments of quiet relaxation.

top: Dormitories of Georgia Tech, which will serve as athlete housing during the Games, rise against the backdrop of the Atlanta skyline.

bottom: In the Village kitchen, staff prepares athlete boxed lunches.

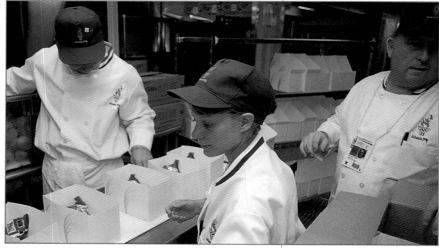

PATRICIA D GOODWIN • TIMOTHY C GOODWIN • TERESA E GOODWIN-TEAGUE • BOB GOODWIN ATC • RENATA L GOODWINE • INDIA A GOODYEAR • LISA A GOODYEAR • LISA A GOODYEAR • MARCUS D GOOGER • SCOTT B GOOGINS • DEBBY GOOLSBY • EMILY J GOOLSBY • TAMIKA GOOSBY • JOHN GOPAUL • KATHY GOPAUL • NIGEL K GOPAUL • JEAN C GORA • MICHAEL J GORA • MARIA E GORANSSON • IRINA F GORB • CAROLYN W GORBY • MICHAEL J GORBY • SARAH T GORDON • ALVIN B GORDON • AMY KAREN GORDON • ANDRE L GORDON • ANN S GORDON • BEATRICE B GORDON • CAROLINE GORDON •

29 JUNE 1996

A member of the crowd salutes the flame with a commemorative plaque.

Huntsville, Alabama, to Birmingham, Alabama

Now well into the heart of the American South, the Olympic Torch Relay begins this day in Huntsville, Alabama—a southern city that is also home to the US Space and Rocket Center. In the shadow of the *Saturn V* rocket that carried the first manned mission to the moon, this day's first torchbearer takes the Olympic flame and heads south toward Decatur. There, a granite memorial has been erected and dedicated to the community heroes from this town who were chosen to share in the Olympic flame's historic journey.

Later today, the Torch Relay arrives in Oakville, Alabama, the boyhood home of Olympic legend Jesse Owens. The announcement earlier this year of the town's inclusion in the torch's journey to Atlanta prompted city leaders to gather support to create a park and monument to honor Owens. This new public area now awaits the arrival of the Olympic flame.

On hand are many of Owens's descendants, who have gathered for a ceremony that salutes the Olympic Movement and the remarkable achievements of an Olympic great whose athletics record stood for more than 50 years.

Upon leaving Oakville, the Torch Relay turns toward Birmingham, where the first stop is the city's Civil Rights Museum. After a moving ceremony, the Olympic flame travels on to Legion Field, the enormous stadium that will host some of the preliminary rounds of Olympic football competition. As today's last stop, the city of Birmingham hosts the Olympic flame's arrival and overnight stay with a celebration.

Atlanta, Georgia—20 days to the Games

Although ACOG's Press Operations staff will not fully occupy the 300,000 sq ft (27,900 sq m) Main Press Center until 3 July, work is already under way on several key areas. Nearing completion is the Kodak Imaging Center—a 20,000 sq ft (1,860 sq m) installation that will be the largest photo processing laboratory in the world during the Games.

Also installed is an area called Main Street, where several thousand members of the accredited press can do their banking, make travel arrangements, receive messages and mail, leave their laundry to be cleaned, rent a variety of telecommunications equipment, send facsimile transmissions worldwide, research Olympic history in a small library, and access a variety of other services. Many of the staff who will provide these services are already at work in the kiosks where they will be stationed, stocking supplies and testing equipment.

Behind the walls and above the ceilings, in the midst of a major trade show, dozens of technicians are installing miles of additional cable and supplemental power sources. As soon as the trade show closes on 3 July, these technicians and many more will attach the thousands of telephones, computers, copiers, facsimile machines, and other equipment needed to serve a common workroom and to outfit 100,000 sq ft (9,300 sq m) of private office space rented to about 95 news agencies. At the same time, teams of movers and construction crews will work 12-hour shifts, 24 hours a day on all of the other aspects of turning vast exhibit halls into one multifaceted, highly complex Main Press Center.

Also of great importance to serving the press and the broadcasters—a constituency of some 15,000 people—is the Media Transportation Mall, which is being constructed a short distance away. This temporary facility will serve as the hub of the system that will transport members of the media to and from their accommodations and the venues. Largely com-

CHERYL GORDON • CLARENCE S GORDON • DENISE GORDON • DUANE A GORDON • EDWARD C GORDON • ERICA L GORDON • GRETA M GORDON • HELEN A GORDON • JAMES GORDON • JAMES GORDON • JAMES D GORDON • JANICE E GORDON • JULIA E GORDON • KRISTIE L GORDON • KRISTIN G GORDON • LAURA GORDON • LAURA J GORDON • LAUREN S GORDON • LAWRENCE R GORDON • LES S GORDON • LESLIE H GORDON • LOUISE H GORDON • MARLENE C GORDON • MATTHEW M GORDON • MAUREEN A GORDON • MELINDA A GORDON • MICHAEL N GORDON • MICHAEL P GORDON • MISHELLE W GORDON •

posed of rows and rows of lanes surrounded by platforms to facilitate loading and unloading the buses, the Media Transportation Mall is being created on a vacant lot the size of a city block that has been leveled, equipped with utilities, and paved. Crews are now finishing construction, which includes installation of a small press center where members of the media will be able to access results and other information while changing from one bus to another.

One of many facilities that has been completed and is now being tested is the Atlanta branch of SmithKline Beecham Clinical Laboratory, Inc. A member of the IOC Medical Commission came to Atlanta early to review this new installation and its processing capabilities. The facility will be certified just prior to the start of the Games.

At Hartsfield Atlanta International Airport, teams of athletes arrive daily and head for the cities throughout Georgia that volunteered to serve as pre-Olympic training and acclimation sites. A total of 65 cities and 103 teams have connected through the Georgia Olympic Train-

ing Alliance, which was established with ACOG's support. Well before they move into the Olympic Village, hundreds of athletes are becoming acclimated in communities throughout Georgia, and their host communities are enjoying an experience that crosses cultural boundaries and creates long-term friendships.

top left: The Kodak Imaging Center, which will be the largest photo processing laboratory in the world during the Games, is almost ready for operations.

bottom left: Athletes' luggage is unloaded at the Airport Welcome Center.

right: Athletes who have arrived early in order to acclimate train at Golden Park in Columbus, Georgia, site of the women's softball competition.

NANCY R GORDON • NICOLE A GORDON • RICK C GORDON • RUTH N GORDON • SHANNON E GORDON • TAYLOR GORDON • TERRI N GORDON • THEODORA P GORDON • VERNA J GORDON • WILLIAM C GORDON • WILLLAM R GORDON • JULIA F GORDY • CHARLES W GORE • DAN GORE • EVITA R GORE • LANCE GORE • MICHAEL J GORE • RICKY S GORE • PAMELA S GORE-EATON • ANDRE'AS GOREE • MEIR GOREN • ROBERT E GORES • KEVIN M GOREY CATC • CLAUDE A GORHAM • JAMES S GORHAM • STEVEN GORIN • BORIS GORINSHTEYN • BARBARA J GORMAN • BRENDAN P GORMAN • CAROLYN C GORMAN

30 JUNE 1996

Birmingham, Alabama, to Montgomery, Alabama

This morning, the Torch Relay leaves Birmingham and travels along the roads of rural Alabama toward Montgomery, the state's capital.

The first stop of the day is in Selma, where ACOG co-chair of the Board and former ambassador to the United Nations Andrew Young preaches a stirring sermon at Brown's Chapel. Three decades ago, this small church reverberated with the words of the Reverend Martin Luther King Jr., as he urged on and inspired civil rights marchers.

At the crest of the bridge, the Olympic flame is passed to a torch carried by Andrew Young, who, as one of King's lieutenants, was present at that earlier march. As Young holds the bright light aloft, 100 children of many races join him in a triumphant crossing that promises a joyous and hopeful future.

The Torch Relay moves into Montgomery and up the steps of the state capitol while 50,000 people throughout the area are poised to begin a joyful celebration of music and dance.

The next stop for the Torch Relay provides a look at the Greek origins of the Olympic Movement. Jasmine

The torch is borne triumphantly across the Edmund Pettus Bridge, a historic site which civil rights marchers were once prevented from crossing.

From Brown's Chapel, the Olympic flame is brought to the steps of the Voting Rights Museum in Selma, a facility dedicated to the memory of the struggle against the disenfranchisement of minorities. Following a historic path, the Torch Relay leaves the museum and heads for Edmund Pettus Bridge, where civil rights marchers were once frustrated in their attempt to cross the bridge on the way to Montgomery.

Hill Gardens, near Wetumpka, Alabama, was created in honor of Olympia, Greece. Today, thousands of visitors flock to this memorial to witness a tribute to the origins of the Olympic Games in a production reminiscent of the lighting of the Olympic flame several months earlier in Greece. Cultural and artistic entertainment, rich with Greek traditions, brings this day to a memorable end.

• GAWAINE GORMAN • HEATHER M GORMAN • HEIDI K GORMAN • KERI A GORMAN • MARTIE GORMAN • NEAL R GORMAN • STEVE J GORMAN • SUSAN E GORMAN • VICTORIA A GORMAN • WILLIAM GORMAN • DENISE M GORMLEY • GLORIA J GORMLEY • WILLIAM A GORNTO • VIKENTI M GOROKHOVSKI • BECCA J GORRELL • AMY L GORRIGAN • MATEO GORRINDO • MACKY M GORTEMOLLER • KATHARINE D GORYCA • JUDITH D GOSA • ANDREW F GOSCH • MARTINA M GOSCHA • NIKOLINA GOSEVA • JIMMIE GOSHEY • KARIN J GOSHINSKI • CALLIE M GOSIER • CHRISTOPHER E GOSS • ELIZABETH A GOSS • KAREN P GOSS

Atlanta, Georgia—19 days to the Games

Athletes and other members of the Olympic Family who are arriving early for the Games can now go directly to the newly opened Airport Welcome Center for accreditation. Because the Atlanta airport lacks sufficient space to accommodate an accreditation center at the main terminal, ACOG rented a nearby airport hangar that was standing vacant and recommissioned it as a mini-terminal for Olympic guests. The exterior of the 71,000 sq ft (6,603 sq m) facility has been repainted the green color of the Look of the Games, and inside, a series of interconnected tents has been erected to provide temporary, air-conditioned space where ultimately, more than 200,000 credentials will be issued.

Outside the hangar, there are designated areas for buses, vans, and cars that will transport Olympic Family members to their accommodations, and holding areas where luggage is held while its owners receive their credentials.

In these first few days of operations, the Airport Welcome Center is open from 7 a.m. to 8:00 p.m. with approximately 94 staff members assigned to the accreditation terminals and help desks, as well as to all the support facilities and services associated with the facility. Well before the peak arrival days of 15–18 July, the schedule will be extended to almost 24 hours a day.

Those arriving early with time to spare from training and executing official duties can choose from a growing number of Olympic Arts Festival programs, including *Wadsworth Jarrell: A Shared Ideology*, *Souls Grown Deep: African-American Vernacular Art of the South* and its companion, *Thornton Dial: Remembering the Road*, and *Out of Bounds: New Works by Eight Southeast Artists*.

Many visit the Atlanta History Center to see the *American South: Past, Present and Future*, which presents both historical and modern views of the region's culture. This multidimensional exhibition uses photos, artifacts, videos, and text to show the influence of everything from barbecues and cotton farming to the civil rights movement, jazz, and William Faulkner.

Another popular stop for a look into the past is Atlanta's Cyclorama, which has just been completely refurbished. This three-dimensional circular mural presents a highly realistic pictorial history of the Battle of Atlanta, one of the last major battles of the US Civil War.

Meanwhile, the local citizenry is extremely concerned with the impact the Olympic Games will have on the city's traffic. For the past several months, ACOG representatives have participated in hundreds of meetings downtown and in areas around the Games venues, talking with business leaders, employees, civic and community groups, and neighborhood residents.

As June ends, a special section of the *Atlanta Journal-Constitution*—produced in cooperation with ACOG—is devoted entirely to Games-time transportation issues, with maps, suggested

left: Depressed, by James Reed, is among 300 works that are presently being refurbished for the opening of *From Rearguard to Vanguard: Selections from the Clark Atlanta University Collection of African American Art* on July 19.

right: Athletes arrive at the Airport Welcome Center at Hartsfield Atlanta International Airport.

routes and travel times, question-and-answer columns, and other reports—all aimed at minimizing the impact on commuters' daily routines. ACOG is distributing 250,000 reprints of the section throughout the city. Copies are distributed among downtown businesses, at MARTA stations, in shopping malls (using ACOG's retail merchandise kiosks), at community centers, and in dozens of other locations.

This publication and dozens of reports on local television and radio—especially WXIA-TV and WGST-Radio, ACOG's official conveyors of Olympic information—help prepare Atlantans for the changes that hosting several million visitors is sure to bring about.

• MARSHALL H GOSS • VIRGINIA N GOSS • WALKER E GOSSAGE JR • DANIELLE E GOSSELIN • MATTHEW R GOSSELIN • GARY DON GOSSETT • KEITH E GOSSETT • LORIN L GOSSETT • MEREDITH GOTLIN • HIDEO GOTO • RACHEL J. GOTT • JILL GOTTESMAN • MICHAEL H GOTTESMAN • ROBERT W GOTTESMAN • MANFRED R GOTTHARDT • MATTHEW A GOTTHARDT • SIDNEY I GOTTLER • ALLEN S GOTTLIEB • JASON M GOTTLIEB • LIDIJA GOTTLIEB • CHARLES A GOTTLOB MD • REGAN D GOTWALT • SHEELA GOUD • ELAINE GOUGE • MICHAEL J GOUGE SR • LINDA L GOUGER • NICHOLAS P GOUGH • RICHARD I GOUGH

3 JULY 1996

St. Petersburg

Gainesville, Florida, to St. Petersburg, Florida

Today, the state that is the mythical home of the Fountain of Youth hosts the Olympic flame. From Gainesville, the Torch Relay takes on new energy as it crosses central Florida into Tampa.

People of the various ethnic groups that live in this Gulf Coast city, many in the clothing of their native lands, have turned out in force. At the civic center in the heart of downtown, thousands of members of the city's Greek population greet the arrival of the Olympic flame with traditional dances. A parade of

national flags follows, and then torchbearers carry the flame from the civic center to the harbor where the sailboat *Peregrine* waits.

The Olympic flame lights a ceremonial cauldron on the boat's aft deck, and the *Peregrine* casts off to sail a loop before thousands of spectators lining the harbor. As gunfire salutes sound from a surrounding flotilla, the *Peregrine* moves across Tampa Bay for the four-hour journey to St. Petersburg.

Upon its arrival, the Olympic flame is carried through the streets of Tampa's sister city before it is returned to the waterfront for a day-end celebration of music and fireworks.

top: Crowds greet the torch as it passes through Tampa.

bottom: The sailboat *Peregrine* brings the flame from the shore of Tampa to St. Petersburg.

Atlanta, Georgia—16 days to the Games

Many Atlantans and several hundred thousand people throughout the US who have purchased tickets to the 1996 Games are now getting a look at the Olympic Transportation System. This information is contained in the 48-page *Guide to the 1996 Olympic Games* that ACOG mailed to ticket holders a few weeks ago.

Along with transportation tips and maps, the guide provides practical information concerning banking services, medical emergencies, and rules and guidelines for spectators. In addition, the guide also provides exciting previews of ceremonies, sports, and Olympic Arts Festival events.

The *Guide to the 1996 Olympic Games* is one of ACOG's largest printing projects, but there are thousands of others. Many are handled at ACOG's copy centers, where large printers are now running almost around the clock. The copy centers produce everything from single-page, black-and-white sheets for rosters and judges' evaluations to operating manuals and reports that run hundreds of pages long and are bound into books. Throughout this month and up to the start of the Games, thousands of different projects will be printed in-house. In addition, a large number of projects are sent to commercial printers. Companies are selected for their ability to bid competitively and meet required deadlines, a factor that is becoming increasingly significant as the Games approach.

With the Fourth of July holiday weekend approaching, ACOG is facing numerous other deadlines, and few staff members plan time off for the traditional barbecues and parades. Many are planning trips, but these are moves from their offices at ACOG headquarters to their venue and operational headquarters in preparation for Games-time. Instead of suitcases, they will pack boxes with their work materials and supplies.

Hundreds of staff members are also eating their first ACOG-provided meals. ACOG's policy is to provide staff and volunteers with one meal per eight-hour shift beginning 1 July. Some meals have also been provided to staff

• STEPHEN T GOUGH • CHARLES W GOULD • JOHN R GOULD • MIMI Y GOULD • STACI O GOULD • WILLIAM T GOULD • DENISE GOULET • MARK P GOULET • NESTOR A GOUNARIS • BRIAN K GOURDIN • MICHELLE GOURGUES • ANDREI G GOUSSAROV • FRAN J GOUZE • SCOTT A GOVE • MEENU GOVIL • BRETT GOWDER • SARAH M GOWDER • BRIAN J GOWDY • KERRY P GOWELL • KEVIN P GOWEN • RICHARD L GOWER • ROY L GOWER • WILLIAM J GOWER III • ASHISH GOYAL • KENNETH R GOYER • VALERIE M GRABB • MICHAEL S GRABER • NEAL B GRABER • KATHY L GRABO • DAVID K GRABOW • MARY J GRABOW • ANN C GRABOWSKY

filling Games-time assignments that begin prior to this date.

By the time the Games end, ACOG Food and Beverage Department will have overseen the delivery of 1.3 million staff meals. Every day for more than 35 days, breakfasts, lunches, and dinners will be assembled at six sites around Atlanta and held in chill rooms until the arrival of refrigerated trucks for delivery to the venues. At the venues, the packaged meals—which contain a variety of cereals, yogurts, sandwiches, salads, fruits, and packaged snacks—are stored in

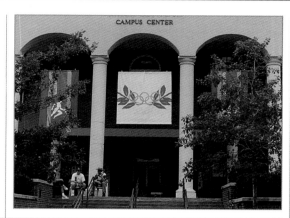

The Look of the Games is applied to competition venues throughout the city, such as Morehouse College (*top*) and the Georgia Dome (*bottom*).

chilled areas before being distributed to staff.

While Food and Beverage planned for a three-day menu rotation schedule, some items appear more frequently than others. Packages of potato chips are especially abundant, thanks to a shipment of nine truckloads of the popular snack.

The start of July also marks the beginning of ACOG's exclusive use period of virtually all Games venues. While final installation, testing of equipment, and completion of all construction and cleaning will require all the time remaining, the venues are almost immediately trans-

formed into sites with an Olympic feel. This overnight change is made possible by the distinctive Look of the Games, which appears everywhere as thousands of volunteers arrive in uniforms adorned with Olympic Rings of blue, teal, gold, and red, and as the colorful Quilt of Leaves banners, markers, and decorations are hung.

• REINHARD H GRABOWSKY • SEBASTIEN GRACCO DE LAY • HEATHER D GRACE • KEN W GRACE • YASMEEN M GRACE • GLENDA J GRADDY • SUSAN S GRADDY • ARGENTINA GRADER • JEROME E GRADER • WESLEY K GRADINGER • RICHARD J GRADKOWSKI • JAY GRADY • MAUREEN F GRADY • ANDREW C GRAEUB • JULIA S GRAF • JEFFREY GRAFF • SUSAN M GRAFF • KIMBERLY A GRAFFEO • MATTHEW H GRAGE • CHERYL GRAGG • JANET S GRAGG • ANGELA R GRAHAM • AUDREY M GRAHAM • BART L GRAHAM • BETH M GRAHAM • BRIDGET L GRAHAM • CHARLES P GRAHAM • CHRISTOPHER I GRAHAM • CLETE C GRAHAM

4 JULY 1996

St. Petersburg, Florida, to Miami, Florida

On this Independence Day holiday, well before the sun rises, the Torch Relay is moving south from St. Petersburg toward Sunshine Skyway Bridge—a new, miles-long span of sparkling steel that soars above the brilliant blue waters of Tampa Bay. Thousands of people watch from the old bridge as a single torchbearer runs up to the peak of the new bridge and passes the Olympic flame to another torchbearer, who follows its downward course to the other side.

The arrival of the flame is met with a Fourth of July breakfast picnic that attracts thousands of people. When the torch leaves this waterside park, it heads south to Sarasota along a course crowded with people starting their Independence Day celebration with a salute to the Olympic flame.

In Sarasota, the Olympic flame is transferred to a ceremonial lantern and put aboard the only operational Short Sunderland Flying Boat in the world. In midafternoon, the boat lifts off from the waters of Sarasota Bay for a 90-minute flight across the legendary Florida Everglades to Miami.

Coming into Florida's largest city, the flying boat passes low over downtown Independence Day celebrations before landing on the water near Dinner Key. On land again, the Olympic flame is brought to City Hall to join in Miami's centennial celebration. From there, the Torch Relay route passes the Orange Bowl that, in two weeks, will host Olympic football competition. Today's final destination is Bayside Park, where nearly one million people are on hand for the lighting of the ceremonial cauldron and an evening of fireworks and laser shows.

The Torch Relay caravan travels over Sunshine Skyway Bridge.

Atlanta, Georgia—15 days to the Games

On this national holiday, Atlanta is emerging as a city of international stature—most audibly, perhaps, at MARTA rail stops, where announcers have begun making rail-station announcements in English, French, German, Spanish, and Japanese. MARTA has also installed multilingual information kiosks at 22 stations.

Today, the most international of the Olympic Arts Festival's events opens to the public. Museums and collectors around the world helped make *Rings: Five Passions in World Art* possible by

Olympic sailors test their courses marked on the Atlantic Ocean off the coast of Savannah, Georgia.

lending Atlanta's High Museum of Art more than 125 masterpieces. After a private opening for Olympic officials and dignitaries, the exhibition is now open to capacity crowds. Many visitors will return several times, and long lines will be common from today until the end of the Games.

Where possible, ACOG is making Games-time fields of play available for training and practice. Many Olympic venues are presently hosting athletes from scores of different nations who have come early in order to acclimate.

One of the sites being used almost continually is the newly built Georgia Tech Aquatic Center. The main pool has been filled with 1 million gal (3.8 million l) of water, and another 600,000 gal (2.3 million l) have been pumped into the diving pool. Swimmers are testing a new design that limits the degree to which

• CONSTANCE L GRAHAM • DAMIEN C GRAHAM • DARNALL A GRAHAM • DARYL B GRAHAM • DAVID GRAHAM • DAVID B GRAHAM • DELLE L GRAHAM • ELLEN S GRAHAM • ELWIN GRAHAM • GAIL M GRAHAM •
GEORGIA J GRAHAM • GERARD H GRAHAM • JANE C GRAHAM • JAWAYNE R GRAHAM • JERUSHIA L GRAHAM • JESSICA GRAHAM • JOHN B GRAHAM • KATRINA P GRAHAM • KAY GRAHAM • KENNETH L GRAHAM •
• LASHONIA SEAN GRAHAM • LINDA J GRAHAM • LISA D GRAHAM • MARY NELL GRAHAM • MARY P GRAHAM • NANCY S GRAHAM • PAMELA H GRAHAM • PENNY C GRAHAM • PHYLISS D GRAHAM •

waves and splashes in one lane can affect other lanes. Divers are trying out the softer landings made possible by a sparger system which blows air bubbles into the pool during practice sessions. As the athletes train, underwater cameras installed to catch the action beneath the surface are being tested.

Preparatory activities are not confined to the Atlanta area. Farther north, on the Ocoee River in Tennessee, water has just been released upstream from the first natural-river Olympic whitewater course. Athletes from several nations are on hand to see the course surge to life and put their vessels into the water for practice runs.

To the south, Olympic sailors are trying the courses marked on the Atlantic Ocean just off the coast of Savannah, Georgia. In the city, local organizers and their staff are preparing for the Opening Ceremony of yachting competition, scheduled for 20 July, which will include a multinational parade of athletes and entertainment programs on picturesque River Street.

Rehearsals and final planning for the Opening Ceremony in Olympic Stadium—which the athletes and officials staying in Savannah will also attend—are under way daily. Performers rehearse music and dance routines, while crews practice detailed procedures to synchronize the movement of thousands of cast members and props onto and off of the field.

At the Atlanta Marriott Marquis, the officially designated Olympic Family Hotel, a distinctive Olympic feature is being added. Working at

night after 11 p.m. to avoid interfering with hotel activities and guests, a crew of six is hanging three enormous ribbon sculptures in the Look of the Games colors in the 50-story atrium. Also enhancing the Olympic feel of this hotel are the special Olympic desks being installed at various locations throughout the hotel's public areas.

This holiday weekend is a popular time for sprucing up neighborhoods and engineering last-minute beautification projects. Several hundred Atlanta families are engaged in preparing their homes for some very special Olympic

visitors—the parents and families of Olympic athletes. In a gesture of true southern hospitality, these Atlanta families are working through an organization called HOST to offer these families free accommodations, breakfast, and transportation to and from the Olympic Transportation System.

top: The *Rings* exhibit, featuring masterpieces from around the world, opens at the High Museum.

bottom: Look of the Games decorations in the lobby of the Atlanta Marriott Marquis help transform the hotel for its Games-time role as the Olympic Family Hotel.

ROBERT C GRAHAM • SARAH L GRAHAM • SONIA C GRAHAM • STACY N GRAHAM • STEWART M GRAHAM • STUART S GRAHAM • SUE I GRAHAM • SUSAN D GRAHAM • SWEETIE D GRAHAM • VANESSA GRAHAM • VIVIAN R GRAHAM • WILLIAM S GRAHAM • WILLIAM A GRAHAM • ALBERT G GRAHAM JR • SAMUEL R GRAISER • LESLIE J. GRAITCER • SAMUEL B GRAITCER • RONALD J GRALEWICZ • ANNA GRALNIK • NANCY L GRAMENZ • BONNIE L GRAMLICH • MICHAEL R GRANBERRY • ROBERT W GRANBERRY • ENID J GRANDISON • BARBARA F GRANDSTAFF MT • SANDRA M GRANE • CLAUDIA S GRANGER •

9 JULY 1996

Savannah

top: The schooner *America* sails up the Savannah River, bringing the flame into the harbor of Georgia's oldest city.

bottom: Georgia Governor Zell Miller lights the cauldron in Savannah.

St. Augustine, Florida, to Savannah, Georgia

The Torch Relay's journey through Florida—which included a stop in Cape Canaveral and a celebration with the astronauts who had taken a torch into space just the week before—is nearing its conclusion. The day begins in St. Augustine, the nation's oldest city. From there, the Torch Relay follows a northward course to Jacksonville, Florida, for a midday celebration that draws thousands of people. Later today, the flame will arrive in Georgia, home state of the 1996 Olympic Games.

to be received by Governor Zell Miller and ACOG CEO Billy Payne.

In a moving ceremony, a cauldron is lit and, in turn, provides the spark for the torch that will start the journey through the historic streets of Savannah, past buildings constructed more than 300 years ago by the first Georgia settlers.

Just past sundown, the Torch Relay's first day in Georgia ends on the lawn of Forsyth Park, where thousands join in a celebration that incorporates Greek and American folk music and dance in a tribute to Greece as the birthplace of the Olympic Movement.

For its trip to Georgia, the Olympic flame travels on the St. John's River to an airstrip, where the flame is secured in a Coast Guard helicopter for the journey up the coast. Near the site of the Olympic yachting course off the coast of Savannah, the flame is transferred to the schooner *America*.

America sets sail on a course up the Savannah River and into the harbor of Georgia's oldest city. The volunteer crew brings the schooner to the banks of Waving Girl Park, where Olympic gold medalists in yachting from the 1992 Games carry the flame ashore

MARK D GRANGER • MARK E GRANGER • DANIEL S. GRANIK • PER GRANKVIST • HUGH M GRANNUM • BILL GRANT • BONI E GRANT • CAY A GRANT • DAVID G GRANT • DAVID M GRANT • DEVON K GRANT • ESTRA G GRANT • FAREED M GRANT • GEOFFREY G GRANT • GLEN E GRANT • ILENE GRANT • JAMES M GRANT • JON S GRANT • LINDA C GRANT • LYNN G GRANT • MARTIN E GRANT • PATRICIA A GRANT • REBECCA T GRANT • REBECCA T GRANT • ROBERT T GRANT • SHAREKA L GRANT • SHEILA M GRANT • SHELLOUISE R GRANT • THOMAS L GRANT • MARSHA L GRANT ATC • BRADLEY C GRANT DO • WILLIAM H GRANT III

Atlanta, Georgia—10 days to the Games

As of today, the Olympic Village is home to more than 800 athletes. Along with their practice and training schedules, athletes arriving early are finding opportunities to enjoy the many amenities available to them. They watch movies at one of the five cinemas in the Village, try out the Internet at the surf shack, visit the day spa, enjoy the recreational pools, get their picture taken with IZZY, and, at night, listen to entertainers at the coffee house or take to the floor of the dance club.

The International Broadcast Center is now fully operational and ready to serve the 10,000 technicians and announcers who will work there at the height of the Games. Meanwhile, the crews of many broadcasting companies are putting the final touches on the studio sets from where their announcers will be seen by viewers around the world. In addition to its studios, editing facilities, and workrooms, the International Broadcast Center offers its own post office, sundry shop, money exchange locations, restaurants, and bar.

The Main Press Center offers similar services to the print journalists and photographers who will be based there. The Main Press Center will also serve as the location for all ACOG and IOC news conferences, as well as dozens of presentations each day by the NOCs, IFs, and other members of the Olympic Family.

Near the High Museum of Art, ACOG has established a separate press center for nonaccredited media members covering the Olympic Arts Festival, which provides many of the same services as the Main Press Center.

Final preparations are still under way at Centennial Olympic Park, which will open to the public on 13 July. All the park's primary structures and features are in place and ready for a series of preview parties hosted by the sponsors. The five electronic kiosks that visitors will use to find their personally inscribed bricks in the park are also ready for operation. Several thousand calls are received daily at a toll-free number ACOG established to assist people in locating their bricks in the Park.

The Coca-Cola Company's Olympic City, a temporary entertainment complex on the south side of the Park, is attracting crowds to its games and exhibits. On the north side of Centennial Olympic Park, work has also been completed on Georgia International Plaza—a 7-acre (2.8 ha) park connecting the Georgia Dome and Georgia World Congress Center. This permanent addition to the area—with its 25 ft (7.6 m) statue of a male gymnast, fountain, and trees—is a park in the air that will serve as a crossroads for the people who will attend the sports competitions.

top: IOC President Juan Antonio Samaranch tries out a virtual reality game during a pre-Games tour of the Atlanta Olympic Village.

bottom: The IOC Executive Board Meeting and 105th Session opens at the Woodruff Arts Center.

Long-term enhancements are also being made to the area around Olympic Stadium, where 300 southern magnolias, crepe myrtles, and laurel oaks are being planted.

At the Olympic Family Hotel, Olympic Family members are arriving for the week-long gathering of the IOC Executive Board Meeting and 105th Session that will begin 11 July. A showcase of the traditional gardens of the American South—and dozens of Cherokee Roses, Georgia's state flower—is being assembled at the Woodruff Arts Center for the IOC Session's opening. Also being created is an edible garden of topiary trees, complete with Georgia peaches.

16 JULY 1996

Young Harris, Georgia, to Franklin, Georgia

With just three days remaining before the Opening Ceremony in Atlanta, the Torch Relay is traveling an average of 22 hours per day. On this warm summer morning, the first torchbearer leaves the center of the town of Young Harris about an hour before the sun rises over the mountains of northern Georgia.

By 8 a.m., the Torch Relay has crossed back into Tennessee for a visit to the Olympic whitewater venue on the Ocoee River. As the torchbearers move along a stretch of the river, kayakers practicing for the Games raise their paddles to salute the flame.

setting, leaders from the eastern and western branches of this Native American tribe come together to pay an unprecedented tribute to the Olympic Movement.

By late this afternoon, the Torch Relay is on its way toward Rome, where city leaders and citizens have turned out in the dress of the ancient Greeks—complete with flowing robes and laurel wreathes—to welcome the Olympic flame.

In every town along the way, the crowds are becoming larger and larger, often numbering three and four times the size of the local population. The culmination is in Franklin, a town of fewer than 5,000, and

A torch celebration on the grounds of New Echota, the one-time capital of the Cherokee Nation, brings together leaders from the eastern and western branches of the tribe.

Back in Georgia, the Torch Relay heads toward the city of Dalton, in the heart of one of the nation's major carpet manufacturing areas. Fittingly, a red-carpet welcome is laid out, with swaths of locally manufactured carpet leading into the city and covering the entire roadway into downtown.

In the midday heat, the Torch Relay turns onto a dusty road that leads to the grounds of New Echota, the one-time capital of the Cherokee Nation. In this historic

the last stopping place of today's journey. Astonishingly, nearly 200,000 people are waiting there, lining the banks of a newly constructed riverside park that residents created as a memorial to the visit of the Olympic flame.

It seems impossible but inevitable that the crowds will grow still larger during the remaining three days of the Torch Relay's journey to Atlanta and onto the field of Olympic Stadium.

ERIC C GRAVITT • LARRY G GRAWBURG • BESSIE M GRAY • BRENDA S GRAY • CAROL GRAY • CHARROLL E GRAY • CHERYL R GRAY • DALE T GRAY • DAVID E GRAY • DEBORAH R GRAY • DORIS W GRAY • DWIGHT D GRAY • ELIZABETH M GRAY • ELLEN L GRAY • FAITH M GRAY • HELEN M GRAY • INGRID S GRAY • JAMES M GRAY • JANE B GRAY • JASON GRAY • JEFFREY W GRAY • JENNIFER J GRAY • JEREMY J GRAY • JIM GRAY • JOEL E GRAY • JOHN R GRAY • KAREN L GRAY • KATHLEEN M GRAY • KIMBERLY A GRAY • LARRY A GRAY • LATANYA C GRAY • LESTER L GRAY • LINDA H GRAY • LINDA L GRAY • LISA M GRAY • LORA J GRAY •

Atlanta, Georgia—3 days to the Games

The first competitions are still four days away, but thousands of spectators are getting a preview of what is to come during podium training sessions for men's and women's gymnastics. A record total of more than 40,000 people attend these three sessions, which are the sports equivalent of a dress rehearsal.

Venue preparations are not going quite as planned at Savannah's Olympic yachting venue, which is returning to normal after being evacuated because of a hurricane. ACOG's emergency

plans were put to the test, but now athletes and boats are back in the water, and the venue's temporary day marina is again fully operational.

Softball officials and umpires give Golden Park, the venue for this new sport in the Olympic programme, high marks in the final inspection of the facility. After a careful tour of the remodeled minor-league ballpark—including an examination of the newly laid infield, outfield fences, and clubhouses—the venue is pronounced ready for Olympic competition.

Atlanta–Fulton County Stadium, the baseball venue, will not require major adaptation. This is fortunate, since the final home game of the Atlanta Braves will not be over until the end of today. With Olympic baseball beginning on 20 July, the staff assigned to operate this facility—many of whom have been on-site making preliminary preparations for the last few weeks—are eager to take exclusive use of the venue.

Yesterday at Olympic Stadium, the Opening Ceremony's final practice before the dress rehearsal was conducted. Families of cast members were invited to this session, which was complete with costumes and props. As will be the case for the final dress rehearsal tomorrow night, the lighting of the Olympic cauldron was not included. The identity of the person or persons who will have this honor remains the most closely guarded secret of the Games, despite the

fact that dozens of reporters are scouting for information, and one is stationed around the clock at the cauldron in the hope of obtaining clues.

In Centennial Olympic Park, hundreds of visitors are especially attracted to the Fountain of Rings, stepping into the shallow pools around the water display to splash and dance. Crowds are also enjoying Southern Crossroads, the Olympic Arts Festival program for the park that features performances on three stages, parades of dance troupes, and a marketplace with southern crafts and food.

Today, the countdown T-shirt auctioned through the Centennial Olympic Games Hanes T-Shirt Auction attracts a final bid of $32,500. Proceeds from this sale—and from those held during the previous 31 days, the final days remaining before the Games, and the 17 days of the Games themselves—will benefit Olympic Aid–Atlanta, a UNICEF program for children in war-torn countries. To help attract contributions, 18 Olympic athletes acting as spokespersons for the program make daily appearances in the park and at other locations.

Most of the athletes who will compete in the 1996 Games have arrived at the Olympic Village. The sundry shop business is booming, especially the sale of postcards. Almost 4,000 are sold today. Athletes are also calling home, using facilities installed exclusively for them at AT&T's Global Olympic Village in the park.

left: **Crowds are already gathering at Centennial Olympic Park.**

right: **To prepare for Games-time, Atlanta–Fulton County Stadium requires only minor adaptations, such as application of the Look of the Games.**

LYNN K GRAY • MARK F GRAY • MARSHALL S GRAY • MARTHA S GRAY • MARTIN B GRAY • MEGAN E GRAY • MICHAEL D GRAY • NANCY A GRAY • NANCY D GRAY • N'DIEYE GRAY • RICHARD H GRAY • ROBERT F GRAY • ROBERT JR GRAY • RONALD P GRAY • ROY GRAY • SARAH H GRAY • STEPHEN M GRAY • STEVEN C GRAY • SUSAN E GRAY • SUSAN H GRAY • SUSAN W GRAY • TARA GRAY • TERRA L GRAY • TERRI P GRAY • TERRY L GRAY • TIMOTHY W GRAY • UNA V GRAY • WILMA M GRAY • EDWARD J GRAY JR • WILLIAM C GRAYBILL II • CORA L GRAYER • PAULINE H GRAYS • ANGELA M GRAYSON • DOROTHY J GRAYSON •

18 JULY 1996

Stone Mountain, Georgia, to Atlanta, Georgia

With the Opening Ceremony set to begin in just 36 hours, the Olympic flame has finally reached the outskirts of Atlanta, arriving in the small village of Stone Mountain. This momentous day began with the flame reaching for the sky, as runners headed to the top of nearby Stone Mountain, the largest outcropping of granite in the world.

Overlooking the venues for archery, cycling, and tennis, the mountaintop also provides a view of metropolitan Atlanta, where crowds have been gathering

to move at its normal pace. Late this afternoon, more than 100,000 people throng the Courthouse Square in Roswell. Many try to follow the flame's progression into Atlanta, but the crowds make this type of movement impossible.

Moving south toward the city of Atlanta, the Torch Relay is an hour behind schedule and losing more time each minute as the pace slows to a crawl. People of all ages claim places along the route as much as six hours before the planned arrival of the flame.

In the popular Buckhead area of Atlanta, it is midnight when the first torchbearer comes into view, and

left: **The crowds that cluster along the path of the Olympic torch are so large that the relay falls an hour behind schedule.**

right: **Around midnight, the Torch Relay reaches the popular Buckhead area, urging crowds of people enjoying Atlanta nightlife to seize this opportunity to join in the Olympic Spirit.**

through the night in anticipation of the arrival of the Olympic flame.

As the Torch Relay descends Stone Mountain, the atmosphere is electric. Today, the flame will travel along a circuitous route through the suburbs—a route that has been well publicized and is already familiar to Atlantans—to give as many residents as possible an opportunity to share in this Olympic experience.

Throughout the day, people cluster so thickly along the route that it is nearly impossible for the Torch Relay

the cars in the caravan must proceed slowly and carefully through the crowd that presses in from all sides. Still, the torchbearers keep the flame moving forward as the ranks of cheering, whistling, and waving fans continue to grow. By dawn tomorrow, more than half of Atlanta's metropolitan-area population of over 3 million will have had the chance to experience the Torch Relay. Most seize the opportunity, taking from it memories that will last a lifetime.

EDWARD P GRAYSON • GINGER GRAYSON • JOSEPH C GRAYSON • LYNNE T GRAYSON • MATTHEW P GRAYSON • WILLIAM J GRAZIANO • NYEEMAH GRAZIER • SULLY F GREABER • KEVIN M GREANEY • BRADY B GREATHOUSE SAT • DENSILL D GREAVES • JAY W GREAVES • JOHN T GREAVES • LEE A GREAVES • MICANEL A GREAVES • ANTHONY J GRECO • DANIELA SABRINA GRECO • RUTH H GRECO • GAIL P GREEAR • PRISCILLA A GREEAR • VANESSA D GREELEY • GAIL M GREELY • AGNES P GREEN • ANNA L GREEN • ANNELISE GREEN • APRIL C GREEN • BARBARA J GREEN • BARBARA Z GREEN • BETHIA GREEN

Atlanta, Georgia—1 day to the Games

Olympic Stadium was nearly filled to its 85,000-seat capacity last night as Olympic Games staff and volunteers attended the Opening Ceremony dress rehearsal. This preview, traditionally performed for those who helped stage the Games, met with overwhelming approval. Fueled by the excitement and emotion of the previous evening, staff members are now eager for the Games to begin.

At Centennial Olympic Park, their enthusiasm is matched by that of the thousands of visi-

tors who are standing in line well before the opening time of 10 a.m. One of the most popular attractions today is the newly opened exhibition at the Swatch pavilion, an *Olympic Portfolio: Photographs by Annie Leibovitz*. The photographs displayed in this exhibition will change daily once the Games begin, as Leibovitz will continue to capture the athletes of the Centennial Olympic Games on film with her unmistakable photographic style.

Atlanta and the world is being provided another look at Olympic athletes and the Olympic Village by NBC-TV's *Today Show*, which has begun broadcasting live from the Village's international zone. The program features panoramic views of the Village and interviews with athletes, who are eager to talk about the experience of living in an international environment.

The weather is warm and humid, making competitors practicing at the Lake Lanier venue for canoe/kayak–sprint and rowing truly appreciative of their sports. They are also enjoying excellent protection from the lightning that sometimes accompanies summer thunderstorms. ACOG has installed a special computer system at the venue to track static activity in the air and

predict when lightning will strike. It sends a warning signal to lake officials who can then evacuate the lake quickly.

In the 100,000 sq ft (9,300 sq m) Atlanta Market Center, the final touches are being put on one of the largest exhibitions of the Olympic Arts Festival. Called *Centennial Collectibles: Olymphilex '96*, it will be the most comprehensive gathering ever of the world's greatest collections of Olympic and sports-related stamps, coins, and memorabilia. IOC President Juan Antonio Samaranch will attend the official open-

ing of the exhibition later today and designate the official poster of the Centennial Games.

Other Olympic Arts Festival programs are already attracting audiences, such as the series of plays and musical performances now opening throughout the city and the dance performances that will soon begin.

The Centennial Olympic Games open tomorrow, and while Atlanta and other Olympic host cities in the Southeast hasten to make final preparations, the scene is more tranquil at the Olympic Youth Camp on the Berry College campus north of Atlanta. A record 458 youngsters from 152 countries have been assigned rooms and introduced to the camp's facilities and are now establishing the bonds of friendship and cross-cultural understanding that are at the heart of the Olympic Movement. During their stay, these campers and their counselors and staff members will leave this peaceful setting to attend sport competitions and events of the Olympic Arts Festival.

far left and center: **Opening Ceremony cast members adjust their costumes.**

right: **IOC President Juan Antonio Samaranch selects the official poster for the 1996 Centennial Olympic Games.**

BETTYE J GREEN • BILLY R GREEN • BONNIE B GREEN • BRADLEY S GREEN • CALVIN M GREEN • CHAD GREEN • CHARLES M GREEN • CLARICE F GREEN • DEBORAH H GREEN • DUEL E GREEN • EARL GREEN • ELAINE F GREEN • ELBERT L GREEN • ELEANOR M GREEN • ELIZABETH A GREEN • ELLABETH THOMAS GREEN • EMILY L GREEN • FREDERICK M GREEN • GLENDA L GREEN • JAMES GREEN • JAMES A GREEN • JAMES L. GREEN • JAMES M GREEN • JASON K GREEN • JEANNETTA B GREEN • JOEL GREEN • JOHN B GREEN • JONATHAN GREEN • JUDITH E GREEN • JUSTINE GREEN • KEITH E GREEN • KEVIN J GREEN •

19 JULY 1996

Atlanta

left: **Coretta Scott King carries the flame near King Chapel at Morehouse College.**

center: **Former Atlanta Mayor Maynard Jackson escorts leaders of the Greek community in Atlanta with the universal beacon—the Olympic torch.**

right: **Atlanta Mayor Bill Campbell receives the torch at City Hall.**

Atlanta, Georgia—Opening Day of the Games

Today, more than seven years of hopes, dreams, plans, preparations in Atlanta and a 16,700 mi (26, 875 km) journey involving 12,467 runners from the hills of ancient Olympia to the modern metropolis of Atlanta will culminate in a Ceremony held tonight at Olympic Stadium to open the 1996 Centennial Olympic Games.

At 6:08 a.m., the final day of the Torch Relay is launched from Hapeville, a small suburb south of Atlanta. Under clear, pre-dawn skies, runners begin to advance the sacred flame on the final leg of its 84-day

journey in the US. It will not reach its ultimate destination for more than 18 hours, when the final runner or runners, whose identity is still kept secret to all but a handful of senior Olympic and broadcast officials, will enter Olympic Stadium and ignite the Olympic cauldron, which will hold the central symbol of the Olympic Spirit throughout the Games.

Throughout this final day of the Centennial Olympic Torch Relay, momentum and excitement build as the size and enthusiasm of the crowds that witness it grow. From a few individuals along some of the less populated stretches of road to the final run into the city, the excitement and anticipation surrounding the flame build throughout the day—mile after mile and wave upon wave. The hot July sun does not keep people from waiting for hours to see and be touched by this symbol of the Olympic ideals—achievement, peace, and unity.

From babes-in-arms to the very elderly, sometimes supported by walkers or wheelchairs, Atlanta-area resi-

dents and those who have come from afar are united in the Olympic Spirit and the euphoria that surrounds the flame. Cheers mingle with tears, pride with awe, and joy with a sense of reverence as the flame winds its way through normally quiet neighborhoods, along ordinarily busy commercial routes, and finally down along Atlanta's spine, Peachtree Street. Wherever the torch goes, people suspend their usual business to contribute their good wishes and collective energy. To be one of the 1.5 million people who form a ribbon of humanity that stretches around and gradually winds its way into the heart of the city is an Olympic experience to cherish for a lifetime.

These final torchbearers seem to float upon the crest of the crowd's excitement as they run their assigned stretch and hand the torch to the next eager runner. These community heroes are overwhelmed by the way their presence seems to inspire all who see them in person or on television. The heroism of these runners prefigures that of the 10,700 Olympic athletes who will embody the Olympic ideals through their athletic performances in the days ahead.

A flurry of official activities throughout the day adds momentum to the already charged atmosphere in Atlanta. In a special ceremony held early in the day, IOC President Juan Antonio Samaranch names 12 new IOC members. He also pays visits to the Main Press Center and the International Broadcast Center, which are now fully operational. Meanwhile, President Bill Clinton, who has just arrived in Atlanta to attend and participate

Atlanta 1996

LEON GREEN • LEWIS E GREEN • LILLIE L GREEN • LINDA A GREEN • LINDA R GREEN • LISA C GREEN • LYNNE GREEN • MAGGIEANN W GREEN • MELANIE GREEN • MICHAEL K GREEN • NAOMI B GREEN • NATHAN L GREEN • NATHANIEL GREEN • NICHOLE GREEN • PHILIP E GREEN • PHILIP R GREEN • PHYLLIS A GREEN • RICARDO R GREEN • ROBERT N GREEN • RONA R GREEN • RONALD M GREEN • SANDRA S GREEN • SANDY F GREEN • SARAH A GREEN • SCOTT T GREEN • SHAGONDA GREEN • SHELIA D GREEN • SHERRY A GREEN • SHIRLEY E GREEN • STACY R GREEN • STANLEY GREEN • STEPHANIE L GREEN •

in the Opening Ceremony, visits the Atlanta Olympic Village to meet the athletes.

Activity at Olympic ticket booths is extremely brisk. At the last moment, more than 2,000 more Opening Ceremony tickets are released for sale, adding to already long lines. Demand for Olympic tickets has never been higher than in Atlanta. With nearly 9 million tickets for sale, ACOG exceeds other Olympic Games' offerings by a substantial margin. Although the availability of most tickets forces scalpers to to sell tickets at or below face value, ticket booths will remain busy throughout the Games.

After more than 11 hours on the road, the Olympic torch, carried by former Atlanta Mayor Maynard Jackson, arrives at Atlanta's City Hall, where it will be on view for several hours before departing for the final leg of its journey. Mayor Bill Campbell is on hand to greet the torch and conduct a brief welcoming ceremony.

The capacity audience that will attend the evening's Opening Ceremony is already making its way to the Olympic Stadium. As the audience begins to sit down, thousands upon thousands of other Olympic fans in Atlanta also begin to take their places—at backyard barbecues, in family rooms, at Atlanta's numerous sports bars and hotels, and in Centennial Olympic Park. The entire city is suspended between a party atmosphere and a feeling of hushed anticipation. Around the world, televisions are turned on, video recorders are prepared, food and drink is set out, and families, friends, and strangers gather to await the grand event. For nearly three hours, over 3.5 billion people throughout the world settle down to watch the most popular program in history.

As the countdown nears zero, audience members within Olympic Stadium rehearse several critical sequences in which they will participate during the evening's festivities. Rehearsals are over for the 10,000 musicians, dancers, twirlers, drivers, and other types of performers who will participate in the Opening Ceremony and are now beneath and around the stadium, preparing for the show.

Across the way, nearly 15,000 athletes, trainers, and other team officials are gathering at Atlanta–Fulton County Stadium to prepare for their traditional march

into the Olympic Stadium. Organized by delegation, this colorful assemblage is larger and represents more countries than ever before.

Just as the ceremony begins, the sun sinks below the horizon and the torch leaves its resting place in City Hall, carried proudly by Olympic gold medal-winner and Georgia native Mel Pender. For the last leg of its journey, the torch will be taken to the historic Martin Luther King Jr. Center for Nonviolent Social Change and then on toward Olympic Stadium where it will appear in a few hours, carried by an as-yet-unnamed individual.

top left: Volunteers place ceremony kits on the seats of Olympic Stadium.

Spectators flock to Olympic Stadium with souvenir tickets in hand *(top right)* to claim their seats for the Opening Ceremony (*bottom left and middle right*).

bottom right: At Atlanta Fulton–County Stadium, athletes prepare for their traditional parade into the Olympic Stadium.

STUART M GREEN • SUBIE B GREEN • SUE C GREEN • TYKNETRA S GREEN • VERONICA L GREEN • VILINDA K GREEN • VIVIAN GREEN • WENDY R GREEN • WILLIAM GREEN • WILLIAM R GREEN • WILLIE A GREEN • WILLIE J GREEN • DAVID T GREEN ATC • ULRICH GREEN JR • JANET L GREEN MT • DAN GREENBAUM • DANIEL GREENBAUM • DAVID R GREENBAUM • JENNIFER L GREENBAUM • JOEL D GREENBAUM • JULIE GREENBAUM • SARA A GREENBAUM • BRAD D GREENBERG • ERIC I GREENBERG • FRANK E GREENBERG • JASON G GREENBERG • JAYNE D GREENBERG • LARRY B GREENBERG • LESLIE R GREENBERG •

CELEBRATING THE GAMES

OPENING CEREMONY
19 JULY 1996

AUDIENCE REHEARSALS and last-minute preparations are complete. A giant digital clock marks two minutes before the show begins, and as the seconds begin to fall away, anticipation grows within the stadium. The final two-minute countdown synchronizes the more than 170 broadcast networks and the more than 3.5 billion people throughout the world who are watching, waiting for the world's greatest peacetime event to begin. At 30 seconds to go, an image from each of the preceding 25 Olympic Games flashes on the screen, one per second, beginning with one from the first modern Games, held in Athens, Greece, in 1896. The first of numerous fireworks displays bursts from behind the giant scoreboard, building the excitement and sending the stadium audience into the first of countless ovations that will be heard throughout the evening.

Three major themes—each of which articulates, illuminates, and celebrates a key message of Atlanta's Olympic Games—link the various segments of the ceremony together: Atlanta, the American South, and its diversity; the centennial of the modern Olympic Games; and the celebration of youth.

To call together the 10,700 athletes of the Centennial Olympic Games and the billions of viewers throughout the world who will watch them compete, the opening segment begins by evoking and celebrating the powerful symbolism of the interlocking Olympic Rings. Representing the five continental associations participating in the Games and the universality of humanity, the five spirits of the Olympic Rings rise above the rim of Olympic Stadium. Emerging as if from enormous flames, each

spirit is draped in huge streamers of flowing fabric matching the color of their respective ring which are thrust skyward by huge wind machines. As they rise in succession, each spirit is accompanied by a distinctive call, drums and percussion representative of the world gathering together to celebrate the Games.

As each spirit emerges from the stadium rim, a huge banner of fabric matching the colors of the Olympic Rings sweeps over the audience and onto the field, triggering the arrival of the tribes of the Olympic Rings. Bursting into the stadium from several entry points, hundreds of these Olympic tribe members, costumed in the

The spirits of the Olympic Rings rise in succession above Olympic Stadium to the percussive sounds that call the world to gather together for the Games.

LINDA A GREENBERG • JOEL A GREENBERG MD • ADRIENNE D GREENE • ALLA Y GREENE • ALMA V GREENE • CORAL GREENE • DECEMBER GREENE • ELIZABETH GREENE • GINNY GREENE • GLENNA L GREENE • GLORIA S GREENE • JAMES H GREENE • JASON C GREENE • JASON E GREENE • JEANNETTE S GREENE • KASUNDRA GREENE • KATHY GREENE • KELLY GREENE • LAVONDA GREENE • MARVA F. GREENE • MATTHEW R GREENE • MELANIE M GREENE • MELINDA M GREENE • NYJA GREENE • PAULA L GREENE • RICHARD L GREENE • RICKEY W GREENE • ROBERT L GREENE • SARALYN GREENE •

colors of the Olympic Rings, pour joyously into the stadium, bearing musical instruments from all over the world and merging into a unifying dance to dramatize the social message of Olympism. The drumbeats of the world, which reverberate from 10-drum towers mounted on a mobile carrier, are supplemented by more than 1,000 percussion instruments played by tribe members.

As the show unfolds, five tribe members, portrayed by US Army Rangers, dramatically sail into the stadium from its top rim, each

top: The Flag Corps of the Atlanta Olympic Band forms a circle surrounding the Centennial Olympic Games logo.

bottom: US President Bill Clinton, accompanied by IOC President Juan Antonio Samaranch and ACOG President and CEO Billy Payne, applauds the US Air Force Thunderbirds.

trailing a stream of fabric that matches one of the colors of the five Olympic Rings.

As the tribes converge to form the interlocking Olympic Rings, 450 Atlanta children, all dressed in white, spill onto the field and form the centennial number "100" beneath the rings. This colorful sequence culminates with the Atlanta Symphony Orchestra's performance of the Olympic Centennial theme, "Summon the Heroes," composed and conducted by John Williams, one of America's most eminent and beloved musicians. During this performance, in a dramatic and emotionally charged transformation that achieves one of the ceremony's most memorable moments, the five tribes unite into a single world family as the children's formation becomes a dove of peace.

In a traditional Olympic ceremony that honors the national government of the host country, the 250-member Flag Corps of the Atlanta Olympic Marching Band parades onto the field bearing large red, white, and blue flags and forms a circle surrounding the Centennial Olympic Games logo. The Joint Services Color Guard, carrying the American flag and the colors of the US Army, Navy, Marine Corps, Air Force, and Coast Guard, joins the flag corps at the center of the field. To the sound of "Ruffles and Flourishes," performed by the US Army Herald Trumpets, US President Bill Clinton enters the stadium and is greeted by IOC President Juan Antonio Samaranch and ACOG President and CEO Billy Payne. Accompanied by the Atlanta Symphony Orchestra, the Centennial Choir—300 singers from Atlanta's top choral ensembles—brings the audience to its feet for the US national anthem, "The Star-Spangled Banner," which is followed by a dramatic stadium flyby from the eight-member US Air Force Thunderbirds in their F-16C Fighting Falcon aircraft.

Now it's Atlanta's turn to welcome the world. The stadium rocks to a contemporary, hip-hop soundtrack that reflects many kinds of southern music, such as country and bluegrass, in an extended, vibrant sequence featuring 1,200 young performers. In a high-powered greeting, reflecting the warmth, hospitality, and effervescent energy of southerners, 500 cheerleaders, 170 precision dancers, 180 steppers, 24 cloggers, and the 300-member Southwest DeKalb High School Marching Band

STEPHANIE Y GREENE • STEVEN B GREENE • THOMAS C GREENE • VENITA W GREENE • WILLIAM R GREENE • DAVID L GREENFIELD • ROBERT T GREENFIELD • WILLIAM H GREENHAW • JANET L GREENHAWK • JANET L GREENHILL • SHANNON L GREENHILL • BARRY D GREENHOUSE • MERYL L GREENHOUSE • GARY A GREENHUT • PAM LUTRICIA GREENLEAF • ANDY GREENLEE • ROBERT GREENLEE • MICHELE R GREENOUGH • JOHN F GREENSLIT • DAVID S GREENSPAN • STACY J GREENSTEIN • STEVEN L GREENSTEIN • DAVID H GREENWALD • JARED L GREENWALD • MICHELLE A GREENWALT • EDWIN R GREENWAY

left and right: Atlanta welcomes the world with a high-energy greeting reflecting southern warmth, hospitality, and energy.

• JOSEPH A GREENWAY • LETITIA M GREENWAY • CHRISTINE GREENWELL • AUDREY GREENWOOD • CHRISTOPHER N GREENWOOD • GIL J GREENWOOD • ANNIE M GREER • BARBARA A GREER • CHARLES A GREER • CHRISTY D GREER • DAVID W GREER • ELIZABETH J GREER • HENRY C GREER • JANE D GREER • JILL S GREER • LYNDA K GREER • MELISSA A GREER • OTHA M GREER • RACHEL E GREER • ROBERT S GREER • ROSE E GREER • SADIE N GREER • SHIRLEY L GREER • SUSAN H GREER • TIFFANY A GREER • TINA E GREER • HAL W GREER III • CARRIE C GREESON • SUSAN M GREFRATH • DELIA M GREGG •

converge on the field. As the music continues to build, the pulsing performers form the word "Atlanta," inspiring the audience to respond by shouting "Atlanta" three times. They repeat this performance with another message, the decidedly southern greeting, "How y'all doin'?" Suddenly, just as the segment seems to reach its peak, 30 chrome trucks zoom onto and encircle the field. The shiny trucks, each of which carries a spotlight to illuminate the festivities, represent an important contemporary icon of the American South. As the minicaravan moves

This beautiful interlude sets the stage for one of the most dramatic and significant artistic segments of the ceremony. It is also Atlanta's opportunity to convey the essence of southern culture and history to the world.

The four-part pageant opens with a segment representing the birth of the southern spirit called "Southern Summer Night." The lush landscape comes to life with nearly 500 performers beautifully costumed as butterflies and fireflies darting through the dark, while the moon rises to meet the new sun and the start

left: **Giant splashes of water move among catfish in "The River," a segment designed to represent the music and traditions of the American South.**

right: **"Southern Summer Night," a segment representing the birth of the southern spirit, comes to life as butterflies and fireflies dart through the dark.**

from position to position in synch with the performers, the trucks sweep their spotlights upward to the audience which, waving colored scarves, performs the "wave," a popular stadium spectator movement known throughout most of the world as the "ola!"

Shifting into a more reflective mood and tempo, this celebratory welcome is warmly enhanced by one of Atlanta's renowned musical superstars, Gladys Knight. Rising majestically from beneath the center of the field, she sings "Georgia on My Mind," the official state song and a perennial favorite.

of the new day. Punctuated by the chattering, buzzing, and humming of a busy insect world and accompanied by a gorgeous soundtrack, this spectacular sequence is dazzling. The beautiful costumes, with their subtle, undulating movement and rich detail, combine to delight the audience and create the second segment, "The River."

Old Man River flows through the southern landscape on a chariot led by four southern catfish, bringing to life the music and traditions of the American South. Giant puppets representing belles, gents, country and jazz dancers, jazz bands, and children all float down

ELLEN S GREGG • JEFFERY R GREGG • JENNIFER A GREGG • NATASHA H GREGG • ROBERT L GREGG • SUSAN L GREGG • TONYA L GREGG • TRACIE M GREGG SAT • ANITA GREGOIRE • ALICE M GREGORY • ANNA RUTH GREGORY • BEVERLY A GREGORY • CHADWICK GREGORY • CHARLOTTE L GREGORY • COLLEEN O GREGORY • FRANK GREGORY • HAGIN S GREGORY • KEN GREGORY • LINDA G GREGORY • LYNN L GREGORY • MARCUS W GREGORY • MARGARET R. GREGORY • MICHAEL E GREGORY • MONIQUE L GREGORY • ROBERT J GREGORY • RON L GREGORY • RUSSELL G GREGORY • SLOAN S GREGORY •

the river, moving to the beat and melody of a lively musical soundtrack that builds in momentum throughout the segment. This marvelous section bubbles with pure joy until suddenly the next segment, "The Storm," erupts.

This segment reflects the periods of turmoil that have tested the South and southerners during the region's history. Led by a gigantic thunderbird, representative of transformation for many Native American cultures, several hundred performers enter the stadium carrying an enormous storm cloud made of thousands of yards of fabric, which depicts the lashing of a storm upon the land. But the South is extraordinarily resilient, and in the final section of this grand production, "Rebirth and Celebration," the storm passes and the southern spirit rises again, triumphant. The chorus breaks into a glorious "Hallelujah" and a climactic version of "When the Saints Go Marching In" as the

giant puppets, butterflies, and fireflies join in a final celebration of the strength of the southern spirit.

With the conclusion of this spectacular celebration of the traditions, spirit, and music of the American South, the program shifts to a celebration of the centennial of the Olympic Games. Opening with a tribute to the origins of the Games in ancient Greece, a solemn procession of temple builders, goddesses, and athletes slowly converges toward a brilliant sacred light in the center of the field. As the procession arrives at the light, the temple builders erect a Temple of Zeus. The enormous temple is created with horizontal classical Greek columns arranged in a huge circle around a central light which are gradually raised to a vertical position. An enormous cloth wall that seems to rise from the ground

The silhouettes of athletes posed in classic Olympic sports positions appear on the walls of an ancient Greek-style temple.

TERRY G GREGORY • TRACY L GREGORY • VIVIAN GREGORY • DEBRA A GREGORY-SUGRUE • HARRY H GREGORY III • SAMUEL GREGORY JR • WOODY GREGORY JR • ADINA S P GREINER • DANIELA GREINER • PAMELA A GREINER • WENDY M GREINER • JUDITH B GRENFELL • INA GRENNES • BETTY R GRENNOR • DENISE S GRENTZ • SIEGFRIED GRENTZ • THOMAS R GRESBACK • JO ANN GRESH • RUTH GRESH • ALBERTA GRESHAM • ALLISON N GRESHAM • AMANDA M GRESHAM • CAROLE J GRESHAM • HAROLD E GRESHAM • HAROLD V GRESHAM • MAXINE GRESHAM • MELINDA G GRESHAM • NANCY C GRESHAM •

61

connects the columns, forming a grand temple within which athletes pose in classic Olympic sport positions, while the sacred light within the temple projects these poses into 50-foot (15-meter) silhouettes on the temple walls. A simulated ancient competition follows, with Greco-Roman wrestling, weightlifting, running, and other sports depicted in silhouette. The entire segment is accompanied by a dramatic, ceremonial musical score.

As the glory of the ancient Games disappears, the image of Baron Pierre de Coubertin, founder of the modern Olympic Games, is projected on screens around the stadium. His voice calls for the creation of the modern Games, which recalls the five Olympic spirits from the ceremony's initial segment. As the spirits rise again from the stadium rim, the vocal calls and percussive sounds heard at the beginning of the ceremony are repeated in a dramatic summons to the nations to revive the Games.

The stadium, which has been darkened, is illuminated again to reveal the track for the first time. A series of runners emerges from the

top: In keeping with tradition, the parade of participants begins with the delegation from Greece, which receives a tremendous welcome from the audience.

bottom: A runner carrying a flag representing the first modern Games held in Athens precedes a succession of runners carrying flags representing the previous Olympic host cities.

center of the field, each carrying a flag representing a previous host city of the modern Games, from Athens to Atlanta. As they join their colleagues, the runners merge into a formation around the stadium's track. The excitement builds until the final runner emerges from an opening in the center of the field bearing the Atlanta flag. The crowd roars as the Atlanta runner, sprinting to reach the group, finally leads them up a long ramp at the north end of the stadium, where the

RICHARD P GRESHAM • RODNEY C GRESHAM • VIRGINIA L GRESHAM • LAMAR W GRESHAM JR • SANDRA L GRESHENFELD • SANDRA L GRESHENFELD • JILL E GRESLEY PT • ILA L GRESSETTE • CAROLYN J GREST • KEITH M GREST • BERNICE A GRETH • PETER GREYLING • VALERIE GREZES • FRANK E GRIBBLE • HERMA JEAN I GRIBBLE • JOEL GRICE • LONNIE T GRICE • VALERIE GRICOURT • LE TINA R GRIDDINE • LINDA ANN GRIEPSMA • CURTIS L GRIER • DEBORAH A GRIER • JAMES O GRIER • LAURA A GRIER • PAUL G GRIESE • BERNARD A GRIESEMER MD • AARON GRIESER • ROBERT H GRIESER JR. • ELEANOR G GRIESHABER

As host country, the American delegation enters last and is welcomed with a thunderous roar that lasts throughout their lap around the stadium.

athletes of the Centennial Olympic Games are ready to make their dramatic entry.

As the flag bearers climb the long ramp extending from the ground to the top of the stadium, the upper section of the ramp suddenly drops away to create an unexpected entryway for the athletes. When the opening at the top of the ramp appears, the first athletes pour over the rim and into the stadium, down the ramp, and onto the track in a spectacular cascade of Olympians that will continue for more than two hours.

Atlanta has seated all the Olympians outside the stadium during the Opening Ceremony so that their entrance into the facility will have the greatest dramatic effect possible. These Olympians have been waiting and watching the proceedings on large video monitors in Atlanta–Fulton County Stadium, which is adjacent to Olympic Stadium.

In keeping with tradition, the delegation from Greece appears first, greeted by a tremendous welcome from the stadium audience. The delegations then follow in alphabetical order,

• JULIA A GRIEST • DEBRA D GRIFFEY • RICHARD D GRIFFEY • AFIYA E GRIFFIN • ALBERT GRIFFIN • ALTHEA R GRIFFIN • AMANDA G GRIFFIN • ANDY M GRIFFIN • ANTHONY L GRIFFIN • BOBBY J GRIFFIN • BRANDON S GRIFFIN • BRIDGET J GRIFFIN • CAROLYN A GRIFFIN • CASEY T GRIFFIN • CHARLES H GRIFFIN • CHERYL A GRIFFIN • CHERYL P GRIFFIN • CINDY C GRIFFIN • COURTNEY M GRIFFIN • CRISTOPHOR M GRIFFIN • DARREN GRIFFIN • DARYLL H GRIFFIN • DAVID S GRIFFIN • DENNIS W GRIFFIN • DONALD L GRIFFIN • DONNA A GRIFFIN • ELIZABETH G GRIFFIN • FRANKLIN R GRIFFIN • HERBERT L GRIFFIN •

63

except for the host nation, which enters last. Following a celebratory lap around the track, the Olympians are led to designated places on the field to await the arrival of their colleagues and the lighting of the Olympic flame.

The largely American audience greets the entry of the American delegation, emerging at the end of the two-hour procession with a thunderous roar that lasts throughout their celebratory lap around the Olympic track.

When athletes from the 197 participating delegations group together, they fill the entire

Eight Olympians carry the Olympic flag around the stadium after the Games are declared officially open.

field. This gathering of almost 11,000 athletes is the largest in Olympic history.

With the athletes gathered, IOC President Juan Antonio Samaranch and ACOG President Billy Payne mount the large platform in the center of the field to make brief opening remarks. US President Bill Clinton then rises from the presidential box to declare the Games of the XXVI Olympiad officially open.

The eight former Olympians selected by ACOG to carry the Olympic flag into and around the stadium make their entrance, accompanied by the traditional, popular Shaker hymn, "Simple Gifts." Composed for the inaugural 1896 Games, the Olympic hymn is performed by the Atlanta Symphony Orchestra and Centennial Chorus as the flag is raised in this dignified, solemn, and pivotal moment

that is a part of each Olympic Opening Ceremony. In a traditional Olympic gesture of peace following the raising of the Olympic flag, 300 symbolic doves—actually dove kites—move through the athletes on the field, carried by 100 Atlanta children.

J FOTHA GRIFFIN • JAMES P GRIFFIN • JEFFREY P GRIFFIN • JENNA E GRIFFIN • JIM GRIFFIN • JOHN L GRIFFIN • JOHN M. GRIFFIN • JOSEPH E GRIFFIN • KAREN D GRIFFIN • KAREN M GRIFFIN • KATHERINE GRIFFIN • KEN GRIFFIN • KENNETH GRIFFIN • KENNETH W GRIFFIN • KENTON G GRIFFIN • KENYA GRIFFIN • LESLEY A GRIFFIN • LINDA C GRIFFIN • LISA D GRIFFIN • LISA R GRIFFIN • MARSHA A GRIFFIN • MARTHA D GRIFFIN • MARY GRIFFIN • MATTIE R GRIFFIN • MEGAN D GRIFFIN • MELINDA C GRIFFIN • MICHAEL A GRIFFIN • PAUL M GRIFFIN • PORTIA T GRIFFIN • RANDY L GRIFFIN • REAGAN L GRIFFIN •

To sustain this important moment dedicated to world peace, Atlanta presents a simple, emotionally stirring tribute to honor the memory and accomplishments of its native son, the Reverend Martin Luther King Jr., a man who dreamed of and worked toward a world united in peace. Portions of King's extraordinary "I Have a Dream" speech are heard, accompanied by projections of his image and a beautiful musical score. Audience members participate in illuminating the stadium with more than 80,000 small flashlights to create a dazzling tribute of light to Dr. King.

The Atlanta Symphony Orchestra and Centennial Chorus perform the Olympic hymn as the Olympic flag is raised.

ROMONA H GRIFFIN • SYDNEY G GRIFFIN • TERRENCE GRIFFIN • TONY GRIFFIN • TORRI L GRIFFIN • WILLIAM J GRIFFIN • WILLIAM T GRIFFIN • GWENDOLYN C GRIFFIN-ODOM • JEFFREY T GRIFFIN ATC • JOHN M. GRIFFIN MD • LETHA Y GRIFFIN MD • KAREN M GRIFFIN PT • AYTEN GRIFFITH • CAREY L GRIFFITH • GAIL GRIFFITH • GERRILL L GRIFFITH • JACK P GRIFFITH • JACKIE B GRIFFITH • JACQUELINE B GRIFFITH • JAMES M GRIFFITH • JULIA A GRIFFITH • KAREN S GRIFFITH • LAURA L GRIFFITH • NAOMI K GRIFFITH • TEDFORD J GRIFFITH • MARCUS C GRIFFITH MD • ANN L GRIFFITHS • JUDITH G GRIFFITHS

The oldest living Olympian,
97-year-old Leon Stukelj
of Slovenia, hops spryly
onto the stage, receiving
a standing ovation
from the crowd.

As a special tribute to all the Olympians who competed during the first century of the modern Olympic era, international sports writers have chosen an outstanding Olympian from each modern Olympic Games to be part of this Opening Ceremony. Those gold medalists able to attend this evening's ceremony are announced and invited onto the large circular stage in the center of the field, surrounded by the centennial athletes. The last to be intro- duced is 97-year-old Leon Stukelj of Slovenia, the oldest living Olympian and a gold medal- ist at the 1920 Games in Belgium. The spry, exuberant Olympian makes his way to the center stage, nearly hopping up the stairs, where he is greeted as a hero by the other Olympians and given a standing ovation by the stadium audience.

LINDA J GRIFFITHS • MAUREEN E GRIFFITHS • GEORGE J GRIFFITHS JR • MATTHEW B GRIFFON • LARRY M GRIGGERS • SHIRLEY G GRIGGERS • AMBER L GRIGGS • DEANDRA GRIGGS • IVA J GRIGGS • JEFFREY GRIGGS • TRACY R GRIGGS • VIRGINIA L GRIGGS • HENRY C GRIGGS JR • REBECCA A GRIGLIONE • DONNY P GRIGSBY • BROOKS GRIGSON • TINA A GRILE • TINA A GRILE • CAROL A GRILL • FRANCIS S GRILLO • DONNA L GRILLO • GLENN N GRILLO • ROBERT G GRILLO • FRANK GRIMALDI JR ATC • CHERYL GRIMES • DENNY R GRIMES • HOLLY J GRIMES • JANET E GRIMES • JANET H GRIMES • JOHN P GRIMES •

The almost 11,000 athletes from the 197 participating delegations fill the entire field, resembling a giant quilt.

The most sacred, dramatic, and anticipated moment of the Opening Ceremony has arrived—the arrival of the Olympic flame. It has been 84 days since its arrival in the United States, which, together with the 16 days of competition to come, will equal a symbolic 100 days. In the US, the flame has traveled more than 16,000 mi (25,749 km) in a journey that will conclude momentarily in Atlanta. The stage is set, and 3.5 billion people around the world, along with the assembled athletes of the XXVI Olympiad, eagerly await the sight of the torch being carried into the stadium by an as-yet unknown runner.

Periodically throughout the evening, updates of the torch's progress have been displayed on large screens inside Olympic Stadium. The final runner, four-time discus gold-medal winner Al Oerter, arrives at the stadium and ignites the torch held by another Olympic

JOSEPH D GRIMES • KATE GRIMES • LESLYN B GRIMES • LETITIA L GRIMES • MARK A GRIMES • MICHAEL C GRIMES • NATHANIEL B GRIMES • PAUL S GRIMES • PEGGY A GRIMES • REGINALD D GRIMES • REGINALD D GRIMES • ROBERT H GRIMES • ROSE MARY GRIMES • SCOTT S GRIMES • SHALANDA L GRIMES • WILLIAM A GRIMES • GERALD A GRIMM • MARGARET H GRIMM • WILLIAM O GRIMM IV • BRIAN D GRIMMESEY • CARTER M GRIMMETT • TONI H GRIMMETT • PHYLLIS J GRIND • FLORA J GRINDSTAFF • JACQUELINE E GRINNAGE • ROY GRINSHPAN • JANE G GRINSTEAD • MARY BETH E GRINWIS • JIMMY V GRINZAID •

great, three-time heavyweight world champion boxer Evander Holyfield, a resident of Atlanta. Holyfield, whose identity as the runner who will enter the stadium with the torch has been kept secret, runs into the tunnel that will take him underground and finally up onto the huge raised platform in the center of the field. His surprise appearance is cheered heartily by the stadium audience and the assembled athletes surrounding the platform. Holyfield leaves the platform and heads for the track, where he beckons runner Voula Patoulidou of

Suddenly appearing to the world, standing confidently at the top, is "The Greatest," the incomparable Muhammad Ali, whose presence draws a collective gasp and then a tumultuous roar from the crowd. Ali, the heavyweight boxing gold medalist at the 1960 Rome Games, is today regarded as the greatest professional heavyweight boxing champion of all time.

Evans touches her torch to Ali's, igniting it. Trembling from the palsy that has gripped his body in recent years, Ali raises the torch triumphantly and is answered by wild, euphoric

left: **Evander Holyfield surprises the crowd when he appears in the midst of the athletes with the torch and joins runner Voula Patoulidou of Greece in a lap around the stadium.**

right: **Janet Evans meets Muhammad Ali, whose appearance comes as a complete surprise to the audience, which erupts in applause as his torch ignites.**

Greece. Together, they carry the torch around the stadium track, where they meet another Olympic great, US swimmer Janet Evans, to whom they pass the torch. Accompanied by the strains of Beethoven's "Ode to Joy," Evans holds the torch high as she begins her lap around the track. The cheers from the capacity crowd swell to a deafening roar, as if to propel Evans toward the long ramp leading up to the top of the north end of the stadium.

The eyes of the world are literally focused on Evans as she begins to climb the long ramp.

cheers from the audience. Then, in a magical sleight-of-hand, Ali slowly lowers his torch to ignite a special self-propelling torch that conveys the flame up a long cable to the waiting cauldron. The mechanical torch is ignited, and begins its journey up the high wire. When it reaches the cauldron's edge, the flame races around the enormous spiral, setting each jet ablaze. Tears of joy flow easily and generously from the eyes of many spectators in the giant Olympic Stadium. This culminating moment, so completely unexpected in its final, emotionally charged twist, enthralls, fortifies, and unites the worldwide audience in a feeling that will be sustained throughout Atlanta's Games.

SAMSON B GRIS • JEANNINE A GRISER • AMY D GRISHAM • EMILY L GRISHAM • PAULA A GRISHAM • THOMAS P GRISHAM ATC • JUDY A GRISSETTE • ERNESTINE GRISSOM • WILLIAM J GRIST • RUBY J GRISWELL • ANGIE C GRISWOLD • GUY C GRISWOLD • GIOVANNI V GRITA • VAUGHN A GRIZZARD • CAROL D GRIZZLE • JENNIFER L GRIZZLE • LEWIS B GRIZZLE • MARSHA M GRIZZLE • STEPHANIE M GRIZZLE • SUMMER L GRIZZLE • JOSEPH E GRNO • THOMAS E GROCE • STEPHEN D GROCER • DENNIS M GROGAN • CHRISTOPHER P GROH • NANCY D GROH • DINAH J GROLLMAN • ROBERT A GROLLMAN • CAROL AGROLNICK •

left: Muhammad Ali ignites the self-propelling torch that will light the Olympic cauldron.

right: The Olympic flame fills the cauldron, where it will inspire participants and spectators alike throughout the Centennial Olympic Games.

The crowd gradually settles down for the final segment of the ceremony, the taking of the Olympic oath, in which athletes and judges proclaim their commitment to abide by all rules and to compete and judge in the true spirit of Olympic competition. The administering of the Olympic oath is one of the highest honors that can be bestowed upon an Olympic athlete and judge, and is a privilege made all the more meaningful because of the centennial of these Olympic Games. US women's basketball player Teresa Edwards takes the oath on behalf of all the athletes. Hobie Billingsly takes the oath on behalf of all Olympic judges to

ANATOLI GROMOV • RAYMOND K GRONEK • KEVIN A GRONER • JOHN B GRONWALL • MARSHA J GROOME • ERIC GROOME • JOAN F GROOME • ALLENE GROOTE • ROBERT GROOTE • ANDREW S GROOVER • JAMES L GROOVER • JOHN B GROSKO • JOHN J GROSKO • SHANNON D GROSKO • ARNOLD GROSS • BARBARA J GROSS • DONALD F GROSS • GILMARA G GROSS • HOLLY M GROSS • JEFFREY H GROSS • KAREN E GROSS • ROBERT M GROSS • SHELLY L GROSS • ABIE GROSSFELD • MARION D GROSSMAN • WILLIAM A GROSSMAN • SCOTT A GROSTEFON • JAMAL E GROSVENOR • SANDRA R GROSVENOR •

69

left: Teresa Edwards of the US women's basketball team takes the Olympic oath on behalf of all the competitors in the Games.

right: International pop music star Celine Dion performs "The Power of the Dream."

officiate and preside fairly and impartially over the outcomes of the many intense competitions to be held in the coming days.

To reinforce the Olympic Spirit that has been generated throughout this long, emotional evening, international pop music star Celine Dion performs a new song with lyrics by Linda Thompson, that evokes powerful feelings of triumph and fellowship, "The Power of the Dream." Accompanied by David Foster, who composed the song with Kenneth "Babyface" Edmunds, Dion sings with support from the Atlanta Symphony Orchestra and Centennial Choir. The song's inspirational refrain is:

Feel the flame forever burn
Teaching lessons we must learn
To bring us closer to the power of the dream
The world unites in hope and peace
Pray that it always will be
It is the power of the dream that brings us here.

In a final grand gesture that concludes the evening as it began, the spirits of the Olympic Rings reappear for a third time, calling out to the athletes on the field and signaling the return of the Olympic tribes with drums and percussion. As the tribes take their places on the track surrounding the athletes, world-renowned opera star and native of Augusta, Georgia, Jessye Norman, ascends from the center of the field to perform "Faster, Higher, Stronger," a new work commissioned for this occasion, composed by Mark Watters with lyrics written by Lorraine Feather. Norman's powerful, sweeping performance incites the athletes to achieve their dreams in the days ahead. The ceremony concludes with a spectacular fireworks display that illuminates Atlanta's nighttime sky and heralds the first day of competition.

STEPHEN P GROTE • LAURA C GROUNSELL • JAMES M GROUTT • LINDSAY A GROVE • MICHAEL L GROVE • ROBERT L GROVE • ROBIN S GROVE • SUE GROVE • ANN M GROVER • MICHAEL A GROVER • MISTY R GROVER • ANNE W GROVES • ROBERT III W GROVES • SUZANNE W GROVES • WILLIAM S GROVES • MACK J GROVES IV • JULIANNE GROW • STEVEN M GROW • DAILY GRUBB • MELINDA M GRUBB • PEGGY M GRUBB • WYNDEE O GRUBB • GENE GRUBBS • JIMMY R GRUBBS • JUDITH A GRUBBS • DAVID B GRUBER • MICHAEL V GRUBER • STACEY GRUBER • THOMAS H GRUBER • JOHN M GRUDZIEN • STEPHANIE M GRUEBBEL •

As the cauldron burns brightly, a spectacular fireworks display ends the Opening Ceremony, illuminating the Atlanta nighttime sky.

RICHARD D GRUEBER • CHARLES E GRUEHN • CHRISTOPHER K GRUEHN • LINDA L GRUEHN • CHRISTINE GRUENHAGEN CATC • ELAINE GRUENHUT • MARIA T GRUEZO • MARY G GRUICH • LARRY D GRULICH • CHRISTINE GRUNEWALD • LEIF G GRUNSETH MT • NORMAN GRUSY • LOUIS GRUVER JR • REID K GRYDER • IRENE GRYNIEWSKI • JILL M GRZANKOWSKI • RENATA E GRZESKOWIAK • IVELISSE GUADALUPE • LAURA D GUADARRAMA • IAN L GUALDONI • JIMMY GUAN • ALICIA GUANDIQUE • ROBERT N GUARINI • PAOLA STARR GUARNERIO • ATTILIO GUARNIERI • NICHOLAS GUASTAFERRO • BLAKE E GUBELI •

71

DAY ONE
20 JULY 1996

Olympic Arts Festival Daily Exhibitions

The Olympic Woman
Souls Grown Deep: African American Vernacular Art of the South
Thornton Dial: Remembering the Road
Rings: Five Passions in World Art
The American South: Past, Present and Future

TODAY'S CALENDAR

Competition

Aquatics—swimming, water polo
Baseball
Basketball
Boxing
Fencing
Football
Gymnastics—artistic
Hockey
Judo
Shooting
Volleyball—indoor
Weightlifting
Wrestling

Olympic Arts Festival

Alliance Theatre Company: *Blues for an Alabama Sky* and *The Last Night of Ballyhoo*
Alvin Ailey American Dance Theater
Atlanta Symphony Orchestra with Itzhak Perlman
Center for Puppetry Arts: *Kudzu Jack and the Giant* and *Frankenstein*
Horizon Theatre Company: *Praying for Sheetrock*
Seven Stages: *When the World Was Green*
Southern Crossroads Festival
Soweto Street Beat Dance Company: *Combo*

IT'S 5:00 A.M. Just a little over four hours since the final, glowing trail of the last skyrocket has dissolved and Olympic Stadium has been emptied of more than 100,000 athletes; production crew, press, and cast members; and spectators, the first Olympians board their buses in the predawn darkness for the first day of competitive events. Waves of buses will leave from and return to the Olympic Village throughout each day in an orchestrated system designed to move thousands of athletes to their assigned venues in plenty of time to check in, prepare for, and compete in their events and return them to the Village when their events are completed. These first buses are the leading edge of an armada of 250 buses that has served the Village each hour since the athletes' arrival and will continue to do so throughout the Games, making an extraordinary total of 154,500 athlete bus trips.

The range of emotions experienced by the athletes on each bus as it leaves the Village for its assigned destination—anxiety, anticipation, hope, determination, and introspection—shifts on the return trip to a more focused atmosphere reflecting the proverbial "thrill of victory and agony of defeat," tempered by the contemplative mood of those who are still competing and have neither won nor lost. This confluence of triumph, heartbreak, hope, and disappointment seems to inhabit these special vehicles throughout the Olympic Games.

Olympians traveling by bus to their venues feel a combination of anxiety, hope, and determination for their competition events.

For some Olympians, this first day of competition will also be the last. The events for which they have arduously trained and carefully prepared will be completed in only a few hours—almost as the Games begin, leaving them either victorious or defeated, but nonetheless on the sidelines for the remaining 15 days. For others, after the thrill of participating in the Opening Ceremony, they must wait and continue to prepare for the events

SHANNON L GUDENKAUF • BARBARA L GUDGER • MARIANNE L GUDINA • JANICE GUDIS • MARK S GUENTHER • GUILLAUME J GUERIN • JENNIFER L GUERIN • RACHEL E GUERNICA • MAURICIO GUERRA • CANDELARIA MA GUERRERO • DOLORES GUERRERO • ELIZABETH L GUERRERO • JAIME N GUERRERO • NICOLE V GUERRERO • NATASHA J GUERRIER • SHARON M GUESS • JO BETH C GUEST • RODNEY M GUEST • ALFREDO O GUEVARA • ANDRES GUEVARA • RAFAEL GUEVARA • WILLIAM S GUFFIN JR • MONICA J GUGEL • WAYNE T GUGEL • DAVID GUGGENHEIM • CELINE C GUIBAT • FRANCIANE GUIBERT •

73

top: **Crowds of spectators fill International Boulevard in downtown Atlanta.**

bottom: **MARTA, Atlanta's bus and rail system, accommodates some of the 17.8 million riders it will serve during the Games.**

scheduled to begin in a few days, a week, or even longer. Adjusting to the competition schedule is as much a part of each athlete's Olympic experience as the competition itself. An athlete's ability to focus and perform at maximum levels on this first day, or to settle into a completely different mental and physical training routine while events unfold and medals are won and lost, can be the difference between victory and defeat.

Almost simultaneously with the first competitors' departure from the Village, Olympic fans armed with tickets, sunscreen, sunglasses, backpacks, and satchels emerge from their homes, hotels, and recreational vehicles to make their way toward the competition venues. This is also the first of 16 days that will push Atlanta's bus and rail system, MARTA, which has been expanded for the Games period with extra cars and a supplemental fleet of more than 1,700 buses, to unprecedented extremes. Over the 17 days of the Games, MARTA will serve 17.8 million riders—the number of riders that would normally be served in a 45-day period. The MARTA schedule has been expanded to operate 24 hours daily, and 500 additional MARTA personnel have been assigned to assist spectators.

As the Games progress, the crowds will grow larger, and fans and operators alike will learn to meet the challenges of spectator transportation. Fortunately, on this first day of competition when both riders and providers are becoming acquainted with the system, not all

SARAH GUIDA • SARA GUIDEBECK • CARLA F GUIDREY • MATTHEW O GUIDRY • LAURA L GUILL ATC • JOHN P GUILLEBEAU • BRIAN R GUILLEMETTE • MICHAEL A GUILLEN • MICHELLE GUILLERMIN • ISRAEL A GUILLOTY • MARY E GUINAN • BARBARA J GUINAND • PETER COLIN GUINEY • DENISE L GUINN • ROBERT M GUINN • MITCHELL GUINYARD • JOHN GUIPE • ANTHONY S GUISASOLA • DEAN GUITE • JULIE L GUITH • MARY ALICE GUITRAU • SUJOY GULATI • DAVID A GULICK • JOHN R GULICK • MONICA GULLATT • SANDRA GULLATT • ELEANOR E GULLEY • PATRICIA J GULLEY • SAMUEL T GULLEY • GABE GULLIA •

venues are in full operation and, since it is Saturday, weekday commuters are not yet adding pressure to the system. Though crowded, the system functions as planned.

This is also the first day of full operation for Atlanta Olympic Broadcasting (AOB), the official host network responsible for capturing every moment of the Games to broadcast to more than 214 countries and territories—by far the largest number in history—and to record for posterity. Today, the AOB team will air the first of more than 3,000 hours of

Olympic drama with the help of 3,200 producers, directors, camera operators, video editors, and other technical and administrative support personnel. The AOB team will link cameras and microphones in a network of more than 568 mi (914 km) of cable, much of which is state-of-the-art fiber optic.

The International Broadcast Center, located at the Georgia World Congress Center in over 500,000 sq ft (46,500 sq m) of specially designed and equipped broadcast space, is home base for AOB as well as the broadcast teams

top: The television wall at the International Broadcast Center shows the various Olympic Games programs being broadcast all over the world.

bottom: The International Broadcast Center is home base for Atlanta Olympic Broadcasting, as well as the international rights-holding broadcasters.

JOHN F GULLO • MELISSA C GULLOTTI • DEBORAH R GULSTON • GARY L GULSTON • JUDY S GUM • TED S GUM • CARMEN Q GUMATAOTAO • NNEKA H GUMBS • JENNIFER L GUMMEL • MONICA K GUMMIG • THOMAS A GUMP • RIKA GUNAWAN • NARMADA R GUNAWARDENA • LINDA E GUNCKEL • SHARRON C GUNDERSON • MICHAEL K GUNDLACH • MICHAEL D GUNDY • ANDREA L GUNN • ANGELA K GUNN • DEBRA B GUNN • KATHY S GUNN • RICHIE V GUNN • SHIRLEY A GUNN • WILDA V GUNN • FRANKIE E GUNNELLS • COLLEEN R GUNNER • ROBERT E GUNNISON • JAMES P GUNNOUD • JENNIFER M GUNSAULLUS •

representing the international rights holders, who will select from and add their own commentary and supplementary material to the AOB feed to create Olympic coverage for their constituents.

NBC, the official Olympic broadcaster for the US, has assembled a huge team to support its extensive coverage of the Centennial Olympic Games. By the end of the Games, NBC's coverage will have reached a total American audience of 209 million viewers, making the 1996 Olympic Games the most watched event in television history. The extraordinary level of interest in the Atlanta Games will boost NBC's ratings 26 percent above ratings for their coverage of the 1992 Barcelona Olympic Games. As a worldwide broadcast event, Atlanta's Olympic Games will set new records throughout the world, attracting a cumulative audience of 19.6 billion viewers. From the Opening Ceremony onward, Japan, Canada, Australia, and virtually every other country in which the Games are broadcast will report record audiences.

The Main Press Center provides support to more than 6,000 reporters and photographers covering the Games.

ROBERT J GUNSON • BYRON K GUNTER • DIANNA L GUNTER • ERNEST GUNTER • PEGGY S GUNTER • XIZHONG GUO • ARUN K GUPTA • MINI GUPTA • RAJESH GUPTA • RUCHI GUPTA • SANJAY GUPTA • VISHAL GUPTA • JAIDEV GUPTE • JOYCE S GUPTON • PHILIP P GURA • RAYMOND P GURA • ADELE L GUREVICH • ROBERT GUREVICH • CARRIE A GURGANUS • KEITH GURIAN • JODY L GURIN • CHRISTOPHER M GURLEY • DEVIN K GURLEY • SANDRA P GURLEY • JOHN A GURN • BARBARA ANN GURNELL • CATHERINE B GURRY • ALP GURSOY • JOHN P GUSDON • CATHERINE M GUSSLER • BETH A GUSTAFSON •

an accomplished journalist's intuition about where the next major story will unfold and who are there to cover it are as amazing in their own field as the athletes they will photograph and write about in stories.

These are the accredited sports press, those whose primary focus is on the Games and competition results. While Olympians and their victories, defeats, and anecdotal experiences are clearly the centerpiece of traditional Olympic coverage, much of what happens in and around any Olympic Games would be left

On this first day, many of the more than 6,000 reporters and photographers will pour from the Main Press Center to begin covering the first of 271 events in 26 sports at 31 competition venues. Many of these top journalists have been in Atlanta since the center opened on 6 July, preparing to cover the Games and covering the last-minute preparations throughout the city.

Simultaneous, rapid-fire developments on and off the field of play challenge even the most experienced Olympic reporters and photographers. With multiple venues operating at peak capacity from dawn until after midnight, the number of potential stories and the flow of results data increase by the hour. Those with

untold if non–sports-related stories were not included. Thus, a completely separate cadre of nonaccredited reporters and photographers will cover the scenes at Centennial Olympic Park, the Olympic Youth Camp, Hartsfield Atlanta International Airport, area shopping malls, restaurants, clubs, sports bars, and the transportation system. Reports on ACOG's

left: **News agencies from around the world work at stations inside the Main Press Center.**

right: **International commentators at the Omni Coliseum describe preliminary indoor volleyball action.**

DEBORAH GRACE GUSTAFSON • KARRN GUSTAFSON • STACY A GUSTAFSON • FRANK W GUSTAFSON PT • LEIF GUSTAFSSON • JUNE P GUSTIN • PAUL R GUSTKE • MARRICUS A GUSTUS • PETER A GUTHERIE • HELENE GUTHERZ • BILLY H GUTHRIE • CAMILLE A GUTHRIE • DAVID S GUTHRIE • DOUGLAS B GUTHRIE • GREGORY A GUTHRIE • GREGORY J GUTHRIE • KEITH R GUTHRIE • MARJORIE D GUTHRIE • PAT GUTHRIE • THOMAS H GUTHRIE • LILIA A GUTIERREZ • PAUL J GUTIERREZ • DONALD G GUTTINGER • WALTER M GUTZKE • JUSTINE GUTZMER • MICHELLE O GUTZMER • BRIAN T GUY • CAROLYN A GUY •

77

management team, technology, southern food and dialects, volunteers, and innumerable human interest stories provide readers and viewers around the world with a vivid sense of the Games atmosphere.

COMPETITION

This first day of competition, like the 15 that will follow, features an extraordinary range of events, each filled with its own dramatic moments that will collectively distinguish the

Renata Mauer of Poland wins the first gold medal of the Games in the women's 10 m air rifle shooting competition.

Atlanta Games from those that have gone before. The cumulative impact of the triumph and disappointment, and the controversy and celebration that occurs in every sport, both on and off the field of play, weaves these individual events together into a unique patchwork quilt of experience.

This centennial gathering of the world's greatest athletes will be a kaleidoscope of men and women competing individually and in teams in 26 different sports, many of which feature competitions in a variety of disciplines and weight classes. From the highly focused, individual performances of archery, kayaking, shooting, and weightlifting, to the power and highly choreographed teamwork of football, hockey, and water polo, the Olympic environment will be a showcase of excellence.

This showcase begins just three hours into the first day of competition at the Wolf Creek Shooting Range, where Renata Mauer of Poland wins the first medal of the Centennial Olympic Games, a gold in the women's 10 m air rifle competition. Mauer's success begins a series of extraordinary athletic achievements and inspirations that will unfold throughout the Games, and which will emphasize the important role of women in the modern Olympic Games and the Olympic Movement.

As in all Olympic Games, surprises and upsets are inevitable. The Republic of China's Yifu Wang, whose lead appears unsurmountable in the men's 10 m air pistol competition, collapses as he takes his last shot to score a 6.5. His final score still wins the silver medal, but his weakened physical condition prevents him from taking part in the medal ceremony.

Another story surfaces at Wolf Creek this morning. In one of the many firsts that will be achieved during these Games, Lida Fariman becomes the first woman from Islamic Republic

DWIGHT W GUY • ERMA L GUY • JEROME P GUY • KATHRYN GUY • LYNDA M GUY • MEGAN K GUY • NAOMI J GUY • PHILIP WILLIAM GUY • VINCENT P GUY • JAMES B GUYNN • MARY O GUYNN • ROY C GUYTON • AMELIA S GUZMAN • DOROTHY E GUZMAN • ISELA M GUZMAN • LATEIA M GUZMAN • TERESA M GUZMAN • JOSE GUZMAN FORTES • LARRY M GWINN • SANG-HEE GWON • MARY C GWYNN • KATHY E GYSELINCK • ANH N HA • SAONG W HA • ANNEMARIE HAAKE • CARRIE C HAAN • CATHLEEN A HAAS • JACOB J HAAS • JASON M HAAS • LLOYD E HAAS • RAYMOND J HAAS • STEPHEN S HAAS • ARTHUR H HAASE •

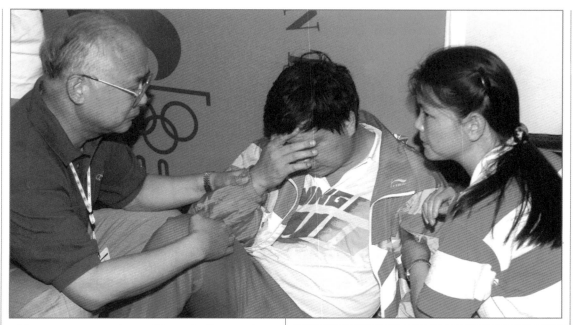

of Iran to compete in an Olympic Games since the Islamic Revolution of 1979.

Across town at the Georgia World Congress Center, a mammoth facility hosting seven sports, Hungarian fencer Ivan Kovacs, seeded 3rd, is challenging the Russian Federation's Aleksandr Beketov, seeded 18th, in the semifinal of the men's individual épée. Kovacs, a favorite for the gold medal, slips and falls from the platform, injuring his ankle. Though hobbled by pain, Kovacs returns to the match, only to be defeated. Later, when asked how he was able to block out the pain, he replies, "There is no pain in the Olympic Games," a sentiment that will be echoed by many other Olympians who will battle injury to continue competing in the days ahead.

Hirokazu Nakamura is the proud father of three sons who are all competing in different weight classes in judo. This is the first time Japan has sent three siblings to a single Olympic Games. Not only do they participate, but Kenzo, the lightweight, and Yukimasa, the half lightweight, will progress to the finals and win gold and silver medals respectively later in this first week of competition.

top: **Yifu Wang of the People's Republic of China recovers from his collapse during the 10 m air pistol competition.**

center: **Aleksandr Beketov of the Russian Federation lunges for Cuba's Ivan Trevejo Perez in the men's individual épée gold-medal match.**

bottom: **Great Britain battles Korea in women's hockey competition.**

By late afternoon, the excitement generated by outstanding performances and unexpected drama at virtually every competition venue is beginning to makes its way onto the street and over broadcasts throughout the world. Across the board, the level of performance is superb, and the quality of the competitions and the operation of the competition venues is outstanding. Many of those who have already purchased tickets are now clamoring for more, and the lines continue to build at Olympic ticket booths throughout the city.

Edgar Padilla of Puerto Rico makes a strong move past Brazil's defenders in men's basketball preliminaries.

After only a few hours of competition, the trend towards outstanding performances by women, initiated by Renata Mauer and Lida Fariman, becomes apparent. From the Athens Games of 1896, when women were not allowed to compete, to the Centennial Games in Atlanta—where 3,779 women, more than 34 percent of the total athlete population and 1,072 (40 percent) more than had competed just four years earlier in Barcelona—generations of women have struggled to be accepted and included as Olympians, and they have achieved a critical mass in Atlanta. Over the next 15 days, the world will come to know and understand the unique contributions made by these remarkable athletes. Their contributions extend far beyond any field of play, touching and inspiring women profoundly in their everyday lives in diverse cultures throughout the world. From extraordinary athletic achievements to stories of intense personal courage and determination, Atlanta's Olympic Games will be enriched by these remarkable women in a succession of events that will unfold throughout these Games.

In the early evening competitions at the Georgia Tech Aquatic Center, three women swimmers help underscore this theme: Irish swimmer Michelle Smith, ranked 41st in the world coming into the Games, wins the first-ever swimming gold medal for her country in the 400 m individual medley. Smith's victory is no fluke, as she will prove in the days ahead, winning two more gold medals in the 400 m freestyle and the 200 m individual medley, and a bronze in the 200 m butterfly. Smith's performance is all the more incredible considering that Ireland does not have a 50 m pool. In order to train, Smith went to the Dutch city of Rotterdam where two-time Dutch Olympic athletics champion Erik de Bruin trained Smith

SYBIL C HADLEY • ROY E HADLEY JR • FABIENNE HADORN • CHARLES K HADSELL • SHARON P HADSELL • DEBORAH J HAERTEL • DIANE V HAERTEL • DAVID L HAET • M LOUIS HAFEZNEZAMI • ABDELKRIM HAFFAD • PATRICK J HAFFEY • WILLIAM B HAFFNER • ALEX HAFFORD • MICHELLE HAFFORD • IDA HAFFORD-BROWN • KHALID A HAFIZ • HEATHER S HAFNER • TOMAS E HAGA • BETTY L HAGAN • CECELIA A HAGAN • JACK S HAGAN • JOAN M HAGAN • LISA L HAGAN • GWENDOLYN S HAGANS • MARY BETH HAGEARTY • RICH D HAGEDORN • ANGELIKA B HAGEL • MARC A HAGEMAN • DAWN M HAGEN • GRANT A HAGEN

using track-related methods that she credited with dramatically improving her swimming performance. But what began as a training exercise has blossomed into romance. Smith and de Bruin married just before the Games and are celebrating their honeymoon while Michelle competes.

American Angel Martino wins the first US medal of the Games, a bronze in the 100 m freestyle. In a dramatic and deeply moving gesture, she gives her medal to Trisha Henry, whose continued work as a volunteer at the

Aquatic Center despite her suffering from cancer inspires Martino's performance. In the days to come, she will win three more medals—a pair of golds as a member of the 4 x 100 m freestyle relay team and the 4 x 100 m medley relay, and a bronze in the 100 m butterfly. Continuing her dominance of the 100 m freestyle event, the People's Republic of China's Jingyi Le wins the gold, fighting off the brave challenges of the silver and bronze winners.

The boisterous crowd at the Aquatic Center also watches Belgium's Fred Deburghgraeve capture his country's first-ever swimming gold medal in the men's 100 m breaststroke. Earlier today, Deburghgraeve set a world record in the

top left: Angel Martino of the US celebrates with Olympic volunteer Trisha Henry, to whom she gave the bronze medal she won in the 100 m freestyle event.

top right: The People's Republic of China's Jingyi Le holds up her bouquet during her gold-medal victory ceremony for the 100 m freestyle.

bottom: Lee McDermott of Great Britain performs on the rings apparatus during the men's gymnastics team competition.

• JENNIFER HAGEN • ANNETTE HAGENBRING • LISA K HAGER • WILLIAM H HAGER II • ONITTA D HAGERMAN • JAY T HAGERMAN JR • CHRIS J HAGERTY • BRIAN D HAGGADONE • PATRICIA P HAGGARD • DONNA B HAGGERTY • JAMES P HAGGERTY • KECIA C HAGGINS • KEVIN C HAGGINS • NANCY HAGGIT • WALTER HAGGIT • MIKKO HAGGOTT-HENSON • JOAN HAGLE • CONSTANCE L HAGLER • JOHN T HAGLER • KATHERINE A HAGLER • RICHARD B HAGLER • CAROLINE HAGLEY • NICOLE HAGNER ATC • ARTHUR T HAGOOD • MARGARET W HAGOOD • NELSON J HAGOOD • ROBERT M. HAGOOD • JAMES F HAGOOD JR •

preliminary heat. His performance this summer is a dramatic reversal of his performance at the Barcelona Games, where he slipped off the starting block and finished in 34th place. New Zealand's Danyon Loader duplicates this feat by capturing his country's first-ever swimming gold medal for his performance in the men's 200 m freestyle. Brazil's Gustavo França Borges takes the silver and Australia's Daniel Kowalski, the bronze.

Olympic action is not restricted to the city of Atlanta. Before a capacity crowd of 83,810

Chinese food, the menu features a marvelous blend of southern favorites and international flavors in honor of this southern city's Olympic guests.

A four-hour drive southeast of Atlanta, historic and picturesque Savannah, host of the yachting competitions, stages its own official Opening Ceremony. "An Olympic love-in, Savannah-style" is what the *Savannah News-Press* calls the Olympic Yachting Opening Ceremony. More than 8,000 people watch, applauding and cheering a warm welcome to 450

top: **Danyon Loader of New Zealand and Daniel Kowalski of Australia congratulate each other after the men's 200 m freestyle.**

bottom: **Fred Deburghgraeve of Belgium celebrates after setting a new world record in the 100 m breaststroke.**

at Legion Field in Birmingham, Alabama, one of four southeastern cities to host the preliminary football competitions, Argentina rallies to defeat the US men's team 3–1.

In addition to an outstanding game, fans are offered an amazing variety of top-quality food. From shrimp Creole to chicken cacciatore, turkey dogs on sticks, Greek gyros, and

top: Members of the Argentinian and US men's football teams vie for the ball in a preliminary game at Legion Field in Birmingham, Alabama.

bottom: The US women's volleyball team blocks the ball against Ukraine's team during a preliminary match at the Omni Coliseum.

athletes and 250 officials from 77 delegations as they march from the Savannah Olympic Village up River Street to where the master of ceremonies, beloved former US broadcaster Walter Cronkite, presides. Many of the athletes' family members have come from around the world to partake in this evening's event and the extraordinary days of Olympic yacht racing ahead. The people of Savannah take these sailors into their hearts, rolling out the welcome mat in the true spirit of southern hospitality, hosting special events over previous weeks for the Austrian, German, Greek, Irish, and Italian teams, among others.

NEHEMIAH HAIRE • SUSAN A HAIRE • DESPINA E HAIRETIS • DOVETTA HAIRSTON • KAREN J HAIRSTON • ROXIE A HAIRSTON • RUBY V HAIRSTON • MARCIA D HAISE • JOHN D HAISLEY • SUSAN E HAISLEY • CATHERINE W HAIST • CARLTON L HAITHCOX • SHERRY C HAIZLIP • MARY ANN HAJDU • DONNA J HAKES • B SHAMAYNE HAKIM • SYLVIA HALASZ • EDWARD A HALBACH • JANE E HALBACH • KRISTEN L HALBERG • LINDA HALBMAN • MICHAEL HALCHAK • BLYTHE A HALDEMAN • ASKIA K HALE • CAROL D HALE • CLIFFORD A HALE • CYNTHIA W HALE • FRANCES E HALE • GREGORY HALE • JAMES A HALE •

left: **Even wet weather doesn't prevent spectators from enjoying Savannah's Opening Ceremony.**

top: **Thousands attend the Opening Ceremony for Olympic yachting competition at its venue in Savannah, Georgia.**

bottom: **The Blues Brothers visit the Olympic Village.**

Spirits are high, but just as festivities get under way, Savannah's skies open up with a tremendous thunderclap, deluging the thousands of assembled Olympians and fans. The band huddles under a nearby tree and continues to play what is almost an anthem in this state, "Georgia on My Mind," as the Dutch team chimes in with their own version of "Singin' in the Rain." In its welcoming of yachting teams and officials, Savannah raises the tradition of southern hospitality to a new level and sets the stage for the competitive events to come.

OLYMPIC VILLAGE AND OLYMPIC ARTS FESTIVAL

Spirits are also soaring at the Atlanta Olympic Village on this first night of competition. Earlier today, the Blues Brothers, clad in their trademark black suits, hats, and ties; white shirts; and sunglasses, stopped by to eat lunch, talk with and wish good luck to Olympians, sign autographs, and pose for pictures. Dan Aykroyd; Jim Belushi, who replaced his late brother John; and the group's newest member, John Goodman, are in Atlanta to open the House of Blues.

Tonight, in a special concert for Olympic athletes, Hootie and the Blowfish, a band that enjoys worldwide popularity, performs at Georgia Tech's Bobby Dodd Stadium. Coming off the European leg of the band's world tour, this talented group, which started as a college band in Columbia, South Carolina, is essentially contributing their performance to the Olympians. The winner of two Grammy awards earlier this year, "Hootie," as the band is known in the music world, has sold millions of albums, making it one of the summer's most popular attractions. Longtime Hootie fan Walter Antonio, a

marksman from Nicaragua, is so thrilled to see one of his favorite musical groups that he takes off his T-shirt and throws it on stage during the concert as a gift to the band. The band has a terrific time as well. Lead singer Darius Rucker tells the crowd, "Never in my wildest dreams did I imagine I would be performing for athletes at the Olympic Village. This is a dream come true for me."

As the hour passes midnight and the end of day one becomes the beginning of day two; as the final competition of the day is completed and fans head toward home, Centennial Olympic Park, or one of hundreds of smaller gathering places throughout the city; and as the last athletes return to the Village to savor or lament their performance, or perhaps to prepare for tomorrow—Atlanta is buoyant. Despite problems with press transportation and the results reporting systems that must be resolved, the tens of thousands charged with the successful operation of these Centennial Olympic Games share a sense of pride and fulfillment.

The dream toward which so many have worked for so long has at last become a reality. Determination mixed with hopeful anticipation permeates ACOG's operational centers as day one's operation is analyzed and schedules and plans are refined to make day two even better.

top left: The Alvin Ailey American Dance Theatre performs at the Atlanta Civic Center.

bottom left: Hootie and the Blowfish entertain athletes at Bobby Dodd Stadium in the Olympic Village.

right: Itzhak Perlman performs with the Atlanta Symphony Orchestra at Atlanta Symphony Hall.

Atlanta 1996.

CHERYL W HALL • CHRISTINE E HALL • CLYDE R HALL • COLLEEN L HALL • CORLIS S HALL • CYNTHIA B HALL • CYNTHIA L HALL • DANIEL HALL • DANIEL B HALL • DARIN S HALL • DARRYL W HALL • DAVID B HALL • DAVID F HALL • DAVID L HALL • DAVID W HALL • DONNA M HALL • DONTHEL D HALL • EDWARD T HALL • ELISABTH F HALL • EMILY R HALL • ERIC E HALL • FELICIA D HALL • FREEMAN S HALL • FRENESA K HALL • GEORGE R HALL • GINGER R HALL • HARRISON K HALL • HATTIE M HALL • IVAN C HALL • JACQUELINE HALL • JAMEELA HALL • JAMES R HALL • JEROME HALL • JOHANNA D HALL • JOHN B HALL •

DAY TWO
21 JULY 1996

Centennial Olympic Park attracts crowds of visitors who come to enjoy the entertainment and celebrate the Olympic Spirit.

IT IS DAY TWO, and the Games are in full swing. Spirits are high. A huge crowd waits patiently for the park to open. With just a single day's experience behind them, the people share a sense of optimism and are eager to get to their respective destinations.

With each morning's sunrise, a large percentage of the tens of thousands of people on their way to the early morning competition sessions start their day with a visit to Centennial Olympic Park. Inspired by the positive impact Barcelona's Plaza de España had on Olympic visitors, ACOG President and CEO Billy Payne felt strongly that Atlanta needed the same kind of central gathering place. But where and how could this be accomplished?

TODAY'S CALENDAR

Competition

Aquatics—swimming,
   water polo
Baseball
Basketball
Boxing
Cycling—road
Equestrian
Fencing
Football
Gymnastics—artistic
Hockey
Judo
Rowing
Shooting
Softball
Volleyball—indoor
Weightlifting
Wrestling

Olympic Arts Festival

Alliance Theatre Company:
   The Last Night of
   Ballyhoo and *Blues for an*
   Alabama Sky
Horizon Theatre Company:
   Praying for Sheetrock
Seven Stages: *When the*
   World was Green
Southern Crossroads Festival
Soweto Street Beat Dance
   Company: *Combo*
World Youth Symphony
   Orchestra

JUAN C HALL • JUDITH A HALL • JULIE E HALL • JULIE M HALL • KATHERINE M HALL • KATHLEEN A HALL • KATHRYN L HALL • KATHRYN R HALL • KEISHA A HALL • KELLY HALL • KENNETH D HALL • KITA L HALL • LAURA L HALL • LINDA HALL • MARINA N HALL • MARQUISETTE E HALL • MARY HALL • MAUREEN M HALL • NANCY R HALL • PATRICIA A HALL • PATRICIA D HALL • PAULA K HALL • PETER J HALL • RACHEL E HALL • RACHEL E HALL • RAMONA D HALL • RECKAY R HALL • ROBERTA HALL • RODNEY A HALL • ROGER E HALL • RUBY HALL • RYAN O HALL • SABRINA HALL •

The answer came one morning as Payne looked out from his office balcony atop ACOG headquarters toward the Georgia World Congress Center, Georgia Dome, Omni Coliseum, and Georgia Tech, the future home of the Olympic Village. In the midst of these key areas of Olympic activity lay an obstacle course of underutilized industrial and warehouse buildings that Olympic visitors would have to navigate to get from one event to another.

In a flash of inspiration, Payne decided to transform this area into both a central gather-

top left: This aerial view, taken September 1994, shows the underdeveloped site chosen to become Centennial Olympic Park.

bottom left: This aerial view of Centennial Olympic Park shows the entertainment pavilions during the Games.

top right: Olympic visitors do the "brick dance" as they search for their personalized bricks in the park.

bottom right: Personalized bricks purchased by Olympic supporters pave walkways in Centennial Olympic Park.

ing place for the Games and a permanent legacy for the city. With less than two full years remaining before 2 million visitors and the world's media and press were to descend upon Atlanta, transforming Payne's vision into reality was a monumental challenge. At a time when ACOG was fully immersed in preparing for the largest Games in history, extraordinary courage was required to commit to this goal.

The story of the creation of Centennial Olympic Park is an epic chapter of its own. Billy Payne's vision resulted in a glorious central gathering place that exceeded even the most optimistic hopes for enhancing the Games while leaving a significant physical legacy for the citizens of Atlanta and future visitors.

From the moment it opens in the early morning until when it closes well after midnight, the park is like a gigantic magnet,

SCOTT HALL • SCOTT E HALL • SHELBY J HALL • SIDONIE A HALL • STACY L HALL • STEVEN O HALL • SUSAN N HALL • THERESA M HALL • TOMMIE L HALL • TONJA S HALL • VIRGINIA L HALL • WALTER HALL • SHARON HALL-JONES • RONALD P HALL II • WILLIAM J HALL II • TYRONE D HALL JR • WORTHAM HALL JR • ALICE C HALL MT • SUSAN J HALL PATCH • JANICE L HALL RN • MELANIE HALL SAT • REBECCA J HALLA • MARY HALLADAY • LAURA J HALLAHAN • LAURA T HALLAM • JOANNA M HALLBERG • JENNIFER A HALLECK • MARGARET M HALLEMAN • PATRICIA E HALLEN • ANN R HALLER

Bagpipers entertain a crowd in front of the Superstore in Centennial Olympic Park.

attracting thousands of visitors going to and from competitions and many more who simply want to relax and enjoy the varied activities and pavilions that fill the park. Many who visit the park come to locate their specially inscribed commemorative Olympic brick among the more than 330,000 that were sold and installed before the Games as pathways and plazas in the south end of the park. Inscribed with one's own name, the name of a loved one, or a favorite phrase—from Bible quotations and witty sayings to marriage proposals—the patchwork of bricks creates a bond

among the people who contributed to the park's construction by participating in the Brick Program.

A special computer, located permanently in the park, directs visitors to the bricks they are seeking. With so many people looking down at their feet in search of their bricks or trying to read what others have inscribed on their bricks, brick hunting is soon labeled the "brick dance." Renewed excitement about the Brick

• ANNE E HALLER • MARGARET A HALLER • KENNETH H HALLER DO • PETER HALLERMANN • CONSTANCE HALLETT • LEANN HALLFORD • TRAVIS P HALLGREN • KATHLEEN S HALLIGAN • FRANCES T HALLIHAN • THOMAS P HALLINAN • ARTHUR H HALLING • JAMES F HALLING • WILLIAM J HALLISEY • DONNA C HALLMAN • FERN HALLMAN • GEORGE G HALLMAN • GERALD D HALLMAN • GERALD W HALLMAN • JEFF H HALLMAN • KENNETH F HALLMAN • LORRAINE K HALLMAN • MARY B HALLMAN • MELANIE R HALLMAN • TOM N HALLMAN • WILLIAM B HALLMAN • GINA P HALLMAN EMT •

left: Siblings splash to keep cool in the reflecting pool in Centennial Park while their mother watches.

top: Children play in the Fountain of Rings in Centennial Olympic Park.

bottom: The Fountain of Rings dances to music.

Program results in orders for more than 100,000 additional bricks to be inscribed and placed in the park after the Games, when the grounds will be groomed into their final, permanent configuration.

Four Olympic sponsor pavilions offering entertainment, exhibits, and refreshments are very popular destinations, as are the three Southern Crossroads stages, where an array of outstanding musicians from the American South perform each day from noon until well past midnight. The Olympic Superstore, nearly an acre in size, sells a large number of Olympic mementos, while the Southern Marketplace offers crafts created by the South's leading artists and artisans.

NATALIE J HALLMARK • ROBERT R HALLMARK • PATRICIA A HALLOCK • ROBERT B HALLOCK II • ELIZABETH A HALLORAN • JAMES H HALLORAN • VERNETHA HALLS • ALTON V HALLUM • AUDREY F HALLYBURTON • PETER H. HALPAUS • SUSAN M HALPERN • ALFRED N HALPHEN • JANET M HALPHEN • JOHN W HALPIN • PATRICIA I HALSELL • BOBBY E HALSTEAD • ELIZABETH D HALSTEAD • JENNIFER L HALSTEAD • MICHELE HALTER • STANTON C HALTER • SUSIE M HALTON • REBECCA A HALTZEL-HAAS • DEBORAH J HALVERSON • CLIFFORD W HALVORSEN • HOLLY L HALVORSON •

A focal point of this 21 acre (8.5 ha) gathering place is the fabulous Fountain of Rings that is the ultimate destination for virtually everyone, especially children. With its huge rings of water dancing to music throughout the day and night, the fountain is filled with merriment, providing not only relief from the heat, but also a fountain of goodwill that seems to emanate from this joyous, lively epicenter of Olympic activity.

More than 250,000 people each day—300,000 on peak days—visit this place to share their Olympic experiences and the spirit that permeates the Games. Though brand new and officially open to the public for the first time just six days before the Opening Ceremony, Centennial Olympic Park exudes a magical atmosphere that connects visitors with family, friends, and strangers alike. As the Games continue, the park will become a living symbol of the Olympic Spirit.

COMPETITION

For those anticipating another day of electrifying competitions, the excitement begins in one of the day's earliest events.

In an 8:00 a.m. baseball game between Japan and Cuba, Japan gives up two runs in the bottom of the 10th inning and loses to Cuba 8–7. A home run by Cuba's Orestes Kindelan flies 521 ft (159 m) into the club level seats in left field, making Kindelan's ball one of the longest ever to be hit in Atlanta–Fulton County Stadium, a facility that will host its final game ever at the close of the current professional baseball season. Afterward, it will be replaced by a retrofitted Olympic Stadium in time for the beginning of the 1997 Major League Baseball season.

While most Olympic competitions are held within fixed facilities, cycling road races are literally taken to the streets, where in midmorning France's Jeannie Longo-Ciprelli leads a field of 58 riders through a grueling 64.8 mi (104.3 km) course (eight laps of an 8.1 mi [13 km]

course) through the streets and hills of Atlanta's exclusive Buckhead neighborhood, made all the more difficult, even treacherous, by intermittent rain. A four-time Olympian and five-time road race world champion, 37-year-old Longo-Ciprelli is the oldest competitor in the race. Cheered on by 50,000 fans, she wins the gold medal that has eluded her throughout her career.

Some of the hottest tickets of the Games are for any women's basketball game. Since becoming an Olympic sport, women's basket-

left: **Jeannie Longo-Ciprielli leads the field of cyclists on her way to win gold.**

right: **Orestes Kindelan of Cuba is congratulated after hitting the longest home run of the Games and winning the game against Japan in the process.**

ball has caught fire throughout the world. With the top teams competing in Atlanta, interest in these games is at an all-time high. At noon, the women of Zaire, playing for the first time in Olympic basketball competition, face a talented and experienced Ukrainian

FRANK HAM • KEVIN Y HAMADA • DEIDRE HAMAGUCHI • YUKI HAMAKAWA • MARNI W HAMAN • LUBNA HAMANA • TOSHIHIDE HAMAZAKI • ANNA G HAMBLEN • D KENT HAMBLEN • DALE G HAMBLEN • J BASIL HAMBLIN • NIGEL D HAMBRICK • GILLIAN E HAMBURGER • CHARLES M HAMBY • MELISSA F HAMBY • MIRIAM M HAMBY • REITA W HAMBY • ROBERT R HAMBY • SALLY W HAMBY • SHARLENE E HAMBY • AMER A HAMDY • JASON M HAMEL • CRAIG HAMER • ROSE MARY HAMER • LINDA A HAMERNIK • ALVIN L HAMES • JENNIFER M HAMES • RODERICK E HAMES • GERRY M HAMILL •

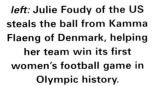

left: **Julie Foudy of the US steals the ball from Kamma Flaeng of Denmark, helping her team win its first women's football game in Olympic history.**

top: **Australian fans at a local restaurant enjoy women's road cycling.**

bottom: **The Atlanta Hawks' Dikembe Mutombo cheers for the team from his native country, Zaire, at women's basketball preliminaries.**

team. The outcome of the game is never in doubt: Ukraine wins 81–65.

The Zairians are talented and enthusiastic, but difficult training conditions at home put them at a disadvantage. Zaire's coach, Mongamaluku Mozingo, notes that in Zaire, a basketball costs the equivalent of two months' salary, and there are no indoor courts, leaving his team to practice outdoors in the blistering sun in an open field with crude goals and only a single basketball. In spite of these challenges, the Zairians display a determined Olympic spirit that sustains them throughout the tournament, enabling them to perform well against far better equipped and supported teams.

In a special gesture of support, Dikembe Mutombo, the Atlanta Hawks' 7 ft 2 in (2.18 m) center and a native of Zaire, helps his fellow Zairians by purchasing uniforms for the team and tickets to the game for the team's

family members. When asked why he did this, Mutombo said, "The score is not important. What was most important was to see the flag of my country waved at the Olympics."

Mutombo's sentiments are reflected everywhere throughout the Games. Inside and outside every competition venue, along the streets,

KATHLEEN A HAMILL • BARBARA A HAMILTON • BENNYCE E HAMILTON • BETSY M HAMILTON • CHARLES R HAMILTON • CHESTER HAMILTON • CHRIS W HAMILTON • CRYSTAL J HAMILTON • GEORGE G HAMILTON • GLENDA R HAMILTON • GLENDINE HAMILTON • HEIDI A HAMILTON • HOLLY J HAMILTON • JACOB A HAMILTON • JACQUELINE HAMILTON • JAMES C HAMILTON • JAMES D HAMILTON • JOHN W HAMILTON • JOYCE H HAMILTON • KATHRYN T HAMILTON • KAY HAMILTON • KEENA I HAMILTON • KENNETH R HAMILTON • LESLIE A HAMILTON • MATTHEW C HAMILTON •

on MARTA trains, in hotel lobbies, in Centennial Olympic Park, and hanging from apartment balconies and the front porches of homes, flags from 197 delegations fly in an exultant declaration that demonstrates the power of this international gathering in a colorful way. The sense of pride in one's national heritage—whether felt by those who have recently moved to the US, Americans who identify with their ancestral heritage, or visitors from other countries who have come to cheer on athletes representing their countries—and the sharing of this

feeling with both friends and strangers, is part of the pulse of every Olympic Games.

Day two is a significant day for football at all venues, especially when it comes to the unexpected. In the men's competition, the big story is in Miami where Brazil, universally acknowledged as the best team in the world, suffers a stunning 1–0 upset at the hands of Japan. Some Japanese sports writers call this the biggest victory in Japanese sports history.

The Japanese victory materializes thanks to a kick by Teruyoshi Ito. With both defenses suffocating play, the game finally breaks for the Japanese with five minutes remaining, when the Brazilian goalie collides with a teammate, leaving both defenders sprawled on the

turf and Ito left alone with an empty goal. Ito seizes this opportunity, striking the ball into the back of the twine for the win. This was Japan's only shot on goal in the second half of the game. Ito commented, "I never even dreamed of scoring the winning goal against the no. 1 team in the world during the Olympics. It's beyond my imagination."

In women's football competition, the US team wins its first game in Olympic Games history, beating Denmark 3–0 in Orlando. Meanwhile, at RFK Stadium in Washington,

DC, the Brazilian team notches a goal in the 90th minute to record a 2–2 tie with the world champions from Norway.

At the cavernous Georgia World Congress Center, minutes before Republic of China's Linsheng Tang is to compete in the men's 59 kg

left: Jose Oliveira of Brazil challenges Japan's Hideto Suzuki for control of the ball.

center: Linsheng Tang lifts his way to a gold medal in the 59 kg weightlifting class.

right: It's up in the air whether Anne Nymark Andersen of Norway (left) or Miraildes Mota of Brazil (right) will gain control of the ball next in women's football competition.

NANCY J HAMILTON • PATRICIA D HAMILTON • ROBERT H HAMILTON • ROBERTA ROBIN A HAMILTON • RUSSELL HAMILTON • SHERRY D HAMILTON • SUSAN G HAMILTON • TERRY T HAMILTON • TIFFANY A HAMILTON • TOM HAMILTON • TONY R HAMILTON • VIVIAN M HAMILTON • WANDA B HAMILTON • JOSEPH F HAMLET • WILLIAM F HAMLET • CLAIRE H HAMLIN • DOROTHY M HAMLIN • WILLIAM H HAMLIN JR • CHARI H HAMM • DONZELLA B HAMM • JAMES F HAMM • JOHNNIE C HAMM • JUDY C HAMM • KATRINA HAMM • ROGER M HAMM • SUSAN M HAMM • THOMAS J HAMM • BOBBY L HAMM SR

top: **Laura Flessel of France defeats Valerie Barlois, also of France, in the women's individual épée final.**

bottom: **Penelope Heyns of South Africa hugs silver-medal winner Amanda Beard of the US after winning the 100 m breaststroke.**

class weightlifting event, he finds a tear in his uniform. Finding another uniform that he can borrow from a fellow competitor proves difficult until Hungarian Zoltan Farkas, who had lifted in an earlier session, comes forward to loan Linsheng Tang his red, white, and green singlet. Sporting the Hungarian uniform, Tang goes on to capture the gold medal. Farkas receives tearful thanks from the Chinese coach.

In the fencing competition, Laura Flessel of France wins the gold in a new Olympic event, the women's individual épée. For the former foil competitor who retired in 1991 after breaking her fencing arm and returned to compete in épée, this is a satisfying win, and she shares the victory podium with teammate and silver medalist Valerie Barlois.

At the Georgia Tech Aquatic Center this evening, two firsts capture the attention of the crowds and press. Costa Rica's Claudia Poll captures her country's first-ever gold medal in the women's 200 m freestyle. During the same session, Penelope Heyns of South Africa wins the first gold medal for her country since 1952, in the 100 m breaststroke. Heyns's victory invigorates South Africa's Olympic efforts and hopes.

OLYMPIC ARTS FESTIVAL

Already in its second full week of peak operation, the 1996 Olympic Arts Festival is attracting large and enthusiastic audiences. The programming is rich and diverse and of consistently high quality, blending and contrasting the festival's two major themes—southern connections and international connections. Of the more than a dozen world premieres commissioned by the Cultural Olympiad, one is performed this afternoon at Atlanta's Symphony

ton, with text by former US Poet Laureate Rita Dove. Renowned conductor Sergiu Commissiona leads the ensemble's 120 gifted young musicians through an emotionally charged performance. The narrative passage, Dove's poem "Each One of Us Counts," is eloquently recited by ACOG co-chair, former Atlanta Mayor, and former UN Ambassador Andrew Young. Singleton's work receives immediate praise from the press.

Across town, the Soweto Street Beat Dance Company, a recent addition to Atlanta's bur-

Hall. The World Youth Symphony from Interlochen Arts Academy in Michigan gives the premiere performance of *Umoja: Each One of Us Counts*, a work for both narrator and orchestra by celebrated American composer Alvin Single-

geoning arts community, performs the second of two performances of a new work created as a festival premiere. The powerful rhythms and high-energy choreography of the piece, entitled *Combo* (Africa is Back), make a bold, colorful impression on the large audiences who attend the performances.

The World Youth Symphony performs at Symphony Hall.

• DELLA H HAMMOND • ERIC E HAMMOND • ERIC K HAMMOND • GUY C HAMMOND • HEATHER C HAMMOND • HERBERT C HAMMOND • KHADIJA S HAMMOND • LANE W HAMMOND • LANORE C HAMMOND • LINDA M HAMMOND • LYNN W HAMMOND • MARJORIE W HAMMOND • MARY F HAMMOND • MYRON D HAMMOND • NICOLAS J HAMMOND • PATRICIA A HAMMOND • PAUL A HAMMOND • RACHEL F HAMMOND • TAMMY S HAMMOND • WILLIAM T HAMMOND • ALLEN L HAMMONDS • DON HAMMONDS • GLADYS P HAMMONDS • GLORIA MARLENE HAMMONDS • JAMES W HAMMONDS •

One of the hottest tickets is for any performance of Alfred Uhry's brilliant new play, *The Last Night of Ballyhoo*, yet another work commissioned for premiere during the Olympic Arts Festival. The celebrated author of *Driving Miss Daisy*, Uhry had not written a new play in 10 years when he was enticed by Atlanta's Alliance Theatre Company to create this new work for the Olympic Games. Every one of the 20 performances is sold out months in advance.

The Olympic Arts Festival's eclectic schedule is comprised of more than 200 music, the-

this page: **Soweto Street Beat Dance Company performs *Combo* at the Martin Luther King Jr. International Chapel at Morehouse College.**

opposite page: **The Last Night of Ballyhoo is performed to a capacity audience at the Alliance Theatre.**

To cover this extraordinary program, several hundred reporters, arts critics, and photographers are in Atlanta, where they operate from a specially equipped ACOG cultural press center near the Woodruff Arts Center. In the days to come, enthusiastic reports of Atlanta's Olympic Arts Festival will be carried in newspapers throughout the world as a significant, positive, and highly successful feature of the Games.

Another event- and emotion-filled day comes to a close with nearly 100,000 people gathered at Centennial Olympic Park to trade

ater, dance, and puppetry performances during the Games, plus more than 20 arts and humanities exhibitions and over a dozen temporary and permanent public artworks, many of which have been commissioned for the Centennial Olympic Games. With the colorful, three-stage Southern Crossroads festival in Centennial Olympic Park celebrating the musical traditions and contemporary interpretations that have their roots in the American South, the cultural component of the Atlanta Games is a major story in itself.

Olympic pins, relax, and enjoy the music coming from stages throughout the park. Day two will soon become day three; for some, it is impossible to imagine how the extraordinary pace that has been established can continue. What records will fall in the days to come? What will be the next upset? What else lies ahead?

Atlanta 1996.

SHERRY A HAMMONDS • WILLIAM M HAMMONDS • HOMER C HAMMONTREE JR • LUCIE F HAMNER • ANN M HAMPSON • WILLIAM G HAMPSON • BONNIE W HAMPTON • DOLORES H HAMPTON • DONALD R HAMPTON • GEORGE R HAMPTON • GERALD T HAMPTON • JERRY R HAMPTON • JESSE R HAMPTON • KELLY B HAMPTON • LARRY W HAMPTON • MARVA E HAMPTON • TARIN T HAMPTON • VIVIAN B HAMPTON • SCOTT G HAMRE • CLAY HAMRIC • ANDREA S HAMRICK • BUD HAMRICK • PAULA S HAMRICK • R KENDALL HAMRICK • HELEN F HAMRYKA • JEFFREY HAN • JIE HAN • LIM S HAN •

DAY THREE
22 JULY 1996

EACH DAY IS FILLED with new records and firsts in virtually every category of athletic competition, but this morning is a first of a totally different kind. It is Monday, the first day of the Games when commuters and spectators will share Atlanta's transportation systems and the day that ACOG's Transportation Department and its affiliates in related government agencies have been anticipating with trepidation. Fingers are crossed throughout the city as the morning rush hour begins. Local radio and television stations, supported by helicopter observers, are poised to provide continuous traffic updates. Fortunately, though this day is filled with events, traffic is significantly lighter than anticipated, precluding any major problems.

The design and successful implementation of a comprehensive Olympic transportation plan is among an organizing committee's most challenging responsibilities. As the Games have grown dramatically in size, scope, and complexity, increasingly large fleets of vehicles, numbering in the thousands, must continue to function efficiently and effectively in a highly choreographed, multilayered network

Banners and lush, green trees line the streets of downtown Atlanta.

ATO Y HAND • FREDRICK HAND • HELEN E HAND • JOSEPH HAND • RICHARD K HAND • SHERRI L HAND • JEAN D HANDELONG • KAREN J HANDLER • DARREN A HANDLEY • DAVID S HANDLEY • GLENNA W HANDLEY • JODI A HANDLEY • WILLIAM M HANDLEY • JAYNE S HANDLIN • CARLOS R HANDY • DIALLO HANDY • JACK A HANDY • VIVIAN F HANDY • KERRI A HANEBRINK • CLAUDETTE A HANEEF • AMY E HANEGAN • JAMES B HANER • DIXIE ANN HANES • MARGAUX G HANES • BARBARA LOIS HANEVOLD • ANNAHITA HANEY • JASON M HANEY • LISSA HANEY • LLOYD E HANEY • SHIRLEY N HANEY • STEVEN R HANEY •

of overlapping systems, each designed to serve a specialized Olympic population. The demand for vehicles and knowledgeable drivers from athletes and officials, the Olympic Family, spectators, staff, broadcasters, the press, and Olympic Arts Festival participants can be overwhelming.

As with the Atlanta Games' two immediate predecessors, Barcelona and Lillehammer, the first implementation of transportation operations of this magnitude creates anxiety for the organizers. Atlanta is no different. Though all

the system a disaster, a burden ACOG will have to bear throughout the Games and beyond.

The operational statistics are staggering: the total fleet of 6,604 vehicles, the largest in Olympic history, consists of more than 2,000 buses, more than 4,000 automobiles and cargo and passenger vans, hundreds of trucks, and numerous specialized vehicles. These vehicles are orchestrated to move athletes, the Olympic Family, media, spectators, staff, and equipment. The media system alone requires in excess of 1.3 million bus trips during the Games;

top left: Fleet vehicles parked at the Olympic Family Hotel are ready to transport Olympic Family members to their destinations.

bottom left: Two of the more than 2,000 buses that support the Olympic Transportation System wait outside the Airport Welcome Center for Olympic Family members.

right: Crowds of people leave a downtown MARTA station on their way to attend Olympic competition events.

systems are running, an adjustment period is inevitable. While the spectator system is working well, there have been some problems with the media transportation system.

Behind the scenes, ACOG's transportation team works feverishly to make the corrections and adjustments necessary to get the system working smoothly. Although the transportation system is working well by the dawn of day three, many journalists have already declared

volunteers and other staff members require an additional 1.5 million trips. The spectator system will make over 3 million stops during the 17 days of the Games. The operation is incomprehensible in its scope, and the concentration of many venues in the Olympic Ring provides a few challenges that initially appear to be insurmountable.

ERWIN A HANGGI • ROSEMARY L HANK • BOYD R HANKE • MARTIN W HANKE • DIANA C HANKINS • MARK D HANKINS • STACIE R HANKINS • NAN HANKS • PHIL HANKS • SEAN P HANLEN • ELLEN HANLEY • JULIA E HANLEY • TRUDY HANLEY • MARK J HANLON • ANIETH L HANNA • CAROLYN B HANNA • DIANE M HANNA • HUGH M HANNA • KATHLEEN I HANNA • JO HANNAFIN MD • PHILLIPS R HANNAFORD • CATHERINE C HANNAH • KAREN E HANNAH • PATRICK D HANNAH • ZACHARY H HANNAH • KEVIN P HANNAN • THOMAS P HANNASCH • DENNIS J HANNEKEN • LARRY E HANNEMAN • KAREN A HANNON •

nickname, "Pocket Hercules," and two gold medals earned at the past two Olympic Games. A hero in his adopted homeland, Süleymanoglu extends his legend in Atlanta to the cheers of 150 devoted fans from his homeland.

He faces strong opposition in the 64 kg class, including familiar opponent Valerios Leonidis of Greece. There is strong competition for the weightlifting medal, which is won in two phases—the snatch, and the clean and jerk. After Jiangang Xiao of the People's Republic of China, who wins the bronze, is elimi-

COMPETITION

On day three, thousands of athletes—some continuing their quest for medals and some competing in their first rounds—sustain the extraordinary level of performance established in the first two days of competition. While some athletes are becoming new legends in their sports, others simply add to their already legendary status.

One legend on this day is Turkish weightlifter Naim Süleymanoglu. The 4 ft 9 in (1.5 m) dynamo enters Atlanta with a well-earned

nated, Süleymanoglu sets the bar for the clean and jerk at a world record weight and lifts successfully, only to see Leonidis top that weight by 2.5 kg (5.5 lb), putting himself in position to win the gold. Pocket Hercules then matches this feat. Leonidis valiantly attempts 190 kg (419 lb), more than he had ever tried even in practice, but misses, and Süleymanoglu claims the new world record, having lifted a total weight of 335 kg (739 lb), and becomes the first weightlifter to win gold at three consecutive Olympic Games.

During the victory ceremony, Süleymanoglu shakes Leonidis's hand and then kisses him on

left: Laurence Modaine-Cessac of France shouts with joy after defeating Germany's Monika Weber-Koszto in the women's individual foil fencing competition.

right: The winners of the 64 kg weightlifting division—Valerios Leonidis of Greece (silver), Naim Süleymanoglu of Turkey (gold), and Xiao Jiangang of the People's Republic of China (bronze)—salute a crowd of fans.

MARTHA R HANNON • MARY E HANNUM • CLEMENT E HANRAHAN • DONNA HANRAHAN • RICHARD HANRAHAN • J.J HANRATTY • EALON S HANSARD • LINDA N HANSCHE • BOB HANSEL • JOEL A HANSEL • CATHERINE C HANSELL • JAY D HANSEN • ALANA J HANSEN • ANDREW R HANSEN • ANNE E HANSEN • BRAD HANSEN • BRETT HANSEN • BRONWYN L HANSEN • CAROL A HANSEN • CAROL J HANSEN • DANNY L HANSEN • DOUGLAS D HANSEN • EDWIN L HANSEN • EVA HANSEN • GERALD R HANSEN • HOLGER HANSEN • JANE L HANSEN • JENNIFER M HANSEN • JENS H HANSEN • JILL M HANSEN •

both cheeks in a moving display of Olympic brotherhood that suspends, for a brief moment, the historical animosity between the two athletes' respective countries.

The power of the Olympic Movement is revealed in another weightlifting story involving determined athlete Marcus Stephen, who competed on the previous day. Stephen's outstanding performance in previous world championships was so impressive that the International Weightlifting Federation's leadership lobbied the IOC to accept his tiny nation, Nauru—an 8.1 sq mi (21 sq km) island in the South Pacific with a population of 10,000—into the Olympic Family.

At one of two Clark Atlanta University hockey fields, the US women's team wins its first Olympic hockey match in 12 years. Scoring with just six seconds left on the clock, the US squad defeats the Korean squad 3–2.

In a late afternoon dramatic finish, completing two incredibly intense days of men's gymnastics team competition, the Russian team comes from behind to defeat the powerful Chinese team and win the gold before a capacity crowd of more than 30,000 at the Georgia Dome.

As the sunlight slowly fades, the triumphs of the Russian Federation Olympians continue as two of Russia's athletes garner gold in the evening's swimming competition. Aleksander Popov defeats American Gary Hall Jr. by .07 seconds to capture the gold in the 100 m freestyle final; Popov's teammate, Denis Pankratov, seizes the gold in the 200 m butterfly. During this event, fans are introduced to Pankratov's controversial "dolphin kick" that enables him to remain underwater for 30 of the pool's 50 m.

left: Anja von Rekowski of Germany is jubilant after defeating Italy's Emanuela Pierantozzi in their 66 kg preliminary match in judo.

right: The US women's hockey team celebrates its win over Korea—the team's first victory in Olympic hockey competition in 12 years.

JOSEPH HANSEN • KATRINA HANSEN • KEITH W HANSEN • KURT A HANSEN • LARRY D HANSEN • LOIS W HANSEN • LYDIA E HANSEN • MARSHA L HANSEN • PATRICIA J HANSEN • PATRICIA M HANSEN • SARAH HANSEN • SARAH N HANSEN • SYRA V HANSEN • STEPHEN P HANSEN SR • MARK T HANSFORD • WILLIAM A HANSFORD • ANDREW C HANSON • ANN T HANSON • BILL C HANSON • BRIDGET E HANSON • DANA J HANSON • EMILY S HANSON • ENID H HANSON • GEORGE W HANSON • GLENDA F HANSON • HILARY R HANSON • JOHN V HANSON • KEN F HANSON • MELVIN M HANSON •

Since its addition to the Olympic roster at the Tokyo Games of 1964, indoor volleyball has become one of the most popular Olympic sports, and is one of the hottest tickets in Atlanta. With virtually every session sold out, the venue is filled with enthusiastic fans. This evening's women's preliminary match promises a particularly exciting game. In a stunning upset in the preliminaries, the talented, highly focused, emotionally charged Brazilian team defeats the world champion Cuban team in three straight sets. Despite Cuba's loss, both teams advance and will meet again in the semi-finals, where Cuba will triumph over Brazil 3–2, and go on to win the gold medal, while Brazil will garner the bronze.

top: The Russian Federation's men's gymnastics team waves to the crowd after receiving their gold medals won in the team competition.

bottom: Gary Hall Jr. of the US rests after winning the silver medal in the men's 100 m freestyle competition.

OLYMPIC ARTS FESTIVAL

Two events dominate this evening's Olympic Arts Festival schedule: An Olympic Celebration of Chamber Music at Atlanta Symphony Hall, and the opening of the Netherlands Dance Theater's three-day run at the Atlanta Civic Center.

Organized by distinguished pianist and Georgia native Charles Wadsworth, founder of the Chamber Music Society of Lincoln Center, An Olympic Celebration of Chamber Music

violists Nobuko Imai and Ida Kavafian; and cellists Lynn Harrell and Sharon Robinson. As brilliant performers in their own right, together these musicians form an ensemble of uncompromising sophistication, depth, and power.

From the opening bars of Moszkowski's Suite in G Minor for Two Violins and Piano, op. 71, the audience is aware of the Olympic nature of this event. The most intimate pearls, such as Frederica von Stade's performance of Leonard Bernstein's "A Little Bit in Love" from

A chamber group of musical luminaries performs Mendelssohn's Octet for Strings in E-flat.

represents an extraordinary and improbable gathering of some of the world's most celebrated musicians. Chamber music concerts, perhaps the most sedate of classical music events, tend to attract knowledgeable connoisseurs. But the Olympic nature of this event, organized and hosted by a native son, makes it far more than a concert. In its own way, tonight's performance is the equivalent of a team final, an event requiring perfect delivery from each performer to achieve a winning score.

What a dazzling team of musical luminaries Wadsworth assembled for this occasion: mezzo-soprano Frederica von Stade; violinists Itzhak Perlman, Pinchas Zukerman, Jaime Laredo, and Georgia native Robert McDuffie;

Wonderful Town, are followed by absolute stillness and then explosive cheers. The evening reaches its climax in a spine-tingling performance of Mendelssohn's Octet for Strings in E-flat. When the opening notes of the magnificent last-movement presto are sounded, the ensemble seems to shift to a level reserved for perfect 10s. As the last chord sounds, the audience leaps to its feet as one in an ovation lasting more than 10 minutes.

For those who wonder why or how art and sport became linked in the Olympic Movement, this concert beautifully illustrates the special bond between these two domains of human achievement. The extraordinary technical virtuosity and physical stamina displayed by the musicians in performances of unsurpassed aesthetic quality underscore that the

CAROL A HARDCASTLE • WILLLAM R HARDCASTLE • S DALE HARDEE • MARYANNE S HARDEMAN • ALBERT J HARDEN • BETTIE B HARDEN • CHARLES A HARDEN • CHRISTINA A HARDEN • CINDY A HARDEN • DANE S. HARDEN • ELIZABETH C HARDEN • GAIL B HARDEN • JABRA HARDEN • LINDA S HARDEN • LOUISE S HARDEN • MARK HARDEN • MARK C HARDEN • MATTHEW J HARDEN • ROSLYN A HARDEN • VALERIE K HARDEN • W JACK HARDEN • WANDA S HARDEN • JAMES HARDEN II • DAVID W HARDER • KARI B HARDER • WAYNE S HARDERS • MOSES HARDIMAN • ALICE J HARDIN • DARIN L HARDIN •

top: The Netherlands Dance Theater performs *Kaguyahime* at the Atlanta Civic Center.

bottom: The Dallas Black Dance Theatre performs at the Martin Luther King Jr. International Chapel at Morehouse College.

outer boundaries of human ability—both in art and sport—are what the Olympic Games are all about.

Long considered one of the world's most adventurous and accomplished contemporary dance companies, the Netherlands Dance Theater was among the first dance companies invited to perform during the 1996 Olympic Arts Festival. Like many of the international companies selected for the festival, this company's Olympic performances are its first in the American South.

Since its creation by the company's artistic director Jiri Kylián in 1988, *Kaguyahime* has become an international signature work for the company. It is a physically challenging, emotionally charged, and visually dazzling work that celebrates the company's multiple strengths. Based on a 10th-century Japanese story of the same name, Kylián's work blends music, dance, and innovative staging and choreography into an organic whole that, in the course of 90 minutes, tells a 1,000-year-old Asian fairy tale.

Throughout the work, the dancers are supported and driven by Circle Percussion, an ensemble of 18 virtuoso drummers whose kalei-doscopic range of percussive textures and rhythms are the heartbeat of the performance. The powerful exchange of energy between the dancers and Circle Percussion seems to grow throughout the work, captivating the audience in a pulsating current of sights and sounds.

Atlanta 1996®

DENISE K HARDIN • FRANCES T HARDIN • HAYLEY E HARDIN • JAMES A HARDIN • JAMES C HARDIN • JEFFREY M HARDIN • JULIA P HARDIN • LISA D HARDIN • MIKE D HARDIN • ROBBIE J HARDIN • RUTH A HARDIN • SALLY A HARDIN • HAMILTON H HARDIN III • WILLIAM G HARDIN III • CAROLE P HARDING • CLARICE P HARDING • BRANDON K HARDISON • BRIAN L HARDISON • WILLIAM V HARDISON • BRYAN T HARDMAN • JACK W HARDMAN • WESLYN E HARDMAN • DAWN D HARDT • DIANE D HARDWICK • GREGORY G HARDWICK • JACQUELINE M HARDWICK • JEFF JR HARDWICK • LISA R HARDWICK •

105

Day Four
23 July 1996

ON DAY FOUR, the competition schedule expands dramatically. From the first morning session through the end of the evening sessions, the nine competition venues clustered around Centennial Olympic Park are all filled to capacity with events and fans. More than 442,000 tickets have been sold to today's events at these venues. The impact on the transportation system, park attendance, security, communications, and every other facet of operations is extraordinary. Fortunately, from what was learned during the first days of the Games, adjustments have been made where necessary and the venues, though at capacity throughout the day, operate without incident.

More than 130,000 volunteers, paid staff, and contracted personnel are operating Atlanta's Olympic Games as a highly synchronized team and are meeting or exceeding expectations. The more than 50,000 volunteers will each log an average of 117.6 hours during the Games period—more than 5.5 million hours of service—in over 250 different positions. The collective efforts of volunteers is the engine that drives every Olympic Games. Volunteerism is a nationwide tradition, but Atlanta's volunteer history and depth of commitment is among the most impressive of any city in the US. The tradition and spirit of volunteerism has permeated and sustained Atlanta's

Volunteers were extensively trained to assist spectators at venues.

Olympic effort since the earliest days of Atlanta's Bid to host the Games, when members of the Bid committee worked as volunteers. Throughout the six years leading up to the Games, Atlanta's organizers relied on the continuing good will and countless hours of service provided by an extraordinary corps of volunteers, some of whom logged in excess of 8,000 hours before the Games even began.

With the Games in full swing, volunteers are the literal backbone of ACOG's operating

PEARCE D HARDWICK • QUINCY L HARDWICK • ANTHONY J HARDY • CARLOS D HARDY • CYNTHIA R HARDY • JOAN T HARDY • KELLY D HARDY • KENNETH D HARDY • MARGARET O HARDY • MARK HARDY • MARTHA B HARDY • MELISSA L HARDY • MICHELLE HARDY • ROY A HARDY • SAM R HARDY • SANDRA E HARDY • SUE R HARDY • TRACY L HARDY • WILLIAM B HARDY • ZAYNE HARDY • ALBERT SID HARDY III • GOLDEN J HARDY III • CORNELIUS C HARE • ELISE D HARE • J C HARE • ZACHARY T HARE • JOHANNA ALANE HAREN • HELEN M HARGETT • HUELL T HARGETT • MARK M HARGETT

107

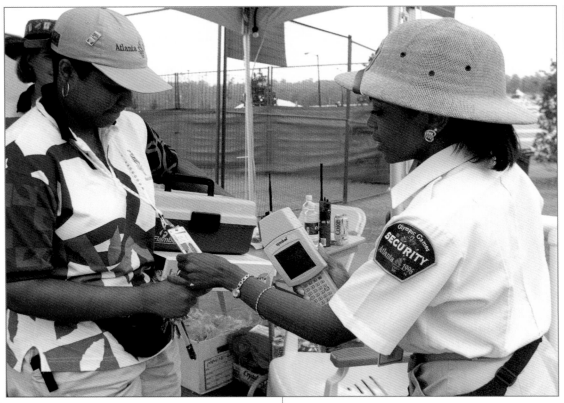

technology operations. Volunteers also support operations at the Main Press Center and International Broadcast Center, warehouses, throughout the airport, in the Olympic Village, at Centennial Olympic Park, at the sponsor hospitality villages, and in innumerable other capacities. Though they have been given a general orientation and an introductory training course, most volunteers must learn their Games assignments on the job—a major challenge for many whose jobs begin during the Games themselves. This talented, committed, and enthusiastic team provides service at an unsurpassed level of quality throughout the Games period.

Two volunteer crews—Olympic envoys and language services specialists—demonstrate the specialized skills and personal qualities required to staff the Games.

A highly skilled, diverse, and dedicated team of 197 specially chosen individuals serves as the corps of Olympic envoys who provide each NOC with vital information, communica-

top: **Security volunteer uses an electronic badge-reader to provide access control to the Stone Mountain Park Tennis Center.**

bottom: **Technically skilled staff at the International Broadcast Center continually monitor the quality of the transmission signal.**

team. This talented group of people of all ages and backgrounds serve side-by-side as ushers, ticket takers, security personnel, drivers, hosts and hostesses, and in a variety of envoy positions, such as communications, logistics, and

• HOWARD M HARGIS • JANETH L HARGIS • LINDA S HARGIS • THOMAS E HARGIS • DAVID R HARGRAVE • ELIZABETH C HARGREAVES • DAVID E HARGROVE • DEBORAH J HARGROVE • DOUGLAS HARGROVE • MERLE HARGROVE • INA H HARIZANOVA • JEFF HARKEY • JOHN P HARKEY • DANIELLE A HARKINS • JAMES R HARKINS • KIMBERLY C HARKINS • LARA E HARKINS • JILL C HARKLEROAD • JERRY A HARKNESS • JODI R HARKNESS • JOHN K HARKNESS • JONATHAN P HARKNESS • KIMBERLY ANNE HARKNESS • PATRICIA C HARKREADER • ROBERT E HARKRIDER • CAROLYN L HARLAN

tion aids, and other logistical support throughout the NOC's stay in Atlanta. Ranging in age from 27 to 73 and speaking 45 languages among them, envoys embody and sustain the Olympic Spirit. Like other volunteers, this select group of individuals began its preparation for the Games in 1994 with weekly training sessions and exams on Olympic history, Games, and Village operations.

Each envoy directs a volunteer team that includes an assistant envoy and drivers for NOC officials. Available 24 hours a day, envoys are the principal contact with ACOG for each chef de mission. Selected for their understanding and appreciation of each nation's distinctive cultural traditions, leadership skills, team spirit, and commitment to Olympic ideals, this corps includes people from many

different backgrounds. They share a deep sense of pride and a profound commitment to delivering service of distinction that assures athletes and officials alike that their time in Atlanta will be of unrivaled quality.

From ACOG's main switchboard to the field of play, the responsibility of providing swift, accurate communication among athletes, officials, judges, and operations personnel from 197 delegations falls to the 5,000 multilingual volunteers who form the Language Services team. Posted at the Atlanta Olympic Village, the Main Press Center, the Olympic Family Hotel, each competition venue, and other key Olympic facilities and locations, ACOG language specialists—some of whom speak three or more languages fluently—are an essential component of Games operations. These volunteers enable cross-lingual communication by providing written translation and interpretative services. During the Games, more than 4.5 million written words will be translated, and interpretative services will be provided in 45 languages at the competition venues and 31 languages at ACOG's switchboard.

Whether they are interpreting a judge's call on the field of play for athletes and team officials or providing simultaneous translation for media briefings and official meetings, every member of this specialized group of volunteers has been tested and certified. In all, more than 3,700 language evaluations have been given in the months leading up to the Games. The languages in highest demand include French, Russian, and Spanish.

A unique asset to the Language Services team, Aberra Aguengnehu is a six-time Olympic volunteer who speaks more than 20 languages and dialects. This Ethiopian-born specialist speaks 12 dialects of Arabic, Amharic, English, French, Hebrew, Italian, Portuguese, and Spanish. Aguengnehu comments, "I don't just learn the language. I'm interested in the culture, the customs, and the history behind the words. When someone speaks to me I can usually pick up the accent right away and can usually respond back in their language. It's my way to make people feel welcome."

Six-time Olympic volunteer translator Aberra Aguengnehu, who speaks more than 20 languages, contributes his skills to the Olympic effort.

• JAYMES J HARLAN • ROBERT M HARLAN • ANNE B HARLAND • RACHELE I HARLESS • DAVID A HARLEY • LINDA D HARLEY • RICHARD C HARLOW • KIMBERLY M HARLOW MT • JOHN W HARM • CHARLOTTE J HARMAN • KATHERINE R HARMAN • LINDA L HARMAN • WILLIAM A HARMAN • ROMAN J HARMEL • JENNIFER A HARMELIN • JOHN M HARMER • PETER A HARMER ATC • VERNON F HARMESON • PATRICIA T HARMEYER • ROBERT E HARMEYER • ANDREW P HARMON • BRENDA HARMON • CAROLYN D HARMON • JAHBAREE A HARMON • JAMES D HARMON • JAMES F HARMON •

109

spectators, she ignores the pain shooting through her leg and again sprints down the runway. This time, she lands cleanly—on one foot—and holds her spot long enough to salute the judges before finally collapsing. She scores a 9.712 for the vault and the US team—Amanda Borden, Amy Chow, Dominique Dawes, Shannon Miller, Dominique Moceanu, Jaycie Phelps, and Kerri Strug—captures gold.

On this day, Olympic history is not made only on the mats. The sands of Atlanta Beach host the debut of a new sport on the Olympic

left: Despite a painful ankle injury, Kerri Strug successfully completes her vault to help the US women's gymnastics team capture its first-ever gold medal in the team competition.

top right: Muene Tshijuka of Zaire gets the tip of a jump ball over Rachael Sporn of Australia during a preliminary women's basketball game.

bottom right: Atlanta Beach hosts the debut of a new Olympic sport— beach volleyball.

COMPETITION

During every Olympic Games, incidents occur which provide tangible examples of the achievement of Olympic ideals. On this fourth day of competition, Kerri Strug provides one of these moments. With the US poised to win its first team gold medal in women's gymnastics history, the competition rests in the hands and feet of the diminutive Strug. After soaring through the air on her first vault attempt, Strug lands, and paints a reluctant smile of elation and relief on her face before she falls to the mat in agony. Strug has torn ligaments in her ankle. Buoyed by the cheers of more than 35,000

JEANNETTE THERESA HARMON • JUDITH L HARMON • KAREN L HARMON • MARTIN HARMON • MATTHEW M HARMON • NANCY B HARMON • PHYLLIS B HARMON • REBECCA J HARMON • SARAH JANE HARMON • STACEY E HARMON • TONYA J HARMON • KATHLEEN M HARMS • CAROL L HARN • DIANNE HARNELL-COHEN • TAMMY M HARNER • BARBARA E HARNESS • MARION F HARNETT • CATHERINE F HARNEY • DAVID M HARNEY • SUSAN H HARNEY • ROBERT J HARNOR • BENTON HAROLD • CHARLES L HAROWITZ JR • CAROLYN M HARP • CHRISTOPHER LEE HARPE • VERONICA A HARPE •

roster—beach volleyball. In the sport's opener, Indonesia's Engel Berta Kaize makes history on two counts: she serves the first ball as well as the first ace. Located about 40 minutes south of downtown Atlanta, the specially designed facility attracts sold-out crowds daily.

Greco-Roman wrestling is filled with drama, both on and off the mats. Shortly after noon, in an unusual "halftime" ceremony following the completion of the morning matches and preceding the afternoon matches, US Greco-Roman assistant coach Bob Anderson weds Judy Munday outside the Georgia World Congress Center. There is no time for the couple to leave for a relaxing honeymoon, however, as Anderson's attention must return to the mats for the afternoon rounds.

Wlodzimierz Zawadzki, a wrestler from Poland in the 62 kg (136.5 lb) class, wins his country's third gold medal before a crowd including Polish president Aleksandr Kwasniewski. In an interview following the match,

top left: A member of the French team wins over his opponent from Germany on the way to France's capture of the bronze medal in the men's team epée.

bottom left: Aleksandr Karelin of the Russian Federation raises three fingers to indicate that he has won a third straight Olympic title in the 130 kg (286 lb) Greco-Roman wrestling division.

right: Anna Maria Solazzi of Italy jumps to block the ball during a preliminary beach volleyball game against Norway.

ALVIN J HARPER • APRIL D HARPER • BEVERLY HARPER • BEVERLY R HARPER • BILL R HARPER • BRIAN A HARPER • BRIAN J HARPER • CATHERINE S HARPER • CHARLES W HARPER • CHRISTOPHER M HARPER • COLLINS W HARPER • DARCY C HARPER • DOROTHY H HARPER • EDNA E HARPER • FOLEY HARPER • FRANK L HARPER • FREDERICK B HARPER • GREGORY A HARPER • HEIDI L HARPER • HILLARY K HARPER • JAN A HARPER • JANICE W HARPER • JEFFREY P HARPER • JENNIFER K HARPER • JIMMY F HARPER • JOELLE M HARPER • KAREN O HARPER • KATHERINE M HARPER •

Zawadzki somewhat immodestly says, "I was very happy because the president doesn't attend all the events, just the big ones."

Later, in an emotional final match between long-time rivals, American Matt Ghaffari challenges Aleksandr Karelin of the Russian Federation in the 130 kg (286 lb) class. The towering Karelin, who weighed an amazing 15 lb (7 kg) at birth, and whose Olympic and World Championship record stands at 44–0 going into this match, defeats the 34-year-old Ghaffari to win his third gold medal. Ghaffari, who desperately wanted to beat Karelin on his home turf, weeps on the victory stand.

In a controversial judo match, underdog Djamel Bouras of France defeats Japan's great half-middleweight, Toshihiko Koga, for the gold medal. The judges in the contest vote 3–0 in favor of Bouras after neither man scores a point for a throw, and the only points scored are those for penalties. Koga's loss is an upset for the traditional judo powerhouse Japan.

This first day of softball competition at the 1996 Games is also softball's debut at the Olympic Games themselves. As a fitting complement to an Olympiad that features the

top left: Djamel Bouras of France combats Toshihiko Koga of Japan in the half-middleweight judo competition.

bottom left: Terry Dewitt of the US team takes aim in the women's double trap shooting preliminaries.

right: A member of Australia's softball team slides into first base during preliminary play against Puerto Rico.

KATHRYN L HARPER • KAY S HARPER • KENT M HARPER • KEVIN L HARPER • LINDA S HARPER • MATTHEW C HARPER • MELISSA B HARPER • MELISSA D HARPER • OSCAR C HARPER • PATRICIA D HARPER • RAYMOND D HARPER • RAYMOND P HARPER • REX S HARPER • RICHARD E HARPER • ROBERT HARPER • ROBERT E HARPER • ROBERT G HARPER • RONALD N HARPER • WARREN H HARPER • HENRY A HARPER III • GERALD I HARPER JR • CORINNE D HARR • ALAN E HARRELL • AMANDA HARRELL • AMY K HARRELL • CHERESE G HARRELL • CHRISTOPHER N HARRELL •

ahead, he will follow through a repeat performance with Nicolas Pereira (no. 75), Thomas Enqvist (no. 10), and Fernando Meligeni (no. 95). While the Games bring new stars to light, they also glorify those who have already earned renown, such as no. 3 ranked Andre Agassi, who turns in a consistently brilliant performance today.

The Georgia Tech Aquatic Center, which has already experienced a large number of thrilling finishes today, is in for more excitement. In a sensational and historic triumph,

most female athletes ever, Olympic softball is exclusively a women's sport. The first of the round-robin softball preliminaries are being held at Golden Park in Columbus, GA. In a game that will prove prophetic of the days to come, Japan meets the US for the first Games in a decisive 6–1 US win. Later, a 2–0 win against Australia causes the Puerto Rican team to rejoice, although it is Australia that will eventually advance to the semifinals.

The first day of tennis competition—the first round of both the men's and women's singles—is being held at the new Stone Mountain Park Tennis Center. Surprises are never far from the field of play, as India's no. 127 ranked Leander Paes eliminates no. 23 ranked Richey Reneberg from the men's singles running. In the days

the US men's 4 x 100 m freestyle relay team, consisting of Josh Davis, Gary Hall Jr., Jon Olsen, and Bradley Schumacher, wins the gold medal—the 100th swimming medal won by the US in 100 years of swimming competition. The US team's dominance of this event is legendary, as it has remained undefeated for the last seven Olympic Games.

Penelope Heyns of South Africa sets a new Olympic record of 2:25.41 while winning the 200 m breaststroke and earning her second gold medal of the Games.

left: **Josh Davis prepares to swim in the men's 4 x 100 m freestyle relay to help the US win its 100th swimming medal in 100 years.**

right: **Jorg Hoffmann of Germany prepares to compete in the men's 400 m freestyle preliminaries.**

DALE F HARRELL • DALE W HARRELL • DIANE C HARRELL • DIANNE F HARRELL • DONNA L HARRELL • DONNA L. HARRELL • FRAN K HARRELL • FRANCES J HARRELL • GERALD E HARRELL • HARRIETT R HARRELL • HENRY E HARRELL • IVAN K HARRELL • JANET E HARRELL • JOLENE A HARRELL • KATY HARRELL • MARTHA D HARRELL • MARY SUE HARRELL • MICHAEL G HARRELL • PATRICIA S HARRELL • PATRICK C HARRELL • SAMUEL R HARRELL • STEPHEN L HARRELL • WILBUR J HARRELL • WILLIAM S HARRELL • ANTHONY B HARRELSON • KATHY D HARRIE • BRIDGET K HARRIGAN •

The Kiss, by Auguste Rodin, is one of the works selected to portray the rubric of love in the *Rings* exhibition.

OLYMPIC ARTS FESTIVAL

A few blocks north and east of the Olympic Village lies the Robert W. Woodruff Arts Center, the heart of Atlanta's cultural life. Home of the Atlanta Symphony Orchestra, the Alliance Theatre Company, the Atlanta College of Art, and the High Museum of Art, the center has just completed a renovation in time to serve the tens of thousands of Olympic Arts Festival patrons expected to attend performances and exhibitions during the Games period. With an of-

Of particular interest is the fabulous exhibition presented at the High Museum of Art, *Rings: Five Passions in World Art*. The centerpiece of the Olympic Arts Festival's visual arts program, *Rings* is a blockbuster. The thematic brainchild of curator J. Carter Brown, distinguished director emeritus of the National Gallery of Art in Washington, DC, this extraordinary exhibition will attract more than 200,000 visitors during its 80-day run.

In his introduction to the catalogue that accompanies the exhibition, Brown writes:

Auguste Préault's *Slaughter* portrays the universal human emotion of anguish.

ficial Olympic box office housed within the center's regular box office operation, the center attracts thousands of additional Olympic visitors who might not otherwise see this impressive focal point of cultural activity. Many of them are encouraged enough by what they see to purchase tickets for one or more of the many Olympic Arts Festival music and theatrical performances being presented during the Games.

In conceiving this exhibition, I have taken, in a metaphorical sense, the concept of interconnectedness that those five rings so graphically embody as the guiding principle for an art exhibition of what we believe to be a wholly innovative kind. Its basis is in the emotional, affective (as distinct from purely cognitive) function of works of art, grouped under five rubrics: Love, Anguish, Awe, Triumph, and Joy.

ASHLEY HARRIS • ASHLEY I HARRIS • BARBARA E HARRIS • BENJAMIN S HARRIS • BERNARD HARRIS • BETTY K HARRIS • BETTYE C HARRIS • BEVERLY L HARRIS • BONNIE J HARRIS • BRENDA A HARRIS • BRESHAWN HARRIS • BRIAN C HARRIS • BRYAN M HARRIS • CAROL W HARRIS • CAROLYN HARRIS • CHARLES E HARRIS • CHARLES E HARRIS • CHARLOTTE R HARRIS • CHERRYL M HARRIS • CHRIS HARRIS • CHRISTAIN HARRIS • CHRISTOPHE HARRIS • COFFEY M HARRIS • DAMIEN J HARRIS • DANIEL N HARRIS • DARNACEA L HARRIS • DAVID A HARRIS • DAVID J HARRIS •

The present exhibition. . .brings together paintings and sculpture as diverse as possible, in scale and materials and originally intended function, objects that span more than 7,000 years of creativity, representing virtually all the major geographic areas and principal religious mainstreams of our world.

Rings, 10 times larger than any exhibition ever presented at the High Museum, is an exhibition of profound thematic structure and sophisticated content, featuring works that range from 4000 BC to the present. From works

by unknown artists from ancient cultures and obscure corners of the world to more recent masterworks by well-known artists such as Caravaggio, Rodin, Picasso, and Matisse, *Rings* is a

kinetic panoply expressive of different essential human emotions. This eclectic confluence of artwork expresses the commonality between all who see it—young and old, local patron and distant traveler, and athlete and fan—uniting them in the Olympic Spirit.

From the moment of its opening, first to major sponsors and donors and then to the public on 4 July, *Rings* sweeps Atlanta off its feet. But not everyone is enthusiastic. As Brown had predicted, the arts press criticizes the thematic concept and some of the objects included in the exhibition, but Cultural Olympiad organizers, High Museum officials, and Brown are not concerned. The long lines outside the museum throughout the exhibition's run and the enthusiastic response of virtually everyone who views the exhibition proclaim *Rings* to be an overwhelming success.

left: Gerrit Van Hothorst's *Merry Fiddler* displays the rubric of joy in the *Rings* exhibition.

right: This monumental female effigy urn from Vera Cruz, Mexico, illustrates the rubric of awe.

DAVID S HARRIS • DAVID W HARRIS • DEANNE E HARRIS • DEBORAH A HARRIS • DEBORAH T HARRIS • DEBRA L HARRIS • DGINA V HARRIS • DON HARRIS • DON HARRIS • DOUG HARRIS • DWAYNE HARRIS • ELAINE M HARRIS • ELAINE S HARRIS • ELAINE S HARRIS • ELLA L HARRIS • ERIC L HARRIS • EUODIA R HARRIS • FAY A HARRIS • FRANCES C HARRIS • GARY A HARRIS • GILFORD HARRIS • GLEN R HARRIS • GREGORY BRYON HARRIS • GREGORY W HARRIS • HAROLD L HARRIS • HELEN L HARRIS • HENRY G HARRIS • HERMAN L HARRIS • IRVING O HARRIS • JADA R HARRIS •

Jean-Auguste-Dominique Ingres's ceremonial portrait of *Napoleon Enthroned* illustrates triumph.

JAMILA HARRIS • JANE H HARRIS • JANE K HARRIS • JANE L HARRIS • JASON HARRIS • JAY HARRIS • JEANNE I HARRIS • JEFFERSIS A HARRIS • JENNIFER HARRIS • JERRI N HARRIS • JIMI R HAR-RIS • JOAN L HARRIS • JOHN HARRIS • JOI R HARRIS • JONATHAN HARRIS • JOSHUA HARRIS • JUAN K HARRIS • JUDITH A HARRIS • JULIAN P HARRIS • KARL W HARRIS • KATHLEEN HARRIS • KATHLEEN W HARRIS • KEITH HARRIS • KEITH E HARRIS • KELLI R HARRIS • KELLY M HARRIS • KIMBERLIE HARRIS • KOREN L HARRIS • LARRY HARRIS • LATOYA J HARRIS • LEONARD G HARRIS

DAY FIVE
24 JULY 1996

DAY FIVE DAWNS with 24 of the possible 26 sports engaged in competitive activity. The sheer quantity of activity—from preliminary to medal rounds—stretches operational and logistical resources to the limit and demands the full attention of ACOG's Venue Management Department, broadcasters, and the press. Fortunately, the many valuable lessons learned in the preceding four days of competition have been applied to every aspect of the Games, and this day is managed without disruption. The various groups that are operating, broadcasting, reporting, attending, and enjoying the Centennial Olympic Games have by now gained enough experience coordinating their activities and moving within the Games environment to meet any challenges that may lie ahead. The anxiety Games staff felt during the first days of competition is being slowly replaced with a sense of relief and enjoyment, coming from the recognition that the systems designed and planned to support the Games work.

Fans and staff, athletes and officials, and the hundreds of millions of viewers around the world who are watching these Games in record numbers voice almost universal praise for Atlanta's Olympic efforts. By contrast, though both press transportation and Games results

Members of the Australian swim team cheer their teammates on at the Georgia Tech Aquatic Center.

systems are now working well, the press corps's criticism of ACOG will continue throughout the Games. Driven by the early and sustained criticism by the press, the clash between these polar extremes of opinion will lead to a continuing debate between an enthusiastic public and the cynical press as to the reliability of some media support services.

TODAY'S CALENDAR

Competition

Aquatics—swimming, water polo
Badminton
Baseball
Basketball
Boxing
Cycling—track
Equestrian
Fencing
Football
Gymnastics—artistic
Handball
Hockey
Judo
Rowing
Shooting
Softball
Table tennis
Tennis
Volleyball—beach, indoor
Weightlifting
Yachting

Olympic Arts Festival

Alliance Theatre Company: *The Last Night of Ballyhoo* and *Blues for an Alabama Sky*
Atlanta Symphony Orchestra with Jessye Norman
Atlanta Symphony Youth Orchestra
Center for Puppetry Arts: *The Hungry Tiger and Other Tales from China*
Netherlands Dance Theater: *Kaguyahime*
Pilobolus Dance Theatre
Seven Stages: *Blue Monk*
Southern Crossroads Festival

• LEWIS N HARRIS • LINDA J HARRIS • LOIS M HARRIS • LORESSA V HARRIS • LOUISE HARRIS • LUCIOUS N HARRIS • LUCY M HARRIS • LULA B HARRIS • MARGARET K HARRIS • MARIA T HARRIS • MARIE HARRIS • MARILYN R HARRIS • MARINE HARRIS • MARK L HARRIS • MARY E HARRIS • MARY E HARRIS • MARY P HARRIS • MELANIE S HARRIS • MICHELLE Y HARRIS • MILLICENT C HARRIS • MYRA C HARRIS • MYRTLE HARRIS • NARVIE HARRIS • NATHA S HARRIS • PAMELA J HARRIS • PAMELA R HARRIS • PATRICIA A HARRIS • QUOVADIS J HARRIS • R PRESSLEY HARRIS • RAMONA H HARRIS • RANDOLPH HARRIS

119

COMPETITION

Outstanding performances are again the order of the day at the Georgia Tech Aquatic Center, where the fifth day of swimming competition is particularly intense. New records are set throughout the day, adding greatly to the audience's enthusiasm.

In a stunning turn of events, Australia's Scott Miller sets a new Olympic record for the 100 m butterfly during his preliminary heat, only to have it swept away in the evening fi-

left: The New Zealand swim team does its traditional "Haka" dance.

right: Australia's Shane Kelly cycles away from the track after his foot slips out of a pedal, causing him to fail to qualify for the medal race.

nals by Denis Pankratov of the Russian Federation, who sets a new world record as he wins his second gold medal of the Games.

In the women's team medley, the US 4 x 100 m medley relay team—which includes Beth Botsford, backstroke; Amanda Beard, breaststroke; Angel Martino, butterfly; and Amy Van Dyken, freestyle—wins Olympic gold after finishing more than two seconds ahead of the second place Australian team.

Despite years of athletes' dedicated training and preparation, sometimes things simply go wrong. At the start of the men's 1 km time trial in track cycling, an event in which even half of a second can make an enormous difference, Australia's cyclist Shane "Minute Man" Kelly's foot slips out of his pedal, causing him

to lose about two critical seconds and ultimately costing him the opportunity to qualify for the medal race. Kelly, the 1992 silver medalist and favorite to win the gold in 1996, is almost energized in defeat, saying, "You'll see me in the year 2000."

Meanwhile, France's Florian Rousseau garners the gold, while American Erin Hartwell and Japan's Takanobu Jumonji take the silver and bronze, respectively.

Two competition stories from the Georgia International Horse Park help to illustrate the

• RAY S HARRIS • RAYMOND J HARRIS • REBA E HARRIS • RICHARD W HARRIS • RITA A HARRIS • ROBERT D HARRIS • ROBERT D HARRIS • ROBERT W HARRIS • ROBIN Y HARRIS • RONNENE M HARRIS • RUTH E HARRIS • SANDRA G HARRIS • SHARON D HARRIS • SHEILA A HARRIS • SHERI HARRIS • SHERRY HARRIS • STANLEY G HARRIS • STANLEY M HARRIS • STEPHANIE HARRIS • SUSAN O HARRIS • SUSAN S HARRIS • SUZANNE C HARRIS • SUZETTE L HARRIS • SYBIL L HARRIS • TAYLOR D HARRIS • TERRELL J HARRIS • TERRY A HARRIS • THOMAS L HARRIS • TODD A HARRIS • TODD A HARRIS • TONYA HARRIS •

top: Australia's equestrian team salutes the crowd after receiving gold medals in the three-day endurance event.

bottom: Members of the US men's hockey team huddle on the field during a game with Argentina.

determination of the athletes and the record-setting performances that continue to dominate Atlanta's Games. Wendy Schaeffer, a 21-year-old rookie from Australia, earns the best score in the jumping phase of the three-day event on her bay gelding, Sunburst, leading Australia to the gold medal.

Only two months before the Games, Schaeffer's Olympic hopes seemed doomed when the young horse upon which she was competing fell, pinning one of Schaeffer's legs against the hurdle and causing it to break. Given a discouraging prognosis for healing in time for the Games, Schaeffer found a surgeon willing to perform an unusual procedure that allowed her to keep riding.

TORRANCE A HARRIS • VERLE D HARRIS • VIRGINIA L HARRIS • VIRGINIA M HARRIS • WALTER J HARRIS • WANDA L HARRIS • WILLIAM C HARRIS • WILLIAM H HARRIS • YUCCA HARRIS • YVONNE HARRIS • KIMBERLY H HARRIS-ADAMS • KATIE V HARRIS-DAVIS • PAMELA R HARRIS-JENKINS • ANGELA Y HARRIS-LEE • JENNIFER A HARRIS-REID • KIMBLEY HARRIS JOHNSON • JAMES R HARRIS JR • ANGELA F HARRISON • ARNETHA E HARRISON • BLAIR D HARRISON • BOBBYE A HARRISON • CAROL A HARRISON • CAROLYN C HARRISON • CHARLES E HARRISON • CHRISTINE C HARRISON • COURTNEY D HARRISON

121

On day five, still recovering from surgery and forced to ice her leg immediately after riding, Schaeffer's gritty determination drives her to help her team win the gold medal.

Also at the horse park, Karen and David O'Connor from the US become the first married couple in Olympic history to ride together on a medal-winning equestrian team. The O'Connor tandem finishes second behind Australia's team to take the silver at the conclusion of the grueling, three-day competition, ahead of a team from New Zealand.

after Erichsen, who comes in ranked no. 1, falls to Olsson 12–15, 15–6, 17–15.

The fans at beach volleyball are numerous, and one of them is just plain large. Sporting a straw hat and a yellow and green shirt, 500 lb (227 kg) Bola Sete, or "Seven Ball," cheers on the Brazilian team. The enthusiastic giant, seen at various venues throughout the Games, becomes an icon, attracting attention from fans and athletes alike wherever he goes.

In the late afternoon, in men's artistic gymnastics individual competition, the People's

top left: Brazil's Bola Sete and other fans cheer at the indoor volleyball competition.

bottom left: Marcos Ondruska of South Africa shows his excitement as he defeats no. 2 seed Goran Ivanisevic of Croatia.

right: Vitaly Scherbo of Belarus performs on the parallel bars in the men's individual artistic gymnastics competition.

Competition begins today in badminton, and the spectators at the Georgia State University Gymnasium are treated to a spectacular men's singles match between Jens Olsson of Sweden, ranked no. 20 in the world, and unheralded Kenneth Erichsen of Guatemala. The two competitors earn a standing ovation

Republic of China's Xiaoshuang Li defeats the Russian Federation's Alexei Nemov to become China's first all-around artistic gymnastics gold medalist. Li takes the lead and wins the gold with his performance on the rings apparatus, scoring a 9.775, while Nemov scores 9.7 on his floor exercise. Li finishes only .049 points ahead of Nemov. The defending Olympic all-around champion, Vitaly Scherbo of Belarus, takes the bronze.

• CRAIG C HARRISON • CYNTHIA M HARRISON • DANA E HARRISON • DANNY K HARRISON • DEBBIE J HARRISON • DENNIS R HARRISON • DERRICK HARRISON • DEXTER B HARRISON • E TRACY HARRISON • EUGENE O HARRISON • FREDDA P HARRISON • GARY E HARRISON • GRACE S HARRISON • HANK D HARRISON • HELEN M HARRISON • INA S HARRISON • J CHRISTOPHER HARRISON • J M M HARRISON • JANE H HARRISON • JANET E HARRISON • JANICE F HARRISON • JODI L HARRISON • JODY HARRISON • JOEL HARRISON • JOHN A HARRISON • JOSEPH S HARRISON • JOSHUA K HARRISON • JUDY C HARRISON •

The Democratic People's Republic of Korea's Hyon Kim concentrates on the ball in her win over Germany's Jie Schopp in a surprising upset in women's table tennis competition.

In its second day of competition, table tennis is a hot ticket. A trio of women athletes from the Democratic People's Republic of Korea, none ranked higher than no. 80 in the world, comes within two points of notching three major upsets. Two of the athletes are able to garner surprising wins as Hyon Kim defeats Germany's Jie Schopp, the world's no. 14 ranked player in the world; and Jong-Sil Tu shocks the Democratic People's Republic of Korea's Ji-Hae Ryu, ranked no. 20 in the world, in two sets. In the other contest, the Democratic People's Republic of Korea's Hyang Kim is leading Jun Hong Jing of Singapore, the no. 16 ranked player in the world, 17–16, in the deciding games of her match when Jing is awarded a point because the judges rule that Kim is shrieking too loudly after winning points. This decision infuriates Kim who, despite leading at game point, loses 22–20.

East of Atlanta, at the magnificent new Stone Mountain Park Tennis Center, boisterous South African fans, black and white alike, join together in song to support team member Marcos Ondruska. The focused support bolsters Ondruska's performance, enabling him to upset no. 2 seed Goran Ivanisevic of Croatia, 6–2, 6–4, in a center-court match before a crowd of more than 12,000.

In a bizarre occurrence at the football competition in Birmingham, Alabama, the Tunisian team shocks the Birmingham Village staff with its urgent request for 40 lb (18 kg) of cold, uncooked turkey meat. The concerned village chef is surprised to learn that the turkey is not to be eaten, but worn inside the competitors' shoes. The Tunisian players will use the turkey meat as shock-absorbing shoe liners to protect their feet from the hard surface of the Birmingham field.

JUSTIN M HARRISON • KAY C HARRISON • KEVIN B HARRISON • KIMBERLY R HARRISON • LAURA G HARRISON • LEE A HARRISON • LEE A HARRISON • MAHALAH J HARRISON • MARGARET A HARRISON • MARK H HARRISON • MATT S HARRISON • MICHAEL L HARRISON • NANCY J HARRISON • PATRICIA A HARRISON • PATRICIA C HARRISON • PAUL D HARRISON • PAULA K HARRISON • PHILIP G HARRISON • REBECCA A HARRISON • RICHARD G HARRISON • RITA B HARRISON • ROBERT A HARRISON • SHANNON HARRISON • SHARON T HARRISON • SHIRLEY C HARRISON • STEPHEN J HARRISON • SUSAN R HARRISON •

Berry College in Rome, Georgia, is a beautiful tree-filled setting for the Olympic Youth Camp.

OLYMPIC YOUTH CAMP

This busy day of competition is an ideal time for the 458 young people, ages 16–18, attending the 1996 Olympic Youth Camp to come to Atlanta to experience some of the excitement firsthand. This talented and culturally diverse group of young men and women, representing 152 participating Olympic delegations, are headquartered on the campus of Berry College, located in the foothills of the Appalachian mountains 65 mi (105 km) northwest of Atlanta in Rome, Georgia.

Established by the IOC at the 1912 Stockholm Games, the Olympic Youth Camp provides a wonderful opportunity for cultural exchange among the young people who have been selected to attend this unique international gathering by their respective National

TERESA D HARRISON • WILLIAM A HARRISON • LANCE H HARRISON JR • LEE HARRISON JR • GREGORY L HARRISON SAT • SCOTT HARRISS • THERESA M HARRON • MONICA HARROW • JOHN A HARSCH •
ANGELA L HART • BETTY L HART • CHARLES E HART • CHRISTOPHER B HART • CINDI L HART • CURTIS D HART • DEASHA Y HART • DIANA O HART • DONALD HART • EDWARD T HART • ELIZABETH A HART •
EMILY A HART • ERSKINE C HART • JANICE M HART • JOHN HART • KEN HART • KENNETH S HART • KRISTIN L HART • MARY ANN HART • MELINDA D HART • MICAH HART • MILDRED C HART • NANCY E HART •

OLYMPIC ARTS FESTIVAL

International opera star Jessye Norman and the Atlanta Symphony Orchestra collaborate in a performance that is also a deeply felt homecoming. The legendary Jessye Norman, a native of Augusta, Georgia, has received universal acclaim for her performances in every international cultural capital. The Atlanta Symphony Orchestra, a fast-rising star in its highly competitive domain, has captivated its hometown audience and garnered significant acclaim

Olympic Youth Camp participants enjoy a multitude of experiences: (left) joining in a discussion at the camp, (top right) visiting with athletes at the Atlanta Olympic Village, and (bottom right) participating in a parade.

Olympic Committees. Activities range from team-building exercises and special projects designed to improve intercultural understanding and cooperation, to a wide range of arts and communications projects.

The fast-paced, stimulating schedule of this two-week program is packed with activity. Camp days start early and run late into the night. Each day is filled with a wide variety of memorable and often challenging experiences. Campers participate in mountain biking, hiking, obstacle courses, and wilderness study; design and create a newspaper, the *Centennial*, and television programs; and perform a series of participatory music and dance recitals. These performances enable talented young people to share the artistic and cultural expressions of their homelands with fellow campers.

Friendships between campers form quickly and run deep. Supported by a carefully chosen staff, a large number of whom are volunteers, Atlanta's Olympic Youth Camp embodies, extends, and reinforces the Olympic Spirit that also brings together the world's greatest athletes and fans.

THE 1996 OLYMPIC YOUTH CAMP
PRESENTED BY swatch

NATASHA S HART • PETER B HART • PRISCILLA A HART • REBECCA S HART • RENEE P HART • RICHARD L HART • RICHARD T HART • ROBERT B HART • FESTONAL HART • RONALD HART • ROSA M HART • SANDRA B HART • STEVEN G HART • SUSAN HART • SUZZANNE P HART • TIMOTHY A HART • TRACY A HART • TREVOR A HART • TERRENCE B HARTE • CAROL P HARTER • NICHOLE A HARTFIELD • DONALD E HARTIG • TIFFANY L HARTING • SHARON L HARTIS • WILLIAM D HARTIS • PAUL J HARTL • JOHN R HARTLAND • ANDREW P HARTLEY • ANTHONY A HARTLEY • BRANDON W HARTLEY • CONNIE R HARTLEY •

left: **Jessye Norman rehearses for her collaborative performance with the Atlanta Symphony Orchestra.**

right: **Richmond Barthé's *Christina*, from the exhibition *From Rearguard to Vanguard*, shows the influence of primitivism as well as abstract expressionism.**

Atlanta Symphony Orchestra. Maestro Levi conducts with supple finesse, colorful detail, and exceptional responsiveness. Miss Norman's delivery is a tour de force achieved not through volume, but through attention to detail and exquisite subtlety, warmth, and spirituality.

The second half of the concert focuses on operatic repertoire. Aria after aria, each seemingly more beautiful than the preceding one, weave a web of vocal magic. The audience responds to each piece with cheers and bravos,

from national and international critics, especially in recent years under the baton of music director Yoel Levi. Bringing these charismatic musical forces together was a top priority from the earliest days of planning for the Olympic Arts Festival. A celebration of Olympic excellence, this memorable collaboration resonates with special significance for the city of Atlanta and the state of Georgia.

Filled to capacity, Atlanta Symphony Hall is buzzing with anticipation. This Olympic audience is a mix of knowledgeable connoisseurs and enthusiastic families, with those from distant lands sitting next to those from Atlanta and its surrounding communities.

The program opens with orchestral and vocal works by Maurice Ravel. The Atlanta Symphony Orchestra performs with technical precision and enthusiasm. A breathless audience awaits the arrival of Jessye Norman, who strides onto the stage, a vision of dignity and beauty that evokes an instant and lengthy ovation. Miss Norman then focuses on her repertoire and her collaboration with the

the ovations growing louder and longer as the evening builds to its climax. At the end of the program, Miss Norman leaves the stage only to be cheered back for five curtain calls. Her choice of encore repertoire is pure Americana—a set of traditional spirituals that brings tears to everyone's eyes, musicians included. This draws the concert to a conclusion that is both reverent and joyful.

An important part of the Olympic Arts Festival is *From Rearguard to Vanguard: Selections from the Clark Atlanta University Collection of African-American Art*, a collection of works the university purchased and gathered between 1942 and 1970. It particularly attracts Games

CYNTHIA H HARTLEY • ELIZABETH A HARTLEY • FRAN D HARTLEY • HELEN C HARTLEY • JAMES J. HARTLEY • KAREN S HARTLEY • KYMBERLY A HARTLEY • LISA K HARTLEY • LOREN G HARTLEY • PATRICIA C HARTLEY • PRISCILLA W HARTLEY • SELWYN T HARTLEY • THOMAS B HARTLEY • ROBERT L HARTLINE • DAVID J HARTMAN • RICHARD D HARTMAN • DEBORAH A HARTMANN • EILEEN M HARTMANN • ESTELLE M HARTMANN • GERRY A HARTMANN • HENRY J HARTMANN • PHYLLIS K HARTMANN • MARSHA W HARTNESS • JILL HARTNETT • PATRICK L HARTNEY • JAMES R HARTON • THOMAS B HARTON III •

left and right: **The highly acclaimed collective, Pilobolus Dance Theater celebrates its 25th anniversary season with performances at the Martin Luther King Jr. International Chapel at Morehouse College.**

visitors who come to Atlanta hoping to discover its roots as a center of African-American ideology and culture. With paintings and sculptures that visually chronicle a critical period of the African-American struggle for identity, the exhibition appeals on historical and political, as well as aesthetic and artistic, levels. Visitors pause before brilliantly colorful, primitive, and radically abstract works, absorbing the impact of a tradition of art that developed largely outside of the establishment. While some are unfamiliar with the more experimental styles, the collection ultimately bears witness to the contributions African-American art has made to the developing art world.

Among the most exciting and important contemporary dance companies, the Pilobolus Dance Theater has been a crucible of choreographic innovation for the past 25 years. Pilobolus's choreographic vocabulary stretches the boundaries of curiosity, creativity, and physical possibility. Pilobolus creates and performs works that appeal to the diverse and eclectic tastes of its audiences, including the intensely acrobatic solo, *Pseudopodia* (1974), the hilarious *Walklyndon* (1971), the political satire, *Pyramid of the Moon* (1995), and a work that explores the deeply emotional side of the human condition, *Sweet Purgatory* (1991). In today's production, each piece and every dancer's performance crackles with a pure energy. The taut focus, flawless execution, and kaleidoscopic range of colors, motions, and physical forms are vivid and entrancing. The energy exchanged between the audience and the stage is palpable.

Atlanta 1996®

DOUGLAS W HARTONG • SUSAN B HARTSFIELD • GREGG A HARTSUFF • NANETTE J HARTUNG • ANA C HARTWIG • BOB M HARTWIG • GEORGE H HARTWIG • MARGARET S HARTWIG • MELANI J HARTWIG • ANA M HARTY • ELLEN HARTZ • DIANE M HARTZELL • RICHARD C HARTZELL • TERRY A HARTZELL • CHRISTIAN W HARTZLER • PHILIP G HARVERSON • ANDREW J HARVEY • BILLIE J HARVEY • DANIEL H HARVEY • DEBBIE HARVEY • DIANE E HARVEY • DORIS L HARVEY • ERICH B HARVEY • GARY H HARVEY • GEORGE HARVEY • HENRI M HARVEY • JAMES A HARVEY • JAMES C HARVEY • JANETTE G HARVEY •

DAY SIX
25 JULY 1996

THE SHEER MAGNITUDE and complexity of the Centennial Olympic Games significantly exceeds that of any prior Olympiad. Even the most cursory review of the operational and logistical statistics proves that, as had been predicted and promised by ACOG from the earliest days of its Bid to host the Games, this is the largest peacetime event in history.

Organizing this endeavor involves networks within networks of the various operations and programs that make the Games of the XXVI Olympiad possible. The network of 31 competition venues that service hundreds of thousands of Olympic ticket holders each day supports highly specialized athletic missions and operational functions at each location. The network of more than 175 additional noncompetition venues provides logistical and functional support for the Games as a whole. To staff all these venues, more than 130,000 people must be managed, uniformed, fed, and supported. A Games-wide security team of nearly 17,000 international, federal, state, and local personnel works together according to a carefully orchestrated network of interlocking jurisdictions. An enormous armada of vehicles is organized into a network of transportation systems that operates 24 hours per day.

Olympic Villages serving athletes in Savannah and Columbus, Georgia; Birmingham, Alabama; Miami and Orlando, Florida; and Washington, DC, each require their own support and operational procedures. The International Broadcast Center and Main Press Cen-

TODAY'S CALENDAR

Competition

Aquatics—swimming
Badminton
Baseball
Basketball
Boxing
Cycling—track
Fencing
Football
Gymnastics—artistic
Handball
Hockey
Judo
Rowing
Shooting
Softball
Table tennis
Tennis

Olympic Arts Festival

Alliance Theatre Company:
  Blues for an Alabama Sky
  and *The Last Night of
  Ballyhoo*
Center for Puppetry Arts: *The
  Hungry Tiger and Other
  Tales from China* and
  Frankenstein
Pilobolus Dance Theatre
Russian National Orchestra
Seven Stages: *Blue Monk*
Southern Crossroads Festival
14th Street Playhouse: *Ali*

Spectators' bags and clothing are inspected by security guards at the entrance to the Georgia International Horse Park.

JENNIFER E HARVEY • JOHN S HARVEY • JOHN S HARVEY • KRISPY C HARVEY • KRISTY V HARVEY • LECIA L HARVEY • LINDRA M HARVEY • MARILYN B HARVEY • MARTHA C HARVEY • MARY G HARVEY • MICHAEL L HARVEY • NEKO D HARVEY • PAMELA C HARVEY • THOMAS G HARVEY • TRACEY C HARVEY • TRACY L HARVEY • WILLIAM B HARVEY • CHERYL D HARVEY-ROSE • GILBERT A HARVILL • TERRI L HARVILLE • KAREN M HARWARD • HILLARY O HARWELL • JEAN C HARWELL • HAYDEE C HARWOOD • PAMELA L HARWOOD • AQUEEL R HASAN • HAKIM HASAN • LERONDA HASAN • TALIAH M HASAN •

129

ter feed televised coverage, news, and information throughout the world 24 hours daily. An Olympic Arts Festival network of more than 40 venues and public art sites is coordinated through its own command center. Centennial Olympic Park meets the requirements of more than 250,000 people per day, 1,000 performers, and the 5 Olympic sponsors whose pavilions lie within the park.

While these are only some of the many elements that make the Games possible, the management of any one of them is an Olympic

The communications systems designed for Atlanta's Games employ the most advanced technology and are the most interconnected ever developed for or used during an Olympic Games. This Games communications system, composed of virtually every available communications platform, is the end product of a multiyear effort among ACOG's technology sponsors. This system is supported by 20,000 telephones, 12,000 radios, 10,000 television sets, 7,700 pagers, 7,000 personal computers, 1,200 cellular phones, 700 facsimile machines,

700 copiers, and an array of specialized electronic support and security equipment. In all, more than 2 million ft (610 km) of fiber-optic cable and 5 million ft (1,524 km) of copper pairs (standard telephone lines) are installed, along with an additional 15,000 telephone lines and an unprecedented 673 video circuits to support this system. During the Games, ACOG's switchboard handles an average of 7,000 calls each day, which is more than 900 per operator per shift.

left: **Press members work in the communications network area inside the Main Press Center.**

right: **The accreditation center at the Airport Welcome Center is a central area of activity for incoming contractors and Olympic Family members.**

challenge. ACOG's challenge is to incorporate these distinct, disparate, and often geographically scattered elements into a single, cohesive operation. In keeping with one of ACOG's central symbols, this essential Games infrastructure is a "patchwork quilt" of communications systems.

Additional communications support is provided by Info'96, a proprietary information system which supplies athletes, officials, the media, Games operations personnel, and other

CHARLES F HASBROOK • TAMARA F HASBROUCK • JOHN S HASCHAK • KYOKO HASEGAWA • FREIDA L HASELDEN • NANCY HASELDEN • THOMAS W. HASH II • MELANIE F HASHAGEN • JANET K HASKELL • VIRGINIA A HASKELL • HARMONY E HASKINS • BENNY G HASLETT • STEVEN R HASLETT • ADEE HASSAN • BINNIE M HASSAN • NITA HASSAN • ROBERT P HASSE • URSULA A HASSEL • MARGARET M HASSELL • SHAILA P HASSELLE • AARON M HASSENBOEHLER • DORIS E HASSENGER • KARIN D HASSENGER • STEVEN D HASSENGER • ROBERT J HASSER • SANDRA E HASSER • SYLVIA W HASSETT •

Olympic Family members with athlete biographies, Games-related data, and other background and operations-related information. Although Info'96 initially suffers from some problems, it supports over 350,000 E-mail sessions and more than 30 million information retrieval requests during the Games. More than 15,000 unique results reports, consisting of over 40 million pages of information, are produced on an average of less than 10 minutes each during the Games.

ACOG's World Wide Web site, the first-ever Olympic Internet presence, provides interested people throughout the world with detailed information about every aspect of the Games. While it is active, ACOG's World Wide Web site receives more than 200 million hits at a rate that accelerates during the Games. On 1 August alone, 16,955,274 hits are recorded. Clearly, the rapid evolution of the Internet as a medium of information exchange is an exciting new development that will become an essential feature of all future Games.

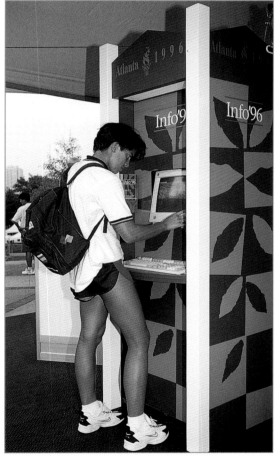

top: Atlanta Olympic Broadcasting staff uses advanced communications systems to televise the Games.

bottom: An athlete sends E-mail using Info'96 at one of the many kiosks located in the Atlanta Olympic Village.

MUHAMMED J HASSIM • JACK P. HASSINGER • NORMA W HASSINGER • L MARTIN HASSON • JILL M HASTIE • ROBERT T HASTIE • BEBE K HASTINGS • HAZEL HASTINGS • MAUREEN P HASTINGS • GILBERT C HASTINGS III • JIM W HASTY • BERTHA P HASWELL • ARTHUR A HASZARD • MIYAKO HATANO • TAKAFUMI HATANO • ELIZABETH A HATCH • ELIZABETH S HATCH • JOI C HATCH • JOSEPH HATCH • KIMBERLY A HATCH • LISA A HATCH • MEREDITH C HATCH • MATTHEW G HATCHELL • DENNIS M HATCHER • PAMELA L HATCHER • SUSAN V HATCHER • GEORGIA M HATCHETT • ANNE-LOUISE D HATFIELD •

131

Kirsten Vlieghuis of the Netherlands, who take silver and bronze, respectively. The torch passes from four-time Olympic medal winner Evans to Bennett and the next generation of young Olympians.

In the men's competition, Gary Hall Jr. of the US, whose father is a three-time Olympian swimmer, is beaten for the second time in these Games by Aleksander Popov of the Russian Federation, who finishes ahead of Hall in the frantic sprint for the 50 m freestyle title. Only .13 second separates the two swimmers.

left: US swimmer Brooke Bennett posts the fastest time in the world this year while winning the gold in the women's 800 m freestyle.

right: Janet Evans leaves the pool after the women's 800 m freestyle event.

COMPETITION

In each Olympic Games, there are events in which past heroes and favorites, despite their best efforts, fail to meet the hopes and expectations of both the athlete and audience. At the same time, among the most exciting aspects of each Olympic Games is the emergence of fresh new faces, bright young stars that appear from obscurity to receive Olympic accolades and capture the hearts of fans throughout the world.

Veteran and perennial favorite US swimmer Janet Evans, who passed the Olympic torch to Muhammad Ali at the climax of the Opening Ceremony a few days ago, needs eight injections of novocaine to numb her broken toe in order to compete in the grueling 800 m freestyle, finishing a disappointing sixth in her final effort to win a medal in Atlanta's Games. In a thrilling finish, however, Evans's teammate, 16-year-old Brooke Bennett, posts the fastest time in the world this year while winning a gold ahead of Dagmar Hase of Germany and

In another dramatic finish, Krisztina Egerszegi of Hungary becomes only the second swimmer to win the same event at three different Olympic Games when she captures gold in the 200 m backstroke. Her Atlanta win, however, sets her apart from all other

BROOKS A HATFIELD • DIAN M HATFIELD • JEREMY I HATFIELD • JILL HATFIELD • LAURA L HATFIELD • LESLEY J HATFIELD • DUAINE E HATHAWAY • KRISTIN M HATHER • DAVID K HATHERLY • EBAN HATHWAY • MELANIE J HATLEY • DAVID L HATMAKER • KATHRYN M HATT • TERRY G HATT • LEONARD/BUD F HATTAWAY • JENNIFER A HATTEN • SHAWANA T HATTEN • ANNE M HATZAKIS • ROXANNE PICKETT HAUBER • CHRISTIAN L HAUCK • LORES M HAUCK • KAWEHI C HAUG • CHARLES HAUGABROOK • KJETIL HAUGAN • DEBRA A HAUGE • CHARLOTTE HAUGEN • MICHAEL W HAUGEN • TIMOTHY J HAUGEN •

swimmers, women and men alike, as she becomes the first swimmer in Olympic history to win a total of five individual gold medals. Egerszegi first emerged at the 1988 Olympic Games in Seoul, where she won the 200 m backstroke despite the fact that she weighed 40 lb (18 kg) less than any other finalist in her event. Her diminutive size and quiet and elusive nature, coupled with the first part of her name, "Eger," which means mouse in Hungarian, have resulted in her nickname, "Mouse." She has incorporated the name into her business at home, a pizzeria, which is called the Mouse Hole.

The women's artistic gymnastics events have moved into the individual rounds. Late this afternoon, Ukraine's Lilia Podkopayeva, the reigning world champion, captures the gold in the individual all-around by a margin of .18 over Romania's Gina Gogean. Simona Amanar and Lavinia Milosovici, also of Romania, share the bronze medal.

At the Georgia Dome, an audience of 31,230—the highest attendance in women's

Lilia Podkopayeva performs for gold in the women's individual all-around artistic gymnastics competition.

JOHN F HAUGH • MAUREEN P HAUGHTON • RHEA M HAUGSETH • RANDALL G HAUK • BETSY A HAUN • DICK D HAUN • MICHAEL GREG HAUN • ROBERT J HAUPT • KEVIN G HAUSCHILDT • JOSEPH S HAUSFELD • GAYLE W HAUSHERR • JOHN M HAUSHERR • JUDITH P HAUSMANN • JURGEN K HAUSMANN • MICHAEL J HAUSMANN • BERTRAND HAUSS • GLORIA J HAUSSER • SANDRA K HAVENS • STEVEN J HAVER • MARY JO HAVERBECK • ELICE D HAVERTY • MICHAEL T HAVIG • SHIRLEY G HAVLAK • JULIA H HAVRON • ALLISON HAWES • ELLEN C HAWES • LISA D HAWES • ANTHONY M HAWK • BOBBIE J HAWK •

The largest audience in women's Olympic basketball history watches as Yelena Pshikova of the Russian Federation (right) gets to the jump ball before Catarina Pollini of Italy (left).

Olympic basketball history—watches the Russian Federation defeat Italy, 75–70, in the first of two games held today. In the second game, the US defeats Zaire, the first African women's basketball squad to compete in the Olympic Games, by a lopsided score of 107–47. Jennifer Azzi leads the US with 18 points.

As the cycling competition moves into the track cycling rounds, the Italian team provides an interesting story. Employing the so-called "superman" riding position, in which riders extend their arms forward on specially designed handlebars, the Italian team has dominated the opening days of track racing. This innovative riding position is proven to be aerodynamically superior to the more conventional riding style

JEROME D HAWK • KATHI C HAWK • SUSAN R HAWK • JANET HAWKES • WILLIAM B HAWKINS • ALAN S HAWKINS • BARBARA N HAWKINS • BEVERLY A HAWKINS • BUDDY A HAWKINS • CAROL R HAWKINS • CAROLYN HAWKINS • CHRISTINA F HAWKINS • CRISTA L HAWKINS • DANA M HAWKINS • DARRELL G HAWKINS • DONALD E HAWKINS • FRANK W HAWKINS • HOPE J HAWKINS • JACKIE HAWKINS • JAYNE HAWKINS • JEAN W HAWKINS • JENNIFER D HAWKINS • JONATHAN E HAWKINS • KELLY G HAWKINS • KEN HAWKINS • LYNDA H HAWKINS • PAUL A HAWKINS • ROBERT B HAWKINS • SARA K HAWKINS •

employed by most other cyclists. Andrea Collinelli, who set a world record in an individual pursuit heat yesterday, goes on to win the gold medal today while his teammate, Antonella Bellutti, sets an Olympic record in the women's pursuit, despite a misstep at the start of her race that cost her a couple of seconds.

American sabre fencer Michael D'Asaro, who accompanies his team today as an alternate, had a special incentive to make the US team. Long before he was named as an alternate to the men's sabre team, D'Asaro purchased one

of the nearly 500,000 personalized engraved bricks sold for Centennial Olympic Park, inscribing it with the message, "Sally Boyle, Marry Me?" The answer? A resounding yes!

Olympic Arts Festival

Formed in the aftermath of the collapse of communism, the Russian National Orchestra has quickly emerged as an institution of uncompromising artistic quality, visceral energy, and polish. This extraordinary ensemble was founded by gifted pianist and conductor Mikhail Pletnev, who won the coveted Tchaikovsky competition in 1978, at the height of the Cold War. Pletnev's courageous decision to pursue a dual career as pianist and conductor, coupled with his desire to create a new orchestra, was bold and visionary. From the moment of its auspicious 1991 debut, the Russian National Orchestra has been recognized as one of the world's most exciting orchestral ensembles, its early recordings have been acclaimed by critics as "definitive," and its at-home and tour performances are always sold out.

The near-capacity audience that fills Atlanta Symphony Hall this evening to hear the orchestra's first Atlanta performance is in for an extraordinary experience. The works Maestro Pletnev has chosen for this evening's performance—Tchaikovsky's Fifth Symphony and Ravel's virtuoso arrangement of Mussorgsky's *Pictures at an Exhibition*—are both familiar and popular pillars of orchestral repertoire.

From the somber, meditative clarinet solo that opens Tchaikovsky's Fifth Symphony onward, Pletnev shapes an inexorable and deeply

Italy's Andrea Collinelli celebrates winning the gold in the men's individual pursuit.

The Russian National Orchestra performs at the the Atlanta Symphony Hall under the expert direction of Mikhail Pletnev.

personal musical statement that is distinctly Russian. This approach is unfamiliar to American ears; but this is a Russian orchestra, an ensemble that welcomes and even celebrates the virtuosity of its members. From beginning to end, this powerfully communicative and intensely cohesive performance intertwines passion with virtuosity. Pletnev's distinctive approach creates a sense of centrifugal evolution that builds throughout each performance,

pulling the audience into the emotional recesses and Russian origins of these majestic works. This is an Olympic concert, and the audience is ecstatic, voicing its approval in a deafening roar accompanied by the loud rhythmic clapping one usually hears at athletic events, only infrequently at the conclusion of a great concert, and never at the end of its first half.

How can the Russian National Orchestra meet, let alone exceed, the expectations of this enthusiastic audience in the second half? The sign of a true champion—indeed, an Olympian —is the ability to go one more round, to raise

• FELICITY A HAYES • ANGELA C HAYES • BENSON D HAYES • BRANDI HAYES • BRUCE HAYES • CARLTON T HAYES • CHARLES C HAYES • CHARMAINE R HAYES • CHRISTINA H HAYES • CHRISTOPHER C HAYES • DANIEL A HAYES • DANIEL J HAYES • DEBORAH W HAYES • DONNA M HAYES • ERNA HAYES • EVELYN J HAYES • FELECIA S HAYES • HEATHER C HAYES • HEATHER R HAYES • JANE D HAYES • JANICE W HAYES • JEFFREY S HAYES • JUANITA C HAYES • KANDICE LEE HAYES • KARIN L HAYES • KATHLEEN M HAYES • KATHRYN H HAYES • KEVIN C HAYES • LISA V HAYES • LORETTA J HAYES • LOY A HAYES • MAURICE E HAYES

Kiev." At the very moment when it seems that it cannot possibly climb the next emotional peak, the orchestra reaches an entirely new level of sonic richness that is sustained through the climactic conclusion of this work.

As the last chord sounds, audience members rise to their feet. For nearly 10 minutes, they clap rhythmically and in unison, demanding more. Their hopes are answered with several brilliant encores.

In pledging to bring distinguished artists of the world to Atlanta, the Cultural Olympiad

the bar one notch higher, to press for a perfect 10 after achieving a 9.98. These occasions are all too rare, and yet that is the challenge the Russian National Orchestra faces as the second half of this concert begins.

Pictures at an Exhibition is a kind of concerto for orchestra, a showcase work in which the entire orchestra, both individually and collectively, gets to show its best. Pletnev knows his players and the strengths and special abilities each possesses, and he plays to them, building toward the grand finale, "The Great Gate of

made a commitment to enrich the experience of local audiences. In the spirit of bringing the best of the world together, the Russian National Orchestra's performance on this special evening demonstrates how cultural exchange, whether through the arts or in sport, can bridge the differences between people throughout the world.

Puppeteer Feng Yang prepares to perform *The Hungry Tiger and other Tales from China* at the Center for Puppetry Arts.

Atlanta 1996

• MICHAEL K HAYES • PARRISH KATHRYN HAYES • REBECCA L HAYES • RICHARD D HAYES • ROBERT D HAYES • ROGER D HAYES • RONALD V HAYES • SARAH C HAYES • SCARLET D HAYES • STEPHANIE A HAYES • SUE HAYES • VICKIE L HAYES • WARREN EDWARD HAYES • JAMES W HAYES JR • JON P HAYGOOD • KARA J HAYGOOD • LISA P HAYGOOD • ANNE N HAYMAKER • ANNETTE B HAYMAN • LARRY W HAYMAN • TERRANCE HAYMAN • LESTER L HAYMAN JR • TAMRA J HAYMANS-BENEDICT • MARYANNA HAYMON • CHRISTINE M HAYNER • ARRON HAYNES • CAROLYN P HAYNES • CHUCK E HAYNES • DAVID C HAYNES •

DAY SEVEN
26 JULY 1996

BY DAY SEVEN, spectators are completely mesmerized by the athletic feats these Games have inspired and the atmosphere of celebration and camaraderie that surrounds them. Contributing to the spectators' experience at Olympic venues is ACOG's comprehensive venue production program that is coordinated with the overall Look of the Games. Atlanta has carefully crafted this effort into a well-orchestrated program of sights and sounds. From a vast collection of many kinds of music to an array of specially produced videos, entertaining and informational scoreboard displays, announcements, and live entertainment, every aspect of each competition venue's production needs has been designed to support and enliven the environment of the Games.

A skilled team of 35 producers has been recruited to design and direct distinct but complementary programs that maximize production values while corresponding to each venue's special atmosphere and operating requirements. The team directs a multilayered schedule filled with a variety of audio, visual, and live entertainment components. Producers may choose to create their customized venue programs using a 32-hour library of music and effects, five special compact discs produced for Atlanta's Games, more than 200 specially produced videos that illustrate the rules and great performances from past Games for each athletic discipline, and live performance elements that can be scheduled for pregame and half-time entertainment. In addition to programming

Entertaining, informative scoreboards at venues enliven the competition environment.

DEBORAH C HAYNES • GEORGE E HAYNES • JILL K HAYNES • PATRICIA P HAYNES • PATRICIA SMITH HAYNES • POWELL J HAYNES • RALPH L HAYNES • RANDALL SHANE HAYNES • STEVEN E HAYNES • WENDY A HAYNES • WILLIAM B HAYNES • WILLIAM J HAYNES CATC • ALLAN M HAYNIE • TINA J HAYNIE PM • YVAN HAYOZ • FRANK J HAYS • FRANKLIN A HAYS • KENNETH HAYS • LAURIE A HAYS • PRESTON A HAYS • RICHARD O HAYS • SHERRY A HAYS • WILLIAM HAYS • DONNA R HAYS ATC • KENNY R HAYSLETT • LORRAINE S HAYSLIP • JOANNE HAYWARD • PAUL R HAYWARD • AMY L HAYWOOD • CHARLES L HAYWOOD

music, video, and supplementary performances, producers are also responsible for all announcements, including the names of athletes and officials, penalties, and other essential information that relates to the field of play. An English-speaking and a French-speaking announcer are assigned to each venue at every competition. Providing play-by-play commentary and ensuring that the correct athlete is announced at the right time for every event is critical to the successful operation of the competitions.

to complement the mood of the moment, keep the mood upbeat, and enhance every spectator's experience at every Olympic event.

In every host city, certain songs catch on with the fans and athletes and become an integral part of the Games. In Atlanta, The Village People's "YMCA"—a 1970s standard and perennial favorite of American sports fans— becomes one of the most enjoyed tunes at Atlanta's Games. Certain songs are played time and again throughout the Games. Sometimes in the most unexpected circumstances; songs

Spectators actively demonstrate their enthusiasm for competition by joining together to participate in songs.

Combining these program elements to fit the atmosphere of each sport and venue is a daunting task. In the case of a rain delay or an emergency time-out, the producer must respond quickly by entertaining the audience with music, a special video, or even an impromptu live performance. The overall plan is

to exhilarate the crowd are sung and danced to with increasing gusto by both athletes and spectators. From US basketball player Charles Barkley leading fans in spelling out the letters of a song at a basketball game to the growing popularity of music at weightlifting and handball venues, songs are heard almost everywhere. Tomorrow, during a women's softball

top: Brazilian fans inspire their country's athletes with hearty cheers.

bottom: Japanese spectators encourage their team at a judo event.

game between Australia and Canada while one of Canada's relief pitchers takes her warm-up tosses, the Australian team will line up in front of its dugout and dance to a song as it blares over the loudspeakers. Energized, the Australian team will go on to win this important game, 5–2. At the conclusion of the special gymnastics gala a few days later, having finished their formal program, the American women will break into an impromptu tumbling routine while leading the capacity audience in a highly animated version of a popular song. The venues are filled with a cheerful, festive atmosphere that reflects and reinforces the spirit of the Games.

VERNETTA L HEAD • YVONNE M HEAD • JAMES M HEAD JR • WILLIAM G HEADINGTON • JANET P HEADLEY • THOMAS C HEALAN • ALMA J HEALD • JUDITH L HEALD • PATRICIA A HEALD • CAROL S HEALEY • THOMAS F HEALEY • BETTY HEALY • CATHERINE L HEALY • JENNIFER S HEALY • MARTIN J HEALY • PAMELA J HEALY • DEBBIE J HEANEY • CARLTON D HEARD • CHARLES HEARD • DEVAUGHN HEARD • EARNEST HEARD • GEOFFREY A HEARD • GERALINE L HEARD • JEFFERY HEARD • NELLIE M HEARD • NELSON M HEARD • SELERY P HEARD • GERALD D HEARLSON • CAROLYN K HEARN • GEORGE W HEARN

COMPETITION

The end of the swimming competition and the opening of the athletics events provide some of the most memorable moments on day seven of this Olympiad.

In a spectacular reprise of her three previous gold-medal finishes, American swimmer Amy Van Dyken upsets world-record holder Jingyi Le of the People's Republic of China in the 50 m freestyle, becoming the first US woman to win four gold medals at a single Olympic Games. Reacting to her win, Van Dyken says, "To all the girls who kind of gave me a hard time in high school, I kind of want to say thank you. This is for all of the nerds out there." In a very productive week, Van Dyken anchored the 400 m freestyle relay team on Monday, won the 100 m butterfly on Tuesday, swam the freestyle leg of her team's winning performance in the 400 m medley relay on Wednesday, and wins the 50 m freestyle today. For any athlete, these feats would be extraordinary, but they are all the more amazing be-

cause this young woman suffers from chronic asthma.

Meanwhile, the US team's highly successful swimming efforts come to a fitting conclusion as the American men's 4 x 100 m medley relay team sprints to Olympic gold in the competition's final event. In the process, Jeff Rouse, Jeremy Linn, Mark Henderson, and Gary Hall Jr. bid the hometown crowd a proper farewell by establishing a new world record at a full two seconds faster than the previous record.

As the curtain descends on the swimming competition, attention turns toward Olympic Stadium on this first of nine days of athletics competition, which is among the Games' most popular events since the dawn of the modern Olympic era. On this day alone, the vast stadium will hold an enthusiastic crowd of

left: Amy Van Dyken of the US shows off her gold medal—one of four gold medals she has won at these Games.

right: Flags representing the 37 delegations competing adorn the badminton venue.

• RUEY N HEARN • CHARLOTTE A HEARON • ELIZABETH C MARNA HEARST • SHERYL L HEASTON • ASHLEY R HEATH • BARBARA M HEATH • BEVERLEY B HEATH • LINDA S HEATH • MARY J HEATH • MAURA F HEATH • MELISSA A HEATH • NANCY M HEATH • ROBERT B HEATH • DIANE L HEATH MD • PAUL L HEATLEY • DAVID W HEATON • DEBORAH S HEBERT • MICHAEL E HEBERT • MICHELLE A HEBERT • GUENTHER H HECHT • KEITH HECHTMAN • DERRIC I HECK • SHELLEY R HECKENBERG • ANDREW T HECKER • JOSIE J HECKERSON • FRANCOISE HECKHAUSEN-EVANS • CARMEN D HECKLER • RON J HECKLER •

80,237 for the morning session and 80,511 for the evening events.

The first athletics medal and Ecuador's first Olympic medal ever is won by Jefferson Pérez for his performance in the 20 km race walk. Pérez, who placed only 33rd in the 1995 World Championships, is as amazed as the fans who cheer his victory. Pérez comments that, when he realized he was in the lead, he felt almost as if he was in a dream. "Then," he said, "I thought, this is my dream. I have to go for it even if I die." His effort stretched him almost

go to accommodate and support Olympic athletes and guests. Rojek, a University of Georgia sociology professor whose volunteer assignment placed him at the DeKalb College track, is concerned that the six Comoran runners do not have running shoes, so he travels to a sporting goods store to buy a pair of shoes for each member of the team.

Sixteen-year-old Rachida Mahamane of Niger, competing in the first heat of the women's 5,000 m race, steals the hearts of the spectators in Olympic Stadium. A few laps

Racewalkers begin the men's 20 km race walk event at Olympic Stadium.

beyond endurance, leaving him totally exhausted and in need of support to leave the field at the conclusion of the race.

The athletics competition attracts perhaps the widest possible range of Olympic delegations—from the largest, best-equipped, and best-trained teams to teams from tiny, underdeveloped countries like Comoros, which struggled to assemble and transport a team to Atlanta.

A story involving the Comoran team and Olympic volunteer Dean Rojek illustrates the lengths to which some ACOG volunteers will

into the race, Mahamane, in her red shoes and shorts, trails the field by a substantial margin. Eventually, the field catches up to and passes her by, and then passes her a second time before Sonia O'Sullivan of Ireland crosses the finish line at 15:15.80 to win the heat. Mahamane, who learned she would be competing for her country only two days before

RONALD M HECKMAN • ANNELI HEDBERG • LINDA R HEDDEN • ALLEN C HEDDEN JR • MARY KATE HEDDERMAN ATC • ELIZABETH L HEDEN • ROBERT I HEDEN • SUSAN L HEDEN • STEVEN J HEDGE • REGINALD D HEDGEBETH • DAYTON W HEDGES • MANDY HEDGES • TRACIE L HEDGES • ROSEMARY HEDIN • JANET B HEDLUND • JENNIFER A HEDLUND • KAIA A HEDLUND • JENNIFER L HEDRICK • LLOYD BILL B HEDRICK • CHUCK HEEGN • SUZANNE R HEER • CARINA HEESTERMANS • BETH A HEFFERNAN • JANE M HEFFERNAN • JAN L HEFFERON • JOHN A HEFFERON • ROBERT J HEFFLEY EMT • KATHARINE M HEFFNER •

she boarded a plane to Atlanta, is running in her first competition of the year.

Determined to finish the race and spurred on by the cheers of the enthusiastic spectators who support her with the wave, the young runner continues to run for another four minutes until she crosses the finish line and collapses into the arms of medical personnel. Aboubacar Agalheir, Niger's National Olympic Committee chef de mission and secretary-general expresses pride in his country's young track star, saying, "She represents the essential

Australian team a shocking 2–1 victory. "I was lucky," Brown says of her clutch hit off of Fernandez, a former UCLA teammate. The seeds of Brown's home run were actually planted in the fifth inning, but Danielle Tyler's apparent home run was not counted because she failed to touch home plate.

The softball competition further illustrates the important role women are playing in these Centennial Games. Female athletes continue to capture some of the most prominent headlines, as stories of one extraordinary accomplishment

top: **Denmark's track cycling team circles the velodrome during the qualifying round of the men's team pursuit.**

bottom: **Germany's Michael Senft (right) and Andre Ehrenberg (left) compete for the bronze in the men's canoe double slalom competition.**

spirit of the Olympic Games, which is to participate, not just to win. We are pleased to be represented at the Olympics and to bring Niger together with the other countries in this spirit."

On the softball diamond, the Australian team finds itself one strike away from a perfect-game defeat at the hands of US hurler Lisa Fernandez. Fernandez strikes out 15 batters and does not allow a runner on base until an Australian player is placed at second base to start the 10th inning as part of the tiebreaker format. However, Fernandez's glee turns to bewilderment with one swing by Joanne Brown. With her team trailing 1–0 in the bottom of the 10th, with two outs and two strikes, Brown slams a pitch over the center field fence, giving the

after another surface throughout the day from a variety of competition venues.

A major story emerges from the women's 48 kg judo competition, where Japan's two-time world champion, Ryoko Tamura, who has won 84 consecutive matches in the extra lightweight division, is defeated at the hands of the Democratic People's Republic of Korea's 16-year-old Sun-Hui Kye, who is competing in her first international tournament. The audience, which is filled with Japanese supporters, all of whom are rooting for their national hero,

is shocked into silence when the virtually unknown Kye becomes the youngest-ever gold medalist in judo and the Democratic People's Republic of Korea's first judo medal winner.

In the individual three-day equestrian event, New Zealand's Blyth Tait, riding the youngest and least experienced horse in the field, clears all 15 jumps in the course without a mistake. Though he starts the day leading the competition, Tait is entered in this event only because his legendary teammate, Mark Todd, was forced to withdraw when his horse was injured. Fellow New Zealand team member Sally Clark's outstanding performance ahead of Tait inspires him to avoid making any mistakes on the 15 required jumps and thus earns the gold.

In a display of feeling for teammate Yifu Wang, who, days earlier, collapsed as he took

his final shot in the 10 m air pistol competition, resulting in his winning the silver medal rather than the gold, the People's Republic of China's Duihong Li is moved to tears as her nation's flag is raised during her medal ceremony. Though she wins her country's first shooting gold medal in the 25 m sport pistol competition, setting a new Olympic record in the process, the 1992 silver medalist says that Wang's "silver is heavier than [her] gold."

In yet another dramatic story that testifies to the importance of women in the Olympic Movement, today the Georgia World Congress Center is rocked by screaming, flag-waving fans

left: **Duihong Li of the People's Republic of China cries as her country's flag is raised at her victory ceremony for winning the gold in the women's 25 m sport pistol competition.**

right: **The Netherlands' Laurien Vermulst and Ellen Meliesie rest after winning their heat in the women's lightweight double sculls competition.**

COLIN HEILMAN • KARL J HEILMAN • SARA L HEILMAN • RICHARD A HEIMBURGER • MARIANNE M HEIMES • MARTIN J HEIMES • JOHN C HEIN • ROSEMARIE A HEINDEL • DANIEL L HEINDL • JAMES R HEINISCH • LISA M HEINISCH • MARGARET B HEINISCH • AMY L HEINL • ANN-MARIE HEINONEN • THOMAS C HEINRICH • KRISTINN I HEINRICHS PT • WHITNEY P HEINSMA • HENRY J HEINTZBERGER • KEVIN S HEINZ • MICHAEL D HEINZ • BETTE HEINZELMANN • JACK HEINZELMANN • MARIA ELENA HEINZEN • PATRICIA A HEINZERLING • SUE A HEISEL • ROBERT L HEISEY • SHARON K HEISEY • CYNTHIA L HEISKELL •

as the People's Republic of China's Yaping Deng and Hong Qiao, the defending world champions and 1992 gold-medal table tennis doubles team, survive two match points in the fifth and final game of the semifinal match to defeat Jing Chen and Chiu-Tan Chen of Chinese Taipei, 23–21. In the epic match, the Chinese Taipei team sends the match into the fifth game by staving off two match points in the fourth set.

The action is certainly not limited to the women's events and performances. In one of the most hotly contested rivalries of the

left: **Fabrizio Nievas of Argentina and Eun-Chui Shin of Korea lean on each other during a 60 kg (132 lb) bout in boxing.**

right: **Juan Dinares of Spain and Steve Jennings of the US struggle for possession of the ball during a preliminary men's hockey match.**

Games, India and Pakistan, two hockey powerhouses, play to a dramatic 0–0 finish before a capacity crowd of 15,000 at Morris Brown College. The dominance of hockey by these longtime political rivals is incredible; of the 17 gold medals ever awarded in Olympic hockey competition, these two teams own 11 of them. Unfortunately for these outstanding teams, today's tie score eliminates both from the medal race.

THE OLYMPIC ARTS FESTIVAL AND CENTENNIAL OLYMPIC PARK

Beginning at noon and extending until at least midnight each day, a smorgasbord of America's musical traditions, called the Southern Crossroads Festival, entertains audiences of more than 115,000 people on three stages in Centennial Olympic Park. Featuring more than 1,100 gifted artists, Southern Crossroads presents a rousing and entertaining panoply of music and dance styles indigenous to the

JAMES M HEISKELL JR • PAUL A HEIST • LEE A HEIZER • JANA J HEJL • JAMES M HELBING • PAMELA J HELBLING • CHRISTINA HELBOCK • JOSE E HELENA • CRAIG A HELF • A J HELGERSON • KAY A HELGERSON • THOMAS G HELLAND • JUDITH A HELLAND • ARNOLD H HELLER • PETER R HELLER • ROBERT B HELLER • SUE A HELLER • THOMAS W HELLER • MICHAEL S HELLERSTEIN • KENNETH C HELLING • KEVIN M HELLIWELL • ERIKA C HELLSTROM • JAY P HELLSTROM • LINDA L HELLSTROM • LINDA B HELLYER • MAUREEN H HELM • PEGGY A HELM • MICHAEL S HELMASE • PATRICK M HELMER

American South. From jazz to gospel, blues to country, bluegrass to Cajun, and Zydeco to rock 'n' roll, the music is lively, fun, and memorable for the millions of people who visit the festival to enjoy the different colors and sounds that emanate from the Southern Crossroads stages. The Southern Music Amphitheater, the Dance Hall stage, and the South on Record stage each present two groups every hour, 14 hours a day. Visitors are encouraged to participate at the Dance Hall stage, where an enormous quilt-patterned dance floor accommodates up to 2,500 dancers at a time. Cajun and Texas two-step, line dancing, square dancing, and even Native American pow-wow dance rituals are featured at various times of the day and night.

Southern Crossroads offers high-quality performances in an informal setting, and is designed to appeal to visitors from Atlanta and

top: **Sounds of Blackness performs at the opening of the Southern Crossroads Festival.**

bottom: **Spectators dance and enjoy music in Centennial Olympic Park.**

DEBBIE HELMKEN • BRENDA T HELMLY • ANGELA R HELMS • CAROL E HELMS • DENISE HELMS • FRANCES M HELMS • FREDRICK E HELMS • JAMIE E HELMS • KELLY M HELMS • PHYLLIS HELMS • KARIN L HELMSTAEDT • DAVID J HELTEBRAN • BLAKE D HELTON • JAMES D HELTON • LILLIAN M HELWICK • THERESA M. HELWIG ATC • CARISSA L HEMBERGER • APRIL K HEMBREE • BECKY HEMBREE • ANTHONY D HEMBRICK • EDWARD HEMBY • JEFF HEMBY • JOHN C HEMBY • ALLISON W HEMINGWAY • GEORGE B HEMINGWAY • JAMES E HEMINGWAY • JUDITH L HEMINGWAY • PATRICIA L HEMINGWAY • JANE R HEMMER

around the world. The audiences are eclectic, enthusiastic, and appreciative, and the performers respond with their own special brand of hospitality and warmth. Whether the Wild Magnolias from New Orleans, whose outrageously colorful, feathery costumes are the talk of the park, or the plainly sung bluegrass of the Appalachian Tunesmiths are performing, the stages at this festival of American music and dance offer something for every taste and interest.

Even to Americans, much of what is presented is unfamiliar. For example, Ulali, a trio of Native American singers, performs both traditional chants as well as a more contemporary three-part harmony, all a cappella. The Sounds of Blackness, an ensemble beginning to gain a significant following throughout the US, performs traditional spirituals as well as many original songs that electrify the crowds that throng to hear them. Steve Riley and the Mamou Playboys kick out traditional Cajun sound that occasionally crosses over into rock 'n' roll, while Maggie Lewis and the Thunderbolts, a rockabilly band from Shreveport, Louisiana, gives audiences an authentic sense of the roots of rock 'n' roll. From the Plainsmen, a Native American dance group, to Othello, a hot band out of Miami that brings the excitement of the Caribbean steel drum together with contemporary funk, the three Southern Crossroads stages are filled with exhilarating musical performances.

The joy and relaxation of Southern Crossroads spills over into the extraordinary atmosphere of Centennial Olympic Park, truly the central gathering place of Atlanta's Games. The park is a place to mingle, share stories from the day's competitions or other Olympic experiences, and meet people from all corners of the world. It is also a place to sample authentic southern foods prepared at a massive food

pavilion called Savor the South or grab a beer at Anheuser-Busch's Budworld. Visitors can also shop for Olympic memorabilia at the Superstore, purchase a craft masterpiece created by one of the South's leading artisans at the Southern Marketplace, visit the Swatch pavilion where renowned photographer Annie Leibovitz's portfolio of Olympians is on display, visit General Motor's futuristic pavilion, or take in a concert at AT&T's magnificent Global Olympic Village stage. Other visitors cool off in and enjoy the merriment that surrounds the

Plainsmen, a Native American dance group, performs at Southern Crossroads.

• JOHN L HEMMER • MARY R HEMMER • CELIA E HEMPHILL • JOHN S HEMPHILL • KATHY D HEMPHILL • TIMOTHY R HEMPHILL • WINIFRED W HEMPHILL • EDGAR HENAO • VIRGINIA R HENCELY • MARK J HENDELSON • JOSEPH A HENDERSHOTT • AMY F HENDERSON • AMY L HENDERSON • BEVERLY C HENDERSON • BRENDA D HENDERSON • CHARLES D HENDERSON • CICILY N HENDERSON • CYNTHIA O HENDERSON • DANIEL S HENDERSON • DAVID C HENDERSON • DAVID R HENDERSON • DEBORAH A HENDERSON • DENISE M HENDERSON • GAIL H HENDERSON • GERALD O HENDERSON •

top: The Southern Music Amphitheater features music that traces its origin to the South.

bottom: Baron Pierre de Coubertin is honored in Centennial Olympic Park by *Gateway to Dreams*, a sculpture by Raymond Kaskey donated by the US Pierre de Coubertin Society.

spectacular Fountain of Rings in the center of the park, or take pictures of each other with the statue of Baron Pierre de Coubertin or one of the other public artworks that have been commissioned for and placed throughout the grounds.

As the close of the seventh day of competition approaches, the thousands of people who have come to the park this evening exude a spirit of generosity, goodwill, and relaxed camaraderie. That such a large body of people, representing innumerable ethnic origins, religious persuasions, political systems, and economic strata can come together and peacefully enjoy each other's company on this summer evening is indeed a tribute to the best of what the Olympic Movement represents. A wish that this spirit could be sustained indefinitely and extended throughout the world is expressed frequently by visitors and staff.

Atlanta 1996

HOWARD M HENDERSON • J ROSS HENDERSON • JAMES A HENDERSON • JAMES B HENDERSON • JANET HENDERSON • JANET M HENDERSON • JOHN E HENDERSON • JOHN M HENDERSON • JUDITH P HENDERSON • JUDY R HENDERSON • KAREN R HENDERSON • KARLYN D HENDERSON • KARON G HENDERSON • KATRINA T HENDERSON • KEISHA L HENDERSON • KELLY J HENDERSON • KYLE HENDERSON • LARHONDE K HENDERSON • LEVI R HENDERSON • LINDA C HENDERSON • LISA R HENDERSON • LLOYD O HENDERSON • LONNIE D HENDERSON • LYNN A HENDERSON • MARGARET C HENDERSON •

DAY EIGHT
27 JULY 1996

AN ANONYMOUS TERROR stuns Atlanta and the world when, at 1:20 a.m., a pipe bomb explodes in Centennial Olympic Park, shattering the peace which has permeated the Games thus far and replacing it with confusion and grief. The explosion that rocks the carefree crowd that had gathered yesterday at the end of the evening to hear the concert at the Global Olympic Village stage takes the life of 1 person and injures 110 others. Another person dies of a heart attack shortly thereafter. The park, which has been such a positive and illuminating force throughout the Games, is suddenly and tragically stunned into silence, emptied of patrons and staff so that an investigation can begin immediately.

Shockwaves reach every part of the Olympic operation, but the determination reached by ACOG and the IOC is forthright and decisive—the Games will go on. ACOG's staff assesses the situation at every venue and prepares for the full day of competition and other events that lie ahead. What ACOG does not know at this early hour is to what extent the park explosion will negatively impact the Games themselves.

How many volunteers will be frightened away? Will all the venues be operational? Will ticket holders come? Will the athletes participate as scheduled? These and many other questions surface in the immediate aftermath of the explosion, throughout the night, and into the early morning hours, when venue teams are scheduled to start their shifts for the day.

In an almost unbelievable demonstration of commitment, dedication, and concern for both the Games as a whole and fellow staff members, the number of volunteers reporting for duty greatly exceeds the number scheduled for

The peace felt in Centennial Olympic Park since the Games began is shattered when a pipe bomb explodes.

MARK A HENDERSON • MARK W HENDERSON • MARY E HENDERSON • MATTHEW J HENDERSON • MIA Q HENDERSON • MICHAEL A HENDERSON • MURRY D HENDERSON • NETTIE M HENDERSON • NINA A HENDERSON • PAUL R HENDERSON • PAUL T HENDERSON • PHILBERT J HENDERSON • ROBERT M HENDERSON • ROBERT T HENDERSON • RODNEY E HENDERSON • ROXANE L HENDERSON • RYAN S HENDERSON • S ELIZABETH HENDERSON • SALADIN HENDERSON • SANDY C HENDERSON • SARAH HENDERSON • SHARON L HENDERSON • SUSAN D HENDERSON • SUZANNE HENDERSON •

this day. Concerned that some of their colleagues might not be able to make it to venues or might be too frightened to come, those who were not scheduled report by the hundreds to virtually every venue to lend their support.

From this time forward, the spirit and operational viability of Atlanta's Games is beyond question. Neither ACOG's dedicated paid and volunteer staff, nor the athletes and team officials, nor the hundreds of thousands of fans who have come to this city for the Centennial Olympic Games will be kept away by this cow-

COMPETITION

In the competitions on the Ocoee River in Tennessee, 17-year-old Michal Martikan of Slovakia, the youngest competitor in the field, wins the gold in the canoe single slalom event, capturing the first gold medal ever for his small central European country which, until 1993, was joined with the Czech Republic as the former nation of Czechoslovakia.

In the cool waters of Lake Lanier, Steven Redgrave and Matthew Pinsent of Great Britain

top: **Great Britain's Matthew Pinsent and Steven Redgrave cross the finish line to take the gold in the men's coxless pair.**

bottom: **Switzerland's Xeno Muller celebrates his gold medal in men's single sculls rowing with Canada's Derek Porter (silver) and Germany's Thomas Lange (bronze).**

ardly and outrageous act. Venues are fully staffed and stands are filled with fans who, in an intense demonstration of the power of the Olympic Spirit, begin each event with a moment of silence. Out of this silence grows powerful, sustained cheers for the athletes that resonate through every venue from this morning and will continue to do so until the close of the Games. Everyone touched by this tragedy shares and carries a deeper understanding of and profound appreciation for the significance and impact of the Olympic vision. This sense of unity will grow with each passing hour as the Games move ahead.

capture gold in the coxless pair event, making Redgrave only the fourth Olympian to win gold in four straight Olympic Games. Immediately after the race, Redgrave announces his retirement from competition, saying, "If you see me anywhere near a boat, shoot me."

After Redgrave's retirement from competition, the silver screen may not be far away. According to Switzerland's single sculls competitor Xeno Muller, both he and Canada's Derek Porter were extras on a California movie set, where the film crew chose Porter over himself for the rowing scenes. In the Olympic setting of today's race, Porter finishes second to Muller, with Germany's Thomas Lange, who won gold in both 1988 and 1992, taking the bronze.

At a morning tennis match at Stone Mountain Park in which Monica Seles of the US team defeats Argentina's star, Gabriela Sabatini, 6–3, 6–3, Seles is so moved by the support of fans that she remains long after the completion of the match to sign autographs. "The fans have been unbelievable, and [their support] definitely pulled me through the second set," she says.

Back in the city of Atlanta, long-standing tension is converted into a table tennis showdown as Korea's Nam-Kyu Yoo meets the Democratic People's Republic of Korea's Gun Sang Li for the first time in six years. After the grueling, 40-minute match, Yoo raises his arms to celebrate a 21–19, 21–14 victory, supported by thousands of cheering, flag-waving Korean fans. During the draw for this competition, Korea protested against the early match with the Democratic People's Republic of Korea. After his win, Yoo offers a unifying theme: "I felt like I had to beat him because he's from North Korea, but now I feel sympathy for him. We're all from one nation, one blood."

Sometimes a match becomes such a mismatch that the contestants decide to have a

little fun. Such was the case in a completely different kind of match-up at the table tennis venue today. Sweden's Jan-Ove Waldner, who built an early and insurmountable lead over Yugoslavia's Ilija Lupulesku, begins hitting high lobs and letting Lupulesku hit smashes back at him. At one point, Waldner leaps over a partition and plays from the adjacent court, allowing Lupulesku to take advantage of his absence from the court to close the gap to 20–16, but Waldner returns to the proper court to win the final point of the match.

left: Touched by the support of her fans, Monica Seles of the US autographs their tickets, remaining long after her victory.

right: Jan-Ove Waldner of Sweden builds an early lead over Ilija Lupulesku of Yugoslavia in the men's table tennis competition.

WALLACE E HENDRICKS • WILBUR C HENDRICKS • WILLIAM F HENDRICKS JR • CARL L HENDRICKS III • KRISTI HENDRICKSON • PAUL W HENDRICKSON • SHARON J HENDRICKSON • BEASEY S HENDRIX • BETTY JANE H HENDRIX • BETTYE J HENDRIX • CATHERINE W HENDRIX • HERBERT G HENDRIX • JACQUELYN M HENDRIX • JAMES S HENDRIX • JARED M HENDRIX • JASON HENDRIX • LOUISE HENDRIX • MARK A HENDRIX • MELISSA B HENDRIX • MYRNA HENDRIX • REBECCA L HENDRIX • ROBERT HENDRIX • DON HENDRIX JR • RONNIE E HENDRIX MD • PETER W HENDRY • BART R HENDRYX •

top: Croatia's water polo team celebrates after winning their first gold medal as an independent Croatian team.

bottom: Two Brazilian teams compete for the gold medal in the women's beach volleyball final.

The two semifinal water polo matches played today determine the teams that will meet tomorrow in the finals. Before a capacity crowd of 4,000, Croatia defeats the defending gold medal team from Italy in a close, hard-fought match, 7–6. In an equally intense and close contest, Spain defeats Hungary with the identical score.

Three members of the Croatian water polo team have won gold medals playing for Yugoslavia, but this is the first time they have competed as an independent country. In an emotional win in the quarterfinals this past Friday, Croatia was assured a medal when its team defeated Yugoslavia, a win they are still celebrating today. Commenting on how he feels about playing for Croatia, former gold-medal winner Dubravko Simenc says, "I've always been a Croat. Then [1988] I was a citizen of Yugoslavia, but now I am a Croat *and* a citizen of Croatia."

On the playing field today, Brazil's Jacqueline Louise Cruz Silva and her partner, Sandra Tavares Pires, win the gold medal in women's beach volleyball and become the first Brazilian women to ever win an Olympic medal.

A beach volleyball pioneer, Silva's on-the-field performance and off-the-field leadership has helped make this sport into the power game it is today. To take the gold, this talented team defeats another outstanding Brazilian team, Adriana Ramos Samuel and Mônica Rodrigues, 12–11, 12–6. Australia's Kerri Ann Pottharst and Natalie Cook take the bronze.

In the evening hours, 34,000 people make their way to the Georgia Dome for women's basketball action. In the fourth game of the day, Brazil improves its record to 4–0, overpowering the People's Republic of China to remain one of only two undefeated teams. In the following game, the other unbeaten squad, the US team, led by guard Teresa Edwards, who has a record 15 assists in the victory, defeats the Australian women 96–79.

In an exciting halftime feature, the Georgia Dome audience leaps to its feet and cheers as the fans watch perennial US favorite Gail Devers on the venue's enormous video screen as she wins gold in the 100 m. By winning this race, Devers becomes only the second woman to win the 100 m in consecutive Games, defeating Jamaica's Merlene Ottey in a photo finish. Ottey, who suffered a similar loss to Devers in the 1993 World Championship in Stuttgart, Germany, files an official protest claiming that it is the torso and not just the head which must cross the finish line first, but the result is not changed.

Devers's coach, Bobby Kersee, husband and coach of heptathlon favorite Jackie Joyner-Kersee, leaps from the stands to embrace Devers after the race. In celebration of her win, Devers and bronze-medal winner and teammate Gwen Torrence take a victory lap, accompanied by the flag-waving and cheering of the capacity audience.

The sprinters continue to take center stage at Olympic Stadium, with the men's 100 m race providing an equally spectacular result. Defending Olympic champion Linford Christie of Great Britain, one of sprinter Donovan Bailey's

Gail Devers crosses the finish line first, becoming only the second woman to win the 100 m in two consecutive Games.

PATRICK J HENRICKS • HENNING K HENRIKSEN • MIRIAM HENRIKSEN • A. PAGE HENRY • BRIAN C HENRY • DEVIE A HENRY • ELIZABETH A HENRY • ELIZABETH J HENRY • FRANKIE L HENRY • JANET E HENRY • JEFFREY HENRY • JILL E HENRY • KAREN E HENRY • KATHY H HENRY • KELLY HENRY • KEVIN G HENRY • LASSELL C HENRY • LISA M HENRY • MAVIS HENRY • MICHELE A HENRY • MIKE HENRY • MIRIAM P HENRY • NICOLE HENRY • RANDY G HENRY • SANDRA S HENRY • SHIRLEY P HENRY • TIMOTHY HENRY • TIMOTHY A HENRY • TRACIE R HENRY • TRISHA L HENRY • TUESDAY HENRY • TYSHAWN A HENRY •

of Canada's main competitors for the gold, is disqualified after two false starts. The Canadians celebrate as Bailey crosses the finish line in the men's 100 m in the world-record time of 9.84 seconds. The race is still a close one, as Frank Fredericks of Namibia and Ato Boldon of Trinidad and Tobago finish just behind Bailey.

With nearly 9 million tickets sold to a variety of events in 31 venues over the course of 17 days—an average of more than 500,000 tickets per day—the sale and servicing of Olympic tickets is unrivaled in complexity and

equipped and staffed vans, sent to resolve problems that cannot be handled by venue box office teams alone.

An occasion to implement this carefully planned system arises this morning when, due to a late change in the sports and television schedule, the morning beach volleyball matches are consolidated from two courts onto the main court. With more than 11,000 tickets already sold to events that were to occur on two courts, approximately 3,000 people will arrive with tickets, but will have no place to sit.

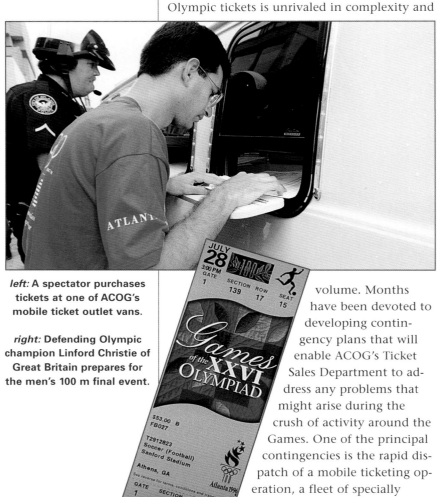

left: A spectator purchases tickets at one of ACOG's mobile ticket outlet vans.

right: Defending Olympic champion Linford Christie of Great Britain prepares for the men's 100 m final event.

volume. Months have been devoted to developing contingency plans that will enable ACOG's Ticket Sales Department to address any problems that might arise during the crush of activity around the Games. One of the principal contingencies is the rapid dispatch of a mobile ticketing operation, a fleet of specially

To avoid making these patrons unhappy, Ticket Sales activates the contingency plan, telephoning all large-volume customers and retrieving 1,200 tickets. This morning, to serve the remaining 1,800 customers who will arrive at the venue, Ticket Sales dispatches four mobile ticket outlet vans capable of selling tickets on-line and a team of 20 customer service specialists to parking lots serving the Atlanta

WAYMOND L HENRY • YVONNE R HENRY • CHARLES L HENRY JR • EUGENE HENRY JR • JOHN D HENRY JR MD • BARBARA K HENSCHEL • CLINTON P HENSEL • PAULA M HENSEL • JAMES D HENSLEY • MARY J HENSLEY • TAMMY L HENSLEY • BART W HENSON • CARL H HENSON • DEBRA A HENSON • DIEDRE M HENSON • JANE E HENSON • LESLIE M HENSON • LINDA J HENSON • PHILLIP L HENSON • RICHARD L HENSON • ROBERT L HENSON • SHARON D HENSON • VICKI D HENSON • VICKIE V HENSON • VERONICA HENSON-PHILLIPS • JACQUELINE S HENSON RN • KATHRYN LOUISE HENTER • MARY W HENTON •

Beach venue. The customer service specialists apprise ticket holders of the situation as they arrive at the lots and offer them a choice of a refund, a ticket to another beach volleyball game, or a ticket-for-ticket swap for a Closing Ceremony ticket. Without this contingency plan and the allocation of equipment and staff to handle such crises, this morning's problem could not have been effectively resolved.

OLYMPIC ARTS FESTIVAL

When asked to describe southern culture, most people, especially southerners, have strong opinions. Southern culture is complex, diverse, and elusive. Whether language, geographic boundaries, food, social customs, architecture,

top: **Great Britain's Bethan Raggatt and Susan Carr tack behind the Norwegian and Finnish teams in the women's double-handed dinghy (470) yachting competition.**

bottom: **Germany's Elisabeth Micheler-Jones makes a run through the Ocoee River in the women's kayak single slalom competition.**

MALIK HEPBURN • E ROBERT HEPFNER • DOUGLAS E HERAKOVICH • DARLENE R HERBERT • EVELYN B HERBERT • JAMA D HERBERT • JAMES C HERBERT • ROBERT C HERBERT • TERI LYNN HERBERT • LARRY R HERBERT JR • JODIE B HERBIG • WILLIAM H HERBIG • WILLIAM L HERBIG • WILLIAM R HERBIG • JARED M HERBST • MARK A HERBST • CAROLYN R HERCHE • JENNIFER B HERDEN • LISA M HERDEN • RALPH B HERDEN JR • VICTOR R HEREC • VLADIMIRA M HERENA • MATTHEW R HERHOLZ • TRES HERIN • ERIK B HERITAGE • JOHN-DAVID HERLIHY • ALLAN HERMAN • ANDREW M HERMAN • BRODIE S HERMAN •

or music is being discussed, consensus on a definition of southern culture is rare, even among the most knowledgeable scholars. Thus, the Atlanta History Center's effort to create a major exhibition to help Olympic visitors understand the intangible qualities of southern culture makes the *American South: Past, Present, and Future* among the most challenging projects presented at the Olympic Arts Festival.

The History Center, one of the South's landmark cultural institutions, has recently expanded its facilities with the addition of a mag-

The American South: Past, Present, and Future exhibition explores the origins of southern culture on many levels, including its agricultural (left) and its cultural (right) heritage.

nificent new building which is the site of this important and intriguing exhibition. Both historical and topical in nature, this exhibition poses as many questions as it provides answers. It leads visitors through a fascinating sequence of historic artifacts, photography, southern dialects, everyday objects, living spaces, social customs, and music in an effort to explore the nature, substance, and spiritual underpinnings of the American South. For southerners and international visitors alike, this exhibition offers numerous messages about southern culture from which the observer can draw his or her own conclusions about the true character of the American South.

Among the most popular features of the exhibit is a video that presents the many styles of music that collectively define the soul of American music and to which the hundreds of musicians who are scheduled to perform on the Southern Crossroads stages in Centennial Olympic Park are connected. As the source for much of what the world knows as American music, the South, through the varied and complex confluence of Native American, African, and European musical traditions, has forged a wide range of musical expressions that, espe-

cially during the past 50 years, have become the most influential and significant export of American culture. The magnetic attraction of southern culture was evident both at the History Center, where scores of people gathered around the television monitor for repeated showings of the video, and in Centennial Olympic Park, where over 100,000 people each

DAVID M HERMAN • DIANN K HERMAN • LAURA E HERMAN • LOUIS R HERMAN • MARGARET J HERMAN • PAUL J HERMAN • MARY J HERMANN • JODIE L HERMANN CATC • DANY J HERMIZ • TOM H HERMSTAD •
ANA MARIA HERNANDEZ • BERNADETTE HERNANDEZ • BOBBY HERNANDEZ • CARLA A HERNANDEZ • CLAUDIA M HERNANDEZ • FELICIA J HERNANDEZ • GLORIA I HERNANDEZ • HECTOR HERNANDEZ •
JESUS A HERNANDEZ • LEOBARDO HERNANDEZ • MARIA HERNANDEZ • MICKEY A HERNANDEZ • RICO HERNANDEZ • ROGER J HERNANDEZ • SAMARA B HERNANDEZ •

top: Performances of *The Hungry Tiger and other Tales from China* at the Center for Puppetry Arts were extremely popular.

bottom: One of the public art focal points of Centennial Park is the sculpture, *Tribute to Olympia*, provided by the American Hellenic Educational Progressive Association.

day visited the Southern Crossroads stages to discover, listen to, dance with, and enjoy the rich variety of uniquely southern cultural contributions. The silence that would engulf the park over the next few days would be in stark contrast to this festive atmosphere.

Atlanta 1996

VICTORIA E HERNANDEZ • WYNNE E HERNANDEZ • AVONNE S HERNDON • JEANETTE M HERNDON • JOEL T HERNDON • JOY L HERNDON • LYNNE B HERNDON • MATT M HERNDON • MIA D HERNDON • PATRICIA L HERNDON • STEPHEN HERNDON • HUGH F HERNON • CATHERINE V HEROLD • LINDA K HEROLD • MICHAEL F HERON • MARLENE S HEROUX • LINDA D HERREN • DANIEL R HERRERA • EDDY A HERRERA • GUSTAVO A HERRERA • JESUS HERRERA • NANCY R HERRERA • OMAR HERRERA • KIMBERLY A HERRES • RICHARD T HERRICK • SANDRA S HERRICK • STELLA K HERRICK • JOAN E HERRIGES •

DAY NINE
28 JULY 1996

BY DAY NINE, many athletes are finished with competition and enjoying the glory or satisfaction of their achievements. An Olympic medal, universally acknowledged as the ultimate prize for excellence and achievement in sport, is the culmination of a lifetime of dedicated preparation and sustained effort. The victory celebrations at which Olympic medals are presented are steeped in tradition recalling celebrations of victory during the ancient Games.

Each host is afforded some creativity in the style in which medals and victory bouquets are presented, but the basic ceremony is structured by the International Olympic Committee. In Atlanta, these celebrations are supported by a select group of young women, all volunteers, who are responsible for carrying the medals and bouquets. Outfitted in cream summer dresses and sun hats, such as might be worn to an afternoon garden party, these lovely young women reflect the spirit of traditional southern hospitality and add a touch of charm and grace to the ceremonies as they accompany presenters to the victory stands with medals and bouquets.

Behind the scenes, a dedicated volunteer team, including a group of senior citizens affectionately called "Flower Power," works overtime to prepare, assemble, and deliver some 2,000 victory bouquets to competition venues. These important components of the victory ceremony are far more than a simple bunch of flowers. Floral designer Mary Jo Means has painstakingly

Volunteers in traditional southern dress deliver medals and victory bouquets to the presenters.

BARBARA A HERRIN • BOYD D HERRIN • CLIFTON C HERRIN • MICHAEL JR P HERRIN • CRAIG HERRING • DOROTHY K HERRING • JESSICA B HERRING • KAREN E HERRING • KIMBERLY A HERRING • KIMBERLY A HERRING • TINA S HERRING • LISA D. HERRING-BIVINS • BRANDON B HERRINGTON • GERALD J HERRINGTON • JOHN M HERRINGTON • LLOYD F HERRINGTON • ROGER HERRINGTON • PENELOPE A HERRIOTT • PATSY HERRMANN • TERRI L HERRMANN • BARBARA R HERRON • GREGORY A HERRON • JILL C HERRON • KEVIN M. HERRON • SYLVIA A HERRON • DAVID C HERSEY • RANDY N HERSH •

created these victory bouquets from a combination of greenery and flowers, each associated with a special meaning or quality that reinforces the themes of celebrating the Olympic centennial and Atlanta's southern hospitality. The greens include laurel for personal glory, an olive branch for peace, palm for victory and success, magnolia for perseverance, and luecothoe for hospitality. The flowers included are cockscomb for immortality, helianthus (sunflower) for loyalty, larkspur for swiftness, tiger lily for pride, and tuberose for love.

Scott Shipley of the US, the world's highest-ranked kayaker, battles the rapids in the men's kayak single slalom finals.

Games were to be a peaceful gathering during which nations could set aside differences and compete in an impartial, apolitical environment. Though keeping track of the winners and losers through a medal count would be a measure of relative performance, the most significant measure of the success of this new enterprise would be the number of participating nations represented at this gathering.

The impact and value of broad Olympic participation is illustrated daily in Atlanta, as it is in every Olympic Games. Every day, at virtually

COMPETITION

Baron Pierre de Coubertin and his colleagues understood that the newly revived Olympic Games could hold a magnetic power and enduring value beyond that of bringing the world's finest athletes together every four years. While clearly focused on the celebration of excellence and achievement, the Olympic

every venue, athletes representing the rainbow of cultures that have come to the Olympic Games at its centennial illuminate and reaffirm de Coubertin's vision by simply taking part. Interacting with one another as individuals and teams and crossing cultural boundaries and political barriers, the men and women who participate inspire observers to extend the Olympic Spirit into their everyday lives.

A marvelous example of the power of this spirit is Samir Karabasic, a slalom kayaker of

place, their fulfillment of the Olympic dream of participation and international friendship is no less glorious than Germany's kayaker Oliver Fix's gold medal score of 141.22 points.

Day nine becomes like many days from past Olympic Games, with Cuba dominating in the sports of baseball and boxing. Before another capacity crowd of 51,223 at Atlanta–Fulton County Stadium, Cuba edges the US baseball team, 10–8 in men's preliminary competition. The US team battles back from an eight-run deficit and brings the winning run to the plate

Bosnia and Herzegovina who survived four years as a combat soldier to return to his sport and represent his country at the Centennial Olympic Games. The best boat his war-ravaged country could provide was a second-hand craft with a hairline crack across the deck that had been patched with duct tape. A crowd of 14,500 is on hand at the Ocoee Whitewater Center for the final day of Olympic slalom competition, where Karabasic beams at cheering fans from a boat given to him by the highest-ranked kayaker in the world, Scott Shipley of the US. While Shipley finishes in a disappointing 12th place, and Karabasic in 41st

in the ninth inning but is turned away by the Cuban team. Miguel Caldes posts five runs batted in, and his home run with two men on base leads his team to win.

From morning until late at night, boxing fans are treated to a series of commanding performances, two of which lift a powerful Cuban

left: The strong arm of Omar Ajete of Cuba contributes to his team's win over the US in men's preliminary baseball competition.

right: Ioannis Melissanidis, Greece's first athlete to win a men's gymnastics medal in 90 years, enjoys his gold-medal victory.

RONALD HESS • TIMOTHY S HESS • LAVADA S HESSER • ROBERT R HESSLER • BARBARA B HESTER • CHERYL A HESTER • DARLA S HESTER • DAVID L HESTER • DOUGLAS L HESTER • JAMES T HESTER • JOANNE O HESTER • JOHN D HESTER • KIMBERLY M HESTER • LISA K HESTER • NANCY S HESTER • ROGER D HESTER • SUSAN G HESTER • THOMAS C HESTER • TYRE HESTER • SUZANNE HESTER-FAHEY • ANN M HESTON • SHAWN L HETH • FRANCES R HETH-FRALIX • JAMES P HETRICK • JOHN S HETTINGER • CHRIS HETTLER • CHUCK W HETTLER • GENE HETZEL • JACK B HETZLER • BARBARA P HEUER •

boxing team's Olympic record to 20–2. Maikro Romero advances to the flyweight 51 kg (112 lb) quarterfinals by defeating Armenia's Lernik Papian, while Hector Vinent, his teammate in the light welterweight 63.5 kg (139 lb) class, defeats Nurhan Süleymanoglu of Turkey who was ranked no. 4 in the world in his weight class coming into the bout.

In one of the most emotional moments of the day, Ioannis Melissanidis becomes Greece's first athlete to win a gymnastics medal in 90 years, taking the gold in the men's floor exercise with a score of 9.850, just ahead of Xiaoshuang Li of the People's Republic of China (9.837) and Alexei Nemov of the Russian Federation (9.800). Commenting on how he prepared for his historic victory he says, "I said to myself, I was not Ioannis Melissanidis, I was Greece."

In the women's artistic gymnastics individual competition, Romania's Simona Amanar wins the vault with a score of 9.825, ahead of the People's Republic of China's Huilan Mo (9.768) and teammate Gina Gogean (9.750).

For Henry Andrade, a 110 m hurdler and the first and only athlete from the tiny island nation of Cape Verde, representing his country in its first Games is a source of profound pride. This determined runner, who worked for 25 years to qualify to compete in an Olympic Games, finally accomplished his dream in March of this year. Just when everything seemed to be heading in the right direction, Andrade ruptured his Achilles tendon during a training session in the Bahamas on his way to Atlanta. "I had a shot to be in the finals," says Andrade. "And that was my goal." But showing the spirit of a true Olympian, Andrade says he is not going to let an injury come between him and the fulfillment of his dream. "I will be at the starting line for my race [today]. You will see my face, and you will see my colors," he says. "If I can only walk, then I'll walk. But if I can run, I will run." Winning is no longer important. "I am here not only for myself. I am here for my country. Cape Verde needs the recognition."

One of two Palestinians competing in the Games, 32-year-old Majed Abu Maraheel, who will compete in the 10,000 m event, brings with him a unique perspective. Having spent 25 years in refugee camps, Abu Maraheel's training has been limited to running along a narrow strip of land on the Mediterranean coast. "I learned to run fast because I was chased everywhere I went," he says. "I told my people, 'Our victory is to represent Palestine in the Olympic Games and, with God's help, I will be one of

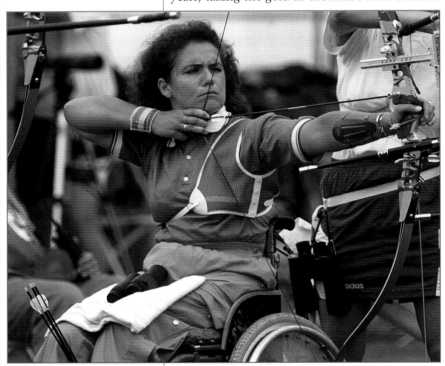

top: Paola Fantato of Italy, the only archery competitor in a wheelchair, draws her bow in the team event.

bottom: Karch Kiraly keeps the ball in play in the all-American beach volleyball final.

gold-medal–winning performance makes Kiraly the first volleyball player to win three gold medals, which he accomplished at three Olympic Games—the other two being at the 1984 and 1988 Games.

Water polo offers fans two outstanding final games. In the gold medal match, Spain, led by five-time Olympian and one of the sport's most proficient players, Manuel Estiarte, defeats Croatia 7–5. The bronze match, preceding the Spain-Croatia contest, features one of the Games' most dramatic contests. Down four

the winners.' Really, I've already won my gold medal just by being in the Village."

Yet another story of Olympic participation unfolds, this time at the Stone Mountain Archery Center, as Italy's Paola Fantato, the Games' only wheelchair-bound athlete, draws her first bow in the team event. The 36-year-old athlete, who contracted polio at eight months of age, fails in her quest for a medal in both the team and individual events, but says, "The most important thing for me is to be recognized as an athlete."

Moving to Atlanta Beach, the volleyball team of Karch Kiraly and Kent Steffes defeats Michael Dodd and Mike Whitmarsh in straight sets, 12–5, 12–8, in an all-American final. The

goals in the final period of play, Italy battles back to take the lead over Hungary with only 49 seconds left. As the clock winds down, the Italian bench, thinking the game is over, dives into the pool to celebrate, but in fact, the clock shows 0.2 seconds left, and the game is far from over. The error gives Hungary a penalty shot, and they take advantage, scoring to tie the game and send it into overtime. In the highest scoring game of the tournament, Italy takes the overtime lead and hangs on to win, 20-18.

left: Jordi Sans of Spain cheers after his team defeats the Croatian team for the gold in water polo.

right: In women's hockey preliminaries, Jill Atkins of Great Britain celebrates her team's win over the team from Germany.

• TONI M HIATT • BETH F HIBBS • CHRISTINA C HIBBS • JEFFREY S HIBSHMAN • LISA B HIBSHMAN • MARK D HICKERSON ATC • CHRISTINE S HICKEY • DIANE P HICKEY • ELLEN A HICKEY • MARIANNE HICKEY • NANCY C HICKEY • PAUL C HICKEY • PRISCILLA K HICKEY • STEVEN D HICKEY • PATRICK T HICKEY JR • JUDSON HICKINBOTHAM • ANDREW D HICKLING • JOYCE H HICKMAN • LON HICKMAN • POWELL E HICKMAN • TERRI L HICKMAN • BONNIE E HICKS • CAROL A HICKS • CAROLE L HICKS • CARRIE L HICKS • CHRISTINA L HICKS • DANETTA M HICKS • DEBRA J HICKS • DON R HICKS • DONNA J HICKS •

The men's and women's top seeds both lose badminton matches today as the world's no. 6 ranked player Rashid Sidek of Malaysia defeats Joko Suprianto of Indonesia, 15–5, 15–12, in the men's competition, while in the women's competition, no. 9 ranked Ji Hyun Kim of Korea defeats the People's Republic of China's Zhaoying Ye, 11–5, 12–11.

A combined crowd of 152,642 morning and afternoon session spectators at Olympic Stadium witness a string of dramatic and exciting men's and women's athletics events. The day begins with the women's marathon. Many of the competitors, anticipating a typical Atlanta summer day, trained for a hot and humid race, but at race time, the air temperature is cool and a slight mist hangs in the air. Favorite Uta Pippig of Germany moves into the early lead but is overtaken at the 16 km (10 mi) mark and eventually drops out of the race after 35 km (21.7 mi). Meanwhile, Ethiopia's Fatuma Roba surges ahead and captures the Olympic title in 2:26:05, two full minutes faster than the silver-medal winner, Valentina Yegorova of the Russian Federation, and the largest margin of victory in Olympic history. Yuko Arimori of Japan takes the bronze.

top: Competitors in the men's lightweight double sculls event compete as the sun glistens on the waters of Lake Lanier.

bottom: Junxia Wang, the only woman to compete in both the 5,000 m and 10,000 m events, captures the People's Republic of China's first athletics gold medal.

FRANCES M HICKS • GERALD W HICKS • H. LEIGH HICKS • JANET S HICKS • JOYCE C HICKS • LILLIAN K HICKS • LISA V HICKS • MARC M HICKS • MARY B HICKS • MARY C HICKS • MATTHEW E HICKS • MAUREEN J HICKS • MAXINE C HICKS • NELSON HICKS • NICOLE C HICKS • PAMELA F HICKS • PENNY M HICKS • RONALD R HICKS • RUSS E HICKS • SAMUEL A HICKS • SHERRY L HICKS • SONJA A HICKS • TIMOTHY P HICKS • TONI A HICKS • TONY L HICKS • WILLIAM A HICKS • DETRA J HICKSON • MICHAEL E HICKSON • TERRENCE HICKSON • MICHAEL J HICKSON MD • WILLIAM R HIDDINK • GAYLE D HIDDLESON •

While the rest of the marathon field may have had trouble keeping up with Roba, Olympic officials had no problem, thanks to a bit of advanced technology. A tiny computer chip, attached to each runner's shoelaces, is being used for the first time in Olympic competition. Programmed with a unique bar code that is transmitted to officials by a micro-transponder, the chip enables race officials to monitor each contestant's progress and prevent the confusion and possible cheating that can occur in a race with a mass start.

An equally important advantage is that the device provides broadcasters and fans with instantly transmitted progress reports on each runner at regular intervals. Though not used to record official times, the chips provide valuable information that would otherwise be impossible to track. Designed in the Netherlands and operated by the official Olympic timekeeper, Swatch, the chips are programmed with each runner's race number and sealed in a plastic disc. Each time a runner passes over one of the special mats located at five kilometer intervals throughout the course, a small antenna picks up the bar code from the disc and transmits it via a weak microwave signal to a computer, where the information is recorded and immediately displayed on the scoreboard at Olympic Stadium.

Later at Olympic Stadium, Jackie Joyner-Kersee's withdrawal from the heptathlon leaves the field open for Syria's Ghada Shouaa, last year's world champion, to win the event and her country's first Olympic gold medal ever with a score of 6,780 points. Shouaa finishes 217 points ahead of the silver medalist, Natalya Sazanovich of Belarus.

Junxia Wang of the People's Republic of China wins the 5,000 m to capture her country's first athletics gold medal. The only woman to attempt both the 5,000 m and the 10,000 m

Hong Kong's Lai Shan Lee celebrates winning the gold medal in the women's yachting mistral class.

in these Games, she will go on to win the silver in the 10,000 m.

At the yachting venue, Hong Kong's tiny Lai Shan Lee, the reigning world champion in the women's mistral class, becomes the first Asian competitor ever to win an Olympic yachting medal, clinching the gold medal after only one race. Upon winning, the 5 ft 5 in (1.65 m), 114 lb (51.7 kg) competitor grabs a bottle of champagne, pops the cork, and takes a big gulp, celebrating her victory and commemorating the last time Hong Kong will compete in the Olympic Games under its own flag, as it will become part of the People's Republic of China on 1 July 1997. In recognition of her victory, the Hong Kong subway company announces that Lee will receive free subway trips for life, and her statue may be erected on the bridge that links the island of Hong Kong to China.

CRYSTAL HIDDLESTON • TISH HIDLE • GEORGE L HIERS • EBBA R HIERTA • ERV HIETBRINK • AMY HIETT • BETTY A HIETT • JEANNE L HIGBEE • KAREN A HIGDON • TRACIE D HIGDON • CRAIG A HIGGASON • CARL L HIGGINBOTHAM • GENE HIGGINBOTHAM • JAMES B HIGGINBOTHAM • PAMELA H HIGGINBOTHAM • RICHARD E HIGGINBOTHAM • TRAVIS HIGGINBOTHAM • BRENNAN S HIGGINS • CHERYL Z HIGGINS • DAVID L HIGGINS • DORIS HIGGINS • ERIN P HIGGINS • GROVER H HIGGINS • JIM E HIGGINS • JOHN M HIGGINS • KEVIN S HIGGINS • MADONNA M HIGGINS • MEREDITH M HIGGINS • PAUL S HIGGINS

167

OLYMPIC ARTS FESTIVAL

The product of a two-year collaborative relationship between the Atlanta-based Ballethnic Dance Company and the Paris-based Compagnie Ebène, this evening's world premiere of *Trouble* by the Parisian company's founder and choreographer Irene Tassembedo is an Olympic Arts Festival milestone. Launched during *Celebrate Africa!*, one of the most ambitious Olympic Prelude programs of the Cultural Olympiad, this dynamic, international collabo-

rative effort has been an extremely gratifying and challenging project.

Founded in 1990 by Waverly and Nena Gilreath Lucas, both former members of the Dance Theatre of Harlem and the Atlanta Ballet, Ballethnic maintains a commitment to reach out to and train young people from minority communities who might not otherwise be exposed to the possibilities of dance. Eager to expand its repertoire, Ballethnic welcomed the opportunity to work with Compagnie Ebène. Combining the powerful rhythms and

The dance group Karas performs *Noiject* at the Atlanta Civic Center, a piece that combines Japanese Buto technique, classical ballet, and modern dance.

• PHILIP W HIGGINS • ROBERT N HIGGINS • SHIRLEY HIGGINS • STEPHEN T HIGGINS • TINA M HIGGINS-DAVIS • THOMAS J HIGGINS ATC • DOUGLAS L HIGGONS • DELORIS V HIGH • MATTHEW S HIGH • THOMAS K HIGH • ANNA B HIGHSMITH • CAROLYN S HIGHSMITH • DARLENE H HIGHSMITH • HELEN E HIGHSMITH • LEMUEL T HIGHSMITH • ROSLYNN B HIGHT • SANDRA S HIGHT • BRENDA J HIGHTOWER • CHRISTOPHER S HIGHTOWER • DEBBIE A HIGHTOWER • DEBORAH HIGHTOWER • GEORGE B HIGHTOWER • HORACE HIGHTOWER • JERRI S HIGHTOWER • JOHN A HIGHTOWER • JOSEFA E HIGHTOWER •

physicality of traditional African dance with the nuance, flexibility, and grace of classical ballet, Tassembedo has created almost an entirely new genre of dance.

As with many multicultural ventures, bringing together artists representing very different cultural backgrounds and parts of the world was a tremendous challenge. Ballethnic's dancers had difficulty absorbing complex, unfamiliar African movements and melding them into Tassembedo's unique choreographic approach, but the end result is worth all the effort.

Tensions are high as the two companies take the stage this evening at the Martin Luther King Jr. International Chapel, but as soon as the work opens, everyone senses that this is one of those rare times when everything will go exactly as planned. The dancers seem to take flight, soaring and whirling with confidence, grace, and power. Tassembedo's towering presence and inventive direction give life to this new work, and Ballethnic gains instant prominence. In keeping with the tradition of discovering bright new athletic stars throughout each Games, this special evening demonstrates that the same kind of glory can be achieved through an Olympic Arts Festival program.

Ballethnic excites the audience with its performance of _Trouble_.

Atlanta 1996

MARY A HIGHTOWER • RAWLS W HIGHTOWER • DORA G HIGHWOOD • JEFFREY L HIGUERA • WILLIAM E HIGY • MIRIAM L HILBERT • STEVEN D HILBUN • ERIN L HILDEBRAND • MARK ALLAN L HILDEBRAND • MARK W HILDEBRAND • JULIE L HILDEBRAND ATC • BOBBY D HILDRETH • WILLIAM P HILDRETH • BETSEY B HILFRANK • BARBARA A HILKE • HERMAN O HILKE • ALVIN J HILL • AMANDA M HILL • ANDREA L HILL • ANDY HILL • BENNA J HILL • BEVERLEY A HILL • BLOISE A HILL • BOBBIE A HILL • BRADFORD HILL • CALVIN HILL • CAROLYN F HILL • CATHY P HILL • CELENA R HILL • CHARLES S HILL • CHRISTINE HILL

DAY TEN
29 JULY 1996

AS MORE ATHLETES in Atlanta are finishing their competitions, most are able to relax and enjoy the atmosphere, activities, and services of the Olympic Village. Located on 270 acres (109.3 ha) of the Georgia Institute of Technology campus, the Atlanta Olympic Village, which protects, houses, and entertains Olympic athletes as well as offering them all the services found in a small town, operates 24 hours daily for more than 30 days. Fulfilling the special needs and complex requirements of Olympic athletes and officials from the 197 participating delegations and many more cultures, ethnic backgrounds, and religious persuasions represents a tremendous task.

In addition to offering housing in refurbished and new dormitory rooms and an almost unlimited menu served around the clock, the Village provides a full range of support services to meet virtually any individual need. The hair salon, for example, does a very brisk business, ultimately providing 4,895 coiffures for those who are either preparing for or hoping to be in the spotlight after capturing a gold medal. The music listening center and sports video viewing and taping facilities are also popular. Internet access is provided to athletes, who are delighted that they can send E-mail to friends at home and receive it from fans in Atlanta who may have just seen them compete. The call center is also busy, placing more than 10,000 calls for athletes during their stay in Atlanta. With Olympians being some of the healthiest people on earth, the Village health club does a very brisk business, hosting 6,300 athlete visits in less than 30 days.

Village residents relax in the residential zone of the Olympic Village.

• CHRISTOPHER H HILL • DAVID D HILL • DEBBIE L HILL • DEBORAH L HILL • DIANE E HILL • DOUG HILL • DUANE G HILL • ELANDA G HILL • ELIZABETH B HILL • ELIZABETH M HILL • ETHEL A HILL • EZEKIEL T HILL • FAYE C HILL • GAIL HILL • GARRY HILL • GEO HILL • HEIDI M HILL • JACQUELYN C HILL • JAMES HILL • JAMES B HILL • JAMES R HILL • JANEEN HILL • JASON PAUL HILL • JAVOYNE HILL • JENNIFER D HILL • JESSIE HILL • JOANNE L HILL • JOSEPH L HILL • JUDSON J HILL • JUDY B HILL • JULIA L HILL • KADIR HILL • KAREN A HILL • KATHY S HILL • KAY HILL • KELLI M HILL • KENT A HILL • KENYETTA R HILL •

Among the most popular Village services, offered to athletes for the first time in Atlanta, is massage therapy. Massage therapists, whose services are available free to every athlete, perform various styles of massage designed to enhance an athlete's training regimen or provide relaxation. Under the auspices of the sports medicine program, 130 therapists were selected from a field of several thousand applicants. "These guys are incredible," says their supervisor Brian Glotzbach, who also staffed the US Track and Field trials in Atlanta earlier this

pore, chooses an elaborate Harley-Davidson tattoo that reads, "Live to Ride, Ride to Live," while Jilma Patrick, who will compete for the Virgin Islands in the 4 x 100 m relay, chooses a more romantic design: a rose and ribbon that entwines the words "True Love."

Athletes' lunches, the result of more than 12 months of careful planning, contain a balanced and flavorful array of 12 components designed to meet the special dietary requirements and high caloric consumption of athletes. With a daily consumption of 8,500–

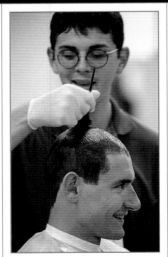

summer. Twenty-five therapists work in the Village's sports medicine center, which is open daily from 7:00 a.m. to 11:00 p.m.

Over 50 athletes line up each day between 5:00 p.m. and 9:00 p.m. to have the "Tattoo Lady," Elizabeth Menzel, decorate them with one of over 300 designs from her collection. The sign above her table in the main recreation center at the Olympic Village reads, "Tattoos so real your mother will faint." Though they look permanent, these tattoos are designed to last only a few days before washing off. Wung Yew Lee, a trap shooter from Singa-

top left and right: The Village health club is consistently popular among Olympians.

bottom: An athlete is coiffed at the Village hair salon.

10,000 calories, Olympic athletes require not just raw fuel, but a precise blend of ingredients that will help maximize their performance.

A team of 36 people works literally around the clock, preparing a daily menu that includes breakfast, lunch, and dinner and rotates on a five-day cycle. Any athlete away from the Village for more than four hours can order a boxed lunch. There is no limit to the number of lunches an athlete may order, so those with bigger appetites are accommodated. Clearly, there are some very big appetites, as approximately 55,000 lunches will be consumed over the 33 days of Village operations.

KIRSTEN HILL • LINDA J HILL • LISA A HILL • LOIS HILL • LUCILLE HILL • MACKENZIE L HILL • MARGARET B HILL • MARILYN A HILL • MARK G HILL • MERILLAT F HILL • MICHAEL D HILL • MICHELLE E HILL • MITCHELL M HILL • MITZI A HILL • PAIGE P HILL • PATRICIA H HILL • PATSY C HILL • PAUL V H HILL • PAULA L HILL • PETER J HILL • PHYLLIS L HILL • RANDALL W HILL • REBECCA C HILL • RENE M HILL • RICHARD H HILL • RICK A HILL • ROBIN L HILL • ROSITA HILL • SAM R HILL • SARA B HILL • SARAH E HILL • SHARON K HILL • SHELLEY Y HILL • SHELLY W HILL • STEPHEN E HILL • SUSAN D HILL • TERRI L HILL

Business is brisk at the Village department store, where athletes and officials purchase large quantities of Olympic merchandise. Especially popular are Olympic pins and postcards, with over 38,000 pins and 65,000 postcards purchased by Village residents. Most popular of all, however, is the video games arcade and laser tag arena, a state-of-the-art facility that is packed all day and night into the early hours of the morning, hosting a total of more than 54,000 visitors during the Games. Photography is also on many athletes' minds, with more

than 8,700 transactions in the Village photo shop, many for multiple rolls of film. There is even a bank, which makes over 12,000 transactions, and a florist, which fills orders for bouquets to congratulate athletes on their triumph or participation.

Atlanta's main Olympic Village and the outlying villages in Savannah, Ocoee (Cleveland, Tennessee), Columbus, and at the five football venues are models of efficient and high-quality operations, offering the athletes the highest level of service and support ever provided at an Olympic Games.

left: The Cardio Theater, equipped with televisions and stereos, energizes the athletes as they work out in the Village healthclub.

right: An athlete takes advantage of the state-of-the-art exercise equipment in the Village health club.

• THOMAS C HILL • THOMAS E HILL • TIM HILL • TONYA D HILL • VALERIE A HILL • VANITA J HILL • VIC B HILL • WILLIAM R HILL • WILLIE B HILL • WILLIE H HILL • WYNETTE F HILL • ELAINE S HILL-SIMPSON • RANDALL W HILL ATC • HENRY J HILL III • BOBBY R HILL JR • GEORGE HILL JR • HOSEA HILL JR • JESSE J HILL JR • JULIE A HILLEBRAND • BONNIE H HILLEGAS • LINDA D HILLEGASS • SARAH HILLER • STEPHAN C HILLERBRAND • HELEN C HILLEY • OLLIE L HILLGARTNER • CARROL M HILLHOUSE • BARBARA F HILLIARD • BETTY J HILLIARD • CALVIN HILLIARD • KELLY S HILLIARD • STEVE G HILLIARD •

COMPETITION

Olympic Stadium is packed with fans and rocks with excitement again today. In a performance that caps one of the most amazing and inspiring Olympic careers of the century, American Carl Lewis leaps into the record books as he soars 8.5 m (27.9 ft) in the long jump. In winning this event—this third of six attempts at these Games to capture his ninth Olympic gold medal—Lewis joins Olympic legend Al Oerter, discus gold medal winner from

Lewis's win would not have been possible without his memorable performance yesterday, when he made a jump that defined the very essence of what it means to be an Olympian. In 15th place after two qualifying rounds, in his last attempt to qualify for the finals, Lewis soared as if on wings to 8.29 m (27.2 ft).

Early in the evening, another memorable drama unfolds. US sprinter Michael Johnson arrived in Atlanta with the hope of becoming the first man ever to win Olympic gold in both the 200 m and 400 m. He achieves his first

top: **Michael Johnson of the US proudly displays his country's flag after winning the gold medal in the 400 m.**

bottom: **Carl Lewis of the US collects the sand he landed in to win the gold medal in the men's long jump competition.**

1956 to 1968, and the only other Olympian to collect four consecutive gold medals in a single event. Today's jump is Lewis's longest since he edged Mike Powell to win the gold medal at the 1992 Olympic Games in Barcelona.

PAULA R HILLIKER • DEBRA M HILLMAN • DELORES HILLMAN • LYN E HILLMAN • WILMA B HILLMAN • JACK HILLMEYER • DESIREE HILLMON ATC • ALVERTA HILLS • DEBORAH A HILLS • GENE HILLS • MICHELLE L HILLS • RICK L HILLS • BRUCE W HILLSTROM • DIANE L HILLSTROM • EMILY A HILLSTROM • STEVEN J HILLSTROM • SUZANNE J HILLSTROM • CARMEN M HILMES • JONI M HILS • SORAYA HILSACA • SUSAN K HILSCHER • WOODY HILSCHER • MICHELLE L HILSE • RUTH D HILSEN • BRIAN HILSON • ROBERT S HILSON • DEBORAH A HILT • COLIN P HILTON • JOHNNIE HILTON • KAREN W HILTON

goal today by sprinting past the field in the 400 m to capture a gold medal in 43.49 seconds. Roger Black of Great Britain takes the silver medal with a time of 44.41 seconds, with Uganda's Davis Kamoga earning the bronze with a time of 44.53 seconds. Almost a full second faster than his nearest competitor, Johnson also sets a new Olympic record for the 400 m in his 55th consecutive competition finals win, a streak that stretches back to the 1989 indoor season.

Meanwhile, in the women's 400 m, France's Marie-Jose Perec, defending Olympic champion, runs the fastest 400 m by a woman in 10 years and sets an Olympic record, winning the gold with a time of 48.25 seconds. Perec, who is poised to match Michael Johnson's try for a second gold in the 200 m on 1 August, is a

top: **Olympic Stadium at night provided a magnificent backdrop for women's athletics competition.**

bottom: **Marie-Jose Perec triumphs as she wins gold in the 400 m, setting an Olympic record in the process.**

top: Baeden Choppy of Australia helps his team advance to a victory over Great Britain.

bottom: Gina Gogean of Romania performs on the balance beam in the women's artistic gymnastics competition.

remarkable athlete whose record-setting performance will go down in Olympic history.

Anticipation for the women's 800 m is great, with the expectation that the contest will be between Maria Lurdes Mutola of Mozambique, winner of 45 consecutive 800 m races, and highly regarded Ana Fidelia Quirot of Cuba. But in yet another upset, the Russian Federation's Svetlana Masterkova, who took three years off from competition to recover from injuries and have a baby, wins the gold medal with a time of 1:57.73. For Quirot, the silver medal is a special victory. "I am not happy with my time, but I am happy with the color of the medal because I was able to upgrade," said Quirot, who won the bronze in this event in Barcelona. Mutola takes home the bronze medal at these Games.

In a morning men's hockey match, Australia secures a place in the semifinals for the third straight Olympic Games with a 2–0 win over Great Britain. In this game, Australian veteran Mark Hager sets a national record by playing in his 228th international match.

Moceanu tumble head-first off the balance beam, scores a 9.862 on the beam to capture her second gold of these Games and her seventh in the last two Olympic Games.

In an exciting finish to the men's vault, a bonus of .02 of a point awarded for distance gives the Russian Federation's Alexei Nemov a score of 9.787, enough to win over Vitaly Scherbo and garner the gold medal. Scherbo wins the bronze, while Korea's Hong-Chul Yeo takes the silver in the best finish ever for any Korean gymnast. In the parallel bars event,

left: A last-second score by Croatia takes the Russian Federation out of the medals in handball.

right: Hye-Young Yoon of Korea qualifies for the second round during the women's individual archery competition.

The gold flows at the gymnastics events as the individual rounds continue in both men's and women's events. Ukraine's Lilia Podkopayeva becomes the first gymnast since Nadia Comaneci (1976) to follow an all-around gold medal up with an individual gold, this time in the floor exercise, where she scores a 9.887. American Shannon Miller, despite having watched her younger teammate Dominique

Rustam Sharipov of Ukraine wins the gold with a score of 9.837, while Jair Lynch of the US wins silver, the first medal for the US on the bars since 1984.

With only four seconds left in a closely contested men's handball match, Croatia scores the decisive goal to defeat the the Russian Federation 25–24 and earn a spot in the semifinal

MICKEY ANN HINOJOSA • GROVER R HINSDALE • JENNIFER L HINSLEA • BEN F HINSON • CARL R HINSON • JAMES A HINSON • JANE C HINSON • KAMELYA D HINSON • MICHAEL R HINSON • PATRICIA A HINSON • RODNEY J HINSON • ALICE J HINTON • AMIE M HINTON • ANDRE S HINTON • BRENDA J HINTON • CARL A HINTON • CONSUELA D HINTON • DAVID R HINTON • EARLETTE M HINTON • KAREN B HINTON • MARILYNN C HINTON • MICHAEL H HINTON • SALLY A HINTON • STEPHANIE A HINTON • VICTOR D HINTON • WINSLOW H HINTON • ZOILA A HINTON • MATTHEW S HINTON ATC • ROSEMARY HINTON CATC

round while Russia, favored by many to capture the gold, is eliminated from the medal rounds. Croatia's bench empties in a jubilant celebration as the final goal is scored and time runs out. Joseph Kaylor, believed to be the lone surviving member of the 1936 US handball team, has been watching matches throughout the week. The game has changed significantly since Kaylor played on an outdoor court with 11 players in the 1936 Berlin Games. Since the 1960s, when the current indoor 12-player version became popular, the outdoor game has all

Zhoucheng Yu, wins the silver, while American Mark Lenzi, who won the event in 1992, takes the bronze. The Chinese team has already won three medals—two gold and one silver—in the first two diving events of Atlanta's Games.

OLYMPIC ARTS FESTIVAL

One of the popular destinations, located on Peachtree Street in the heart of the Olympic Ring, is the Merchandise Mart, Atlanta's original showcase for home furnishing manufactur-

IOC President Juan Antonio Samaranch poses at the *Centennial Collectables* exhibition with Hong Kong artist Nina Kung Wong.

but disappeared. To the delight of spectators, 60 years after becoming an Olympian, Kaylor is honored today by a special ceremony given by the International Handball Federation.

Diver Ni Xiong of the People's Republic of China, who won silver and bronze medals at the 1988 and 1992 Olympic Games, completes his medal set by winning the gold in the men's 3 m springboard event. Xiong's teammate,

ers. During the Games, the largest presentation of Olympic collectibles ever assembled for an Olympic Games is being shown here in a space of nearly 100,000 sq ft (9,300 sq m).

A large exhibition of historic Olympic memorabilia is always a popular attraction, but the opportunity to see the *Centennial Collectibles* exhibition in the midst of the Centennial Olympic Games makes it especially inviting. This exhibition, which has been four years in the making, is designed to offer some-

• EVELYN A HINTZE • MICHAEL J HINTZE • REINHART G HINTZE • HANNAH E HIOTT • JULIAN E HIPKINS III • JOHN E HIPP • MARK R HIPP • PIERRE A HIPPOLYTE • MICHAEL S HIPSHER • YUTAKA HIRANO • REBECCA J HIRE • SHIMOMURA HIROMI • YUKA HIROSE • ANNA HIRSCH • JOSEPH E HIRSCH • JOSH HIRSCH • LAURENCE G HIRSCH • PAUL HIRSCH • ROBERT B HIRSCH • ROCHELE H.C HIRSCH • PAT E HIRSCHBERG • THEODORE M HIRSCHFELD ATC • MARC HIRSCHHEIMER • PAUL HIRSCHHEIMER • RICK A HIRSEKORN • MARCY E HIRSHBERG • NANCY H HIRSHBERG H • DAVID R HIRST • NOELA G HIRST •

thing for every level of interest, knowledge, and experience—from an introductory display of stamps for children to displays of the rarest of stamps, coins, and other Olympic memorabilia. More than 40 dealers are on hand to show, buy, sell, and trade items from their collections. There is even an auction held for each category of collectibles. Gold, silver, and bronze medals, torches from each of the Games, and all kinds of badges, certificates, tickets, programs, and of course, Olympic pins are available. This exhibition, one of more

The intimate, 100-seat Second Stage Theater at the 14th Street Playhouse is the site of a world premiere presentation by ART Station of Stone Mountain, Georgia, one of the metropolitan-Atlanta area's most dynamic and successful arts organizations. In addition to producing theatrical works, ART Station maintains a strong presence in and support for the visual arts and serves more than 100,000 people annually through extensive outreach and training programs in the arts for children and adults.

left: Young people talk to more experienced collectors at the *Centennial Collectibles* exhibition.

right: This graphic look was developed for *Olymphilex '96*.

than 15 free Olympic Arts Festival exhibitions, attracts over 5,000 people per day, among them beginning collectors, knowledgeable enthusiasts, and serious collectors.

Centennial Collectibles' central feature is an official, international competition for stamp collectors called *Olymphilex '96*, organized under the auspices of the International Federation of Philately. Entrants from all over the world have submitted their collections to compete for highly prized awards that will be bestowed on 3 August by a distinguished international jury of experts.

As part of the Cultural Olympiad's Southern Play Project—a successful, multiyear program to commission and develop new plays by southern playwrights about the American South for premiere during the 1996 Olympic Arts Festival—ART Station's artistic director David Thomas wrote a theatrical version of "Harmony Ain't Easy," a short story by Ferrol Sams, one of the South's most beloved writers.

Generous in spirit, featuring characters whose warmth and wit are distinctly southern, the production is a marvelous showcase

SUZANNE T HIRST • DEBRA J HISBON-LEE • BETTY G HISCOCK • CHARLES G HISCOCK • ROBERT G HISCOCK • TRICIA L HISE • JAMES HISSAM • EVEMARIE D HITCHCOCK • GAIL R HITCHCOCK • GREGORY V HITCHCOCK • JOHNATHON C HITCHCOCK • PATRICIA M HITCHCOCK • ROBERT L HITCHCOCK • ROBERT S HITCHCOCK • ROGER D HITCHCOCK • SUSAN B HITCHCOCK • VARA V HITCHCOCK ATC • RANDALL H HITCHENS • CHERYL A HITCHINGS ATC • MICHAEL J HITCHYE • JASON B. HITNER • CHRISTOS G HITOPOULOS • JERRY L HITT • ROBERT T HITT • BRETT M HIVELY • CATHY L HIX • DONALD G HIX • ELLYN HIX •

***Harmony Ain't Easy,* adapted from a short story by beloved southern author Ferrol Sams, shares southern spirit and values with its audience.**

reflect the special qualities of a long relationship. The audience's close physical proximity to the cast provides Thomas with numerous opportunities to incorporate knowing glances and quick asides that draw the audience into the play. Thomas's attention to detail and focus on language and cultural values make *Harmony Ain't Easy* an especially significant and appealing way to share the spirit and values of the South.

Both critical and audience response is warm and enthusiastic. Within a few weeks of *Harmony*'s world premiere, ART Station will receive requests from theaters throughout the country to produce Thomas's play in their communities, confirming the power and reach of positive Olympic exposure.

The discovery of unfamiliar cultures is one of the most exciting opportunities afforded by the Olympic Arts Festival. The Royal Thai Ballet is giving its first performances in Atlanta, and tickets for this performance have been selling well from the moment they became available. Anticipation is high as the curtain rises on a gloriously colorful and beautifully performed evening. The program includes major segments from the Ramayana legend, a historic epic that is an essential aspect of many Asian cultures. Exquisitely costumed and featuring an instrumental ensemble that performs on a variety of instruments, most of which sound unfamiliar to western ears, the Royal Thai Ballet is a company of sophistication and extraordinary grace. Attending the Royal Thai Ballet presentation is like experiencing a new cuisine, new flavors to which one's palate must adjust and grow accustomed. At the conclusion of the performance, spirits are high on both sides of the footlights: the company feels warmly welcomed, and the audience is enriched by this encounter, which has brought one of the world's leading dance companies to its first Olympic audience.

for ART Station, the Cultural Olympiad, and the New South. Performed without intermission, the fast-paced play focuses on a variety of humorous collision points between Dr. Ferrol Sams and Helen, his wife of more than 40 years, that individually reveal and collectively

TIMOTHY R HIX • JENI G HIXON • KIMBERLY L HIXON • REBECCA A. HIXON • ROBERT S HIXON • TRACY L HIXON • VIVIAN L HIXON • TARRA T HIXSON • JULIE A HIXSON-WALLACE • THERESA M HIZER • STINE HJERTVIK • LOUIS S HLAD • MICHELLE A HLAVACEK • THOMAS E HLAVACEK • DOREDA L HLLDEBRAND • CAROLINE KAYEE HO • JOSEPH C HO • LANCE S HO • RAY HO • SHIRLEY L HO • THERESA D HO • TRINH C HO • TRUNG V HO • ZHANYING STACY HO • CHARLES P HOAG • TED P HOAGLAND • ALLYN B HOAK • PAMELA S HOBACK • MARY HOBBIE • JANET B HOBBINS • CAROLINE E HOBBS • DELRIE L HOBBS •

The Royal Thai Ballet gives a graceful and sophisticated performance of *Khon* to an audience at the Atlanta Civic Center.

DIANE E HOBBS • GENE O HOBBS • JOSEPH HOBBS • KIMBERLY A HOBBS • NANCY D HOBBS • THOMAS W HOBBS • CHRISTOPHER D HOBBS PM • REDRICK T HOBBY • CHARLES F HOBGOOD • W. SANDS HOBGOOD • DOLORES A HOBRLE • JOHN W HOBRLE • BOYD A HOBSON • CHANCE W HOBSON • KARRI L HOBSON • MICHAEL HOBSON • ELIZABETH A HOCEVAR • DAVID B HOCH • JOHN D HOCH • JAMES K HOCHGERTLE • JODI HOCHSCHILD • ALEXANDER I HOCK • DEBORAH O HOCK • HOLLY HOCK • FOSTER A HOCKETT • ROBERT S HOCKETT • LYNNELLE D HOCKRIDGE • NEIL E HOCKSTEIN • JOHN D HOCUTT

181

DAY ELEVEN
30 JULY 1996

Andrew Young moves the audience with his remarks at the memorial service in Centennial Olympic Park.

AFTER HAVING BEEN closed for three days for an investigation of the early-morning bomb blast that struck on 27 July, Centennial Olympic Park reopens today at 8:00 a.m. Thousands of people are on hand, waiting from before dawn for the gates to open in an unprecedented display of support for the athletes, one another, and the Olympic Spirit. The turnout this morning demonstrates what so many expressed in the bomb's aftermath— that an act of cowardly terrorism will not be allowed to destroy the tremendously positive spirit of these Games.

By the time the gates open, the crowd has swollen to more than 20,000 people, and thousands more are on their way. A memorial for the victims of the blast is scheduled for 10:00 a.m., by which time the park holds nearly 100,000 people. Standing shoulder to shoulder under the bright summer sun, the huge crowd falls silent as jazz musician Wynton Marsalis steps to the center of the vast AT&T stage, lifts his trumpet, and plays an unaccompanied version of a tune from his native New Orleans,

TODAY'S CALENDAR

Competition

Aquatics—diving, synchronized swimming
Archery
Badminton
Baseball
Basketball
Boxing
Canoe/kayak—sprint
Cycling—mountain bike racing
Football
Gymnastics—artistic
Handball
Hockey
Modern pentathlon
Softball
Table tennis
Tennis
Volleyball—indoor
Weightlifting
Wrestling
Yachting

Olympic Arts Festival

Alliance Theatre Company: *Blues for an Alabama Sky* and *The Last Night of Ballyhoo*
ART Station: *Harmony Ain't Easy*
Center for Puppetry Arts: *Bathtub Pirates*
Olympic Jazz Summit with Wynton Marsalis
Royal Thai Ballet: *Khon*
Southern Crossroads Festival

• SARAH HODA • SYED S HODA • GEOFFREY C HODAPP • NANCY N HODAPP • LYDA S HODDER • ACIA M HODGE • BETH E HODGE • BONNIE L HODGE • CHRISTINE M HODGE • JIM B HODGE • PAMALA J HODGE • ROXAN HODGE • VICKIE Y HODGE • FRAN G HODGES • JAMES J HODGES • JIM HODGES • KIM HODGES • MARK D HODGES • MELISSA H HODGES • MONLEESE HODGES • OLIVIA I HODGES • RENEE C HODGES • RICHARD P HODGES • ROBERT D HODGES • ROBERT J HODGES • SUE P HODGES • TIM HODGES • JEFFREY P HODGES ATC • JACK K HODGKIN JR • ELENA H HODGSON • JOAN S HODGSON • LINDSAY M HODGSON

183

top: Thousands of people attend the memorial service held in Centennial Olympic Park for the victims of the bombing.

bottom: The tragedy unites people in the aspiration toward world peace.

"Just a Closer Walk with Thee." ACOG president and CEO Billy Payne welcomes everyone and introduces the Reverend Andrew J. Young, ACOG's co-chair, Atlanta's former mayor, and the former US ambassador to the United Nations, whose remarks move the audience deeply.

"We are not here to wallow in tragedy, but to celebrate a triumph, a triumph of human spirit. So we say to those who suffered here, we assure your suffering was not in vain," Young said. This brief, eloquent moment of reflection in the midst of the Games has a powerful impact that will be felt at every Olympic venue throughout the end of the Games.

The atmosphere around the park and the attitude of the people within it are unspoiled by the tragedy that occurred a few days ago. If

Mountain bike racing makes its Olympic debut.

COMPETITION

anything, the sense of goodwill that character-ized this gathering place seems to reach a new level of value, intensity, and meaning as the crowd disperses after the memorial. It is this special quality that attracts the largest crowds ever from today and it will continue to do so until the close of the Games; everyone, it seems, wants to be a part of or touched by the park.

COMPETITION

Olympic events have evolved much over this first century of modern Olympic competition. Some events, such as athletics, gymnastics, and swimming, have always been part of the master programme of sports, while others have come and gone over time. In Atlanta, for example, several new sports have been added, such as beach volleyball, mountain bike racing, and softball, bringing the total number of sports in the Centennial Olympic programme to 26.

This morning opens with the modern pen-tathlon, an event that has been part of the Games for 84 years and which tests a combina-tion of five different skills—shooting, fencing, swimming, riding, and running. In past Games, the modern pentathlon has been held over several days, but Atlanta brings all its seg-ments together on this one day, making the grueling event even more challenging.

The competition requires transportation for the athletes, support staff, and media to sev-eral venues, starting with shooting and fencing at the Georgia World Congress Center, then moving to the Aquatic Center for swimming, and ending with the riding and running seg-ments at the Georgia International Horse Park. After 12 hours of competition, Alexandre Paryguin of Kazakhstan fends off 1992 bronze

DAVID M HOFELE • LLOYD M HOFER • D DEAN HOFF • MICHELLE M HOFF • LIZI HOFFBAUER • AGNES A HOFFMAN • ALLISON L HOFFMAN • CAROLE J HOFFMAN • CAROLYN E HOFFMAN • D GRANT HOFFMAN • DARYL L HOFFMAN • GEORGE A HOFFMAN • GEORGE ANN HOFFMAN • JENNIFER A HOFFMAN • JOANNE J HOFFMAN • JOHN A HOFFMAN • KATHRYN HOFFMAN • KENNETH A HOFFMAN • LAUREN S HOFFMAN • MARIAN S HOFFMAN • MAUDE E HOFFMAN • SHERIE N HOFFMAN • TERRY J HOFFMAN • TIMOTHY R HOFFMAN • VIRGINIA HOFFMAN • HENRY C HOFFMAN III • JOSEPH I HOFFMAN JR MD • ANN K HOFFMANN

medalist Eduard Zenovka of the Russian Federation by a score of 5,551–5,530 to take the gold medal. János Martinek of Hungary, who won the gold medal in 1988, takes the bronze.

Earlier on this day, the horse park hosted cyclists from around the globe for the first and only day of competition in mountain bike racing, a new Olympic discipline. Mountain bike racing has taken the cycling world by storm in the past decade. Combining the dangers of off-road terrain with power, balance, and endurance, this sport has attracted much attention in Atlanta. In the first-ever Olympic mountain bike race over a tough 48.7 km (30.3 mi) course, the Netherlands's Bart Brentjens, 1995 world champion, bolts to the lead and sets a blistering, unmatchable pace for the field of 43 riders. He never looks back, completing the course in a total elapsed time of 2:17:38, winning the gold medal, and setting an Olympic record. Crossing the finish line 0:02:36 later, Thomas Frischknecht of Switzerland wins the silver medal.

In early afternoon, the women compete in their first mountain bike racing event. Italy's Paola Pezzo overcomes painful leg cramps in her final lap of the 31.8 km (19.8 mi) course to take the gold, her country's fourth cycling gold medal of these Games. Alison Sydor of Canada, the reigning world champion, and Susan De-Mattei of the US take the silver and bronze medals, respectively.

top: France's team begins its technical routine in the synchronized swimming competition.

bottom: Men's doubles table tennis winners—People's Republic of China's Lin Lu and Tao Wang (silver), People's Republic of China's Linghui Kong and Guoliang Liu (gold), and Korea's Chul-Seung Lee and Nam-Kyu Yoo (bronze)—wave from the victory stand.

• ROSALIND E HOFFMANN • RUSSELL E HOFFMANN • HENRY L HOFFMANN JR • DENISE A HOFMANN • JACK W HOFMANN • APRIL M HOGAN • BRIAN N HOGAN • DEBORAH L HOGAN • KATHLEEN A HOGAN • KRYSTLE M HOGAN • MICHAEL G HOGAN • VICKEY W HOGAN • JAMES D HOGAN JR • CHAD M HOGE • GEORGE A HOGE • JOHN HOGE • JOYCE P HOGE • KATHRYN L HOGE • GRANT W HOGG • BRENDA E HOGGARD • LORI K HOGLE • JOSEPH T HOGLEN • BOYD P HOGLUND • EDWARD W HOGSHEAD • THOMAS F HOGSHEAD • KAREN K HOGUE • LOUIS J HOHMAN PT • MELANIE B HOIT • WESLEY A HOKE •

On the first day of synchronized swimming competition, US fans are out in force to cheer for their home team, which performs to near perfection. But stellar performances are also delivered by the Canadian, Japanese, and Mexican teams, all of which receive enthusiastic cheers from the crowd. Mexico's team, performing to lively mariachi music, gets the spectators roaring in approval, then protesting loudly when scores are lower than they anticipated. At the close of the day, the US team holds a commanding lead over second-place Canada, thanks to a routine that earns three perfect 10s.

Back at the Georgia World Congress Center, the teams from the People's Republic of China continue their successful run on the tables in the men's table tennis competition, but exactly who contributes to this success is a bit surprising. Coming into today's competition, the 1992 Olympic gold-medal–winning doubles team of Tao Wang and Lin Lu has lost only one table tennis match in five years. But today, the duo is defeated in the gold-medal match by fellow teammates Linghui Kong and Guoliang Liu. This victory comes on the heels of a gold-medal victory by Yaping Deng and Hong Qiao of the People's Republic of China in the women's doubles yesterday.

On the wrestling mats, there is no question that the winner of the important second-round match in the 82 kg (180.5 lb) freestyle class will bear the name of Jabrailov. The only question is whether Elmadi Jabrailov of Kazakhstan or his older brother and coach, Lucman Jabrailov of the Republic of Moldova, will be triumphant. Both were originally from Chechnya and both are former world champions in their weight class. When the final buzzer sounds, Elmadi has defeated Lucman by a 10–8

score. After the contest, the brothers giggle as Elmadi explains, "[Lucman] usually wins because he's my coach. Before the match we talked about it and already knew what the outcome would be. Except it turned out different this time. Afterward we joke about it."

On the final day of weightlifting competition, a tournament in which 15 world records will be set, the super heavyweights are in charge and continue breaking world records in an amazing display of raw power. Germany's Ronny Weller is an athlete who has had to

top: Yevhen Braslavets and Ihor Matviyenko of Ukraine race their double-handed dinghy in the 470 class yachting competition.

bottom: Kazakhstan's Elmadi Jabrailov defeats the US's Les Gutches to advance and compete against his brother, Lucman, in the 82 kg class in freestyle wrestling.

CHRISTOPHER E HOLABIRD • CAMILLA C HOLADAY • CHARLES E HOLAWAY • DOROTHY M HOLAWAY • CONNIE W HOLBERT • CAMILLE I HOLBROOK • CHARLES E HOLBROOK • DANIEL L HOLBROOK • SALLY C HOLBROOK • STEPHEN E HOLBROOK • TODD C HOLBROOK • VIRGINIA A HOLBROOK • JOSEPH A HOLBROOKS • BRIAN G HOLCOMB • CAROLE A HOLCOMB • GEORGE HOLCOMB • KENT HOLCOMB • LISHA D HOLCOMB • MARK S HOLCOMB • MICHAEL V HOLCOMB • REBECCA L HOLCOMB • SHEILA L HOLCOMB • THOMAS T HOLCOMB • WILLIAM R HOLCOMB • ZACHARY T HOLCOMB • DIANE R HOLCOMBE •

conquer not only his competitors, but also the consequences of a tragic auto accident in 1989 that claimed the life of his girlfriend and left him in a coma for five days with a fractured skull and other injuries. Battling back to competitive shape only 15 months after the accident, Weller won the 1992 gold medal in the 110 kg (242.5 lb) division. Today, Weller sets a world record in the clean and jerk by lifting 225 kg (496 lb), but the mark hardly has time to dry in the record book before the Russian Federation's super heavyweight Andrey

left: Magalys Carvajal of Cuba goes for a shot against Tammy Liley of the US to help Cuba advance to the semifinals in women's indoor volleyball.

right: The US women's softball team's pitcher, Lisa Fernandez, celebrates her team's victory over the People's Republic of China in the gold-medal game.

Chemerkin bests Weller's achievement by an incredible 5 kg (11 lb) to set a new clean and jerk world record and capture the gold. Chemerkin also sets a world record for his total lift weight of 457.5 kg (1,008.6 lb). Chemerkin celebrates by playfully lifting his team coach,

to the delight of the more than 7,000 spectators in attendance.

In the evening hours, a capacity crowd of 8,750 fans at the softball diamond in Columbus, Georgia, chants, "USA! USA! USA!" to spark the women of the US team to a 3–1 victory over a talented team from the People's Republic of China, and its first-ever gold medal in Olympic softball. The gold is the crowning achievement for a team that entered the tournament with a record of 110–1 against international competition since 1986.

This game, however, does brew some controversy. Batting in the third inning, 34-year-old Dorothy (Dot) Richardson, the US team

JAMES H HOLCOMBE • MICHAEL HOLCOMBE • MOLLY M HOLCOMBE • REBECCA L HOLCOMBE • RICK HOLCOMBE • VICKI Y HOLCOMBE • VICTORIA M HOLCOMBE • WILLIAM F HOLCOMBE • JAMES G HOLDEN • JENELL D HOLDEN • JENNIFER L HOLDEN • KATHLEEN A HOLDEN • MERTON F HOLDEN • TARA HOLDEN • TERRESA T HOLDEN • JOHN HOLDEN JR • DONNA T HOLDER • ESTHER J HOLDER • KEVIN HOLDER • LOUISE I HOLDER • MALEIKA C HOLDER • MICHELLE S HOLDER • ROSEMARY CASSIDY HOLDER • SUSAN E HOLDER • RICHARD M HOLDREN • SHELLY D HOLDREN • MAUREEN E HOLEN • LYNN M HOLEVINSKI

captain and shortstop, hits a disputed, two-run home run down the right field line to put her team ahead for good. The team from the People's Republic of China protests vigorously that the ball passed outside the right-field foul pole, but the hit and the score stand. Lisa Fernandez, whose unrivaled combination of power and control make her an awesome, almost unstoppable pitcher, protects the American lead and gold medal victory for the remainder of the game. After the victory ceremony, Richardson, who took a year off from her job as an or-

thopedic surgeon in Los Angeles County so she could compete, says, "My three big Olympic dreams happened. The first was to hit a home run in my first Olympic at bat—well, it came on my fourth. The second was to hit a home run in the gold medal game. The third was to get on the podium to get the gold medal."

Basketball continues to draw capacity crowds. With the medal rounds just ahead, interest intensifies. In a stunning upset in the quarterfinal rounds, Australia's men's basketball team rallies in the closing minute to defeat

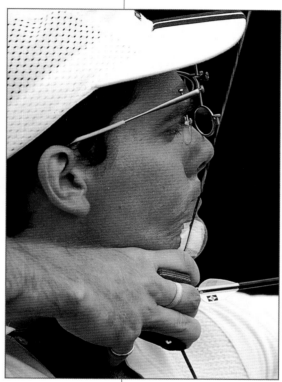

left: Toni Kukoc of Croatia protects the ball before Australia wins in the closing minute of a men's basketball semifinal game.

right: Simon Fairweather of Australia takes careful aim during a preliminary round of the men's individual archery competition.

Croatia, the defending 1992 silver medal team, 73–71. This earns them the right to play in the semifinals, where they will meet the US team, which defeated Brazil, 98–75, in its quarterfinal match. Australia's four-time Olympian, Andrew Gaze, comments that Australia's win is "the biggest win in Australian basketball history." In a very different kind of victory, Yugoslavia scores more than twice the points of the People's Republic of China, 128–61, and moves on to face Lithuania, which defeats Greece, 99–66, in the other semifinal game.

leads all countries with 9 boxers, while the US advances 7. Seven of 8 boxers from Germany and 7 of 9 from the Russian Federation are still competing for an opportunity to show their best in the ring. Kazakhstan has 5 boxers still competing; Algeria and Thailand each have 4; Korea has 2 boxers; Canada sends 3 boxers; Spain, Croatia, and Turkey each have a single boxer in the mix. All will compete in today's rounds.

In a rematch at the University of Georgia's Sanford Stadium in Athens, before a capacity

left: **France's Rachid Bouaita ducks a punch delivered by Cuba's Arnaldo Mesa during their quarterfinal match in the bantamweight class of boxing.**

right: **The Russian Federation's Vera Ilyina gives a star performance to lead in the women's 3 m springboard diving preliminary competition.**

Boxers from 40 delegations have treated fans at Georgia Tech's Alexander Memorial Coliseum to an incredible series of matches over the past several days. As of today, Cuba

LEE M HOLLAND • MARY L HOLLAND • MAURICE G HOLLAND • MONIQUE HOLLAND • PAMELA A HOLLAND • ROBERT E HOLLAND • RUBY N HOLLAND • SANDRA E HOLLAND • SHARON HOLLAND • SUSAN C HOLLAND • VIRGINIA A HOLLAND • WESLEY W HOLLAND • WILLIAM W HOLLAND • VIRGINIA HOLLAND-DAVIS • GAYLE C HOLLAND MOSS • BOB HOLLANDER • RICHARD A HOLLANDER • JAMES D HOLLANDSWORTH • ANNA S HOLLARAN • PAULA D HOLLCROFT • BRAD A HOLLENBACH • MARY D HOLLENBACK • BONNIE L HOLLER • ANN L HOLLEY • DANA L HOLLEY • DIANE S HOLLEY • FRANCIS M HOLLEY

crowd of 78,212 that pushes football attendance over the 1 million mark, Argentina
edges Portugal 2–0. Though they outshoot the
Portuguese 14–2 in the first half, Argentina is
unable to score until 10 minutes into the second half, when Hernán Jorge Crespo heads in
a cross by Claudio Javier López. Crespo adds
another goal in the 62nd minute of the game
to seal the win. Reaching the semifinal game
with Argentina is still a victory for the Portuguese, who have been absent from Olympic
football competition since 1928.

With its win, Argentina earns a spot in the
finals against Nigeria, which records a stunning upset of tournament favorite Brazil in the
other semifinal contest. Behind 3–1 with less
than 15 minutes left in regulation play, Nigeria
scores two goals to tie and another goal in
overtime to achieve a stunning 4–3 upset.

top: **Jose Antonio Chamot of
Argentina assists his team
in triumphing over the
Portugese team to advance
to the men's football finals.**

bottom: **Mikko Kolehmainen
of Finland races to
qualify for the semifinals
in the men's single
kayak competition.**

• HARRIETT N HOLLEY • RONALD L HOLLEY • VIVENE L M HOLLEY • COOK LOYCE HOLLIDAY • MARY L HOLLIDAY-FRAZIER • DAVID G HOLLIFIELD • CARLA M HOLLINGS • DORIS JOYCE HOLLINGSWORTH •
JONATHAN D HOLLINGSWORTH • KELLEY D HOLLINGSWORTH • LIBBY M E HOLLINGSWORTH • LYN G HOLLINGSWORTH • M. R. HOLLINGSWORTH • MARTIN A HOLLINGSWORTH • STEPHANIE L
HOLLINGSWORTH • BRIAN G HOLLINS • EUGENE R HOLLINS • MICHELLE C HOLLINS • ADRIENNE L HOLLIS • ALTHEA M HOLLIS • CASSANDRA D HOLLIS • CHRISTOPHER J HOLLIS • EMILY H HOLLIS •

OLYMPIC VILLAGE AND OLYMPIC ARTS FESTIVAL

The Olympic Village's dance club rocks tonight as a huge number of athletes gather for what is becoming one of the athletes' most popular social activities, the T-shirt swap. Held for the first time at the Lillehammer Winter Games of 1994, event-sponsor Champion was so pleased with the bonds of friendship generated by this special exchange between athletes that they decided to try it in Atlanta. Each athlete re-

T-shirt swapping and signing is a favorite activity among athletes at the Olympic Village.

ceives three free T-shirts from Champion to keep or trade, and most also bring their own T-shirts, which they can also swap with fellow athletes. The dance floor buzzes with activity as Olympians trade T-shirts and stories, dance, laugh, and autograph one another's shirts until the club finally closes.

Also tonight, Wynton Marsalis, a performer of rare ability and uncommon generosity of spirit and the most acclaimed and popular jazz musician of his generation, is performing at Atlanta Symphony Hall. He is an artist who is equally at home in the worlds of both jazz and classical music. Although he is now only in his mid-30s, his career took off so early and he has garnered such extraordinary success that it seems as if he should be twice his age. As a performer, Marsalis approaches everything he does with purpose, dedication, a commitment to challenging the boundaries of what has been done before, and extraordinary dignity. He is not only an unmatched musician, but is also the leader of an entire generation of musicians.

Jazz has declined in popularity in the past two decades in its native country while flourishing in Europe, Asia, and other parts of the world. While it is the most homegrown of American musical genres, jazz is not always the most accessible of music's many languages. At its core, jazz relies on improvisation. This intuitive but semistructured interaction, which is at the very heart and soul of great jazz, is what Wynton Marsalis has so magnificently absorbed and communicates to audiences.

Marsalis attracts musicians of like spirit and mind to perform and create with him on every new project he tackles. For the Olympic Arts Festival, he has created a new, 10-movement suite that explores the idiom of the Big Band and the Afro-Cuban roots and contemporary expressions of jazz. This is not what most of his fans have anticipated. He has even elected to include dancers in his program, making this trio of jazz concerts most unusual.

The musicians of the ensemble are true Olympians, able to leap over the highest musical hurdles with ease, and play faster, stronger, and higher than one could possibly imagine. Marsalis is also at his best, leading the ensemble through a magnificent tour de force that

FRAZIER HOLLIS • RHONDA L HOLLIS • THOMAS G HOLLIS • COUTIES D HOLLIS JR • GENE E HOLLIS JR • DEBRA L HOLLISTER • MARK W HOLLMANN MD • JEFFREY P HOLLOBAUGH • BETTY HOLLOMAN • KATHRYN Y HOLLOMAN • HORACE C HOLLOMAN JR • WILLIAM E HOLLOMAN JR • JOHN G HOLLORAN • ANNETTE Y HOLLOWAY • ARNOLD R HOLLOWAY • DOROTHY G HOLLOWAY • ESTHER F HOLLOWAY • GLORIA I HOLLOWAY • JOE L HOLLOWAY • JOSEPH C HOLLOWAY • LAYNNE L HOLLOWAY • LEE L HOLLOWAY • LENDA P HOLLOWAY • LOIS A HOLLOWAY • RONNIE HOLLOWAY • SUNNY HOLLOWAY •

electrifies the audiences privileged to hear and see this incredible musical event. This is jazz composition and performance at its finest—extraordinary individual musicianship that, while retaining its spontaneity, is buoyant, focused, free-spirited, and powerfully compact. The evening's pure, penetrating musical energy builds from the first notes through the end of the concert, bringing the audience to its feet to cheer a truly gold-medal performance.

top: Wynton Marsalis rehearses the extraordinary 10-movement jazz suite that will be performed tonight.

bottom: These puppets are the stars of today's performance of *Bathtub Pirates* at the Center for Puppetry Arts.

Atlanta 1996.

SYBIL Y HOLLOWAY • TIMOTHY N HOLLOWAY • TODD O HOLLOWAY • FRANCINE L HOLLOWELL • JOHN F HOLLOWELL • JANE M HOLLSTEGGE • GRACE R HOLLY • DAVID S HOLLYDAY • CAROL A. HOLM • DAVID HOLMAN • DAWN M HOLMAN • LAURA G HOLMAN • LORRA J HOLMAN • PAMELA C HOLMAN • ROBERT HOLMAN • SHERMAN P HOLMAN • REBECCA C HOLMBERG • ROBERT M HOLME • ANDREW E HOLMES • BERNICE HOLMES • BEVERLY M HOLMES • BRIAN HOLMES • DEBORAH M HOLMES • DIANE D HOLMES • EDWARD JR A HOLMES • GLEN HOLMES • JACQUELINE J HOLMES • JAMES HOLMES • JUDY R HOLMES

193

DAY TWELVE
31 JULY 1996

INJURIES ON THE field of play have taken their toll throughout the Games so far, and today is no exception. Five-time Olympian, world-record holder, and 1988 Olympic champion pole vaulter Sergey Bubka of Ukraine, suffering from an Achilles tendon injury, is forced to withdraw before attempting a single vault. He joins Sonia O'Sullivan of Ireland and Jackie Joyner-Kersee of the US as gold medal favorites who are held back by injury or illness. Distance runner O'Sullivan drops out of the 5,000 m final because of a stomach virus; weakened by the virus and suffering from dehydration, she fails to qualify in the 1,500 m. Joyner-Kersee, who was forced to drop out of the heptathlon competition because of an aggravated hamstring, battles pain to compete in the women's long jump, capturing a bronze medal, the sixth medal of her career.

The task of providing medical assistance to these athletes and their more than 10,000 fellow competitors is the responsibility of an extraordinary team of nearly 1,000 athletic trainers, as well as numerous physicians, medical technicians, and paramedics. The polyclinic at Olympic Village operates 24 hours a day and is staffed by a team of 142 doctors and 35 nurses.

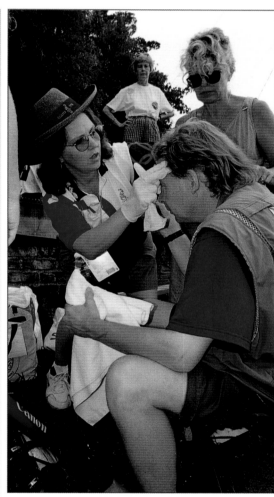

Medical staff member provides assistance to an injured photographer.

TODAY'S CALENDAR

Competition

Aquatics—diving
Archery
Athletics
Badminton
Basketball
Boxing
Canoe/kayak—sprint
Cycling—road
Equestrian
Football
Handball
Hockey
Table tennis
Tennis
Volleyball—indoor
Wrestling
Yachting

Olympic Arts Festival

Alliance Theatre Company: *Blues for an Alabama Sky* and *The Last Night of Ballyhoo*
ART Station: *Harmony Ain't Easy*
Australian Youth Orchestra and Atlanta Symphony Youth Orchestra
Center for Puppetry Arts: *Bathtub Pirates*
Jomandi Productions: *Hip 2: Birth of the Boom*
Southern Crossroads Festival

• LINDA M HOLMES • MARILYN E HOLMES • MARY H HOLMES • MELVIN C HOLMES • MICHAEL E HOLMES • MICHAEL F HOLMES • PAT L HOLMES • RANDY HOLMES • RICHARD L HOLMES • SHARRON D HOLMES • SHARYL HOLMES • SHEILA L HOLMES • SHIRLEY M HOLMES • TAURUS L HOLMES • TECHUMSHEA HOLMES • TERESSA C HOLMES • V. GAIL HOLMES • VARNER B HOLMES • VICKI M HOLMES • WILLIAM D HOLMES • WINSTON A HOLMES • ZAKIYA HOLMES • GENE HOLMES JR. • MARGARET HOLMES KING • JOHN N HOLMGREEN • JEFFREY C HOLMSTROM EMT • DIANE HOLOWESKO • PAUL J HOLRITZ • JACK M HOLSTAD

Located at Georgia Tech's Student Health Center, the clinic houses medical records for all Games participants and offers a full range of medical services, including dentistry, gynecology, internal medicine, ophthalmology, orthopedics, and radiology, as well as a pharmacy. In addition, sports medicine stations and ambulances are located near the field of play at each venue to render any aid that may be needed.

The final operating program includes a network of hospitals that are prepared to efficiently and effectively respond to any kind of or magnitude of medical emergency that might occur. Specialists in virtually every medical area are included among the small army of physicians who have volunteered their time for the Games—from general practitioners to allergists; dentists; dermatologists; ear, nose, and throat specialists; infectious disease specialists; ophthalmologists; and surgeons.

Among the specialized medical support programs provided by ACOG is the Olympic sensory performance center, a facility in the Olympic Village where athletes can have their hearing and sight reflexes tested. The audio-response tests enable athletes to see their eardrums on a computer screen. Audiologists then measure hearing ability and reaction time to recognizable stimuli, such as a starter's gun. Using each hand and foot, athletes react to noises by punching buttons, and their reaction time is recorded from the release of the button to the next time it is touched.

Next door, optometrists perform a far more revealing test on vision performance than the static vision test which is most often administered. "An athlete's vision is typically more stable at a higher level," says Dr. Michael Pier, chief director of the vision center. "If I test 100 people like me, maybe 5 will have exceptional visual abilities. But if I test 100 athletes, 85 will be exceptional."

Uniting this summer in a spirit of peace to help the millions of children caught in the crossfire of war, Olympians from around the world have joined the Olympic Aid Team for Children to advocate Olympic Aid–Atlanta, a cooperative effort among ACOG, the United Nations Children's Fund (UNICEF), and the US

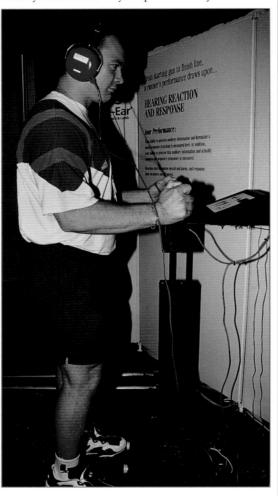

Weightlifter Jaroslav Jokel of Slovakia tests his hearing reaction and response in the Olympic Village.

• PENNY HOLSTAD • F LEE HOLSTON • ISABELLE HOLSTON • ANNA A HOLT • BETTY H HOLT • CARL P HOLT • CYNTHIA A HOLT • CYNTHIA K HOLT • DAVID E HOLT • DAVID R HOLT • DIANE K HOLT • DONNA B HOLT • FAITH C HOLT • GEORGE L HOLT • GEORGE M HOLT • GERALDINE B HOLT • HANNAH J HOLT • JAMES P HOLT • KAYE G HOLT • KELLY MARIE HOLT • MICHAEL A HOLT • PEGGY A HOLT • SPENCER M HOLT • TIMOTHY HOLT • VIRGINIA B HOLT • JOYCE M HOLTE ATC • THOMAS J HOLTERHOFF • ROBERT B HOLTON • JANET F HOLTON • PATRICK B HOLTON • RAY O HOLTON • THOMAS W HOLTON ATC • MAGGIE HOLTZBERG •

Committee for UNICEF. "As athletes, we can use our positions as role models as a platform to change children's lives," says Johann Olav Koss, a five-time Olympic medal-winner in speed skating and the spokesperson for the program. "All of us together can use the spirit of the Olympic Games to bring hope to or realize a dream for a child." Olympic Aid–Atlanta is bringing much-needed medicine, immunizations, counseling, and educational programs to nearly 18 million children in war-torn regions of the world.

left: Centennial Olympic Games Hanes T-shirt auctions are held each day to raise funds for Olympic Aid–Atlanta.

right: Five-time Olympic medal-winner in speed skating and Olympic–Aid Atlanta spokesperson Johann Olav Koss encourages athletes to use their positions as role models to benefit children.

ADRIAN W HOLTZMAN • CHAD D HOLVENSTOT • NANCY L HOLVENSTOT • KATHRYN HOLWILL • DONALD A HOLYFIELD • DONNA M HOLYFIELD • MARIKA S HOLZENDORF • RAYMOND M HOM • JENNIFER A HOMA • JOHN M HOMA • DON R HOMBROEK • GERALD HOMICK • URS HONAUER • LAWRENCE R HONE • AMANDA E HONEYCUTT • DEAN L HONEYCUTT • DEBORAH C HONEYCUTT • JANET G HONEYCUTT • LEAH A HONEYCUTT • JI SEON HONG • KELLY A HONG • MIN OAK HONG • SEUNG-YOUN HONG • SHUGUANG HONG • SUH YOUNG HONG • SUZI HONG • RUTH J HONIG • CYNTHIA S HONSSINGER • JOYCE CHOOBLER

COMPETITION

While injuries have halted some of the Games' most remarkable athletes, new heroes blossom each day in the competitions. In the fastest men's 800 m race in history, with four runners finishing in under 1:43, Vebjørn Rodal becomes only the second athlete from Norway to win a gold medal in athletics, the previous win having occurred some 40 years ago. Rodal's Olympic-record time of 1:42.58 is all the more remarkable given his unusual training regimen.

The injury bug finds kayaker Heidi Lehrer, who paddles for her island nation of Antigua and Barbuda. Lehrer will have to paddle in pain today in her 500 m singles kayak race because of injuries suffered in an accident. Although she finishes eighth in her heat, a full minute slower than the rest of the field, she still qualifies for the repechage.

Trailing by 13 points going into the finals of the women's 3 m springboard competition, the People's Republic of China's diving phenomenon, Mingxia Fu, overtakes Irina Lashko of the

left: **Nico Motchebon of Germany congratulates Vebjørn Rodal of Norway, who has just won the 800 m final.**

right: **Ruiping Ren of the People's Republic of China lands after a triple jump.**

Unlike most of his competitors, he often trains indoors because of the long Norwegian winters, and runs back and forth in an underground tunnel that is only 1,148 ft (350 m) long. In another historic moment, Hezekiel Sepeng becomes the first black South African to win an Olympic medal, capturing the silver.

In athletics competition, the women's first triple jump gold medal is awarded to Inessa Kravets of Ukraine on a leap of 15.3 m (50.2 ft), achieved on her penultimate attempt. Though short of the world record set at the 1995 World Championships, Kravets's performance is ahead of the rest of the field by a quarter of an inch.

Russian Federation to capture her second gold medal of the Games. Several days ago, she outdistanced her nearest competitor by more than 40 points—a huge margin in an Olympic diving competition—to win the gold medal in 10 m platform diving, a competition she also won at the 1992 Games. In yet another first for Atlanta's Games, Fu becomes the first woman since 1960 to win both the platform and springboard events in a single Olympic Games. Just 17 years old, Fu has now won a total of three gold medals in a sport in which no one has ever won more than four.

Today, two boxing matches—featherweight and super heavyweight—capture a great deal of attention. In the featherweight bout, Floyd

• ANGELA B HOOD • CATHERINE W HOOD • CHERYL L HOOD • CHESTER L HOOD • DAVID HOOD • DAVID C HOOD • DEBRA A HOOD • GLORIA L HOOD • MARSHA M HOOD • MARTHA T HOOD • QUAJULAN HOOD • RENEE A HOOD • RITA L HOOD • SANDRA T HOOD • SHIRLEY HOOD • SUSAN E HOOD • WENDY M HOOD • CHARLES G HOOD JR • ROBERT H HOOD JR • RONNIE HOOF • JAMES J HOOGERWERF • FREDRICK J HOOGLAND • WILLEM N HOOGSTRATEN • CHARLES W HOOKER • KRISTEN F HOOKER SAT • CAROLYN D HOOKS • GAIL G HOOKS • LYNN HOOKS • MICHELLE A HOOKS • TIMOTHY N HOOKS • WILLIAM S HOOKS •

Mayweather becomes the first US Olympic boxer to defeat a Cuban boxer since 1976.

In the super heavyweight class of boxing, Alexis Rubalcaba of Cuba meets Tonga's Paea Wolfgram. Rubalcaba's punch packs an incredible amount of power; in an earlier bout, he hit his opponent hard enough to knock him into a backward somersault. In today's match, however, the 141 kg (311 lb) Wolfgram wins easily. After his win, Wolfgram says that the entire population (90,000) of his tiny island nation in the South Pacific fasted and prayed for him today, and that he received a good luck message by facsimile transmission from King Taufa Ahau to spur him to victory. Later in the Games, Wolfgram will capture the silver, Tonga's first-ever Olympic medal, while Rubalcaba will finish in seventh place.

After 221.9 km (137.9 mi) and five hours, the men's road cycling race comes down to less than a wheel-length, as Switzerland's Pascal Richard streaks past Denmark's Rolf Sorensen at the finish line to win the gold medal. Both men are credited with the same time—4:53:56—but Richard's last spurt of energy drove him across the finish line just ahead of Sorensen. "When I saw two laps to go, I did not think I could make it," Richard says. "My legs did not feel too good. Victory was the only thing that interested me." In a magnanimous gesture, Richard dedicates his race to his family and his father, an Olympic cyclist who died when he

Floyd Mayweather of the US (right) defeats Cuba's Lorenzo Aragon—the first time a US boxer has beaten a Cuban boxer since 1976.

was 18, and to Italy's Fabio Casartelli, the 1992 Olympic gold medalist who died in a cycling crash in last year's Tour de France.

At Stone Mountain Park, Korea's team continues its dominance in archery as Kyung-Wook Kim wins the women's individual title. Her victory marks the fourth consecutive gold medal achieved by Korea in the women's individual competition.

At the nearby tennis venue, fans witness a battle of friends as the US's Mary Joe Fernandez drops a straight set decision, 6–2, 7–6 (8–6), to

Lindsay Davenport, also of the US, in the women's singles semifinals. As the players meet and shake hands at center court, Davenport apologizes to her friend and teammate. Later, she expands, "On top of being the biggest match of my life so far—going for the gold—I was playing someone who I never really want to see lose."

Men's indoor volleyball has a new champion in 1996 as a fired-up team from Yugoslavia outlasts the defending 1992 Games champion, Brazil, in a grueling, five-set quarterfinal match.

top left: **Courtenay Becker-Dey sails her way to become the first US athlete to win a medal in yachting—a bronze in the Europe class of the yachting competition.**

bottom left: **Archers are right on target at the women's individual archery finals.**

• CHRIS HOPKINS • CHRIS HOPKINS • DANIEL D HOPKINS • DAVE HOPKINS • DEAN A HOPKINS • DOYAL C HOPKINS • ELLEN HOPKINS • FRANK E HOPKINS • HAL T HOPKINS • JACK E HOPKINS • JOHN C HOPKINS • KATHY HOPKINS • KELLY A HOPKINS • LUKE A HOPKIT'S • MARCIA A. HOPKINS • MARGARET E HOPKINS • MARILYN G HOPKINS • MARION D HOPKINS • MARSHALL I HOPKINS • MARY J HOPKINS • PATRICIA G HOPKINS • RACHEL L HOPKINS • RICHARD N HOPKINS • ROSILYNN Y HOPKINS • STEPHEN P HOPKINS • WHITNEY L HOPKINS • YVONNE H HOPKINS • NANCY L HOPKINSON • JEFFREY M HOPP •

Up by two games, 15–6, 15–5, in what appears to be headed for a three-set match victory for Yugoslavia, the Brazilian team battles back, winning the next two games 15–8, 16–14 to even the match and force a fifth and final game. The momentum seems to have shifted in Brazil's favor, but the team from Yugoslavia regains its composure and strikes back, scoring a 15–10 victory which sends the team to the semifinal round against Italy.

At the Georgia World Congress Center, the atmosphere in the table tennis venue is posi-

tively electric as the only two women to win gold medals in previous Olympic singles competitions—the People's Republic of China's Yaping Deng and Jing Chen of Chinese Taipei—meet in Atlanta's gold medal game. Deng, the 1992 Olympic champion, though only 4 ft 8 in (1.4 m), is an aggressive and powerful player. She takes command from the first point, taking the first two games from her former teammate and 1988 gold-medal winner, Chen, 21–14 and 21–17. Chen, who is attempting to win Chinese Taipei's first Olympic gold medal, is deter-

center spread: **Pascal Richard of Switzerland pushes past Rolf Sorensen of Denmark to win the gold medal in men's road cycling.**

right: **Arantxa Sanchez Vicario of Spain celebrates after winning the semifinal match in women's singles tennis.**

Yugoslavia's men's volleyball team advances to the semifinals, defeating the defending Olympic champion team from Brazil.

mined and fights back. Trailing 19–20 in the third and what could be the final game of the match, Chen rallies to win 22–20. Sparked by her win in the third game, she takes the fourth game 21-17 to even the match at two games apiece. The capacity crowd, filled with vocal supporters for both players, cheers almost non-stop throughout the match, rising in a

death weighs heavily on his mind as he goes to work in this critical contest for the gold medal. The wrestlers battle to a 1–1 tie, but in a controversial decision, the judge awards Angle the victory. Jadidi protests vehemently and files a formal protest, but Angle's victory prevails. After the victory ceremony, Angle weeps as he pays a heartfelt tribute to Schultz, saying, "Dave has had a big impact on my life. That's who I was thinking about when I was up there. Now I know what he felt like when he won in 1984. He was my idol."

crescendo as the fifth and decisive game gets under way. Calling on her extraordinary reserves of energy and concentration, Deng charges back, stunning Chen in the final game, 21–5, to win her second gold in the singles competition.

At the Georgia World Congress Center arena, the US freestyle wrestling team is inspired and saddened by the memory of a beloved teammate. Team members wear black bands on their singlets in memory of Dave Schultz, who was killed in January. Schultz, who won a gold medal at the 1984 Olympics, aspired to make this year's team after finishing fifth at the 1995 World Championships.

Emotions are especially intense in freestyler Kurt Angle of the US as he steps onto the mat to meet the Islamic Republic of Iran's Abbas Jadidi in the 100 kg (220 lb) weight class before more than 7,000 vocal fans. Schultz's tragic

left: **The People's Republic of China's Hong Qiao serves up to win a bronze medal in the women's singles table tennis competition.**

top right: **Stein Jorgensen and John Mooney of the US race to qualify for the semifinal of the men's 500 m kayak doubles competition.**

bottom right: **Kendall Cross of the US triumphs over the Democratic People's Republic of Korea's Yong Sam Ri on his way to winning a gold medal in the 57 kg (125.5 lb) class of freestyle wrestling.**

JOYCE H HORNOR • DENISE B HORNSBY • ANGELA F HORRISON-COLLIER • MAURICE L HORSEY IV • DEAN L HORSTMAN • THOMAS R HORSTMAN • JASON C HORTMAN • BRYAN A HORTON • DARRYL T HORTON • DAVID HORTON • DONALD J HORTON • ERICA L HORTON • EUSTACE M HORTON • FREDDIE HORTON • GAYLE D HORTON • JAMES A HORTON • JANICE W HORTON • KAREN M HORTON • KELLY H HORTON • KIMBERLY A HORTON • KONIQKION C. HORTON • LEO BETH A HORTON • LINDELLE HORTON • MELISSA G HORTON • PAUL W HORTON • PHILLIP G HORTON • ROGER D HORTON • SANDRA K HORTON •

OLYMPIC ARTS FESTIVAL

Cultivating dialogue and encouraging friendship between young role models—heroes and heroines through whom millions of others may better understand the importance of working together toward world peace—is an infrequently publicized but essential function of all Olympic Games, and Atlanta's Games are no exception. In this spirit of celebrating cross-cultural collaboration and understanding, the Cultural Olympiad has brought the Atlanta

falls silent. The Atlanta Symphony Youth Orchestra rewards the audiences with a stellar performance of Stravinsky's Suite from *The Firebird* (1919 version), a tour de force for any orchestra. The performers are at the top of their form, responding to conductor Jere Flint's direction with equal measures of power, grace, suppleness, and virtuosity. The finale literally shakes the rafters, and the enthralled audience responds with an explosive, sustained ovation.

Next, the Australian Youth Orchestra takes its place on stage under the direction of guest

The Atlanta Symphony Youth Orchestra, together with the Sydney-based Australian Youth Orchestra, stuns the audience with its passionate performance.

Symphony Youth Orchestra, an accomplished ensemble of Atlanta's brightest and best young artists, together with the Sydney-based Australian Youth Orchestra, an ensemble of internationally recognized artistry. Both orchestras have already performed individual concerts in the series which were well attended and received positive notice from the press.

Tonight's concert gives each ensemble an opportunity to perform alone before being brought together for the exciting finale. The many families and young people attending this matinee performance are particularly animated as they take their seats. As the Atlantans take the stage and begin to tune, the audience

conductor, Christopher Seaman. The average age of its musicians is a few years senior to that of its Atlanta colleagues, and the orchestra performs with maturity and polish. Their selection, The Moldau from Smetana's *Mâ Vlast*, demands flexibility, a wide dynamic range, and the conveyance of a real sense of drama. The orchestra delivers a magnificent performance which receives an enthusiastic ovation.

When the audience reenters the hall after intermission, a mega-orchestra of 230 enthusiastic, talented, and committed young musicians fills every corner of the stage, making a cacophony of sounds as it warms up to perform Tchaikovsky's Fifth Symphony. As conductor Christopher Seaman makes his way to the stage, the concertmasters of these two mar-

SHEILA D HORTON • STEPHEN J HORTON • SUZANNE B HORTON • THERESA E HORTON • THERESA M HORTON • WYOLENE HORTON • ANDRAS HORVATH • DEENA L HORWATH • DAVID M HORWATH JR • ELLA R HORWITZ • HELEN HORWITZ • LAURA E HOSBEIN • ANGELA Y HOSCH • ERIC HOSCH • SUZANNE M HOSCH • TIMOTHY M HOSEA • ALVIN D HOSFORD • MAGGI HOSH • ISAKO HOSHINO • LINDA L HOSIE • JILL L HOSKINS • CAROL R HOSKINSON • ELIZABETH B HOSKINSON • HARRIET HOSKYNS-ABRAHALL • ROGER L HOSLER • TREON HOSLEY • COURTNEY ELIZABETH HOST • PAMELA S HOST • JEFFREY D HOSTERMAN

velous young orchestras exchange instruments, as if to physically intertwine and visibly link their ensembles. From the mournful tones of the clarinet solo that opens the performance to the final, resounding chord at the end of the last movement, this young orchestra plays with tremendous power, depth, passion, and skill as a single, unified ensemble.

The capacity audience, overwhelmed by the stunning virtuosity and passionate performance they have just experienced, leaps to its feet in an ovation that matches what they

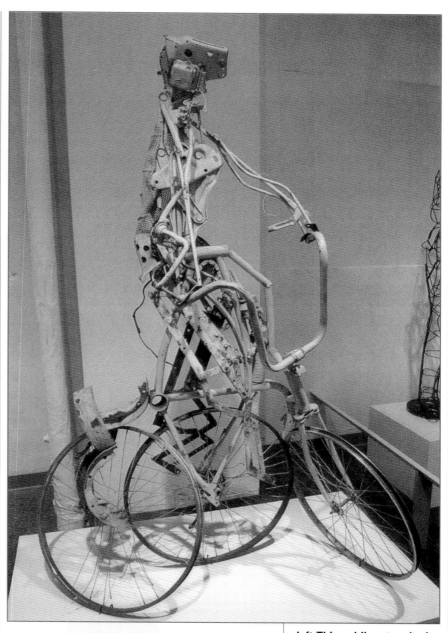

have just experienced. The musicians on stage hug one another and shake hands; a number are moved to tears. This memorable occasion symbolically passes the cultural torch from Atlanta to Sydney. It also demonstrates the power of cross-cultural artistic collaboration, a theme upon which Atlanta's cultural program was built.

left: This public artwork, the *Sacrifice of Isaac,* was installed as part of the Cultural Olympiad.

right: This wire sculpture is one of the many works of art made of found objects in the exhibition *Souls Grown Deep.*

Atlanta 1996.

• ALAN A HOSTETLER • TARA L HOSTETLER • ALBERT C HOSTETTER • KAREN A HOTZ • MARGOT K HOUCHINS • RICHARD A HOUDEN • CRAIG HOUGEN • AMANDA M HOUGH • AMITY M HOUGH • DAVID D HOUGH • JOHN W HOUGH • LESLIE S HOUGH • PALMER F HOUGH • SHARON A HOUGH • RAMONDA HOUGHTON • ROBERT M HOUGHTON • CAROL H HOULE • RAYMOND J HOULE • SHARON HOULE • WALTER D HOULE • BARBARA L HOULIHAN • KEVIN R HOULIHAN • ETHEL L HOUMAN • JESSICA BROOK HOUPPERT • JAMES F HOURIGAN JR • JONATHAN E HOUSCH • ABBEY J HOUSE • ANTWAN HOUSE • CATHERINE A HOUSE •

205

DAY THIRTEEN
1 AUGUST 1996

FOR THE PAST few days, spectators have gathered at Olympic Stadium to watch athletics events. Today, anticipation is high for the women's and men's 200 m events. Of the many facilities designed and built to accommodate sports competitions and athletes for the Games and to remain as a legacy to the city afterwards, none are as visible as Olympic Stadium. Although it appears to be permanent in its Games-time, 85,000-seat capacity configuration, Olympic Stadium will be converted after the Games into the new 49,714-seat home of the Atlanta Braves baseball team.

After the Games, a stadium built at Clark Atlanta University—one of two hockey stadia ACOG built at the Atlanta University Center Complex—will become the permanent home of the athletics track. This will be the first time that an Olympic track has been moved after the Games. "Our selection to receive the actual Olympic track on which numerous world records are expected to be broken is a unique opportunity for our institution to share in the lasting legacy of the 1996 Olympic Games," said Clark Atlanta University President Thomas W. Cole Jr.

Another important Olympic legacy, the magnificent Georgia Tech Aquatic Center, contains two pools, seating for 13,000 spectators, a

The Olympic Stadium track will be given to Clark Atlanta University after the Games as a permanent legacy to the school.

state-of-the-art, computer-controlled lighting system that reduces glare on the water, and a silver-paneled, photovoltaic roof that generates its own electricity. The main competition pool, which holds more than 1 million gal (3.8 million l) of water, has been equipped with a movable floor to adjust water depth, the first

CHARLOTTE S HOUSE • GERALDINE HOUSE • JENNIFER J HOUSE • JOHN C HOUSE • KIRK A HOUSE • KYLE HOUSE • LAURA HOUSE • LILLIAN D HOUSE • MARTHA HOUSE • PATRICIA A HOUSE • PAULA P HOUSE • ROY W HOUSE • SANDRA E. HOUSE • SUSAN M HOUSE • WILLIAM E HOUSE • MITCHEL P HOUSE III • ANITA B HOUSER • LUCY C HOUSER • ROBIN HOUSER • WILLIAM HOUSER • LYNNE HOUSLEY • THOMAS W HOUSLEY • TIPAWAN HOUSMANS • AKIL HOUSTON • COURTNEY P HOUSTON • CYNTHIA B HOUSTON • DAVID A HOUSTON • DEBRA M HOUSTON • ELNORA C HOUSTON • GAIL S HOUSTON • GARY L HOUSTON

207

Dormitories constructed to house athletes and officials will provide student housing for the Georgia Institute of Technology and Georgia State University after the Games.

of its kind in the US. The water circulation system is the most advanced and sophisticated available, providing the best water conditions for athletes and making this the fastest pool in the world. The diving pool, which holds 700,000 gal (2.65 million l) of water, is outfitted with three diving towers and a sparger system that blows air bubbles into the pool to soften landings during practice. Georgia Tech researchers have also installed an electronic sensor plate on the 10 m tower that records the force with which divers push off the platform. Data collected from the sensor plate is

being used in ergonomic studies. The third pool, for water polo, is located adjacent to the main facility. This configuration enabled ACOG to place all aquatic events at the same venue for the first time in Olympic history.

The eight new dormitories that have been built to help accommodate the approximately 16,000 Olympic athletes and officials on the campus of Georgia Tech will fulfill their long-term mission of providing additional student housing for Georgia Tech and nearby Georgia

• HERMIE HOUSTON • JACK E HOUSTON • JACQUELYN A HOUSTON • MARTIN W HOUSTON • MARY W HOUSTON • MICHAEL HOUSTON • PAUL N HOUSTON • PHILIP L HOUSTON • TERESA A HOUSTON • TYRONE P HOUSTON • CECILIA M HOUSTON-TORRENCE • KARL J HOUTCHENS • MICHAEL D HOUTZAGER • LAURA HOVATTER • ZANE B HOVATTER III • PAMELA D HOW • JAN F HOWAH • ALECHIA A HOWARD • ALISA K HOWARD • AMY M HOWARD • BARRY L HOWARD • BETTY P HOWARD • BILLY HOWARD • BRENT R HOWARD • CHARLES L HOWARD • COLLEEN C HOWARD • DEIRDRA L HOWARD • DONALD W HOWARD

State University immediately after the Games. ACOG's plan has balanced Olympic needs with those of community partners, thus producing a meaningful legacy of outstanding facilities that support Olympic requirements and survive to serve community needs and sports interests.

Along with these impressive permanent facilities, an incredible range of new specialized facilities has been created for the Games. In all, more than 2.5 million sq ft (232,500 sq m) of new construction, both permanent and temporary, has been built and equipped to support

Olympic Stadium. In all, more than 35 mi (56 km) of temporary fencing is installed around and within competition and noncompetition venues and sites. Power systems to support broadcasting, timing and scoring, communications, lighting, and critical backup systems are provided by 25 MW of portable generator power—enough to light a small city. Additionally, the heat and humidity of Atlanta summers also requires the installation and full-time application of 1,500 tons (1,361 t) of portable air-conditioning systems.

top and bottom: **Numerous temporary structures were constructed and equipped to provide support for Atlanta's Games.**

Atlanta's Games. A considerable portion of this space was built to house operations and support staff. For example, more than 520 office and specialty trailers—comprising enough space to house a town of 2,000 people—has been provided by ACOG's construction team. Venues and sites require more than 175,000 temporary seats, 40,000 of which are at

• DONNA C HOWARD • DONNA M HOWARD • DONNIE R HOWARD • FREDERICK R HOWARD • GEORGIA L HOWARD • HARRIET B HOWARD • JAMES A HOWARD • JASON N HOWARD • JEAN F HOWARD • JEANETTE H HOWARD • JEANETTE S HOWARD • JERRY HOWARD • JOAN S HOWARD • JOHN H HOWARD • JOHN W HOWARD • JOHN W HOWARD • JOHN W HOWARD • KEVIN L HOWARD • KEVIN V HOWARD • KRISTIN K HOWARD • LEONARD HOWARD • LINDA H HOWARD • LINDA M HOWARD • M SCOTT HOWARD • MARIAN A HOWARD • MARILYN C HOWARD • MARJORIE F HOWARD • MARK HOWARD • MARVIN L HOWARD • MARY LEE HOWARD

COMPETITION

Whether the motivation for his achievement was inspired by the the frenzied crowd of 83,000, the quality of the Olympic Stadium track, or his desire to become the first man in history to win the vastly different 200 m and 400 m events, Michael Johnson of the US joins the pantheon of Olympic heroes this evening as he sweeps past the field in the 200 m final to win the gold. He achieves his coveted second gold-medal victory, setting a world record

son set in June on this track during the US Olympic trials. What makes his new mark even more incredible is that he stumbled out of the blocks and felt a twinge in his right hamstring five meters before reaching the finish line. The victory is especially sweet because only four years ago at the Barcelona Games, Johnson failed to make it out of the 200 m semifinals due to illness.

For all the significance of Johnson's accomplishments, he is not the only Olympian to complete a 200/400 double on this day.

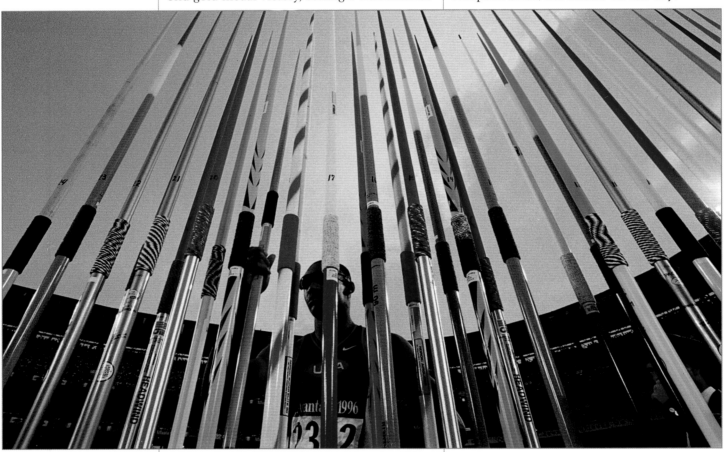

Chris Huffins of the US selects the javelin he will use in the decathlon competition.

of 19.32 seconds in the process. "The world record is a bonus," Johnson says. "The most important thing was making history. A lot of people held a world record. I held one before I came here. But nobody else can say they made history, the first to win the 200 and 400." The previous world record, 19.66, is a mark John-

France's Marie-Jose Perec matches Johnson by winning the women's 200 m to score dual gold medal victories in the 200 m and 400 m, the second time this double victory has been achieved in women's Olympic competition. The silver medal is won by Merlene Ottey of Jamaica, an extraordinary athlete who is the first runner in history to reach the finals in the

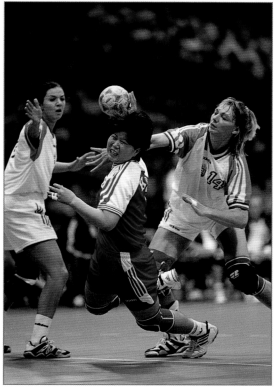

same event at five Olympic Games. Also the winner of the silver in the women's 100 m, Ottey has won four bronze and two silver medals during her Olympic career. Her habit of finishing in third place has earned her the nickname "Miss Bronze." In a statement of camaraderie and Olympic Spirit, Perec expresses her mixed feelings about beating Ottey, saying,

top left: Canada's Mike Smith clears the bar in the decathlon pole vault as the Olympic cauldron burns in the background.

bottom left: In women's handball competition, a Korean team member dodges a block from Hungry to help her team win this semifinal. game.

right: Jamaica's Merlene Ottey makes a strong start and captures the silver in the women's 200 m.

WILLIAM P HOWARD • BERTHA D HOWARD-BRAY • JANET HOWARD-JOSEPH • BROOKE HOWARD-SMITH • LORI C HOWARD ATC • BENNIE HOWARD III • JOHN R HOWARD JR • LOUANNE HOWARD MT • LISA E HOWARD WOOTEN • DORIS L HOWE • JOHN W HOWE • KIRSTEN A HOWE • LENORE A HOWE • RANUSIA G HOWE • ADELAIDE S HOWELL • ADRIENNE Y HOWELL • BARRETT HOWELL • BESSIE A HOWELL • BETTY C HOWELL • BURTON R HOWELL • CARLEASE S HOWELL • DOROTHY A HOWELL • EVAN H HOWELL • FRANCES S HOWELL • GENE W HOWELL • GRANT E HOWELL • HENRY L HOWELL • JAMES HOWELL

Fans from the People's Republic of China support their team in the women's football finals.

"When I passed the finish line, I was quite happy, but also inside I was a little bit sad. I think you could see on my face I was not over-joyed because I admire Merlene a lot."

In a dramatic reversal of fortune, US decath-lete Dan O'Brien rebounds from his failure to qualify for the 1992 Games by winning the gold medal today, scoring 8,824 points over the 10 events. Going into the final event, O'Brien holds a 209 point lead over Germany's Frank Busemann and needs only to finish within 32 seconds of Busemann to win the gold. Since the 1,500 m is O'Brien's greatest challenge, he pulls out all the stops in this gru-eling event, straining to keep up with his clos-est rival. Inspired by a stadium full of adoring, cheering fans, he manages to cross the finish

line just 14.48 seconds behind Busemann to secure his gold medal and become the first American decathlon champion since Bruce Jenner in 1976.

In a story that hits close to home, Derrick Adkins becomes the first Atlantan to win an Olympic gold medal in his hometown. A grad-uate of Georgia Tech, Adkins wins the men's 400 m hurdles in 47.54 to capture a gold medal. To win, Adkins defeats his friend and rival, Zambia's Samuel Matete. Another Ameri-can, Calvin Davis, a converted 400 m sprinter who ran his first hurdles race in April 1996, wins the bronze.

Meanwhile, the largest crowd ever to watch an Olympic men's or women's football match—more than 76,000 people strong—is on hand to see one of the most memorable gold medal matchups in history as the US and People's Republic of China's women's football teams battle one another during 90 minutes of suspense.

• JAMES D HOWELL • JUDY A HOWELL • JULIA C HOWELL • KATHRYN B HOWELL • KELLIE N HOWELL • KYM L HOWELL • LORETTA L HOWELL • MARGARET ANNE HOWELL • MARIANNE R HOWELL • MISTY M HOWELL • MONA L HOWELL • PATSY N HOWELL • PHILLIP L HOWELL • RAYMOND HOWELL • TERESA HOWELL • THAMARA J HOWELL • TOM D HOWELL • TRICIA I HOWELL • VICTOR H HOWELL • WILLIAM B HOWELL • ALAN J HOWELL CATC • EARL S HOWELL JR • DAINA C HOWERTON • ELIZABETH P HOWERTON • KENTON J HOWERTON • BARBARA J HOWERY • ROBEN E HOWERY • TRACY R HOWK • ANNESLEY HOWLAND •

A pair of exciting semifinal games on 28 July sets up this gold-medal showdown. In one game, the People's Republic of China's Haiying Wei scored two goals in the final 10 minutes to lead China past Brazil's powerful team, 3–2. In the other semifinal, the Americans defeated the world champion Norwegian team, 2–1, with an overtime goal chipped in by late substitute Shannon MacMillan.

In today's contest, both sides run each other ragged, but the US team takes a 2–1 lead on Tiffeny Milbrett's goal in the 68th minute and holds on to capture the gold medal. Shannon MacMillan, who was cut from this team in December but who successfully earned her place back and scored the first American goal says, "Oh my gosh, it's the best feeling in the world. It took 90 minutes to wear these guys down." The level of physical exertion for both teams as they battle for the gold is absolute. In the final minute of the game, Mia Hamm of the US, suffering from the extreme physical play and total exhaustion, is carried from the field on a stretcher.

Most of the fans who have come to the Georgia Dome today have come to watch the US men's basketball team compete with Australia in one of two semifinal men's matches. The other semifinal also provides exciting action, as Yugoslavia and Lithuania battle for the opportunity to advance to the gold medal game. In the most intense game of the tournament, Yugoslavia holds Lithuania scoreless in

top: Australia's Shane Heal guards the ball from John Stockton of the US during the semifinals of men's basketball.

bottom: Tiffany Milbrett of the US women's football team and Huilin Xie of the People's Republic of China vie for the ball in the finals.

JOHANNE M HOWLAND • PAM A HOWLAND • WILLIAM S HOWLAND JR • MCKENZIE B HOWLE • JOHN T HOWSON • JULIE W HOWSON • THOMAS HOWSON • CYNTHIA R HOWZE • DYLAN L HOWZE • RICHARD T HOY • SHELLY M HOY • SUSAN HOY • EDDIE W HOYAL • LORI P HOYE • WALTER B HOYE II • DOUGLAS W HOYEM • JILL M HOYLA • JESSICA K HOYNOWSKI • ANN W HOYT • CHARLES E HOYT • EARL H HOYT • SARAH C HOYT • WILLIAM D HOYT • GORDON HRIBERNICK • CAROLINE S HSU • JENNY H HSU • JOHN H HSU • PAULA W HSU • PING-YUN HSU • CHEN HU • LI-HSI T HU • MINH T HUA • ALICE Y HUANG •

top: The German equestrian team members show their medals after winning the gold in a grueling 12-hour jumping competition.

bottom: The Australian women's hockey team celebrates after defeating Great Britain's team to win the gold medal.

the final 3:22 of play to hang on for a 66–58 win. The Yugoslavian team members react jubilantly to their victory in this semifinal game. Meanwhile, the US defeats Australia 101–73 to advance to the gold medal game, with Charles Barkley shooting a perfect 7 for 7 from the field, scoring 24 points, and pulling down 11 rebounds.

The Australian women's hockey team, extending their remarkable unbeaten string of 40 games, beats an excellent team from Korea 3–1 to take the gold medal. The Dutch team wins the bronze, defeating the British team 4–3 on penalty strokes after neither team scores during regulation play.

The equestrian venue has received rave reviews throughout the competition from athletes, fans, and media. The obstacles used for

CHRISTOPHER HUANG • GAN HUANG • KERYN I HUANG • LISA L HUANG • NINGSHENG HUANG • TSAI C HUANG • TZU-CHUAN J HUANG • YAO-WEN HUANG • CHARMAINE W HUBBARD • EBONY HUBBARD • ELAINE Y. HUBBARD • JOANNE C HUBBARD • JOHN H HUBBARD • JOYCE L HUBBARD • KATHLEEN H HUBBARD • MAKEDAH S HUBBARD • MALVA L HUBBARD • MARILYN D HUBBARD • NANCY F HUBBARD • SARA E HUBBARD • SHELBY J HUBBARD • WLLLIAM R HUBBARD • LINDA P HUBBARTT • STEVEN K HUBBARTT • JAMES S HUBBLE • LORETTA J HUBBLE • PENNY L HUBBLE • LAURIE B HUBBS • ROBERT G HUBBS •

today's team jumping competition, for example, represent icons from American life and form a kind of "ride across America" for the riders. From the Statue of Liberty water jump to the Georgia Peach Oxer and the Hawaiian Bamboo double combination, the variety of colorful obstacles make this a beautiful event to watch. Germany's Ludger Beerbaum, defending 1992 individual jumping gold medalist, with his near-perfect performance aboard his mount Ratina, leads his team to victory ahead of the US and Brazilian teams, which

take the silver and bronze medals, respectively, in the grueling, two-round, 12-hour team jumping competition. In the midst of the lengthy, demanding competition, one of Atlanta's frequent summer thunderstorms drops an inch of rain in 30 minutes, drenching competitors and spectators and forcing a delay in the competition.

Both men's and women's gold medal badminton singles finals offer enthusiastic fans extraordinary displays of power and dexterity. In the men's contest, Denmark's Poul-Erik Hoyer

Larsen wears a pair of 8-year-old "lucky" shoes as he defeats China's Jiong Dong 15–12, 15–10. In the women's gold event, Korea's Soo Hyun Bang continues the dominant style of play that has brought her to this final match, defeating Indonesia's 16-year-old Mia Audina 11–6, 11–7. Bang has not lost a game in the tournament, overpowering many of her opponents, even defeating one competitor 11–0, 11–0 in a match that lasted only 10 minutes.

It is another all-Chinese final in table tennis, as 20-year-old Guoliang Liu defeats his

left: Yumiko Shige of Japan is elated after winning the women's double-handed dinghy with teammate Alicia Kinoshita.

right: Ireland's Jessica Chesney rides Diamond Exchange in the first round of the team jumping competition.

LINDORA S HUBEL • ALBERT C HUBER • ALICE A HUBER • DAVE C HUBER • DONALD E HUBER • GERALDINE C HUBER • JOHN Y HUBER • LILLIAN F HUBER • MARGARET L HUBER • PHYLLIS M HUBER • RUSSELL C HUBER • SARA A HUBER • SYLVIA C HUBER • THOMAS C HUBER • WERNER HUBER • WILLIAM F HUBER • WILLIAM R HUBER • IVEY L HUBERT • HAROLD D HUBERT SAT • VICTORIA L HUBERTUS • LESLIE G HUBL • LORI A HUBL • ROSALEE M HUBL • DOUGLAS JOHN HUBRICH • MARK C HUBRICH • BARBARA E HUCK • KELLY M HUCK • MICHAEL V HUCK • JOHN M HUCKABY • SCOTT A HUCKABY • JIHAD A HUD •

teammate Tao Wang, 28, to win the men's singles championship in a five-set match on this final day of table tennis competition. The capstone of an incredible string of victories, Liu's win brings China's medal total to eight: golds in all 4 singles and doubles competitions, 3 silvers, and 1 bronze, a level of dominance virtually unequaled by any country in any sport.

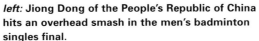

left: **Jiong Dong of the People's Republic of China hits an overhead smash in the men's badminton singles final.**

top right: **Guoliang Liu of the People's Republic of China concentrates on winning the men's table tennis final.**

bottom right: **Spectators enjoy the action in the all-Korean mixed doubles finals in badminton.**

Almost unknown among international archers, Justin Huish from the US is an Olympian who emerges from the shadows to strike gold. In a streak of consistently superior performances, the ponytailed, reversed baseball-capped archer from California gives his competitors a lesson as he advances through the quarterfinals to the semifinals and ultimately wins the gold medal.

In the men's quarterfinals, tied at 112 with Italy's Michele Frangilli, Huish responds to the challenge by hitting consecutive center bull's-eyes to press past Frangilli into the semifinals. The young archer then defeats Paul Vermeiren of Belgium by nine points in the semifinal and edges Magnus Petersson of Sweden by five points in the final to capture the gold in one of the most surprising finishes of the Games.

Justin Huish of the US takes aim in the men's individual archery quarterfinals.

OLYMPIC ARTS FESTIVAL

The Atlanta Symphony Orchestra has been an important and featured ensemble throughout ACOG's four-year Cultural Olympiad. During this Olympic period, beginning with the first event presented by the Cultural Olympiad in February 1993, the Atlanta Symphony Orchestra, one of the nation's finest, has been an especially visible representative of Atlanta's arts community. As the orchestra on the stadium field throughout the Opening Ceremony of the Games, it was seen by a worldwide audience of 3.5 billion people, easily the largest audience ever to see an orchestra perform. The orchestra's earlier performances in the Olympic Arts Festival have already received high marks from critics.

Today's performance is especially important to the orchestra and its noted musical director, Yoel Levi. Along with the Atlanta Symphony Orchestra Chorus, a powerful, polished ensemble that is among America's finest symphonic choruses, the orchestra performs Mahler's

Yoel Levi directs the Atlanta Symphony Orchestra in a performance that brings the classical music series to a fitting close.

• ADIEL HUERTAS • CARLOS HUERTAS • MYLAN N HUET • EVA N HUETER • JENNIFER A HUETTER • CHARLES M HUEY • CYNTHIA G HUEY • MARGIE L HUEY • NANCY F HUEY • ALEXIS A HUFF • ARLETHA M HUFF • BOB HUFF • CARLTON HUFF • CHRIS P HUFF • CORNELIA C HUFF • DARLEN G HUFF • IVY S HUFF • LARRY R HUFF • MARY B HUFF • MARY E HUFF • NANCY J HUFF • WILLIAM H HUFF • WILLIAM J HUFF • ROSA M HUFFER • GERALD H HUFFMAN • SUZANNE L HUFFMAN • WILL HUFFMAN • THOMAS M HUFFMAN JR • LINDA J HUFFMYER ATC • MATT W HUFFORD • FRANK R HUFFSCHMIDT • JOAN L HUFFSTETLER •

magnificent Symphony no. 2, "The Resurrection." Mahler's masterpiece is a fitting close to the Olympic Arts Festival's classical music series. Enhancing today's performance is mezzo-soprano Jennifer Larmore, a native of nearby Marietta, Georgia, and one of the hottest new international opera stars. Larmore has a voice of extraordinary depth, warmth, range, and power. She is joined by soprano Margaret Jane Wray, another gifted rising star whose voice complements Larmore's beautifully.

Levi's performance embraces and communicates the vastness of Mahler's musical architecture and the depth of this great work's spiritual content. The chorus performs with clarity, warmth, and an uncommon energy that brings the piece to its overwhelming conclusion. The commitment of and outstanding performance by this gifted, hometown ensemble are rewarded with an especially vocal and sustained response from the near-capacity audience.

The Atlanta Ballet is the oldest regional ballet company in the US. Under the company's new artistic director, John McFall, the Atlanta Ballet has focused its artistic mission and captured audiences with its energy and artistic quality. The final program of its Olympic Arts Festival dance series showcases the company's contemporary repertoire. *Read My Hips* is a flashy, electric work that is young in spirit, accurately reflecting the soul of Atlanta. The gifted and celebrated American choreographer David Parsons contributes an astonishing and fascinating work, *Caught*, a dance that uses strobe lights to create the effect that the solo male dancer is continually suspended in space. The electronic music that accompanies the choreography adds to the otherworldly quality of the piece, which elicits an overwhelming response from the audience for the athleticism and gymnastic control of the dancer. *Yellow-tailed Dogs*, a work commissioned by the Atlanta Ballet for performance during the Olympic Arts Festival combines text, music, theater, visual effects, and unusual choreography to create a mixed-media whole. Following

Mezzo-soprano Jennifer Larmore, a Georgia native, performs with the Atlanta Symphony Orchestra.

MICHAEL J HUFNAGEL • DWIGHT MAURICE HUGGET • DAVID "HUGGINS • DEBORAH L HUGGINS • JACK B HUGGINS • JOHN E HUGGINS • KIMBERLY J HUGGINS • LISA P HUGGINS • MARGARET S HUGGINS • NATASHA M HUGGINS • TIA HUGGINS • JAMES HUGGINS III • AARON C HUGHES • ANDERSON L HUGHES • ANNE R HUGHES • ARLEEN HAWKINS HUGHES • BLAINE HUGHES • BONNIE A HUGHES • CAROLYN W HUGHES • CHRISTOPHER L HUGHES • DANNY R HUGHES • DARRELL R HUGHES • DAVID G HUGHES • DEBRA E HUGHES • DORIS HUGHES • DWAYNE S HUGHES • DWIGHT HUGHES • EMMA L HUGHES

219

top: Jomandi Productions performs *Hip 2: Birth of the Boom*, an extraordinary tour de force by the company's artistic director, Thomas W. Jones II, to a capacity audience.

bottom and opposite page: The Atlanta Ballet presents the dance technology project, *Drastic Cuts*, the result of a collaborative effort with Georgia Tech.

the paths of three characters from the early 1800s to 1996, the piece weaves a complex series of images and ideas into a cohesive work that moves from quiet, reflective, and poetic moments to abrasive urban outbursts. Audience reaction is tempered enthusiasm, but the work has the impact choreographer David Rousseve desired: that is, inspiring the audience to think about the meaning of the work and react to more than just the quality of the choreography and physical performance.

The final piece is a stunningly beautiful, evocative work set in Heaven. Written as a lament for a lost friend by choreographer Lila York, *Rapture* combines a superb ensemble, captivating choreography, and the larghetto from Prokofiev's Piano Concerto no. 5 to produce an ethereal, reverent atmosphere. The audience, clearly moved by this remarkable finish, is suspended in reflection rather than roused to tumultuous applause.

ERIC J HUGHES • GARY V HUGHES • GINA M HUGHES • IRIS R HUGHES • JACK HUGHES • JACK HUGHES • JACK H HUGHES • JAMES F HUGHES • JAMES M E HUGHES • JAMES R HUGHES • JAMES R HUGHES • JANE E HUGHES • JANE T HUGHES • JOHNNIE R HUGHES • JOHNNY HUGHES • JUANITA S HUGHES • JULIANA HUGHES • KERWIN D HUGHES • LAURA M HUGHES • LILLIE R HUGHES • LINDA K HUGHES • LINDA L HUGHES • LOUISE I HUGHES • LYNN HUGHES • MARCELLA M HUGHES • MARLENE HUGHES • MARY ANN A HUGHES • MARY V HUGHES • MICHAEL C HUGHES • MICHAEL F HUGHES • MICHAEL G HUGHES •

DAY FOURTEEN
2 AUGUST 1996

Spectators find creative ways to fend off Atlanta's hot summer weather.

ATLANTA'S SUMMER HEAT and humidity, of concern to the organization since the Bid process, has fortunately been milder than anticipated, especially during this second week of competition. Preparing for the anticipated heat has been an integral part of ACOG's planning from the organization's earliest days. Providing proper support and facilities to service athletes, spectators, and staff has occupied various ACOG departments and teams of people, including the medical advisory committee and competition venue operations.

While some press coverage during the first days of the Games dubs spectators "southern fried fans," the decision to plan for the most extreme possibilities has allowed for prompt and appropriate attention to all heat-related problems. Misting stations, roller-skating "heat busters" carrying portable sprayers, Salvation Army water canteens at venues and parking lots, Red Cross tents equipped with first-aid supplies, roving medical teams at outdoor venues, and hundreds of thousands of gallons of free water at Olympic venues and other key locations within the Olympic Ring keep the effects of the heat at bay. A fleet of emergency vehicles, including several specially equipped golf carts, provide additional safety precautions.

DAVID P HULBERT III • HELEN S HULEN • WILLIAM E HULEN • KELLY J HULETT • MELVIN D HULETT • LEANN R HULETTE • SHARON L HULETTE • HANNELORE S HULICK • ALEC A HULL • DON HULL • EVELYN A HULL • GERRY G HULL • GERRY G HULL • JANET K HULL • JOHN E HULL • JULIE L HULL • KIRSTEN E HULL • MITCHELL C HULL • PATRICIA S HULL • PATRICIA S HULL • TODD W HULL • BONNIE P HULL RN • ANGELA S HULLIBERGER • JOSEPH J HULLINGS • SUSAN C HULSCHULZE • JEANNE E HULSEN • DEBORAH L HULSEY • MARTHA G HULSEY • MICHAEL E HULSEY • PAMELA K HULSEY • ROBERT L HULSEY •

Centennial Olympic Park visitors cool off in the reflecting pool.

Athletes, spectators, and staff have also made their own preparations, knowing that the hot weather would very likely be a challenge. Most spectators are well prepared to brave the weather. They are armed with chill packs, water bottles, canteens, wet "neckerchiefs," sunscreen, hats of every possible description, including some with personalized electric fans mounted on top of or suspended from them, and thousands of handheld fans, like those traditionally used in the South before air-conditioning was available.

Hundreds of thousands of pounds of ice—amounting to an expected total of several million tons during the Games—are needed to service each day's vast rate of ice consumption. That most prized commodity of all, air-conditioning, is plentiful in buildings and also in numerous air-conditioned tents and other portable structures and trailers located throughout the Olympic Ring, providing another level of relief.

If all attempts to keep cool fail, spectators can go to the Fountain of Rings and large reflecting pool in Centennial Olympic Park. These places attract tens of thousands of people, day and night, who stand, sit, or lie in the water to cool off.

The weather cooperates for the most part, and ACOG's preparations prove judicious. Coping with the hot weather simply becomes an integral part of the Olympic experience.

COMPETITION

On the baseball diamond, few teams have been able to thwart the awesome power and depth of the Cuban team. Today, cementing its place as the top team in amateur baseball, Cuba downs the Japanese, 13–9, to capture the gold medal. Cuba's third baseman, Omar Linares, slugs three home runs and drives in six runs to lead Cuba's onslaught. Linares finishes the tournament with a .476 batting average after hitting a total of eight home runs and driving in 16 runs. The Americans score a 10–3 victory over Nicaragua to capture the bronze. This has been Nicaragua's best Olympic performance in any sport, improving on an 11th place finish achieved by a weightlifter in the 1992 Games.

A few miles north at the Georgia World Congress Center, Bulgaria's Valentin Dimitrov Jordanov, a 52 kg (114.5 lb) freestyle wrestler, is on his way to capturing his first Olympic gold medal, scoring a controversial takedown to win 4–3 in overtime over Azerbaijan's Namik Abdullayev before a capacity crowd of more than 7,000. The win gives Jordanov 12 world and Olympic medals, including seven world titles. Reacting to what he perceives as an unjust call, Abdullayev refuses to shake officials' hands at the end of the match.

top: **Cuba's pitcher Pedro Luis Lazo and catcher Juan Manrique celebrate after their team wins the gold medal in baseball.**

bottom: **David Pichler of the US competes in the men's 10 m platform diving competition.**

WENDY E HUMPHREY • WILLIAM D HUMPHREY • DONA S HUMPHREYS • GARDNER K HUMPHREYS • ROBERT T HUMPHREYS • DORIS G HUMPHRIES • NANCY D HUMPHRIES • PAUL E HUMPHRIES • JULIA A HUMPTON • DOUGLAS H HUNCZAK • FAY B HUNCZAK • PHILLIP E HUNDLEY • IMOGENE W HUNDLY • ASHLEY W HUNDT • SHEILA W HUNDT • MICHAEL W HUNEKE II • JOANNE HUNER • JIMMY L HUNEYCUTT • DANIEL H HUNG • JEANNE M HUNGERPILLER • JOHN C HUNGERPILLER • TZU WEI HUNG • ANITA Y HUNNICUTT • EMILY A HUNNICUTT • JEAN P HUNNICUTT • LAURA R HUNNICUTT • MARIE HUNNICUTT •

Despite an upset in the preliminary round, US super heavyweight and two-time gold-medal–winning wrestler Bruce Baumgartner earns a bronze medal. His winnings now include 13 world or Olympic medals, surpassing the record of Jordanov and long-standing Soviet hero, Alexander Medved.

Capacity crowds continue to be the norm at Olympic Stadium, where the attendance figures for today's two sessions are over the 1 million mark. With another day of competition still to come, the athletics attendance at Atlanta's

left: **Bruce Baumgartner of the US earns a bronze in the 130 kg (286 lb) wrestling competition.**

right: **Robert Korzeniowski of Poland is elated after winning the men's 50 km race walk.**

Games will exceed the records set in Melbourne and Los Angeles and stand as the largest audiences to witness athletics competition in Olympic history.

Fan support is also evident today in the streets of Atlanta, as crowds gather to watch the men's 50 km race walk event, won by Poland's Robert Korzeniowski. "I don't think I could have been better," said Korzeniowski of his performance. "I didn't make any mistakes, and I didn't die! It was the best race of my life." Indeed, Korzeniowski's performance this time-out is almost perfect, as the 1996 gold-medal winner completes the demanding course in 3:43:30, overcoming a devastating disqualification in Barcelona after he entered the stadium in the lead for the final kilometer. He met the same fate and disappointment at the 1993 World Championships, where he received a third "red card" (two are allowed each runner) in this sport in which the rules

CAROL C HUNSBERGER • CHRISTINA M HUNSICKER • DAVID E HUNSINGER • BELINDA A HUNT • BETTIE HUNT • BRUCE O HUNT • CHARLES K HUNT • DEBORAH A HUNT • DEBRA HUNT • DELWIN M HUNT • EDGAR S HUNT • ELISE M HUNT • GWYNNE C HUNT • HERMAN T HUNT • HYLAND HUNT • JANE C HUNT • JEFFREY W HUNT • KATHLEEN M HUNT • KENNETH HUNT • KERENSA E HUNT • KYLIE R HUNT • LAVERNE E HUNT • MALCOLM S HUNT • MARINA HUNT • MARY M HUNT • MARY V HUNT • MIRIAM T HUNT • MONIKA HUNT • NANCY M HUNT • NAOMI R HUNT • PAMELLA M HUNT • PATTI A HUNT • TIMOTHY J HUNT •

of form are strictly enforced. Winning the gold medal at the Centennial Olympic Games is an exhilarating experience for this gifted and determined Olympian.

Having already won the gold in the women's 5,000 m, Junxia Wang of the People's Republic of China seems on her way to an unprecedented second win in distance racing, as she heads into the lead of the 10,000 m race. But Portugal's Fernanda Ribeiro—the world-record holder in the shorter, faster 5,000 m distance who chose to race only in the 10,000 m

The Olympic record is broken again and again throughout the competition. In the end, three vaulters clear 5.92 m (19.42 ft), a centimeter better than Bubka's previous record. The tie among three vaulters means that France's Jean Galfione, who has missed the fewest attempts during the event, captures the gold, while Russia's Igor Trandenkov and Germany's Andrei Tivontchik take silver and bronze, respectively.

Bubka's disappointment in having to withdraw from the hunt for gold is somewhat abated by his election to the IOC Athletes

left: Participants in the men's 50 km race walk press toward the finish line.

right: Chioma Ajunwa of Nigeria performs the winning long jump to earn a gold medal.

in the Games—foils Wang's attempt by outsprinting her in the final meters, winning the race in an Olympic-record time of 31:01.63 seconds. Wang finishes less than one second behind Ribeiro to take the silver medal.

With world-record holder Sergey Bubka of Ukraine forced to withdraw from the pole vault event, the field is left completely open.

TOM L HUNT • TRACY R HUNT • WILLIE P HUNT • ROBERT W HUNT JR • APRIL D HUNTER • BECKY E HUNTER • BOBBY HUNTER • BONITA R HUNTER • CALVIN HUNTER • CAROL N HUNTER • CHRISTOPHER D HUNTER • CHUCK HUNTER • D FRASURE HUNTER • DEBORAH A HUNTER • DONNA M HUNTER • ELEANOR L HUNTER • EVAN J HUNTER • GLENDA F HUNTER • GWENDOLYN E HUNTER • JAN B HUNTER • JANA L HUNTER • JANET A HUNTER • JAYSON D HUNTER • JOHN HUNTER • JOHN J HUNTER • JULIE V HUNTER • KARA M HUNTER • KAREN J HUNTER • KATRINA C HUNTER • KEITH C HUNTER • LEE A HUNTER •

volleyball captain Bob Ctvrtlik, Algeria's middle distance runner Hassiba Boulmerka, and rower Roland Baar of Germany.

In a semifinal contest between the US and Australian women's basketball teams before a huge crowd of 32,000 in the Georgia Dome, the US team, which trailed by as many as eight points in the first half, ultimately wins, 93–71, to earn a spot in the gold-medal game. Australia's Michele Timms turns in an outstanding 27-point game in the loss, but the US, led by Lisa Leslie's 22 points and Teresa Edwards's

left: **Maria Paula Gonçalves da Silva hugs Mareia Angelica Gonçalves da Silva after Brazil's semifinal win in women's basketball.**

center spread: **Spain's rhythmic gymnastics team gives a spectacular performance which garners the gold medal.**

Commission by his fellow athletes. Bubka is the athlete with the highest number of votes in the special election, in which only athletes in the Olympic Village vote. This honor is also extended to six other highly respected and popular athletes: swimmer Aleksander Popov of the Russian Federation, the Czech Republic's javelin-thrower Jan Zelezny, runner Charmaine Crooks of Canada, American indoor

LISA B HUNTER • LISA B HUNTER • MARIETHA Y HUNTER • MARION N HUNTER • MARTHA I HUNTER • MARTINE HUNTER • MARY J HUNTER • NELLA HUNTER • PAULETTE V HUNTER • RHONDA HUNTER • RICHARD A HUNTER • ROBERT E HUNTER • SHEILA A HUNTER • STEPHEN A HUNTER • STUART L HUNTER • THOMAS N HUNTER • TIFFANY E HUNTER • TONYA S HUNTER • TRECINIA T HUNTER • TRICIA K HUNTER • CONWAY W HUNTER III • RONALD E HUNTER SR • ANDREA L HUNTEY • LESLIE HUNTINGTON • DEBORAH T HUNTLEY • MYRNA H HUNTLEY • CHRISTOPH HUPACH • JEAN A HUPP • JESSICA HUPP •

eight assists, powers back in the second half to win the game.

In the other women's basketball semifinal, a confident team from Brazil earns the right to oppose the US in the gold-medal game by handily defeating Ukraine's team, 80–61.

The Australian men's tennis doubles team of Mark Woodforde and Todd Woodbridge defeats Neil Broad and Tim Henman of Great Britain to capture the gold medal. Lindsay Davenport of the US triumphs over Spain's Arantxa Sanchez Vicario in today's women's singles

top: **Every competition venue continues to attract capacity crowds.**

bottom: **The women's archery team from the Democratic People's Republic of Korea wins the gold medal.**

defeats Mary Joe Fernandez of the US 7–6 (8–6), 6–4 to become the first Czech Republic woman to win an Olympic medal.

Meanwhile, Spanish athletes achieve an extraordinary upset, edging the heavily favored Bulgarian rhythmic gymnastics team by just .067 of a point to capture the team gold medal in the team event's Olympic debut.

In the men's hockey finals, Spain's team gives the Netherlands' team a mighty battle before losing 3–1 in front of nearly 14,000 frenzied fans at Morris Brown College. Spain is actually leading the match 1–0 when the favored Dutch squad comes from behind and pumps in a flurry of goals to post the gold-medal–winning victory.

At the Georgia Tech Aquatic Center, the US synchronized swimming team earns all perfect 10s, the first perfect score in international synchronized swimming competition, in an awe-inspiring display of talent. They capture the

top: **Jan Hempel of Germany (silver), Dmitri Saoutine of the Russian Federation (gold), and Hailiang Xiao of the People's Republic of China (bronze) acknowledge the crowd during the medal ceremony for the men's 10 m platform diving event.**

bottom: **The US synchronized swimming team earns all perfect 10s to win the gold.**

gold-medal match, 7–6 (8–6), 6–2. Reflecting on her win, Davenport says, "That was definitely the most proud I've ever been in my life, not only for myself, but for my country." In the bronze-medal match, Jana Novotna

first-ever team gold medal in this event, while the Canadian team earns the silver medal and Japan wins the bronze.

top: The German yachting team of Jochen Schuemann, Thomas Flach, and Bernd Jaekel celebrates after winning the gold medal in the soling class.

bottom: Costars Arnold Schwarzenegger and Vanessa Williams visit the Olympic Village for the premier of the movie *Eraser*.

Later, China's hopes for a clean sweep in all diving events are dashed as Russia's Dmitri Saoutine captures the gold in the men's platform event ahead of Germany's Jan Hempel and Hailiang Xiao of China.

Today, competition concludes at the yachting venue in Savannah, where Germany wins the soling class with Russia and the US, taking home the silver and bronze respectively. During the course of the wide-open competition, 22 different countries garner Olympic medals.

OLYMPIC VILLAGE AND OLYMPIC ARTS FESTIVAL

Hollywood superstar Arnold Schwarzenegger is in Atlanta this evening to host the world premiere of his newest thriller, *Eraser*, presented to Olympic athletes on a four-story screen at Georgia Tech's Bobby Dodd Stadium. "I was a competitive athlete before becoming an actor, so I am particularly proud to have the world's greatest athletes as special guests for this premiere," says Schwarzenegger. He is joined on stage prior to the movie's start by costars Vanessa Williams and James Caan. The pop

band Goo Goo Dolls performs a high-energy segment before the movie begins. Mexican swimmer Carlos Arena says, "It's cool to think that an athlete like Arnold would choose the Village for his premiere," a sentiment echoed

DENNIS E HUTCHESON • JIM W HUTCHESON • LAURENE HUTCHESON • SKYLAR C HUTCHESON • THOMAS I HUTCHESON • JEFF C HUTCHINGS • BROWN B HUTCHINS • DAVID M HUTCHINS • DONNIE E HUTCHINS • GINGER S HUTCHINS • JOYCE M HUTCHINS • LINDA R HUTCHINS • MICHAEL V HUTCHINS • RUTH A HUTCHINS • SHANA K HUTCHINS • BONNIE S HUTCHINSON • DOUGLAS P HUTCHINSON • GENE L HUTCHINSON • GEORGE B HUTCHINSON • GERALD F HUTCHINSON • HARRY B HUTCHINSON • JASON B HUTCHINSON • JILL E HUTCHINSON • JOAN M HUTCHINSON • JOHN P HUTCHINSON •

231

by thousands of his fellow athletes as they cheer their appreciation for the world-famous actor and bodybuilder.

At the very beginning of the High Museum of Art's marvelous photographic essay on the American South, *Picturing the South, 1860– Present*, visitors encounter a small, profoundly touching portrait of a female slave taken in 1860. The woman stares intensely, looking directly into the camera and drawing the viewer into this deeply moving photograph and into the exhibition.

The Smithsonian Jazz Masterworks Orchestra performs at Atlanta Symphony Hall.

tivity of a wide range of gifted photographers, both named and anonymous, the exhibition follows the South from the conflagration of the Civil War through Reconstruction, the beginnings of urbanization, and the civil rights clashes of the 1950s and 1960s to the present. The series of more than 100 images reveals major themes and concepts and explores the inner struggles and triumphs of individuals.

Some photographs are familiar, especially those of the civil rights leader Reverend Martin Luther King Jr. and his colleagues. Others are

This beautiful exhibition is the result of exhaustive research and a painstaking curatorial approach. It weaves together several overarching themes to provide a penetrating vision of the evolution of the American South from the beginning of the Civil War to the present. Through the discerning eye and aesthetic sensi-

shocking, and still others are subtle and thought-provoking. The juxtaposition of images, content, and themes has a significant cumulative impact on the viewer, an impact which is fully realized only after completing a circuit through the entire exhibition. While each photograph stands on its own as a work of depth and quality, one is left at the end with a distinct impression of the exhibition as a whole.

Among Atlanta's most prominent, creative, and innovative cultural institutions, the

KATHERINE E HUTCHINSON • MARCUS HUTCHINSON • SARAH M HUTCHINSON • THOMAS M HUTCHINSON • ALBERT L HUTCHINSON JR • HELEN L HUTCHISON • LOREN D HUTCHISON • MARGARET E HUTCHISON • PAT D HUTCHISON • CHARLES J HUTHMAKER • FRANK M HUTHNANCE • CHRISTOPHER M HUTKO • LOIS P HUTKO • ELAINE M HUTSELL • MARIA J HUTSICK ATC • HEATHER L HUTSON • JANICE S HUTSON • KELLE D HUTSON • MICHAEL D HUTSON • SHERMAN HUTSON • MARISA L HUTTENBACH • CHRISTINE M HUTTO • DAVID A HUTTO • EVERETT E HUTTO • FRAN L HUTTO • HERBERT T HUTTO •

top: John Ludwig presents a new adaptation of Mary Shelley's *Frankenstein* at the Center for Puppetry Arts.

bottom: The High Museum of Art was one of the best attended cultural venues during the Olympic Arts Festival.

Center for Puppetry Arts annually performs for more than 1 million people at its home in a converted elementary school building. With two theaters, including a 350-seat auditorium for children and a 35-seat theater for adult audiences, a workshop, classrooms, a marvelous museum, and a special space in which to exhibit traveling and temporary shows of all kinds, the center is active nearly every day of the year. While the center's audiences are primarily children, productions for older audiences are also offered.

Puppetry is a time-honored tradition and art form that appears in virtually every culture. As the current headquarters for the international puppetry movement, Atlanta's Center for Puppetry Arts is perhaps known even better internationally than it is in its own community. But with hundreds of thousands of young people and their parents visiting the center on a regular basis throughout the year, it has become one of the most popular cultural destinations in Atlanta.

Among the most distinguished and celebrated creative forces in the world of contemporary puppetry is the center's renowned creative genius, John Ludwig. Commissioned by the Cultural Olympiad to create a new work for the 1996 Olympic Arts Festival, Ludwig elected to tackle the tale of *Frankenstein*. Because it will be performed in the tiny theater for adult audiences, a ticket to *Frankenstein* is among the most difficult festival tickets to obtain.

Frankenstein is filled with special effects and gallows humor, both noted Ludwig specialties. His puppets are astonishing in their quality, and the production glows with originality and wit. Audience reaction is universally positive.

Atlanta 1996®

NANCY P HUTTO • ALICIA M HUTTON • ELIZABETH A HUTTON • KATHRYN S HUTTON • MARGIE J HUWIG • DENISE D HUYNH • BENO HVALA • JI-YEON HWANG • SAMUEL S. HWANG • YOUNG HWANGBO • ALEX K HYATT • ERAN F HYATT • RICHARD A HYATT • ROBERT P HYATT • STAN HYATT • VERONICA HYATT • HARVEY N HYATT JR. • CARL M HYDE • HERSHEL E HYDE • MARK A HYDE • MELINDA S HYDE • MELODY W HYDE • MORGAN HYDE • JOHN C HYDER • MARIE A HYDER • LEE HYE-JIN • GWEN HYER • LARRY R HYGH • ROY HYINK • CHARLES J HYLAND • MARKUS HYLLA • PATRICK A HYLTON • THERESA L HYLTON • CAROLYN J HYMAN •

DAY FIFTEEN
3 AUGUST 1996

SUSPENSE HAS BEEN building for today's finals in a number of team sports—men's football and basketball and women's volleyball and handball. The atmosphere of excitement and festivity that dominates the competition venues that host these, as well as other, sports is enhanced by coordinated decorations and signage. These elements, known as Atlanta's Look of the Games, appear throughout all areas of Olympic activity.

Creating and implementing this graphic design system was an incredibly complex task that occupied a focused staff for more than three years. A team of design firms was responsible for designing the many components that give Atlanta its unique and distinctive Look. This team worked to develop a Look that would express hospitality, friendship, and the city of Atlanta's ambiance. The Look elements defined by these teams radiated from the central symbol of the Quilt of Leaves and the central color—the deep, rich Georgia green. The list of components that were designed and produced in keeping with the Look is staggering. It includes buttons and pins, exterior bus wraps, more than 14,000 banners ranging in size from 2 x 6 ft (.61 x 1.83 m) to 50 x 50 ft (15.2 x 15.2 m), entryways and exits

The Quilt of Leaves, centerpiece of ACOG's Look of the Games, expresses hospitality, friendship, and unity.

for every competition and noncompetition facility, and parking lot and other transportation-related signs. In all, hundreds of individual designs—variations on the primary logo and thematic elements and color palettes—were designed and fabricated.

Packaging the multiple individual components required to support each of hundreds of previously identified locations and organizing the installation of the packages according to a

TODAY'S CALENDAR

Competition

Athletics
Basketball
Boxing
Canoe/kayak—sprint
Cycling—road
Equestrian
Football
Gymnastics—rhythmic
Handball
Tennis
Volleyball—indoor

Olympic Arts Festival

Alliance Theatre Company: *Blues for an Alabama Sky* and *The Last Night of Ballyhoo*
Atlanta Ballet: *Drastic Cuts*
Center for Puppetry Arts: *Bathtub Pirates* and *Frankenstein*
Jomandi Productions: *Hip 2: Birth of the Boom*
Southern Crossroads Festival

DAVID HYMAN • RANDY E HYMAN • CAROLYN A HYMES • SEAN HYNES • PEGGY M HYNOTE • BRADLEY C HYRE • RANDAL M HYRE • WESLEY HYRE • JAMAL HYSAW • ALICIA J HYSINGER • STEPHANIE IACONO • JAMES W IAMS • JOSEPH P IANDOLI • ANDREW J IBBOTSON • CHUKS N IBEKWE • OZOEMENA O IBEZUE • KADIDJA IBN-IAHOUCINE • ABDUL IBRAHIM • NADEER IBRAHIM • LINDA G IBSEN • NICOLE ICE • STANLEY R ICE • MICHELLE L ICENOGLE • YUMIKO ICHISE • DIANE S IDE • LOGAN IDE • LUCIENNE M IDE • ALEX IDICHANDY • KIMBERLY IEMMA • FREDERICK C IFFLAND • STEVEN J IGARASHI •

emblazoned with Look elements and used to wrap platforms and fences and other large obstacles—is an enormous undertaking.

In addition to fabric components such as banners, flags, and signs, the Look design team also incorporated a wide array of supplemental plants and trees at hundreds of Games locations to enhance walkways, plazas, and other gathering places. The key Look element, leaves, was translated into 128 tractor loads of plant materials, including 632 shade trees, 1,077 crepe myrtle trees, 1,133 planter pots, and more than 150,000 lb (68,000 kg) of wildflower seed. Once installed, these plants need to be watered and maintained. A team of 65 people use eight water trucks to distribute more than 200,000 gal (757,080 l) of water each day, prune and trim as necessary, and even replant. As they go about their work, this team of unsung heroes become important ambassadors, spreading southern hospitality and teaching Olympic visitors something about the native horticulture of this lush region.

Among visual elements Games organizers must develop for each Olympic Games is a system of unique icons that identify each of the 26 sport disciplines. Called pictograms, these important components of the Look are designed with care and are subject to review by the IOC. In keeping with its commitment to

left: Hundreds of variations of the Look are used on the banners that hang at the competition venues and throughout Atlanta.

right: Five intersecting circles of flowers represent the Olympic Rings at the equestrian jumping course.

precise schedule was an awesome task that required months of detailed planning. Allowances for breakage, theft, and other possible problems that could arise during the Games meant that supplemental components had to be ready in case they were needed.

A team of people checks every Look installation each day and night to ensure that all installed components remain intact, clean, and attractive. The size of this task is monumental; inspecting and maintaining the fence covering alone—more than 80,000 ft (25,000 m) of fabric

OFELIA J IGASAKI • DANA M IGLESIAS • GAY E IGLESIAS • REGINO T IGNACIO • ALGIS J IGNATONIS • OBINNA C IHEME • RONALD M IHNOT • TAD R IHNS • JOHN IHRIG • KEITA IIDA • ARCHIBALD A IKANENG • ALBERT W IKEDA • JASON P IKEDA • MAIKO IKEDA • DOUGLAS C IKELMAN • RAYMOND IKEMAN • HIDEKAZU IKEMOTO • IBANGA E IKPE • PATRICK L ILABACA • GLORIA A ILAGAN • ELI ILANO • RAOUL MOYNAN ILAW • IGOR ILIC • LILIANA A ILICA • ALLA O ILINA • GURSEL ILIPINAR • LUBA ILIYN • PETER JOHN ILIYN • CLEMENT KOLA ILUGBO • ROLAND ILZHOFER • HEE-JUNG IM • JI WON IM • WALTER M IMAHARA • SABURI IMARA •

celebrate athletic achievement and convey the personal quality of the South, Atlanta's pictograms employ the human form for the first time at a modern Olympic Games. These pictograms are used on signage as wayfinding devices to help spectators who speak any language find their venue destinations.

COMPETITION

Today marks the finale of the most popular Olympic football tournament in history. More than 1 million fans have filled the five football venues during the 13 days of competition—more than twice the total attendance for football competition at the 1992 Games. The men's gold-medal match continues the trend of thrilling games, as 86,100 fans watch a determined Nigerian team achieve a controversial 3–2 victory over Argentina.

The controversy erupts in the 89th minute of play when the referee fails to call Nigeria's midfielder, Emmanuel Amunike, offside as he scores the go-ahead and winning goal. The

Pictograms of the sport(s) being competed decorate each competition venue.

WILLIAM R IMES • MARGARET A IMHOF • DOUG C IMIG • PAULINE B IMLAY • EARL J IMMEL • IRMGARD S IMMEL • KAREN K IMMEL • ELISABETH INACKER • ROBERT W INACKER • ANTHONY J INCAMPO • FRANK S INCORVAIA • HOLLY A INCORVAIA • ANN W INDERBITZIN • ROBERTO C INFANTE • HEATHER A INFANTRY • MELANIE R INFINGER • FRANCIS A INGALSBE • MARGARET A INGALSBE • WILLIAM E INGALSBE III • JOSEPH INGE • HELEN INGEBRITSEN • STEPHEN R INGELS • AMY B INGHAM • LISA J INGHAM • DOUG P INGLE • LAURA L INGLE • PATTI L INGLE • PAUL H INGLE • RICHARD A INGLES • JOE INGLIMA •

237

inflamed Argentines swarm the referee and demand the offside call, but the referee holds firm and the score stands. The Nigerian team members, whose style of play is more offense-oriented than the traditional defensive style of football played in countries like Argentina and Italy, win the African continent's first Olympic medal in football competition.

The crowds also flock to Olympic Stadium. Today, before 83,300 fans—the largest crowd to watch any of the athletics sessions of the Games—the Canadian men's 4 x 100 m relay

left: A determined Nigerian team defeats Argentina to win gold in the men's football finals.

right: Noureddine Morceli of Algeria finishes in front to win the gold medal in the men's 1500 m.

team defies history by surpassing the US to capture the gold medal. Anchored by Donovan Bailey, the Canadian team sets a blistering pace and wins the gold in a time of 37.69 seconds.

Meanwhile, Atlanta's Gwen Torrence anchors the women's 4 x 100 m relay and captures her first gold medal of the Games in a time of 41.95, the fastest relay of the year, and the US's fourth consecutive gold medal in the women's sprint relays. Pauline Davis, who runs the anchor leg for the Bahamas team, has a faster split than Torrence, but is unable to catch up to her longtime friend and training partner down the stretch. "I told her I was running like a madwoman to catch her," says Davis, who was ecstatic about the island nation's first-ever track medal, the silver. Torrence later laughed, "I said, 'Pauline, you aren't going to walk me down in my hometown.'"

Trained and entered in the 1996 Games as a 1,500 m runner, Venuste Niyongabo of Burundi relinquishes his place in the 1,500 m to teammate Dieudonne Kwizera, whom Niyongabo credits with having brought their war-torn country to the Games. Later, Niyongabo competes in the men's 5,000 m race and paces the field to capture his country's first Olympic medal in history, a gold, in 13:07:96. He

JOSEPHINE D INGLIMA • ARTIE V INGLIS • GEORGE ANNE INGLIS • JOYE A INGLIS • WILLIAM T INGLIS • EVA I INGMAN • LARS C INGMAN • IVAN INGRAHAM • RONWYN M INGRAHAM • SUSAN P INGRAHAM • DOLORES ELIZABETH INGRALDI • JOEY INGRALDI • JEROME INGRAM • CRISTY A INGRAM • DOROTHY T INGRAM • EMILY K INGRAM • EVELYN A INGRAM • GERI B INGRAM • GLORIA J INGRAM • JAMES D INGRAM • JAMES R INGRAM • JENNIFER A INGRAM • JILL R INGRAM • JUDITH A INGRAM • LINDA INGRAM • LINTON E INGRAM • LORA J INGRAM • MATTIE C INGRAM • PATRICIA G INGRAM • PATRICIA J INGRAM •

quickly dedicates his medal to the cause of peace in his tiny African homeland, which is presently engulfed in civil war.

Bulgaria's 1995 defending world champion high jumper, Stefka Kostadinova, sets a new Olympic record on her way to the gold medal, turning in an incredible leap of 2.05 m (6.73 ft) in one of the greatest women's high jump competitions ever, with more women clearing 1.93 m (6.33 ft) and 2.01 m (6.59 ft) than ever before. Kostadinova was the world's top high jumper in the 1980s until breaking her foot

and having a baby kept her out of competition. As she leads an extraordinary field of competitors, it is clear that she has regained her winning form.

The first man to repeat as javelin gold-medal winner since 1924, the Czech Republic's Jan Zelezny outdistances his competition with a throw of 88.16 m (289.24 ft). Zelezny's rocket-like throw attracts the attention of professional baseball scouts and fans alike.

There are some surprises in the course of the US men's basketball team's 95–69 gold-medal

Atlanta native Gwen Torrence anchors the US women's 4 x 100 m relay and captures gold.

RAYFORD L INGRAM • RONALD L INGRAM • ROSA M INGRAM • SUSAN D INGRAM • CREOLA INGRAM DAVIS • ALISON INGVOLDSTAD • PATRICIA D INGVOLDSTAD • WESLEY W INGWERSEN • BARRY O INMAN • CARLTON B INMAN • DARRYL D INMAN • MARK A INMAN • MARY INMAN • RUSSELL L INMAN • WILLIAM P INMAN JR • JAMES W INNES • JOHN P INNES II • HIROYUKI INOUE • LILY S INSIXIENGMAY • ALEXANDRA A INSLEY • LUCIO INTELLIGENTE • MELISSA A INTVELDT • ROY R IOANNIDES • ROBERT IONTA • ANNETTE T IOVOLI • CARROLL H IRBY • ELIZABETH B IRBY • KENNETH F IRBY • CAROLE N IRELAND

victory over an aggressive Yugoslavian team in the final. Before an Olympic record-setting crowd of 34,600 at the Georgia Dome, Yugoslavia trails by only one point, 51–50, with 14 minutes remaining in the contest. But when Vlade Divac, Yugoslavia's star center, fouls out, the middle is left open for American David Robinson, who pumps in a game-high 28 points to lead his team to victory. A three-time Olympian, Robinson is now the US's all-time leading scorer in Olympic men's basketball competition, with 270 points.

left: Anette Hoffman of Denmark takes a shot during her team's handball final match with Korea.

right: David Robinson of the US dunks the ball on his way to a game-high 28 points in the gold-medal game in men's basketball.

In a special ceremony held at halftime, IOC President Juan Antonio Samaranch awards Muhammad Ali a gold medal to replace the medal Ali won in 1960, but later lost. As Samaranch places the medal around Ali's neck, Ali kisses him on both cheeks and then kisses the medal. This moving tribute to Ali, "The Greatest," recalls the special role he played in the Opening Ceremony.

Also within the Olympic Ring, more than 15,300 fans pack the Omni Coliseum for the women's volleyball final, an outstanding match between two dynamic teams, Cuba and the People's Republic of China. During the culmination of yet another thrill-packed tournament, the Chinese initially take the upper hand, winning the first game of the match 16–14. But the Cubans, the long-dominant

• JACK W IRELAND • JOAN E IRELAND • MELVIN L IRELAND • TRAVIS R IRELAND • MARJORIE IRION • MILDRED B IRIONS • WAYNE G IRIONS • DENISE IRISH • JOHN R IRISH • TERESA A IRISH • TERRY D IRONS • GEORGIA A IRRE • GREGORY A IRVIN • SUSAN D IRVIN • BARBARA J IRVINE • JOAN P IRVINE • ROBERT C IRVINE JR • LEROY IRVING • LEROY IRVING • PEARLYNE IRVING • TRISHA J IRVING • BILLY H IRWIN • LEIGH A IRWIN • MARK M IRWIN • MICHELE E IRWIN • NATASHA D IRWIN • SARA P IRWIN • ELIZABETH A ISAAC • MARIO M ISAAC • MONIFA K ISAAC • SAJU M ISAAC • CAROL B. ISAACS • GEORGE R ISAACS •

top left: **Muhammad Ali stands with the US men's basketball team at a special half-time ceremony.**

top right: **Ali kisses the gold medal presented to him to replace the one he lost.**

bottom: **Cuba battles the People's Republic of China to win the gold medal in the women's volleyball final.**

power of women's volleyball, lean on their long-time star, 28-year-old Luis Mireya, and power back to win the next three games, 15–12, 17–16, 15–6, and the gold medal. Mireya paces her team by hammering 31 kills in the winning effort.

In the earlier bronze-medal game, Brazil outlasts the Russian Federation in a five-set match to keep the Russian team from winning a medal for the first time in the eight Olympic Games in which the team has competed.

In a surprising and thrilling victory, Denmark's first women's Olympic handball team holds on in a dramatic overtime shootout to defeat the favored Koreans in a 37–33 victory. In what may be the noisiest game on record, Korean supporters crash cymbals and gongs and bang on inflatable yellow "sticks" while Denmark's fans—joined by the large and lively Norwegian crowd that came to cheer its team

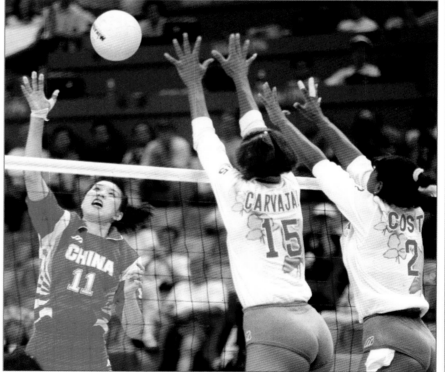

JOHN A ISAACS • KIMBERLY A. ISAACS • MARK R ISAACS • PATRICIA A ISAACS • ROSE D ISAACS • SETH E ISAACS • VERNA M ISAACS • DORIS ISAACS STALLWORTH • MARTHA J ISABEL • THOMAS E ISABEL • ANGELA T ISABELL • RALPH G ISAK • CRUZ G ISAURA • NICKIE C ISBEL • REGINA J ISBEL • STEVEN M ISBELL • NANCY ISENBERG • TOMMY A ISENHOUR • ANNE ISENHOWER • TOMO ISHIZUKA • ALLISON L ISHMAN MT • MIR S ISLAM • KENNETH D ISLER • FLEXNER ISLEY • LORI P ISLEY • SYED ISMAIL • ANTHONY C ISOM • BARBARA M ISOM • CAROLE W ISOM • DONALD L ISOM • TRACEY S ISOM • DAIRO ISOMURA

top: The bronze-medal–winning Hungarian women's handball team congratulates the gold-medal winners from Denmark.

bottom: Russia's Oleg Saitov (left) wins the 67 kg (147 lb) welterweight final over Cuba's Juan Hernandez (right).

each bout, Cuba's dominance seems to fade. Of the first six gold medals awarded, only two go to Cuba, while the others are won by Algeria, Bulgaria, Hungary, and the Russian Federation. While Cuba's boxers are having some unexpected trouble with their opponents, virtually everyone—coaches, athletes, and fans—is unhappy with the new scoring system that governs Olympic boxing under International Boxing Federation rules. Russian coach Nikolai Khromov says the system "has made these Olympics very difficult. Fighters are uncertain when they have won or lost. It has put a lot of pressure on them."

In a new Olympic road cycling event called time trials, Spain's indomitable Miguel Indurain completes the 32.4 mi (52.2 km) Atlanta course at an average speed of 30.3 mph (48.8 kph), 12 seconds ahead of his teammate, Abraham Olano, and well ahead of 36 other racers to capture the first-ever gold medal in the individual time trial.

Indurain enters this competition on the heels of his most disappointing racing season in which he failed to win his sixth straight

in the earlier bronze medal game—a game Norway lost to Hungary, 20–18—clang on cowbells throughout the game.

At the Alexander Memorial Coliseum, perennial powerhouse Cuba appears unstoppable going into boxing's gold medal bouts. But with

victory in the Tour de France, finishing 11th. "The [1996] tour was a low point in my career. Now I appear to have recovered." Indeed, Indurain, whom his rivals and the press call "superhuman," is in extraordinary condition; at rest, his heart beats a remarkable 28 times each minute. IOC President Samaranch presents the medals to his fellow countryman in person.

In the women's individual time trial, the Russian Federation's Zulfiya Zabirova wins the first gold by 20 seconds over French cycling legend Jeannie Longo-Ciprelli, completing the

nally clears, Agassi dazzles the fans and his opponent in an incredibly brief, 77-minute, three-set victory—6–2, 6–3, 6–1—to capture the gold medal. After hitting a forehand winner for match point, Agassi throws his racket into the air and the crowd leaps to its feet to cheer his victory. Though he has won every grand slam event except the French Open, Agassi says of today's victory, "To me this is the greatest thing I've accomplished in the sport. I'd keep this over all of them." He embraces his fiancée and coaches, and then heads

16.22 mi (26.1 km) course in 0:36:40 at an average speed of 26.5 mph (42.7 kph). The time trial course, the same course used for the earlier road race competition, is lined with tens of thousands of fans who cheer the riders to the finish.

Spain's Sergi Bruguera and the US's Andre Agassi, as well as the capacity crowd on hand to watch them play the men's tennis singles gold-medal match, are forced to wait through a three-hour rain delay. When the weather fi-

top: Igor Bonciukov of the Republic of Moldova races in the individual time trial finals of road cycling.

bottom: Miguel Indurain of Spain (right) celebrates his gold medal in road cycling with his family.

NORMA L IWANE • YUMIKO IWATA • ELAINE A IWUOHA-YOUNG • SHAILA IYER • DEBBIE M IZA • JOSE L IZAGUIRRE • LESZEK M IZDEBSKI • GWENDOLYN R IZELL • CEDRIC IZILEIN • RAUL IZQUIERDO MT • HIRONORI IIZUMI • ROBERT A IZZO • J. GARY REDDING • FREDA P JABBAR • STEPHEN M JABLECKI • ADAM R JABLONOWSKI • MICHAEL J JABLONSKI • GEORGE T JACAK • CYNTHIA C JACENTY • JEFFREY W JACENTY • JANELLE M JACK • LARRY L JACK • MARTHA JACK • NICOLA N JACK • SUSAN L JACK • STEFANI E JACKENTHAL • MARILYN R JACKLICH • STEPHANIE S JACKS • ADRIENNE N JACKSON • ALEX JACKSON

Like Agassi, Paes has a family lineage that provides him with the makings of an Olympian. His father was on the Indian hockey team that won the bronze in 1972, and his mother was captain of India's women's basketball team.

Fifty-five miles north of Atlanta at Lake Lanier, powerful men's and women's teams from Germany continue their winning ways in the first day of finals in the canoe/kayak–sprint competition. The German teams capture three gold medals and a bronze in the first six races and place fourth in two other races.

OLYMPIC ARTS FESTIVAL

Souls Grown Deep: African American Vernacular Art of the South, an exhibition of extraordinary quality, depth, and scope, is the largest and most important exhibition of its kind ever presented to the public. Most of the self-taught African-American artists who created the 450 works included in this exhibition have been, until recently, relatively unknown beyond the limited circle of collectors and scholars who have followed their work over the past 20–30 years. Organized by Emory University's Michael C. Carlos Museum and presented in a

left: Leander Paes, ranked no. 127 in the world, wins the men's singles tennis bronze medal to become India's first Olympic medal winner in 16 years.

right: Andreas Dittmer and Gunar Kirchbach of Germany win the gold medal in the men's pairs 1000 m canoe–sprint competition.

for his father, Mike Agassi, who boxed for Iran in the 1948 and 1952 Olympic Games. "It was a memorable embrace we'll have forever," said Agassi of his father's hug. "I let him get closer to the gold than he ever got."

Unseeded Leander Paes, who entered the competition ranked no. 127 in the world, collects himself after dropping the first set and wins the men's singles bronze medal to become India's first Olympic medal winner in 16 years.

• AMANDA JACKSON • AMANDA L JACKSON • AMELIA JACKSON • AMY L JACKSON • ANDREA L JACKSON • ANGELINA JACKSON • ANNA L JACKSON • ANNETTE F JACKSON • ANNETTE M JACKSON • ANNIE LEE JACKSON • ANTHONY JACKSON • ANTHONY R JACKSON • ARTHUR D JACKSON • AUBREY M JACKSON • BARBARA J JACKSON • BARBARA K JACKSON • BENJAMIN H JACKSON • BENJAMIN L JACKSON • BEVERLY L JACKSON • BOB W JACKSON • BRENDA J JACKSON • BRYAN A JACKSON • CALVIN A JACKSON • CAMIE L JACKSON • CAMILLE JACKSON • CANDICE E JACKSON • CARLISS F JACKSON • CAROL W JACKSON •

new, 30,000 sq ft (2,800 sq m) space within City Hall East, *Souls Grown Deep* has attracted significant and enthusiastic attention from the press, especially from the international press, which had been largely unfamiliar with this kind of work.

Curated by Dr. Robert C. Hobbs of Virginia Commonwealth University, this extraordinary exhibition is a landmark presentation of paintings, sculptures, and works on paper by the 30 leading self-taught artists from the South. Nearly all the exhibited works were drawn from the collection of William Arnett, a full-time collector whose early passion for and commitment to work by self-taught artists led him to assemble an extensive collection of the highest quality.

The collective impact of the exhibition is extremely powerful, but it is the opening that so effectively grabs the attention of visitors. A collection of "yard art," with works by several

artists, most notably Lonnie Holly, is presented in a marvelous re-creation of the environment one might encounter along the backroads of the South, where most of the exhibition's artists live and work. An almost overwhelming collection of sculptures—made of everything from old hubcaps to garden tools, that most people would classify as just junk—is arranged along either side of a lengthy pathway. From fantastic sculptures made of found objects to wood carving and works on paper in ink, crayon, magic marker, and other, unusual writ-

ing implements, the range of emotions, subject matter, and treatments is extraordinary.

A companion piece to this exhibition is a smaller display of the creations of Thornton Dial, located at the Michael C. Carlos Museum. Many consider Dial the dean of the aesthetic genre of using found objects in works of art. Dial's physically imposing and spiritually provocative paintings seem to transcend the two- and three-dimensional world of art they inhabit, generally incorporating found objects. Viewers can spend a long time trying to unearth the hidden ideas and masked metaphors contained in these remarkable works.

left: The Alliance Theatre Company revives the highly acclaimed *Blues for an Alabama Sky* by famed African-American playwright Pearl Cleague, which stars Deidre Henry (left) and Phylicia Rashad (right).

right: Souls Grown Deep, an exhibition of over 450 painting, sculptures, and works on paper by 40 contemporary self-taught African-American artists from the South, is shown at City Hall East.

Atlanta 1996®

CAROLYN JACKSON • CATHERINE A JACKSON • CHARLES E JACKSON • CHERYL A JACKSON • CHERYL J JACKSON • CHRISTINA M JACKSON • CHRISTINE A JACKSON • CHRISTOPHER D JACKSON • CHRISTOPHER H JACKSON • CHRISTOPHER T. JACKSON • CONNIE JACKSON • CONNIE L. JACKSON DEBRA L LEFKOWITZ • BILLIE J LEFLER • CAREY LEE LEFLER • LEE M LEFLER • STEFANI LEGALL • THOMAS C LEGAN • WAYNE LEGG • WILLIAM A LEGGETT • SCOTT A LEGGIO EMT • ELLEASHIA L LEGINGTON • CHRISTOPHE R LEGLAND • DEYANIRA J LEGOAS • ERIC L LEGOME • JACQUES LEGRAND • JOHN A LEGRAND

Day Sixteen
4 August 1996

Today's Calendar

Competition

Athletics
Basketball
Boxing
Canoe/kayak—sprint
Equestrian
Gymnastics—rhythmic
Handball
Volleyball—indoor

Olympic Arts Festival

Southern Crossroads Festival

**Centennial Olympic Games
Closing Ceremony**

Pin trading, a favorite Olympic pastime, is enjoyed by children and adults alike.

MOST FIRST-TIME Olympic spectators are baffled by all the hoopla surrounding Olympic pins and the activity of pin trading. It seems like almost everyone is either trading or buying pins. Pin trading is infectious, catching on with virtually everyone, even those who claim they have no interest in becoming serious pin collectors. Every host organization licenses the right to design and produce pins to one or more companies. Sponsors are entitled to produce their own pin series, and the National Olympic Committees, International Federations, official broadcasters, and some other entities also have the option of producing and selling these popular Olympic commodities. The sheer quantity of pin designs is so great that even those responsible for monitoring the approval process are pressed to keep up. The total number of pins manufactured and distributed is in the millions.

Two giant pin-trading centers, hosted by The Coca-Cola Company, attract thousands of visitors each day. The volume of activity in these two locations—one at the old Georgia Freight Depot near Underground Atlanta, the other in Centennial Olympic Park—means lines of people are frequently kept waiting. Inside, thousands upon thousands of pins of every possible description overwhelm and excite even the most experienced traders.

P • CONSTANCE K JACKSON • CORA E JACKSON • CYNTHIA Y JACKSON • DANNTON C JACKSON • DAVID A JACKSON • DAVID E JACKSON • DEBORAH J JACKSON • DEBORAH R JACKSON • DIANE E JACKSON • DONNA L JACKSON • DORIS L JACKSON • DYNAH C JACKSON • EDWIN L JACKSON • ELAINE R JACKSON • ELIZABETH C JACKSON • ELIZABETH S JACKSON • ERNESTINE M JACKSON • EVELYN JACKSON • EVELYN B JACKSON • FELICIA G JACKSON • FREDERICK P JACKSON • GAIL P JACKSON • GALE P JACKSON • GARY P JACKSON • GENA C JACKSON • GEORGIA F JACKSON • GERALD D JACKSON • GERTHA DEAN JACKSON

Newcomers are stunned by the mind-boggling range of choices. But these two spots are not the only places pin traders gather. Impromptu streetside trading tables set up by serious, experienced collectors and traders attract crowds instantly.

The methods visitors use to display pins vary widely, from those who wear virtually every pin they own to those who display only one or two prize pins. Some carry their collection in their belt-pack, some around the brim of or entirely covering their hat. More experi-

Kids are quick to catch on and are natural traders, sure of what they like and which pins they are willing to part with to get a coveted new pin. Pin trading by its very nature inspires the Olympic Spirit and often leads to conversations and exchanges of Olympic tales—many in the tall-tale category. This highly social and inexpensive hobby fuels the spirit of exchange between people and extends interest in the Olympic Games as every collector carries home mementos of their Olympic experience.

Impromptu pin-trading displays attract instant crowds.

enced collectors often wear special pin vests that are covered with an enormous number of pins, front and back. When these individuals meet a potential trader, they can quickly pull off the vest and lay it out on a flat surface to create an instant trading table.

Bartering is the essential skill required for successful pin trading, and it can sometimes become intense. The level of trading sophistication escalates as more and more people are swept up by the pin exchange frenzy, but for the most part, pin trading is just pure fun.

COMPETITION

The men's marathon, which is traditionally held just prior to the beginning of the Closing Ceremony, is moved to 7:05 a.m. on this final day of competition to compensate for anticipated heat and humidity that might negatively affect the runners later in the day. Far more than a long foot race, this event embodies and vividly recalls the spirit of the ancient

Park to become acclimated to Atlanta's heat and humidity. Now that he has had the time to adapt, Keleketu feels that he is ready for today's race, but victory is not to be his.

In the closest men's marathon finish in history, South Africa's Josia Thugwane and the Democratic People's Republic of Korea's Bong-Ju Lee enter Olympic Stadium almost at the same time for the final lap. The first black South African to win an Olympic gold medal, Thugwane crosses the finish line first in 2:12.36, only three seconds ahead of Lee. Kenya's Eric

left: Runners in the men's marathon run down Capitol Avenue in downtown Atlanta.

right: Athletes file out of Olympic Stadium at the beginning of the men's marathon.

Games. This centennial marathon delivers the most thrilling and historically significant finish in modern Olympic history.

"Nobody starts a marathon as a champion," says Botswana's Benjamin Keleketu. "Everybody has a chance. Anything can happen, and I am hoping to win." The diminutive marathoner has come to Atlanta to try again after the 1992 Games, when he struggled to the finish line racked by pain and suffering but determined to reach the end. "Only two things can happen: win or lose," he says. "Doing your best is what is important." Though he finished in last place in 1992, Keleketu returned to his homeland something of a hero. Since his arrival in Atlanta, he has become a popular figure who is often seen working out in Piedmont

KEITH M JACKSON • KEITH T JACKSON • KELLIE J JACKSON • KERRI M JACKSON • KIMBERLY JACKSON • LAMONICA JACKSON • LARRY D JACKSON • LATRICE S JACKSON • LATRICIA JACKSON • LAWRENCE M JACKSON • LEE C JACKSON • LERLINE JACKSON • LESIA A JACKSON • LINDELL JACKSON • LISSA J JACKSON • LOIS I JACKSON • LORI L JACKSON • LYDIA S JACKSON • MADESTA D JACKSON • MARSHA D JACKSON • MARY L JACKSON • MATTHEW J JACKSON • MELVIN JACKSON • MICHAEL J JACKSON • MONROE JACKSON • NANCY T JACKSON • PAMELA D JACKSON • PAMELA F JACKSON • PANSY E JACKSON •

249

top: A competitor clears the first jump, signifying Atlanta, in the equestrian individual jumping finals at the Georgia International Horse Park.

bottom: David Reid of the US knocks out Cuba's Alfredo Duvergel in a come-from-behind win in light middleweight boxing.

Wainaina comes in just five seconds after Lee to capture the bronze medal, his country's first Olympic medal in the marathon event. Reflecting on the significance of his victory, the 5 ft 2 in (1.58 m), 99 lb (45 kg) Thugwane says, "What the medal means to me is our problems are over in our country. We are free to run and be part of the international community. We are back in the fold and will be counted as part of the world community." Thugwane's gold pushes South Africa's total medal count in Atlanta to five—2 gold and 1 bronze in swimming and 1 silver in the 800 m, in addition to the marathon gold.

In an almost unbelievable come-from-behind win, light middleweight boxer David Reid of the US trails Cuba's Alfredo Duvergel 16–6, but knocks him out in the third round to earn the US's only boxing gold medal in these Games. The series of final bouts is interrupted when Muhammad Ali unexpectedly enters the Coliseum. The fans break into a unified chant of "Ali! Ali!" as "The Greatest" blows kisses to the crowd. When action resumes, gold medals are won by light welterweight Hector Vinent and flyweight Maikro Romero, both of Cuba.

In a rematch of a preliminary men's handball game between Sweden and Croatia won by Sweden 27–18, Croatia fights back to take a

PATRICIA G JACKSON • PATRICIA J JACKSON • PATRICIA L JACKSON • PHILIPPA JACKSON • PRINCETON L JACKSON • QUEEN E JACKSON • R MARK JACKSON • RANATA M JACKSON • RAY P JACKSON • REGINA A JACKSON • RENATTA T JACKSON • RICHARD A JACKSON • RICHARD L JACKSON • ROBERT E JACKSON • ROBERT L JACKSON • RON A JACKSON • RUBY A JACKSON • SANDRA JACKSON • SANDRA D JACKSON • SEBASTIAN D JACKSON • SHARI L JACKSON • SHELLEY D JACKSON • SHERRY JACKSON • SHERRY L JACKSON • SHIRLEY M JACKSON • SILVIA M JACKSON • SONIA D JACKSON • STEPHEN C JACKSON •

top: Sweden's Thomas Sivertsson and Magnus Wislander try to block Croatia's Goran Perkovac's pass in the men's handball gold-medal game.

bottom left: The Ukrainian team's Oksana Dovgalyuk moves the ball down the court in the women's bronze-medal basketball game.

bottom right: The US women's basketball team celebrates after defeating Brazil and capturing the gold medal.

27–26 victory in the final. The Georgia Dome crowd, estimated at 30,000, watches as Croatia takes an early lead and then holds off a furious rush by Sweden in the closing two minutes to retain the lead and claim victory. "We know everyone in the country was standing behind us," said Croatia's captain Goran Perkovac.

"We knew we could go all the way." And indeed they did, as Croatia wins the first gold medal in the history of this young country.

Later in the evening, the Georgia Dome hosts the women's final basketball match. A raucous capacity crowd of 33,000 roars approval as the US squad defeats Brazil, 111–87. The gold-medal victory was the first for the Americans since 1988 and avenged a 110–107

STUART A JACKSON • SUE JACKSON • SUSAN R JACKSON • SYLVIA JACKSON • SYLVIA K JACKSON • TAMARA N JACKSON • TAYLOR N JACKSON • TEDDY JACKSON • TELLIS JACKSON • TERESA A JACKSON • TERRI L JACKSON • TERRI W JACKSON • TOM V JACKSON • VALERIE D JACKSON • VALERIE V JACKSON • VI LYNNE JACKSON • VIOLA C JACKSON • WILLIAM-ADAM P JACKSON • WILLIAM D JACKSON • WILLIAM J JACKSON • WILLIAM R JACKSON • WILLIE L JACKSON • WILLIE LEE JACKSON • WILMA J JACKSON • YEVETTE JACKSON • YVONNE A JACKSON • YVONNE C JACKSON • LENA A JACKSON-WILLIAMS •

defeat at the hands of Brazil during the world championships in 1994. Repeating their outstanding performances in the semifinal game against Australia, 6 ft 5 in (1.96 m) center Lisa Leslie leads the US team, shooting 12 of 14 for 29 points and six rebounds, while teammate Teresa Edwards, the only three-time Olympic basketball gold medalist in history and former University of Georgia All-American, makes 10 assists in the victory.

The results of today's game are also significant for Brazil, as the 1994 world champions

match is the longest of the tournament, lasting nearly three hours. In the earlier medal game, Yugoslavia defeats Russia to take the bronze medal.

At Lake Lanier, Antonio Rossi of Italy and the Czech Republic's Martin Doktor put on impressive displays for the fans in the final rounds of the canoe/kayak–sprint competition, each taking home two gold medals. After teaming up with his countryman, Daniele Scarpa, to capture the gold in the double kayak 1,000 m on Saturday, Rossi wins gold today in

The Netherlands' team defeats Italy's team for the gold in a hard-fought men's volleyball final.

earn their first Olympic medal in women's basketball. Australia turned in a medal-winning performance in an earlier game, capturing the bronze by defeating the Ukrainians 66–56.

In a replay of the 1996 Volleyball World League Championship final in June, the Netherlands defeats Italy in a hard-fought, lead-swapping, five-set match—15–12, 9–15, 16–14, 9–15, 17–15—to win the Olympic gold medal in the men's division. This dramatic

the men's singles kayak 500 m race. Doktor won his second gold medal by capturing the men's singles 1,000 m canoe event on Saturday. Scarpa scores another medal today as he teams with Beniamino Bonomi to take a silver in the 500 m double kayak.

In a totally unexpected finish to the equestrian individual jumping final, Germany's Ulrich Kirchhoff is the only rider to clear every jump in the two-round event, giving Germany gold medals in both dressage and jumping. Kirchhoff, who is relatively new to international competition, replaces his two teammates,

DEBRA J JACKSON ATC • MELVIN JACKSON II • RICHARD L JACKSON JR • ROBERT TOUSSAINT JACKSON JR • LORRAINE A JACOB • VERNAL J JACOB • HOWARD L JACOBI • NICOLE M JACOBITZ • ANNA A JACOBS • ANNE E JACOBS • CARL M JACOBS • CAROLYN G JACOBS • DARRION T JACOBS • HERMAN JACOBS • HOWARD G JACOBS • JEANETTE F JACOBS • JEFFREY A JACOBS • JEFFREY D JACOBS • JENNIFER L JACOBS • JOYCE JACOBS • LAFAVERIAN J JACOBS • MARA L JACOBS • MICHAEL A JACOBS • NORMAN F JACOBS • PRICE C JACOBS • SARAH L JACOBS • SCOTT R JACOBS • SCOTT R JACOBS • SHERILYN C JACOBS •

Ludger Beerbaum and Franke Sloothaak, both top riders worldwide, who are forced to withdraw from competition when Beerbaum's horse is injured and Sloothaak is hurt in a fall during a qualifying round. Willi Melliger of Switzerland takes the silver; Alexandra Ledermann of France, the bronze.

Earning the all-around gold medal in rhythmic gymnastics, Kateryna Serebryanska of Ukraine scores sufficient points in the first three rounds to offset a potentially disastrous loss of her ribbon when it is swept from her grasp by the air-conditioning system during the final round of competition. Serebryanska's teammate, Olena Vitrichenko, takes the bronze while Ianina Batrychinko of the Russian Federation captures the silver.

The last competing athletes of the 1996 Olympic Games leave the final victory ceremonies with a variety of sentiments. Some are flushed with pride in their achievements, whether their athletic skills earned them a medal or the satisfaction of having shone amongst the most talented athletes in the world. Others are already burning to return to practice, so they can redress a failed attempt at the next Olympiad. Still others, often accomplished veterans of more than one Olympiad, are looking forward to retiring from competition and entering a new phase of their lives.

Despite this variety of emotions, there is a new sense of peace and unity on the buses returning to the Atlanta Olympic Village—a feeling that comes with the knowledge that competition is over. Athletes that left the Olympic Village earlier today as rivals return as colleagues and friends.

With the pressure of competition eliminated, athletes can now reflect on the meaning of saying "good-bye." Back at the Village, athletes are exchanging telephone numbers and addresses with the friends and associates they have made in the past 16 days, which have been among the most intense days in their lives. The real good-byes, however, will be said at the biggest party of their stay in Atlanta—the Closing Ceremony.

The skill of Kateryna Serebryanska garners the gold in rhythmic gymnastics competition.

TERESA JACOBS • TERRY F JACOBS • THOMAS JACOBS • TONI P JACOBS • VICKI K JACOBS • CHRIS JACOBSEN-HARM • JAMES R JACOBSON • JARED S JACOBSON • JOAN R JACOBSON • KRISTIN D JACOBSON • LAURA ELIZABETH JACOBSON • MARCIA N JACOBSON • PAULINE M JACOBSON • TEDDI J JACOBSON • KRISTEN JACOBUS • DAVID SCOTT JACOBY • RENEE JACOKES • BRANDON C JACQUES • MAE R JACQUES • ONDRE M JACQUES • VALERIE D JACQUES • MICHAEL A JACUBENTA • JOETTA S JAEGER • MARIA JAEGER • SHIRLEY A JAEGER • THOMAS E JAEGER • THOMAS E JAEGER JR • HAMID S JAFARI •

The *Olympic Woman* exhibition portrays women's early struggles and recent triumphs in the modern Olympic era.

OLYMPIC ARTS FESTIVAL

The occasion of the Centennial Olympic Games provides numerous opportunities to explore and celebrate various aspects of Olympic history. Among the most compelling and emotionally captivating themes in the first century of the modern Olympic era has been the early struggle and more recent triumph of women's participation in and enrichment of the Olympic Games.

The Cultural Olympiad made an early commitment to chronicle and celebrate this remarkable and inspiring story during the Olympic Arts Festival. Multi-Media Partners,

Ltd. of Washington, DC, painstakingly researched and organized the *Olympic Woman*, a historically comprehensive, interactive, and inspiring exhibition that has attracted audiences of all ages and garnered significant positive notice from the international sports press.

The exhibition's opening on the morning of 23 June was led by ACOG President and CEO Billy Payne, whose remarks honored the contributions women have made to the Olympic Movement. Olympians Aileen Riggen Seoule, Alice Coachman, and Joan Benoit Samuelson, each representing a different era of Olympic history, took part in the opening festivities, leading attendees through the exhibit. Their connection to some of Olympic history's most meaningful moments added significantly to the immediacy and highly personal approach of the exhibition.

The exhibition is organized as a walk through Olympic history that highlights achievements within the social and political contexts of the various eras. An introductory scene, which describes the little-known involvement of female athletes in ancient Greece, sets the tone for what follows. Then the *Olympic Woman* moves on to capture the drama, the underlying social advancement

uses a movie-reel approach to highlight the earliest participation of women in the modern Olympic Games; *Marvelous Mama* contrasts the social role of women after World War II with the expanded role of women athletes in the Olympic Games of that period; *Breaking Barriers* highlights the extraordinary history and spectacular achievements of African-American women during the 1960s; *Eastern Bloc Athletes* emphasizes the dominant role and contributions of Eastern Bloc female athletes for almost three decades; and *Winter Symphony* pays trib-

Olympian Aileen Riggen Seoule attends the *Olympic Woman* exhibition at Georgia State University with her family.

campaign, and the historic details behind the scenes from Victorian days to current times.

Memorabilia—including medals, shoes and other athlete equipment, photographs and newspaper clippings, and soundclips—provide a wealth of material for visitors to explore. In addition, five videos, produced for the exhibit, provide a historic context for key exhibition themes and messages. The first of the videos

ute to the accomplishments of female Olympians in the Winter Olympic movement.

The exhibition's grand finale is a spectacular three-screen video, *Passion to Excel*, that celebrates Olympic women throughout the modern Olympic Era. By contrasting moments of triumph and exaltation with those of defeat and despair, the video's rich visual content, beautifully enriched by an inspiring and emotional musical score, moves many viewers to tears.

Atlanta 1996.

PATRICK H JAMBE • STACY J JAMBE • VÉNITA D JAMERSON • A CAMILLE JAMES • ALAN JAMES • ALMA F JAMES • ANGELA A JAMES • BEVERLY R JAMES • BRENDA J JAMES • BYRON C JAMES • BYRON O JAMES • CARLA A JAMES • CARLA R JAMES • CARLOS A JAMES • CECELIA S JAMES • CHARLENE M JAMES • CHESTER JAMES • CLARA A JAMES • DALE L JAMES • DAWN L JAMES • DEVORAH JAMES • DOROTHY E JAMES • ELAURA Q JAMES • ELIZABETH R JAMES • ELLEN J JAMES • ERIC H JAMES • ERNEST JAMES • ESTELLE F JAMES • FLEMING JAMES • FRANKIE M JAMES • GLORIA GUNTER JAMES • JAMIN J JAMES • JANICE E JAMES

255

CLOSING CEREMONY
4 AUGUST 1996

Closing Ceremony volunteer cast members hold silk squares above their heads to form an Olympic quilt symbolizing unity.

LET THE FINAL celebration begin! The Centennial Olympic Games—by far the largest Games in Olympic history, attracting holders of 8.6 million sport and more than 228,000 Olympic Arts Festival tickets—have filled the past 16 days to overflowing with an extraordinary and unprecedented array of athletic and artistic achievements, countless dramatic moments, tens of thousands of new cross-cultural friendships that will outlast these Games. Underlying all these experiences and events is the essence of the Olympic Ideal, the idealistic statement of purpose Baron de Coubertin put into words at a reception held in 1908 when he quoted the following passage from a sermon delivered by Bishop Talbot:

> The important thing in the Olympic Games is not winning but taking part, for the essential thing in life is not conquering but fighting well.

The quilt, selected by ACOG to serve as the omnipresent icon and metaphor for the Centennial Olympic Games during this Olympiad, has been transformed from a beautiful symbol to a living presence within every aspect of this incredible world gathering. This historically rich and meaningful cultural expression of the American South, in which the pieces of patchwork composed of many different fabrics and patterns are brought together to form a unified whole that comforts and warms its owner, is the embodiment and manifestation of these Olympic Games. Innumerable threads of shared experiences—from spectators in the stands to athletes on the field of play and broadcast audiences, some of whom have witnessed and shared in the Games from

• JEANNIE A JAMES • JENNIFER JAMES • JIMMY A JAMES • JOHN C JAMES • KATHLEEN S JAMES • LILLIAN R JAMES • LYNORRIS JAMES • MARY B JAMES • MELISSA JAMES • MICHEAL W JAMES • PEGGY A JAMES • RANDALL H JAMES • ROBERT E JAMES • RODERICK B JAMES • SHERI E JAMES • STEPHANIE M JAMES • TERRENCE B JAMES • TERRI S JAMES • VANESSA D JAMES • JANET K JAMES ATC • MARCIA JAMES GLUZ • ANDREW JAMESON • DAVID H JAMESON • ELIZABETH H JAMESON • JANE N JAMESON • WALTER JAMESON • ALICE L JAMIESON • DARRYL C JAMIESON • JOHN JAMIESON • JUDY J JAMIESON • SUZANNE G

top: **Athletes celebrate while watching the victory ceremony for the men's marathon in Olympic Stadium.**

bottom: **An Olympic Games staff member joins the crowd in celebration as the fireworks begin at the Closing Ceremony in Atlanta.**

half the world away—have sewn a macro-quilt, uniting the very world.

During the Opening Ceremony 16 days ago, when 3.5 billion people around the world watched as the world's greatest athletes marched into Olympic Stadium to form a multicolored patchwork quilt representing a microcosm of humankind, an Olympic bond was forged. Since that magnificent occasion, hundreds of events have taken place. Those who have achieved victory and those who have not, those who have attended the Games in person and those who have looked in and experienced the Games from afar—all have shared a common experience through participating in this extraordinary journey of discovery.

The journey has been emotional for each participant and observer—either celebratory or disappointing, depending on the outcome of each event. For a brief moment, it had seemed as if Atlanta's Olympic journey might be curtailed. But the power of the Olympic Ideal overcame the pain and fear of the bombing in Centennial Olympic Park, and the Games did indeed go on. In the aftermath of tragedy, the

JAMIESON • WILLIAM J JAMIESON • BRETT D. JAMISON • BRIAN C JAMISON • EMILY B JAMISON • ANGELA C JAMISON JOHNSON • HELEN M JANCIK • JAMES F JANCIK • CAROL D JANDRLICH • CATHERINE M JANDRLICH • ROBERT L JANDRLICH • RONNA RENEE JANES • BEATRICE JANEX • INSICK JANG • JOON JANG • YOUNG JANG • YOUNG-JEE JANG • COLLEEN A JANICH • SALLY C JANICK • RICHARD F JANICKI • CHARLOTTE H JANIS • LAUREN A JANIS • LILI R JANKO • ROBERT S JANKO • DANIEL M JANKOWSKI • MARTHA JANKOWSKI • LAURA S JANN • CARL P JANNETT • MARLENE J JANOS • DANAJANOVSEK • MARK C

Olympic flame, which so eloquently embodies the spirit of humankind, seemed to burn more brightly from the cauldron at Olympic Stadium. As if invoking the spirit of Atlanta's history, the phoenix, the Games rose out of the darkness of that moment to foster an even deeper sense of commitment to the Olympic Spirit among athletes, spectators, and staff.

The celebratory nature of the Closing Ceremony contrasts with the more formal atmosphere of the Opening Ceremony. The Closing Ceremony reunites the thousands of athletes

whose outstanding performances, record-setting achievements, commitment to excellence, determination, and dedication to the Olympic Spirit have thrilled the world. This festival of friendship also provides an opportunity to release emotions and extend the goodwill generated during these Centennial Olympic Games in a renewal of commitment to the Olympic Ideal.

The Closing Ceremony begins with a stirring rendition of composer John Williams's "Summon the Heroes" by the Cadets of Bergen County, the oldest and most honored drum and bugle corps in the world. In an expression of appreciation to the host country, the internationally acclaimed popular vocal group Boyz II Men follows immediately with a richly harmonized performance of "The Star-Spangled Banner," setting the stage for an evening of performances by some of the most popular musical artists in the US.

In a break from tradition, the men's mara-

thon, which historically finishes immediately before or during the beginning of the Closing Ceremony, was held earlier today to take advantage of cooler temperatures. The marathon victory ceremony, however, was scheduled to take place now, amid the fanfare of the Closing Ceremony. As a televised replay of the finish is shown on screens throughout the stadium, the winning athletes are decorated with medals and victory bouquets, generating a rousing cheer from the more than 85,000 fans who have come to witness this historic finale

of the Centennial Olympic Games.

The audience is astonished as the Cadets of Bergen County take the field during the opening flourish of activity and begin to perform a precision marching routine conducted by comedian Bill Irwin. America's long tradition of enhancing important events with marching bands, generally formal and ceremonial in their deportment, is treated humorously as the inept conductor is literally run down by this "band on the run."

This brief transition sets up a special tribute to the Olympians who have given the world 16 days of outstanding performances. Stadium spectators raise cards to form a giant laurel wreath based on ACOG's Quilt of Leaves pattern as the song "Faster, Higher, Stronger,"

left: The Cadets of Bergen County begin the Closing Ceremony with a performance of "Summon the Heroes."

right: The medal-winners of the men's marathon—Josia Thugwane of South Africa (gold), Bong-Ju Lee of Korea (silver), and Eric Wainaina of Kenya (bronze)—celebrate their victory at Closing Ceremony.

JANOWSKI • AMY W JANSEN • BEVERLY R JANSEN • LAURA C JANSEN • MELVA D JANSEN • EMMANUEL C M JANSSEN • LARS D JANSSON • GWENDOLYN JANUARY • RIMA J JANULEVICIUS • STEPHEN A JANUSESKI • CHIP JANVIER • MICHAEL L JANZEN • ANDRES V JARAMILLO • MARTY JARAMILLO ATC • MARY RUTA JARAS • WILLIAM A JARMON • ELIZABETH A JARNAGIN • EVA JAROMIRSKI-PRITCHETT • CHRIS D JAROS • ANITA M JARRARD • CYNTHIA H JARRARD • DENNIS L JARRARD • BRIAN E JARREL • REX B JARRELL • CHERYL L JARRETT • DEBORAH L JARRETT • NANCY J JARRETT • PAUL A JARRETT • ROGERS G

premiered by Jessye Norman at Opening Ceremony, is performed by the talented Atlanta Symphony Youth Orchestra and the Morehouse College Glee Club.

Superstar vocalist Gloria Estefan gives a powerful performance of "Reach," a song she wrote as an inspirational tribute to Olympic athletes that seems to rouse an exultant mood in the people throughout the stadium. As Estefan's song concludes, an array of young mountain bikers, skateboarders, in-line skaters, BMX

top: The Morehouse College Glee Club joins the stars as they salute the athletes with song.

bottom: The audience raises cards to form a giant laurel wreath in Olympic Stadium.

bikers, and daring gymnasts cascades onto the field to perform an "extreme ballet" on the ramps of a street course erected almost instantly in the center of the field. Propelling themselves as high as 24.9 ft (7.6 m) in the air, these daring and gifted athletes reflect the dynamic energy of youth in an extended routine performed to a score by Michael Kamen, one of Hollywood's top composers. Atlanta native Ann Marie McPhail sings "On Wings of Victory," playing the part of an extreme diva to open the performance.

JARRETT • WILLIAM J JARRETT • WILLIAM H JARRETT II • VICTORIA A JARRETT SAT • BERNIE F JARRIEL SR • ADRIENNE L JARVIS • ERNIE R JARVIS • SUSAN D JARVIS • DAVID R JASINEK • DONALD A JASLOW • BRENDA C JASON • JAMES E JASPER • SUZANNE L JASPER • JAMES JATCKO • DEANNA K JATKO • JEFFREY E JAUDON • CARLOS JAURIGUE • LESLIE S JAVETZ • CAROL A JAVORSKY • HEATHER J JAVORSKY • JUDITH A JAVORSKY • SHAUNTE M JAVORSKY • ADAM J JAY • CAROL M JAY • JENNIFER H JAY • JO ANNE H JAY • ROBERT L JAY • SATEESH B JAYAPRAKASH • SUMATI S JAYARAMAN • BETTY F JAYNES • HAROLD

Audience reaction to this captivating sequence is enthusiastic and loud, and a roar of approval erupts as the routine comes to its climactic finish. This tribute to the daring, skill, and achievement of Olympic athletes is followed by a parade of 197 flags, each carried by an athlete selected by his or her National Olympic Committee to represent the delegation, marches into the stadium and around the track. This colorful tapestry of cultures is woven together to the strains of another Kamen score written especially for this occasion, "The Sacred Truce," performed by the Atlanta Symphony Youth Orchestra and the Atlanta Olympic Band. In keeping with Olympic tradition, the procession is led by the International Olympic Committee flag, first used for the 1920 Games in Antwerp, and concludes with the entry of the host country's national flag.

top left: An array of bikers, skateboarders, and in-line skaters entertain the crowd with daring routines.

bottom left: Gloria Estefan performs "Reach," a song she wrote as an inspirational tribute to Olympic athletes.

right: The Atlanta Olympic Band performs "The Sacred Truce," written by Michael Kamen for this occasion.

L JEAN • LILIAN JEAN • PAULA H JEANE • BARBARA B JEANNERET • KIMBERLY K JEANS • CURTIS L JEANS JR • FRANCOIS JEANSON • ANN JEFFCOAT • CAROLYN G JEFFERIES • KIM L JEFFERIES • MARY L JEFFERIES • MAURICE JEFFERIES • ROBERT K JEFFERIES • FITCH B JEFFERIES III • FITCH B JEFFERIES JR • DONALD J JEFFERS • PETER JEFFERS • PETER M JEFFERS • THERESA N JEFFERS • JACKIE L JEFFERSON • JACQUELINE JEFFERSON • JONATHAN K JEFFERSON • LINDA CLEAVES JEFFERSON • LOYLENE JEFFERSON • MARCIA N JEFFERSON • MARY F JEFFERSON • RODRIQUES M JEFFERSON •

Flag-bearing athletes representing each participating delegation march into the stadium.

In honor of the origins of the Olympic Games and in anticipation of the Sydney Games of 2000, this ceremony of flags concludes with the raising of the national flags of Greece and Australia, accompanied by their respective national anthems—"Hymn of Freedom" and "Advance Australia Fair."

International Olympic Committee President Juan Antonio Samaranch and ACOG President and CEO Billy Payne address the audience briefly, thanking all those who took part and who made the Games possible. President

Many are moved to tears when a warm, glowing, and very familiar voice penetrates the stillness of the summer evening, singing, "Imagine there's no heaven. It's easy if you try. . ." It is rock 'n' roll legend Stevie Wonder singing John Lennon's famous song of peace, "Imagine." Many lock arms and sway quietly to the music; others sing along. In this moment of reflection, there is a sense that the quest for unity that lies at the heart of the Olympic Movement has been achieved. As the song concludes, President Samaranch

International Olympic Committee President Juan Antonio Samaranch and ACOG President and CEO Billy Payne thank those who took part in the Games and those who made them possible.

Samaranch breaks his long-standing silence on terrorism and the Olympic Movement to denounce the bombing in Centennial Olympic Park and the murder of 11 Israeli athletes during the 1972 Olympic Games in Munich. He says, "No act of terrorism has ever destroyed the Olympic Movement and none ever will. More than ever are we fully committed to build a better and more peaceful world in which all forms of terrorism are eradicated." Samaranch then calls for a moment of silence in honor of those who died or were injured in the park bombing and the Munich tragedy.

declares the Games of the XXVI Olympiad officially closed.

Atlanta Mayor Bill Campbell and Sydney Mayor Frank Sartor join Payne and Samaranch on the central stage to complete the formal closure of Atlanta's Olympiad. Mayor Campbell waves the Olympic flag one last time before passing it to Mayor Sartor as the crowd cheers for both Atlanta and Sydney, host of the next Olympic Games in September 2000.

• BENJAMIN F JENKINS • BRYAN JENKINS • CAROLYN S JENKINS • CHARLES JENKINS • CHARLES E JENKINS • CHERI J JENKINS • CHRIS JENKINS • CORINNE F JENKINS • DANA K.B. JENKINS • DORIS J JENKINS • GARY C JENKINS • HOLLY S JENKINS • HUNTER S JENKINS • IESHIA K.L. JENKINS • IRIE B JENKINS • JACKIE P JENKINS • JAMIE E JENKINS • JENNIFER C JENKINS • JEOFFREY S JENKINS • JOANNE E JENKINS • JOEL R JENKINS • KORI M JENKINS • KRISTINA JENKINS • KYLE V JENKINS • LENA D JENKINS • LINDA L JENKINS • LINDA L JENKINS • LINDA S JENKINS • LYN E JENKINS • MARY C JENKINS •

In keeping with tradition, the next host city responds to its acceptance of the Olympic flag with a brief performance. Sydney presents a colorful, lighthearted sequence that highlights its aboriginal culture and features many traditional icons of Australia, such as inflated kangaroos that enter the stadium mounted on the backs of bicycle riders, cockatoos, flowers, and the world-famous profile of the Sydney Opera House.

The lowering and departure of the Olympic flag at the conclusion of each Olympic Games

Watkins, along with ACOG co-chair Andrew Young, carry the Olympic flag down the track and out of the stadium, visibly moved by the honor bestowed upon them.

ACOG's emphasis on youth as a key ingredient of the Games, featured especially in the Opening and Closing Ceremonies, gives the children of Atlanta their own opportunity to bid the athletes farewell. Building from a single child, Rachel McMullin, who walks onto the field singing "The Power of the Dream," the field is gradually filled with 600 other

left: Syndey portrays Australian aboriginal culture through a sequence which includes performers playing digeridoos.

right: Large inflated balloons represent the profile of the world-famous Sydney Opera House.

is a time-honored tradition. The 10 individuals who originally joined Billy Payne to form Atlanta's Bid committee back in 1987 were honored for their volunteer efforts to win the Games for Atlanta and service in the years since by being asked to perform this important Olympic task. Atlanta-born mezzo-soprano and Atlanta Metropolitan Opera star Jennifer Larmore performs the traditional "Olympic Hymn" as Charles Battle, Peter Candler, Tim Christian, Cindy Fowler, Robert Rearden, Charles Shaffer, Horace Sibley, Linda Stephenson, and Ginger

children, ages 6–12. In a special gesture of harmony and goodwill, the audience joins in at the end of the song.

As the Atlanta Symphony Youth Orchestra performs an instrumental version of John Jarvis's "The Flame," highlights from the Games are projected onto large broadcast screens and special cards held by audience members.

The Olympic flame, which has been burning throughout the Games since it was first lit by Muhammad Ali 17 days ago, embodies the highest aspirations of the world's greatest athletes. The flame is also an expression of hope

MELISSA M JENKINS • NANCY A JENKINS • NANCY J JENKINS • NICK J JENKINS • PERRY L JENKINS • RANDALL J JENKINS • REGIENA C JENKINS • RICHARD P JENKINS • RONN JENKINS • SEREATHA A JENKINS • SHARON B JENKINS • SHIRLEY T JENKINS • SIMMS JENKINS • STEPHANIE JENKINS • SUE A JENKINS • VANTONY A JENKINS • WILLIAM W JENKINS • MAURICE E JENKINS JR • DAVID M JENKINSON • DANELLE M JENKS • JOSEPH A JENKS • MARY A JENKS • NOEL L JENKS • JANET L JENNESS • BOBBY G JENNINGS • BRENDAN D JENNINGS • CAROLYN J JENNINGS • DEBORAH K JENNINGS • DONALD J JENNINGS •

for peace, enlightenment, and goodwill among humankind, representing the spirit of the Olympic Ideal that has brought the world together for this momentous gathering.

The capstone of the ceremonial portion of the Closing Ceremony, the extinguishing of the Olympic flame, brings the Games to completion. As the atmosphere within the stadium is hushed with anticipation and with over 3.5 billion people around the world watching, Atlanta country music star Trisha

Yearwood appears high on the steps of the Olympic cauldron, just below the giant flame, to sing "The Flame" a cappella. As the stadium falls silent after the last echo of her voice dies out, the flame is extinguished.

The quiet, reflective, almost somber mood in the stadium is brought back to life by a swinging New Orleans–style funeral procession complete with jazz musicians and dancers with black umbrellas. Spirits begin to soar as the rollicking rhythms and lively character of the many American genres of music that have their roots in the South combine in a gigantic musical jamboree.

top: The original members of Atlanta's Bid committee take the Olympic flag on its final journey in Atlanta.

bottom: Carrying lit candles, 600 children fill the field of Olympic Stadium, singing "The Power of the Dream."

GAIL JENNINGS • HAROLD F JENNINGS • LINDA F JENNINGS • NATALYN E JENNINGS • OTHERIA R JENNINGS • PATRICIA J JENNINGS • RICHARD H JENNINGS • ROBERT M JENNINGS • SHERRY L JENNINGS • WANDA C JENNINGS • TRACYEE A JENNINGS-SCOTT • THOMAS M JENNINGS ATC • BJARKE G JENSEN • DANNY D JENSEN • DAVID W JENSEN • JENEEN K JENSEN • KAREN R JENSEN • KOHLER A JENSEN • KRISTA L JENSEN • KRISTEN A JENSEN • LARS BOE JENSEN • MARY N JENSEN • ROBERT C JENSEN • ROBERTA J JENSEN • SCOTT JENSEN • TRACY L JENSEN • MELANIE A JENSEN EMT • MARGOT R JENSON

265

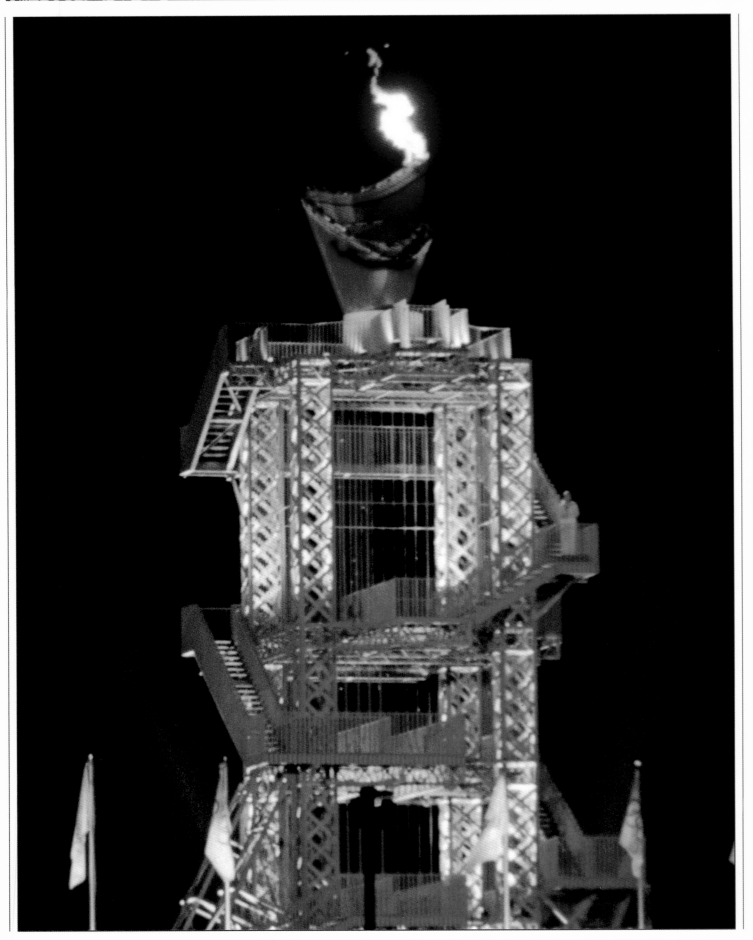

• RENEE H JENSRUD • SABINE B JENTSCH • GARRY E JEOFFROY • WON SEOK JEON • YOUNG A JEON • JIN-HONG JEONG • JEFFREY P JERDEN • GERRY JEREMIE • KAREN L JERG • PHILLIP JERG • JANET S JERITZA
• AARON J JERMUNDSON • ERIN M JERNIGAN • GENE JERNIGAN • HELEN L JERNIGAN • HENRY O JERNIGAN • JANE B JERNIGAN • KAREN E JERNIGAN • MARK A JERNIGAN • PAT S JERNIGAN • SANDRA F.
JERNIGAN • SHERRI L JERNIGAN • TERRIE ANN HARRIS JERNIGAN • ISAIAH JERNIGAN JR. • DELINDA JEROME • PAUL A JERRAM • AARON JERRELLS • LISA D JERVES • CAROL P JERVIS • RENISON F JERVIS •

Led by keyboardist and arranger Paul Shaffer and noted Broadway music director Harold Wheeler, the evening's entertainment segment opens with trumpeter Wynton Marsalis, the most popular and acclaimed jazz musician of his generation, who bursts onto the scene to start the party. Marsalis is followed by some of the music industry's greatest exponents of other musical styles, including multiple Grammy winners; legendary fiddler, guitarist, and mandolin player Mark O'Connor; and Faith Hill, one of country music's hottest young female vocalists. Rhythm and Blues stars Al Green, B.B. King, and the Pointer Sisters raise the temperature of the already heated stadium with each tune they perform.

Gloria Estefan returns with Latin percussionist Tito Puente and popular music vocal sensation Sheila E. to rock the stadium with the energized beat of the music of southern Florida. A performance given by rock 'n' roll legend Little Richard, the original "wild man," ignites the crowd of spectators and athletes. In the midst of the upward spiraling energy that has engulfed the stadium, Buckwheat Zydeco, a popular band from the Louisiana bayou, strikes up a spicy Creole jumbo of dance music that pulls the audience members who are not already dancing to their feet.

Spirits are high as, one after another, the members of this cast of musical luminaries honor the athletes with their finest performances. Unable to contain themselves, the athletes pour out onto the field to shout, dance, and gyrate to the music. The tone throughout the rest of the stadium is much the same. Spectators are on their feet clapping, dancing, embracing, singing along, and crying in a jubilant celebration of the Games.

In a concluding gesture of appreciation, the audience rises on cue to take snapshots of this last moment in a wave that wraps the entire stadium in a brilliant ring of light that ripples with the popping of flashbulbs. This light display erupts into the finale of the Games, an extended fireworks extravaganza.

Though the Closing Ceremony is over, the party seems to go into full swing as the stars all move to a central stage to continue performing for the thousands of athletes who have gathered on the field.

facing page: The flames burning within the Olympic cauldron are extinguished section by section until the cauldron is dark.

this page: A New Orleans–style funeral procession begins the conclusion of the ceremony, bringing the audience to its feet.

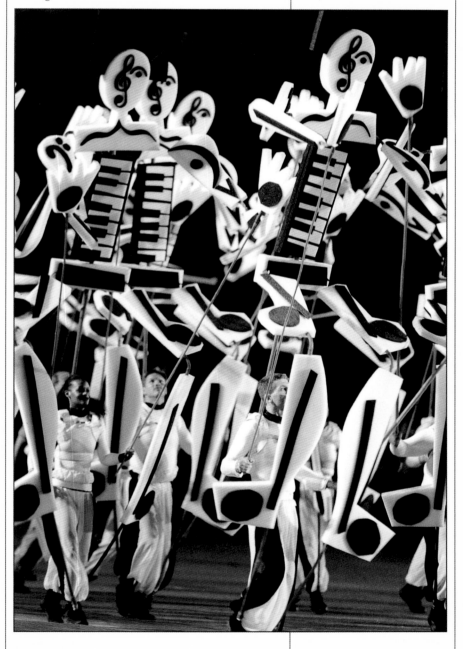

The Centennial Olympic Games are now officially complete. "The Power of the Dream" that captured the mind and heart of one Atlantan in 1987 and became his personal quest has, in the ensuing years, grown to reach out to and be shared by nearly two-thirds of the world's population tonight. The threads of experience woven together in the hearts and minds of these gifted athletes and the millions upon millions of spectators who have watched, listened, and shared in this grand event forge an unbreakable bond, a patchwork quilt and cultures together. The countless threads of individual Olympic memories that will travel home with athletes, staff, and spectators, while meaningful and alive this evening, will gain in significance in the weeks, months, and even decades following these Games. Those who have contributed to or experienced the Games directly will undoubtedly share their own personal threads—their stories—in this enormous living quilt of Olympic adventures with families, friends, and colleagues, adding to and passing along the Spirit of these Games.

top: Athletes pour onto the field to sing and dance to the music.

of humankind, that has been strengthened and energized by the flame.

For those committed to the message and values that are at the foundation of the Olympic Movement, the Olympic Games symbolize a common striving after excellence and unity that brings people from different backgrounds

At the threshold of the modern Olympic Movement's second century, the Games have achieved a level of maturity, a quality of community, and a depth of penetration that Baron de Coubertin could never have envisioned when he founded the Olympic Movement in 1894. Certainly, no one can predict what new levels of athletic and artistic achievements may

MAC INNIS JIMMY • SEOKJOON JIN • BECKY B JINKS • JILL K JINKS • DAVID JOB JR • LISA A JOBE • PATRICIA V JOBE • DEAN R JOBKO • KATHY K JOCKISCH • THEODORE I JOCKISCH • ALAN A JOE • CARA LINN JOE • CAROL P JOE • CONSTANCE E JOE • HERBERT P JOE • JEAN D JOE • DENISE M JOEHL • LYONS B JOEL • DEAN W JOELSON • HEGE JOHANNESSEN • BOB L JOHANNS • FRANK JOHANSEN • RUNAR JOHANSEN • KARL E JOHANSSON • ALBERT F JOHARY • CHRIS D JOHN • JENNIFER A JOHN • MELL JOHN • RAYMOND JOHN • GENIE K JOHNDROW • JUANITA H JOHNIGAN • HARRY M JOHNQUEST • AMANDA K JOHNS •

be possible in the second Olympic century. Beyond athletic performance, the Olympic Games must continue to focus on and cultivate the movement's idealistic underpinnings—inclusiveness, international understanding, and world peace.

top left: Athletes from around the world bid the Games of the XXVI Olympiad good-bye.

bottom left: Spectators gaze in wonder as the last fireworks erupt over Olympic Stadium, filling the Atlanta sky.

right: A spectacular fireworks display closes the Centennial Olympic Games in Atlanta.

Atlanta 1996

FRED L JOHNS • GREG JOHNS • JUDITH A JOHNS • KIMBERLY A JOHNS • LORIE D JOHNS • MARGUERITE E JOHNS • PHYLLIS E JOHNS • ROGER M JOHNS • YVONNE I JOHNS • TOM O JOHNS MD • DANIEL T JOHNSON • JOHN F JOHNSON • NANCY A JOHNSON • AARON J JOHNSON • AKEMA R JOHNSON • ALAN W JOHNSON • ALEXA A JOHNSON • ALEXIS JOHNSON • ALICIA L JOHNSON • ALLENA G JOHNSON • ALONZO S JOHNSON • ALTHEA JOHNSON • AMY C JOHNSON • ANGELA J JOHNSON • ANGELA M JOHNSON • ANGELIQUE Y JOHNSON • ANN K JOHNSON • ANNETTE L JOHNSON • ANNIE B JOHNSON •

LIVING THE DREAM

Aquatics—Diving

Venue Used:
**Georgia Tech
Aquatic Center**

Days of Competition: **8**

Medals Awarded: **12**
Gold 4
Silver 4
Bronze 4

Number of Nations: **39**

Number of Officials: **36**

Officiating Federation:
**International
Amateur Swimming
Federation (FINA)**

AQUATICS

A TOTAL OF 1,143 ATHLETES took part in the four aquatics disciplines: diving, swimming, synchronized swimming, and water polo. These competitors created some of the grandest moments of the Centennial Olympic Games.

VENUE

For the first time in Olympic history, events for all four aquatics disciplines were held at the same venue—the Georgia Tech Aquatic Center, located on the campus of the Georgia Institute of Technology adjacent to the Atlanta Olympic Village.

This state-of-the-art open-air facility, which was built especially for the 1996 Olympic Games, included a permanent, 15,000-seat outdoor stadium covered with a roof 110 ft (33.5 m) above the pool to provide shade. Within this main complex, there was a main swimming pool, a diving well, and a warm-up pool. Thirty-three feet (10 m) of the floor of the main pool could be raised or lowered up to 10 ft (3 m). This unique feature, as well as the pool's wide lanes and gutters, was designed specifically to create opportunities for faster performances.

The adjacent second area of the Aquatic Center contained a temporary outdoor pool for water polo with 4,000 seats.

The diving well was 79 x 75 ft (24 x 22.75 m) with a minimum depth of 15 ft (4.5 m) and featured three 1 and 3 m springboards and 1, 3, 5, 7.5, and 10 m platforms. The swimming pool was 164 x 82 ft (50 x 25 m) with a minimum depth of 10 ft (3 m). The synchronized swimming competition was held within the main swimming pool in a 98 x 82 ft (30 x 25 m) area at a depth of 10 ft (3 m). The water polo pool was 108 x 72 ft (33 x 22 m) with a depth of 7 ft (2.2 m).

Set against the backdrop of the downtown Atlanta skyline, the Aquatic Center was a unique and popular venue. A roof over the main complex, as well as beautifully decorated sun shades on both ends of the stadium, ensured ideal competition conditions. The computer-controlled lighting system reduced glare on the water. Scoreboards, as well as the competition area, could be easily seen from every seat, and for the first time in Olympic history, the scoreboards provided information such as notations of national and area records. The Aquatic Center is one of the enduring legacies of the Centennial Olympic Games that will benefit the Atlanta area well into the next century.

ARLESTER J JOHNSON • AUNDRIA C JOHNSON • AYEOLA B JOHNSON • BARBARA B JOHNSON • BARBARA J JOHNSON • BENJAMIN L JOHNSON • BENKEI JOHNSON • BETTY J JOHNSON • BONNIE L JOHNSON • BRENDA C JOHNSON • BRENDA D JOHNSON • BRENDA W JOHNSON • BRETT D JOHNSON • BRIAN L JOHNSON • BRIDGET L JOHNSON • BRUCE H JOHNSON • BRYANT O JOHNSON • BYRON E JOHNSON • CARL J JOHNSON • CARMEN B JOHNSON • CAROL JOHNSON • CAROLINE J JOHNSON • CAROLINE R JOHNSON • CAROLYN A JOHNSON • CAROLYN E JOHNSON • CHAN'NEL L JOHNSON • CHERYL A JOHNSON

DIVING

The diving competition was held over eight days (26 July–2 August). A total of 122 divers (66 men and 56 women) from 39 countries competed in the 3 m springboard and 10 m platform events. Every session was sold out.

COMPETITION

Each of the diving events consisted of preliminaries, semifinals, and finals. The 18 divers with the highest scores in the preliminaries advanced to the semifinals. The scores received in the preliminaries and semifinals were added together to determine the 12 divers who would compete in the finals.

3 m Springboard. In the men's 3 m springboard competition, Ni Xiong of the People's Republic of China won the gold medal in his third Olympic medal-winning performance. After winning the silver in 1988 and the bronze in 1992, 22-year-old Xiong completed his medal set by garnering the gold with a score of 701.46. Xiong took the lead in the preliminaries and never looked back. Xiong's teammate, Zhuocheng Yu, won the silver (690.93) thanks in part to his third-round dive, when he scored 47.25 on a three and one-half somersault, his most difficult dive in the competition. Mark Lenzi of the US, the defending gold medalist from the 1992 Games in Barcelona, returned from a 20-month retirement to win the bronze (686.49).

Perhaps the biggest surprise of the diving competition came in the preliminaries for the women's 3 m springboard, when World Champion Tan Shuping of the People's Republic of China missed on her third and fifth dives, finishing 23rd as a result. In the finals, the People's Republic of China's Mingxia Fu, 17, overcame a 33-point deficit to win the gold (547.68). The Russian Federation's Irina Lashko won the silver medal (512.19) for the second consecutive Olympiad, while Canada's Annie Pelletier captured the bronze (509.64).

top: Ni Xiong of the People's Republic of China competes in the men's 3 m springboard semifinals.

bottom: The People's Republic of China's Mingxia Fu salutes the crowd after receiving the gold in the women's 3 m springboard.

• CHESTER R JOHNSON • CHRISTINE M JOHNSON • CHRISTOPHER A JOHNSON • CHRISTOPHER L JOHNSON • CHRISTOPHER RICHARD JOHNSON • CHRISTOPHER RICHARD JOHNSON • CLARISSA R JOHNSON • CLAS A JOHNSON • CLAUDINE JOHNSON • COLLEEN A JOHNSON • CONNIE L JOHNSON • CONSTANCE D JOHNSON • CRAIG W JOHNSON • CURTIS S JOHNSON • CYNTHIA D JOHNSON • CYNTHIA K JOHNSON • CYNTHIA L JOHNSON • CYNTHIA L JOHNSON • DANETTE JOHNSON • DANIEL L JOHNSON • DANNY JOHNSON • DARYL C JOHNSON • DAVID C JOHNSON • DAVID E JOHNSON • DAVID R JOHNSON

10 m Platform. After finishing fifth in the men's 3 m springboard competition, Dmitri Saoutine of the Russian Federation, the Olympic favorite and world's no. 1 ranked diver, established his dominance in the men's 10 m platform competition. En route to his gold medal (692.34), the 22 year old received a perfect mark of 10, the first awarded at the Centennial Olympic Games. Germany's Jan Hempel won the silver medal (663.27), and 19-year-old Hailiang Xiao of the People's Republic of China, who was second after both the preliminaries

made her the youngest diver to win both diving events in the same Olympic Games, and the first woman since 1960 to accomplish this feat. Germany's Annika Walter, who entered the finals in fifth place, won the silver medal (479.22). Mary Ellen Clark, 33, became the oldest US diver to win a medal. The 1992 Olympic bronze medalist not only overcame a year-long bout with vertigo, which sidelined her for the previous season, but she also rebounded from a 12th-place showing in the preliminaries to earn the bronze (472.95).

left: A computer graphic description of the decorations for the diving platform is shown.

right: The Russian Federation's Dmitri Saoutine performs his final dive in the men's 10 m platform semifinals.

far right: Back in form, the US's Mary Ellen Clark completes the first of her four dives in the semifinals of the women's 10 m platform event.

and semifinals, took home the bronze medal (658.20).

Mingxia Fu became the first woman to win back-to-back platform titles since the 1950s by capturing gold in the women's 10 m platform (521.58). Fu's double gold-medal performance, which began on the women's 10 m platform and was completed on the 3 m springboard,

CONCLUSION

Several athletes left their mark on the Centennial Olympic Games' diving competition. In the men's 3 m springboard, the third time proved to be the charm for the People's Republic of China's Ni Xiong, who finally won gold in his third Olympic appearance. The Russian Federation's Dmitri Saoutine received a perfect

• DAVID S JOHNSON • DEANNE L JOHNSON • DEBORAH A JOHNSON • DELLA B JOHNSON • DEMETRIUS C JOHNSON • DENISE S JOHNSON • DEREK E JOHNSON • DERNESSA L JOHNSON • DIANA K JOHNSON • DIANE JOHNSON • DIANE A JOHNSON • DIANE L JOHNSON • DIANNE C JOHNSON • DISA A JOHNSON • DOLORA L JOHNSON • DON J JOHNSON • DONNA R JOHNSON • DOROTHY B JOHNSON • DOROTHY M JOHNSON • DOUGLAS P JOHNSON • DOUGLAS W JOHNSON • DOYLE M JOHNSON • DREW M JOHNSON • EATHAN C JOHNSON • EBONY JOHNSON • ELIZABETH E JOHNSON • ELIZABETH G JOHNSON •

mark of 10 during his gold-medal performance in the men's 10 m platform event. On the women's side, 17-year-old Mingxia Fu became the youngest diver to win both diving events in the same Olympic Games.

Hailiang Xiao's bronze-medal showing in the men's 10 m platform event enabled the People's Republic of China to medal in all four diving events at the Centennial Olympic Games. With Fu's double-gold performance, the People's Republic of China firmly established itself as the dominant team in women's

diving. Over the last three Olympiads, the People's Republic of China has won all six women's gold medals. Xiong's gold-medal victory in the men's 3 m springboard competition gave the People's Republic of China its second gold medal in men's diving (the first was at the Barcelona Games in 1992).

SWIMMING

There were several first-ever aspects of the Centennial Olympic Games swimming competition. For the first time in Olympic history, the swimming events stretched over seven consecutive days (20–26 July), with no rest day in the middle of competition. The 1996 Games also introduced the women's 4 x 200 m freestyle relay into Olympic competition, bringing the total number of medal events to 32. In another Olympic first, countries entered swimmers based on two levels of qualifying standards (A and B). As a result, in order for a country to enter two swimmers, both swimmers had to meet the faster A standard. Otherwise, countries could enter just one athlete per men's and women's event. Furthermore, in addition to recognizing world and Olympic records, the scoreboard indicated when national and area records were broken. The notation of an NR (national record) or AR (area record) by the swimmer's name was particularly meaningful for athletes who did not qualify for the finals, but who recorded the fastest time in their country's history.

COMPETITION

The general competition format for swimming remained unchanged, with preliminaries and A and B finals in all events. Exceptions were the 800 m freestyle, 1,500 m freestyle, and the relay events, for which there were only preliminaries and A finals.

The swimming competition was divided into the following events: 50 m freestyle, 100 m freestyle, 200 m freestyle, 100 m breaststroke, 200 m breaststroke, 100 m backstroke, 200 m backstroke, 100 m butterfly, 200 m butterfly, 200 m individual medley, 400 m individual medley, 400 m freestyle, 800 m freestyle (women), 1,500 m freestyle (men), 4 x 100 m freestyle relay, 4 x 200 m freestyle relay, and 4 x 100 m medley relay.

Aquatics—Swimming

Venue Used:
Georgia Tech
Aquatic Center

Days of Competition: 7

Medals Awarded: 96
Gold 32
Silver 32
Bronze 32

Number of Nations: 119

Olympic Records: 14

World Records: 4

Number of Officials: 72

Officiating Federation:
International
Amateur Swimming
Federation (FINA)

The Aquatic Center at Georgia Tech hosted the diving, swimming, synchronized swimming, and water polo events.

ELIZABETH T JOHNSON • ELMORE G JOHNSON • EMILY M JOHNSON • ERIC M JOHNSON • ERIC R JOHNSON • ERIN G JOHNSON • ESTELLA J JOHNSON • ESTELLA M JOHNSON • FELICIA V JOHNSON • FELTON M JOHNSON • FRANCES M JOHNSON • GAIL JOHNSON • GAIL C JOHNSON • GARY D JOHNSON • GARY O JOHNSON • GENE R JOHNSON • GEORGE ANN PONDER JOHNSON • GERTRUDE B JOHNSON • GLORIA D JOHNSON • GREG L JOHNSON • GRETCHEN T JOHNSON • GWENDOLYN A JOHNSON • HAROLD B JOHNSON • HAROLD L JOHNSON • HEATHER C JOHNSON • HEATHER M JOHNSON • HEINZ H JOHNSON •

50 m Freestyle. Olympic-record holder Aleksander Popov of the Russian Federation defended his Olympic title in the men's 50 m freestyle with a winning time of 22.13. "If you win your first Olympics, you become famous," said Popov, who has not lost a major international 50 m or 100 m freestyle race since 1991. "If you win your second Olympics, you become great." And with his goal of winning the gold again at the 2000 Olympic Games in Sydney, Australia, he concluded, "If you win your third Olympics, you become history." Placing

behind Popov was silver medalist Gary Hall Jr. of the US, who touched at 22.26. Brazil's Fernando de Queiroz Scherer finished third, only .03 behind Hall at 22.29.

The women's 50 m freestyle completed an outstanding competition for Amy Van Dyken. Van Dyken became the first US woman to win four gold medals in one Olympic Games when she upset world-record holder Jingyi Le of the People's Republic of China. Before winning the 50 m freestyle, Van Dyken had previously won the 100 m butterfly and had been a part of two

relays. Van Dyken, 23, finished first with a US-record time of 24.87. Le won the silver with a second-place time of 24.90, while bronze medalist Sandra Voelker of Germany finished at 25.14.

100 m Freestyle. World-record holder Aleksander Popov became the first Olympic swimmer since 1928 to win consecutive 100 m freestyle gold medals. Popov won the men's

left: Look of the Games banners with the swimming pictogram decorated the Georgia Tech Aquatic Center.

middle: The US's Amy Van Dyken rejoices after winning the women's 50 m freestyle event.

right: The Russian Federation's Aleksander Popov reacts after winning the gold in the men's 100 m freestyle.

100 m freestyle race by .07, finishing with a time of 48.74. Silver medalist Gary Hall Jr. of the US finished with a time of 48.81, followed by bronze medalist Gustavo França Borges of Brazil (49.02).

World-record holder Jingyi Le of the People's Republic of China won the women's 100 m freestyle in an Olympic-record time of 54.50, just edging out silver medalist Sandra Voelker of Germany, who finished at 54.88. Angel Martino of the US won the bronze medal (54.93).

200 m Freestyle. Two athletes brought home their countries' first-ever gold medals by winning the 200 m freestyle. Danyon Loader captured New Zealand's first gold, finishing first in the men's 200 m freestyle with a time of 1:47.63. Gustavo França Borges of Brazil won the silver with a time of 1:48.08, while Australia's Daniel Kowalski won the bronze with a time of 1:48.25.

In the women's 200 m freestyle, Claudia Poll placed Costa Rica on the top of the victory podium for the first time after surprising world-record holder Franziska van Almsick of Germany. Poll bested silver medalist van Almsick, who at the age of 14 won four medals at the 1992 Barcelona Games, by .41 (1:58.16 to 1:58.57). Germany's Dagmar Hase took home the bronze (1:59.56).

100 m Breaststroke. Belgium's Fred Deburghgraeve captured his country's first swimming gold medal by winning the men's 100 m

breaststroke. His time of 1:00.65 in the finals was bested only by his world-record time of 1:00.60 in the morning preliminaries. Finishing behind Deburghgraeve were silver medalist Jeremy Linn of the US (1:00.77) and bronze medalist Mark Warnecke of Germany (1:01.33).

In the women's 100 m breaststroke, South Africa's Penelope Heyns set a world record in the morning preliminaries (1:07.02) and followed it with an evening gold-medal swim (1:07.73). Finishing behind Heyns were 14-year-old Amanda Beard of the US (1:08.09),

who took the silver, and bronze medalist Samantha Riley of Australia (1:09.18).

200 m Breaststroke. Hungary's Norbert Rózsa won the men's 200 m breaststroke with a time of 2:12.57. Rózsa beat out teammate Károly Güttler, second at 2:13.03, and bronze medalist Andrey Korneyev of the Russian Federation (2:13.17).

Penelope Heyns captured her second gold medal of the Games by winning the women's 200 m breaststroke in an Olympic-record time

left: Costa Rica's Claudia Poll starts off the block in the women's 200 m freestyle heat.

right: Hungary's Norbert Rózsa goes for the gold in the men's 200 m breaststroke.

JEAN C JOHNSON • JEANETTE A JOHNSON • JEANIE D JOHNSON • JEANNE P JOHNSON • JEFFREY E JOHNSON • JEFFREY P JOHNSON • JENNIFER E JOHNSON • JENNIFER L JOHNSON • JEREMIAH P JOHNSON • JEREMIAH W JOHNSON • JEREMY S JOHNSON • JEROME R JOHNSON • JESSICA K JOHNSON • JETTIE MAE JOHNSON • JOANN JOHNSON • JOANNE L JOHNSON • JOANNE L JOHNSON • JOHN A JOHNSON • JOHN DARWIN JOHNSON • JOYCE A JOHNSON • JOYCE E JOHNSON • JOYCE L JOHNSON • JOYCE M JOHNSON • JOYCE Y JOHNSON • JOYCE Y JOHNSON • JOYCELYN M JOHNSON •

277

stroke with a time of 54.10. Placing behind Rouse were two Cuban athletes, silver medalist Rodolfo Falcon (54.98) and bronze medalist Neisser Bent (55.02).

In the women's 100 m backstroke, 15-year-old Beth Botsford of the US finished first with a time of 1:01.19. Botsford won over teammate Whitney Hedgepeth (1:01.47), the silver medalist, and bronze medalist Marianne Kriel (1:02.12) of South Africa.

200 m Backstroke. Brad Bridgewater of the US finished first in the men's 200 m backstroke with a time of 1:58.54. Bridgewater finished ahead of silver medalist Tripp Schwenk of the US, second at 1:58.99, and bronze medalist Emanuele Merisi of Italy, third at 1:59.18.

World- and Olympic-record holder Krisztina Egerszegi of Hungary became the second swimmer in Olympic history to win the same event at three straight Olympic Games when she successfully defended her title in the women's 200 m backstroke. The win also gave her a total of five individual gold medals, the most ever earned by an Olympic swimmer. Finishing behind Egerszegi (2:07.83) were silver medalist Whitney Hedgepeth of the US (2:11.98) and bronze medalist Cathleen Rund of Germany (2:12.06).

left: Swimmers begin heat five of the women's 100 m backstroke preliminaries.

right: The Russian Federation's Denis Pankratov wins the gold in the men's 100 m butterfly.

of 2:25.41. Once again, Heyns edged out silver medalist Amanda Beard, who finished second at 2:25.75, while Hungary's Agnes Kovács was third (2:26.57).

100 m Backstroke. World-record holder Jeff Rouse of the US won the men's 100 m back-

JOY E L JOHNSON • JUDD L JOHNSON • JUDY A JOHNSON • JUDY J JOHNSON • JULIA T JOHNSON • JUNE E JOHNSON • JUNE K JOHNSON • KAREN S JOHNSON • KATHIE E. W. JOHNSON • KATHLEEN M JOHNSON • KATHRYN JOHNSON • KATHRYN JOHNSON • KATHRYN TERESA JOHNSON • KATIE S JOHNSON • KATY C JOHNSON • KECIA L JOHNSON • KEINON JOHNSON • KEITH E JOHNSON • KELLEY JOHNSON • KEN A JOHNSON • KENNETH A JOHNSON • KRISTA S JOHNSON • KRISTINA E JOHNSON • KRYSTAL D JOHNSON • LADAWN S JOHNSON • LANDY B JOHNSON • LARA C JOHNSON • LARRY M JOHNSON •

In the tightest race of the Olympic swimming finals, Amy Van Dyken of the US swam 59.13, finishing .01 in front of the People's Republic of China's Limin Liu (59.14) to win the women's 100 m butterfly. Angel Martino of the US finished third at 59.23.

200 m Butterfly. World-record holder Denis Pankratov won the men's 200 m butterfly with a time of 1:56.51. Placing behind gold medalist Pankratov were silver medalist Tom Malchow of the US (1:57.44) and bronze medalist Scott Goodman (1:57.48) of Australia.

100 m Butterfly. In the spotlight on day five was the Russian Federation's Denis Pankratov, who established a world record in the men's 100 m butterfly with a winning time of 52.27. Following Pankratov were silver medalist Scott Miller of Australia (52.53) and bronze medalist Vladislav Kulikov of the Russian Federation (53.13).

Ireland's Michelle Smith's bid to become only the third Olympian to win four individual gold medals in one Games came up short on the seventh and final day of competition. Australia's Susan O'Neill won the gold in the women's 200 m butterfly with a time of 2:07.76, while Smith captured the bronze with a time of 2:09.91. "This was the greatest week of my life," said Smith, whose native country of Ireland does not even have an Olympic-sized (50 m) pool. "The biggest medal was the first one. To win that medal, to stand on the podium with the national anthem, that was what I always had dreamed about. That was the

top: Scott Miller of Australia swims to silver in the men's 100 m butterfly.

bottom left: An underwater view shows a competitor in the women's 100 m butterfly finals.

bottom right: Gold medalist Susan O'Neill of Australia competes in the women's 200 m butterfly preliminaries.

LERLEAN N JOHNSON • LINDA JOHNSON • LINDA JOHNSON • LINDA EILEEN JOHNSON • LISA L JOHNSON • LISA M JOHNSON • LISA P JOHNSON • LORI L JOHNSON • LORI T JOHNSON • LORRAINE A JOHNSON • LOUIS JOHNSON • LOUIS JOHNSON • LUCIE M JOHNSON • LYNNE G JOHNSON • MABLE JOHNSON • MAGDALENA T JOHNSON • MALCOLM L JOHNSON • MAMIE R JOHNSON • MARGARET L JOHNSON • MARGARET PEGGY B JOHNSON • MARIAN JOHNSON • MARIE-PIERRE L J JOHNSON • MARILYN JOHNSON • MARILYN R JOHNSON • MARK JOHNSON • MARK E JOHNSON • MARY E JOHNSON •

279

one I wanted. The rest were extra." O'Neill's teammate, Petria Thomas, won the silver medal by finishing at 2:09.82.

200 m Individual Medley. Hungary's Attila Czene finished first in the men's 200 m individual medley with an Olympic-record time of 1:59.91. Finishing behind Czene were Finland's Jani Sievinen, second at 2:00.13, and Canada's Curtis Myden, third at 2:01.13.

Two days before capturing the bronze in the 200 m butterfly, Michelle Smith was in the spotlight when she received her third gold medal

left: **Hungary's Attila Czene celebrates his world-record time in winning the men's 200 m individual medley.**

right: **Michelle Smith of Ireland raises her arms in victory after winning the gold in the women's 200 m individual medley.**

of the Games by winning the women's 200 m individual medley with a time of 2:13.93. Canada's Marianne Limpert won the silver (2:14.35), and the People's Republic of China's Li Lin won the bronze (2:14.74).

400 m Individual Medley. Despite suffering from exercise-induced asthma, which affords him only 20 percent of the oxygen intake of the average person, Tom Dolan garnered the first gold medal for the US at the Centennial Olympic Games. Dolan, 20, captured the men's 400 m individual medley with a time of 4:14.90, almost 3.0 off his world-best mark. Dolan's teammate, Eric Namesnik, finished a close second at 4:15.25 to win the silver, and Canada's Curtis Myden took home the bronze (4:16.28).

In the women's 400 m individual medley, Michelle Smith began what would be one of

MARY E JOHNSON • MARY L JOHNSON • MARY L JOHNSON • MARY LYNNE JOHNSON • MARYLOU JOHNSON • MEIKAEL JOHNSON • MICHAEL C JOHNSON • MICHAEL D JOHNSON • MICHAEL E JOHNSON • MICHELLE A JOHNSON • MIKE JOHNSON • MIKE C JOHNSON • MILDRED D JOHNSON • MILTON E JOHNSON • MINNIE L JOHNSON • MONICA U JOHNSON • MONIQUE D JOHNSON • MONTE R JOHNSON • MORRIS Q JOHNSON • MYRTLE F JOHNSON • NANCY J JOHNSON • NATHAN DALE JOHNSON • NORMAN R JOHNSON • OUIDA W JOHNSON • PAMELA G JOHNSON • PAMELA L JOHNSON • PAMELA Y JOHNSON

the top individual performances of the Games with the opening day's biggest upset. Shaving an amazing 13.5 off her previous best, Smith captured Ireland's first-ever gold medal, posting a time of 4:39.18. Silver medalist Allison Wagner of the US finished nearly 3.0 later (4:42.03), while Hungary's Krisztina Egerszegi earned the bronze (4:42.53).

400 m Freestyle. Danyon Loader of New Zealand captured his second gold medal of the Games by finishing first in the men's 400 m freestyle with a time of 3:47.97. Finishing behind Loader were silver medalist Paul Palmer of Great Britain (3:49.00) and bronze medalist Daniel Kowalski of Australia (3:49.39).

Michelle Smith turned in her second stunning performance of the Games on day three of the competition. The blossoming Irish legend was approved as a late entry in the women's 400 m freestyle, which eventually eliminated four-time Olympic gold medalist Janet Evans of the US from the finals for the first time in her three Olympic performances. In the finals, Smith upset defending Olympic champion Dagmar Hase of Germany. Smith's winning time of 4:07.25 was an astounding 19.0 improvement in 15 months from her Irish-record time of 4:26.18. Hase won her second medal of the Games by finishing with a time of 4:08.30 to take home the silver, and Kirsten Vlieghuis of the Netherlands captured the bronze (4:08.70).

800 m Freestyle. Brooke Bennett, 16, of the US won the women's 800 m freestyle with a time of 8:27.89. Germany's Dagmar Hase won the silver medal (8:29.91), while the Netherlands' Kirsten Vlieghuis took home the bronze (8:30.84).

1,500 m Freestyle. World-record holder Kieren Perkins of Australia successfully defended his gold medal in the men's 1,500 m freestyle with a time of 14:56.40. Placing behind Perkins in the men's 1,500 m freestyle were teammate Daniel Kowalski, second at

15:02.43, and Great Britain's Graeme Smith, third at 15:02.48.

4 x 100 m Freestyle Relay. Two Olympic records were set in the final event on day four of the competition in the men's 4 x 100 m freestyle relay. First, Gary Hall Jr. prevailed against Aleksander Popov by swimming the fastest 100 m split in history (47.45) while anchoring the US men's team. Hall, who one

top: Tom Dolan of the US swims to gold in the men's 400 m individual medley.

bottom: Kieren Perkins of Australia takes a breath during his gold-medal swim in the men's 1,500 m freestyle.

· PAT H JOHNSON · PATRICE J JOHNSON · PATRICIA K JOHNSON · PATRICIA R JOHNSON · PAUL JOHNSON · PAUL JOHNSON · PAUL A JOHNSON · PAUL M JOHNSON · PAUL R JOHNSON · PAUL T JOHNSON · PAULA F JOHNSON · PAULA L JOHNSON · PEGGY JOY A JOHNSON · PETER S JOHNSON · PHYLLIS A JOHNSON · PHYLLIS J JOHNSON · PIERRE B JOHNSON · PRENTICE JOHNSON · QUINTEN R JOHNSON · RACHEL A JOHNSON · RALPH A JOHNSON · RALPHALETTA V JOHNSON · RANDELL G JOHNSON · RAY L JOHNSON · RAYFORD K JOHNSON · RAYMOND L JOHNSON · REBECCA H JOHNSON ·

281

night earlier had lost to Popov by .07 in the men's 100 m freestyle, teamed with Josh Davis, Jon Olsen, and Bradley Schumacher to win the gold medal in an Olympic-record time of 3:15.41. Popov was a member of the silver-medal Russian team (Popov, Vladimir Predkin, Vladimir Pyshnenko, and Roman Yegorov) that finished at 3:17.06. Germany (Mark Pinger, Christian Troeger, Bengt Zikarsky, and Bjoern Zikarsky) won the bronze (3:17.20).

The US team of Catherine Fox, Angel Martino, Jenny Thompson, and Amy Van Dyken

The US men's 4 x 100 m medley relay team holds up a sign thanking fans following a world-record performance.

facing page: **The US team performs its gold-medal routine.**

won the gold in the women's 4 x 100 m freestyle relay with an Olympic-record time of 3:39.29. The People's Republic of China (Na Chao, Jingyi Le, Yun Nian, and Ying Shan) won the silver (3:40.48), and Germany (Antje Buschschulte, Simone Osygus, Franziska van Almsick, and Sandra Voelker) took the bronze (3:41.48).

4 x 200 m Freestyle Relay. The US team of Ryan Berube, Josh Davis, Joe Hudepohl, and Bradley Schumacher won the men's 4 x 200 m freestyle relay with a time of 7:14.84. Sweden

(Lars Frolander, Anders Holmertz, Anders Lyrbring, and Christer Wallin), second at 7:17.56, and Germany (Aimo Heilmann, Christian Keller, Christian Troeger, and Steffen Zesner), third at 7:17.71, finished out the medal contingent.

In the women's 4 x 200 m freestyle relay, the US won with an Olympic- and US-record time of 7:59.87. Jenny Thompson teamed with Trina Jackson, Sheila Taormina, and Cristina Teuscher in the record-setting performance. The win was Thompson's third relay gold medal of the Games, giving her a total of five gold medals over the last two Olympic Games. Placing behind the US were silver medalist Germany (Dagmar Hase, Kerstin Kielgass, Anke Scholz, and Franziska van Almsick), 8:01.55, and bronze medalist Australia (Julia Greville, Emma Johnson, Susan O'Neill, and Nicole Stevenson), 8:05.47.

4 x 100 m Medley Relay. In the final swimming race, the US men's 4 x 100 m medley relay team bid a fond farewell to the Centennial Olympic Games in world-record fashion. Before a highly supportive audience at the Aquatic Center, the foursome reached the pinnacle of the event as they won the gold with a world-best time of 3:34.84. The team of Gary Hall Jr., Mark Henderson, Jeremy Linn, and Jeff Rouse electrified the frenzied, full-capacity crowd by finishing more than 2.0 ahead of the previous world record, which was set by the US eight years ago at the Seoul Games. The Russian Federation (Stanislav Lopukhov, Denis Pankratov, Aleksander Popov, and Vladimir Selkov) was second (3:37.55), and Australia (Steven Dewick, Michael Klim, Scott Miller, and Philip Rogers) was third (3:39.56). In appreciation of the vocal spectators, after the awards ceremony, the US foursome posed for pictures taken by the fans in the stands and walked around the pool while holding a

REBECCA L JOHNSON • REBECCA SUE JOHNSON • RENEE M JOHNSON • RICHARD C JOHNSON • RICHARD E JOHNSON • RICHARD E JOHNSON • RICHARD H JOHNSON • RICHARD W JOHNSON • ROB JOHNSON • ROBERT E JOHNSON • ROBERT G JOHNSON • ROBERT L JOHNSON • ROBIN JOHNSON • ROGER W JOHNSON • RONALD C JOHNSON • RONALD L JOHNSON • ROY JOHNSON • ROY L JOHNSON • RUBY S JOHNSON • RUE S JOHNSON • RUGENIA H JOHNSON • RUTHIE W JOHNSON • SAMANTHA R JOHNSON • SAMUEL C JOHNSON • SAMUEL L JOHNSON • SANDRA B JOHNSON • SANDRA R JOHNSON •

banner that read, "Thanks America for a dream come true."

In the final event of day five of the swimming competition, the US team of Amanda Beard, Beth Botsford, Angel Martino, and Amy Van Dyken won the gold in the women's 4 x 100 m medley relay with a time of 4:02.88. Australia (Susan O'Neill, Samantha Riley, Sarah Ryan, and Nicole Stevenson) took the silver (4:05.08), and the People's Republic of China (Huijue Cai, Yan Chen, Xue Han, and Ying Shan) received the bronze (4:07.34).

SYNCHRONIZED SWIMMING

Synchronized swimming became a team sport for the first time in Olympic history in 1996. In the three previous Olympic Games, synchronized swimming had two events: solo and duet. At the Centennial Olympic Games in Atlanta, however, 80 women (eight teams of 10) competed over two days (30 July and 2 August) in the single medal event. The competi-

Aquatics—Synchronized Swimming

Venue Used:
Georgia Tech Aquatic Center

Days of Competition: 2

Medals Awarded: 3
Gold 1
Silver 1
Bronze 1

Number of Nations: 8

Number of Officials: 28

Officiating Federation:
International Amateur Swimming

CONCLUSION

The men's 4 x 100 m medley relay gold medalists provided a fitting climax to seven days of competition in which the US swept all six relays en route to winning 13 gold, 11 silver, and 2 bronze medals. While the US led many races, four athletes brought summer gold to their countries for the first time: Ireland's Michelle Smith, New Zealand's Danyon Loader, Belgium's Fred Deburghgraeve, and Costa Rica's Claudia Poll. In all, a total of 119 nations were represented, 985 athletes competed, 4 world records were established, and 14 Olympic records were set during the swimming competition at the Centennial Olympic Games.

tion format was also modified, as the traditional figures competition was replaced with a 2:50 technical routine. In the technical routine, required elements were executed in a prescribed order and, with the exception of one required cadence action, synchronized. However, the music and choreography during the required elements varied from team to team. The second day was the five-minute freestyle routine, which allowed the teams to perform without any figures or strokes restrictions. Separate scores for technical merit and artistic impression were awarded during both the technical and freestyle routines. Both sessions of the synchronized swimming competition were held before full-capacity audiences.

SANDY U JOHNSON • SEAN K JOHNSON • THANA B JOHNSON • SHANITA JOHNSON • SHEILA A JOHNSON • SHERRY A JOHNSON • SHERRY M JOHNSON • SHIRLEY J JOHNSON • SIBYL E JOHNSON • SONJA F JOHNSON • SONJA F JOHNSON • SONYA L JOHNSON • STANLEY F JOHNSON • STELLA J JOHNSON • STEPHANIE JOHNSON • STEPHANIE L JOHNSON • STEPHEN J JOHNSON • STEVEN JOHNSON • STEVEN A JOHNSON • STEVEN R JOHNSON • SUSAN JOHNSON • SUSAN A JOHNSON • SUSAN B JOHNSON • SUSAN H JOHNSON • SUSAN L JOHNSON • SUSAN M JOHNSON • SUZANNE H JOHNSON •

COMPETITION

Eight teams qualified for the synchronized swimming competition: Canada, France, Italy, Japan, Mexico, the People's Republic of China, the Russian Federation, and the United States. The results of the 1996 competition, however, followed an already established pattern: since synchronized swimming became an Olympic sport in 1984, every gold and silver medal has been won by either the United States or Canada.

10 judges awarded perfect scores of 10.0 (the highest and lowest scores were dropped, giving the US all 10.0 scores). This Olympic-record perfect score, the highest ever awarded in international synchronized swimming competition, secured the gold medal for the US, which finished with a total score of 99.720. Performing to prerecorded orchestra music, the US swimmers illustrated the playing of violins as they hung upside down in the water while drawing one leg across another. In addition, the routine was filled with risky lifts, power kicks, and

left: **En route to placing fourth, the Russian Federation's team performs one of its two routines.**

right: **Japan performs its technical routine on the opening day of the synchronized swimming competition.**

In the opening technical routine, the no. 1 ranked US team received the day's only perfect score. Before an enthusiastic crowd, the host team received a pair of perfect scores of 10.0 for technical merit and a third for artistic impression. As a result, the US held first place after the technical routine with a score of 99.200, followed by Canada (97.933) and Japan (97.667).

On day two, in the freestyle routine, the United States received a perfect score as 9 of the

high-speed maneuvers that made it the most difficult of all the routines. "Where we differed was the intensity and difficulty level," said US coach Chris Carver, whose team had been working on the routine as much as eight hours a day, six days a week since January. "Our routine was more taxing than the others."

"I think for all of us it was a perfect moment, and we'll always remember this night that way," team member Emily Porter LeSueur said. Led by Becky Dyroen-Lancer, the world's no. 1 ranked individual synchronized swimmer, the members of the US team were Suzannah Bianco, Tammy Cleland, Emily Porter

SUZANNE M JOHNSON • SYLIVIA M JOHNSON • SYLVIA C JOHNSON • TAMICA S JOHNSON • TANYA A JOHNSON • TANYA L JOHNSON • TERI L JOHNSON • TERRENCE K JOHNSON • TERRY-TERRENCE O JOHNSON • TERRY D JOHNSON • THADDEUS J JOHNSON • THEA A JOHNSON • THEOPOLIS W JOHNSON • THOMAS A JOHNSON • THOMAS G JOHNSON • THOMAS R JOHNSON • THOMAS T JOHNSON • THOMAS W JOHNSON • TIM W JOHNSON • TODD JOHNSON • TOM JOHNSON • TONI JOHNSON • TONI H JOHNSON • TONICA JOHNSON • TRACY L JOHNSON • TRAVIS JOHNSON • VALENCIA JOHNSON •

Schneyder, Heather Simmons-Carrasco, Jill Sudduth, and Margot Thien.

Canada (98.367) won the silver medal on the strength of a heartfelt routine that dramatized the country's secession controversy. "We wanted to give a message of unity within our team, within our country, and ultimately within the world," said Canada team member Erin Woodley. Joining Woodley on the Canadian team were Lisa Alexander, Janice Bremner, Karen Clark, Karen Fonteyne, 1992 individual co–gold medalist Sylvie Frechette, Valerie

top: A computer graphic illustrates the pool used for the synchronized swimming competition.

bottom: The Canadian synchronized swimming team rejoices on the medal stand.

Hould-Marchand, Kasia Kulesza, Christine Larsen, and Cari Read.

Japan swam an elegant freestyle routine based on *The Four Seasons* to capture the bronze medal (97.753), .493 in front of the no. 3 ranked Russian Federation. Japan's team consisted of Raika Fujii, Mayuko Fujiki, Rei Jimbo, Miho Kawabe, Akiko Kawase, Riho Nakajima, Miya Tachibana, Kaori Takahashi, Miho Takeda, and Junko Tanaka.

CONCLUSION

Although the Centennial Olympic Games marked the first time synchronized swimming was contested as a team event, the United States and Canada still maintained their stronghold in the sport. Following a perfect score in the freestyle routine, the United States received the gold. Canada, on the strength of its powerful and dramatic freestyle routine, earned the silver. In a surprise finish, Japan rounded out the medal stand placement by winning the bronze over the Russian Federation.

VALERIA L JOHNSON • VALERIE JOHNSON • VALERIE I JOHNSON • VELMA N JOHNSON • VICTOR L JOHNSON • VICTORIA N JOHNSON • VIRGINIA A JOHNSON • VIRGINIA L JOHNSON • WALLACE C JOHNSON • WALTER L JOHNSON • WAYNE D JOHNSON • WENDELL L JOHNSON • WENDY E JOHNSON • WILLIAM C JOHNSON • WILLIAM JR O JOHNSON • WILLIAM L JOHNSON • WILLIAM R JOHNSON • WILLIAM T JOHNSON • WILLIE C JOHNSON • WILLIS JOHNSON • WILMA G JOHNSON • ZYLPHIA JOHNSON • MARY A JOHNSON-PRATT • SHERRY J JOHNSON-WILKES • RALPH D JOHNSON JR • JARUIS M JOHNSON EMT

WATER POLO

A total of 156 men (12 teams of 13) competed in water polo, which was introduced in 1900 as the first team sport in the modern Olympic Games. The majority of the competition took place in the water polo pool, which was adjacent to the main complex of the Georgia Tech Aquatic Center. In the medal rounds, the action shifted to the larger swimming pool in the main complex, which seated 15,000 for the finals.

COMPETITION

In the preliminary rounds, the 12 teams were divided into two groups of six, with each group participating in a round-robin format. The top four teams from each group advanced to the quarterfinals in a single-elimination round to decide the gold medal winner.

The top six finishers from the IX men's water polo World Cup and the top six teams from the Olympic Games' qualifying tournament, which was held in Berlin in February 1996, qualified for entry into the 1996 Games. The 12 teams that qualified were Croatia, Germany, Greece, Hungary, Italy, the Netherlands, Romania, the Russian Federation, Spain, Ukraine, the United States, and Yugoslavia.

Most of the first round went as expected, with the top two teams—Italy and Hungary—dominating the five-game round-robin. But the competition intensified on the final day of the first round when archrivals Hungary and Yugoslavia battled for pool supremacy. The match pitted the sport's once-dominant team Hungary, which had won medals in 12 Olympiads up through the 1980 Games in Moscow, against Yugoslavia, the gold-medal winner in both the 1984 and 1988 Olympic Games. Led by Tibor Benedek's three goals, the Hungarians notched a 12-8 victory to finish the first round

top: Serguei Evstigneev of the Russian Federation and Spain's Salvador Gomez battle for the ball in their preliminary match.

bottom: Look of the Games banners decorated the spectator areas for the water polo competition venue.

facing page: Italy's Alberto Angelini prepares to score on Hungary's goalkeeper Zoltan Kosz in Italy's bronze-medal victory.

• HARRY L JOHNSON II • EDWARD O JOHNSON III • JOHN JOHNSON III • ROBERT H JOHNSON III • WESLEY JOHNSON IV • ARLANDUS JOHNSON JR • AUBREY R JOHNSON JR • CONEY H JOHNSON JR • FARRIS T JOHNSON JR • FRANK W JOHNSON JR • JOHN J JOHNSON JR • MARCUS A JOHNSON JR • JAMES R JOHNSON MT • LARRY K JOHNSON PM • KEVIN R JOHNSON SR • TAMMY JOHNSTON • ANNA M JOHNSTON • B K JOHNSTON • BRUCE JOHNSTON • CURTIS L JOHNSTON • DIANNE JOHNSTON • GLENNA C JOHNSTON • GREG W JOHNSTON • HARRY B JOHNSTON • JANELLE JOHNSTON • JANICE W JOHNSTON •

COMPETITION

All competition arrangements were determined by ACOG and the International Archery Federation (FITA). For the fourth straight Olympic Games, the competition format was modified to make archery more appealing to the spectators in attendance, as well as to the broadcast audience around the world. In an Olympic first, countries could qualify up to three archers for individual competition. In addition, the cumulative scoring round, in which archers shot at targets from four different distances, was eliminated, and a single-elimination match format was introduced.

Under the Games' modified competition format, archers shot from a single distance of 230 ft (70 m) at a 4 ft (1.22 m) target face divided into 10 scoring rings. Rings were

top: Olympic archers train at the Stone Mountain Park Archery Center on 28 July.

bottom: France's Lionel Torres releases an arrow during the men's quarterfinals.

CRAIG G JONES • CURTISJEAN JONES • CYNTHIA JONES • CYNTHIA G JONES • CYNTHIA L JONES • CYNTHIA P JONES • CYNTHIA T JONES • DALE A JONES • DALE D JONES • DANELLE P JONES • DANETTE M JONES • DANIEL S JONES • DAVID JONES • DAVID G JONES • DAVID P JONES • DAVID W JONES • DAWATHA JONES • DAWN M JONES • DEAN JONES • DEBORAH L JONES • DEBRA JONES • DEBRA S JONES • DENISE L JONES • DESHONDA D JONES • DEVON A JONES • DOLORES A JONES • DONNA M JONES • DONNA W JONES • DOROTHY L JONES • DOROTHY M JONES • DOROTHY V JONES • DOVE JONES • DUNCAN L JONES

291

worth fewer points the farther they were from the center. The outer ring was worth 1 point; the inner ring, called a "gold," was worth 10 points.

The archers began the competition with the ranking round, which was shot on the 22-lane practice field. In this opening round, each athlete shot 72 arrows to determine his or her ranking in the tournament. The athlete with the highest total score in the ranking round was seeded no. 1, while the lowest-scoring athlete was ranked no. 64.

Italy's Michele Frangilli sets an Olympic record in the men's individual quarterfinals.

Based on their total scores earned in the ranking round, athletes were placed in brackets and began the individual, single-elimination tournament. For this Olympic round phase, the athletes carried their bows and quivers into the main arena, where the competition took place. The first three elimination rounds (1/32, 1/16, 1/8) consisted of one-on-one 18-arrow matches (each archer shooting 18 arrows). In the quarterfinals, semifinals, and finals, all matches were one-on-one 12-arrow matches.

Individual. As the men's individual competition began, fate seemed to be pushing Italy's Michele Frangilli firmly toward the top step of the medal stand. After opening with an Olympic-record ranking round (684), Frangilli set another Olympic mark in the 1/8 round. The Italian bowman shot an 18-arrow match score of 170 in a driving rainstorm to advance to the quarterfinals. But when facing the tournament's no. 9 ranked competitor, the US's Justin Huish, Frangilli found fate unkind. In a dramatic tiebreaker, Huish calmly shot two win-or-lose arrows, and both were perfect center gold bull's-eyes. As a result, the 21 year old from the US advanced to the semifinals.

Gaining momentum from his upset effort, Huish defeated Belgium's Paul Vermeiren in the semifinals and earned a gold-medal date with Sweden's Magnus Petersson. Huish excelled in the limelight of the finals. Sporting a ponytail and donning his baseball cap backward, Huish continually energized the capacity crowd of more than 5,000 and rode their enthusiasm to a 112-107 gold-medal victory over Petersson. "I'm stoked," Huish said. "Every time they [the crowd] cheered for me, they gave me the score I needed." Despite the fact that much of the boisterous crowd was cheering for Huish in the gold-medal match, Petersson, who took home the silver medal, said of the moment, "I think it was just as much fun for me."

On the strength of an Olympic-record–setting performance, Korea's Kyo-Moon Oh, the world's no. 2 ranked men's archer, earned the individual bronze medal by defeating Vermeiren 115-110. In the process, Oh also established the men's individual 36-arrow finals combined world record with a three-round score of 338.

In the women's individual competition, Lina Herasymenko of Ukraine posted an Olympic-

• EDWARD M JONES • ELAINE F JONES • ELAINE J JONES • ELIZABETH JONES • ELIZABETH JONES • ELIZABETH P JONES • ELLA SHIRLENE JONES • ELLEN JANE JONES • EUGENE L JONES • EUNICE F JONES • FRANCES L JONES • GARY K JONES • GAYLE JONES • GERTRUDE JONES • GLENN A JONES • GLORIA J JONES • GREG R JONES • GWENDOLYN B JONES • HARLEY T JONES • HEATHER M JONES • HENRY D JONES • HENRY D JONES • HERMAN D JONES • HERMAN S JONES • HOLLY L JONES • IRENE C JONES • ISABELL B JONES • JACK K JONES • JACK P JONES • JACKIE JONES • JACQUELINE G JONES • JACQUELINE P JONES

record score of 673 (out of a possible 720) in the ranking round to earn the tournament's top seed. But Herasymenko's tournament ended suddenly after a second-round (1/16 round) defeat at the hands and bow of the People's Republic of China's Xiaozhu Wang.

Another major tournament upset came a round later (1/8 round) when Germany's Barbara Mensing defeated the Republic of Moldova's Natalia Valeeva, the bronze medalist in Barcelona. Valeeva, who entered the tournament as the world's no. 1 ranked female archer

before finishing the ranking round as the no. 7 seed, lost the 163-158 match to no. 42 ranked Mensing. Mensing's victory celebration, however, was short-lived. One round later in the quarterfinals, Mensing completely missed the target with her first arrow and subsequently lost to 19-year-old Ying He of the People's Re-

public of China. Things continued to progress nicely for He, as she advanced to the women's individual gold-medal match.

After five grueling rounds of competition, the Olympic finals belonged to a 25-year-old Olympic rookie. Competing in her first Olympic Games, Kyung-Wook Kim of Korea

top: The Republic of Moldova's Natalia Valeeva takes aim in the women's individual preliminary round.

bottom left: Korea's Kyo-Moon Oh shoots to win the men's individual bronze.

bottom right: Colorful banners and pictogram representations adorned the entrance to the Stone Mountain Park Archery Center.

· JAMES D JONES · JAMES E JONES · JAMES RAYMOND JONES · JAN J JONES · JAN P JONES · JANAY S JONES · JANE J JONES · JANUARY JONES · JAY D JONES · JEANNE E JONES · JEANNETTE G JONES · JEFFREY B JONES · JEFFREY P JONES · JENNIFER JONES · JENNIFER A JONES · JENNIFER M JONES · JERRY L JONES · JERRY V JONES · JOHN JONES · JOHN A JONES · JOHN B JONES · JOHN C JONES · JOHN D JONES · JOHN R JONES · JOHNNY JONES · JOSEPHINE E JONES · JOYCE D JONES · JOYCE L JONES · JOYCE M JONES · JUANASHA C JONES · JUDY C JONES · JULIANA H JONES · JULIE A JONES ·

293

defeated silver medalist He 113-107 to capture the gold medal. In the 12-arrow championship match, Kim shot six center gold bull's-eyes, twice with such precision that she damaged the target cam resting inside the center ring of the target. Kim also established a women's individual 36-arrow finals combined world record with a three-round score of 330. Ukraine's Olena Sadovnycha captured the bronze medal by defeating Turkey's Elif Altinkaynak, the world's no. 2 ranked female archer entering the tournament, 109-102.

Thanks to a world-record total in the ranking round (2,031), Korea earned the men's tournament's top ranking and with it, a first-round bye. The ranking seemed appropriate, as Korea marched into the gold-medal matchup by defeating Slovenia in the quarterfinals and Australia in the semifinals. The semifinal victory was particularly impressive because Australia's bowmen entered the semifinals fresh off a quarterfinal victory over Sweden, where they had set both world and Olympic records by posting a score of 253 (out of 270).

left: **The US men's archery team of Justin Huish, Rod White, and Richard Johnson works together to capture the gold medal.**

right: **Kyung-Wook Kim of Korea celebrates on the medal stand after winning the women's individual gold.**

Team. The ranking round was also used to determine the eligibility and pairings for the team competition. Teams consisted of three archers, whose scores from the individual ranking round were totaled to determine their team's score in the ranking round. The men's and women's teams with the top 16 scores advanced to compete in the head-to-head, single-elimination team competition. All team competition consisted of 27-arrow matches in which each team member shot nine arrows.

In the other half of the bracket, the United States squad surprised the tournament's no. 2 ranked team, Italy, to earn a spot in the finals.

With the tense final match pitting the no. 1 and no. 3 ranked squads against each other, the resulting tiebreaker was hardly a surprise, but the victor may have been. After the judges '

KAREN C JONES • KAREN S JONES • KARLETHIA T JONES • KATHY A JONES • KELLEY S JONES • KELLY W JONES • KENDRA M JONES • KIMBERLY H JONES • LARRY D JONES • LARRY G JONES • LARRY P JONES • LARRY W JONES • LAURA JONES • LAURA N JONES • LEIGH F JONES • LEONARD W JONES • LINDA A JONES • LINDA M JONES • LINDA S JONES • LISA JONES • LISA S JONES • LOTTIE Y JONES • LOUISA G JONES • LYN C JONES • LYNN M JONES • M LYNN JONES • MALIKAH B JONES • MAMIE L JONES • MARCELLE E JONES • MARGARET M JONES • MARGARET M JONES • MARGARET T JONES • MARIAN A JONES •

CONCLUSION

When the final arrow had punctured the target and the last medal had been awarded, the archers of the Centennial Olympic Games had established 15 Olympic records and 4 world records. The stellar performances were also well received by the fans, as all competition sessions (28 July–2 August) were sold out, pushing the total attendance figure for the six days of competition to approximately 42,000.

official scoring of the arrows, the US (Justin Huish, Richard Johnson, and Rod White) captured the team gold 251-249 over silver medalist Korea (Yong-Ho Jang, Bo-Ram Kim, and Kyo-Moon Oh). In the bronze-medal match, Italy (Matteo Bisiani, Michele Frangilli, and Andrea Parenti) clipped Australia 248-244.

In the women's team competition, Korea (Kyung-Wook Kim, Jo-Sun Kim, and Hye-Young Yoon) not only dominated the opening rounds of competition, but also walked away with the gold medal. After starting the competition with a world record in the ranking round (1,984), Korea nabbed another Olympic record in the quarterfinals by scoring 249 (out of a possible 270) against Sweden. Catapulted by its record-setting performances and top ranking, Korea eased into the gold-medal round. In the final, Korea defeated silver medalist Germany (Barbara Mensing, Cornelia Pfohl, and Sandra Wagner) 245-235 to take home the gold. With its winning score in the championship match, Korea also established the 54-arrow finals combined world record with a two-round score of 490. Despite a no. 12 ranking following the ranking round, Poland (Iwona Dzieciol, Katarzyna Klata, and Joanna Nowicka) captured the women's team bronze medal by edging Turkey 244-239.

left: **Barbara Mensing takes aim in the German team's quarterfinal win over the Italian team.**

right: **Jo-Sun Kim helps the Korean team target an Olympic-record score in its quarterfinal win over Sweden.**

Atlanta 1996.

MARLYNN R JONES • MARTIN W JONES • MARY I JONES • MARY J JONES • MARY K JONES • MARY S JONES • MARYHELEN B JONES • MEG JONES • MICHAEL JONES • MICHAEL JONES • MICHAEL A JONES • MICHAEL D JONES • MICHAEL D JONES • MICHAEL R JONES • MICHAEL R JONES • MICKEY JONES • MURIEL J JONES • NADINA F JONES • NAN B JONES • NANCY L JONES • NATASHIA V JONES • NEAL E JONES • NEKOOSA N JONES • ORADELL JONES • OTIS C JONES • PATRICIA A JONES • PATRICIA B JONES • PATRICIA C JONES • PATRICIA J JONES • PATRICIA K JONES • PAULA JONES • PAUL S JONES • PENNY L JONES

ATHLETICS

OF THE 197 OLYMPIC delegations that participated in the Centennial Olympic Games, 193 were represented in the athletics competition. During the nine-day event, Olympic Stadium hosted 2,259 athletes (1,407 men and 852 women) as a total of 44 medal events (24 men's and 20 women's) were contested, including several events that were part of the programme of the Olympic Games for the first time.

VENUES

As the site of the athletics competition as well as the Opening and Closing Ceremonies, Olympic Stadium served as the centerpiece for the 1996 Centennial Olympic Games. Located in the Olympic Ring, 2.7 mi (4.3 km) from the Atlanta Olympic Village, the athletics venue was constructed especially for the Games.

Olympic Stadium provided a magnificent backdrop for athletics—the direct descendant of the original Games of ancient Greece and one of the largest competitions of the modern Games. Within the beautiful 85,000-seat facility, dramatic record-setting performances established their place in the 100-year legacy of the modern Olympic Games. Record attendance added to the atmosphere, with 1,134,558 spectators passing through the Olympic Stadium gates during the nine days of athletics compe-

tition (26 July–4 August, with a rest day on 30 July).

Featured within Olympic Stadium was a 400 m Mondo track that was literally built for speed: the baked-rubber surface was made as hard as international standards would allow for the sprints and distances. The oval track contained eight lanes, each 4 ft (1.22 m) wide, with a ninth lane on the sprint straightaway. Within the turf area inside the track were two long jump/triple jump runways, two high jump areas, three pole vault runways, two javelin runways, one hammer throw circle, two discus circles, and four shot put circles.

The marathon and race walk events used Atlanta city streets as a venue. Between starting and finishing in Olympic Stadium, courses wound past several historic sections and monuments of Atlanta, including the Martin Luther King Jr. Center for Nonviolent Social Change.

COMPETITION

The athletics events were 100 m, 200 m, 400 m, 800 m, 1,500 m, 5,000 m, 10,000 m, 100 m hurdles (women), 110 m hurdles (men), 400 m hurdles, 3,000 m steeplechase (men), 10 km race walk (women), 20 km race walk (men), 50 km race walk (men), 4 x 100 m relay, 4 x 400 m relay, marathon, high jump, long

• PRECIOUS B JONES • PRINCESS V JONES • RAHFIYA A JONES • RALPH E JONES • REBECCA L JONES • REBEKAH K JONES • REINA JONES • RICHARD JONES • RICHARD B JONES • RICHARD L JONES • RICHARD M JONES • RITA A JONES • ROBBIE L JONES • ROBERT C JONES • ROBERT L JONES • RONALD E JONES • ROSALYNE J JONES • ROSETTA JONES • SAMUEL K JONES • SANDRA E JONES • SARA L JONES • SARAH M JONES • SAYURI JONES • SCHALYSE JONES • SCOTT T JONES • SELMA J JONES • SHALONDA D JONES • SHANNON L JONES • SHANTERRIA Y JONES • SHARON L JONES • SHARON M JONES

jump, triple jump, pole vault (men), shot put, discus throw, javelin throw, hammer throw (men), heptathlon (women), and decathlon (men).

Two nonmedal events were also added: men's 1,500 m wheelchair and women's 800 m wheelchair.

The International Amateur Athletics Federation (IAAF) made two schedule modifications for the Centennial Olympic Games. The modifications changed the time of the men's and women's 200 m to enable athletes to enter both the 400 m and the 200 m and changed the start time of the men's marathon from 6:30 p.m. to 7:30 a.m.

Track Events

100 m. In the first round, 106 athletes competed in the men's 100 m. After a second round and the semifinals, Canada's Donovan Bailey claimed the title of "world's fastest human" by winning the event in a world-record time of 9.84. "My start was not all that great, but my acceleration phase was very good," Bailey said after becoming the second straight Jamaican-born sprinter to win gold in the event. Prerace favorite Frank Fredericks of Namibia won the silver medal with a time of 9.89, while Trinidad and Tobago's Ato Boldon took the bronze at 9.90.

Fifty-six women competed in round one of the women's 100 m. After two rounds and the semifinals, Gail Devers of the US became only the second woman to win consecutive Olympic sprint titles (the US's Wyomia Tyus was the first) when she defeated Jamaica's Merlene Ottey in a photo finish to capture the gold in the women's 100 m race. Devers and silver medalist Ottey both crossed the line at 10.94, while Atlanta's Gwen Torrence finished a fraction behind at 10.96 to take the bronze.

100 m Hurdles. In round one of women's 100 m hurdles, 44 athletes competed. In the

top: **Look of the Games structures greeted spectators at the entrance to Olympic Stadium.**

middle: **Gail Devers of the US edges out Jamaica's Merlene Ottey in the women's 100 m final.**

bottom: **Canada's Donovan Bailey celebrates after winning the gold and breaking the world record in the men's 100 m.**

final, after two rounds and a semifinal, Sweden's Ludmila Engquist accelerated in the last 10 m to win the gold, squeezing past Slovenia's Brigita Bukovec by .01, 12.58 to 12.59. France's Patricia Girard-Leno edged out Gail Devers in a photo finish for the bronze, 12.65 to 12.66.

110 m Hurdles. Out of a field of 62, US hurdler Allen Johnson swept through both his qualifying-round heats, as well as his semifinal heat, en route to winning the gold in the men's 110 m hurdles with an Olympic-record

time of 12.95. Teammate Mark Crear finished second at 13.09, while Germany's Florian Schwarthoff held off world-record holder Colin Jackson of Great Britain to win the bronze, 13.17 to 13.19.

400 m Hurdles. Fifty-five men started out in the men's 400 m hurdles. There were three rounds: preliminaries, semifinals, and the final. In the most intense rivalry of the men's intermediate hurdles, Atlanta native Derrick Adkins maintained an early lead to defeat his longtime friend and rival Samuel Matete of Zambia, 47.54 to 47.78. Entering the Games,

Matete had beaten Adkins in four of five 1996 meetings to take a 22-15 lead in their head-to-head series, which dates back to their college days. Adkins, however, won the biggest race in the rivalry as he captured the gold before a hometown crowd of 82,884. Adkins said afterward, "I fantasized about this moment, but it's something I didn't know would happen. It's one of the greatest feelings in my life."

The US's Calvin Davis recovered after colliding with the first hurdle to take the bronze at 47.96.

In the women's 400 m hurdles, 30 competitors started out in the preliminary round, which was followed by a semifinal round. In the final, Jamaica's Deon Hemmings led from the start and defeated world-record holder Kim Batten of the US. Hemmings's winning

left: Atlanta native Derrick Adkins of the US clears the final hurdle in his gold-medal victory in the 400 m hurdles.

right: Samuel Matete of Zambia sprints around the Olympic Stadium track in the men's 400 m hurdles.

which consisted of two preliminary rounds, a semifinal round, and the final, began with 62 competitors.

The women's event, which also consisted of two preliminary rounds, a semifinal round, and the final, began with 49 competitors. France's Marie-Jose Perec saved her best performance for the final as she raced to the women's 400 m gold in an Olympic-record time of 48.25. Perec improved her personal-best time by defeating the fastest Olympic women's 400 m field ever: six runners finish-

time of 52.82 established an Olympic record, breaking the mark (52.99) Hemmings had set just two days earlier in the semifinals. Placing behind silver medalist Batten (53.08) was teammate Tonja Buford-Bailey, who was third at 53.22.

400 m. Michael Johnson of the US won his first individual gold medal of the Games by breaking away decisively in the men's 400 m final. In the last 150 m of the race, Johnson left the eight-man field in his wake as he blazed around the turn and down the backstretch. Johnson finished with an Olympic-record time of 43.49 (the fourth-fastest time ever), giving him three of the four fastest 400 m times in history and extending his 400 m finals winning streak to 55. Placing 8 m back at 44.41 was silver medalist Roger Black of Great Britain, while Uganda's Davis Kamoga won the bronze with a time of 44.53. The event,

ing under 50.0. Silver medalist Catherine Freeman of Australia also bested the previous Olympic record (48.65) by finishing with a time of 48.63. Falilat Ogunkoya won Nigeria's first-ever individual athletics medal with her bronze-medal finish at 49.10.

200 m. The US's Michael Johnson etched his name in the Olympic history books by winning the men's 200 m in a stunning world-

left: France's Marie-Jose Perec explodes from the starting blocks during her gold-medal performance in the women's 400 m final. Perec later attained double-gold status by capturing the 200 m event.

right: Athletes competing in the men's 200 m preliminaries race by the steeplechase water jump.

JONES III • WILLIAM E JONES III • WILLIAM F JONES III • G FRANKLIN JONES JR • HARRY J JONES JR • KENN JONES JR • ROBERT C JONES JR • VERN L JONES JR • WILLIAM G JONES JR • RICHARD E JONES JR • NOVELLA JONES SHERMAN • BOYCE A JONES SR • A J JONESCO • DONNA G JONSSON • EVA H JONSSON • DAVID A JONUSKA • HEUI YUN JOO • SANG-HYUN JOO • YOUNG S JOO • CHRISTIAN JOOS • ANNA CLYDE JORDAN • ANTHONY T JORDAN • BELINDA JORDAN • BRENDA JORDAN • BUTTONS JORDAN • CARLA R JORDAN • CAROLYN R JORDAN • CHRISTOPHER S JORDAN • DANIELLE K JORDAN •

The US's Michael Johnson breaks the world record in the men's 200 m final.

record time of 19.32, becoming the first man ever to win both the 200 m and 400 m titles at the same Olympic Games. "I've always wanted to bring the two events together in a way that nobody else had ever done," Johnson said. "The world record is a bonus, but nobody else can say they made history, the first to win the 200 and 400."

Johnson literally coasted through the field of 78, breezing through the two qualifying heats and actually slowing at the finish of the semifinal. In the final, he accelerated out of the turn and left the rest of the eight-man field far behind. "Coming off the curve, I felt I was running faster than I'd ever run before in my life," he said.

Although he stumbled coming off the starting blocks, Johnson still managed a split time of 10.12 for the first 100 m of the race. Sport-

ing the gold shoes for which he will forever be remembered, he then blasted out of the turn and accelerated to an amazing 9.20 split time in the final 100 m of the race. Silver medalist Frank Fredericks of Namibia ran the third-fastest 200 m ever but finished second at 19.68.

"Michael is now the world's fastest human," said bronze medalist Ato Boldon of Trinidad and Tobago, who finished third in the 100 m and third behind Johnson in the 200 m at 19.80. After smashing his own world record, 28-year-old Johnson kneeled to give thanks and kissed the track.

In the women's 200 m, 47 athletes began the event, which consisted of two preliminary rounds, a semifinal round, and the final. Prior to Johnson's historic feat, Marie-Jose Perec

DAVID D JORDAN • ELIZABETH A JORDAN • HILL R JORDAN • HUBERT J JORDAN • IRMELA JORDAN • JAMES D JORDAN • JAMES R JORDAN • JEAN G JORDAN • JEFFERY R JORDAN • JENNIFER C JORDAN • JOANNE G JORDAN • JOHN P JORDAN • JULIE J JORDAN • KELLEY J JORDAN • KEVIN M JORDAN • LACEY K JORDAN • LINDSEY S JORDAN • MALAIKA E JORDAN • MARYNOEL M JORDAN • MATTHEW E JORDAN • MICHELLE L JORDAN • MICHELLE P JORDAN • MIRIAM JORDAN • PATSY JORDAN • PEARLIE T JORDAN • RANDY JORDAN • REBECCA M. JORDAN • ROBERT L JORDAN • SCOT R JORDAN • SCOTT R JORDAN •

became the first woman to win gold in both the 200 m and 400 m events at the same Olympic Games. Perec won the 200 m with a time of 22.12, as she overtook Jamaica's Merlene Ottey in the final 10 m to claim the top spot on the medal stand. "The 200 was like the icing on the cake for me," Perec said.

Ottey made some history of her own by becoming the first runner in Olympic history to reach the final of the same event in five Olympic Games. With her silver-medal time of 22.24, Ottey captured her sixth Olympic medal. Nigeria's Mary Onyali finished at 22.38 to earn the bronze.

800 m. Fifty-six men took part in the preliminary round of this event, followed by a semifinal and the final. Led by Norway's Vebjørn Rodal, four runners in the men's 800 m surpassed the Olympic record and broke the 1:43 barrier, marking the first time more than two runners in the same race have done so. Rodal finished first with an Olympic-record time of 1:42.58, becoming just the second Norwegian gold medalist in athletics and his country's first medalist since 1956. Hezekiel Sepeng became the first black South African to win an Olympic medal by finishing second with a time of 1:42.74, and Kenya's Fred Onyancha was third at 1:42.79.

The women's competition also consisted of one preliminary round, a semifinal, and the final, with 36 athletes making up the field. A major upset occurred in the women's 800 m as the Russian Federation's Svetlana Masterkova took the lead in the first lap and closed with a powerful sprint to capture her first international title, taking the gold with a time of 1:57.73. After taking three years off because of injuries and to have a baby, Masterkova made her grand return by stunning race favorites Ana Fidelia Quirot of Cuba, the reigning world champion and 1992 bronze medalist, and

Mozambique's Maria Lurdes Mutola, who had won 45 consecutive 800 m races. Quirot, who had completed her recovery from a near-fatal experience in a house fire, went on to win the silver with a time of 1:58.11, while Mutola took the bronze at 1:58.71.

1,500 m. In the preliminary round of the men's 1,500 m, 57 athletes competed. There was one semifinal, leading to the final round. World-record holder Noureddine Morceli of Algeria finally added an Olympic gold medal to his impressive résumé, as the world's greatest

Norway's Vebjørn Rodal crosses the finish line ahead of South Africa's Hezekiel Sepeng in the men's 800 m.

SHELBY W JORDAN • SHERYL A JORDAN • STACY JORDAN • STEVEN A JORDAN • SUSAN JORDAN • SUSAN O JORDAN • TERRENCE R JORDAN • THOMAS M JORDAN • WILLIA H JORDAN • WILLIAM A JORDAN •
SALLY S JORDEN • JOHN H JORDON • DEBORAH A JORGENSEN • KENNETH D JORGENSEN • KIMBERLEY S JORIS • MATTHEW JOSCELYNE • ALWYN D JOSEPH • ANSELM F JOSEPH • CHARLETT R JOSEPH •
DOUGLAS JOSEPH • ESSEC R JOSEPH • FRANK R JOSEPH • GEORGE JOSEPH • HERB C JOSEPH • MARILYN JOSEPH • MARY LYNN JOSEPH • PAMELA E JOSEPH • RAND JOSEPH • VELANDE JOSEPH •

middle-distance runner defeated defending Olympic champion Fermin Cacho of Spain and Kenya's Stephen Kipkorir in the men's 1,500 m. Morceli overcame a spike wound to his Achilles tendon to win the race in 3:35.78. Cacho took the silver at 3:36.40, and Kipkorir took the bronze at 3:36.72.

In the women's 1,500 m event, Svetlana Masterkova was even more impressive than in her 800 m win, as she sprinted her final lap of the race in 60.01 to claim her second gold medal of the Games. Masterkova won with a

time of 4:00.83 over 20-year-old silver medalist Gabriela Szabo of Romania (4:01.54) and Austria's Theresia Kiesl (4:03.02), who earned the bronze medal. Thirty-two competitors made up the field in the preliminary round, which was followed by the semifinal and final rounds.

5,000 m. For Burundi's Venuste Niyongabo, the decision to move up from the 1,500 m to the 5,000 m proved golden, as he earned his country's first Olympic medal by winning the men's 5,000 m with a time of 13:07:96. Kenya's Paul Bitok took the silver at 13:08.16, and Morocco's Khalid Boulami finished with the bronze (13:08.37). The 37 athletes competed in a preliminary round, semifinals, and the final.

In the women's 5,000 m, 46 women competed in a single preliminary round and then the final. Junxia Wang of the People's Republic of China claimed her country's first athletics gold medal by winning the inaugural women's 5,000 m event with a time of 14:59.88. Kenya's Pauline Konga was on the medal stand to receive the silver with a time of 15:03.49. Italy's Roberta Brunet joined them to receive the bronze with a time of 15:07.52.

10,000 m. For the men's 10,000 m event, 46 athletes took part in the preliminary round. In the final, Haile Gebreselassie of Ethiopia shattered the Olympic record by more than 14.0, winning the gold medal with a time of 27:07:34. Gebreselassie, who owns five world records and is nicknamed "the emperor," maintained his rule in the distance event with a burst of speed over the final 1,000 m of the race. Kenya's Paul Tergat took the silver in 27:08.17, and Morocco's Salah Hissou took home the bronze at 27:24.67.

In the women's 10,000 m event, Junxia Wang faced a field of 35 in the opening round. In the finals, however, she came up short in her bid for double-gold status as Portugal's

top: Athletes make the turn in the men's 5,000 m.

bottom: The Russian Federation's Svetlana Masterkova and Algeria's Hassiba Boulmerka compete in the women's 1,500 m preliminaries.

Fernanda Ribeiro sprinted past her in the last 15 m to win the gold in an Olympic-record time of 31:01.63. Wang's silver-medal time of 31:02.58 also broke the former Olympic mark, while Ethiopia's Gete Wami placed third to take the bronze at 31:06.65. Ironically, Ribeiro holds the world record in the 5,000 m race that Wang won, and Wang holds the world record in the 10,000 m race, won by Ribeiro.

3,000 m Steeplechase. Thirty-five men began competition in the first of three rounds in the men's 3,000 m steeplechase. Kenya's

top left: Haile Gebreselassie of Ethiopia celebrates after establishing an Olympic record in the men's 10,000 m event.

top right: Kenya's Joseph Keter leads Italy's Alessandro Lambruschini in the finals of the 3,000 m steeplechase.

bottom: Portugal's Fernanda Ribeiro rejoices in her victory in the women's 10,000 m.

Joseph Keter broke away on the final lap to earn the gold at 8:07.12, defeating his team-mate and training partner and three-time World Champion Moses Kiptanui, who won the silver (8:08.33). Italy's Alessandro Lambruschini took the bronze (8:11.28).

4 x 100 m Relay. Anchored by the men's 100 m sprint champion, Canada ended the

MARSHA H JOYNER • MICHAEL T JOYNER • MICHAEL T JOYNER • ROWANNE E JOYNER • SUSAN B JOYNER • CHARLES E JOYNES • JASON JUAN • KARIM A JUAN • PALOMA JUAREZ • MATT M JUBITZ • DOROTHY JUBON • REBECCA L JUBON • LEE R JUCKETT • BRIAN T JUDD • ELAINE L JUDGE • ELIZABETH K JUDGE • JUDITH K JUDGE • VICKEY A JUDKINS • KATHRYN L JUDSON • NICOLAAS F JUDSON • KIMBERLY JUDY • SHEILA K JUDY • ALLEN R JUE • WILLIAM A JUERGENS • KRISTIN A JUERGENS ATC • JOHN P JUGENHEIMER • MONIKA JUHASZ-NAGY • GREGORY B JUHL • OLIVIER JUINO • MICHAEL JULA • NANCY JULIA •

303

US's dominance in the men's 4 x 100 m relay. The Canadian team of Donovan Bailey, Robert Esmie, Glenroy Gilbert, and Bruny Surin turned in a 4 x 100 m relay time of 37.69 to win the gold. Despite raising his hands in victory while running the last 15 m, Bailey still quelled the American challenge with the fastest 100 m split time (8.95) in the race. At 38.05, the US foursome of Jon Drummond, Tim Harden, Michael Marsh, and Dennis Mitchell earned the silver. Brazil (Edson Luciano Ribeiro, André Domingos da Silva, Arnaldo de Oliveira Silva, and Robson Caetano da Silva) claimed the bronze in 38.41. Thirty-seven countries competed in the event.

The US won its fourth consecutive women's 4 x 100 m relay gold medal as the team of Gail Devers, Chryste Gaines, Inger Miller, and Gwen Torrence finished first with a time of 41.95. Running the anchor leg before a hometown crowd of 83,313, Atlanta native Torrence held off closing charges by the Bahamas' Pauline Davis and Jamaica's Merlene Ottey for the victory. The Bahamas' team of Eldece Clarke, Pauline Davis, Sevetheda Fynes, and Chandra Sturrup took the silver in 42.14, while Jamaica's Juliet Cuthbert, Michelle Freeman, Nikole Mitchell, and Merlene Ottey earned the bronze at 42.24. For Ottey, who had the fastest 100 m split in the race with an electrifying 9.83 anchor run, the bronze gave her a career total of seven Olympic medals (two silvers and five bronzes), which put her in a tie for the most medals won by a female athletics competitor. "I've been running nonstop for 16 years, so it's a great accomplishment for me," said 36-year-old Ottey. Twenty-two countries were represented in the event.

4 x 400 m Relay. The men's 4 x 400 m relay, the final relay of the 1996 Games, saw 35 countries vying in the preliminary round, followed by a semifinal round and the final. In front of one of the largest athletics crowds of the Atlanta Games (83,313), the US (Alvin Harrison, Anthuan Maybank, Derek Mills, and LaMont Smith) captured the gold medal with a time of 2:55.99, the third-fastest time in history and the fastest ever on US soil. Great Britain (Jamie Baulch, Roger Black, Mark Richardson, and Iwan Thomas) claimed the silver with a European-record time of 2:56.60, and Jamaica (Davian Clarke, Gregory Haughton, Roxbert Martin, and Michael McDonald) took the bronze at 2:59.42.

top: Canada's 4 x 100 m relay team takes a victory lap while holding Canadian flags.

bottom: The relay exchange takes place in the women's 4 x 400 m relay final.

BILL JULIAN • JACK W JULIAN • OPAL P JULIAN • RUSSELL ELRICH JULIAN • EDWARD L JULIANO • MARY NICOLE JULIAS • PERRY H JULIEN • WONDRA JULIEN • JEREMY M JULIN • GILBERT L JULLIEN • BARBARA B JULYAN • JULIA N JUMBELIC • MARILYN M JUMP • HOKYONG J JUN • SO YEON JUN • JOSEPH A JUNCA • LYNN M JUNCA • CHEW J JUNG • CONNIE F JUNG • DAEHOON JUNG • ELEANOR H JUNG • ELLEN J JUNG • HYUN JOO JUNG • HYUN SUK JUNG • JAE-HEE JUNG • JENNIFER S JUNG • LORI M JUNG • MARTHA S JUNG • MARY JUNG • SHINN Y JUNG • STEVEN JUNG • SUK-HEE JUNG • WALTER JUNG •

Sparked by the third relay leg of Kim Graham, the US captured its second gold medal ever in the women's 4 x 400 m relay event. When Graham took the baton, the US trailed Nigeria by nearly 10 m. When Graham handed off for the final leg, however, the US had a 7 m lead. Staked to that lead, the US team of Kim Graham, Maicel Malone, Jearl Miles, and Rochelle Stevens posted a winning time of 3:20.91. Silver medalist Nigeria (Bisi Afolabi, Falilat Ogunkoya, Charity Opara, and Fatima Yusuf) finished at 3:21.04, while Germany (Grit Breuer, Linda Kisabaka, Uta Rohlaender,

and Anja Rucker) clocked in at 3:21.14 to take the bronze medal. Fourteen nations competed in the event.

Field Events

High Jump. The US's Charles Austin sprang to an Olympic record of 7 ft 10 in (2.39 m) to capture the gold medal in the men's high jump. Austin had missed twice at 7 ft 9.25 in (2.37 m), but cleared the record height on his third attempt to defeat Artur Partyka of Poland, who had cleared 7 ft 9.25 in (2.37 m) on his second attempt to earn the silver medal. Great Britain's Steve Smith took home the bronze with 7 ft 8.67 in (2.35 m). Thirty-seven competitors participated in the preliminary round, and 14 took part in the final.

Divided into two groups, 31 women took part in the qualifying round of the women's high jump. In the final, world-record holder and 1995 World Champion Stefka Kostadinova of Bulgaria established an Olympic record as she leaped 6 ft 8.75 in (2.05 m) to win gold in the best Olympic women's high jump competition ever. A record 14 women cleared 6 ft 4 in (1.93 m), and a record 3 women surpassed 6 ft 7 in (2.01 m). Kostadinova cleared her first seven heights without a miss. Niki Bakogianni of Greece won the silver medal with a personal-best jump of 6 ft 8 in (2.03 m), while Inha Babakova of Ukraine claimed the bronze at 6 ft 7 in (2.01 m).

Long Jump. The US's Carl Lewis literally jumped into the Olympic history books. Lewis, 35, overcame tremendous odds to capture a record fourth consecutive men's Olympic long jump title, making him only the second Olympian ever to win an athletics event four times and just the fourth athlete in the 100-year history of the Games to win nine gold medals.

left: The US's Carl Lewis leaps to his fourth straight long jump gold medal.

right: Great Britain's Steve Smith clears the bar in the men's high jump qualifying round.

In an upset, Lewis qualified for the US Olympic team by a mere 1 in (2.54 cm). In the qualifying round, he aborted at takeoff on his second attempt, leaving him in 15th place with one last chance to qualify for the final (the top 13 in the field of 52 advanced). "No way I wanted that to be my last experience in the Olympic Games," he said of his botched second attempt. On his third and final attempt, Lewis stunned the field with a best jump of 27 ft 2.5 in (8.29 m) to move into first place heading into the final.

He stood in second place after a 26 ft 8.5 in (8.14 m) jump on his second attempt in the final. With the eyes of 82,773 spectators upon him, Lewis soared into the Atlanta night air amidst thousands of glittering camera flashes. He landed in the sand at the gold-medal mark

of 27 ft 10.75 in (8.50 m). Jamaica's James Beckford won the silver at 27 ft 2.5 in (8.29 m), and the US's Joe Greene took the bronze at 27 ft .5 in (8.24 m). "The ninth one is the most special," Lewis proclaimed. "It took the most focus, the most pain, and it could not have happened without a ton of support."

Out of a field of 48 athletes in the women's long jump, 12 qualified for the final. Nigeria's Chioma Ajunwa, a former football player, captured the gold medal with a jump of 23 ft 4.5 in (7.12 m). Italy's Fiona May won the silver at 23 ft .5 in (7.02 m). The injury-hampered Olympic-record holder, Jackie Joyner-Kersee of the US, took third place on the medal stand to receive the bronze with her jump of 22 ft 11.75 in (7.00 m).

Triple Jump. On the same night his girlfriend Gail Devers successfully defended her 100 m title, the US's Kenny Harrison made a mark of his own as he smashed the Olympic

left: Gold and green banners reflecting the Look of the Games as well as the athletics pictogram decorated Olympic Stadium.

middle: The US's Jackie Joyner-Kersee takes flight in the women's long jump qualifying round.

right: The US's Kenny Harrison establishes an Olympic record while winning the men's triple jump.

RONALD C KAASE • STEVEN J KABDEBO • OSMAN KABIA • KEIKO KABURAKI • PATRICIA A KACENA • THOMAS F KACHEROSKI • CAROLYN C KACHMANN • TAD KACZOR • STACY M KADER • DAMIR I KADIJA • SCOTT B KADISON • MARIKAY L KADLEC • VAUNE M KADLUBEK • ADEGBOYEGA J KADREE • JASON KADUSHIN • LUCIA KAEMPFFE • DAGMARA E KAFAROVA • NANCY L KAFSKY • JEREMY H KAGAN • OSAMU KAGAWA • ERIC R KAGERER • LEAMOR KAHANOV ATC • CAROLINA C KAHL • MICHAEL KAHLEN • ALAN H KAHN • JENNIFER E KAHN • KEVIN M. KAHN • LAUREN KAHN • LAWRENCE G KAHN • MAGDA R KAHN •

record to win the men's triple jump at 59 ft 4.25 in (18.09 m). World-record holder and favorite Jonathan Edwards of Great Britain never found his timing as he missed four of his six attempts in the final and took home the silver with 58 ft 8 in (17.88 m). Cuba's Yoelbi Quesada jumped 57 ft 2.75 in (17.44 m) to win the bronze. A total of 43 athletes competed in the men's triple jump.

World-record holder Inessa Kravets of Ukraine, the 1992 Olympic long jump silver medalist, leaped 50 ft 3.5 in (15.33 m) to win

the gold in the Olympic debut of the women's triple jump competition. She outdistanced the Russian Federation's Inna Lasovskaya and the Czech Republic's Sarka Kasparkova, who both jumped 49 ft 1.75 in (14.98 m). Lasovskaya took the silver because of a better second-best jump, and Kasparkova won the bronze.

Thirty-two athletes competed in the women's triple jump.

Shot Put. On his sixth and final attempt, world-record holder and 1988 Olympic silver medalist Randy Barnes of the US launched a throw of 70 ft 11.25 in (21.62 m) to beat teammate and reigning World Champion John Godina, 68 ft 2.5 in (20.79 m), in the men's shot put. Ukraine's Oleksandr Bagach secured the bronze on his sixth attempt with a distance of 68 ft 1 in (20.75 m). After earning the top two spots among the field of 36 athletes competing

in the event, Barnes and Godina took a victory lap to a standing ovation and chants of "USA! USA!"

In the women's shot put, Germany's Astrid Kumbernuss extended her winning streak to 38 by capturing the gold with a throw of 67 ft 5.5 in (20.56 m). The People's Republic of China's Xinmei Sui took silver at 65 ft 2.75 in (19.88 m), and the Russian Federation's Irina Khudorozhkina seized the bronze at 63 ft 6 in (19.35 m). Twenty-five athletes competed in the women's shot put.

Discus. Bulgaria had two of the three medalists in the men's discus event, but Germany's Lars Riedel took top honors, capturing the gold with an Olympic-record throw of 227 ft 8 in (69.40 m). Bulgaria's Vladimir

left: Ukraine's Inessa Kravets goes airborne in the women's triple jump.

right: The Russian Federation's Irina Khudorozhkina throws the shot put in her bronze-medal performance.

NOAH D KAHN • PHYLLIS J KAHN • JAMES R KAHRS • RONALD A KAHRS • SARAH A KAHRS • SHEILA O KAHRS • SUSAN A KAHRS • CHRISTOPHER S KAIGLER • RONNIE A KAIGLER • DONNA L KAIN • RON KAIPUS • NADEEM KAISER • PENELOPE A KAISER • SARAH R KAISER • STACY W KAISER • AMANDA S KAISER ATC • DEBRA KAISERMAN • VIKRAM H KAJI • BATENGA N KAJUMBA • KSHAMA A KAKADE • CELSO A KALACHE • VASUDEVAN M KALADI • KRISTEN L KALAHAR • KRISTIN L KALAR • STACEY KALBERMAN • JOSEPH L KALCSO • ALBERT KALEN • JOE KALER • MATTHEW E KALER • KEITH G KALET • RHONDA L KALETZ •

Dubrovshchik won the silver at 218 ft 6 in (66.60 m), and teammate Vasiliy Kaptyukh secured the bronze at 215 ft 10 in (65.80 m). Forty athletes competed in the men's discus competition.

Using a special strategy, Germany's Ilke Wyludda easily captured the women's discus gold medal with a throw of 228 ft 6 in (69.66 m). "I will tell you my secret: for six weeks, I have not eaten ice cream," she said. Then, with the gold medal in hand, Wyludda, ready for some ice cream, jubilantly proclaimed, "Let's start now!" The Russian Federation's Natalya Sadova won the silver at 218 ft 1.3 in (66.48 m), and Bulgaria's Elyna Zvereva took the bronze at 218 ft 4.25 in (65.64 m). A total of 39 athletes competed.

Javelin. World- and Olympic-record holder Jan Zelezny of the Czech Republic became the first athlete in 72 years to repeat as the men's javelin champion. Zelezny successfully defended his gold medal with a winning throw of 289 ft 3 in (88.16 m). Great Britain's Steve Backley took the silver at 286 ft 10.52 in (87.44 m),

top left: Germany's Ilke Wyludda begins a throw in the women's discus competition.

top right: Hungary's Balázs Kiss exalts in his winning hammer throw.

bottom: Gold medalist Jan Zelezny of the Czech Republic competes in the men's javelin final.

and Finland's Seppo Raty hit the bronze at 285 ft 4.4 in (86.98 m). Thirty-four athletes competed in the men's javelin competition.

In the women's javelin competition, Finland's Heli Rantanen garnered the gold with her initial throw in the finals of 222 ft 10.8 in (67.94 m). Australia's Louise McPaul won the silver with a throw of 215 ft 0.3 in (65.54 m), while Norway's Elsa Katrine Hattestad took the bronze with a distance of 213 ft 2.27 in (64.98 m). Thirty-two athletes competed in the women's javelin event.

Hammer Throw. Hungary's Balázs Kiss survived a last-throw challenge from the US's

GAIL KALEY • LINDA KALEY-LOVELETTE • ELAINE M KALIFEH • RON J KALIL • INGA A KALINICHENKO • YURI S KALININ • SUSAN G KALISHMAN • TAMARA N KALISON • ROBERT G KALKREUTER • AUGUSTINE F KALLAI • LAURA L KALLAM • CLINTON C KALLBREIER • JUDY S KALLBREIER • WILLIAM L KALLBREIER • WILLIAM L KALLBREIER III • FREDERICK B KALLMEYER • DAVID H KALMAN • GEORGE N KALNIN • SANJAY KALRAY • MARGARET J KALVELAGE • KEVIN KALVITIS • LEE KALWERISKY • ENID L KAM • HAL A KAM • RITESH KAMAL • LAKSHMI KAMALANATHAN • STEPHANIE S M KAMAN • CAROL E KAMARA

the world-record holder, withdrew from the qualifying round because of an injured Achilles tendon. A total of 37 athletes competed.

Combined (Track and Field) Events

Decathlon. World-record holder Dan O'Brien of the US claimed the gold medal in the men's decathlon with a determined finish in the final heat of the 1,500 m—the competition's 10th and final event. Having held the lead since the third event (shot put), in order to win, O'Brien needed to finish the heat within 32 seconds of

left: France's Jean Galfione soars to gold in the pole vault.

right: The US's Dan O'Brien celebrates after winning the decathlon.

Lance Deal to win the gold medal in the men's hammer throw. Kiss's third throw of 266 ft 6.4 in (81.24 m) earned him the gold medal. Deal's final attempt came up silver at 266 ft 2.1 in (81.12 m). Ukraine's Oleksiy Krykun won the bronze with a distance of 262 ft 6.4 in (80.02 m). Thirty-seven athletes competed in the event.

Pole Vault. All three medalists in the men's pole vault broke the Olympic record held by Ukraine's Sergey Bubka, as each vaulted 19 ft 5 in (5.92 m). France's Jean Galfione won the gold based on fewer misses, followed by the Russian Federation's Igor Trandenkov, who re-peated as the silver medalist, and bronze medalist Andrei Tivontchik of Germany. Bubka,

Germany's Frank Busemann, who was second in the overall standings. Although O'Brien fin-ished eighth in the 10-man heat, he crossed the finish line only 14.48 behind Busemann and captured his much sought-after Olympic cham-pionship. O'Brien's winning tally of 8,824 points was the sixth-highest decathlon score of all time. Busemann won the silver with 8,706 points, while the Czech Republic's Tomas

EVELYNE M KAMAT • NIKHIL M KAMAT-MHAMAI • RANDALL H KAMAY • DANIEL W KAMBEL • KEITH G KAMBEROS • MIHIR M KAMDAR • YUKO KAMEI • RUDOLPH J KAMENICK • ANTHONY K KAMENJUH • ANITA J KAMENZ • RUSSELL S KAMER MD • JAMIE M KAMIN • EDWARD W KAMINSKI • LEE KAMINSKI • LEONARD KAMINSKI • URSULA A KAMINSKI • JULIE B KAMINSKY • KIMBERLY KAMINSKY • LIZANNE R KAMINSKY • LORRAINE KAMISKY • ELIZABETH D KAMMER • KATHERINE N KAMMER • PETE L KAMMER • ALEXANDRA I KAMPER • CARL A KAMPPI • CINDY L KAMRADT • DAVID S KAN • MELANIE J KANAKA • JOHN M KANALY

Dvorak secured the bronze with 8,664 points. Thirty-one athletes competed in the decathlon.

Heptathlon. World Champion Ghada Shouaa won the Syrian Arab Republic's first-ever Olympic gold medal when she captured the women's heptathlon with 6,780 points. Standing in second place following the fifth event, Shouaa finished strong, as she won the javelin and finished in the top 10 of the 800 m. Natalya Sazanovich of Belarus won the silver with 6,563 points, and Great Britain's Denise Lewis passed Poland's Urszula Wlodarczyk in

line at 2:12:36, 3.0 ahead of Korea's silver medalist Bong-Ju Lee (2:12:39) and 8.0 in front of bronze medalist Eric Wainaina of Kenya (2:12:44). The men's marathon saw 124 athletes compete.

Ethiopia's Fatuma Roba, a farmer's daughter who prior to the Centennial Olympic Games had never even seen the Olympic Games on television, won the women's marathon with the greatest margin of victory in the history of the event. Roba easily ran away with the gold with a winning time of 2:26:05. Defending Olympic champion Valentina Yegorova of the Russian Federation finished in 2:28:05 to take the silver. Japan's Yuko Arimori, the silver

top: South Africa's Josia Thugwane, on his way to marathon gold, moves ahead of silver medalist Bong-Ju Lee of Korea and bronze medalist Eric Wainaina of Kenya.

bottom left: Rita Inancsi of Hungary and World Champion Ghada Shouaa of the Syrian Arab Republic clear the hurdles in the heptathlon competition.

bottom right: Ethiopia's Fatuma Roba kisses the track after her victory in the women's marathon.

the 800 m to take the bronze with 6,489 points. Twenty-five athletes competed in the heptathlon.

Road Events

Marathon. In the most competitive men's marathon in Olympic history, Josia Thugwane became the first black South African to win an Olympic gold medal. He crossed the finish

• DEBORAH KANAR • EMI KANAYAMA • LOUIS KANDEL • MINDY R KANDEL • PHILIP H KANDEL • THOMAS S KANDUL • CHRISTOPHER J KANE • COURTNEY S KANE • KARIN J KANE • MICHAEL M KANE • KATHLEEN H KANE ATC • EDWARD J KANE PT • EUI-KYU KANG • HONG KYU KANG • HYEON U KANG • NATALIE A KANIEL • YAEL D KANIEL • MORA C KANIM • JOHN S KANIPE ATC • BURT KANNER • JOSEPH E KANSAO • CAROLE A KANT • WENDY K KANTER MT • JAMAAL M KANTEY • ANDREW P KANTOR • HEIDI S KANTOR • MARK A KANTOR • STEPHEN J KANTOR • JAMIE KANTROWITZ • KRISTIN KANY • CHIUNG-HWA C KAO •

medalist in Barcelona, took the bronze at 2:28:39. A total of 86 athletes competed in the women's marathon.

10 km Race Walk. World-record holder Yelena Nikolayeva of the Russian Federation lowered the Olympic-best time in the women's 10 km race walk by almost 3:00, claiming the gold medal in 41:49. Italy's Elisabetta Perrone finished second at 42:12, and the People's Republic of China's Yan Wang came in third at 42:19. Forty-four athletes competed in the 10 km race walk.

20 km Race Walk. Jefferson Pérez gave Ecuador its first Olympic medal ever by winning the men's 20 km race walk with a

top: The pressure is on at the start of the women's marathon.

bottom: Yelena Nikolayeva of the Russian Federation sets a new Olympic record and wins the women's 10 km race walk.

Competitors push forward at the start of the men's 20 km race walk.

time of 1:20:07. The Russian Federation's Ilya Markov took the silver medal at 1:20:16, and world-record holder Bernardo Segura of Mexico earned bronze in 1:20:23. Sixty-one athletes competed in the event.

50 km Race Walk. Poland's Robert Korzeniowski won the gold medal in the men's 50 km race walk at 3:43:30. The Russian Federation's Mikhail Shchennikov took the silver with a time of 3:43:46, and Spain's Valentin

Massana earned the bronze at 3:44:19. Fifty-two athletes competed in the 50 km race walk.

Nonmedal Events

In one of the two nonmedal competitions, France's Claude Issorat won the men's 1,500 m wheelchair event with a time of 3:15.18, followed by Scot Hollonbeck of the US (3:15.30) and Switzerland's Franz Nietlispach (3:16.41).

Australia's Louise Sauvage captured the women's 800 m wheelchair event with a first-place time of 1:54.90, ahead of the US's Jean Driscoll (1:55.19) and Cheri Becerra (1:55.49).

ROBERT L KARANTZ • NICOLE G KARDELL • RANA KARDESTUNCER • SUSAN H KARELS • LISA J KARGAUER • CHRISTA F KARI • CAROLYN M KARIBO • ALLAUDDIN J KARIMI • MARY F KARINEN • EVA KARLINER • JERROLD KARLINER • ASA KARLSSON • ULRICA M KARLSSON • PAUL E KARLZEN • REBECCA S KARLZEN • ALBERT A KARMAKAR • LORRAINE L KARMONOCKY • JOHN A KARN • RAHUL KARNANI • ANNE KARNBROCK • ALLAN L KARNITZ • DANIELLE M KAROSAS • CHERYL L KARP • HEATHER L. KARP • JORDAN KARP • STEVEN L KARP • YATIN S KARPE • JESSE L KARR • PAULA J KARR • ANDREAS J KARRAS •

CONCLUSION

The track in Olympic Stadium proved to be one of the fastest ever constructed. Two world records, 17 Olympic records, 25 area records, and 282 national records were set on the surface. In the premier 100 m event, all three men's medalists broke Carl Lewis's Olympic record (9.92) set at the Seoul Games in 1988.

In the women's 100 m, Gail Devers earned the crown of world's fastest woman for a second time, but she was unable to win a second medal in the women's 100 m hurdles. "I did better than [at] Barcelona," said Devers, who has overcome Graves' disease, a condition that nearly resulted in the amputation of one of her feet. "I was fourth [in the hurdles], and I finished on my feet."

Following the Games, Olympic Stadium was converted into a state-of-the-art baseball stadium, and in 1997, it became the home of major league baseball's 1995 world champions, the Atlanta Braves.

Australia's Louise Sauvage crosses the finish line first to win the women's 800 m wheelchair event.

MARTHA D KARRAS • ROSE KARRELS • BARBARA I KARSCH • ROBERT KARSCH MD • KIMBERLY A KARSIAN • LEA ANN A KARSTEN • RICK KARSTEN • SARAH A KARTMAN • TEA S KARVINEN • KIMBERLY D KARVONEN • SUSAN H KASATE • SHIRA R KASH • HEATHER KASHNER • VIPUL Y KASHYAP • BEVERLY A KASHYCKE • JOHN KASHYCKE • JUSTIN P KASIAN • SIMON E KASIEWICZ • ANDREA L KASPAR • EDYTA A KASPRZYCKI • PETER ROBERT KASPRZYCKI • SARA A KASS • RIKKE H KASSE • JONATHAN M KASSEL • CISLYN J KASSIE • KATHLEEN B KASTEN • CHRISTINE A KASTING • CHRISTINA N KASTRITIS •

313

BADMINTON

Venue Used:
Georgia State University
Gymnasium

Days of Competition: 9

Medals Awarded: 15
Gold 5
Silver 5
Bronze 5

Number of Nations: 37

Number of Officials: 72

Officiating Federation:
International Badminton
Federation (IBF)

WITH THE SHUTTLECOCK reaching speeds of up to 200 mph (322 kph) and the world's best players putting on an amazing display of athleticism, footwork, and quickness, the competition at the Centennial Olympic Games was more intense than any badminton game ever played at a summer backyard barbecue or picnic gathering.

A record number of athletes and countries participated in the Atlanta Games competition. Thirty-seven nations were represented by 96 men and 96 women in the five medal events.

VENUE

The Olympic badminton competition was held indoors at the 3,500-seat gymnasium on the campus of Georgia State University, 2 mi (3.3 km) from the Olympic Village. The venue featured three competition courts, each measuring 20 x 44 ft (6.1 x 13.4 m), and two warm-up courts.

COMPETITION

For the first time in Olympic history, the badminton competition included mixed doubles. The other four events in the nine-day competition schedule (24 July–1 August) were men's and women's doubles, and men's and women's singles. All were contested in a single-elimination tournament consisting of best of three sets matches. In another Olympic first, playoffs determined third place, while the fourth- through eighth-place finishers received diplomas.

MIKI KASUGA • LOPA D KATARIA • DEBRA E KATCOFF • JASON P KATCOFF • KAREN L KATELEY • LISA C KATICH • YASUKO KATO • SUSAN E KATRIN • MARK KATS • OLGA KATSNELSON • ALAN L KATTERHENRY • CYNTHIA W KATTERHENRY • BARBARA B KATZ • DARREN J KATZ • DORIS KATZ • JANET C KATZ • MATTHEW L KATZ • MEIRA P KATZ • PATSY KATZ • PAULA J KATZ • ROBERT A KATZ • SHEILA M KATZ • SHERI D KATZ • JANET S KATZENBERGER • REID S KATZUNG • BARBARA B KAUFFMAN • JOHN KAUFFMAN • JUANITA S KAUFFMAN • RYAN M KAUFFMAN • CINDY B KAUFMAN • CYNTHIA D KAUFMAN • HAROLD M KAUFMAN •

Singles. The men's singles competition sizzled from the outset. In what was almost a shocking upset, Sweden's Jens Olsson, ranked no. 19 in the world, held off Guatemala's Kenneth Erichsen, ranked no. 119, to post a thrilling 12-15, 15-6, and 17-15 win. Following the match, both players received a standing ovation.

The trip through the second round was easier for the globe's top-ranked players. After receiving a first-round bye, no. 1 ranked Jiong Dong of the People's Republic of China and no. 2 ranked Poul-Erik Hoyer Larsen of Denmark advanced in straight sets, while no. 4 seed Allan Budi Kusuma of Indonesia opened his defense of his 1992 gold medal with a victory.

For one of the favorites, however, domination turned to defeat in the quarterfinal round.

The tournament's top seed, Joko Suprianto of Indonesia, was overwhelmed by no. 7 seed Rashid Sidek of Malaysia and lost in straight sets. In addition, the quarterfinals witnessed the end of Kusuma's quest for a second gold, as he was eliminated by Hoyer Larsen. Dong and Indonesia's Heryanto Arbi advanced with Sidek and Hoyer Larsen.

The semifinals proved to be a testament to comfortable, if a bit worn, shoes. Having lost seven of his previous nine matches against Arbi, Hoyer Larsen decided a change was afoot and donned the same pair of 1989-vintage shoes that he had worn when he won the 1995 and 1996 All-England Championships. The result was a 15-11 and 15-6 victory. Dong defeated Malaysia's Sidek 15-6 and 18-16 in the other semifinal match.

Hoyer Larsen's tattered pair of lucky shoes carried him to the championship. Defeating Dong in two sets, the Dane became the first European to win an Olympic gold medal in badminton. And what of his shoes? "I hope to be able to put some rubber on them and make them last a few more years," said Hoyer Larsen, who after the 15-12 and 15-10 gold-medal victory, wrapped his country's flag around his neck like a cape and danced for the celebrating Danish fans in the stands. Dong took home the silver, while Sidek won the bronze with a 5-15, 15-11, and 15-6 win over Arbi.

Early round highlights of women's singles included a rare shutout turned in by 1992

facing page: **Poul-Erik Hoyer Larsen of Denmark proudly displays his gold medal.**

left: **1993 World Champion Joko Suprianto of Indonesia eyes a return in his preliminary-round win.**

right: **Look of the Games banners with the badminton pictogram decorated the Georgia State University Gymnasium.**

KATHRYN C KAUFMAN • TRACY F KAUFMAN • ALICE H KAUFMANN • CAROLINE R KAUFMANN • ROBERT S KAUFMANN • TIM KAUFMANN • PUSHKAR N KAUL • PAUL G KAUS • ROBERT F KAUS • RAKESH KAUSHISH • NANCY KAVANAUGH • CAROL S KAVIS • DUSTIN R KAWA • ERNESTO R KAWAMOTO • ZAZUTADA KAWAMURA • FRANK T KAWE • ANGELA M KAY • GEORGE P KAY • JANET L KAY • MARY W KAY • NANCY B KAY • PAMELA J KAY • SCOTT T KAY • STEVE J KAY • WILLIAM S KAY • JUDITH LYNN KAY-MONAGHAN • SELIM KAYALI • BENJAMIN J KAYE • BRIAN G KAYE • HOLLY L KAYE • LARRY J KAYE • RAYMOND KAYE •

left: Indonesia's Mia Audina hits a return in her semifinal win.

right: Women's singles gold medalist Soo Hyun Bang of Korea waves to the crowd during the medal ceremony.

of China lost in two sets to Korea's Ji Hyun Kim. The no. 2 seeded player was also in dire straits, but Indonesia's Susi Susanti rebounded from an opening game defeat to knock out no. 5 seeded Jingna Han of the People's Republic of China in three sets. Audina and Bang also advanced into the semifinals.

Indonesian and Korean athletes went head-to-head in the semifinals, a round that seemed to foreshadow the finals. Bang earned Korea's place by defeating defending gold medalist Susanti 11-9 and 11-8. Amid loud chants of

silver medalist Soo Hyun Bang of Korea. She needed just 10 minutes to defeat Nigeria's Obigeli Olorunsola 11-0 and 11-0. Meanwhile, Indonesia's 16-year-old sensation Mia Audina, ranked no. 11 in the world, was impressive in defeating no. 18 ranked Christine Magnusson of Sweden 11-6 and 11-1. The win by the small, dynamic Audina raised Indonesia's record in the first three days of competition to 8-0.

As in the men's event, the quarterfinal round proved unkind to the tournament's top seed as Zhaoying Ye of the People's Republic

"Mia, Mia, Mia," Audina defeated 21-year-old Kim in three sets, 11-6, 9-11, and 11-1, to earn Indonesia's finals berth.

In the gold-medal match, Bang capped her marvelous run with an 11-6 and 11-7 win over Audina. On her way to the gold, Bang was unstoppable; she never lost a single game. Susanti defeated Kim 11-4 and 11-1 to win the bronze.

RODERICK F KAYE • SYLVIA KAYE • BEN L KAYHART • DEBORAH J KAYLOR • EILEEN F KAYLOR • JEANNE H KAYLOR • JULIA W KAYNE • MARION R KAYS • SANDRA F KAYS • SKIP KAYS • DAVID W KAZANOWSKI • CLARENCE MARION KAZMIER • LORETTA H KAZMIER • HELEN M KAZMIERCZYK • GWENDOLYN H KAZUNAS • ALEX KE • TREY KEADLE • JOHN A KEANE • PATRICIA A KEANE • SIOBHAN M KEANE • ELISA K KEARNEY • ELIZABETH L KEARNEY • JAY T KEARNEY • JOANNE M KEARNEY • STEPHEN J KEARNEY • STEPHEN P KEARNEY • MARY CLARE KEARSE • JEFF T KEAS • HELEN W KEATEN • BONNIE M KEATING •

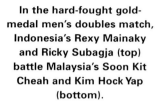

In the hard-fought gold-medal men's doubles match, Indonesia's Rexy Mainaky and Ricky Subagja (top) battle Malaysia's Soon Kit Cheah and Kim Hock Yap (bottom).

Doubles. Early in the men's doubles tournament, Great Britain's Simon Archer and Chris Hunt won their match against Hong Kong's Siu Kwong Chan and Tim He in straight sets. The British duo advanced to the quarterfinals before dropping a straight-set decision to Beng Kiang Soo and Kim Her Tan of Malaysia.

Also advancing into the all-Asian semifinals were Indonesia's Rexy Mainaky and Ricky Subagja, Malaysia's Soon Kit Cheah and Kim Hock Yap, and Indonesia's Antonius Ariantho and Denny Kantano. The semifinal matches proved to be mismatches. Before a loud contingent of Indonesian fans, Mainaky and Subagja defeated Soo and Tan 15-3 and 15-5, while no. 2 seeded Cheah and Yap advanced over no. 3 seeded Ariantho and Kantano 15-10 and 15-4.

The men's doubles final, however, was an evenly matched contest. Losing the first game 5-15, Mainaky and Subagja rallied to seize the final two games—and the gold medal—15-13 and 15-12 over Cheah and Yap, who won the silver. In the third game of the competitive 89-minute match, the score was tied nine times. After falling behind 10-12, Mainaky and Subagja won five straight points to take the title.

HOWARD J KEATING • JOAN M KEATING • PATRICIA M KEATING • COSANDRA D KEATON • MERAT KEBEDE • LYNN KEBLINGER • MICHAEL S KECHRIOTIS • ARIC L KECK • DON W KECK • MARK F KECKLER •
TOMMIE S KEEBAUGH • LISA R KEEBLE • STEVEN KEEFER • AMY T KEEFNER • ANN L KEEFNER • LAUREN A KEEGAN • PIER KEEGAN • ROBIN L KEEGAN • LOU R KEEHN • CHRIS KEEHNER • JOEL C KEEL •
MICHAEL C KEELEY • BRYAN E KEELING EMT • BEVERLY H KEEN • CARROLL P KEEN • CHELIN KEEN • JACK N KEEN • JERRY KEEN • MELISSA C KEEN • PAUL T KEEN • JIM R KEENAN • JOSEPH R KEENAN •

317

The People's Republic of China's Jun Gu and Fei Ge congratulate each other during their gold-medal victory.

Ariantho and Kantano, the no. 3 seeded team, claimed the bronze over Soo and Tan with a 15-4, 12-15, and 15-8 win.

The women's doubles competition opened with a double dose of Olympic sisters. Korean sisters Mee-Hyang Kim and Shin Young Kim defeated Japan's sibling duo of Aikiko Miyamura and Aiko Miyamura 15-12 and 18-13 in the first-round contest.

In quarterfinal action, all top four seeds advanced to the semifinals. To advance to the semifinals, the People's Republic of China's no. 2 seeded team of Fei Ge and Jun Gu ousted another pair of sisters, Indonesia's Eliza Zelin and Rosiana Zelin. Other winners included Korea's Young Ah Gil and Hye Ock Jang, the no. 1 seeds; the no. 3 seeded team of Helene Kirkegaard and Rikke Olsen of Denmark; and no. 4 seeds Yiyuan Qin and Yongshu Tang of the People's Republic of China.

STEPHANIE KEENAN • JACQUELINE P KEENAN-KINCAID • BRENDA D KEENE • ELIZABETH A KEENE • MICHELLE L KEENE • MILLIE A KEENE-SCHUMACHER • BRIAN P KEENER • CONNIE T KEENER • MARY L KEENER • SANDRA K KEENER • STACEY L KEENER • JULIA C KEENEY • LINDA B KEENEY • CHARLOTTE E KEENOY • REBECCA J KEENUM • GLENN G KEES • JAMES L KEES • MIDGE E KEES • KELLY A KEESEE-JONES • DEE M KEETON • KATHERENE Z KEETON • LINDA R KEETON • LORELEI T KEETON • DEBRA A KEEZELL • KIMBERLY K KEFFER • MARA W KEGGI • ANDREW B KEGLER • SUSAN B. KEGLEY • BRIAN KEHINDE

After semifinal victories, the top tournament seeds met in a historic battle for the gold. The tandem of Ge and Gu captured the People's Republic of China's first gold medal in badminton with a 15-5 and 15-5 upset win over top seeds Gil and Jang. "A gold medal is definitely a breakthrough," Gu said afterward. In the bronze-medal match, Qin and Tang defeated Kirkegaard and Olsen 7-15, 15-4, and 15-8.

Mixed Doubles. The mixed doubles tournament opened with a remarkable upset win by Indonesia's unseeded team of Nimpele Flandy

and Rosalina Riseu over no. 6 seeds Simon Archer and Julie Bradbury of Great Britain 15-5 and 15-6. Flandy and Riseu reached the quarterfinals before being eliminated by Jianjun Liu and Man Sun of the People's Republic of China.

The road for Liu and Sun, however, ended in the semifinals with defeat in two sets at the hands of Korea's Joo-Bong Park and Kyung Min Ra. Korea completed a semifinal sweep when

Dong Moon Kim and Young Ah Gil defeated the People's Republic of China's Xingdong Chen and Xingyong Peng in two sets.

In a contest between teammates, Gil and Kim dropped the first game against Park and Ra 13-15 before rallying to win the next two games 15-4 and 15-12 to capture the title. The bronze-medal match also pitted teammates against each other: the People's Republic of China's Liu and Sun defeated Chen and Peng 13-15, 17-15, and 15-4.

CONCLUSION

All sessions for badminton, which is hailed by the International Badminton Federation as the "world's fastest racket sport," were sold out. The enthusiastic crowd supported the players by beating drums, chanting, singing, stomping their feet, and waving flags.

Much of the excitement at the Games was created by the Asian players and fans. Indicative of the passion demonstrated by the sport's top countries, Indonesia's government had awarded Susanti and Kusuma substantially for their gold-medal efforts in 1992. This time, however, Indonesia's passion was not able to overcome the strength of Korea's efforts. Among the nations represented in the Centennial Olympic Games badminton competition, Korea had the best showing, winning two gold and two silver medals. Following Korea were the People's Republic of China and Indonesia, both of which won one gold, one silver, and two bronzes, and Malaysia, which tallied one silver and one bronze.

Korea's gold-medal mixed doubles team of Dong Moon Kim and Young Ah Gil rejoice after scoring a point during their semifinal match.

Atlanta 1996

• MATTHEW KEHNER • MARYANNE D KEHOE • STACY LORRAINE KEHOE • EMILY E KEHRBERG • BRIAN A KEICHER ATC • DAVID KEIDEL • EDWIN C KEIFFER • KATIE KEIGHER • BOB H KEIL • CAROL J KEIM • JOHN R KEIM • KARI KEISER • LYNNE C KEISER • NATALLIE JOANN KEISER • WALTER E KEISER • SCOTT KEIT • DAMAFING KEITA • MARY S KEITH • AMY L KEITH • JANET B KEITH • JUDY B KEITH • MARY J KEITH • SHAWN C KEITH • STANLEY G KEITH • TOMMY H KEITT • CHRISTOPHER R KELCO • LISA MARIE KELCOURSE • TERRI D KELDIE • MARCIA L KELEMEN • CAROLYN J KELFER • ELIZABETH J KELHOFFER •

BASEBALL

Venue Used:
Atlanta–Fulton
County Stadium

Days of Competition: 12

Medals Awarded: 3
Gold 1
Silver 1
Bronze 1

Number of Nations: 8

Number of Officials: 65

Officiating Federation:
International Baseball
Association (IBA)

THE BASEBALL TOURNAMENT of the 1996 Olympic Games took place from 20 July to 2 August. In excess of 1.13 million tickets were sold, more than tripling the attendance record set in 1984. Admission to the baseball tournament was also the most inexpensive of all Games sports, with some tickets priced as low as $7.

VENUE

Atlanta–Fulton County Stadium, the site of four of the last five World Series, was the host venue for the Centennial Olympic Games baseball competition. The 30-year home of the city's major league baseball team—the 1995 World Champion Atlanta Braves—the 54,000-seat facility holds a regulation baseball field with an outfield fence measuring 330 ft (100.6 m) to left and right fields, 385 ft (117.3 m) to the power alleys, and 402 ft (122.5 m) to center field. The stadium was located 2.7 mi (4.3 km) from the Atlanta Olympic Village.

COMPETITION

A total of 160 athletes (20 per team) took part in the eight-team, 28-game, round-robin tournament. The countries that competed were Australia, Cuba, Italy, Japan, Korea, the Netherlands, Nicaragua, and the United States. The top four teams advanced to the semifinals, where the winners competed in the gold-medal

game, and the third- and fourth-place teams played for the bronze.

Opening tournament play, Australia gave gold-medal favorite Cuba a battle before dropping a 19-8 decision to the defending gold medalist. The teams combined for the most runs in a single Olympic game (previously 20). After being briefly ahead 4-2, the Australian team members found themselves in an 8-8 deadlock in the sixth inning before Cuba awoke and plated eight runs in the inning. Cuba's designated hitter, Orestes Kindelan, led the late onslaught with two home runs and six runs batted in (RBIs), while second baseman Antonio Pacheco knocked in seven RBIs with hits that included two home runs, a single-game high for Olympic competition. The duo became the first Olympic teammates to hit multiple home runs in the same game.

On the second day of competition, the no. 1 seeded Cubans found themselves close to losing only their second nonexhibition international tournament game in 13 years. But Cuba scored two runs at the bottom of the 10th inning to pull out an 8-7 win over Japan. The game featured Kindelan's gigantic 521 ft (159 m) home run, the longest measured in the history of Atlanta–Fulton County Stadium. Later in the preliminaries, Kindelan hit another 500 ft (152 m) shot and finished with an individual record of nine home runs in the tournament.

At the halfway point in the round-robin, Cuba and the US were the only undefeated

JANET E KELHOFFER • JOHN W KELL • KARA L KELLAM • VETA W KELLAM • ANN MARIE KELLER • CHUCK H KELLER • CLAYTON A KELLER • DAWN A KELLER • DEBRA D KELLER • ELAINE M KELLER • ERNEST E KELLER • GARY R KELLER • GINNIE A KELLER • JEFFREY R KELLER • L ANNE KELLER • MARY A KELLER • TR KELLER • ARTHUR L KELLERMAN • KIMBERLY A KELLETT • ALEXIS C KELLEY • BOBBIE M KELLEY • CYNTHIA K KELLEY • DAMON KELLEY • DAVID M KELLEY • DONALD J KELLEY • ERICA KELLEY • FRANCES E KELLEY • JAMES K KELLEY • JOHN KELLEY • JOHN G KELLEY • JONNIE C KELLEY • KIMBERLEY A KELLEY

top: The US's Troy Glaus connects on a home run in Cuba's preliminary-round win.

bottom: Nicaragua's shortstop Bayardo Davila Montiel looks for the call after tagging Korea's Jae-Ho Back in a preliminary game.

teams. Surprisingly, Korea, a pre-Games medal contender, was virtually eliminated from contention after opening with four straight losses.

In front of a sold-out crowd of 51,795 on the sixth day of preliminary play, the US batters pounded seven home runs in a 15-5 win over Japan. The game was shortened to seven innings because of the 10-run lead "mercy rule" used in international play: if a team is trailing by 10 or more runs after batting seven innings, the game is declared over. In the contest, the US set three home-run marks for Olympic competition: most home runs in an inning (five); most consecutive home runs (four); and most home runs in a game (seven).

On the eighth day of competition, the much-anticipated showdown between the tournament's only unbeaten teams materialized when Cuba faced the US. Another sold-

• LINDA K KELLEY • MARSHA A KELLEY • MARTHA B KELLEY • MARY B KELLEY • MICHAEL J KELLEY • PAT KELLEY • PAUL B KELLEY • RONALD G KELLEY • RUTH S KELLEY • SANDRA L KELLEY • SEAN F KELLEY • THOMAS R KELLEY • TONY R KELLEY • WILLIAM A KELLEY • FORREST E KELLEY SR • JONATHAN A KELLNER • GILLIAN S KELLOGG • MARY J KELLOGG • MARY M KELLOGG • TAMMY M KELLOGG • CYNTHIA D KELLUM • SALLY D KELLUM • SIMONE D KELLUM • ALISON E KELLY • ALMA J KELLY • BERNARD KELLY • BETSY M KELLY • CAROL ANNE KELLY • DAVID A KELLY • DAVID R KELLY • DEBBIE K KELLY • DEBRA A KELLY

out crowd watched both teams put on their usual display of offensive firepower, but it was Cuba that capitalized with runners in scoring position to post a 10-8 win. The victory gave Cuba a record of 6-0 in the tournament and the no. 1 seed in the upcoming four-team medal round. At 5-1, the US clinched the no. 2 seed.

After the preliminary games, Cuba (7-0), the US (6-1), Japan (4-3), and Nicaragua (4-3) advanced to the tournament semifinals. Though Italy (2-5) and the Netherlands (2-5) did not qualify for the medal round, they became the first European teams to win more than one game in Olympic baseball play. Leading the way for Italy were Luigi Carrozza, the leading hitter in the tournament with a .571 batting average (12 for 21), and pitcher Roberto Cabalisti, who was at the top in strikeouts with 17. The Netherlands' Eric de Bruin was among the tournament's leading hitters, finishing with a .471 batting average.

In the opening game of the semifinals, Cuba moved into the gold-medal contest with a solid 8-1 win over Nicaragua, whose pitching staff

left: Massimo Fochi pitches for Italy, one of the first European teams to advance past the first round in Olympic play.

right: The Netherlands' shortstop Evert-Jan 't Hoen leaps over Australian first baseman Andrew Scott to complete a double play in the Dutch team's win.

• DIA D KELLY • DONNA P KELLY • ELIZABETH KELLY • ERIN KELLY • FRANK A KELLY • GAIL E KELLY • GERARD J KELLY • GLORIA M KELLY • GRAHAM T KELLY • GUSSIE M KELLY • HENRY A KELLY • JAMES M KELLY • JAMES W KELLY • JOHN P KELLY • JOSEPH L KELLY • JOYCE M KELLY • JULIE A KELLY • LESLIE M. KELLY • MARGARET P KELLY • MARGO F KELLY • MATTIE W KELLY • MAXINE KELLY • MELISSA A KELLY • MICHELLE N KELLY • PATRICK M KELLY • PAUL E KELLY • PAUL G KELLY • ROBERT KELLY • ROBERT A KELLY • SCOTT E KELLY • SCOTT W KELLY • STEVE P KELLY • SUSAN E KELLY • TERRI L. KELLY • THOMAS J KELLY •

entered the medal round with a tournament-best earned run average (ERA) of 3.88. Just three days earlier, Cuba had had to rally four times before beating Nicaragua 8-7.

In the other semifinal game, Japan became the only country to earn a medal in each of the last four Olympic Games baseball competitions when it pulled off a stunning 11-2 upset over the United States. In the preliminaries, the US had drilled seven home runs in a 15-5 win over Japan, but this time, Japan clubbed five home runs while the US had only one.

top: Nicaragua's shortstop Jorge Luis Avellan dives for the ball during a game with Italy.

bottom left: US catcher A. J. Hinch watches Hideaki Okubo hit a home run in Japan's win.

bottom right: Look of the Games structures enhanced the entrance to Atlanta–Fulton County Stadium.

TIM M KELLY • VIOLA KELLY • WILLIAM N KELLY • WILLIE M KELLY • YOLANDA KELLY • THERESA KELLY-GEGEN • KAREN KELLY-NELSON • KATHRYN D KELLY ATC • EILEEN KELLY BERRY • HENRY N KELLY JR • MARILYN B KELM • JENNIFER N KELSCH • ELAINE M KELSEY • PATRICK E KELSEY • JENNIFER J KELSO • DAVID E KELTERBORN • ANNE A KELTY • PAIGE L KELTY • SUSAN A KEMETER • COURTNEY KEMMERER • SARAH C KEMMERER • SHERRIE O KEMMERER • SUZANNE M KEMMERER • KELLY S KEMMERLIN • ALAN E KEMP • ANITA KEMP • DEBORAH D KEMP • DONALD B KEMP • DONALD G KEMP • DONNA O KEMP •

In a rematch of the 8-7 extra-inning thriller from the second day of tournament play, unbeaten Cuba (8-0) faced Japan (5-3) in the gold-medal game before a crowd of 44,221. Given the number of home runs that had been hit in the tournament (122), it was only appropriate that the championship game turned into an exciting long-ball hitting contest. A total of 11 home runs was hit as Cuba held on for a 13-9 win. Cuba blasted eight of the game's 11 round-trippers, and leading the way was third baseman Omar Linares, who hit three two-run

top: Japan's Yasuyuki Saigo slides safely into home plate past Cuba's catcher Juan Manrique during the gold-medal game.

bottom: Omar Linares *(right)* is greeted at home plate by teammates Antonio Pacheco *(left)* and Luis Ulacia *(center)* after his first-inning home run in Cuba's gold-medal win.

homers. Linares also extended his hitting streak to 18 games—hitting safely in all nine games in each of the last two Olympic Games. Cuba's team members were Omar Ajete, Miguel Caldes, Jose Ariel Contreras, Jose Estrada, Jorge Fumero, Alberto Hernandez, Rey Isaac, Orestes Kindelan, Pedro Luis Lazo, Omar Linares, Omar Luis, Juan Manrique, Eliecer Montes de Oca,

GAYLE N KEMP • HARRY T KEMP • KENNETH L KEMP • KEVIN O KEMP • LISA M KEMP • ROBERT E KEMP • TERRELL D KEMP • SHERI M KEMPEL • DENNIS E KEMPER • GARY W KEMPER • MARILYN E KEMPER • SUZANNE M KEMPINGER • ANDREW W KENDALL • BRADLEY J KENDALL • FREDERICK C KENDALL • JAMES A KENDALL • JAMES R KENDALL • JENTRY R KENDALL • SHARON L KENDALL • SUSAN G KENDALL • TODD H KENDALL • LINDA M KENDIG • SUSAN B KENDRA • ALAN S KENDRICK • ANITA V KENDRICK • ASHLEY E KENDRICK • LISA KENDRICK • MARGARET K KENDRICK • VIRGINIA W KENDRICK •

Antonio Pacheco, Juan Padilla, Eduardo Paret, Osmany Romero, Antonio Scull, Luis Ulacia, and Lazaro Vargas.

The silver-medal Japanese team consisted of Kosuke Fukudome, Tadahito Iguchi, Makoto Imaoka, Takeo Kawamura, Jutaro Kimura, Takashi Kurosu, Takao Kuwamoto, Nobuhiko Matsunaka, Koichi Misawa, Masahiko Mori, Masao Morinaka, Daishin Nakamura, Masahiro Nojima, Hideaki Okubo, Hitoshi Ono, Yasuyuki Saigo, Tomoaki Sato, Masanori Sugiura, Takayuki Takabayashi, and Yoshitomo Tani.

Loyd, Warren Morris, Augie Ojeda, Jim Parque, Jeff Weaver, and Jason Williams.

CONCLUSION

On the field, defending gold medalist Cuba, which went 9-0 in tournament play at the 1992 Barcelona Games, continued its winning streak. This baseball-crazed country once again went undefeated in Olympic tournament play, going 9-0 and hitting 38 home runs en route to winning a second straight Olympic gold medal.

top: Takayuki Takabayashi leads the Japanese team from the podium following the silver medal presentation.

bottom: The interior and exterior of the baseball venue were decorated with Look of the Games elements.

In the bronze-medal match, the US hit four home runs, including two in a four-run first inning, en route to a 10-3 win over Nicaragua. The members of the US team were Chad Allen, Kris Benson, R. A. Dickey, Troy Glaus, Chad Green, Seth Greisinger, Kip Harkrider, A. J. Hinch, Jacque Jones, Billy Koch, Mark Kotsay, Matt LeCroy, Travis Lee, Braden Looper, Brian

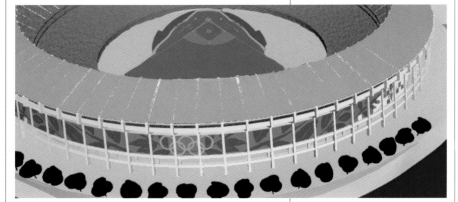

Atlanta 1996

WAYNE M KENDRICK ATC • PATSY J KENDRIX • ROY S KENEDA • JANICE P KENEMER • KATSUO KENMOCHI • JOHN A KENNEALLY • ADRIENNE KENNEDY • ANN KENNEDY • ANNE E KENNEDY • ANNE T KENNEDY • AUSTIN O KENNEDY • BARBARA A KENNEDY • CATHRINE L KENNEDY • COLIN J KENNEDY • COLLEEN F KENNEDY • DANIEL M KENNEDY • DAVID C KENNEDY • DEATRICE L KENNEDY • DEBRA E C KENNEDY • EILEEN N KENNEDY • ELISA KENNEDY • ERICA J KENNEDY • FRANCES G KENNEDY • JIM L KENNEDY • JOHN A KENNEDY • JOHN M KENNEDY • JOHN W KENNEDY • KELLY F KENNEDY • LAIR T KENNEDY •

BASKETBALL

Venues Used:
Georgia Dome

■

Morehouse College
Gymnasium

Days of Competition: 16

Medals Awarded: 6
Gold 2
Silver 2
Bronze 2

Number of Nations: 19

Number of Officials: 90

Officiating Federation:
International Basketball
Federation (FIBA)

FOR THE FIRST TIME in Olympic history, the basketball competition included an equal number of men's and women's teams. Four teams were added to the women's tournament, and a total of 144 men (12 teams of 12) and 144 women (12 teams of 12) representing 19 countries competed in identical pool-play formats.

VENUES

Two venues hosted both the men's and women's basketball competitions at the Centennial Olympic Games: the Morehouse College Gymnasium and the Georgia Dome. The 6,000-seat Morehouse College Gymnasium, which was designed to become the new home of the school's men's and women's basketball teams after the Games, was located approximately 2.2 mi (3.5 km) from the Atlanta Olympic Village and hosted 26 of the preliminary-round games played 20–30 July. The Georgia Dome was located approximately 1.9 mi (3 km) from the Atlanta Olympic Village and hosted the remaining preliminaries as well as the quarterfinals, semifinals, and finals (20 July–4 August).

The main site for the 1996 Centennial Olympic Games basketball competition was the 69,000-seat Georgia Dome, the largest cable-supported stadium in the world. In addition to basketball, this facility hosted artistic gymnastics and the men's handball finals. To facilitate this, the Georgia Dome was divided in half by a soundproof curtain, and the seating capacity for basketball was 34,500 spectators.

COMPETITION

The preliminary round of competition consisted of two pools of six teams that played in a round-robin. The top four teams in each group advanced to the quarterfinals.

Men

The men's competition began with one of the tournament's most exciting games as Lithuania came from behind in an 83-81 double-overtime win over Croatia. The match showcased Arvydas Sabonis of Lithuania and Toni Kukoc of Croatia—both of whom play professionally in the National Basketball Association (NBA). Sabonis led Lithuania with 20 points and 14 rebounds before fouling out with 2:16 left in the second overtime. Kukoc scored a game-high 33 points for Croatia.

After opening wins over Argentina (96-68) and Angola (87-54), the United States team defeated Lithuania 104-82 in its first major test of the tournament. The US then advanced past the People's Republic of China (133-70) before tuning up for the quarterfinals with an impressive 102-71 win over Croatia. Croatia was led by Zan Tabak (19 points) and Kukoc (10 points and 10 assists). Mitch Richmond (16 points) and

LIONEL W KENNEDY • MARJORIE P KENNEDY • MARTI J KENNEDY • MARY JANE B KENNEDY • MERRILL E KENNEDY • MICHELLE R KENNEDY • PATRICK J KENNEDY • PATSY P KENNEDY • PEGGY L KENNEDY • PEGGY P KENNEDY • SANDRA KENNEDY • SANDRA L KENNEDY • STEPHANIE KENNEDY • SUELLAN C KENNEDY • TAMMY P KENNEDY • TIMOTHY KENNEDY • TINA KENNEDY • W L KENNEDY • GREGORY J KENNEDY MT • CHERYL C KENNELLY • AMY M KENNERK • CHRIS KENNERLY • ANNA L KENNEY • CARROLL S KENNEY • CATHY G KENNEY • MARK L KENNEY • NANCY H KENNEY • SORAYA M KENNEY •

Charles Barkley (14 points and 12 rebounds) led the US in the victory.

Going into the quarterfinals, both the US and Yugoslavia were undefeated at 5-0. The other teams advancing to the quarterfinals were Australia (4-1), Croatia (3-2), Greece (3-2), Lithuania (3-2), Brazil (2-3), and the People's Republic of China (2-3).

In the men's quarterfinals, both the US (winner of Pool A) and Yugoslavia (winner of Pool B) remained undefeated at 6-0. Yugoslavia advanced over the People's Republic of China 128-61, while the US defeated Brazil 98-75. In the loss to the US, Brazil's five-time Olympian, 38-year-old Oscar Schmidt, scored 26 points and became the first player in Olympic history to score an accumulated 1,000 points.

Also in the quarterfinals, Lithuania defeated Greece 99-66, and Australia rallied from a 64-56 deficit and pulled off the biggest upset of the tournament with a shocking 73-71 win over Croatia, the silver medalist at the 1992 Games in Barcelona. "This is probably the biggest win in Australian basketball history," Australia's four-time Olympian Andrew Gaze said. The victory sent Australia straight into a match with the US in the semifinals.

Before a crowd of 34,069 at the Georgia Dome, the US recorded its 100th win in Olympic

basketball history by defeating Australia 101-73. Leading the US in its milestone win was Barkley, who made all seven of his field-goal attempts and finished with a team-best 24 points and 11 rebounds. In the loss, Gaze sparked Australia with a game-high 25 points.

In the other semifinal game, Predrag Danilovic scored 6 of his 19 points in the final 79 seconds to boost Yugoslavia to a 66-58 win over Lithuania. In the loss, Lithuania's Rimas

left: **Argentina's Juan Espil shoots over Arijan Komazec during Croatia's preliminary-round win.**

right: **Banners and other elements utilizing the Look of the Games were used to decorate the basketball venue at the Georgia Dome.**

STEVEN T KENNEY • WILLIAM C KENNEY • ROSALIND A KENNISON • JOHN D KENNON • ALICE G KENNY • LOUIS A KENNY • NANCY A KENNY • PATRICK KENNY • AD KENT • ALICIA M KENT • BARBARA L KENT • BILL E KENT • CHARTRAE J KENT • GARY KENT • JAMES F KENT • KAREN KENT • LINDA C KENT • RONALD J KENT • SILVANA KENT • SUSAN A KENT • SUSAN C KENT • THOMAS I KENT • VICKI E KENT • TINA M KENT SHUPE • LAWRENCE K KENTERA • RICHARD G KENTWELL • TIM D KENWORTHY • JASON D KEOUGH • ROBERT W KEOWN • UROS KEPIC • JOAN R KEPPLER • MILENA N KERBA • KEVIN A KERBER •

Kurtinaitis hit five out of seven three-point shots and scored a game-high 22 points.

An Olympic-high basketball crowd of 34,500 gathered at the Georgia Dome to watch the US capture the gold medal with a 95-69 win over Yugoslavia, which took home the silver. Riding the momentum of a 7-0 Olympic winning streak and a 16-game international competition streak, a physical Yugoslavia team cut the United States's lead to 51-50 in the second half, before US center David Robinson scored 10 of his game-high 28 points in a 19-4 run that put

the game away. In the win, two honors were bestowed upon Robinson: becoming the all-time leading scorer in US Olympic men's basketball history, with a career total of 270 points, and being the most decorated men's basketball player in US Olympic history, with three gold medals.

The members of the US gold-medal team were Charles Barkley, Anfernee Hardaway, Grant Hill, Karl Malone, Reggie Miller, Shaquille O'Neal, Hakeem Olajuwon, Gary Payton, Scottie Pippen, Mitch Richmond, David Robinson, and John Stockton.

The members of Yugoslavia's silver-medal team were Miroslav Beric, Dejan Bodiroga, Predrag Danilovic, Vlade Divac, Aleksandar Djordjevic, Nikola Loncar, Sasa Obradovic, Zarko Paspalj, Zeljko Rebraca, Zoran Savic, Dejan Tomasevic, and Milenko Topic.

left: The US's Charles Barkley goes up for a basket over Yugoslavia's Zarko Paspalj and Vlade Divac in the gold-medal game.

right: Lithuania's Arturas Karnisovas looks to shoot over Australia's Scott Fisher in Lithuania's bronze-medal victory.

LUCY W KERMAN • MICHAEL G KERMAN • ASHLEY L KERN • E LEE KERN • JESSICA C KERN • JOSH I KERN • MARIAN R KERN • TONYA M KERN • HILARY B KERN MD • MARTHA E KERNAN • WILLIAM J KERNEY III • SHEREE W KERNIZAN • JAMES E KERNS • KATHERINE KERNS • LARRY M KERNS • ROBERT Z KERNS • SANTHA S KERNS • DALE KERR • DOUGLAS G KERR • JACQUELINE P KERR • JUDY A KERR • MARY FRANCES KERR • ROBERT R KERR • THOMAS J KERR • MICHAEL G KERRIGAN • BOB KERSCH • KATA KERSCHBAUM • ART KERSEY • CORNELE H KERSEY • SHARON A KERSHBAUM • JUDITH KERSHOW •

In the third-place game, Lithuania won its second straight bronze medal with a 80-74 win over Australia.

The players on the bronze-medal team from Lithuania were Gintaras Einikis, Arturas Karnisovas, Rimas Kurtinaitis, Darius Lukminas, Sarunas Marciulionis, Tomas Pacesas, Arvydas Sabonis, Saulius Stombergas, Rytis Vaisvila, Eurelijus Zukauskas, and Mindaugas Zukauskas.

Women

Following a 52-0 training record, the US women opened Olympic play with a 101-84 win over Cuba, followed by a 98-65 win over Ukraine, the defending European champion. Guard Ruthie Bolton led the US past Ukraine, making 7 out of 10 shots and finishing with a game-high 21 points. Also on the second day of tournament play, defending World Champion Brazil defeated defending Olympic champion the Russian Federation 82-68. In the win, Hôrtencia de Fátima Marcari Oliva scored a game-high 20 points for Brazil, while Irina Rutkovskaya led the Russian Federation with a team-best 18 points.

Brazil and the US finished the preliminaries undefeated (5-0). The other teams advancing to the quarterfinals were the Russian Federation (4-1), Australia (3-2), Italy (3-2), Ukraine (3-2), Cuba (2-3), and Japan (2-3).

Before 31,070 spectators at the Georgia Dome, the US's 6 ft 5 in (1.96 m) center Lisa Leslie stood out, literally, in her team's 108-93 quarterfinal win over Japan. Playing against a Japanese squad that did not have any player taller than 6 ft (1.8 m), Leslie scored a US women's basketball record of 35 points (just four less than the women's record in Olympic competition). Also in quarterfinal action, Australia survived a heated battle to win 74-70 over the Russian Federation. Trailing 73-70, the Russian Federation team came away with a crucial

jump ball; the referees, however, awarded the ball to Australia on a controversial jump-ball violation, and the Australian team held on for the victory. The other two quarterfinal winners were Brazil, a 101-69 winner over Cuba; and Ukraine, a 59-50 victor over Italy.

In the semifinals, the tournament's two undefeated women's teams continued on their gold-medal collision course. Brazil, led by its pair of veteran guards—Oliva, 36, and Maria Paula Gonçalves da Silva, 34—beat Ukraine 81-60. In the win, Brazil's talented guard duo

US guard Ruthie Bolton heads upcourt in the United States's win over Japan in the quarterfinals.

SCOTTIE KERSTA-WILSON • MEERA KESAVAN • AMINA A KESHODKAR • BARBARA A KESKE • KATHY KESKENY • LEVENT KESKINTEPE • SUHA KESKINTEPE • DOUGLAS R KESKULA PT • BARBARA M KESLER • HENRY N KESLER • PATRICIA D KESMODEL • JOAN P KESSEL • JOHN L KESSEL • AKWASI B KESSIE • JOSEPH F KESSIE • DONNA R KESSINGER • ALLYSON F KESSLER • AMY L KESSLER • COLLEEN M KESSLER • DAVID A KESSLER • DAVID B KESSLER • ETIENNE KESSLER • JOANN C KESSLER • JOANNE W KESSLER • LINDA S KESSLER • SANDY A KESSLER • TODD A KESSLER • TRAUDI KESSLER • ROSEMARY A KESTELOOT

combined for a 44-point, 9-assist performance. On the other side of the semifinal bracket, the US defeated Australia for a second time in tournament play, shooting 59 percent from the field and out-rebounding Australia 48-25 in the 93-71 win.

Brazil met the United States in front of the largest crowd to see an Olympic women's basketball game, 32,997 (the sixth straight 30,000-plus audience for the US women). Shooting an astounding 66 percent from the floor, the US set a new high for points scored in a gold-

Australia's Sandy Brondello looks for an opening during her team's bronze-medal win over Ukraine.

medal game with its 111-87 win. Leslie led the US with a game-high 29 points, while US guards Bolton (15 points) and Nikki McCray held Oliva and da Silva to a combined total of 18 points. The silver-medal showing earned Brazil its first medal in women's basketball.

Earlier in the tournament, Australia captured its first medal in either men's or women's basketball with a 66-56 win over Ukraine in the bronze-medal game.

With the US gold, forward Teresa Edwards—the first US basketball athlete to compete in four Olympic Games—became the most-decorated US basketball athlete with four medals (three golds and one bronze).

The gold-medal team from the US comprised the following members: Jennifer Azzi, Ruthie Bolton, Teresa Edwards, Venus Lacey, Lisa Leslie, Rebecca Lobo, Katrina McClain, Nikki McCray, Carla McGhee, Dawn Staley, Katy Steding, and Sheryl Swoopes.

Brazil's silver-medal-winning team members were Janeth dos Santos Arcain, Roseli do Carmo Gustavo, Silvia Andrea Santos Luz, Hortência de Fátima Marcari Oliva, Alessandra Santos de Oliveira, Claudia Maria Pastor, Ariana Aparecida dos Santos, Cintia Silva dos Santos, Maria Angélica Gonçalves da Silva, Maria Paula Gonçalves da Silva, Leila de Souza Sobral, and Marta de Souza Sobral.

Australia's bronze-medal team consisted of Carla Boyd, Michelle Brogan, Sandy Brondello, Michelle Chandler, Allison Cook, Trisha Fallon, Robyn Maher, Fiona Robinson, Shelley Sandie, Rachael Sporn, Michele Timms, and Jennifer Whittle.

CONCLUSION

The gap in basketball between the US and the rest of the globe has narrowed. Many of the US men's games were closer than expected, and the squad's average margin of victory fell 11 points from the 1992 tournament. "The days of winning by 40, 50, or 60 points are over," said Barkley, who for the second straight Olympic Games was the US's leading scorer (12.4 points per game) and the 1996 team's leading rebounder (6.6 per game).

• THAD KESTEN • THOMAS A KESTER • JAMES A KESTON • AJIT K KESWANI • NANDITA KESWANI • PURNIMA KESWANI • LISA A KESWICK • BETHANY R KETCHEN • CARLYE N KETCHUM • STACEY L KETCHUM • KELLY KETNER • PATRICK A KETNER • LANCE KETTERING • ALAN KETZES • WADE N KEUNG • ANNE P KEY • ARTHUR J KEY • DAVID W KEY • DIANNE KEY • ERICA L KEY • ERNEST D KEY • HERMAN A KEY • JOHN W KEY • MARY A KEY • MATTHEW W KEY • MILTON K KEY • TERESA M KEY • TISH S KEY • WILLIAM S KEY • BEN W KEY JR • GWENDOLYN KEYES • RONALD W KEYES • CHRISTOPHER C KEYLON • FLAY M KEYS •

Meanwhile, the US women's team, which formed more than a year before the Centennial Olympic Games, impressively captured the gold and in the process garnered new fans for women's basketball. The women's tournament posted the largest spectator attendance in its Olympic history. Men's and women's competitions combined, the 1996 Games set an Olympic high for basketball attendance at 1,068,032.

left: The US's Lisa Leslie tries for a rebound against Brazil's Marta de Souza Sobral and Alessandra Santos de Oliviera in the gold-medal game.

top right: Look of the Games banners decorated the entryways to the Morehouse College Gymnasium and the Georgia Dome.

bottom right: Players from the US women's basketball team celebrate their gold-medal victory.

Atlanta 1996.

KIMBERLY M KEYS • CRAIG W KEYWORTH • WAJEEHAH KHABEER • FOUAD N KHALIL • JOSEPHINE P KHAMISI • FAKIHA KHAN • FAZAL Z KHAN • HAZEL E KHAN • ISHTIAQ A KHAN • ISLAM W KHAN • KIREN S KHAN • QAMAR R KHAN • ROY A KHAN • SAFI A KHAN • SHIREEN A KHAN • ZESHAN Q KHAN • NIKKI D KHANNA • ANUJA V KHAROD • BHAIRAVI V KHAROD • DIVYA V KHAROD • AQUENDINE KHASIDIS • MANOUCHEHER KHATIBI • BASEM T KHAYAT • JULIE N KHEIR • AMAN K KHESHGI • KEVIN KHO • KIMBERLY A KHO • MEIRAMKUL K KHODJASHOVA • ALICE J KHOL • KAY HOCK KHOO • MARILYN A KHOURY •

BOXING

Venue Used:
**Alexander Memorial
Coliseum**

Days of Competition: **15**

Medals Awarded: **48**
Gold 12
Silver 12
Bronze 24

Number of Nations: **101**

Number of Officials: **98**

Officiating Federation:
**International Amateur
Boxing Association (AIBA)**

ONCE KNOWN AS the "noble art of self-defense," boxing is one of the older and more popular sports in the Olympic programme. Its continuing appeal was evident during the 1996 Centennial Olympic Games, which featured capacity audiences—more than 162,000 tickets were sold—that routinely broke into cheers of support and encouragement during the 15 days of boxing competition. A total of 101 nations were represented as 355 boxers showcased their talent.

VENUE

Near the Atlanta Olympic Village on the campus of the Georgia Institute of Technology, the newly renovated Alexander Memorial Coliseum was no stranger to fierce competition. Home to Georgia Tech's basketball teams, the venue proved an ideal setting for the enthusiastic crowds that packed the 10,000-seat arena to witness the boxing competition.

COMPETITION

The competition in Atlanta featured an electronic scoring system, first used at the 1992 Barcelona Games, in which five judges use keypads to record the punches scored by each boxer. In order for a punch to be counted, three of the five judges had to press the button

on their pads within one second of the punch being landed. Although designed to standardize scoring procedures and provide impartiality, the system was a point of contention when the results of close matches seemed affected by the slow reflexes of the judges.

Medals were contested in 12 weight classes: light flyweight, 48 kg (106 lb); flyweight, 51 kg (112 lb); bantamweight, 54 kg (119 lb); featherweight, 57 kg (125 lb); lightweight, 60 kg (132 lb); light welterweight, 63.5 kg (139 lb); welterweight, 67 kg (147 lb); light middleweight, 71 kg (156 lb); middleweight, 75 kg (165 lb); light heavyweight, 81 kg (178 lb); heavyweight, 91 kg (201 lb); and super heavyweight, +91 kg (+201 lb).

The competition took place in a single ring. Each match consisted of three three-minute rounds with a one-minute break between rounds. The winner of each match advanced to the next round in the single-elimination

HUSAM J KHREIM • ANUJA KHURANA • WOO KYONG KI • JUDY P KIANG • AMY L KIBBE • LISA M KIBBE • DEBBIE L KIBBEE • CATHERINE KIBLER • JANET A KIBLER • PAMELA F KIBLER • THOMAS C KIBLER • MAHAN J KICK • MARK L KICK • SOODI KICK • LUKE A KICKLIGHTER • ALICE LL KIDD • ANN I KIDD • ANTHONY W KIDD • COLBY KIDD • DONNA L KIDD • JANE V KIDD • JEFF B KIDD • JOSEPH M KIDD • KELLY M KIDD • LAUREL M KIDD • PATRICIA M KIDD • THOMAS I KIDD • ERNEST J KIDD MT • MARK L KIDDIE • SANDY KIDDIE • DANIEL T KIDWELL • PAUL KIEBLESZ • SUSAN M KIEFFER • ROBERT E KIEFFER JR • MARY JO S KIEHLE •

format, with matches progressing within each weight category from the preliminary rounds to the quarterfinals, semifinals, and finals. The winning and losing finalists received the gold and silver medals, respectively, while the third- and fourth-place semifinalists were both awarded bronze medals.

Light Flyweight, 48 kg (106 lb). In the light flyweight category, Mansueto Velasco's dreams of delivering the Philippines its first gold medal were dashed by reigning world champion and 1992 silver medalist, Bulgaria's Daniel Petrov Bojilov. Velasco began competition by handing perennial boxing power Cuba its first loss in the tournament, as he defeated Yosvani Aguilera 14-5. In the final, however, Bojilov led from the start and beat Velasco 19-6 to take the gold. Velasco received the silver. Semifinalists Oleg Kiryukhin of Ukraine and Rafael Lozano of Spain took home the bronze medals.

Flyweight, 51 kg (112 lb). Cuba's Maikro Romero needed every second possible to defeat Kazakhstan's Boulat Djoumadilov for the gold medal in the flyweight classification. Trailing 8-5 after the second round, Romero relied on his swiftness to land seven punches as he rallied for a close 12-11 victory. Receiving bronzes were semifinalists Albert Pakeev of the Russian Federation and Zoltan Lunka of Germany.

Bantamweight, 54 kg (119 lb). Bantamweight István Kovács gave Hungary its first Olympic boxing gold medal in 24 years when he defeated Cuba's Arnaldo Mesa 14-7. In the quarterfinals, Mesa had left the US's Zahir Raheem facedown on the canvas with 45 seconds left in the first round. In the semifinals, Mesa advanced over World Champion Raimkul Malakhbekov of the Russian Federation in a tiebreaker after the judges scored their contest a 14-14 draw. In the gold-medal match, however, silver medalist Mesa's strong left hand

could not overcome Kovács's superior hand speed and strength. Malakhbekov and Thailand's Vichairachanon Khadpo were the recipients of the bronze medals.

Featherweight, 57 kg (125 lb). In featherweight action, Somrot Kamsing of Thailand easily advanced to the finals, outscoring his first four opponents by a combined total of

top: Kazakhstan's Boulat Djoumadilov connects with a punch to Germany's Zoltan Lunka in the flyweight semifinals.

bottom: Thailand's Somrot Kamsing hugs his coach after winning gold in the featherweight class.

facing page: The Philippines' Mansueto Velasco punches Spain's Rafael Lozano in the light flyweight semifinal bout.

BRIAN C KIEL • THOMAS A KIELY • ARNOLD KIEN • GERALD A KIENITZ • GEORGE W KIERMAS • ADRIENNE C KIES • KENNETH O KIESLER • TRACY M KIETT-LYNN • GARY L KIFER • JAMES KIFFMEYER • RONALD L KIGER • RAYMOND H KIGKLIGHTER • ESTHER W KIHARA • PERTTI H KIIRA • ELIZABETH A KIKER • LINDA A KIKER • KAHA KIKNAVELIDZE • KIYOMI KIKUCHI • SHOKO KIKUCHI • YUKA KIKUCHI • KOICHI KIKUSHIMA • ANN KILANDER • CHARLES C KILANDER III • BARBARA W KILBOURNE • SCOTT D KILBOURNE • ANNA W KILBURN • RICHARD A KILBURN • EILEEN C KILCOYNE-BARROW • MAR-DE P KILCREASE

top: Algeria's Hocine Soltani drops to his knees after winning the gold over Bulgaria's Tontcho Tontchev in the lightweight competition.

bottom: Cuba's Hector Vinent squares off with Germany's Oktay Urkal in the light welterweight final.

58-21. At the other end of the bracket, two-time World Champion Serafim Todorov of Bulgaria advanced after defeating the US's Floyd Mayweather in a controversial 10-9 upset in the semifinals. In the battle for the gold, Todorov fought well but could not match Kamsing's blows in the 8-5 decision. Placing behind silver medalist Todorov were bronze medalists Mayweather and Pablo Julio Chacón of Argentina.

Lightweight, 60 kg (132 lb). Hocine Soltani won Algeria's first-ever boxing gold medal when he beat Bulgaria's Tontcho Tontchev in a tiebreaker after a 3-3 draw. Only four scoring punches were thrown in the final, as Soltani dodged his way to a 3-3 decision. Earning bronze medals were Terrance Cauthen of the United States, who lost a controversial 15-12 decision to Tontchev in the semifinals, and Romania's Leonard Doroftei.

Light Welterweight, 63.5 kg (139 lb). In the light welterweight classification, two-time

Vinent continued the pounding in the last two rounds and won by a score of 20-13. The bronze medals were captured by Bolat Niazymbetov of Kazakhstan and Fathi Missaoui of Tunisia.

Welterweight, 67 kg (147 lb). In welterweight action, the Russian Federation's Oleg Saitov defeated Cuba's Juan Hernandez, the 1992 silver medalist and three-time world champion, 14-9 to take the gold medal. Earning bronze medals were semifinalists Marian Simion of Romania and Daniel Santos of Puerto Rico.

Atlanta 1996

left: **Gold medalist David Reid of the US dodges a punch thrown by Cuba's Alfredo Duvergel in the light middleweight final.**

right: **Look of the Games banners decorated Alexander Memorial Coliseum during the boxing competiton.**

World Champion Hector Vinent of Cuba easily captured his second straight Olympic gold medal. Vinent overpowered his last four opponents by a combined total score of 81-27. Armed with a devastating right-left combination, Vinent scored a knockdown in the first round of the finals against opponent Oktay Urkal of Germany, who took home the silver.

Light Middleweight, 71 kg (156 lb). En route to a 12-4 semifinal win in the light middleweight category, David Reid of the United States knocked down Uzbekistan's Karim Tulaganov in the second round. The excitement continued when Reid met Cuba's Alfredo Duvergel for the gold medal. Duvergel led 16-6

ERMA KILLINGS • ANN E KILLORIN • ARTHUR W KILLOUGH • AZIZE WILLIAMS KILPATRICK • BARBARA M KILPATRICK • MICHAEL O KILPATRICK • THOMAS G KILPATRICK • WILLIAM B KILPATRICK • BRIAN M KILROY • AE S KIM • ALICE KIM • ASHLEY H KIM • CHANGSUK KIM • CHONG S KIM • CHRISTIN J KIM • CURTISS KIM • DANIEL K KIM • DONG KIM • EUGENE D KIM • EUISUK KIM • EUN-HWA KIM • EUN-RA KIM • EUN HEE KIM • EUN SOOK KIM • GYUHEUI KIM • HEE-KYOUNG KIM • HEE-SEUNG KIM • HONG SEOCK KIM • HYE JIN KIM • HYUN-SANG KIM • HYUN H KIM • HYUN JOO KIM • ILNAE KIM • INHYE KIM • JAE-SOO KIM •

early in the match. Reid rallied, however, and 36 seconds into the third round he landed a powerful right that knocked out Duvergel. Reid's victory gave the US its only gold medal in boxing at the Centennial Olympic Games. Tulaganov and Ermakhan Ibraimov of Kazakhstan were the bronze medalists.

Middleweight, 75 kg (165 lb). Cuba's Ariel Hernandez lived up to his billing as the best pound-for-pound amateur boxer in the world by successfully defending his Olympic middleweight title. In the tournament, Hernandez

light heavyweight division. Boxing with the painful injury, Jirov used his repetitive step-and-stab style to outscore Seung-Bae Lee of Korea 17-4 in the final. Placing behind silver medalist Lee were bronze medalists Antonio Tarver of the US and Thomas Ulrich of Germany.

Heavyweight, 91 kg (201 lb). In heavyweight action, Cuba's Felix Savon, the defending Olympic gold medalist and five-time world champion, maintained his 10-year undefeated international record when he captured his second Olympic heavyweight title. In

left: Cuba's Ariel Hernandez is declared the victor in the middleweight gold-medal match.

right: Kazakhstan's Vassili Jirov connects with a punch during his win over Korea's Seung-Bae Lee in the light heavyweight final.

outscored his five opponents 59-21. Hernandez became a two-time Olympic gold medalist by defeating Turkey's Malik Beyleroglu 11-3. Silver medalist Beyleroglu became Turkey's first Olympic boxing finalist. Bronze medals went to Mohamed Bahari of Algeria and Rhoshii Wells of the US.

Light Heavyweight, 81 kg (178 lb). Vassili Jirov of Kazakhstan did not let a swollen black eye stand in his way of a gold medal in the

the final bout, Savon forced Canada's David Defiagbon into a standing-eight count in the second round before winning a 20-2 decision; Defiagbon took the silver. For the entire tournament, Savon conceded a total of only nine points. Receiving bronze medals were semifinalists Nate Jones of the United States and Luan Krasniqi of Germany.

Super Heavyweight, +91 kg (+201 lb). In the super heavyweight classification, Tonga's Paea Wolfgram blasted his way into the final to capture the first Olympic medal of any kind for

JAMES S KIM • JANE KIM • JEANNIE LEE KIM • JEESUN KIM • JEONGIM KIM • JUNG Y KIM • KI HONG KIM • KUM H KIM • KYUNG W KIM • LESLIE F KIM • MEERA KIM • MI-OCK KIM • MIN-JUNG KIM • MIN K KIM • MOON K KIM • NAM-MYUNG KIM • NOOLIE L KIM • PATRICIA J KIM • PAULA D KIM • PETER KIM • PETER H KIM • SANG K KIM • SANG T KIM • SARA J KIM • SEONG E KIM • SERAN KIM • SEUNG-HWAN KIM • SEUNG H KIM • SEUNG JUN KIM • SO-HEE KIM • STEPHEN KIM • SUN-KEE KIM • SUNG HEE KIM • SUSAN J KIM • TOICHI KIM • WAN-JIN KIM • YANG-MI KIM • YONG S. KIM • YOUNG-JU KIM • YOUNG K KIM • YUNG HEE KIM •

his country. The fans at Alexander Memorial Coliseum took notice of Wolfgram when he defeated Cuban big man Alexis Rubalcaba in the quarterfinals. Earlier, Rubalcaba had displayed his strength by sending one opponent rolling in a backward somersault. The winner of the super heavyweight division, however, turned out to be Ukraine's Volodymyr Klychko, who defeated silver medalist Wolfgram 7-3 to take the gold. Semifinalists Alexei Lezin of the Russian Federation and Duncan Dokiwari of Nigeria earned the bronze medals.

top: Tonga's Paea Wolfgram is declared the victor over Cuba's Alexis Rubalcaba in the super heavyweight quarterfinals.

bottom: Cuba's Felix Savon defeats Canada's David Defiagbon in the heavyweight gold-medal match.

CONCLUSION

Although Cuba, with four gold and three silver medals, continued to be the dominant force in Olympic boxing, spectators saw the competition divide its 48 medals widely among 22 countries.

Boxing proved to be one of the most well-attended and popular sports of the Centennial Olympic Games, with tickets to most sessions selling out well in advance. Seating in the venue was full to capacity with zealous fans who had come to support their favorite boxers.

ANTHONY P KIMANI MWANGI • CINDY S KIMBALL • EUGENE L KIMBALL • JULIE A KIMBALL • KATHARINE H KIMBALL • LINDA L KIMBALL • MYRTLE L KIMBALL • SUZANNE L KIMBALL • STEPHANIE D KIMBELL • KELLY M KIMBERL • TERRY H KIMBERLIN • RICHARD L KIMBERLING • SOPHIE F KIMBLE • KATHY A KIMBLE RN • CHARLOTTE A KIMBRELL • SHERRY L KIMBRO CATC • ANN L KIMBROUGH • AUDREY KIMBROUGH • JAMES EDWARD KIMBROUGH • JAMES M KIMBROUGH • LATOYNA KIMBROUGH • DARYL R KIMCHE • MONTE A KIMES • WILLIAM K KIMES • ERICH J KIMMEL • MICHAEL TODD KIMMEL • VICTOR S KIMMEL •

337

CANOE / KAYAK

Canoe / Kayak—Slalom

Venue Used:
Ocoee Whitewater Center

Days of Competition: 3

Medals Awarded: 12
Gold 4
Silver 4
Bronze 4

Number of Nations: 31

Number of Officials: 81

Officiating Federation:
International Canoeing
Federation (FIC)

A **PAIR OF SCENIC** outdoor venues hosted the events of the two canoe/kayak disciplines. The Ocoee River near Cleveland, Tennessee, was the home of the slalom competition, while Lake Lanier near Gainesville, Georgia, hosted the sprint athletes. A total of 485 athletes and 312 boats competed in the two disciplines. Thirty-one countries were represented in the slalom events, and 45 in the sprint events.

SLALOM

The canoe/kayak–slalom competition at the Atlanta Games was held over three days, from 26 to 28 July. A total of 135 athletes (105 men and 30 women) in 120 boats challenged the raging waters of the Ocoee River for a shot at Olympic gold.

VENUE

For the first time in Olympic history, canoe/kayak–slalom athletes maneuvered the white-water rapids of a natural river. Arguably the most beautiful venue at the Centennial Olympic Games, the Ocoee Whitewater Center featured a rugged course along the Ocoee River near Cleveland, Tennessee, 130 mi (209 km) from the Olympic Village in Atlanta.

The course ran through a beautiful rocky river gorge among the Appalachian Mountains in the Cherokee National Forest. It stretched approximately 1,362 ft (415 m), with a gradient of 30 ft (9 m) and a water flow of 1,200 cu ft per second (34 cu m per second). This world-class Olympic course also had carefully designed artificial enhancements to further challenge the white-water paddlers.

The Olympic course was a refreshing return to a time when all white-water races were held on powerful rivers. The foaming and crashing venue truly represented the thundering power of a raging wild river for the competitors, while bleachers positioned on the narrow riverbank provided the capacity crowds of approximately 14,400 spectators with a close-up scenic view of the white-water experience in the wilderness.

"This is without a doubt the most fantastic white-water slalom course in the world," said Albert Woods, International Canoeing Federation Slalom Committee chair. "It combines the best of a natural river with the best of an artificial course."

COMPETITION

In each event, the Olympic athletes navigated through 25 slalom gates, frequently having to pass through the gates while traveling against the churning current. Olympic racers were allowed one official training run and then competed in two timed runs down the course, with the lower score counting as the final score. The time of the run in seconds, plus penalty points,

SUSAN P KIMMEY • REBECCA J KIMPSON • WAYMAN D KIMPSON • ANNETTE KIMSEY • HOLLY A KIMSEY • JANELLE KIMSEY • SONJA KIMSEY • TRAVIS L KIMSEY • KENTA KIMURA • YUMI KIMURA • JUSTIN R KINARD • TERESA G KINCAID • CYNTHIA A KINCEY • WILLIAM K KINCH • MICHAEL S KINDBERG • BETTY KINDER • KARIN L KINDER • BARBARA L KINDRED • WILLIAM T KINDRED • BRIAN M KINDZIA • ALAN R KING • ALEXANDRA A KING • AMANDA JOY KING • AMY M KING • ANGELA KING • AVETA M KING • BARBARA KING • BARBARA M KING • BENJAMIN L KING • BERNARD KING • BEVERLY KING • BIEACE B KING • BOB KING •

equaled the total score. A 5-point penalty was assessed for each touched gate, and a 50-point penalty was given for each missed gate. Athletes competed in four medal events: men's and women's kayak single, men's canoe single, and men's canoe double.

Kayak Single. A crowd of 14,421, the largest crowd ever to watch a white-water slalom race, was on hand for the final day of the Olympic slalom competition. In the men's kayak single race, the crowd witnessed 1995 World Champion Oliver Fix of Germany seize the gold with

top: The Look of the Games decorated the bridge over the slalom course of the Ocoee Whitewater Center.

bottom left: Spectators watch men's kayak single action in the slalom competition.

bottom right: New Zealand's Owen Hughes makes his run down the men's kayak single slalom course.

BRANDON J KING • CAROL M KING • CAROL T KING • CAROLINE Y KING • CASEY N KING • CELIA M KING • CHARLES E KING • CHUCK D KING • CLAIRE A KING • DANA C KING • DAVID KING • DAVID C KING • DAVID E KING • DAVID L KING • DIANETRA S KING • EDWARD J KING • ELAINE KING • ELIZABETH A KING • ELIZABETH J KING • EMILY K KING • GLENDA W KING • GRACIE M KING • GREG A KING • GREGORY W KING • GUY KING • HARRY L KING • HUGH KING • HULEN G KING • IVA L KING • JAN JO C KING • JANE L KING • JENNIFER L KING • JERMAINE T KING • JESSICA K KING • JONATHAN D KING • JONATHAN S KING • JOY E KING •

a first-place score of 141.22 points. Fix clocked in with an impressive best-run time of 2:16. No. 13 seed Andraz Vehovar of Slovenia won the silver medal, finishing with a score of 141.65, while no. 8 seed Thomas Becker of Germany captured the bronze after posting 142.79.

The race for gold in the women's kayak single slalom competition came down to a tale of two runs. Stepanka Hilgertova of the Czech Republic and Dana Chladek of the United States finished with identical top scores of 169.49

points. In the tiebreaker, however, Hilgertova posted a better second run score, so the Czech Republic paddler garnered the gold. "The course was easy, but the white water was hard," the gold medalist said afterward. Chladek, the bronze medalist at the Barcelona Games in 1992, came into the 1996 Games following a severe shoulder injury that had sidelined her for the entire 1995 season. Her silver-medal comeback made her the only repeat medalist in the women's slalom competition.

Former World Champion Myriam Fox-Jerusalmi of France won the bronze medal by finishing with a score of 171.00. The medal was the first for Fox-Jerusalmi with her husband, Richard Fox, a former world champion, as her coach. After flipping on her first run, current World Champion Lynn Simpson of Great Britain turned in a second run that would have been fast enough for the gold had she not barely missed a gate—resulting in a 50-point penalty.

Canoe Single. Seventeen-year-old Michal Martikan won the first-ever Olympic gold medal for Slovakia in the men's canoe single slalom event. Before the roaring cheers of the full-capacity crowd, Martikan turned in a

top left: Slovakia's Michal Martikan blasts through the rapids on his gold-medal run in the men's canoe single event.

bottom left: France's Patrice Estanguet navigates the rapids on his way to a bronze-medal finish in the men's canoe single event.

right: Stepanka Hilgertova of the Czech Republic paddles to gold in the women's kayak single.

JUDY S KING • JULIE A KING • KARI R KING • KAYE KING • KENNETH L KING • KEVIN C KING • KEVIN D KING • LA CHELLE B KING • LAMONT KING • LENORA KING • LINDA W KING • LISA M KING • LORIS O KING • M. ANN KING • MARCUS V KING • MARIA J KING • MELISSA J KING • MICHAEL J KING • MICHAEL J KING • MIKE KING • MILTON K KING • MINDI A KING • NANCY H KING • NANCY M KING • NANCY R KING • PATRICIA KING • PATRICIA J KING • PATSY L KING • PAUL H KING • PHILIP M KING • PHILLIP W KING • REBECCA J KING • RENEE KING • RICHARD F KING • ROBERT KING • ROBERT C KING • ROBERT K KING • ROBIN M KING

blazing run to overtake defending gold medalist Lukas Pollert of the Czech Republic. The
youngest paddler competing in the slalom
competition, Martikan finished in the top spot
with a score of 151.03. "He [Martikan] is beautiful on the water," said an impressed Pollert
after the winning run.

Pollert, the gold medalist at the Barcelona
Games in 1992, won the silver medal with a
score of 151.17, and bronze medalist Patrice
Estanguet of France was third at 152.84. At 37,
David Hearn of the US was the oldest athlete
in the competition. Hearn, the defending
world champion, finished ninth with a score
of 162.51.

Canoe Double. In raging rapids that would
swallow average paddlers, the men's canoe
double pair of Wilfrid Forgues and Frank Adisson dramatically won France's first slalom gold
medal. The stage was set when the pair of
French paddlers were about to miss gate 18,
which would have eliminated them from
medal contention. "We made a big, big mistake," Forgues said. "We had to be on the right
side very slow. But we were on the left side
very fast. In a millisecond I said, 'We must
back-paddle.'" Against the powerful Ocoee
rapids that had tormented all 15 of the world's
best canoe teams, Forgues and Adisson began
the formidable task of back-paddling. As they
did, the crowd erupted into cheers, inspiring
the 11-year partners to make it through the
gate. From there, Forgues and Adisson sliced
through the course en route to the gold. The
former world champions and 1992 Olympic
bronze medalists finished with a golden score
of 158.82.

The Czech Republic's Miroslav Simek and
Jiri Rohan, silver medalists at the Barcelona
Games in 1992, won their second straight sil-
ver medal, finishing with a score of 160.16.

Placing third was Germany's bronze-medal
team of Andre Ehrenberg and Michael Senft
(163.72).

CONCLUSION

Against a backdrop of regal mountains, the
Czech Republic, France, and Germany dominated the slalom competition by winning 9 of
the 12 medals at the Centennial Olympic
Games. The Ocoee River, however, left its
mark on most of the competitors. The major-

ity of athletes found it difficult to make a
clean run—a trip down the course passing
through all 25 gates without hitting the gate
poles. In the opening practice runs, all three
female medalists from the 1992 Games were
among the dozen or more paddlers who cap-
sized; one even got caught in the vortex
created by 4 ft (1.2 m) waves at the rapids
nicknamed "Humongous."

**Navigating the Ocoee River
Olympic course, the Czech
Republic's Miroslav Simek
and Jiri Rohan pass a gate
on their silver-medal run
in the canoe double
slalom event.**

Canoe / Kayak—Sprint

Venue Used:
Lake Lanier

Days of Competition: 6

Medals Awarded: 36
Gold 12
Silver 12
Bronze 12

Number of Nations: 45

Number of Officials: 35

Officiating Federation:
International Canoeing
Federation (FIC)

SPRINT

Unlike its white-water counterpart, the canoe/kayak–sprint competition is a straight race of speed to the finish line that does not involve passing gates or navigating around obstacles. Consequently, one of the differences between the two disciplines is the length of the boat used in competition. Built for straight-line speed, canoe/kayak–sprint boats are longer and sleeker than canoe/kayak–slalom boats and have V-shaped hulls.

VENUE

The world-class canoe/kayak–sprint competition course was located at scenic Lake Lanier, a beautiful Georgia resort area near the city of Gainesville, 55 mi (88 km) north of Atlanta. The venue's innovative design, which incorporated the natural beauty of its surroundings, placed spectators on the south side of the lake and technical and support facilities on the north side. Permanent facilities included two boathouses and a finish tower with a scoreboard and video boards that enabled the spectators to be involved in the competition, even when the athletes were out of sight on the course. In addition, the facility included a temporary athlete day village. "It's the best venue for sprint in the United States," said Sergio Orsi, president of the International Canoeing Federation (FIC).

Temporary grandstands resting on a floating platform on the surface of the lake provided seating for 17,300. All athlete and event support services were on the opposite bank.

The facility, which also hosted the Olympic rowing competition, became an enduring legacy designed to benefit the region well into the next century. The venue's permanent facilities were given to the city of Gainesville and Hall County for use in holding future national and international competitions.

COMPETITION

In the canoe/kayak–sprint competition, a total of 350 athletes (250 men and 100 women) with 192 boats competed in 12 medal events (three women's and nine men's) between 30 July and 4 August. The women's events were 500 m kayak single, 500 m kayak double, and 500 m kayak fours. The men's events were 500 m canoe single, 1,000 m canoe single, 500 m canoe double, 1,000 m canoe double, 500 m kayak single, 1,000 m kayak single, 500 m

kayak double, 1,000 m kayak double, and 1,000 m kayak fours.

500 m Canoe Single. On the final day of competition, the Czech Republic's Martin Doktor established himself as the world's top sprint canoeist when he won his second gold medal of the Centennial Olympic Games. Doktor captured the men's 500 m canoe single race with a

MARSCIDA D KINLAW • SETH J KINLEY ATC • ROBERT L KINNAIRD • PAUL KINNALY • MARGARET KINNEAR • TODD E KINNEBREW MD • CARLA C KINNETT • CHARLES E KINNETT • MICHELE L KINNETT • JAMES C KINNEY • LEE A KINNEY • VANESSA A KINNEY • STEPHANIE L KINNICK • DAVID KINNISON • ANDREA M KINSEL • JEAN A KINSER • NANCI A KINSER • ROLAND E KINSER • BRUCE F KINSEY • LAUREL J KINSEY • STEPHANIE J KINSEY • VALERIE D KINSEY • DAVID B KINTZING • SUSAN G KINTZLER • KELLIE A KINZER • GLEN A KINZLY • THERESA R KINZLY • PATRICIA M KIPHART • PATTY M KIPP • MARK P KIRACOFE •

time of 1:49.934. "In my town, I will be a hero," said Doktor, whose gold-medal performances in flat-water canoe racing were the first for the Czech Republic in 44 years, when it existed as Czechoslovakia. Slavomir Knazovicky of Slovakia won the silver (1:50.510), and Imre Pulai of Hungary earned the bronze (1:50.758).

1,000 m Canoe Single. Before taking the gold in the 500 m canoe single, Martin Doktor won his first gold medal in the men's 1,000 m canoe single race with a time of 3:54.418. For the second straight Olympic Games, Ivan

Nikolai Juravschi and Victor Reneischi of the Republic of Moldova won the silver with a close second-place finish of 1:40.456, while Romania's Gheorghe Andriev and Grigore Obreja captured the bronze (1:41.336).

1,000 m Canoe Double. Germany's pair of Andreas Dittmer and Gunar Kirchbach won the men's 1,000 m canoe double final with a time of 3:31.870. Romania's Antonel Borsan and Marcel Glavan won the silver (3:32.294), and Hungary's Csaba Horváth and György Kolonics took the bronze (3:32.514).

left: Romania's Antonel Borsan and Marcel Glavan win the first heat of the men's 1,000 m canoe double event.

top right: Germany's Thomas Zereske paddles to the finish line at Lake Lanier in the men's 500 m canoe single preliminary competition.

bottom right: Italy's Antonio Rossi competes in heat 3 of the men's 500 m kayak single before going on to win the gold.

facing page: The Czech Republic's Martin Doktor is triumphant after winning gold in the men's 1,000 m canoe single.

Klementjevs of Latvia won the silver (3:54.954), and Hungary's György Zala captured the bronze (3:56.366).

500 m Canoe Double. Hungary added to its medal total when the team of Csaba Horváth and György Kolonics, the reigning world champions, won the gold in the men's 500 m canoe double, finishing first with a time of 1:40.420.

500 m Kayak Single. In the gold-medal race of the men's 500 m kayak single, Italy's Antonio Rossi led from start to finish and won with a time of 1:37.423. Knut Holmann of Norway, the 1992 bronze medalist, won the silver (1:38.339), and Poland's Piotr Markiewicz secured the bronze (1:38.615).

In the women's race, Hungary's Rita Köbán, the 1995 world champion and 1992 silver

ANNIE M KIRBY • CYNTHIA A KIRBY • DIANE A KIRBY • ELIZABETH ANN KIRBY • ELLIS G KIRBY • JAMES A KIRBY • KEITH W KIRBY • KELLIE C KIRBY • KRISTINE M KIRBY • LYNN W KIRBY • MARY ANN T KIRBY • MEGAN L KIRBY • PHYLLIS KIRBY • RACHELLE L KIRBY • RONALD D KIRBY • SCOTT W KIRBY • SEAN M. KIRBY • SHANNON L KIRBY • TIMOTHY N KIRBY • VIVIAN D KIRBY • JULIE KIRBY-FARMER • JANET H KIRCH • RENATE KIRCHGESSNER • ELIZABETH A KIRCHNER • BONNY F KIRIN-PEREZ • ARLENE KIRK • BILLY KIRK • CASSANDRA KIRK • DOROTHY S KIRK • GEOFFREY P KIRK • JANE KIRK • JOE A KIRK • JOYCE L KIRK

top: **Germany's Kay Bluhm and Torsten Gutsche paddle to victory in the men's 500 m kayak double semifinals.**

bottom: **Paddling in sync, Daniela Baumer and Ingrid Haralamow of Switzerland qualify for the 500 m kayak double sprint final.**

Italy were a mere .032 behind at 1:28.729. Australia's Daniel Collins and Andrew Trim won the bronze (1:29.409).

In the women's 500 m kayak double final, Sweden's team of Agneta Andersson and Susanne Gunnarsson improved on their silver-medal showing at the Barcelona Games with a gold-medal victory in 1996. Andersson and Gunnarsson clocked in with a time of 1:39.329, while Germany's 1992 gold medalist Ramona Portwich teamed with Birgit Fischer to win the silver at 1:39.689. Australia's team of Katrin Borchert and Anna Wood captured the bronze (1:40.641).

1,000 m Kayak Double. Kay Bluhm and Torsten Gutsche again reached the finals, but they were not as fortunate in the men's 1,000 m kayak double race. Antonio Rossi and Daniele Scarpa of Italy defeated Germany's defending gold medalists with a time of 3:09.190. Bluhm and Gutsche took the silver (3:10.518), and Bulgaria's Andrian Dushev and Milko Kazanov earned the bronze (3:11.206).

500 m Kayak Fours. Germany's Birgit Fischer, Manuela Mucke, Ramona Portwich, and Anett Schuck adjusted to the wind conditions and easily won the gold-medal race of the women's 500 m kayak fours with a time of 1:31.077. "We had to change our race plan due to the wind coming from behind us," Fischer said. "But we trained under a variety of conditions, so that was no big problem." Switzerland (Daniela Baumer, Sabine Eichenberger, Ingrid Haralamow, and Garbiela Müller) won the silver with a time of 1:32.701. Sweden (Agneta Andersson, Ingela Ericsson, Anna Olsson, and Susanne Rosenqvist) repeated as the bronze-medal winner(1:32.917).

medalist, finished first with a time of 1:47.655. Canada's Caroline Brunet won the silver at 1:47.891, and Italy's Josefa Idem (1:48.731) defeated Germany's Birgit Fischer (1:49.383), the 1992 gold medalist, for the bronze.

1,000 m Kayak Single. World Champion Knut Holmann of Norway led the final men's 1,000 m kayak single race from start to finish to capture the gold with a time of 3:25.785. Italy's Beniamino Bonomi won the silver at 3:27.073, and the 1992 gold medalist, Australia's Clint Robinson, took the bronze (3:29.713).

500 m Kayak Double. In the men's 500 m kayak double race, Germany's duo of Kay Bluhm and Torsten Gutsche successfully defended its Olympic gold medal, winning with a time of 1:28.697, while silver medalists Daniele Scarpa and Beniamino Bonomi of

1,000 m Kayak Fours. Germany's quartet of Detlef Hofman, Thomas Reineck, Olaf Winter, and Mark Zabel captured the gold in the men's 1,000 m kayak fours with a winning time of 2:51.528. Hungary (Attila Adrovicz, Ferenc Csipes, Gábor Horváth, and András Rajna) repeated as the silver-medal winner in the event (2:53.184), and the Russian Federation

• KATHLEEN G KIRK • KEITH C KIRK • KIMBERLY S KIRK • LASUNDRIA W KIRK • MICHELE P KIRK • MIKE S KIRK • PATRICIA A KIRK • RONALD KIRK • STANLEY C KIRK • STEVEN H KIRK • WAYNE A KIRKBRIDE • MARIANNE KIRKEBO • LEWIS J KIRKEGAARD • RENAE E KIRKHART • ELIZABETH C KIRKLAND • JEFFREY KIRKLAND • JESSICA D KIRKLAND • MARY K KIRKLAND • MIRTA L KIRKLAND • MONICA KIRKLAND • RHONDA KIRKLAND • SUSAN R KIRKLAND • ELIZABETH K KIRKLAND MT • CHARLES H KIRKMAN • GAIL S KIRKPATRICK • JIMMY C KIRKPATRICK • KELLI L KIRKPATRICK • MARJORIE M KIRKPATRICK •

(Oleg Gorobiy, Anatoliy Tishchenko, Georgiy Tsybulnikov, and Sergey Verlin) won the bronze (2:53.996).

CONCLUSION

Overall, Germany led the sprint medal count at the Centennial Olympic Games with four gold and two silver medals. Italy was second with two golds, two silvers, and a bronze. Hungary followed with two gold, a silver, and three bronze medals.

In addition, Germany's Birgit Fischer tied an Olympic mark. The 34 year old's gold- and silver-medal performances in the 1996 Games gave her a lifetime total of eight Olympic medals (five gold and three silver), which tied her with Sweden's Gert Fredriksson as the most decorated sprint paddler in Olympic history.

top: Athletes race from the start of the qualifying round for the semifinals of the women's kayak fours.

bottom: Men's kayak fours speed to the finish at Lake Lanier.

Atlanta 1996

SIDNEY H KIRKPATRICK • CRAIG KIRKSEY • JEFFREY M KIRKSEY • NANCY S KIRKSEY • JERRIANN KIRKWOOD • PATRICIA A KIRN • MIKIAS KIROS • PAUL KIRSCH • RICHARD KIRSCH • ROBIN E KIRSCH • WILLIAM P KIRSCH • KATIE KIRSCHBAUM • THOMAS J KIRSCHE • NANCY G KIRSCHMANN • KEITH A KIRSCHNER • VILIA KIRVELAITIS • JOE KISER • MICHAEL KISER • RESTA KISER • SAM J KISER • SCOTT E KISER • STEPHANIE A KISER • ANITA I KISHORE • CINDY KISIDA • YEVETTE Y KISIL • EDITH J KISS • ELIZABETH KISS • LEONARD N KISS • NANCY B KISS • SANDOR KISS • FRANCIS I KISSEL • SABINE KISSING

CYCLING

Cycling—Mountain Bike

Venue Used:
Georgia International Horse Park

Days of Competition: **1**

Medals Awarded: **6**
Gold 2
Silver 2
Bronze 2

Number of Nations: **30**

Number of Officials: **30**

Officiating Federation:
International Cycling Union (UCI)

WITH EVENTS LOCATED at three separate venues—the Georgia International Horse Park, the streets of Atlanta, and Stone Mountain Park—and athletes numbering more than 500, the Centennial Olympic Games cycling competition electrified fans throughout the Atlanta area for 9 of the Games' 16 days of competition.

MOUNTAIN BIKE

The 1996 Centennial Olympic Games marked the first time that mountain bike racing was recognized as an official discipline of the sport of cycling. A total of 44 men and 29 women representing 30 countries competed. Both the men's and women's races were held on 30 July.

VENUE

The venue for this inaugural Olympic event was the Georgia International Horse Park, a 1,139 acre (461 ha) site in Rockdale County near Conyers, Georgia, that was approximately 33 mi (53 km) east of the Atlanta Olympic Village. Racing took place on the park's equestrian endurance course. In addition to mountain bike racing, the horse park hosted the Olympic equestrian competition and both the riding and running events of the modern pentathlon.

Over terrain that included wooded trails, dirt roads, steep inclines and descents, single-track sections, and open-track sections, the course offered elevation gains per lap of ap-

proximately 700–800 ft (213–244 m). Despite the absence of long, sustained climbs, the course was highly technical, featuring short, steep climbs and varying terrain.

• MYRNA C KISSINGER • MARYELLEN KISSMAN • AKEMI KITAJIMA • NATTSU KITAMURA • EIKO KITAZAWA • BRUCE N KITCHELL • PAUL M KITCHEN • ELAINE KITCHENS • NEALE B KITCHENS • SUE Y KITCHENS • WILLIAM C KITCHENS • PHYLLIS C KITCHINGS • CHARLES KITE • JEAN R KITE • WALTER G KITE • KARLANE B KITT • STEVEN D KITTELL • DELMAR F KITTENDORF JR • JEFFREY R KITTLE • SHAIDU W KIVEN • JULIA KIVASHKO • MARICY Y KIYOKAWA • LAURA M KIZER • LINDA KIZZART • ANNA LENA KJELLMAN • ERLEND KJELLSTAD • LINE SOFIE KJENSTAD • SIGBJOERN N KJENSTAD • JENNIFER L KLAAS • DEAN KLAHR •

COMPETITION

The mountain bike racing competition consisted of two events—men's and women's cross-country races. Each lap of the competition's figure eight–shaped course measured approximately 6.6 mi (10 km). The men's race consisted of four and one-half laps (30.3 mi /48.8 km), and the women's race consisted of three laps (19.8 mi/31.9 km).

Cross Country. The Netherlands' Bart Brentjens, the reigning men's world champion, set a blazing pace and never looked back, winning the men's cross-country race with a time of 2:17:38. "I told my wife this morning that after the first half-lap, they would never see me again," he said afterward. Setting an early blistering pace, Brentjens did not swelter from the Georgia heat. In preparation for the race, he had trained for such conditions by riding an indoor bike inside a hot, steamy room. Brentjens's performance was so outstanding that he finished almost 3:00 ahead of silver medalist Thomas Frischknecht of Switzerland, who finished second at 2:20:14. France's

Miguel Martinez finished third at 2:20:36 to take the bronze.

In 91°F (33°C) heat, Italy's Paola Pezzo overcame a fall and leg cramps to win the women's race with a time of 1:50:51. After the race, Pezzo dedicated her victory to former fallen Italian teammate Fabio Casartelli, a 1992 Olympic gold medalist who died in a wreck during last year's Tour de France. "This win is for Fabio Casartelli," said Pezzo, who crashed in the opening lap of the mountain bike competition, only to come back and take the lead just a

few miles later. Finishing behind Pezzo were silver medalist Alison Sydor (1:51:58) of Canada, the reigning world champion, and bronze medalist Susan DeMattei (1:52:36) of the US.

CONCLUSION

The rookie Olympic sport of mountain bike racing, with its pair of inaugural champions— the Netherlands' Bart Brentjens and Italy's Paola Pezzo—enjoyed frenzied support from the fans during the one-day competition. Almost 28,000 people attended the men's and women's cross-country events, which featured a challenging outdoor course. The six medals of the competition were distributed evenly, with six different countries taking top honors.

facing page: **Reigning men's World Champion Bart Brentjens of the Netherlands rides alone in front of his competitors en route to winning the gold medal.**

left: **Canada's Alison Sydor and the US's Susan DeMattei battle for position in the women's mountain bike race.**

top right: **Gold medalist Paola Pezzo of Italy races to victory in the women's mountain bike racing competition.**

bottom right: **Switzerland's Thomas Frischknecht rides to silver ahead of bronze medalist Miguel Martinez of France in the men's mountain bike competition.**

KRISTEN C KLAKULAK • JOSHUA M KLAPPER • GARY E KLAR • DAVID M KLATER • KATHLEEN C KLATER • MICHAEL E KLATT • ANDREW M KLATT • DAVID N KLATT • MAYA V KLAVORA • DEBRA A KLAYMAN • DON A KLAYMAN • SUZETTE KLAYMAN • JAMES E. KLEBAU • SCOTT B KLEBER MD • WILLIAM J KLECKLEY • ANDREW T KLEE • HELEN N KLEIBER • FRANK KLEIER • DAVID W KLEIMAN • DEBORAH G KLEIMAN • MARGARET A KLEIMAN • SCOTT G KLEIMAN MD • ANN L KLEIN • DIANE P KLEIN • DONALD E KLEIN • EDWARD W KLEIN • ELIZABETH B KLEIN • JEFFERY T KLEIN • KATHERINE M. KLEIN • KATHLEEN J KLEIN •

Cycling—Road

Venue Used:
Streets of the city of Atlanta

Days of Competition: **3**

Medals Awarded: **12**
Gold 4
Silver 4
Bronze 4

Number of Nations: **61**

Number of Officials: **30**

Officiating Federation:
**International Cycling
Union (UCI)**

ROAD

Cycling has been included in every modern Olympic Games. At these Centennial Olympic Games, the road cycling competition included two Olympic firsts: professional riders were allowed to compete, and individual time trials were added to the programme. A total of 189 men and 60 women from 61 countries competed in the four road cycling medal events. The competition began with the women's road race on 21 July, followed by

cated less than 10 mi (16 km) from the Atlanta Olympic Village. The course stretched through the Buckhead community, a historic residential and shopping district in Atlanta. The start/finish area of the course was located in front of three 100-year-old churches. From there, the course proceeded through the Buckhead shopping district before winding through a tree-lined residential area featuring stately mansions and the home of Georgia's governor. Flags from the various countries represented in the race were hanging from

the men's road race on 31 July, and both the men's and women's individual time trials on 3 August.

VENUE

Racers pedaled within the Olympic Ring through the streets of Atlanta on a course approximately 8.1 mi (13 km) in length and lo-

the balconies of these beautiful homes, and residents who lived along the route held parties in their front yards to watch and cheer on the racers.

Spectators gathered all along the course route, and a temporary seating section was located at the competition's start/finish area. Admission to the road cycling competition was free and open to the public.

KAY KLEIN • KEITH H KLEIN • LARISSA A KLEIN • LISA A KLEIN • LUCILLE R KLEIN • MARC A KLEIN • RICHARD P KLEIN • ROBERT A KLEIN • SARAH F KLEIN • SUSAN A KLEIN • WADE KLEIN • STEPHANIE A KLEIN-DAVIS • KATHLEEN KLEIN RN • ELIZABETH KLEINE • KEVIN D KLEINE • SUSAN F KLEINE • DAVID G KLEINMEYER CATC • RICHARD A KLEINOVINK • KATHY W KLEINSTEUBER • BRUCE H KLEMENS • KRISTINE M KLEMM • LAURA K KLENKE • DOUGLAS D KLENOVICH • MELISSA G KLEPPE • PAUL J KLEPPER • JOSEPH O KLIM • SCOT KLINBILE CRU • BONNIE S KLINE • JON T KLINE • MARK D KLINE • MICHELLE L KLINE •

COMPETITION

In the mass-start road race, the cyclists raced over a distance of 17 laps (137.85 mi/221.85 km) for men and 8 laps (64.87 mi/104.4 km) for women. In the individual time trials, where cyclists started individually from a starting ramp at 90-second intervals, the men raced four laps (32.4 mi/52.2 km), and the women raced two laps (16.2 mi/26.1 km).

Road Race. Among a field of 184 in the men's road race, Switzerland's Pascal Richard outsprinted Denmark's Rolf Sorensen in the last 60 ft (18 m) and won the gold by less than a wheel-length (both riders were credited with the same time of 4:53:56). "When I saw two laps to go, I did not think I could make it," Richard said. "My legs did not feel too good." Richard, however, prevailed, later saying, "Victory was the only thing that interested me."

"To be so near is something that will stay with me for a very long time," said silver medalist Sorensen, whose father raced in the 1960 Olympic Games in Rome. "I did everything I could, but Pascal had a stronger sprint finish." Taking the bronze was Great Britain's Maximilian Scjandri (4:53:58).

An estimated crowd of 50,000 was on hand for the women's road race, as Jeannie Longo-Ciprelli of France survived a three-bike breakaway to win the gold with a time of 2:36:13. Italy's Imelda Chiappa finished second for the silver medal at 2:36:38. Clara Hughes, who was a junior national speed skating champion before she took up cycling at age 18, won Canada's first medal of the Centennial Olympic Games by finishing third for bronze at 2:36:44.

At age 37, Longo-Ciprelli was not only one of the oldest competitors in the 58-rider field, but she was also one of the most accomplished. One title that had eluded this 10-time world and 18-time French national champion, however, was that of Olympic champion. A competitor in each Olympic Games since women's cycling made its debut in 1984 in Los Angeles, Longo-Ciprelli's best showing had been her silver-medal finish at the 1992 Games in Barcelona. With that in mind, she was determined not to finish second again. "My career would have absolutely been incomplete if I had not won an Olympic gold medal," said Longo-Ciprelli.

top right: **Banners decorated in the Look of the Games were hung at the start and finish lines of the cycling courses.**

bottom right: **The men's road race passes fans along the course through the streets of Atlanta.**

left: **Silver medalist Imelda Chiappa of Italy is closely followed by bronze medalist Clara Hughes of Canada in the women's road race.**

facing page: **The women's road race wheels through the Buckhead shopping district.**

NORMAN C KLINE • PAUL E KLINECT • VICKI L KLINGE • SUSAN K KLINGELHAFER • WILLIAM J KLINGENER • JANN KLINGER • KORA L KLINGER • CRAIG S KLINGLER • KAHLILA M KLINGLER • ROBERT F KLINGLER • JOSEPH S KLINGMAN • BEVERLEY A KLIPPERT • KATE KLITENIC • LOIS O KLITSCH • MATTHEW B KLOBUKOWSKI • PAUL C KLOCEK • MITCHELL KLODER • MICHAEL J KLODNICKI • JANET M KLOEPFER • LISA K KLOEPFER • MELANIE L KLOES • CAROLINE J KLOMPMAKER • NOMIKI N KLONARIS • MOLLY R KLOPFENSTEIN • ROBERT K KLOPFENSTEIN • NINA L KLOSS • DAVID A KLOSSNER • ANN E KLOSTERMANN •

top: Five-time Tour de France winner and 1996 gold medalist Miguel Indurain of Spain completes the first of four laps in the men's individual time trial.

bottom: The Russian Federation's Zulfiya Zabirova goes for the gold medal in the inaugural women's individual time trial event.

Individual Time Trial. In the race against the clock—a true test of competitors' times—Spain's Miguel Indurain, a five-time winner of the Tour de France, won the men's individual time trial. Indurain averaged a remarkable 30.3 mph (48.8 kph) as he won in a time of 1:04:05. "Winning the Olympics is a historic achievement," said 32-year-old Indurain, whose superior cardiovascular system has a heartbeat of 28 times a minute at rest. Following Indurain in the 40-man field was Spanish teammate Abraham Olano, silver medalist at 1:04:17, and Great Britain's Chris Boardman, who won the bronze at 1:04:36. During the medal ceremony, IOC President Juan Antonio Samaranch personally awarded his fellow countrymen—Indurain and Olano—their medals.

In the first-ever Olympic women's individual time trial, the Russian Federation's Zulfiya Zabirova, 22, won the gold, while France's Jeannie Longo-Ciprelli earned a silver medal, and Canada's Clara Hughes took the bronze. Zabirova won the race with a time of 36:40. "I have never ridden so smoothly, so calmly in my life," said Zabirova, who averaged 26.5 mph (42.6 kph). Longo-Ciprelli clocked in at 37:00, and Hughes finished at 37:13.

CONCLUSION

In the road cycling competition, fans found a bit of everything in the four events. In the women's events, spectators saw four-time Olympian Jeannie Longo-Ciprelli win her first gold medal and witnessed the inaugural individual time trial. On the men's side, cycling enthusiasts experienced the drama of the road race being won by a matter of inches. In the time trial, they enjoyed watching Spain's Miguel Indurain add an Olympic gold medal to his remarkable cycling résumé.

TRACK

The track competition rounded out the three cycling disciplines. For five days, from 24 to 28 July, a total of 152 men and 54 women from 45 countries competed for gold on the newly constructed Olympic velodrome.

VENUE

The track cycling competition at the Centennial Olympic Games was held against the magnificent backdrop of 825 ft (252 m) high Stone Mountain, the world's largest exposed granite monolith. The Stone Mountain Park Velodrome, located in beautiful 3,200 acre (1,295 ha) Stone Mountain Park, approximately 16.5 mi (26.6 km) from the Atlanta Olympic Village, consisted of a temporary 5,200-seat velodrome with a revolutionary new wooden surface. The 820 ft (250 m) oblong track, featuring 42° banking in the turns and 13° banking along the straightaways, had a surface of plywood panels covered by a textured surface called Teak Skidguard—a smooth, slip-resistant resin that also reduced moisture on the track. The temporary open-air venue was constructed especially for the 1996 Olympic Games. At the conclusion of the Games, the facility was removed to a site in Florida, and the area was restored to its natural state.

COMPETITION

Among the modifications for the Atlanta Games was the addition of the women's point race. This brought the number of medal events contested in the track cycling competition to eight: men's and women's sprint, individual pursuit, and point race; and men's 1 km time trial and team pursuit. All sessions were sold out well in advance of the Games. In keeping with the spirit of the competition, an average

ANN F KLOUSER • VERNA KLUBNIKIN • JANET A KLUG • KATHARINE N KLUTTZ • SUSAN K KLUTTZ • MARY E KLUTZ • ALAN KMIECIK • MARJORIE C KNAP • DONNA M KNAPP • DOREEN R KNAPP • HEATHER M KNAPP • JAMES L KNAPP • JULIE N KNAPP • ROBERT A KNAPP • SARA B KNAPP • HOWARD KNAPP II • RAYMOND G KNAPP IV • CHRISTINA KNAPPITSCH • KATHY O KNAPPITSCH • PETER E KNAUP • JOHN T KNECHT • SHANNON L KNEELAND • IRA E KNEISE • RICHARD KNEISEL • AMY L KNEISS • RICHARD F KNERR • CHARLES E KNESEL • SHEREL A KNESEL • BARBARA E KNIAT • KENNETH S KNIAT • JEANE KNICK

Olympic-record time of 1:02.712. Erin Hartwell of the US, the 1992 bronze medalist in Barcelona, was close behind Rousseau at 1:02.940. The silver-medal showing was a personal victory for Hartwell and was also important to the US Cycling Federation, which had developed the sleek, 17 lb (7.7 kg) Superbike II Hartwell was riding. Finishing behind Rousseau and Hartwell was Japan's Takanobu Jumonji (1:03.261), who took the bronze.

Individual Pursuit. In preliminary competition on day one of the track cycling events, the

crowd of 4,700 watched as Italy's Andrea Collinelli twice set a world and Olympic record in the men's 4,000 m individual pursuit. Early in the day, Collinelli set the world and Olympic record with a heat time of 4:19.699—breaking the Olympic mark (4:21.295) France's Philippe Ermenault had established earlier. Later, however, he eclipsed his own performance with a new world- and Olympic-record time of 4:19.153.

On day two of the competition, Collinelli failed to match the world-record time he had established a day earlier, but he did capture the gold medal in the men's individual pursuit with a winning time of 4:20.893. Finishing behind Collinelli were silver medalist Ermenault (4:22.714) of France and Bradley McGee (4:26.121) of Australia. "It was pure pleasure

left: The track cycling competition took place at the Stone Mountain Park Velodrome, a temporary facility built especially for the Games.

right: Italy's Andrea Collinelli rides to world and Olympic records in the men's individual pursuit qualifying round.

of about 100 spectators cycled to the velodrome on each day of the track cycling events.

1 km Time Trial. One world record and four Olympic records were set on the first day of the track cycling competition. In the men's 1 km time trial, France's Florian Rousseau won the first gold medal of the competition in an

Cycling—Track

Venue Used:
Stone Mountain Park Velodrome

Days of Competition: 5

Medals Awarded: 24
Gold 8
Silver 8
Bronze 8

Number of Nations: 45

Olympic Records: 13

World Records: 2

Number of Officials: 30

Officiating Federation:
International Cycling Union (UCI)

• TOMAS KNICK • SUSAN P KNICKERBOCKER • SUSAN J KNIES • BONNI S KNIGHT • BRENDA H KNIGHT • CHRISTOPHER L KNIGHT • CYNTHIA KNIGHT • ELAINE KNIGHT • ELIZABETH A KNIGHT • GAYLE L KNIGHT • GEORGE D KNIGHT • JENNIFER A KNIGHT • LAIRD A KNIGHT • LARRY E KNIGHT • LINDA A KNIGHT • LYNN S KNIGHT • MICHAEL J KNIGHT • NATALIE P KNIGHT • PATRICIA E KNIGHT • PHILIP R KNIGHT • RANDOLPH R KNIGHT • RICHARD F KNIGHT • SHEILA M KNIGHT • SUSAN F KNIGHT • WALKER L KNIGHT • WALTER L KNIGHT • WILLIAM B KNIGHT • JAMES L KNIGHT JR •

to the eyes to see a human being move that quickly on a bicycle," bronze medalist McGee said of Collinelli's performance.

In the women's individual pursuit qualification round on day two of track cycling, three riders—Germany's Judith Arndt, Antonella Bellutti of Italy, and France's Marion Clignet—bettered the Olympic mark of 3:41.509, which had been set in Barcelona. Leading the way was Bellutti, who shattered the earlier mark in establishing an Olympic-best time of 3:34.130. Both Collinelli and Bellutti used Italy's "super-

left: The Netherlands' Ingrid Haringa races during the women's 200 m sprint time trial qualification round.

right: France's Felicia Ballanger races ahead of Australia's Michelle Ferris in the women's sprint final.

man" riding position—a new aerodynamic position in which the arms are stretched out fully in front on specially designed handle bars.

Bellutti came back on day three and broke the Olympic record she had set on day two. She established a new Olympic mark in the 12-lap race with a blazing time of 3:32.371.

In the finals, Belluti finished first to win the gold medal in the women's individual pursuit with a time of 3:33.595, defeating France's Clignet, who earned the silver (3:38.571). Amid tears of joy, Bellutti waved an Italian flag while taking a victory lap. Germany's Arndt (3:38.744) won the bronze.

Sprint. Germany's Jens Fiedler successfully defended his 1992 Olympic gold medal in the men's sprint race. Before an enthusiastic crowd of 6,696, Fiedler defeated Olympic favorite and 1994 World Champion Marty Nothstein of the US, who won the silver medal, in two straight sprints in the best-of-three format. Fiedler's winning times were 10.664 and 11.074. Canada's Curt Harnett announced his retirement from international competition after he defeated Olympic-record holder Gary Neiwand of Australia 10.947 and 10.949 to win the bronze. On the opening day of the track cycling competition, Neiwand had established an Olympic record with a time of 10.129.

Michelle Ferris of Australia set an opening-day Olympic record with a time of 11.212 in the women's 200 m sprint time trial. In the fi-

DEWAYNE C KNIGHT MD • TAVIS L KNIGHTEN • ROBERT C KNIGHTON • ROBERT L KNIGHTON • YASMIN M KNIGHTON • MARIANNE M KNISLEY • STEVE KNITTEL • MARIANNE R KNIZEWSKI • JUDITH E KNOEBEL • BEVERLY D KNOECHEL • WALTER R KNOECHEL • CHARLES M KNOLES • CARLA K KNOLL • JAMES H KNOLL • SANDRA T KNOLL • DAVID E KNOPE • CAROL B KNOPKA • CAROLYN R KNOPP • VIRGINIA W KNORR • ALEXANDER KNOTT • DORIS M KNOTT • CHRISTOPHER J KNOWLES • DEBORAH J KNOWLES • DOROTHY L KNOWLES • ELIZABETH C KNOWLES • G RENE KNOWLES • JOANNE P KNOWLES • PAUL L KNOWLES

nals, France's Felicia Ballanger defeated Ferris 11.903 and 12.096 to win the gold, while Ferris took home the silver. The Netherlands' Ingrid Haringa outsprinted Germany's Annett Neumann 12.074 and 11.782 to win the bronze.

Team Pursuit. The Russian Federation set an Olympic men's team pursuit record of 4:08.785 on day three of the track cycling competition. On the following day, however, France's team of Christophe Capelle, Philippe Ermenault, Jean-Michel Monin, and Francis Moreau topped that by defeating the Russian Federation with a gold-medal–winning, Olympic-record time of 4:05.930. The Russian Federation silver medalists (Anton Chantyr, Eduard Gritsun, Nikolay Kuznetsov, and Aleksey Markov) bettered their previous record time by finishing at 4:07.730. Australia (Bradley McGee, Stuart O'Grady, Timothy O'Shannessey, and Dean Woods) won the bronze with the next fastest time in the semifinals (4:07.570).

Point Race. On the final day of competition, Italy captured the gold in the men's point race when Silvio Martinello won with 37 points, defeating silver medalist Brian Walton of Canada (29 points) and bronze medalist Stuart O'Grady of Australia (25 points).

France, meanwhile, won its fourth gold medal in track cycling at the Centennial Olympic Games. In the women's point race, France's Nathalie Lancien finished first with 24 points, followed by Ingrid Haringa of the Netherlands (23 points) and Australia's Lucy Tyler-Sharman (17 points).

CONCLUSION

During the five-day track cycling competition, 2 world records and 13 Olympic records were established. France led the medal count with six medals—four gold and two silver. Italy followed with three gold medals. Also placing among the European cycling powers was Australia, which finished with five medals—one silver and four bronze. The US track cycling team won two silver medals.

top: **Positioned to win, France's Nathalie Lancien prepares to take the gold in the women's point race.**

bottom: **France's Francis Moreau, Christophe Capelle, Philippe Ermenault, and Jean-Michel Monin finish in first place during the men's 4,000 m team pursuit semifinals.**

• ROD KNOWLES • SCOTT D KNOWLES • STEVEN L KNOWLES • JULIE M KNOWLES ATC • CHRISTOPHER M KNOWLTON • ELAINE H KNOWLTON • REED KNOWLTON • ANSLEY M KNOX • BETTY KNOX • BRIAN P KNOX • CHINAETTA Y KNOX • DAVID J KNOX • HOYT L KNOX • JANNELL KNOX • JEANNE B KNOX • NATALIE M KNOX • ROBERT G KNOX • SALLY Y KNOX • MARSHALL G KNOX III • MARY WOODY KNUDSEN • TOR HENNING R KNUDSEN • ERIC D KNUTSON • JOYCE C KNUTSON • WILHO J KNUUTI • CHING-CHIA KO • CHING-TZY KO • KEVIN E KOBAYASHI • MASAKO KOBAYASHI • SHIGEKI KOBAYASHI • TATSUYA KOBAYASHI

Venue Used:
Georgia International Horse Park

Days of Competition: 13

Medals Awarded: 18
Gold 6
Silver 6
Bronze 6

Number of Nations: 33

Number of Officials: 75

Officiating Federation:
International Equestrian Federation (FEI)

EQUESTRIAN

THE 33 COUNTRIES that qualified for the Centennial Olympic Games equestrian competition comprised a field of 255 horses (all required to be at least seven years old) and 225 riders. More than 350,000 tickets were sold.

VENUE

All three disciplines of the equestrian competition were held at the Georgia International Horse Park. The horse park was a 1,139 acre (461 ha) site located within the Yellow River valley in Rockdale County near Conyers, Georgia, approximately 33 mi (53 km) east of the Atlanta Olympic Village. The horse park also hosted the mountain bike racing competition, as well as the riding and running phases of the modern pentathlon. As one of the permanent sports arenas built especially for the Games, the horse park is now part of a multiuse recreational park operated by the city of Conyers.

Shaped and constructed from a natural bowl in the red Georgia clay, the park's magnificent 32,000-seat main arena featured a 198 x 66 ft (60 x 20 m) rectangular sand dressage piste and a 328 x 476 ft (100 x 145 m) rectangular sand jumping area. The main arena was surrounded by pristine open countryside, which contained a 25-obstacle, 700 acre (283 ha) endurance course. In addition, the park included stables (five barns with 92 stalls each), a covered arena, a hacking field with grass dressage and jumping

areas, a track course, trails, a steeplechase oval, 11 sand training areas, a complete veterinary clinic, a grooms' housing complex with accommodations for 300 people, an athlete lounge and locker room, and administrative offices.

COMPETITION

Divided into three disciplines (three-day event, dressage, and jumping), the Olympic equestrian competition spanned a 15-day period (21 July–4 August, including two rest days) with six medal categories. Team and individual medals were awarded in all three disciplines.

THREE-DAY EVENT

When the three-day event was introduced at the 1912 Olympic Games, the competitors were strictly cavalry officers. That, however, was not the case at the 1996 Games, as a total of 89 athletes from 24 countries qualified for the three-day event. All athletes were required to be at least 18 years old. Each country could enter a maximum of seven riders and horses in the event.

For the first time in Olympic history, the three-day event (21–26 July) was held as two separate competitions: a team event followed

• ARI G KOBB • JACK KOBEDA • TANYA R KOBEK • CANDI M KOBETZ • RICHARD A KOBLE • SARA B KOBLEGARD • SAMANTHA L KOBRIN • DEANA R KOBRYNSKI • WILLIAM E KOBUS • EILEEN KOCA • KEITH L KOCA • ALAN D KOCH • DAVID J KOCH • DEREK A KOCH • GREGORY M KOCH • GUENTHER M KOCH • JANE E KOCH • JOHN H KOCH • JOSHUA M KOCH • JUDY D KOCH • KIM A KOCH • LINDA M KOCH • MELITH KOCH • MICHAEL B KOCH • MONICA L KOCH • PAMELA H KOCH • PEGGY KOCH • TINA S KOCH • TODD A KOCH • RACHELLE J KOCHANSKI • ERIC G KOCHER • LISA M KOCON • RUMIKO KODERA • MARK SKOEBERNIK •

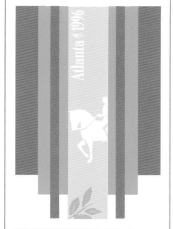

by an individual competition. Both competitions in this all-around test of horsemanship challenged the horse and rider on dressage, endurance, and jumping. Penalty points were assessed for mistakes in each of the three tests.

Dressage involved 20 movements designed to test the horse's obedience, flexibility, and harmony with the rider. The endurance portion of the event required riders to complete all four phases—short roads and tracks, steeplechase, long roads and tracks, and cross country—plus jumping the obstacles in the steeplechase within time constraints. The scenic cross-country course had obstacles based on historical themes involving Georgia and the southern US. The final portion of the three-day event was jumping, which again challenged the horse and rider with obstacles.

Team. The first two days of the three-day event team competition involved two rounds of dressage. The United States rested in first place as all four riders posted their best-ever scores in this event. On the opening day of competition, the US rode its way to the top behind the husband and wife duo of Karen and David O'Connor, who produced the second- and fourth-best dressage scores of the day on Biko and Giltedge, respectively. Thanks to the O'Connors' showing, the US team led with a score of 80.40. The top individual performance was demonstrated by Great Britain's Ian Stark and his mount Stanwick Ghost, who turned in a 35.20 penalty-point showing to guide Great Britain to second place in the standings (84.20). On the second day, the US widened its lead with the performance of five-time Olympian and double gold medalist Bruce Davidson and his mount

left: **Kerry Millikin of the US rides Out and About against an Olympic ring of flowers which accented the Georgia International Horse Park's dressage piste.**

top right: **Look of the Games banners decorated the competition venue.**

bottom right: **The US's David O'Connor rides Custom Made in the three-day event endurance test.**

KRISTI L KOEHN • JAN M KOEHN-SELMAN • KELLY J. KOELKER • NEIL C KOENEMAN • ANNE L KOENIG • CAROLINE KOENIG • CHRISTOPHER J KOENIG • HELEN M KOENIG • JODI L KOENIG • JUNE KOENIG • KAREN KOENIG • KARLA Y KOENIG • KIPP C KOENIG • KURT KOENIG • LIBBY THACKER KOENIG • MARGIE A KOENIG • MARK E KOENIG • PATTI J KOENIG • RICHARD L KOENIG • RONALD H KOENIG • SARAH E KOENIG • JAIN S KOEPKE • RONALD L KOERBER • CHRISTI L KOERNER • STACEY L KOERTS • BONNIE R KOETHER • CAROLYN S KOFA • CATHERINE D KOFA • JEANNETTE D KOFA • ANNE D KOFFEY •

Phillip Dutton on True Blue Girdwood (8.80) and Wendy Schaeffer on Sunburst (11.60) helped Australia to jump five places in the overall standings. France moved up to fourth place thanks to a remarkable performance by Jacques Dulcy on Upont—the only horse and rider that finished the endurance test without any penalty points.

Olympic rookie Jill Henneberg and her horse Nirvana of the United States crashed and were eliminated from the remainder of the three-day event. As a result, the US fell to second (244.60)

in the overall standings, and was virtually eliminated from gold-medal contention. Elsewhere in the overall standings, New Zealand remained third (255.80); Great Britain fell from second to sixth place (298.40); and Canada, which was fourth after the dressage test, was eliminated when two of its riders failed to complete the endurance course.

Australia successfully cleared the final hurdle of the three-day event—the jumping test—and repeated as the team gold medalist, finishing with a total score of 203.85 penalty points. Leading the way for Australia was Schaeffer, the

left: **France's Jacques Dulcy and mount Upont ride to a penalty-free performance in the endurance test of the three-day event.**

right: **Bruce Davidson and his horse Heyday take part in the United States's silver-medal team in the three-day event team competition.**

Heyday. Davidson, 46, and Heyday turned in a career-best score of only 42.60 penalty points.

The US lead was short-lived, however, as later that day, Australia moved into first place after the endurance test with an overall score of 183.60. Andrew Hoy and his mount Darien Powers led Australia with a team-best endurance ride of 6.80 penalty points. Teammates

THOMAS J KOFFOLT • EMMANUEL A KOFIE • PETER T KOGAN • ANDREAS M KOGELNIK • MICHAEL KOGER SR • PAMELA K KOHER • DIANE M KOHL • GERSON F KOHLER • MARY P KOHLER • SHARON F KOHLER • JACK L KOHLMEIER • JAMES A KOHM • ROBERT N KOHMESCHER • JACKIE KOHN • JAMES A KOHN • JENNIFER E KOHNEN • JENNIFER L KOHNEN • JESSICA L KOHNEN • DIANE V KOHRMAN • ROBERT L KOHRMAN • ANNE N KOHTALA • PHYLLIS J KOIWAI • ALFRED B KOJIMA • HIKARU KOJIMA • KATSUNORI KOJIMA • SEAN E KOKKO • BARBARA A KOKOTEC • DAWN M KOKOWSKI • KARI K KOLANOSKI •

Zealand's duo of riders Blyth Tait on Ready Teddy and Sally Clark on Squirrel Hill galloped their way to the top of the standings in the endurance test. Tait and Ready Teddy turned in a fast time with just 5.20 penalty points to take over first place (56.80), while Clark completed one of the best rides of her career on Squirrel Hill to move into second place (60.40).

Just 12 penalty points separated the top five horses and riders heading into the jumping test of the three-day event individual competition. After Clark and Squirrel Hill rode flaw-

top overall rider in the three-day event team competition. Despite breaking her leg in a fall just two months before the Olympic Games, Schaeffer rode her bay gelding Sunburst to the lowest total score of penalty points (61.00). "People break their legs all the time," the 21-year-old Olympic rookie said. "They just don't normally do it two months before the Olympics." Following Schaeffer were Dutton on True Blue Girdwood (69.40) and Hoy on Darien Powers (73.45).

The O'Connors made Olympic history when they became the first married couple to ride together on a medal-winning equestrian team. Karen (105.60) and David (76.00) O'Connor teamed with Davidson (79.50) to lead the successful silver-medal charge for the United States (261.10). The New Zealand team of Blyth Tait on Chesterfield (70.10), Vaughn Jefferis on Bounce (97.80), and Andrew Nicholson on Jagermeister II (100.65) won the bronze with a total of 268.55 penalty points.

Individual. In the individual competition, Great Britain's Mary King and her mount King William led after the dressage test with a score of 31.60 penalty points. David O'Connor of the US on mount Custom Made were in second place (37.60), and Australia's Nikki Bishop on Wishful Thinking was third (40.00). New

left: Andrew Hoy and Wendy Schaeffer of Australia ride as they celebrate their gold-medal win in the three-day event team competition.

right: New Zealand's Andrew Nicholson competes on Buckley Province in the individual three-day event.

top: **New Zealand's Blyth Tait guides Ready Teddy to individual gold in the three-day event.**

bottom: **The US's Michelle Gibson, aboard Peron, executes her freestyle routine during the individual dressage competition.**

lessly through the stadium jumping course to secure at least the silver medal, the pressure to make a mistake-free run through the 15-jump course switched to teammate Tait and Ready Teddy. During Tait's ride, one of Ready Teddy's hooves hit a rail with such force that the loud impact caused the full-capacity crowd to gasp. The spectators, as well as Tait, knew that just one rail knockdown would mean the difference between gold and silver. "The jump went 'klunk' and so did my heart," Tait said of the hit. "I thought I'd lost it."

The rail, however, stayed up, and Tait and Ready Teddy leaped their way to an individual gold medal with 56.80 penalty points. Tait's mount, 8-year-old Ready Teddy, was also the youngest and least-experienced horse in the competition. "He's just got the biggest heart of any horse I've ever ridden," Tait said. New Zealand teammate Clark riding Squirrel Hill won the silver medal (60.40), and Kerry Millikin riding Out and About (73.70) took the bronze for the US.

DRESSAGE

A total of 50 athletes (required to be at least 16 years old) and mounts competed in the team and individual dressage events at the Centennial Olympic Games. Within the beautifully decorated rectangular dressage piste in the center of the main arena, the difficulty of the maneuvers was illustrated by the circular and diagonal patterns etched by the horses' hooves in the white sand. Conceived from its military background as a method of training war horses, the sport of dressage is a subtle ballet in which the horse and rider attempt to flawlessly execute a series of maneuvers that beautifully demonstrates a combination of artistic and athletic equestrian skills.

The horses' highly refined but natural maneuvers are based on three gaits: canter, trot, and walk. Riders demand that the maneuvers be done in a certain order, at specific places, and with proper rhythm, while making it appear as if no commands are being used. Within the show ring, 12 letters are marked to designate where moves should start and end.

In the Olympic grand prix (27–28 July), horses were required to excel at five difficult maneuvers: piaffe, a tight, elevated trot without forward movement that gives the impression that the horse is marching in place; passage, a suspended trot in slow motion while moving forward that appears as if the horse is pausing in midair; pirouette, a rhythmic rotation in place while either cantering or walking; half pass, a crossing of the legs while in a canter or trot that causes the horse to move both sideways and forward; and flying change, a changing of the horse's leading front leg every fourth, third, second, and single stride that gives the appearance that the horse is skipping.

Every rider followed the same two test sequences of complex moves in the grand prix and grand prix special tests. The grand prix test

is composed of 38 compulsory movements that test the rider's command and the horse's agility, grace, and obedience. The top three scores from each country in the grand prix test (each country is allowed to enter up to four horses and riders) were combined to determine the team medal winners. In the individual competition, the top 24 horse and rider pairs in the grand prix test advanced to the more difficult grand prix special test, a mandatory 32 compulsory movement exam. The top 12 from the grand prix special test advanced to the first-ever Olympic musical grand prix freestyle test—a three-minute final segment ridden to music with steps chosen by the competitors. Equal weight was given to all three tests as a

panel of five judges positioned around the show ring scored the riders on the horses' quality of movements. Penalty points were given for mistakes, poor style, and resistance by the horse.

Team. Germany established a commanding lead on the opening day of the grand prix test. Leading the way for Germany (3,708) was Isabell Werth and her mount Gigolo, who had the opening day's top individual score during team competition of 1,915. Following Germany in the team competition were the Netherlands (3,544) and the US (3,529).

Those team standings, which were the same as the team results at the 1992 Olympic Games, remained the same at the end of the two-day team competition. Germany (Klaus Balkenhol, Martin Schaudt, Monica Theodorescu, and Isabell Werth) finished with a gold-medal total of 5,553 points, while the Netherlands (Tineke Bartels-de Vries, Gonnelien Rothenberger, Sven Rothenberger, and Anky van Grunsven) successfully defended its silver medal (5,437), and the US (Robert Dover, Michelle Gibson, Steffen Peters, and Guenter Seidel) repeated as the bronze winner (5,309).

Individual. In the individual competition, the world's top two dressage riders began jockeying for the gold in the second test—the grand prix special. The Netherlands' Anky van Grunsven and her spirited mount Bonfire took over the lead by finishing with a combined score of 153.44. Isabell Werth and Gigolo made two critical mistakes, which dropped the defending Olympic silver medalist to second (152.09).

The final dressage test—the musical grand prix freestyle—made a popular debut as the spectators responded enthusiastically to the individually choreographed routines ridden to musical accompaniments. In the battle for the

left: **Germany's Isabell Werth, aboard Gigolo, reigns supreme in the Olympic equestrian individual dressage competition.**

right: **The Netherlands' Anky van Grunsven, who rode Bonfire, displays her individual dressage silver medal.**

gold, Werth and Gigolo came out on top with a total score of 235.09, while van Grunsven and Bonfire took the silver (233.02). During the medal ceremony, a large contingent of spirited German fans waved more than a dozen flags while chanting, "Gigolo, Gigolo, Gigolo." "To me, it's the greatest victory of my life," Werth said after winning her first individual gold medal. Van Grunsven's teammate Sven Rothenberger and mount Weyden took the bronze (224.94).

JUMPING

The jumping competition (25, 29 July and 1, 4 August) was held in the rectangular jumping area in the main arena. Beautifully designed, the course of colorful jumps made of rails featured themes from Georgia and the historic southern landscape, US landmarks, and cities that have hosted the modern Olympic Games. Within a certain time limit, each horse and rider team was required to complete the test while knocking down as few rails as possible (points were added for each knockdown). A total of 83 athletes (required to be at least 18 years old) and 27 countries (each country could enter a maximum of four competitors and six horses) qualified for the competition.

The lone format modification involved qualification for the individual competition. The team results dictated the individual qualifiers, as scores from the qualifying competition, held prior to the team event, were combined with the scores from the first two rounds of the team event to determine which competitors were eligible for the individual jumping event. As a result, only the 45 riders with the best scores qualified for the semifinals of the individual event, from which only the top 20 advanced to the finals, held on the last day of the Games.

left: The Netherlands' Sven Rothenberger rides Weyden in the team dressage competition.

right: Germany's Ulrich Kirchhoff and his horse Jus de Pommes jump for gold in both individual and team jumping.

The qualifying competition began with the event favorite setting the pace. Germany's Ludger Beerbaum, winner at both the 1993 World Cup and the 1992 Barcelona Games, rode his horse Ratina through a clean round (0.00). Six other riding pairs also finished the individual jumping qualifying round with zero penalty points.

Team. On the final day of the team jumping competition, the course design represented landmarks on a journey across the United States, beginning with the "Statue of Liberty" water jump and ending with the "Hawaiian Bamboo" double combination. The different course design, however, failed to distract Beerbaum and his 14-year-old mare Ratina from a near-perfect ride. The pair, which tied Spain's Fernando Sarasola riding Ennio for the top individual score after the first two rounds (0.25),

ANTON G KORT • KIMBERLY A KORT • PHILIPPA A KORT • VALERIE A KORT • CINTHIA R KORTE • BROOKE A KOSAKA • ROBERT KOSAKOSKI • SUSAN L KOSCHAK • BETTY S KOSCO • BILL KOSCO • CAROLINE L KOSCO • CAROLYN B KOSEL • PAUL A KOSHEWA • VICTORIA J KOSIENSKI • CHARLES V KOSIOR • LINDA L KOSKELA • KURT A KOSMOWSKI • MARK E KOSON • ARTHUR A KOSTARAS • STEPHEN J KOSTECKI • JOHN F KOSTER • EUGENE E KOSTIUK • DONNA L KOTANKO • NAPOLEON D KOTEY • ALAN R KOTH • DELY J KOTLAN • ELAINE A KOTLER • DANNYE M KOTT • MARY SUSAN B KOTTKAMP • DANIEL K KOUAME •

led gold medalist Germany to its first team medal in jumping since the 1964 Games. The other horse and rider pairs on the winning German team were Ulrich Kirchhoff with Jus de Pommes, Lars Nieberg with For Pleasure, and Franke Sloothaak with Joly. Germany won the gold with a total of 1.75.

The US became the only team to win a medal in all three equestrian disciplines when it captured the silver. In addition, by winning its fourth medal in the six-medal sport, the US posted its best Olympic equestrian showing

and Tomboy clinched the bronze with a strong round that sent the Brazilian fans into a jubilant uproar.

Individual. Ulrich Kirchhoff and Jus de Pommes of Germany were the only pair to clear every jump in the final two individual rounds, which earned the Olympic rookie his second gold medal of the Games. Placing behind Kirchhoff were Switzerland's Willi Melliger on Calvaro, who won the silver, and France's Alexandra Ledermann on Rochet M, who took home the bronze.

left: **Lars Nieberg rides For Pleasure to help the German team win the jumping gold medal.**

right: **France's Alexandra Ledermann rides Rochet M to take the individual jumping bronze.**

ever. The members of the US team and their mounts were Leslie Burr-Howard with Extreme, Anne Kursinski with Eros, Peter Leone with Legato, and Michael Matz with Rhum. The team finished with a total score of 12.00.

Finishing behind Germany and the US in the 19-country team competition was Brazil (Luiz Felipe de Azevedo with Cassiana, André Bier Johannpeter with Calei, Álvaro Affonso de Miranda Neto with Aspen, and Rodrigo de Paula Pessoa with Tomboy), which won its first-ever equestrian medal (17.25). Pessoa, 23,

CONCLUSION

Overall, the German fans had the most reason to celebrate, as Germany won individual and team gold medals in two—dressage and jumping—of the three equestrian events. Germany also featured two double-gold pairs: Ulrich Kirchhoff and Jus de Pommes, winners of individual and team gold in jumping, and Isabell Werth and Gigolo, gold recipients in individual and team dressage. Australia and New Zealand supporters reveled over the other two gold-medal winners in the three-day event. Boisterous US fans cheered the American team medalists in all three disciplines, and Brazilian flags appeared among the crowd in the team jumping competition as fans rejoiced over that country's first equestrian medal.

Atlanta 1996.

JEAN E. KOUCH • HILARY T KOUHANA • MICHELLE L KOULETIO • ANTHONY KOUNUKLOS • MICHAEL D KOURY • MICHAEL E. KOVAC • CAROLE L. KOVACH • DIANE L KOVACS • KIM KOVACS • MICHAEL R KOVACS • LOUIS S KOVACS JR • CHRISTINE E KOVAL • JONATHAN KOVAL • ALEXANDER G KOVALIOV • EDWARD J KOVARIK • MANDI E KOWAL • KATHRYN P KOWALCZJY • MALGORZATA M KOWALIK • CARL M KOWALSKI • CATHERINE M KOWALSKI • JANET KOWALSKY • ALLAN C KOYANAGI • KRIS C KOZAK • SUSAN L KOZAK • EUGENE W KOZIATEK • KEITH R KOZICKI • JENNIE KOZICKI • DENNIS T KOZIEL • WALTER J KOZIK •

FENCING

Venue Used:
Georgia World
Congress Center

Days of Competition: 6

Medals Awarded: 30
Gold 10
Silver 10
Bronze 10

Number of Nations: 46

Number of Officials: 82

Officiating Federation:
International Fencing
Federation (FIE)

FENCING AT THE Centennial Olympic Games featured many innovations to the sport witnessed in 1896 by Baron Pierre de Coubertin, the founder of the modern Games and a fencer himself. Fencers in Atlanta dueled under brilliant spotlights while uniformed from head to toe in protective clothing and connected electronically to a high-tech scoring machine. Each weapon was wired with a body cord running from the base of the sword, up the fencer's sleeve, out of the back of the uniform, and into the scoring system.

VENUE

The fencing events took place in Hall F of the Georgia World Congress Center, located 1.9 mi (3 km) from the Olympic Village. Competition took place on a custom-made, elevated field of play known as a piste. The fencing athletes competed on one of five competition pistes, each measuring 59 x 7 ft (18 x 2 m). More than 5,000 spectators attended the fencing matches daily from 20 through 25 July.

COMPETITION

Fencers competed in single-elimination rounds in each discipline during the six days of events. Pairings were determined by World Cup rankings. Each bout ended after three three-minute periods or when one fencer scored 15 points.

A hit, or a touch, was worth one point, and fencers were also awarded points if they forced an opponent off the piste.

Competition took place in three different weapon categories: foil, épée, and sabre. The foil, a light and flexible weapon, was originally used for practicing combat. In competition, only blade-point touches made on the torso count, and fencers must follow a certain sequence of movements called conventions. Hits in épée, or dueling sword, must be made with the tip of the rigid 3 ft (.9 m) triangular blade, but can be scored over the entire body. In sabre—the only weapon that can be used with a cutting motion—the target area is above the hips, much as it was for combatants using cavalry swords from horseback.

Men competed in individual and team events in all three categories, while women competed in individual and team foil and épée. A total of 233 Olympic fencers (140 men and 93 women) came to Atlanta seeking Olympic gold.

Because fencing officials wanted to strengthen the international status and visibility of one of the few sports contested at every modern Olympic Games, new elements enlivened the competition and enhanced fencing's visual impact: the debut of women's individual and team épée, and the use of modified

TANYA S KOZIMER • SARA A KOZINSKY • SUE A KOZISEK MT • BRIAN S KOZLOWSKI • VITALI B KOZLOYSKI • GWEN B KRAATZ • MARSHA A KRAATZ • DALE J KRACH ATC • SUSAN J KRACHT • JOHN D KRAFKA • JULIE A KRAFLZENK • CAROL W KRAFT • IRIS B KRAFT • KENNETH M KRAFT • SHIRLEY J KRAFT • WALTRAUD KRAFT • SUSAN L KRAHAM • JASON D KRAHN • JORI GAILE KRAINC • PHIL KRAJEC • ANNETTE K KRAMER • CAROLYN M KRAMER • CELIA L KRAMER • CHERYL M KRAMER • EARL J KRAMER • JAMES R KRAMER • JOHN H KRAMER • MARGARET KRAMER • MATTHEW C KRAMER • MELANIE D KRAMER • SUSAN W KRAMER

Plexiglas masks that allowed a fencer's face to be seen during competition.

Individual Foil. In the men's individual foil competition, which began with 45 participants, the top three seeds were all eliminated by the third round of the preliminaries. In the medal round, Italy's Alessandro Puccini (no. 7) captured the gold with a victory over Lionel Plumenail (no. 5) of France, who earned the silver medal in the hard-fought 15-12 contest. France's Franck Boidin won the bronze by defeating Germany's Wolfgang Wienand 15-11.

defeated the world's no. 4 ranked player, Italy's Diana Bianchedi, in the preliminary rounds. When the semifinalists put down their weapons, Badea had captured the gold by defeating silver medalist Vezzali 15-10. Trillini defeated Modaine-Cessac 15-9 to win the bronze.

Team Foil. The men's foil teams from Austria, Cuba, Poland, and the Russian Federation advanced through two preliminary rounds to reach the semifinals and the finals. The Russian Federation's team of Ilgar Mamedov,

left: Laura Badea of Romania scores a hit against Giovanna Trillini of Italy to win the women's individual foil semifinal.

right: Look of the Games banners with the fencing pictogram decorated Hall F of the Georgia World Congress Center.

The women's individual foil competition neatly followed the pre-event seedings, as the three top-ranked players in the world advanced through four rounds to the semifinals: Italy's Valentina Vezzali (no. 1 seed); 1992 gold medalist Giovanna Trillini (no. 2), also from Italy; and Romania's Laura Badea (no. 3). Taking the fourth semifinal spot was France's Laurence Modaine-Cessac (no. 13), who

Vladislav Pavlovich, and Dmitriy Shevchenko upset no. 1 seed Cuba 45-44 in the semifinals before defeating Poland (Piotr Kielpikowski, Adam Krzesinski, Jaroslaw Rodzewicz, and Ryszard Sobczak) 45-40 in the match to determine the gold and silver medals. Austria, which upset no. 2 seed Italy to reach the semifinals, fell to Cuba (Oscar Manuel Garcia Perez,

• TIMOTHY KRAMER • WILLIAM J KRAMER • KENNETH G KRAMP III • ROMAN S KRAMPL • BARBARA M KRANTZ • DIANNE P KRANTZ • MICHAEL J KRANTZ • RUSSELL W KRANTZ • JODIE L KRASEVEC • JOSEPH KRASEVEC • SHARON L KRAUN • ADRIANE M KRAUS • ALEX KRAUS • BRUCE R KRAUS • JOHN W KRAUS • KELLY G KRAUS • PETER ALAN KRAUS • TODD KRAUS • FRED E KRAUSE • LYNNE J KRAUSE • ROBIN R KRAUSE • SUSAN KRAUSE • VICKI D KRAUSE • DANIEL R KRAUSS • JEFFREY A KRAUSS • MONIKA KRAUSZ • CARL F KRAUTH • DARBIE A KRAUTH • DENISE A KRAUTH • LAUREL A KRAUTH • NANCY L KRAUTH •

363

Elvis Gregory, and Rolando Samuel Tucker Leon) 45-28 in the bronze-medal match.

Following two preliminary rounds and the semifinals, the remaining teams in the women's team foil were Germany, Hungary, Italy, and Romania. After beating no. 4 seed Hungary 45-42, no. 1 seed Italy defeated no. 3 seed Romania 45-33 to capture its second consecutive gold medal in women's team foil. In the final, all three Italians—Francesca Bortolozzi Borella and individual medalists Valentina Vezzali and Giovanna Trillini—went undefeated (3-0) in their

top: The Russian Federation's Dmitriy Shevchenko and Cuba's Rolando Samuel Tucker Leon battle in men's team foil competition.

bottom: Italy's Francesca Bortolozzi Borella is congratulated by teammates and coaches after winning the women's team foil gold-medal match.

matches against Romania (Laura Badea, Roxana Scarlat, and Reka Szabo-Lazar). No. 2 seed Germany (Sabine Bau, Anja Fichtel-Nauritz, and Monika Weber-Koszto) won the bronze with a 45-42 win over Hungary.

Individual Epée. In the men's individual epée competition, the Russian Federation's Aleksandr Beketov eliminated a pair of defending medalists and then survived a 15-14 marathon bout (in which the score was tied nine times) with Cuba's Ivan Trevejo Perez to win the gold medal. Perez then became the silver medalist. A tumble from the fencing strip in the semifinal round dashed the gold-medal hopes of Hungary's Ivan Kovacs. Attempting to back away from an attack by Beketov, Kovacs slipped and injured his right ankle. Medics taped the ankle, and Kovacs hobbled through the remainder of the bout. He departed amidst a resounding ovation. Later, in the all-Hungary bronze-medal match, Géza Imre defeated teammate Kovacs 15-9.

Women's individual épée made its Olympic debut in Atlanta, and French athletes won both the gold and silver medals. In the quarterfinals, France's Valerie Barlois upset no. 1 seed Timea Nagy of Hungary. In the final, however, Barlois lost to French teammate Laura Flessel 15-12. Flessel captured the gold, while Barlois took home the silver. Despite Nagy's loss, Hungary appeared on the medal stand when Hungarian Gyöngyi Szalay captured the bronze in a 15-13 win over Italy's Margherita Zalaffi.

Team Epée. Italy's men's épée team of Sandro Cuomo, Angelo Mazzoni, and Maurizio Randazzo lived up to their top seeding. In the final, the Italian trio won the gold 45-43 over the Russian Federation (Aleksandr Beketov, Pavel Kolobkov, and Valeriy Zakharevich), which received the silver medal. No. 2 seed

RICHARD S KRAUZE · ROGER E KRAVA · ERIC T KRAVITZ · EVAN R KRAVITZ · JENNIFER E KRAVITZ · CHRISTOPHER S KRAWCZYK · SILVIE KRAWCZYKOVA · ERIC L KREBS · JAMES A KREBS · HEATHER M KREGER · JOHN L KREIMEYER · MARK S KREINER · JANA F KREISBERG · JOHN J KREITNER · KARCH L KREITZ · ZOLTAN J KREKO · DONNA J KREMER · GRACE A KREMER · HAROLD R KREMER · RAY ANN Y. KREMER · SARAH A KRENEK · VENESSA L KRENEK · JYLYNN I KRENTZ · JENNIFER L. KREPS · MARC K KREPS · JAMES J KRESL · MARILYN KRESS · BARBARA J KRESSEL · MATTHEW O KRESSEL · MARIAN B KRETSCHMER

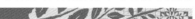

France (Jean-Michel Henry, Robert Leroux, and Eric Srecki) took the bronze with a 45-42 victory over Germany.

Armed with the individual épée gold and silver medalists, France easily captured the women's team epée gold medal in the debut of this event at the Olympic Games. Sophie Moresee-Pichot teamed with Valerie Barlois and Laura Flessel to defeat Italy (Laura Chiesa, Elisa Uga, and Margherita Zalaffi) 45-33 in the final. In the battle for the bronze, the Russian Federation (Karina Aznavuryan, Yuliya Garayeva, and Mariya Mazina) upset no. 1 seed Hungary by one point, 45-44.

Individual Sabre. Although no. 1 seed Grigoriy Kiriyenko of the Russian Federation was eliminated by an upset loss in the preliminaries, the men's individual sabre gold-medal match was still an all–Russian Federation showdown. No. 2 seed Stanislav Pozdnyakov took the gold 15-12, while his teammate, no. 5 seed Sergey Sharikov, won the silver. France's Damien Touya upset no. 3 seed József Navarrete of Hungary 15-7 to earn the bronze.

Team Sabre. On a quest for satisfaction after losing gold to the Russians four years earlier, Hungary's efforts again came up silver in Atlanta. Kiriyenko teamed with individual gold

medalist Pozdnyakov and silver medalist Sharikov to give the Russian Federation a 45-25 gold-medal victory over Hungary (Csaba Köves, József Navarrete, and Bence Szabó). In the bronze-medal match, Italy (Raffaello Caserta, Luigi Tarantino, and Tonhi Terenzi) defeated Poland 45-37.

CONCLUSION

Known as the "chess game" of Olympic sports, fencing continued its proud tradition of strat-

egy and athleticism in Atlanta. Tradition also applied to the medal count, as long-time fencing superpowers the Russian Federation (four golds, two silvers, and one bronze), Italy (three golds, two silvers, and two bronzes), France (two golds, two silvers, and three bronzes), and Hungary (one silver and two bronzes) dominated the medal stand. Meanwhile, a newly enhanced competition environment and record attendance totaling more than 24,000 kept this noble contest exciting.

left: The Russian Federation's Stanislav Pozdnyakov defeats Spain's Fernando Medina en route to winning the gold in the men's individual sabre.

top right: Italy's men's epée team of Sandro Cuomo, Angelo Mazzoni, and Maurizio Randazzo wave to the audience after winning the gold.

bottom right: France's Laura Flessel and Italy's Margherita Zalaffi face off in the women's team epée final.

Atlanta 1996.

• BRIAN W KREUTTER • JULIAN A KREVERE • CHRISTINE A KREY • WALTER J KRICKICH • CAROL A KRIDER • GEORGIA KRIDER • KERR J KRIDER • CARRIE L KRIEG • CHRISTINE N KRIEG • JONATHAN P KRIEG • DOLORES J KRIEGER • PHERIS G KRIEGER • SHEILA H KRIESEL • BEVERLY J KRIEWALD • ANDREW C KRIKELAS • SUSAN H KRILL • DEBORAH B KRILLA • MARK E KRISE • GLORIA J KRISEL • ARUN KRISHNAMOORTHY • KAYLA L KRISS • LOFTUR G KRISTJANSSON • NATHANIEL KRISTY • MARIE T KRIZ • SHARON Y KRIZ • LADISLAN KRNAC • PATRICIA J KROC • DANA H KROEGER • KACEY J KROEGER •

FOOTBALL

Venues Used:
Florida Citrus Bowl

Legion Field

Orange Bowl

Robert F. Kennedy
Memorial Stadium

Sanford Stadium

Days of Competition: 12

Medals Awarded: 6
Gold 2
Silver 2
Bronze 2

Number of Nations: 21

Number of Officials: 179

Officiating Federation:
International Association
Football Federation (FIFA)

THE CENTENNIAL OLYMPIC Games football tournament ushered in a new era as women competed for the first time in Olympic play. There were 416 athletes (288 men and 128 women) representing 21 nations taking part in the football competition. During the 12 days of tournament play, 20 July–3 August with three rest days, more than 1.2 million fans jammed five venues, making football the highest-attended sport during the 1996 Games.

VENUES

Five different venues hosted football competition. Preliminary rounds took place at the Florida Citrus Bowl in Orlando, Florida, with a seating capacity of 65,000 and located 321 mi (517 km) from Atlanta; Legion Field in Birmingham, Alabama, with a seating capacity of 81,700 and located 148 mi (238 km) from Atlanta; the Orange Bowl in Miami, Florida, with a seating capacity of 72,700 and located 668 mi (1,075 km) from Atlanta; and Robert F. Kennedy (RFK) Memorial Stadium in Washington, DC, with a seating capacity of 56,500 and located 640 mi (1,030 km) from Atlanta. The Orange Bowl and Legion Field also hosted the men's quarterfinals. All four outlying venues

Atlanta 1996

Birmingham

Washington D.C.

South Florida

Orlando

celebrated with Opening Ceremonies, and each had its own Village to house the athletes.

The fifth venue was the University of Georgia's Sanford Stadium in Athens, Georgia, with a seating capacity of 86,100 and located 65 mi (105 km) from Atlanta. Sanford Stadium hosted all the semifinals and finals of the competition.

M ELLEN KROEGER • TERRY J KROGEN • JOSEPHINE S KROGER • RHAWN KROGH • KELLY E KROHN • DOUGLAS L KROHN ATC • MARK D KROMREI • TAMMY L KROMREI • MARILYN R KRONE • CELESTE M KRONEN • ERICA A KRONEN • REGINA M KRONEN • RONALD C KRONEN • DEBRA L KRONENBITTER • GARY L KRONICK • TOBY KRONICK • YVONNE M KRONLAGE • BARBARA K KROPF • DAWN M KROPF • FRANK J KROPF • HENRY R KROPINSKI • AMANDA KRUEGER • ERIC C KRUEGER • ERIKA M KRUEGER • JOEL S KRUEGER • LEROY A KRUEGER • MARY M KRUEGER • MICHAEL D KRUEGER • JACK N KRUG •

COMPETITION

In the preliminaries of both the men's and women's tournaments, teams competed in a round-robin. The 16 men's teams were divided into four groups of four, with the top two teams from each group advancing to the single-elimination quarterfinals. The eight teams in the women's tournament were divided into two groups of four, with the top two teams in each group advancing to the semifinals.

In the preliminaries, teams were awarded three points for each win and one point for each tie. At the end of the round-robin, ties in points were resolved by calculating the difference between the number of goals scored and the number of goals allowed, with the team with the greater differential advancing. If still tied, the team with the greater number of goals scored received the higher ranking. In the event of a tie at the end of regulation play in the men's quarterfinals and the men's and women's semifinals and medal rounds, teams played up to two sudden-death extra time periods. The first team to score won. If the score remained tied, a penalty-kick shoot-out decided the winner.

Men

On the strength of just one victory and two ties each, Argentina and Portugal advanced to the quarterfinals out of the Group A field that also included Tunisia and the United States. Portugal's lone victory over Tunisia was the country's first win in 68 years, while Argentina defeated the US 3-1 before an opening-day crowd of 83,110 at Legion Field.

In Group B, France and Spain advanced by defeating both Australia and Saudi Arabia and battling to a 1-1 tie in head-to-head competition. All four teams in Group C—Ghana, Italy, Korea, and Mexico—managed just one win each. Mexico, however, claimed the top spot with one win and two ties. Both Ghana and

Korea finished with records of one win, one loss, and one tie; however, despite Korea's 1-0 victory over Ghana in the head-to-head meeting, Ghana advanced because of its higher goal differential.

Action in Group D—Brazil, Hungary, Japan, and Nigeria—featured one of the tournament's biggest upsets: Japan's 1-0 victory over medal favorite Brazil. Brazil, Japan, and Nigeria all finished with identical 3-1 records, but Brazil and Nigeria won the quarterfinal berths based on goal differentials.

Ghana's Christian Sabah and Mexico's Manuel Sol attempt to gain control of the ball in preliminary action at RFK Memorial Stadium.

facing page: Coordinating Look of the Games banners decorated the corrals at each stadium.

JENNIFER J KRUG • JOYCE KRUG • MATTHEW J KRUG • PAMELA L KRUG • JEFFREY K KRUGER • SANDRA J KRUGER • DAVID A KRUKE • NEIL D KRULL • DEBBRA D KRULL • STEPHEN P KRUM • PAULA KRUMBACH • BELINDA J KRUPCALE • JOHN W KRUPILIS • MARILYN D KRUPILIS • JACK KRUPNICK MD • KARLA E KRUSE • NORMAN C KRUSE • ROGER J KRUSE MD • AMY M KRUSZKA • STACEY L KRUZIC • AMY E KRYGIER • CHARLOTTE L KRYGIER • JANE E KRYGIER • THOMAS J KSIONZYK • IVY A KU • KAI MAN KUAN • JOHN J KUBIS • MARY ELLEN KUBIS • DEBRA A KUBLY • MASAKO KUBOTA • ROBBIE G KUCHAR • ROBERT A KUCHAR

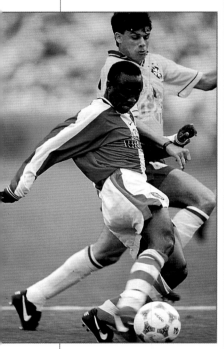

left: Forward Tijani Babangida of Nigeria advances the ball past defender Ronaldo Guiaro of Brazil in Nigeria's stunning semifinal victory.

right: Argentina's Matias Jesus Almeyda makes a play for the ball in Argentina's semifinal win over Portugal.

In the quarterfinals, Argentina knocked out Spain 4-0, Portugal advanced past France 2-1, Nigeria blanked Mexico 2-0, and Brazil was a 4-2 winner over Ghana.

Before a semifinal crowd of 78,212 at Sanford Stadium, Argentina overcame a stubborn Portugal defense as Hernán Jorge Crespo scored twice within a seven-minute span in the second half to advance Argentina to the gold-medal match with a 2-0 win. These same teams had fought to a 1-1 tie in the preliminary round.

Playing a day later before 78,587 fans, Nigeria rallied from a 3-1 second-half deficit to stun Brazil 4-3 in the other semifinal match. Nigeria's team captain Nwankwo Kanu celebrated his 20th birthday a day early by scoring the game's final two goals within five minutes.

The game-winning goal came later, in the 94th minute of play.

In the thrilling final match, Nigeria defeated Argentina 3-2 to become the first African nation to win a gold medal in football. With the score tied at 1-1, Crespo scored on a penalty kick five minutes into the second half to give Argentina the lead. The goal also gave Crespo the tournament scoring title with 21 points (six goals and three assists). Nigeria's Daniel Amokachi made the score 2-2 in the 74th minute of play, setting the stage for his teammate Emmanuel Amunike to score the winning goal. With one minute remaining in regulation play, Argentina attempted an offside trap on a free kick from the edge of the penalty area, but

• KEVIN KUCKEL • LOUISE A KUDRO • THOMAS G KUDRO • SARAH E KUEHL • TIMOTHY J KUEHLMAN • GAIL L KUEHN • WENDY F KUEHN • CHERYL M KUEHNE • DIANNE M KUEHNEMUND • CHRISTINA KUEHNLE • GARY M KUFAHL • LAURA G KUFFREY • LARRY T KUGLAR • LYNN H KUGLAR • MARK P KUGLITSCH • DOROTHY M KUHLMAN • ALANNA V KUHN • ANDREW L KUHN • JOHN KUHN • KAREN S KUHN • KATHRYN E KUHN • KATHY J KUHN • KORNELIA KUHN • TAMARA L KUHN • DAVID L KUHN PT • RICHARD S KUHNE • HARRIET A KUHR • PAVAN KUKREJA • DONNA J KULA • MEREDITH L KULA • GILBERT B KULERS •

Amunike beat the trap and struck a volley into the lower-right corner of the net. While Argentina protested in vain for an offside call on the play, the Nigerian "Super Eagles" celebrated their historic victory.

The gold-medal-winning Nigerian team had the following members: Daniel Amokachi, Emmanuel Amunike, Tijani Babangida, Celestine Babayaro, Emmanuel Babayaro, Joseph Dosu, Teslim Fatusi, Victor Ikpeba, Nwankwo Kanu, Garba Lawal, Abiodon Obafemi, Mobi Obaraku, Kingsley Obiekwu, Augustine Okocha, Sunday

Sensini, Diego Pablo Simeone, and Javier Adelmar Zanetti.

In the bronze-medal match, the crowd witnessed a hat trick (three goals scored in one game by a single player) by Brazil's forward José Roberto Gama Oliveira in Brazil's decisive 5-0 victory over Portugal. The Brazilian team members were Flávio da Conceição, José Marcelo Ferreira, Rivaldo Victor Borba Ferreira, Oswaldo Giroldo Junior, Luiz Carlos Goulart, Ronaldo Guiaro, Danrlei de Deus Hinterhloz, Ronaldo Luiz Nazario Lima, Alexandre da Silva Mariano,

top: Players from the Argentinian and Nigerian teams converge on the ball in the men's gold-medal game.

bottom: Sweden's Annika Nessvold controls the ball in front of the People's Republic of China's Qingmei Sun in China's preliminary-round win.

Oliseh, Wilson Oruma, Okechukwu Uche, and Taribo West.

The members of the Argentinian team were Matias Jesus Almeyda, Roberto Fabián Ayala, Christian Gustavo Bassedas, Carlos Gustavo Bossio, Pablo Oscar Cavallero, José Antonio Chamot, Hernán Jorge Crespo, Marcelo Alejandro Delgado, Marcelo Daniel Gallardo, Claudio Javier López, Gustavo Adrián López, Hugo Alberto Morales, Arnaldo Ariel Ortega, Pablo Ariel Paz, Hector Mauricio Pineda, Roberto Nestor

TIMOTHY J. KULKA • ASHOK B KULKARNI • SANDY M KULKIN • CHERYL P KULL • CLAYTON J KULL • FREDERICK J KULL • MARGARET A KULLMAN • JANE KULLMANN • JUSTIN W KULPA • BRIAN S KULT • MARINA K KULUBERIS • ANIL KUMAR • LAKSHMI KUMAR • MUTHU KUMAR • PRASAD KUMAR • RAJIV KUMAR • USHA KUMAR • RANIL KUMARA • CHARU KUMARHIA • SHINJA/JENNY MOON KUME • IRENE A KUMMERER • KEVIN L KUMMERER • MARSHA KUMMINS • RYAN J KUMMINS • LINDA M KUNDELL • ANTO I KUNDUKULAM • MARKUS KUNERT • JUDY KUNIANSKY • KILHAK L KUNIMOTO • REBECCA L KUNIMOTO •

José Elias Moedim Junior, André Luiz Moreira, José Roberto Gama Oliveira, Sávio Bortolini Pimentel, Aldair Nascimento Santos, Narciso dos Santos, Nelson de Jesus Silva, Roberto Carlos Silva, and Marcelo José de Souza.

Women

In the preliminaries of the women's tournament, the People's Republic of China and the United States advanced to the semifinals out of Group E with two wins and one tie each. Both teams defeated Sweden and Denmark before

left: **The People's Republic of China's Ailing Liu and US forward Shannon MacMillan vie for the ball.**

right: **Brazil's Miraildes Maciel Mota and Marianne Pettersen of Norway chase down the ball in Norway's bronze-medal victory.**

meeting one another in a scoreless head-to-head draw.

Defending World Champion Norway secured the top spot in Group F with two wins and one tie. Brazil, which finished preliminary play with one win and two ties, earned the other berth in the semifinals by finishing ahead of Germany and Japan.

Brazil was in position to upset the favored People's Republic of China in the semifinals, but Haiying Wei scored twice in the final seven minutes to propel the Chinese into the women's final with a 3-2 victory. Playing before 64,196 ecstatic fans in the other semifinal match, the US posted a dramatic 2-1 win over Norway in sudden-death overtime. Norway's Linda Medalen—who won the women's tournament scoring title with 15 points (four goals and three assists)—put her team in front at the 18-minute mark by scoring the game's first goal. In the 76th minute of play, Michelle Akers, the all-time leading scorer for the US women, tied the game 1-1 on a penalty kick. The teams remained deadlocked until the 100th minute of play, when the US scored the winning goal off the foot of Shannon MacMillan.

Ironically, both medal-round pairings were rematches between teams that had tied each other in head-to-head confrontations in the preliminaries. In the battle of the two unbeaten teams, the United States broke a scoreless tie from its earlier encounter with the People's

EIJI KUNISAWA • RINAKO KUNISAWA • KARL H KUNISCH • LOUISE R KUNISCH • MARY L KUNKA • MICHAEL J KUNKA • KARISSA KUNKEL • WENDY R KUNKEL • JAMES A KUNTZ • RYAN KUNTZ • AYDIN A KUNUTKU • GLENDA H KUNZ • JULIANA KUNZE • KLONIE M KUNZEL • ROBERT H KUNZLER • CHENGFANG KUO • CHUNG-CHENG KUO • JAMES A KUO • JOHN C KUO • SUPRIA B KUPPUSWAMY • DAVID M KUPSKY • STEPHEN K KUPSOV • BARBARA A KURDELMEIER • DONNA J KURDELMEIER • GARY R KURDELMEIER • BARBARA A KURDZIEL • ROBERT E KURDZIEL • TOMOKO KURIHARA • HIROKO KURIMOTO • MASAO KURIMOTO •

Republic of China and posted a 2-1 win to capture the first-ever Olympic gold medal in women's football. In front of a Sanford Stadium crowd of 76,481 fans—the largest crowd ever to attend a women's football match—MacMillan put the Americans ahead by scoring in the 19th minute after a scramble in front of China's goal. Later, the People's Republic of China tied the score 1-1 on Wen Sun's goal, only the third given up by US goalkeeper Briana Scurry in the five-game tournament. In the second half, US forward Tiffeny Milbrett received a pass from Joy Fawcett and deposited the ball in China's goal, electrifying the crowd with what turned out to be the game-winning shot.

The members of the US team were Michelle Akers, Brandi Chastain, Joy Fawcett, Julie Foudy, Carin Gabarra, Mia Hamm, Mary Harvey, Kristine Lilly, Shannon MacMillan, Tiffeny Milbrett, Carla Overbeck, Cindy Parlow, Tiffany Roberts, Briana Scurry, Tisha Venturini, and Staci Wilson.

The silver-medal-winning People's Republic of China team consisted of Yufeng Chen, Yunjie Fan, Hong Gao, Ailing Liu, Ying Liu, Guihong Shi, Qingxia Shui, Qingmei Sun, Wen Sun, Liping Wang, Haiying Wei, Lirong Wen, Huilin Xie, Hongqi Yu, Lihong Zhao, and Honglian Zhong.

On the strength of two first-half goals from midfielder Ann Kristin Aarønes, Norway posted a 2-0 victory over Brazil to claim the bronze medal.

The members of the Norwegian team were Ann Kristin Aarønes, Agnete Carlsen, Gro Espeseth, Tone Günn Frustol, Tone Haugen, Linda Medalen, Merete Myklebüst, Bente Nordby, Anne Nymark Andersen, Nina Nymark Andersen, Marianne Pettersen, Hege Riise, Brit Sandaune, Reidun Seth, Tina Svensson, and Trine Tangeraas.

CONCLUSION

Historical references are common when referring to the Olympic Games, but few can match those made by the champions of the Centennial Olympic Games football competition. In a sport that has been dominated by the Europeans, Nigeria's gold-medal victory in the men's tournament not only welcomed a new power to the football stage, but also introduced a new attack style of play.

Meanwhile, the women's gold medalists did more than just open up another sport for women. The US team's gold-medal run made another form of "football" more familiar to the host country; and this global version of football was a success, nearly tripling the attendance figures from the Barcelona Games and averaging more than 40,000 spirited fans each game. Football at the 1996 Games was enjoyable for fans and players alike.

US forward Mia Hamm takes control of the ball in the gold-medal final.

Atlanta 1996.

RICHARD KURIN • GINGER C KURMANN • AUDREY J KUROWSKY • DIANE B KURTZ • GLENN M KURTZ • RAYMOND M KURYLA • ROSEANN L KURYLA • KAREN A KURZ • JOSEPH T KUSCHELL PHARM D • LINDA D KUSHNIR • GLORIA K KUSMIK • JOSEPH N KUSMIK • MARY S KUSMIREK • ANITA V KUSNOOR • KOURTNEY KUSS • PATRICIA R KUSS • ADAM JONATHON KUTAS • ALEXANDER KUTIKOV • STEPHEN R KUTNER • STEPHEN S KUTNER • PADDY H KUTZ • PRITI KUVADIA • KAZUYA KUWATA • GARY R KUZARA • DANIEL J KUZIO • HEE-SOO KWAK • ROBERT J KWAK • YEUN-HEE KWAK • RONALD KWAN • JAMES L KWATER

GYMNASTICS

Gymnastics—Artistic

Venue Used:
Georgia Dome

Days of Competition: 8

Medals Awarded: 45
Gold 14
Silver 16
Bronze 15

Number of Nations: 36

Number of Officials: 70

Officiating Federation:
International Gymnastics
Federation (FIG)

TWO DISCIPLINES—artistic and rhythmic—comprised the gymnastics competition of the Atlanta Games. The most striking difference between the two disciplines concerns the equipment used by the athletes during the events. Artistic gymnastics traditionally utilizes a hand apparatus, while rhythmic gymnastics is based on dance and is performed using other types of equipment, including balls, hoops, and ribbons. The two disciplines of gymnastics drew a combined total of more than 518,000 fans over the total 12 days of Olympic competition.

ARTISTIC

During the eight days of artistic gymnastics competition (20–25 and 28–29 July), 218 athletes (113 men and 105 women) representing 36 nations displayed their power, strength, agility, and grace. More than 470,000 tickets were sold to artistic gymnastics events.

VENUE

The artistic gymnastics competition was held in the largest gymnastics venue ever: the 69,000-seat, 27-story Georgia Dome, the largest cable-supported stadium in the world. The Georgia Dome was located within the Olympic Ring, approximately 1.9 mi (3 km) from the Atlanta Olympic Village. For the Centennial Olympic Games, a soundproof curtain separated the space into two 34,500-seat sections. One section housed the basketball competition, while the other section hosted the men's handball finals and the artistic gymnastics events. Carpeting, banners, and design motifs exhibiting the Look of the Games dressed the field of play and surrounding arena areas. The competition field of play included the gymnastics podiums and production table, which were located within a corral (fence) measuring 202 x 136 ft (61.6 x 41.5 m). Each podium was 37 in (94 cm) high and staged an apparatus for the men's and women's artistic gymnastics competition.

COMPETITION

Fourteen medals were awarded in three event categories for both men and women: team, individual all-around, and apparatus finals. Medals were awarded for individual performances in the apparatus finals in the following events for men: floor exercise, pommel horse, rings, vault, parallel bars, and horizontal bar; and for women: vault, uneven bars, balance beam, and floor exercise. In addition, for the first time in Olympic history, ticketed sessions for artistic gymnastics included podium training, which occurred prior to the start of the Games, and the Gala Exhibition (30 July).

KATHRYN M KWECH • ROBERT W KWECH • SUSANNA L KWITNY • JEFFFEY C KWOK • PETER C KWOK • CARY S KWON • DAVID U KWON • DO YOON KWON • GRACY M KWON • HAE-WON KWON • HYON C KWON • JUNG HYUN KWON • MIKE C KWON • OH-IL KWON • FRANCIS A KWONG • KATHARINE P KYANNE • KELLY KYBURZ • STANLEY KYEYUNE • CAROLYN S KYLE • EMILY K KYLE • JAMES M KYLE • JEROME S KYLE • KEVIN R KYLE • LARRYETTE M KYLE • WILLIAM KYLES • BAERBEL KYPER • ALEXANDER V KYRIAS • CHRISTIANA S KYRILLOU • BRIAN KYZER • JOY A KYZER • JOHN A LA ARGO • CURTEIS J LA BOY •

For both the men's and women's competitions, 12 teams took part in compulsory and optional rounds (the Atlanta Games were the last in which compulsories were judged, ending the mandatory routine). The top 36 gymnasts from the team competition squared off for the individual all-around title, with the top eight scorers in each event qualifying for the individual apparatus finals. Six judges scored each apparatus while taking into consideration the degree of difficulty of a gymnast's program.

For each individual routine, gymnasts began with a base score (9.000 for men, 9.400 for women) and earned bonuses for exceptional performances (a possible 1.000 bonus for men, a possible .400 bonus for women). The highest and lowest of the six scores were discarded, and the rest were averaged. Although six gymnasts from each team took part in the team competition, only the scores of the top five athletes on each apparatus were factored.

Team. In the men's team competition, Alexei Nemov dominated the individual standings in leading a strong team from the Russian Federation (Sergei Charkov, Nikolay Krukov, Alexei Nemov, Eugeni Podgorni, Dmitriy Trush, Dmitri Vasilenko, and Alexei Voropaev) to win the gold. The Russian Federation (576.778) finished more than one point ahead of the silver medalist, the People's Republic of China (Bin Fan, Hongbin Fan, Huadong Huang, Liping Huang, Xiaoshuang Li, Jian Shen, and Jinjing Zhang) with 575.539, and more than five points ahead of bronze medalist Ukraine (Igor Korobchinski, Oleg Kosiak, Grigory Misutin, Vladimir Shamenko, Rustam Sharipov, Alexandre Svetlichnyi, and Yuri Yermakov) with 571.541.

In what will remain as one of the most enduring images of the Atlanta Games, the United States captured its first-ever gold in the artistic gymnastics women's team event. With the team title on the line, the US's Kerri Strug, who was hobbled by two torn ligaments in her ankle, gallantly stuck the landing in her final vault to secure the US team's 389.225 winning score over the Russian Federation (388.404) and Romania (388.246).

The US, which was in second place behind the Russian Federation after the compulsories, took the lead in the optionals. The US's Dominique Dawes successfully completed a reverse Hecht and a Hindorff on the uneven parallel bars, posting a team-best 9.850. The next stop was the balance beam, where the

left: **Huilan Mo competes for the People's Republic of China on the balance beam during the women's team competition.**

top right: **Eugeni Podgorni performs on the parallel bars to help the Russian Federation win the gold in the men's team competition.**

bottom right: **Armenia's Norayr Sargysian approaches the vault in the men's team compulsories.**

CAROL L LA CHAPELLE • DIANE M LA CHARITE • WINKIE LA FORCE • JULIO A LA FROSSIA • JAMIE LA JOIE • MARIA I LA MONT • LAURIE M LA PORTE • MAGUY LA ROCHELLE • DIANE F LA ROSS • DANIEL J LAAK • ANTHONY J LABADIA • MAURA C LABARRE • CATHY A LABATE • CHRISTINA E LABELL • KARREN E LABENNE • FLORENCE A LABENSKI • THOMAS J LABISCH ATC • GLENN E LABODA • JEAN R LABOSSIERE • DOMINGO A LABOY • EDWARD A LABRECK • VIRGINIA L LABRECK • WILLIAM P LABRUNA JR ATC • BRIAN LABUDDE • NOLA K LABUDDE • JANEEN LACASSE • KAREN B LACASSE • MICHELE M. LACEN •

US's Shannon Miller scored a team-high 9.862. Dominique Moceanu ended a 9.837 floor exercise routine with a flawless two and one-half twisting salto, and the US led the Russian Federation by nearly one full point. Each team, however, was able to drop its lowest score on each apparatus, and as a result, the Russian Federation was still mathematically within striking distance.

With the stage set, Strug stepped up to the vault as the last US athlete. "She had the gold, the silver, the bronze in her hands," coach Bela Karolyi said afterward. Landing awkwardly on her first vault and twisting her left ankle, Strug hobbled tenuously back to the top of the runway. With a crowd of 32,040 anxiously watching, she turned and sprinted full-speed into her second vault: a perfect Yurchenko one and one-half twist in the layout position, landing on both feet. As she lifted the injured ankle off the ground, her teeth were clenched in agony as the audience erupted into roaring cheers. Strug's score of 9.712 was enough to give the US the gold.

Later, with her foot in a temporary splint and tears streaming down her face, Strug received her gold medal with the team. She was subsequently withdrawn from the individual competition because of the injury.

The US team members were Amanda Borden, Amy Chow, Dominique Dawes, Shannon Miller, Dominique Moceanu, Jaycie Phelps, and Kerri Strug.

The Russian Federation, which took the silver, had the following team members: Svetlana Chorkina, Elena Dolgopolova, Rozalia Galiyeva, Elena Grosheva, Dina Kochetkova, Eugenia Kuznetsova, and Oksana Liapina.

The bronze-medal-winning Romanian team was comprised of Simona Amanar, Gina Gogean, Ionela Loaies, Alexandra Marinescu, Lavinia Milosovici, and Mirela Tugurlan.

Individual All-Around. World Champion Xiaoshuang Li became the People's Republic of China's first men's gymnastics individual all-

top left: The US women's team gold medalists salute a supportive crowd.

bottom left: Men's individual all-around gold medalist Xiaoshuang Li of the People's Republic of China displays his strength during his horizontal bar routine.

right: Ukraine's Lilia Podkopayeva leaps to women's all-around gold with her near-flawless floor exercise routine.

CURTIS E LACEY • DENISE I LACEY • JOANNE LACH • MILISSA A LACHAUSSEE • BENJAMIN G LACHER • MICHAEL W LACHER • ALYSON M LACHMANW • JOEL B LACKEY MARK S LACKEY • CHRISTINE A LACKOWSKI • MARRIETTA LACLAIR • PAULETTE M LACOMBE • BRANDON J LACOV • CRAIG B LACOV • JUSTIN S LACOV • LAURIE T LACOV • COURTNEY J LACROIX • CRAIG LACROSS • SHARON A LACRUISE • ALLAN R LACY • CAROL J LACY • CLARENCE A LACY • JAMES W LACY • SHELBY J LACY • VIRGINIA LACY • ARCHIE E LADD • MARTHA W LADD • VYONNE S LADD • IRV LADDIN • GARY N LADEN • MONA A LADHA •

Nemov, who won top scores on the pommel horse (9.800), parallel bars (9.762), and horizontal bar (9.800), led after the first two rotations and then again after the fifth. On his sixth and final rotation, however, the 20 year old missed a move in the middle of his floor exercise routine and subsequently scored a 9.700 to slip narrowly into the silver-medal slot in what was the third-closest Olympic all-around contest ever. At the end of competition, Li captured the gold with 58.423, while Nemov received the silver with 58.374. Belarus's Vitaly Scherbo, winner of six gold medals at the Barcelona Games, garnered the bronze (58.197).

In the women's individual all-around competition, World Champion Lilia Podkopayeva extended her gymnastics reign when she won Olympic gold. The 17-year-old gymnast from Ukraine soared from third to first place with a near-flawless 9.887 floor exercise. The routine included a risky double flip with a half-twist. In capturing the gold, Podkopayeva became the first gymnast to hold concurrent world and Olympic titles since 1972, when the Soviet Union's Lyudmilla Turischeva accomplished this feat. Romania's Gina Gogean took the silver, finishing 0.150 behind Podkopayeva's winning total of 39.225 with 39.075. Romania's Simona Amanar and 1992 bronze medalist Lavinia Milosovici tied for third (39.067). Huilan Mo of the People's Republic of China shared the lead going into the last rotation, but finished in fifth place. As a result, the Chinese women, ranked no. 2 in the world, were shut out in both the women's team and all-around competitions.

Apparatus Finals. Despite being edged out for the gold in the men's individual all-around, Alexei Nemov won the most medals of the competition: six, which included four medals

around Olympic winner, earning the gold with a remarkably consistent performance, placing no lower than seventh on any apparatus among the 35 finalists. He was first on the vault (9.812), second on both the rings (9.775) and horizontal bar (9.787), and third on the floor exercise (9.687). After receiving his score on the horizontal bar to finish a mere 0.049 ahead of the Russian Federation's Alexei Nemov, Li jumped into the arms of his coach in celebration of his golden moment.

left: **Romania's Simona Amanar performs on the balance beam during the compulsories.**

right: **The Russian Federation's Alexei Nemov vaults to gold in the men's apparatus finals.**

in the individual apparatus events. In addition to team gold and all-around silver, Nemov captured the gold in the vault with a score of 9.787 and earned bronze medals in the floor exercise, pommel horse, and horizontal bar. Placing behind Nemov in the vault were Korea's Hong-Chul Yeo (9.756) and Belarus's Vitaly Scherbo (9.724).

Four-time world champion Yuri Chechi of Italy scored a 9.887 in the rings event to achieve his goal of winning an Olympic title. The silver was split between Romania's Dan

Burinca and Hungary's Szilveszter Csollány, who each finished with a mark of 9.812.

Germany's Andreas Wecker took top honors on the horizontal bar (9.850), followed by silver medalist Krasimir Dounev (9.825) of Bulgaria and a trio of bronze medalists at 9.800: the People's Republic of China's Bin Fan, Nemov, and Scherbo.

On the parallel bars, Ukraine's Rustam Sharipov won gold with a score of 9.837. Placing behind Sharipov were silver medalist Jair Lynch of the US (9.825) and bronze medalist Scherbo (9.800).

It was a long, 13-year odyssey for Switzerland's Donghua Li, the Chinese-born Swiss who lost his spleen and kidney in training, tore both Achilles tendons in competition, and endured a five-year wait to compete for his adopted country. Li capped his painful journey with a dazzling pommel horse routine that earned him a gold-medal victory with a score of 9.875, 0.050 over the silver medalist, Romania's Marius Urzica (9.825). "I never gave up despite all of my injuries," said Li. "This is an incredible accomplishment for me." The Russian Federation's Nemov secured the bronze (9.787).

top left: World Champion Andreas Wecker of Germany soars to gold in the men's horizontal bar final.

bottom left: Donghua Li became the first Swiss gymnastics champion in 40 years when he won the gold in the men's pommel horse final.

right: Yuri Chechi of Italy has a hold on gold in the men's rings exercise.

In the floor exercise routine, Ioannis Melissanidis won Greece's first Olympic gymnastics medal in 90 years (since the 1906 rope-climbing competition). His gold-medal score of 9.850 was also his highest score in any major competition. Placing behind Melissanidis were Switzerland's Li (9.837) and the Russian Federation's Nemov (9.800).

All the favorites came through in the individual apparatus finals of the women's gymnastics competition. Lilia Podkopayeva received a score of 9.900 (out of a possible 10.000) from

four of the six judges and won the floor exercise routine. In the process of capturing her second gold medal of the Games, Podkopayeva became the first gymnast since Nadia Comaneci in 1976 to follow up an all-around gold medal with a gold medal in an individual apparatus event. Placing behind Ukraine's Podkopayeva (9.887) were silver medalist Simona Amanar of Romania (9.850) and bronze medalist Dominique Dawes of the US (9.837).

Prior to the floor exercise final, Romania's Amanar won the women's vault gold medal with a score of 9.825, finishing ahead of the People's Republic of China's Huilan Mo (9.768) and Romania's Gina Gogean (9.750).

Two-time world champion Svetlana Chorkina of the Russian Federation captured the women's uneven bars crown with a score of 9.850, edging co–silver medalists the People's

Republic of China's Wenjing Bi (9.837) and the US's Amy Chow (9.837).

With her first-place finish on the balance beam, the US's Shannon Miller earned her second gold in Atlanta, and in the process became the second all-time leading women's medal winner (with seven) in US Olympic history. The five-time medalist at the Barcelona Games has a total of two gold, two silver, and three bronze medals in two Olympic Games. Placing behind Miller (9.862) on the balance beam were Podkopayeva (9.825) and Gogean (9.787).

CONCLUSION

With the tension of eight days of competition behind them, the athletes joined together for a lighter affair—the Olympic Games' first artistic gymnastics Gala Exhibition. In this newest gymnastics event, every medal winner (individual and team) performed various routines, some of which were dramatic while others were comedic, in celebration of the sport. With yet another capacity crowd of more than 33,000, the exhibition provided a proper ending to what will be remembered as one of the greatest artistic gymnastics competitions in the history of the sport.

left: The US's Shannon Miller won her seventh Olympic medal when she earned the gold on the women's balance beam.

top right: Suspended in midair, the People's Republic of China's Wenjing Bi performs her silver-medal routine on the uneven bars.

bottom right: The Georgia Dome was decorated with Look of the Games banners for the artistic gymnastics competition.

JUDITH LAMARSH • JUDITH A LAMAS • THOMAS J LAMAS • ROSEANN LAMATTINA • ALISON H LAMAY • DAVID J LAMAY • BRENDA J LAMB • CLARK LAMB • ELIZABETH R LAMB • MICHAEL M LAMB • MILFORD C LAMB • NANCY R LAMB • RICHARD B LAMB • RICK M LAMB • ROSANNA Z LAMB • SHARON LAMB • RONALD J LAMBE • JOYE S LAMBERSON • KEITH A LAMBERSON • BRIAN LAMBERT • DELOIS A LAMBERT • EDDIE E LAMBERT • FLORA LAMBERT • GERARD W LAMBERT • JACK LAMBERT • JAY LAMBERT • KEELEY M LAMBERT • LATIECE M LAMBERT • LAUREN A LAMBERT • LYDIA F LAMBERT • LYNN E LAMBERT •

Gymnastics—Rhythmic

Venue Used:
**University of Georgia
Coliseum**

Days of Competition: **4**

Medals Awarded: **6**
Gold 2
Silver 2
Bronze 2

Number of Nations: **22**

Number of Officials: **43**

Officiating Federation:
**International Gymnastics
Federation (FIG)**

RHYTHMIC

Rhythmic gymnastics gained medal status in 1984 with the individual competition. The team competition, however, made its debut as an Olympic event in Atlanta. A total of 90 women representing 22 nations took part in the team and individual all-around competitions, with 37 women participating in the individual all-around events, and 53 women (eight teams of six and one team of five) taking part in the team competition.

VENUE

The 10,000-seat University of Georgia Coliseum, located 65 mi (105 km) northeast of Atlanta in Athens, Georgia, hosted the rhythmic gymnastics competition, which was held 1–4 August 1996. The facility, which also hosted some of the preliminary men's and women's indoor volleyball competition, was normally used by the university's gymnastics and basketball teams and received extensive renovation in preparation for the Games.

MELVENA E LAMBERT • PETER W LAMBERT • RAYMOND C LAMBERT • TIFFANY A LAMBERT • VICTORIA E LAMBERT • LORI P LAMBERTH • BUENA S LAMBETH • ELIZABETH R LAMBLE • GEORGE LAMBOUSIS JR • HEATH J LAMBRIGHT • ANNA V LAMBROS • SCOT J LAMERS • DEB MARIA LAMIA • M G LAMISON • SANDRA K LAMM • JOHN C LAMMERS • PETRA LAMMERS • JANICE H LAMMERT • JOHN H LAMMERT • JOHN S LAMMERT • FRANK H LAMONS • CHRISTOPHE J LAMOR • ANTHONY M LAMORTE • BRIGITTE LAMOUREUX • VERONICA P LAMOY • KAROL L LAMPE • IVAN L LAMPKIN • LIZ LAMPKIN • WILLIAM T LAMPL •

top: Bulgaria claims the silver on the strength of its team hoops routine.

middle: Members of the bronze-medal-winning Russian Federation team perform during the balls and ribbons team final.

bottom: Banners displaying the Look of the Games surrounded the rhythmic gymnastics field of play.

facing page: Spain performs its gold-medal routine in the hoops team final at the University of Georgia Coliseum.

The rhythmic gymnastics field of play was 139 x 76 ft (42 x 23 m) and featured two 43 x 43 ft (13 x 13 m) individual- and team-competition carpet areas. The field of play was surrounded by a corral, which enclosed the two competition carpets and seating for the competition officials.

COMPETITION

Different from the artistic discipline, rhythmic gymnastics is based on dancelike movements and the use of special equipment. During competition at the Centennial Olympic Games, athletes displayed strength, agility, beauty, and grace as they threw, caught, and danced with five types of equipment—balls, clubs, hoops, ribbons, and rope.

In the team competition, five women performed at one time on the gymnastics mat. Teams performed two exercises, one featuring three balls and two ribbons, and the other featuring five hoops. The goal of the gymnasts was complete synchronization. In the individ-

ual all-around competition, gymnasts performed four exercises: one with a ball, one with clubs, one with ribbon, and one with rope.

The base score for the group exercise was 19.20, with a possible bonus of up to .80 for an exceptional performance. In the individual all-around competition, the base score was 9.60, with a possible bonus of up to .40 for an exceptional performance. Deductions by the judges were made for such infractions as dropping equipment or letting it continually touch

TARA R LAMPLEY • ROBERT BRUCE LAMUTT • AMY L LANCASTER • CAREY LANCASTER • DAY LANCASTER • DONNA L LANCASTER • JAMES E LANCASTER • MARC O LANCASTER • MARY S LANCASTER •
MELISSA DAWN LANCASTER • VALARIE H LANCE • LISA B LANCEY • SCOTT L LANCILOTI • BETSY A LAND • BEVERLY C LAND • MARY J LAND • SUSAN H. LAND • LESLIE C LANDEN • GERALD J LANDERS •
JENNIFER R LANDERS • LEE LANDERS • LIBBIE K LANDERS • OLLIE LANDERS • GISELE LANDERS-GRIGGS • DAVID A LANDES • DONNA L LANDES • JO A LANDES • PATRICIA A LANDES • KEN D LANDESS •

the body. Two panels, one for composition and the other for execution, judged each routine.

Team. Spain upset reigning World Champion Bulgaria by .067 to win the first Olympic gold medal in team rhythmic gymnastics. Trailing Bulgaria 39.016 to 38.966 after the preliminaries, Spain performed its final hoop routine to an all-American medley—including "Everything Good in America" and "I've Got Rhythm"—that had the audience clapping along in unison. The Spanish team—Marta Baldo, Nuria Cabanillas, Estela Gimenez,

Spain's victory was greeted by shouts of "Olé! Olé!" from appreciative spectators. "We have oftentimes been very close, but not quite so close, so this time we feel very happy," said Spain's coach Emilia Boniva.

Individual All-Around. The Russian Federation and Ukraine battled for individual honors, as each had two of the top four performers. Trailing teammate Olena Vitrichenko after the preliminaries of the individual all-around competition, Ukraine's Kateryna Serebryanska took the lead in the semifinals and never looked

Ukraine's Kateryna Serebryanska leaps to individual all-around gold with top scores in three routines, including rope.

Lorena Gurendez, Tania Lamarca, and Estibaliz Martinez—then gave an impressive performance with the balls and ribbons, finishing with a total of 38.933.

Bulgaria (Ina Deltcheva, Valentina Kevlian, Maria Koleva, Maya Tabakova, Ivelina Taleva, and Vjara Vatachka) finished with a score of 38.866 to earn the silver. The Russian Federation (Evguenia Botchkareva, Olga Chtyrenko, Irina Dziouba, Angelina Iouchkova, Ioulia Ivanova, and Elena Krivochei) took home the bronze with 38.365.

back. In the finals, she earned perfect scores of 5.00 in composition for each of her four routines and finished with a 39.683 to win the individual all-around gold medal. Serebryanska, 18, earned scores of 9.95—the highest score of the competition—on her rope, ball, and club routines. "I think all the athletes here are queens of this sport," Serebryanska said. "But with the gold medal in hand, maybe I think I'm a little princess."

The Russian Federation's Ianina Batrychinko, who leapt from 13th after the preliminaries to 3rd after the semifinals, won the silver with a score of 39.382. With the exception of one 4.90

TOM A LANDGRAF • CAROL M LANDGREBE • PHILIP A LANDGREBE • MARK A LANDGREEN • ROBERT F LANDIN • LARISSA C LANDINEZ • LEE ANN LANDIS • MARILYN A LANDIS • BILL LANDISS • AVITAL S LANDMAN • KEREN Z LANDMAN • SAUNDRA L LANDON • JENNIFER S LANDRAM • EDWARD D LANDRETH • AUDREY W LANDRUM • DOUGLAS G LANDRUM • HUGH B LANDRUM • JACK M LANDRUM • MCDANIEL W LANDRUM • PATRICIA C LANDRUM • CAROL J LANDRY • EMILY M LANDRY • ROBERT P LANDSTROM • SUSAN O LANDSTROM • PAMELA A LANDT • TIMOTHY L LANDT • TOM LANDY • JANICE L LANE •

in the ribbon routine, Batrychinko received perfect scores of 5.00 in composition for each of her four routines.

Despite being the only gymnast to hit all 12 of her routines in the four-day competition, Ukraine's Vitrichenko took home the bronze with a score of 39.331.

CONCLUSION

The highlight of the rhythmic gymnastics competition was the first-ever Olympic team

left: Balanced on her ball routine, the Russian Federation's Ianina Batrychinko earns individual all-around silver.

right: Ukraine's flexible Olena Vitrichenko ends her clubs routine in the preliminaries of the individual all-around competition.

event, in which Spain received the gold after upsetting two-time defending World Champion Bulgaria. More than 46,000 tickets were sold, and following the event, US coach Rossitza Todorova echoed the sentiments of many rhythmic gymnastics enthusiasts as she said with genuine elation, "We showed everyone a new and great sport."

ARTHUR LANE • CHARLES R LANE • CHARLES S LANE • CHRISTINA E LANE • DANIEL T LANE • ESSIE LEE LANE • GAVIN J LANE • JACI LANE • JAMES E LANE • JANET L LANE • JANET L LANE • JERRY LANE •
JOSEPH M LANE • LYNDA S LANE • MAMYEE LANE • MICHAEL E LANE • MICHELLE M LANE • PEARCE ROCKY A LANE • REMER Y LANE • RICHARD K LANE • ROBERT LANE • SCOTT A LANE • SHERRYL E LANE •
SHIRLEY O LANE • TRACY C LANE • VIRGINIA M LANE • WENDY M LANE • WILLIAM C LANE • JULIETTE LANE-HAILEY • EDDIE B LANE ATC • SUSAN A LANEY • WILLIAM B LANEY • PATTI C M LANFORD •

381

HANDBALL

Venues Used:
Georgia Dome

Georgia World
Congress Center

Days of Competition: 12

Medals Awarded: 6
Gold 2
Silver 2
Bronze 2

Number of Nations: 18

Number of Officials: 64

Officiating Federation:
International Handball
Federation (IHF)

HANDBALL TEAMS representing 18 countries converged in Atlanta to compete in this fast-paced, high-scoring sport that combines elements of football, lacrosse, and basketball. Although handball was first invented in the early 1900s by Danish football players looking for a form of indoor winter exercise, it was modified into an outdoor sport by the Germans. When Olympic competition began at the 1936 Berlin Games, handball was played outdoors with 11 players on each side. In 1972, handball returned to the Games as an indoor sport with seven players per side.

A total of 319 athletes (191 men and 128 women) on 12 men's and 8 women's teams participated in the 12-day tournament (24 July–4 August).

VENUE

The women's competition and the men's preliminaries, semifinals, and placement finals were all held in Hall G of the Georgia World Congress Center, located in the heart of the Olympic Ring, approximately 1.9 mi (3 km) from the Olympic Village. The men's medal matches were held in the Georgia Dome, also located within the Olympic Ring, the largest cable-supported domed stadium in the world. Hall G of the Georgia World Congress Center had seating for approximately 7,300 spectators, while the largest crowd in handball history—estimated at 30,000—witnessed the men's finals at the neighboring Georgia Dome. The fields of play at both venues were 131 x 66 ft (40 x 20 m) courts.

COMPETITION

In Atlanta, the men's competition was divided into two six-team groups. Each group competed in a round-robin format, with the top two teams in each group advancing to the semifinals. For the women's competition, teams were divided into two groups of four, each group competing in a round-robin format with the top two squads in each group advancing to the semifinals.

WILLIAM T LANFORD • HERBERT A LANFORD JR • BOBBY L LANG • CHARLES A LANG • DANIEL J LANG • DARA M LANG • JENNIFER B LANG • JOHN M LANG • KENT LANG • OLIVER S LANG • ROBERT F LANG • SISSIE I LANG • SONJA R LANG • SUSAN B LANG • SUZANNE A LANG • TODD J LANG • FRANK G LANG JR • JOHN P LANGDON • LINDA K LANGDON • ANDREW J LANGE • DEBORAH M LANGE • EMMETT R LANGE • HENNING LANGE • J HARRY LANGE • JAMES A LANGE • SCOTT A LANGE • STEVE E LANGE • MELISSA LANGENBACH • ROSS K LANGENBACH • ARLENE G LANGER • HILKE LANGER • LAWRENCE LANGER •

A change in rules gave players a breather at the Atlanta Games. While teams previously engaged in 30-minute nonstop halves, under the new rules, each team was given a one-minute time-out per half. In preliminary rounds, games could end in a tie, but in the semifinals and finals, one or two 10-minute overtime periods were added when necessary. If a game was still tied after double overtime, a five-shot shoot-out took place, with teams alternating attempts. A game that was still tied after a shoot-out went into a sudden-death shoot-out.

Men

In the final round of the men's preliminaries, Spain and Egypt squared off with a spot in the semifinals at stake. Spain's Alberto Urdiales scored a game high of eight goals, but it was Talant Dujshebaev's fourth goal with two minutes remaining that advanced the Spaniards into the semifinals with a 20-19 win.

Spain, however, lost its semifinal game with Sweden. Pierre Thorsson scored on seven of eight shots in leading the Swedes to a 25-20 win. In the other semifinal, a rematch of the 1995 world championship, which the French won, Croatia defeated the defending bronze medalist 24-20. Patrik Cavar scored eight goals in leading Croatia to the victory, while

France's Stephane Stoecklin scored eight goals in the loss.

In the Georgia Dome, Croatia and Sweden faced each other for the second time during the Games, this time to determine who would win Olympic gold and silver. Competing under its own flag for the first time in Olympic history, Croatia edged Sweden 27-26 for the gold

left: Goalkeeper Mohamed Bakir positions himself to block Brazil's Milton Pelissari's shot in Egypt's preliminary-round win.

top right: Mateo Garralda shoots over defender Klaus-Dieter Petersen of Germany to score one of his four goals in Spain's preliminary-round win.

bottom right: Salvador Esquer goes airborne for a shot past Egypt's Ahmed Ali in Spain's win in the preliminaries.

facing page: Colorful Look of the Games banners decorated the venues used for the Olympic handball competition.

SCOTT G LANGERMAN • VICTORIA E LANGERMAN • GWENDOLYN F LANGFORD • JACKIE S LANGFORD • JANICE G LANGFORD • JOHN S LANGFORD • RHONDA M LANGFORD • ROBERT H LANGFORD • PERRY L LANGHAM • HANS G LANGHOUT • LYNN M LANGILL • ANGELA E LANGIONE • KLAUS LANGKILDE • CARLA N LANGLAND • ANNE E LANGLEY • CAROLE B LANGLEY • GARY W LANGLEY • GERALDINE S LANGLEY • SCOTT LANGLEY • VERNON L L ANGLEY • DEBORAH L LANGLEY-PALMER • ANN S LANGSTON • ELLEN LANGSTON • EVELYN A LANGSTON • EVELYN J LANGSTON • JAMES E LANGSTON • JAMES R LANGSTON

left: Demetrio Lozano fights for the ball with France's Jackson Richardson in Spain's bronze-medal win.

right: Bozidar Jovic prepares to score one of his six goals in front of Sweden's Per Carlen during Croatia's gold-medal victory.

medal—more than redressing its 27-18 loss to Sweden in the preliminaries.

Croatian fans sang throughout much of the game and waved their nation's red and white checkered flag and bundles of red and white balloons. Thriving on the fans' enthusiasm, Croatia took advantage of a series of early Swedish turnovers to build a 6-1 lead within the first 10 minutes. The Croatians extended their lead over the defending silver medalist to as much as seven goals in the second half, before a late rally brought the Swedes within one goal of a tie. As the final buzzer sounded, Croatian players flung themselves to the floor and bodysurfed along the court in jubilation.

"This is the greatest achievement in Croatian sport," said Cavar, who scored three goals in the win and finished as the tournament's top scorer with a total of 43 goals (7.2 per game). "This means an incredible amount to

• MARGIANNA LANGSTON • RICHARD A LANGSTON • WILLIAM L LANGSTON • JOHN A LANHAM • HARRY K LANIER • JUSTIN L LANIER • KIMBERLY M LANIER • LAFONDRAETTA LANIER • LAURA E LANIER • MARY LOUISE LANIER • PRICE M LANIER • RENE LANIER • TRACY LANIER • BRUCE N. LANIER III • MORTON R LANING JR • JOHN C LANK • BONNIE B LANKARD • JUANITA F LANKFORD • RYAN D LANKFORD • SANDRA P LANKFORD • TAMMERA G LANKFORD • ROBERT H LANNING • GORDON C. LANNOU JR • PATRICIA M LANSDELL • ROBERT A LANSDELL JR • NICHOLE LANSDON • RONDA M LANSFORD • LUCILE LANSING •

our people and to our country." Croatians Bozidar Jovic, Goran Perkovac, and Irfan Smajlagic each scored six goals in the final victory, while Thorsson garnered eight goals for silver medalist Sweden.

The gold-medal-winning Croatian team consisted of Patrik Cavar, Valner Frankovic, Slavko Goluza, Bruno Gudelj, Vladimir Jelcic, Bozidar Jovic, Nenad Kljaic, Venio Losert, Valter Matosevic, Zoran Mikulic, Alvaro Nacinovic, Goran Perkovac, Iztok Puc, Zlatko Saracevic, Irfan Smajlagic, and Vladimir Sujster.

In another exciting finish, Demetrio Lozano scored five second-half goals, including one made with 10 seconds left, as Spain beat France 27-25 to capture the bronze medal. Lozano's late goal helped Spain hold off a furious comeback by the French, who had trailed 24-17 with 12 minutes left. Pascal Mahe's goal with 33 seconds remaining pulled France to within one goal at 26-25. Spain, however, worked down the clock before getting the ball to Lozano, who fired the clinching goal. Lozano, Urdiales, and Salvador Esquer each

In women's preliminary action, Gitte Madsen scores one of her seven goals in Denmark's win over the People's Republic of China.

The Swedish team members were Magnus Andersson, Robert Andersson, Per Carlen, Martin Frandesjo, Erik Hajas, Robert Hedin, Andreas Larsson, Ola Lindgren, Stefan Lövgren, Mats Olsson, Staffan Olsson, Johan Peterson, Thomas Sivertsson, Thomas Svensson, Pierre Thorsson, and Magnus Wislander.

tallied five goals for Spain, while Stephane Cordinier led the French with seven.

The Spanish team members were Talant Dujshebaev, Salvador Esquer, Aitor Etxaburu, Jesus Fernandez, Jaume Fort, Mateo Garralda,

STANLEY B LANSKY • THOMAS E LANSLEY • PEGGY M LANTHIER • ELAINE M LANTZ • JOHN H LANTZ • LELA M LANTZ • REBECCA LYNN LANTZ • WILLIAM D LANUM • WLLLIAM H LANUM • JASON F LANYON • JAMES R LANZER • SOPHIE M LAPAIRE • GORDON A LAPEAN • XAVIER LAPIE • MELISSA J LAPIN • KATARZYNA LAPINSKA • DAVID LAPIOLI • JENNIFER LAPIOLI • STEVEN J LAPLACE • FREDERICK L LAPLANTE ATC • LINDSAY L LAPOLE • JULIE LAPOMARDO • HEATHER LAPORTE • BURTON M LAPP • JILL M LAPP • JOHN P LAPP • MICKEY S LAPP • THOMAS G LAPPIN • FRANK J LAPSLEY • NATIVIDAD C LAPUT •

Raul Gonzalez, Rafael Guijosa, Fernando Hernandez, Jose Hombrados, Demetrio Lozano, Jordi Nunez, Jesus Olalla, Juan Perez, Inaki Urdangarin, and Alberto Urdiales.

Women

With a string of victories stretching so far back that coach Hyung-Kyun Chung admittedly could not remember the last time his team was defeated in international competition, Korea seemed poised for a third straight Olympic women's handball gold medal. In the semifi-

Korea's Jeong-Ho Hong attempts to score against Denmark in the women's gold-medal game.

nals, the Korean team claimed a fast-breaking win over Hungary. Sparking Korea in the 39-25 victory were Jeong-Ho Hong (nine goals) and Seong-Ok Oh (eight goals). Denmark earned the other berth in the gold-medal game by beating long-time rival Norway, 23-19. In the semifinal win, Denmark was led by a pair of Andersens, Camilla and Anja Jul, who accounted for seven and nine goals, respectively.

In the final, the Danish athletes doused the Korean team's hot streak and laid claim to their country's first women's handball medal. Paced by Anja Jul Andersen's 11 goals, Denmark's team triumphed over the highly favored Korean team in a thrilling 37-33 overtime victory. "We deserved to win this gold medal," Andersen said. "We beat the best team in the world." Although competing in Denmark's first-ever Olympic women's handball tournament, the team played like anything but rookies. With 1:11 remaining in regulation play, Camilla Andersen scored to tie the game 29-29 and send the battle into overtime. In the extra period, Heidi Astrup netted three goals as Denmark defeated the two-time defending Olympic champions.

The Danish team was comprised of Anja Jul Andersen, Camilla Andersen, Kristine Andersen, Heidi Astrup, Tina Bottzau, Marianne Florman, Conny Hamann, Anja Byrial Hansen, Anette Hoffman, Tonje Kjaergaard, Janne Kolling, Susanne Lauritsen, Gitte Madsen, Lene Rantala, Gitte Sunesen, and Anne Dorthe Tanderup.

O-Kyeong Lim turned in a sensational performance for Korea, scoring a game-high 15 goals in the loss. Though they took home the silver medal, the Koreans dominated the tournament's final statistics—boasting the tournament's leading scorer in Lim, with 41 goals (8.2 per game), and top assist leader in Oh (4.6 assists per game).

The members of the Korean team were Eun-Hee Cho, Sun-Hee Han, Jeong-Ho Hong, Soon-Young Huh, Cheong-Shim Kim, Eun-Mi Kim, Jeong-Mi Kim, Mi-Sim Kim, Rang Kim, Hye-Jeong Kwag, Sang-Eun Lee, O-Kyeong Lim, Hyang-Ja Moon, Seong-Ok Oh, Yong-Ran Oh, and Jeong-Rim Park.

Hungary and Norway took to the court to determine the bronze medalist. Hungary's balanced attack, in which Erzsebét Kocsis, Beatrix Kökény, Eszter Mátféi, and Beáta Siti each scored three goals, captured the bronze over Norway 20-18. In the loss, Kjersti Grini led Norway with eight goals.

KATHLEEN M LAQUALE ATC · JOAQUIN M LARA · CHARLES W LARCOM · DAMIAN J LARCOMBE · JOHN H LARDAS · SAM LARDNER · STEPHANIE G LARDSCHNEIDER · JOSEPH R LAREAU · CHARLES L LARGAY · BARBARA F LARGENT · HELEN MARY LARGENT · HURBERT E LARGENT · MATTHEW C LARGENT · TORY A LARGENT · JASON T LARGEY · JEFFREY R LARGEY · TAMMY A LARGIN · JOHN D LARIMER · BARBARA T LARIMORE · NANCY M LARIOS · MICHAEL L LARISCY · CHRISTOPHER J LARIVIERE · CHUCK LARKIN · JON C LARKIN · KATHIE M LARKIN · LINDA O LARKIN · MYRA J LARKIN · STEPHEN M LARKIN ·

The bronze medal–winning Hungarian team consisted of Éva Erdõs, Andrea Farkas, Beáta Hoffmann, Anikó Kántor, Erzsebét Kocsis, Beatrix Kökény, Eszter Mátféi, Auguszta Mátyás, Anikó Meksz, Anikó Nagy, Helga Németh, Ildikó Pádár, Beáta Siti, Anna Szantó, Katalin Szilágyi, and Beatrix Tóth.

CONCLUSION

Every Olympic Games has its share of storybook endings, and in 1996, team handball's finale was among Atlanta's most gripping. Backed by a legion of ardent fans, both the men's and women's championship squads marched to the victory podium for the first time. In addition, narrow overtime wins and record crowds (nearly 187,000 tickets were sold) produced perhaps the most thrilling chapter yet in Olympic handball history.

top: **Denmark's players celebrate their gold-medal win over Korea.**

bottom: **Hungary's Erzsebét Kocsis goes for the ball against Norway's Tonje Larsen for a bronze-medal victory.**

Atlanta 1996

TIMOTHY J LARKIN • AARON D LARKINS • JOYCE R LARKINS • KATHLEEN R LARKINS • LAWRENCE O LARKINS • MICKEY L LARKINS • VERNA M LARKINS • ROLAND R LARMORE • GREER G LARNED • ANNA M LAROCCA • ELEANOR LAROCCO • MARIA LAROQUE • CAROLINE LAROSE • CLEVELAND A LAROSE • GLORIA A LARROCHE • BRADLEY E LARRONDO • LOWRY T LARRY • CHARLES W LARSEN • DONALD LARSEN • ELIZABETH C LARSEN • HERB LARSEN • JESPER LARSEN • ROBERT M LARSEN • SHAUNA C LARSEN • ALAN L LARSON • BARBARA H LARSON • COLLEEN P LARSON • DARREN A LARSON

HOCKEY

Venues Used:
Clark Atlanta
University Stadium

Morris Brown
College Stadium

Days of Competition: 14

Medals Awarded: 6
Gold 2
Silver 2
Bronze 2

Number of Nations: 12

Number of Officials: 108

Officiating Federation:
International Hockey
Federation (FIH)

HOCKEY IS THE OLDEST known ball and stick game, dating back more than 4,000 years. At the 1996 Olympic Games, 12 nations were represented by a record 318 athletes (190 men and 128 women). The 14-day Centennial Olympic Games hockey competition extended from 20 July to 2 August.

VENUES

Two venues—Clark Atlanta University Stadium and Morris Brown College Stadium—hosted the hockey competition. Both newly built stadia are adjacent facilities in the Atlanta University Center, a six-college area located in the Olympic Ring within 2.2 mi (3.5 km) of the Atlanta Olympic Village. The preliminary matches were played at the 5,000-seat Clark Atlanta University Stadium, while the finals were staged at the 15,000-seat Alonzo Herndon Stadium, located on the campus of Morris Brown College. Each venue featured a new synthetic-turf competition field.

COMPETITION

In the men's event, the 12 teams were divided into two pools of six in which they competed in a round-robin before the semifinal round. The top two teams in each pool advanced to the semifinals, while the remaining teams competed in classification matches for places 5 through 12. In the finals, the winners of the two semifinal matches competed for the gold

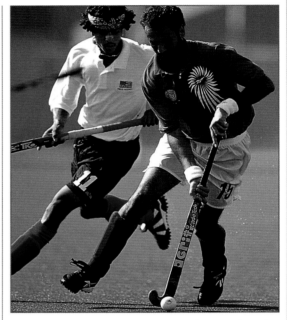

India's Ramandeep Singh moves upfield against the US's Nick Butcher in India's preliminary-round win at Morris Brown College.

and silver medals, while the losing teams played for the bronze medal.

In the women's event, all eight teams competed in a round-robin before the semifinals. The top two teams from the preliminaries battled in the match for the gold and silver medals, while the third- and fourth-place teams played in the bronze-medal match.

Men

Perhaps the most compelling showdown of the men's tournament took place in the preliminaries, as defending World Cup champion and Barcelona silver medalist Pakistan faced Olympic hockey rival India. Entering the

388

JOHELEN B LARSON • LINDA B LARSON • LINDA C LARSON • MARY S LARSON • MELINDA G LARSON • RICHARD G LARSON • STEPHEN F LARSON • STEVEN P LARSON • TIMOTHY J LARSON • EUNICE J LARSON MD • BRENDA J LARUE • JOHN A LARUE • MARY M LARUE • ANN E LARY • DENISE A LARZELERE • RESIL LASAM • JANET LASATER • BARBARA J LASCODY • PAULA M LASH • JENNIFER M LASHER • CONNIE M LASHLEY • LANA LASHOFF • COLEEN M LASKEY • CORINNE R LASKEY • MELANIE A LASOFF • LEA LASOI • GLORIAJEAN LASOTA • DEBRA M LASSITER • SHELBY J LASSITER • MAXINE LASTER •

match, the two traditional powerhouses of hockey together had won 11 of the 17 Olympic hockey gold medals awarded. Chants echoed throughout the stadium from the dozens of Pakistani fans waving their country's green-and-white flags. A group of fans from India wearing orange scarves around their heads countered with cheers of support for their team. In the end, India and Pakistan battled to a 0-0 draw. Later in the tournament, however, both were shut out of medal contention for only the fourth time in Olympic history.

At the conclusion of the preliminaries, Spain (4-1) and the Netherlands (4-0-1) stood alone at the top their respective pools, while Germany and Australia, which both finished with identical 3-1-1 marks, secured the other two berths in the semifinal round. In the semifinals, Spain defeated Australia 2-1, while the Netherlands, led by Taco van den Honert's three goals, defeated Germany 3-1.

In the gold-medal match, an early goal by Spain's Victor Pujol quickly quelled the enthusiasm of the hundreds of orange-clad Dutch fans in attendance. Spain did not have much time to celebrate, however. In the next 10 minutes, the Dutch scored two goals en route to ending

nearly 70 years of Olympic frustration by earning their first-ever team gold medal in hockey. The Netherlands' goals came off penalty corners by Floris Jan Bovelander in the 52nd and 54th minutes of play. Later, Bram Lomans sealed the victory by scoring off a penalty corner with just two minutes remaining. The Netherlands won with a score of 3-1.

The members of the Dutch team were Floris Jan Bovelander, Jacques Brinkman, Maurits Crucq, Marc Delissen, Jeroen Delmee, Leo Klein Gebbink, Taco van den Honert, Ronald Jansen,

Erik Jazet, Bram Lomans, Tycho van Meer, Teun de Nooijer, Wouter van Pelt, Stephan Veen, Guus Vogels, and Remco van Wijk.

The Spanish team consisted of Jaime Amat, Pablo Amat, Javier Arnau, Jordi Arnau, Oscar Barrena, Ignacio Cobos, Juan Dinares, Juan Escarre, Xavier Escude, Juantxo Garcia-Maurino, Antonio Gonzalez, Ramon Jufresa, Joaquin Malgosa, Victor Pujol, Ramon Sala, and Pablo Usoz.

In the bronze-medal match, Australia, which took silver in a 1992 gold-medal loss to Germany, reversed the outcome in 1996 with a

left: **Australia and Germany battle in the bronze-medal match at Morris Brown College.**

top right: **Shin-Heum Park of Korea scores through the outstretched arms of goalkeeper Lachlan Dreher in Australia's preliminary-round win over Korea.**

bottom right: **Look of the Games structures decorated the entrances to the competition venues**

VIVIAN LASTER • PATRICIA E LATCH • BRENT W LATHAM • JACQUELYN C LATHAM • KINARD L LATHAM • SUZETTE LATHAM • TRICIA A LATHAM • VAN LATHAM • WILEY G LATHAM • MILLIE H LATHAN • ROB LATHAN • ROBERT X LATHAN • STEWART LATHAN • KYLE S LATHON • FRANK J LATHRON • SCOTT S LATHROP • RHONDA C LATIF • CAROLYN S LATIFF • VINCENT J LATIGUE • GLENN E LATIMER • JIM W LATIMER • LORI LATIMER • MARGARET G LATIMER • STEVEN M LATIMER • RICHARD J LATIMER ATC • MARTHA I LATIMORE • MELISSA V LATORRE • CLAUDINE LATOUCHE • DARNELDA L LATSON • SHERRELL A LATSON

thrilling 3-2 win over Germany. Oliver Domke put Germany ahead 2-1 on a running shot in the 46th minute, but Australia's Jason Stacy scored his second goal of the game off a penalty corner, evening the score at 2-2. The winner came with just one minute remaining, as Baeden Choppy tipped in a penalty corner for the third-place finish for Australia with a score of 3-2. The members of the Australian team were Stuart Carruthers, Baeden Choppy, Stephen Davies, Damon Diletti, Lachlan Dreher, Lachlan Elmer, Brendan Garard, Paul Gaudoin, Mark Hager, Paul Lewis, Grant Smith, Matthew Smith, Daniel Sproule, Jason Stacy, Kenneth Wark, and Michael York.

Women

In women's preliminary play, the host team finally quenched its thirst for a victory. In a thrilling early tournament match, the United States defeated Korea 3-2 on Barb Marois's last-second, game-winning goal from the penalty corner. The win was the Americans' first victory in the last 12 years of Olympic play. At the conclusion of the seven rounds of preliminary games, Australia was at the top of the standings with a 6-0-1 mark. The team responsible for the one tie (3-3) on Australia's record was Korea, which earned the remaining place in the gold-medal final with a 4-1-2 record.

Playing in the gold-medal match before a capacity crowd at the Morris Brown College Stadium, the two teams were tied again at 1-1 after the first half of play. Early in the second half of the action, forward Alyson Annan of Australia scored her second goal of the game as she pumped in the eventual game-winning shot on a penalty stroke for a 2-1 lead. Australia clinched the gold on Katrina Powell's goal in the 3-1 win. With her two goals, Annan set a record for the most goals scored in an Olympic championship, and she tied Korea's Eun-Jung Chang for most points scored in an Olympic tournament (eight in eight games). With the victory, Australia became the second women's hockey team to win two Olympic gold medals and, in the process, extended its 40-game winning streak.

top: Spain's Xavier Escude controls the ball in front of Dutch player Bram Lomans in the Netherlands' gold-medal win.

bottom: Dutch players celebrate their gold-medal win over Spain.

• ALAN LATTA • COLLEEN A LATTA • ELIZABETH A LATTA • JORAUN LATTA • REGINALD LATTA • WILLIAM F LATTA • JACQUELINE R LATTIMER • ERIN B LATTIMORE • STEVEN M LATTIZORI • ARLINE LATTURAL • KEVIN C LATTY • CORINNE A LAU • GARVIN FRANCIS A LAU • HUGH LAU • JOHN J LAU • MELISSA A LAU • RONALD J LAUBER • XAVIER A LAUCIRICA • DOLORES H LAUDERDALE • JENNIFER C LAUDERMILCH • VON R LAUDERMILCH • JOHN E LAUER • BRIAN S LAUGHHUNN • ERIN M LAUGHLIN • JEFF R LAUGHLIN • KIMBERLY P LAUGHLIN • THOMAS D LAUNDER • REBECCA L LAURENS • VINCENT J LAURENT •

Lee, Ji-Young Lee, Jeong-Sook Lim, Seung-Shin Oh, Hyun-Jung Woo, and Jae-Sook You.

In one of the more evenly matched games of the tournament, Great Britain and the Netherlands faced off in the bronze-medal final. Fittingly, the two teams, which finished the preliminaries with identical 3-2-2 records, were tied 0-0 at the end of regulation play. The Netherlands eventually captured the bronze with a 4-3 victory in penalty strokes.

The Netherlands' team members were Stella de Heij, Wietske de Ruiter, Fleur van de Kieft,

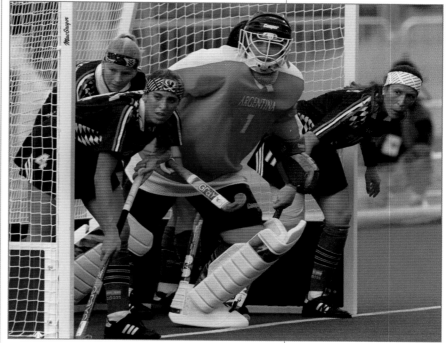

top left: Olympic tournament leading scorer Alyson Annan of Australia celebrates with teammates Juliet Haslam and Jennifer Morris after scoring one of her two goals in Australia's

Australia's team members were Michelle Andrews, Alyson Annan, Louise Dobson, Renita Farrell, Juliet Haslam, Rechelle Hawkes, Clover Maitland, Karen Marsden, Jennifer Morris, Jacqueline Pereira, Nova Peris-Kneebone, Katrina Powell, Lisa Powell, Danielle Roche, Kate Starre, and Liane Tooth.

Korea's silver-winning team consisted of Eun-Jung Chang, Eun-Jung Cho, Eun-Kyung Choi, Mi-Soon Choi, Young-Sun Jeon, Deok-San Jin, Myung-Ok Kim, Soo-Hyun Kown, Chang-Sook Kwon, Eun-Kyung Lee, Eun-Young

Dillianne van den Boogaard, Suzan van der Wielen, Myntje Donners, Willemijn Duyster, Noor Holsboer, Nicky Koolen, Ellen Kuipers, Jeannette Lewin, Suzanne Plesman, Florentine Steenberghe, Margje Teeuwen, Carole Thate, and Jacqueline Toxopeus.

CONCLUSION

The Dutch men (6-0-1) and the undefeated Australian women (7-0) dominated the 14 days of the Centennial Olympic Games hockey competition as they captured the Olympic crowns. The Spanish men, however, gave the tournament its biggest surprise. Spain matched its previous best finish—a silver medal in the 1980 Moscow Games—by finishing at 5-2-0 and upsetting Australia, Germany, and Pakistan before losing in the gold-medal final.

bottom left: Great Britain's Kathryn Johnson and the Netherlands' Dillianne van den Boogaard scramble for the ball during preliminary play.

right: Argentina defends its goal in Germany's preliminary-round win.

LOUIS J LAURIA • HARRY LAURIE • ROCHELLE D LAURINO • JOHN T LAURY • MOSES W LAURY • MARSHA C LAUSMAN • VANCE A LAUSMANN • GEORGE W LAUTER • THOMAS P LAUTH • BRADLEY R LAUX • BROWN S LAVADA • GEORGE A LAVALLEE • PAUL F LAVALLEE • INES R LAVELLE • MARC B LAVELLE • PATRICIA A LAVELLE • CATHERINE LAVENDER • EDITH B LAVENDER • EUGENE E LAVENDER • JAMES A LAVENDER • SIMMIE R LAVENDER • SUZANNE A LAVENDER • JOHN D LAVENDER ATC • THERESA L LAVERGNE • DARCEY J LAVERTY • MAIA LAVILLE • JAY LAVIN • EVA M LAVINE • MARCIA LAVINE •

JUDO

Venue Used:
Georgia World
Congress Center

Days of Competition: 7

Medals Awarded: 56
Gold 14
Silver 14
Bronze 28

Number of Nations: 92

Number of Officials: 86

Officiating Federation:
International Judo
Federation (IJF)

JUDO WAS INTRODUCED into the Olympic programme at the 1964 Tokyo Games, and the Atlanta Games marked just the second time that the women's competition was a medal event. A total of 392 athletes (241 men and 151 women) representing 92 nations participated. More than 76,000 tickets were sold for the competition, which spanned seven days, 20–26 July.

VENUE

Judo was one of seven sports housed in the halls of the Georgia World Congress Center, the second-largest convention center in the United States. Located in the heart of the Olympic Ring, approximately 1.9 mi (3 km) from the Olympic Village, this facility, along with the neighboring Omni Coliseum and Georgia Dome, formed the Olympic Center—the most concentrated cluster of competition venues within the Olympic Ring. The Centennial Olympic Games judo competition took place in Hall H of the Georgia World Congress Center.

Two competition tatamis—covered mats of pressed foam that served as the competition area—were laid together over an elevated wooden platform, which offered clear and favorable viewing for the competition officials and approximately 7,300 spectators. Temporary walls separated the athlete area from the fields of play, providing a dramatic presentation.

COMPETITION

Both the men's and women's competitions were divided into seven categories. The classifications were extra lightweight, 60 kg (men), 48 kg (women); half-lightweight, 65 kg (men), 52 kg (women); lightweight, 71 kg (men), 56 kg (women); half-middleweight, 78 kg (men), 61 kg (women); middleweight, 86 kg (men), 66 kg (women); half-heavyweight, 95 kg (men), 72 kg (women); and heavyweight, +95 kg (men), +72 kg (women).

By means of a draw, athletes in each weight class were divided into two pools, where they competed in an elimination system with double repechage. The elimination system determined which two finalists would compete for the gold and silver medals, while the double repechage allowed athletes who lost a match to reenter the

TERESA A LAVOIE • VALERIE LAVOYER • EDITH L LAW • HENRY W LAW • JACK E LAW • KARI A LAW • LINDA K LAW • STEVE JOSEPH LAW • DANA M LAW-MCKENZIE • KEITH E LAWDER • SELENA LAWHORN • DIANNE B LAWHORNE • ANNE W LAWING • JOHN S LAWLER • AN. TA J LAWLER • DAVID R LAWLER • DEVIN LAWLER • JAMES N LAWLER • MICHAEL F LAWLER • CRYSTAL D LAWLER RN • WILLIAM P LAWLER JR • DANIEL R LAWLESS • JOAN LAWLESS • JOHN JOSEPH LAWLESS • GARY W LAWLEY • JULIE M LAWLOR • MARY LAWLOR • BARBARA B LAWRENCE • BOUCHRA LAWRENCE • CALVIN D LAWRENCE •

competition in the repechage bracket and compete for third and succeeding places. The two top finalists from the repechage brackets each received bronze medals.

One referee and two judges officiated the contests, awarding scores based on the effectiveness of the techniques applied. Players scored through throws and mat holds, with submissions achieved by joint locks and strangling techniques. The first contestant to score a full point won. If a full point was not scored, the contestant with the highest score was declared the winner. In the case of a tied score or no score, a "majority of three" decision from the officials determined the winner.

Extra Lightweight (60 kg, men / 48 kg, women). Tadahiro Nomura of Japan dominated the men's extra lightweight competition en route to winning the gold. In the final, Nomura defeated Italy's Girolamo Giovinazzo, who won the silver medal. Germany's Richard Trautmann and Mongolia's Dorjpalam Narmandakh won the bronze medals.

The women's competition provided a monumental upset as 16-year-old Sun Hui Kye of the Democratic People's Republic of Korea defeated Japan's Ryoko Tamura for the gold. Tamura, who had won 84 consecutive matches since losing the gold-medal match in Barce-

left: Gold medalist Tadahiro Nomura of Japan throws Italy's Girolamo Giovinazzo in the men's extra lightweight final.

right: Up in arms, Sun Hui Kye of the Democratic People's Republic of Korea celebrates her gold-medal win over Japan's Ryoko Tamura in the women's extra lightweight final.

facing page: Colorful Look of the Games banners decorated Hall H of the Georgia World Congress Center, the site of the judo competition.

CAROLYN J LAWRENCE • DUANE LAWRENCE • EDDIE M LAWRENCE • EDNA Y LAWRENCE • ERNEST L LAWRENCE • JAMES F LAWRENCE • JO A LAWRENCE • KARLENE K LAWRENCE • KENNETH DAVID LAWRENCE • LEONARD B LAWRENCE • MARY J LAWRENCE • MIMI R LAWRENCE • NICK N LAWRENCE • RONALD LAWRENCE • SHIRLEY A LAWRENCE • STEPHANIE B LAWRENCE • STEPHEN LAWRENCE • TERRY S LAWRENCE • THOMAS E LAWRENCE • TIFFANY C LAWRENCE • VIRGINIA R LAWRENCE • WILLIAM A LAWRENCE • RON M LAWRENCE MD • KRISTINE V LAWRIE • RICHARD V LAWRY •

Iona, lost to Kye on points to take the silver. The bronze medalists were Cuba's Amarilis Savon and Spain's Yolanda Soler.

Half-Lightweight (65 kg, men / 52 kg, women). Germany's Udo Quellmalz, a two-time world champion and the 1992 Olympic bronze medalist, triumphed over Japan's Yukimasa Nakamura on a judges' decision to win the men's half-lightweight gold medal. Quellmalz scored four ippons on his way to the title. Nakamura garnered the silver, while bronze medals went to Cuba's Israel Hernandez

Lightweight (71 kg, men / 56 kg, women). Japan's Kenzo Nakamura evened the score in the final 10 seconds of the men's gold-medal match and was then awarded a 2-1 judges' decision. Nakamura, one of three brothers competing for Japan, captured the lightweight division by defeating Korea's Dae-Sung Kwak, who became the silver medalist. James Pedro of the US and France's Christophe Gagliano earned the bronzes.

In the women's lightweight category, world champion and 1992 bronze medalist Driulis

left: Victory in hand, France's Marie-Claire Restoux waves from the medal stand after winning Olympic gold in the women's half-lightweight division.

top right: Marisabel Lomba of Belgium defeats the People's Republic of China's Chuang Liu on her way to claiming the bronze in the women's lightweight competition.

bottom right: Overwhelmed by emotion, Germany's Udo Quellmalz drops to his knees after winning the gold in the men's half-lightweight class.

Plana and Brazil's Henrique Carlos Serra Azul Guimarães.

In the women's half-lightweight event, World Champion Marie-Claire Restoux of France outscored Korea's Sook-Hee Hyun to win the gold. Hyun took home the silver. Japan's Noriko Sugawara and Cuba's Legna Verdecia seized the bronze medals.

WILLIAM LAWS • HEATHER E LAWSKY • ABRAM V LAWSON • CAROL A LAWSON • CHERIS M LAWSON • COURTNEY L LAWSON • DANA T LAWSON • GODFRIED L LAWSON • JAMES D LAWSON • JESSIE J LAWSON • KRISTI L LAWSON • MICHAEL A LAWSON • RHODA A LAWSON • YVONNE S LAWSON • YYOKKIA LAWSON • MARY A LAWSON-BENJAMIN • OWEN M LAWSON IV • DOUGLAS J LAWTON • LYNNORE S LAWTON • MARY BETH LAWTON • TERRY L LAWTON • TOBIAS K LAWVER • ROBERTA I LAXER • BILLY R LAXTON ATC • CHARLTON E LAY • DEIRDRE C LAYAGUE JOHNSON • JAMES DOUG LAYE • LINDA LAYE

Gonzalez of Cuba claimed the gold in a points decision over Korea's Sun-Yong Jung, who received the silver. Belgium's Marisabel Lomba and Spain's Isabel Fernandez won the bronzes.

Half-Middleweight (78 kg, men / 61 kg, women). Djamel Bouras of France scored an upset victory over Japan's Toshihiko Koga to win the gold in the men's half-middleweight class. Koga, the 1992 gold medalist in the lightweight class, took silver, losing in a 3-0 judges' decision. Bronze medals went to Georgia's Soso Liparteliani and Korea's In-Chul Cho.

top left: Georgia's native Soso Liparteliani controls Brazil's Flavio Canto in a match Liparteliani won before taking the bronze in the men's half-middleweight division.

bottom left: Gella Vandecaveye of Belgium flips Yuko Emoto during the gold-medal match in the women's half-middleweight division.

right: Ki-Young Jeon of Korea defeats Armen Bagdasarov of Uzbekistan in the men's middleweight division.

In the women's competition, first-time Olympian Yuko Emoto of Japan triumphed over defending gold medalist Catherine Fleury-Vachon of France and then captured the gold by defeating Belgium's Gella Vandecaveye, who took home the silver. Claiming the bronze medals were Korea's Sung-Sook Jung and Jenny Gal of the Netherlands.

Middleweight (86 kg, men / 66 kg, women). Athletes from Korea won both the men's and women's middleweight classifications. Ki-Young Jeon won the men's division, defeating Armen Bagdasarov of Uzbekistan, who took the silver. On his way to the title, Jeon recorded four ippons in five matches. Germany's Marko Spittka

• WILLIAM K LAYE • CAMILLE LAYERS • CATHRYN C LAYFIELD • CAROLYN S LAYMAN • DYMPLE D LAYMAN • MILLIE J LAYMAN • BRENDA K LAYMANCE • CARLTON R LAYNE • CHRISTOPHER C LAYNE • LESLIE J LAYNE • ALLEN W LAYSON JR • ANDREW B LAYTON • JAMES A LAYTON • RANDY O LAYTON • RICK G LAYTON • SHIRLEY A LAYTON • JOAN R LAZAR • LAURA N LAZAR • OLGA LAZAREVA • CAROLE L LAZAROU • PHYLLIS G LAZARUS • RICHARD W LAZARUS • GABRIELLA P. LAZEA • MARK W LAZENBY • ALLEN LAZERSON • NATASA LAZETIC • KATHLEEN M LAZOUR • TONY LAZZARO • CRAIG LAZZERETTI

395

and Mark Huizinga of the Netherlands won the bronze medals.

In the women's division, Korea's Min-Sun Cho defeated Aneta Szczepanska of Poland to determine the gold and silver, respectively. Like Jeon, Cho was at the top of her category with four recorded ippons. The People's Republic of China's Xianbo Wang and the Netherlands' Claudia Zwiers took the bronze medals.

Half-Heavyweight (95 kg, men / 72 kg, women). Despite suffering from a neck injury, Poland's Pawel Nastula flipped Korea's Min-Soo

top: **Poland's Pawel Nastula takes down Korea's Min-Soo Kim in the half-heavyweight gold-medal final.**

***bottom:* Women's middleweight bronze medalist Claudia Zwiers of the Netherlands defeats the US's Liliko Ogasawara in a second-round match at the Georgia World Congress Center.**

Kim and immobilized him for 30 seconds to claim the gold in the men's half-heavyweight class. Nastula, a three-time European champion and the 1995 world champion, displayed diverse technical skills in defeating his opponents, and achieved two victories by throws. Kim became the silver medalist. Stephane Traineau of France, who recorded the fastest decision in the half-heavyweight competition, and Aurélio Fernandes Miguel of Brazil won the bronzes.

In the women's half-heavyweight division, Belgium's Ulla Werbrouck, who suffered a broken knee in Barcelona, won the gold by defeating Japan's Yoko Tanabe, who took the silver. Italy's Ylenia Scapin, the 1995 world champion, and Cuba's Diadenis Luna Castellano won the bronzes.

Heavyweight (+95 kg, men / +72 kg, women). In the men's heavyweight class, France's three-time world champion David Douillet captured

France and Johanna Hagn of Germany were awarded the bronzes.

CONCLUSION

The Centennial Olympic Games judo competition was dominated by three countries: Japan, France, and Korea. In the 14 events, Japan captured eight medals—three golds, four silvers, and one bronze. France also won three gold medals as well as three bronzes, for a total of six medals. Korea matched Japan with eight medals: two golds, four silvers, and two bronzes.

top left: Gold medalist David Douillet of France takes down Spain's Ernesto Perez in the men's heavyweight final.

the gold medal over silver medalist Ernesto Perez of Spain by turning him and holding him to the mat less than halfway through the bout. Germany's Frank Moeller and Harry Van Barneveld of Belgium took the bronze.

In the women's heavyweight division, the People's Republic of China's Fuming Sun won the gold by defeating Cuba's Estela Rodriguez, who captured the silver. Christine Cicot of

bottom left: The People's Republic of China's Fuming Sun wins the gold over Cuba's Estela Rodriguez in the women's heavyweight classification.

right: Bronze medalist Frank Moeller of Germany prepares to throw the Russian Federation's Sergey Kosorotov in the men's heavyweight division.

Atlanta 1996

• MEREDYTH G LEAPTROT • BRIAN LEARY • JACK T LEARY • JAY LEARY • MYLEEN M LEARY • DONALD E LEAS • MICHELE D LEASOR • DAN S LEASURE • E BISHOP LEATHERBURY • MARCUS F LEATHERMAN •
• MARK D LEATHERMAN • CYNTHIA LEATHERS • JAMIE F LEATHERS • JUDY G LEATHERS • GERALDINA LEAVITT • PAUL LEAVITT • THOMAS W LEAVITT • GARY H LEAZER • VIKKI C LEB • KATHLEEN A LEBEAU •
• JENNIFER A LEBEL EMT • THOMAS LEBETTRE • BERNADETTE K LEBLANC • DEBRA C LEBLANC • JAMES C LEBLANC • LINDA LEBLANC • NELSON O LEBLANC • STEVE M LEBLANC • SYLVIA M LEBLANC •

397

Modern Pentathlon

Venues Used:
Georgia International Horse Park

∎

Georgia Tech Aquatic Center

∎

Georgia World Congress Center

Days of Competition: 1

Medals Awarded: 3
Gold 1
Silver 1
Bronze 1

Number of Nations: 22

Number of Officials: 61

Officiating Federation:
International Modern Pentathlon and Biathlon Union (UIPMB)

FOR THE FIRST TIME in its 84-year Olympic history, modern pentathlon was held in one day. This demanding Olympic event, which is traditionally spread over five days, was held on day 11 of the Games. The competition took place at three venues: the Georgia World Congress Center, the Georgia Tech Aquatic Center, and the Georgia International Horse Park. A total of 32 athletes representing 22 nations were required to shoot, fence, swim, ride, and run as they competed in this grueling 12-hour test of skill and endurance. More than 10,600 tickets were sold.

VENUES

The shooting and fencing events were held in two separate sections of Hall F of the Georgia World Congress Center, which was located 1.9 mi (3 km) from the Olympic Village. Each section seated approximately 2,000 spectators. The shooting area included a 10 m shooting range with electronic standing targets and scoreboards that showed the athletes' competition numbers, names, and scores. The fencing side of the hall featured eight electronic competition pistes, with two alternate pistes, set in an H-shaped configuration. Scoreboards on each strip showed the names of the fencing pentathletes, with the winner of each bout

clearly indicated. A nine-cube video wall gave spectators up-to-the-minute rankings.

Following the shooting and fencing competitions, pentathletes and staff were transported by air-conditioned buses to the 15,000-seat Georgia Tech Aquatic Center, which was adjacent to the Olympic Village. The covered center featured a 165 ft (50 m) pool with eight lanes and electronic timing. Competitors' numbers were placed on the starting blocks to help spectators identify the pentathletes competing in the 300 m freestyle.

The final two phases of modern pentathlon—riding and running—were held at the Georgia International Horse Park. The pentathletes were transported 33 mi (53 km) from the

JACQUES E LEBON • MARCIA S LEBOS • BETH S LEBOWITZ • JEAN L LEBRUN • KATHLEEN E LECADRE • KAREN C LECATES • MIEKA L LECLAIR • VIOLET LECLAIR • ANN D LECLAIR-ASH • UVEDIA S LECOUNTE • BETTY J LECROY • BILLY D LECROY • RETHA L L'ECUYER • ALAN C LEDBETTER • JANIE H LEDBETTER • LARRY K LEDBETTER • SCOTT E LEDBETTER • TIMOTHY E LEDBETTER • ZACHARY S LEDBETTER • MATTHEW C LEDDY • MICHEAL J LEDDY • ADRIENNE P LEDER • GERALYNN M LEDERHOS • GILBERT L LEDERHOS JR • CYRIL LEDERMAN • CHRIS D LEDFORD • MICHELLE C LEDFORD •

Aquatic Center to the world-class horse park in specially designed buses that also served as locker rooms. Inside these buses, athletes had the opportunity to change clothes, relax, rehydrate, and have refreshments. The riding competition took place in the 32,000-seat main arena, which featured a beautifully designed modern pentathlon course. The jumps on the course were decorated with a traditional motif representing the South, featuring an abundance of flowers and foliage.

Several enhancements were made to the running portion of modern pentathlon. The running course began and ended in the center of the main stadium arena at the venue. Each of the four 1,000 m loops of the course passed through the specially prepared track inside the arena for approximately 400 m and then left the arena to continue on an adjacent, relatively level grass field.

COMPETITION

Points were compiled after each event in the modern pentathlon competition. The running event, the last event of the competition, provided a dramatic close to the day's activities. The pentathletes started the running event at intervals corresponding to the total number of points they differed from the leader. Therefore, the first three men to cross the finish line became the three highest scorers and therefore the medal winners. A newly developed audio computer start system allowed the competitors to use two lanes instead of the traditional three.

Shooting. Modern pentathlon began at 7:00 a.m. on 30 July at the Georgia World Congress Center with the shooting competition. Pentathletes fired 20 shots (slow fire) from a 4.5 mm air pistol on a 10 m air pistol range. The competitors were seeded based on their international ranking prior to the Games. After the first event, however, Switzerland's marksman Philipp Waeffler had fired his way to the top of the standings. Waeffler's near-perfect

The shooting phase opens the competition as pentathletes stand on the firing line at the Georgia World Congress Center.

facing page: Banners adorned with Look of the Games elements and the modern pentathlon pictogram decorated the three competition venues.

SUE LYNN M LEDFORD • AMBER D LEDOUX • RICHARD D LEDOUX • JIM LEDVINKA • ALICE A LEE • ALLAN M LEE • ANGELA C LEE • ANGELA M LEE • ANITA G LEE • ASHLEY M LEE • BARBARA S LEE • BARRY S LEE • BETSY W LEE • BETTY J LEE • BEVERLY K LEE • BILL M LEE • BONNIE C LEE • BRONSON H LEE • CARENE E LEE • CAROL A LEE • CHARLES M LEE • CHOUNG I LEE • CHRISTINA U LEE • CHRISTINE L LEE • CINDY LEE • CURTIS E LEE • DANAH M LEE • DANNY LEE • DAVID R LEE • DEANNA K LEE • DEBBIE F LEE • DEBORAH H LEE • DEBORAH O LEE • DINO T LEE • DONALD W LEE • DONALD W LEE •

399

score of 185 on 20 10 m targets put him in first place with 1,156 points.

Fencing. Moving to the other side of the hall, the pentathletes engaged in the fencing portion of the competition, which began at 8:30 a.m. This event, conducted as a round-robin, required each pentathlete to fence 31 one-minute, one-touch bouts of épée. After three hours of bouts, Kazakhstan's Alexandre Paryguin and Ukraine's Heorhiy Chymerys captured the fencing portion of modern pentathlon, as each finished with 21 victories.

top: Italy's Cesare Toraldo takes a break between fencing matches.

bottom: Overwhelmed with elation, Mexico's Sergio Salazar celebrates his victory over Lithuania's Andriejus Zadneprovskis in the fencing phase.

DONG HYEON LEE • EDITH N LEE • ELIZABETH LEE • ELIZABETH A LEE • ELLIS I LEE • EMING R. LEE • EMMALYNN S LEE • ERIN E LEE • EUN HYE LEE • EVAN E LEE • FAY LEE • FITZROY A LEE • GARY A LEE • GERALD D LEE • GLORIA V LEE • GRACE D LEE • HEATHER LEE • HEE JUNE LEE • HYE EUN LEE • HYUN LEE • IL-GYU LEE • IMARI E LEE • IMOGENE M LEE • JACQUELINE J LEE • JAE MAN M LEE • JAMES H LEE • JAMIE B. LEE • JANG MI LEE • JAQUADA S LEE • JASON LEE • JEANNE H LEE • JEFFREY S LEE • JENNIFER G LEE • JENNIFER S LEE • JIN S LEE • JOAN P LEE • JOHN J LEE • JOHN S LEE • JONG H LEE •

After two events, Paryguin was in first place overall with a total of 2,042 points, while Chymerys stood in fifth place with 1,982.

Swimming. At 1:00 p.m., the pentathletes entered the pool at the Georgia Tech Aquatic Center for the 300 m freestyle swimming event. A rousing crowd from an earlier synchronized swimming competition remained in the stands and provided cheers of support during the four heats of eight competitors each. Georgia's Vakhtang Yagorashvili won the swimming event with a time of 3:15.04; however, in the overall standings at the end of the first three events, Italy's Cesare Toraldo was in first place with 3,284 points.

Riding. After the refreshed pentathletes arrived at the horse park, a random computer draw selected the riders' mounts for the equestrian jumping event. The pentathletes were allowed 20 minutes to get acquainted with their mounts and practice on the 350 m course of 12 obstacles. Competition began at 5:15 p.m. A crowd of about 10,000 watched the final two events.

Three pentathletes completed the riding phase with no penalties (points are deducted for falls, refusals, knockdowns, or riding too slowly): Hungary's János Martinek, the gold medalist at the Seoul Games in 1988; Richard Phelps of Great Britain; and Poland's Igor Warabida. Martinek, riding a horse named

top: The US's Michael Gostigian swims in the third phase of modern pentathlon.

bottom: Claud Cloete of South Africa clears a jump during the riding competition.

JOSEPH S LEE • JUANITA S LEE • JUDY S LEE • JUNG SIM LEE • KAREN K LEE • KAREN M LEE • KEITH E LEE • KENNY Y LEE • KI-TAE LEE • KITTY W LEE • KYOUNG-SUK LEE • KYUNG-IL LEE • LARRY B LEE • LAURA T LEE • LINDA S LEE • LORRAINE R LEE • LOTTA H LEE • LOUISE G LEE • MARILYN L LEE • MARTHA M LEE • MARY E LEE • MARY ELLEN LEE • MARY M LEE • MATTHEW S LEE • MEE-YOOK LEE • MICHAEL D LEE • MICHAEL R LEE • MICHELLE C LEE • MOON Y LEE • NAT LEE • NELL R LEE • PAMELA B LEE • PATRICIA H LEE • PATRICIA M LEE • PEARL LEE • PEGGY S LEE • PETER LEE • RENUNDA S LEE • RICHARD T LEE

Mike, navigated the jumps in 65.65 seconds with no penalties to pull into third place overall with 4,258 points. Italy's Toraldo remained the overall leader with an impressive performance on Kirby, an unruly horse that caused another pentathlete to withdraw from the competition. After four events, Toraldo led with a total of 4,324 points, while Kazakhstan's Paryguin was second with 4,278 points.

Running. The day-long pentathlon competition culminated in the 4,000 m cross-country run at 7:00 p.m. When Paryguin sprinted to the finish line ahead of the Russian Federation's Eduard Zenovka, the gold medal became his. Despite starting 15.33 seconds later in the staggered start, Paryguin easily passed Toraldo before narrowly holding off Zenovka for the victory. Paryguin finished with a total of 5,551 points. Zenovka, the bronze medalist at the Barcelona Games in 1992, won the silver medal with a total of 5,530 points after finishing the run with a time of 12:21.487—the fastest actual time without regard to the handicapped start. Hungary's Martinek began and

Hungary's János Martinek rides Mike through the jumping test with no penalties to move into third place in the overall standings.

• RICO LEE • ROBERT A LEE • ROBERT E LEE • ROBERT E LEE • ROBERT EDWARD LEE • ROBIN A LEE • RONNIE LEE • ROSEMARY E LEE • SAK LEE • SAK LEE • SANDRA K LEE • SANDRA P LEE • SANG H LEE • SARA A LEE • SEIJUNG LEE • SEOKYOUNG LEE • SHANA LEE • SHERRIE N LEE • SHERYL D LEE • SHUK UAN AGNES LEE • STACEY N LEE • STEPHEN H LEE • STEPHEN S LEE • SUK-MIN LEE • SUN-YOUNG LEE • SUNG-CHAN LEE • TARA M LEE • TERESA J. LEE • TERESA R LEE • TERRY B LEE • TIEN C LEE • VELETA E LEE • VICTOR LEE • VIVIAN K LEE • WILLIAM B LEE • WILLIAM C LEE • WILLIAM R LEE • WING LEE •

ended the running event in third place, finishing with a total of 5,501 points, which garnered him the bronze.

CONCLUSION

Modern pentathlon is rich in Olympic history and tradition. Conducting all five events on a single day of competition gave special significance to this ultimate test of athletic ability and endurance. The new format also increased ticket sales. Transportation was included in the ticket price, heightening public interest by enabling more people to see the event in its entirety while visiting three different venues.

Support for the pentathletes could be seen throughout the competition. IOC President Juan Antonio Samaranch joined spectators at the horse park, and a dedicated group of cheering, flag-waving, and singing fans from Mexico followed the competitors to all three venues.

top left: Georgia's Vakhtang Yagorashvili begins the final phase with the staggered start of the running test at the Georgia International Horse Park.

bottom left: Kazakhstan's Alexandre Paryguin sprints to the finish line to take modern pentathlon gold.

right: After five grueling phases, the Russian Federation's Eduard Zenovka (silver), Kazakhstan's Aleksandre Paryguin (gold), and Hungary's János Martinek (bronze) are awarded the medal honors.

Atlanta 1996.

YIM M LEE • YOON J LEE • DAVID B LEE ATC • JOHN H LEE JR • ROBERT E LEE JR • RYALS E LEE JR • DOOHI LEE MD • WILLIAM N LEECAN • KENNETH R LEECH • STEPHEN R LEEDS • CHALIS N LEEPER • DOROTHY LEEPER • JULIE M LEES • DIANNE CHRISTENA LEESON • DIANNE CHRISTENA LEESON • CAROL P LEETH • CARON S LEFF • GAYLE B LEFF • LISA MEREDITH LEFF • SHEILA LEFF • SCOTT L LEFFEL • MARTIN S LEFFLER • • JACQUES LEGRAND JR • MICHEL J LEGROS • JASON C LEHBERGER • DOUGLAS LEHMAN • KEVIN W LEHMAN • RHONDA G LEHMAN • SETH M LEHMAN • JEANETTE MARIE LEHMANN

ROWING

Venue Used:
Lake Lanier

Days of Competition: 8

Medals Awarded: 42
Gold 14
Silver 14
Bronze 14

Number of Nations: 45

Number of Officials: 76

Officiating Federation:
International Rowing
Federation (FISA)

THE EIGHT-DAY rowing competition (21–28 July) showcased a record number of 597 athletes (392 men and 205 women) from 45 countries competing in 139 races in 14 events (8 for men and 6 for women).

VENUE

Situated on picturesque Lake Lanier, a popular recreation destination 55 mi (88 km) northeast of Atlanta near Gainesville, Georgia, this world-class Olympic rowing and canoe/kayak–sprint venue featured a permanent cabling system and lane markers (which retract to allow recreational use of the lake), a permanent finish tower, two permanent boathouses, boat ramps and docks, and a permanent storage building. Construction for the site began in November 1994, and the legacy left at Clark's Bridge Park was given to the city of Gainesville and Hall County following the Games.

As many as 17,300 spectators literally sat on Lake Lanier to view the Olympic competition each day. Seating was provided on a four-story grandstand rising from a massive 650 x 300 ft (198 x 91 m) temporary dock that extended 425 ft (129.5 m) into the water, adjacent to the finish line. Located on the east side of the lake,

opposite the athlete areas and boat launch, the platform was positioned 4 ft (1.2 m) above the lake at full pool, 1,071 ft (326 m). It rested on steel pilings 80 ft (24 m) in length, which were hammered into the bottom of the channel. Also found on the spectator platform were concessionaires, spectator services, and a broadcast media grandstand. After the Games, the entire temporary-seating platform was dismantled. On the west side of the lake, a day village for the athletes—complete with private team tents, rest lounges, lockers, showers, and recreation areas—was provided alongside the dock areas and practice courses.

COMPETITION

The Atlanta Games were the first to use a new Agsostart automated starting system—an audible tone and visual indicator at the starting line of the 2,000 m course—that provided for fewer false starts and initiated the timing of the races.

A trio of lightweight events premiered at the 1996 Games: men's lightweight double sculls, men's lightweight coxless four (replacing men's

SETH M LEHMAN • JEANETTE MARIE LEHMANN • JOHN L LEHMANN • MARILYN E LEHMANN • PEGGY S LEHMBERG • KAREN R LEHNER • TRUDY CP LEHNER • CAROLYN A LEHR • JENNIFER A LEHR • TAMARA L LEHR • LINDA C LEHSTEN • MARY E LEIBLE • STEPHEN D LEICHT • MARLENE LEICHTER • JOEL E LEIDER • KIRK V LEIDY • CAROLINE LEIGH • JAMES H LEIGH III • LESLIE S LEIGHTON • JOHN A LEIGHTY • BONNIE A LEIKAM • CHRISTOPHER W LEINER • JOAN E LEININGER • CYNTHIA S LEIPMAN • CYNTHIA N LEIPOLD RN • HELEN T LEISHMAN • DONALD E LEITCH • KRISTEN BESS LEITCH • THOMAS E LEITCH •

four with coxswain), and women's lightweight double sculls (replacing women's four with coxswain). The remaining events were single sculls, double sculls, quadruple sculls, coxless pair, coxless four (men), and eight.

Athletes who did not advance in the preliminary heats entered repechage races to try to qualify for the semifinal and final races.

Single Sculls. In the men's single sculls, his third race in the competition, Switzerland's Xeno Muller claimed the gold with a time of 6:44.85 over silver medalist Derek Porter of Canada (6:47.45) and two-time defending champion Thomas Lange of Germany, who took the bronze (6:47.72).

On the women's side, Ekaterina Khodotovich of Belarus (7:32.21) sprinted to an upset victory over Canadian national hero and favorite Silken Laumann (7:35.15) for the prestigious race's gold medal. Finishing behind Laumann's silver, Denmark's Trine Hansen garnered the bronze (7:37.20).

Double Sculls. In the finals, the third race for all three pairs, Agostino Abbagnale and

top: Olympic rowing spectators enjoy the view at Lake Lanier.

bottom left: Look of the Games structures with pictograms welcomed spectators at the entrance to the rowing venue.

bottom right: Silver medalist Silken Laumann of Canada wins her opening heat in the women's single sculls competition.

ANJA LEITENBERGER • GORDON A LEITER • DAVID K LEITSON • MICHAEL E LEITZEL • PATRICE M LEIVO • LAURA A LEJARZAR • JOANNE C LELEKATCH • CAROLINE MARIE LELEU • LUCIA LELII • DAPHNE K LEMAIRE • DENNIS M LEMAN • BILL N LEMASTER • PATRICIA T LEMAY • MARY ANNE B LEMBO • ROBERT E LEMCKE JR • ELIZABETH C LEMER • TIMOTHY C LEMKE • JANET L LEMLE • MARSHA H LEMLEY • RODNEY A LEMLEY • JOHN R LEMMON • LINDA K LEMMON • SARAH M LEMMON • ROBERT M LEMON • CATHERINE LEMONS • GEORGE E LENAEUS • SUSAN M LENAEUS • FRANCES C LENCH •

Davide Tizzano of Italy (6:16.98) edged Steffen Skår Størseth and Kjetil Undset of Norway (6:18.42) to take the gold in the men's double sculls. Størseth and Undset garnered the silver, while France's Samuel Barathay and Frederic Kowal took the bronze (6:19.85).

Canadians Kathleen Heddle and Marnie McBean, who were double gold medalists in Barcelona, added another gold to their collection by winning the women's double sculls (6:56.84) in what was the third race for all the pairs. Mianying Cao and Xiuyun Zhang from the People's Republic of China (6:58.35) and Irene Eijs and Eeke van Nes from the Netherlands (6:58.72) won the silver and bronze, respectively.

Lightweight Double Sculls. Pairs in the men's lightweight double sculls event took part in four preliminary heats, repechages, and semifinals. Switzerland's Markus Gier and Michael Gier (6:23.47) dominated the finals from the opening sprint and defeated the silver and bronze medal–winning duos Pepijn Aardewijn and Maarten van der Linden from

top: Canada's duo of Kathleen Heddle and Marnie McBean stroke to Olympic gold in women's double sculls.

bottom: Norway's Steffen Skår Størseth and Kjetil Undset row their way to silver in men's double sculls.

the Netherlands (6:26.48) and Anthony Edwards and Bruce Hick from Australia (6:26.69) by more than 3.00 to capture Olympic gold.

In the women's lightweight double sculls competition, Constanta Burcica and Camelia Macoviciuc from Romania (7:12.78) earned Olympic gold by overtaking the US squad of Teresa Z. Bell and Lindsay Burns (7:14.65), who won the silver. Rebecca Joyce and Virginia Lee of Australia (7:16.56) earned the bronze

TIMOTHY S LENCZOWSKI • JOHN D LENIHAN • ANITA R LENKEIT • WILLI A LENKEIT • LYDIA F LENNON • PATRICK LENNON • NATHALIE LENOBLE • CHARISSE S LENOIR • JOYCE J LENOIR • RUTH E LENOIR • GUENTER J LENSGES • JO A LENYK • BRIAN T LENZIE • LAULII L LEOFO • AMY P LEON • JEAN LEON • BETTY LEONARD • DANNIE W LEONARD • GLADYS J LEONARD • GREGORY LEONARD • JEANNE M LEONARD • JENNIFER MAE LEONARD • JOHN LEONARD • JOHN W LEONARD • KAREN E LEONARD • KAY T LEONARD • LINDA LEONARD • LORI M LEONARD • MICHELLE R LEONARD • PATRICK D LEONARD •

medal. The finals were the third race for all three teams.

Quadruple Sculls. In the finals, the third race for each of the foursomes, Germany's crew of Andreas Hajek, Andre Steiner, Stephan Volkert, and Andre Willms (5:56.93) won gold in the men's quadruple sculls. The United States (Jason Gailes, Brian Jamieson, Eric Mueller, and Tim Young) earned the silver medal (5:59.10), and Australia (Duncan Free, Boden Hanson, Janusz Hooker, and Ronald Snook) finished third to take the bronze medal (6:01.65). On the awards dock, IOC member Anita DeFrantz, a bronze-medal rower for the US in 1976, awarded the medals.

Setting a blistering pace, Germans Kathrin Boron, Kerstin Koeppen, Katrin Rutschow, and Jana Sorgers (6:27.44) won the gold in the women's event. The silver and bronze medalists were from Ukraine (Inna Frolova, Svitlana Maziy, Dina Myftakhutdinova, and Olena Ronzhina), 6:30.36, and Canada (Laryssa Biesenthal, Kathleen Heddle, Marnie McBean, and Diane O'Grady), 6:30.38, respectively.

Coxless Pair. Great Britain's Matthew Pinsent and Steven Redgrave, winners of three straight world titles and the 1992 Olympic gold medal, reigned supreme in the men's coxless pair event with a final time of 6:20.09. With the gold-medal victory, Redgrave earned his fourth medal in as many Olympic Games, joining the elite group of Olympians who have already managed this feat.

Crossing the finish line, Redgrave's arms collapsed on his oars. "I am absolutely knackered," he proclaimed after the pair's victory lap. "They were never going to catch us." Robert Scott and David Weightman of Australia captured the silver (6:21.02), and France's Michel Andrieux and Jean-Christophe Rolland took the bronze (6:22.15).

In the closest racing final of the 1996 Olympic Games, defending World Champions Kate Slatter and Megan Still of Australia won the gold in the women's coxless pair event by

just .39 with a time of 7:01.39, as they held off the final sprint of Karen Kraft and Missy Schwen of the US (7:01.78). Schwen and Kraft garnered silver medals. France's Helene Cortin and Christine Gosse took the bronze (7:03.82).

left: World Champions Kate Slatter and Megan Still of Australia defeat Karen Kraft and Missy Schwen of the US to win the gold in the women's coxless pair event.

top right: Teams compete in women's quadruple sculls action at Lake Lanier.

bottom right: Great Britain's Steven Redgrave and Matthew Pinsent repeat as the Olympic gold medalists in the men's coxless pair event.

PEGGY P LEONARD • RICHARD LEONARD • ROBERT R LEONARD • RUTH S LEONARD • SHERYL H LEONARD • STEPHANIE M LEONARD • SUZANNE K LEONARD • VERONICA MECHELL LEONARD • JAMES C. LEONARD MD • WALLACE LEONARO • ANTHONY M LEONE • LISA A LEONHARDT • JEFFREY J LEPAK • HEATHER F LEPESKA • CHRISTOPHE G LEPIGEON • MICHAEL E LEPIS • DANIELLE K LEPLEY • DAVID A LERCH • JASON P LERCH • YVONNE D LERMA • JOSEPH N LERNER • MARK S LERNER • ADRIANE M LEROY • COLLEEN M LEROY • PEGGY A LEROY • PHILIP N LEROY • SHARON P LEROY • RANDALL J LESCAULT

Coxless Four. Coming out on top after three races each, Australia, France, and Great Britain took medals in the final round. The Australian foursome of Drew Ginn, Nicholas Green, Michael McKay, and James Tomkins (6:06.37) took the gold in the coxless four event. France (Gilles Bosquet, Daniel Fauche, Olivier Moncelet, and Bertrand Vecten), 6:07.03, came in second to win the silver, finishing .25 ahead of Great Britain (Timothy Foster, Rupert Obholzer, Greg Searle, and Jonny Searle), 6:07.28, which captured the bronze.

Eight. The Netherlands' team of Michiel Bartman, Jeroen Duyster, Ronald Florijn, Koos Maasdijk, Nico Rienks, Diederik Simon, Niels van der Zwan, Niels van Steenis, and Henk-Jan Zwolle (5:42.74) claimed the gold medal in the men's eight competition in the finals, their second race. The Olympic victory capped an outstanding season for the Dutch team that included besting the world's fastest time in the eight event. As their team crossed the finish line, a few excited Netherlands fans cheered before jumping into Lake Lanier in celebration.

left: Alone in first place, Denmark's team celebrates its gold-medal triumph in the men's lightweight coxless four competition.

right: Australia's coxless four rowing team rows to gold at the Centennial Olympic Games.

Lightweight Coxless Four. With only 500 m left in the final, their third race of the competition, Denmark's foursome of Eskild Ebbesen, Victor Feddersen, Niels Laulund Henriksen, and Thomas Poulsen (6:09.58) tapped their reserve energy to capture Olympic gold in the lightweight coxless four competition by overtaking silver medalist Canada (David Boyes, Gavin Hassett, Jeffrey Lay, and Brian Peaker), 6:10.13. The US team (William Carlucci, David Collins, Jeff Pfaendtner, and Marc Schneider) earned the bronze (6:12.29).

Placing behind the Netherlands was silver medalist Germany (Roland Baar, Wolfram Huhn, Detlef Kirchhoff, Mark Kleinschmidt, Frank Richter, Thorsten Streppelhoff, Peter Thiede, Ulrich Viefers, and Marc Weber), 5:44.58, and the Russian Federation (Nikolay Aksyonov, Anton Chermashentsev, Andrey Glukhov, Aleksandr Lukyanov, Sergey Matveyev, Pavel Melnikov, Roman Monchenko, Dmitriy Rozinkevich, and Vladimir Volodenkov), which took the bronze (5:45.77).

After finishing fourth in each of the last three Olympic Games, Romania's women's eight team, which won the 1990 and 1993 world championships, easily took the gold in

• SUSAN M LESCHER • ARTHUR E LESESNE • EDNA M LESESNE • MICHELE A LESHAN • LAWRENCE A LESHER • TRACY W LESIEUR • JOAN LESLEY • BONNALEE B LESLIE • BRENDA M LESLIE • DAVID H LESLIE • DICK W LESLIE • FRANCES A LESLIE • GLORIA G LESLIE • SHEILA R LESLIE • TONY M LESLIE • WILLIAM F LESLIE • WILLIAM T LESLIE • CRAIG S LESSER • ERIK S LESSER • LAURENCE M LESSER • MICHAEL F LESSNER • PHYLLIS C LESSNER • SHERRY F LESSNER • AMANDA L LESTER • CHRISTA LESTER • ELLEN B LESTER • JOHN F LESTER • KIM N LESTER • LAMAR A LESTER • PATRICIA A LESTER •

the 1996 Games, winning both of its races. The crew of Vera Cochelea, Liliana Gafencu, Elena Georgescu, Doina Ignat, Elisabeta Lipa, Ioana Olteanu, Marioara Popescu, Doina Spircu, and Anca Tanase (6:19.73) bolted from the start line and finished more than a length ahead of silver medalist Canada (Alison Korn, Theresa Luke, Maria Maunder, Heather McDermid, Jessica Monroe, Emma Robinson, Lesley Thompson, Tosha Tsang, and Anna van der Kamp), 6:24.05. Securing the bronze was Belarus (Tamara Davydenko, Natalya Lavrinenko, Yelena Mikulich,

competition, as calm winds and smooth water provided excellent racing conditions, capacity crowds watched the competition from a closer proximity than ever before.

The venue was especially productive for Australia, which won a pair of golds, a silver, and four bronze medals; Canada, which netted a gold, four silvers, and a bronze; and Romania, which won three gold medals in the women's competition. In all, 16 nations earned medals in the Centennial Olympic Games rowing competition.

Aleksandra Pankina, Yaroslava Pavlovich, Valentina Skrabatun, Natalya Volchek, and Marina Znak), 6:24.44.

CONCLUSION

British rowing team manager David Tanner summed up the sentiments of those who participated in and watched the rowing competition when he called Lake Lanier "the greatest rowing venue ever." During the eight-day

top: Men's eight teams are synchronized at the start of the qualifying heat for the semifinals.

bottom: The finish tower at Lake Lanier was decorated with Look of the Games patterns to complement the rest of the venue.

Atlanta 1996.

ROBERT W LESTER • STEVE LESTER • SUSAN C LESTER • TODD L LESTER • TRACEY S LESTER • JOHN A LESTER III • CHRIS LETARES • DOUG E LETHCO • JOANNE LETKY • JOHN LETKY • AMY LETOURNEAU • PAT M LETSON ATC • CELIA E LETT • MARTINA LETTOVSKA • BRYAN R LETURGEZ • STEFAN LETZ • AMY LEUGERS • DONNA LEUNG • LILLIAN LEUNG • MAX K LEUNG • AMY M LEURART • JUDY LEUTY • ALVINA A LEVA • RONALD L LEVAN • MARTIN E LEVANDOSKI • JOEY M LEVASSEUR • ZELDA D LEVAY • BARBARA L LEVEDAHL MT • LAURA M LEVEILLE • PATRICIA M LEVENBURG • VICTORIA E LEVENE •

Venue Used:
Wolf Creek
Shooting Complex

Days of Competition: 8

Medals Awarded: 45
Gold 15
Silver 15
Bronze 15

Number of Nations: 100

Olympic Records: 27

World Records: 1

Number of Officials: 55

Officiating Federation:
International Shooting
Union (UIT)

SHOOTING

THE FIRST MEDAL ceremony of the Centennial Olympic Games took place at the shooting competition venue. In an Olympic first, the medal ceremonies for shooting were held on the ranges themselves at the conclusion of each final, allowing athletes to fully enjoy the praise of the spectators.

VENUE

The shooting competition was held 20–27 July at the 7,500-seat Wolf Creek Shooting Complex, located 21 mi (33.7 km) from the Atlanta Olympic Village. The venue included three separate air-conditioned rifle and pistol buildings and three combined skeet and trap fields, all constructed around a common spectator plaza, which created an observer-friendly environment. One of the permanent buildings held a 50 m rifle and pistol range with 60 firing positions and a 2,500-seat finals pavilion. The second building housed a 10 m air rifle and pistol range with 60 positions and a 10 m running target range with three firing positions and a dry fire range. The third building contained a 25 m pistol range with 10 firing positions.

The outdoor clay target range provided a combination of three fields: skeet, trap, and double trap. The range was equipped with phonopull releases for all targets and featured a 5,000-seat spectator grandstand. Following

the Games, the venue—one of the few sites in the US capable of hosting world-class shooting competitions—was given to Fulton County for use by the public.

COMPETITION

The Wolf Creek Shooting Complex featured the most modern target and results system ever installed in a shooting range. For the first time in Olympic history, electronic targets rather than the conventional paper targets were fired upon in the rifle and pistol events. As a result, every shot was instantly scored and displayed on electronic monitors and scoreboards so that shooters, coaches, and spectators could see the results immediately.

Further enhancements were added to make the competition more enjoyable for the spectators. These enhancements included using music before and after each competition; supporting all athlete introductions with each competitor's biographical information, which was displayed on video boards; and providing programs to inform the spectators about the events, equipment, and competitors.

Shooting consisted of 10 men's events and 5 women's events. Two new Olympic clay target events—men's and women's double trap—were contested for the first time in Atlanta. A total of 295 men and 128 women competed in the events. This total represented an Olympic record of 100 nations, eclipsing the previous record of 80 set at the 1992 Games.

ADAM P LEVENSALOR • SANDRA F LEVENT • DARREN W LEVERENZ • BETTYE T LEVERETT • RICHELLE M LEVERETT • LARRY D LEVERMANN • LAURA H LEVEROOS • TED H LEVEROOS • TRACIE A LEVERT • DARRYL LEVETTE • DEBORAH K LEVEY • ROBIN L LEVEY • DEBBIE L LEVI • JOHN LEVI • NICOLE LEVI • SUSAN J LEVI • SUZANNE E LEVI • BRENDA R LEVIN • JEREMY LEVIN • JEREMY LEVIN • NITA E LEVIN • ADAM L LEVINE • BILLY L LEVINE • BRETT G LEVINE • DAVID L LEVINE • EDWARD LEVINE • GERDA M LEVINE • JAMES D LEVINE • JULIAN A LEVINE • KENNETH C LEVINE • LEA M LEVINE • RITA S LEVINE •

All athletes entered in an event competed in the qualification round. The eight highest scoring competitors in all rifle, pistol, and running target events advanced to the final rounds. In the clay target events, the six highest-scoring athletes in the qualification rounds advanced to the final rounds.

Rifle Events

The following rifle events were held at the 1996 Centennial Olympic Games: 10 m air rifle, 50 m standard rifle 3 position (women),

50 m free rifle prone (men), 10 m running target (men), and 50 m free rifle 3 position (men).

10 m Air Rifle. Firing an Olympic-record final score of 695.7, the Russian Federation's Artem Khadzhibekov won the men's 10 m air rifle event. Austria's Wolfram Waibel Jr. (695.2) finished with the silver, and France's Jean-Pierre Amat (693.1) received the bronze.

The honor of being the Centennial Olympic Games' first gold-medal winner was bestowed on Renata Mauer of Poland. Mauer fired a near-perfect final shot to win the women's 10 m air rifle event with a score of 497.6. Before a standing room–only crowd, IOC President Juan Antonio Samaranch presented Mauer with the first gold medal awarded at the 1996 Games. Germany's Petra Horneber (497.4) won

top: **Poland's Renata Mauer, the first gold medalist of the 1996 Centennial Olympic Games, proudly displays the gold medal she won in the women's 10 m air rifle competition.**

bottom: **Bronze medalist Jean-Pierre Amat of France takes aim in the men's 10 m air rifle event.**

right: **Look of the Games structures welcomed spectators at the entrance of the Wolf Creek Shooting Complex.**

ROBIN S LEVINE • TODD L LEVINE • VIVIAN R LEVINE • ALLAN LEVINE MD • MICHAEL S LEVINE MD • BRENDA J LEVINS • CAROL LEVITT • CHARLES D LEVITT • GARY E LEVITT • IAN LEVITT • ROSE M LEVITT • IRINA LEVTOV • TERRIE B LEVULIS • ANN S LEVY • BOHDAN J LEVY • FREDERICK P LEVY • JACQUELINE A LEVY • JENNIFER B LEVY • NEILAN B LEVY • PAMELA J LEVY • ROBYN J LEVY • CAROLYN B LEVY MT • ARON LEW • SARA E LEW • DORIS L LEWALLEN • JOHNNY V LEWALLEN • CHRISTOPHER E LEWALLEN PM • BERTRAM C LEWARS • MICHAEL D LEWIN • LEAH LEWINE • RACHEL LEWINE • KASIA LEWINSKA

the silver medal, and Yugoslavia's Aleksandra Ivosev (497.2) earned the bronze.

50 m Standard Rifle 3 Position. In the women's 50 m standard rifle 3 position, Aleksandra Ivosev and Renata Mauer swapped positions in the medal order, with Ivosev winning the gold by posting an Olympic-record score of 686.1, and Mauer (679.8) winning the bronze. The Russian Federation's Irina Gerasimenok (680.1) garnered the silver.

50 m Free Rifle Prone. Germany's Christian Klees won his country's first gold medal of the

left: **The People's Republic of China's Ling Yang aims for gold in the men's 10 m running target event.**

right: **In the women's 10 m air rifle competition, sharpshooter Petra Horneber of Germany competes for the silver medal.**

Games by establishing both a world and Olympic record en route to winning the men's 50 m free rifle prone event. Klees hit the gold with a world-best score of 704.8, while out-

shooting Kazakhstan's Sergey Belyayev (703.3), who won the silver, and Slovakia's Jozef Gonci (701.9). Gonci's bronze was the first-ever Olympic medal for Slovakia, which became an independent nation in 1992. "I am very proud because [the medal] will be part of my country's history," Gonci said.

10 m Running Target. Gold-medal favorite Ling Yang of the People's Republic of China improved on his third-place preliminary showing by firing an Olympic-record total score of 685.8 to win the men's 10 m running target. Ling's teammate Jun Xiao (679.8) won the silver, and the Czech Republic's Miroslav Janus (678.4) won the bronze.

50 m Free Rifle 3 Position. Shooting an Olympic-record score of 1,273.9, France's Jean-Pierre Amat won the men's 50 m free rifle 3 position by edging out Kazakhstan's Sergey Belyayev (1,272.3). Austria's Wolfram Waibel Jr. (1,269.6) took the bronze.

Pistol Events

The pistol events contested at the Games were 10 m air pistol, 50 m free pistol (men), 25 m rapid fire pistol (men), and 25 m sport pistol (women).

10 m Air Pistol. The People's Republic of China's Yifu Wang, a diabetic, lost his lead in

• RAFAL Z LEWINSKI • ALBERT Z LEWIS • ALLAN L LEWIS • ALLEN G LEWIS • ANDREA L LEWIS • ANGELES P LEWIS • ANITA M LEWIS • BILL LEWIS • BLANCHE-NICOLE LEWIS • BOB J LEWIS • BOBBY O LEWIS • CAROL A LEWIS • CHARLES M LEWIS • CHARLOTTE W LEWIS • CHARMAYNE A LEWIS • CLARE H LEWIS • CLOREADIA P LEWIS • COREY LEWIS • CRYSTAL J LEWIS • CURTIS A LEWIS • CYNTHIA L LEWIS • CYNTHIA M LEWIS • DANA O LEWIS • DARIEN L LEWIS • DARRYL S LEWIS • DELORES S LEWIS • DIANE M LEWIS • DIONNE D LEWIS • DON R LEWIS • DONNA E LEWIS • DOROTHY P LEWIS • EDGAR V LEWIS

the men's 10 m air pistol event on his last shot when he became ill and fainted. The misfire by the defending gold medalist, who earlier set an Olympic qualifying round record, allowed Italy's Roberto di Donna (684.2) to come from behind and edge out Wang (684.1), who won the silver, while Bulgaria's Tanu Kiriakov took the bronze (683.8).

The Russian Federation's Olga Klochneva established an Olympic record in winning the women's 10 m air pistol event. Klochneva fired an Olympic-best score of 490.1 to edge out teammate and defending gold medalist Marina Logvinenko (488.5). Logvinenko took the silver by winning a shoot-off with bronze medalist Mariya Grozdeva of Bulgaria (488.5).

50 m Free Pistol. Olympic history was made in the men's 50 m free pistol competition. Although Sweden's 62-year-old Ragnar Skanaker, a four-time medalist, did not win a medal at the 1996 Games, this Olympiad marked the seventh time he made an appearance at an Olympic Games. In the competition, the Russian Federation's Boris Kokorev fired an Olympic-record total score of 666.4 to win the gold, followed by Belarus's Igor Basinski (662.0), who won the silver, and Italy's Roberto di Donna (661.8), who took the bronze.

25 m Rapid Fire Pistol. One day after firing a score of 298 (out of a possible 300) to lead the preliminary round, Germany's Ralf Schumann successfully defended his title in the men's 25 m rapid fire pistol event by shooting an Olympic-record score of 698.0 points, breaking his previous Olympic record. Bulgaria's Emil Milev (692.1) took the silver, while Kazakhstan's Vladimir Vokhmyanin (691.5) captured the bronze.

25 m Sport Pistol. In the women's 25 m sport pistol event, the People's Republic of China's Duihong Li won the gold with an Olympic-record total score of 687.9. Trailing Li were Bulgaria's Diana Jorgova (684.8), the silver medalist, and 1992 gold medalist Marina Logvinenko (684.2), who took the bronze.

top: Double medalist Wolfram Waibel Jr. of Austria won silver in the men's 10 m air rifle competition and bronze in the 50 m free rifle 3 position event.

bottom: In the men's 10 m air pistol competition, Italy's Roberto di Donna comes from behind to win Olympic gold.

ELIZABETH M LEWIS • ELYTHIA M LEWIS • ENID E LEWIS • ERIC W LEWIS • ERIKA LEWIS • ESTHER V LEWIS • FRANCES D LEWIS • HEATHER J LEWIS • JACQUELINE D LEWIS • JACQUELINE R LEWIS • JAMES R LEWIS • JAMES S LEWIS • JEANETTE LEWIS • JEFFREY D LEWIS • JENNIFER S LEWIS • JEWEL J LEWIS • JIMMY LEWIS • JOHN C LEWIS • JOHN M LEWIS • JON K LEWIS • KAREN J LEWIS • KAREN L LEWIS • KAYAMMA M LEWIS • KELLEY V LEWIS • KEVIN M LEWIS • KIANDA M LEWIS • LAURA D LEWIS • LAURA J LEWIS • LESLIE H LEWIS • LINDA LEWIS • LINDA M LEWIS • LINDSAY H LEWIS • LISA L LEWIS •

Shotgun Events

In addition to the two new events of men's and women's double trap, the shotgun events at the 1996 Games consisted of trap (men) and skeet (men).

Trap. Australia's John Maxwell, Germany's Karsten Bindrich, and Korea's Chul-Sung Park all fired a perfect 75 during the first three preliminary rounds of the men's trap competition. None, however, placed in the finals, as Australia's Michael Diamond shot a perfect score (25 out of 25) in the final round en route to

left: **Diana Jorgova of Bulgaria wins silver in the women's 25 m sport pistol event.**

right: **Italy's Albano Pera celebrates his silver-medal performance in the men's double trap competition.**

winning the gold with an Olympic-record score of 149. Diamond was the first Australian to capture a gold medal in shooting since 1900. A pair of US athletes rounded out the top three spots, as both Josh Lakatos and Lance Bade finished with identical scores of 147 (Lakatos won the silver in a shoot-off; Bade took home the bronze).

Double Trap. In winning the men's double trap event, Australia's Russell Mark shot an Olympic-record score of 189 to defeat Italy's Albano Pera and the People's Republic of China's Bing Zhang, both of whom fired scores of 183 (Pera took the silver by winning a shoot-off; Zhang took the bronze).

The US's Kim Rhode, 17, made the most of her Olympic debut by winning the first-ever Olympic women's double trap event. Firing an Olympic-record score of 141 points, Rhode finished just ahead of Germany's Susanne Kiermayer and Australia's Deserie Huddleston, both of whom fired a score of 139 (Kiermayer won the shoot-out to capture the silver; Huddleston received the bronze).

Skeet. In front of another standing room-only crowd, the shooting competition ended with an Olympic record set in the men's skeet

final. Italy's Ennio Falco and Poland's Miroslaw Rzepkowski both turned in error-free performances in the preliminary rounds, firing three perfect 25 target rounds. Falco, however, was slightly better in the finals, and he won the gold by finishing with an Olympic-record score of 149 (out of a possible 150). Rzep-

MARCIA L LEWIS • MARIE A LEWIS • MARIE P LEWIS • MARSHA K LEWIS • MARVIN E LEWIS • MARY LEWIS • MARY E LEWIS • MARY M LEWIS • MELANIE K LEWIS • MELISSA A LEWIS • MICHELE LEWIS • MIKE LEWIS • NANCY P LEWIS • PAMELA R LEWIS • PATRICIA A LEWIS • PAULINE E LEWIS • REBECCA L LEWIS • REGINA M LEWIS • RICKY L LEWIS • ROB LEWIS • ROBERT LEWIS • ROBERT E LEWIS • RODNEY LEWIS • RONALD L LEWIS • RONDA L LEWIS • SAM R LEWIS • SANDRA L LEWIS • SHARON A LEWIS • SHARON L LEWIS • SHELBY F LEWIS • SHELBY R LEWIS • SHOSHANNA E LEWIS • STEFFANIE J LEWIS •

kowski (148) took the silver, and Italy's Andrea Benelli (147) won a shoot-out with Denmark's Ole Rasmussen to capture the bronze.

CONCLUSION

The Olympic shooting competition was the first event of its type to sell out in the United States, with standing room–only crowds in addition to seated spectators at six of the eight finals. Overflowing crowds for the eight-day competition set US attendance records at all three shooting events.

Inside the ranges at the Wolf Creek Shooting Complex, the Olympic athletes' marksmanship established new records. During the eight-day competition, the shooting was so precise that Olympic records fell in every event, two world records were matched, and one new world record was set. The Russian Federation garnered the most gold medals with three, but a total of nine different delegations captured Olympic gold.

top: Seventeen-year-old Kim Rhode makes history by winning the inaugural Olympic women's double trap event with an Olympic-record score of 141.

bottom: Poland's Miroslaw Rzepkowski celebrates after winning the silver medal in the men's skeet competition.

Atlanta 1996.

STEPHANIE V LEWIS • STEVE H LEWIS • STEVEN A LEWIS • STEVEN K LEWIS • SVETLANA V LEWIS • TANYA LEWIS • TERRENCE A LEWIS • THADDEUS B LEWIS • THOMAS G LEWIS • TIMOTHY D LEWIS • TIMOTHY D LEWIS • TORRANCE LEWIS • VALERIA LEWIS • VALERIA D LEWIS • VIRGINIA L LEWIS • WALTER C LEWIS • ZENZEL LEWIS • GENON LEWIS JR • I. RICK LEWIS JR • JOE Z LEWIS JR • MARIA L LEWIS VMD • MELITTA K LEWITIN • STANLEY D LEWTER • NATHAN A LEY • KAREN J LEYDON • STEPHEN A LEYDON • PETTER LEYRA • GWENDOLYN S LEYS • RICHARD J LEYS • ALICE-ANGEL M LEYVA •

415

SOFTBALL

Venue Used:
Golden Park Stadium

Days of Competition: 9

Medals Awarded: 3
Gold 1
Silver 1
Bronze 1

Number of Nations: 8

Number of Officials: 60

Officiating Federation:
International Softball
Federation (ISF)

THE CENTENNIAL OLYMPIC Games marked the long-awaited and much-anticipated debut of women's softball as an Olympic sport. A total of 120 female athletes competed in the tournament. The nine-day tournament was held 21–30 July, with a rest day on 28 July.

VENUE

The site chosen to host the Olympic softball tournament was 8,800-seat Golden Park Stadium in Columbus, Georgia. Located along the Georgia/Alabama border on the banks of the scenic Chattahoochee River, Golden Park—currently the home of minor league baseball's Columbus Red Stixx—was approximately 105 mi (169 km) southwest of the Atlanta Olympic Village.

After extensive work, the stadium was remodeled to fit a standard fast pitch softball field, which featured a skinned infield and an outfield fence at 200 ft (61 m). The satellite Village for the athletes and officials involved in the Olympic softball competition was located at Henry Hall on the US Army base at Fort Benning, Georgia.

COMPETITION

Eight fast pitch teams (Australia, Canada, Chinese Taipei, Japan, the Netherlands, the People's Republic of China, Puerto Rico, and the United States) competed in a round-robin of seven games, with the top four teams progressing to the semifinals and medal-round games.

Sporting a 110-1 record in international play prior to the Games, the US was heavily favored entering the Olympic tournament. In the opening contests, the Americans did little to disprove this ranking. In the first four games, the United States recorded three shut-outs, surrendered a total of only nine hits, and outscored its opponents 29-1.

As an example of the tournament's outstanding pitching, the People's Republic of China's Liping He and Yaju Liu combined for a no-hitter in a 8-0 win over the Netherlands on the fifth day of the preliminary round. Together, the duo struck out 9 of the 22 batters they faced, while walking none.

On the sixth day of tournament play, first baseman Haruka Saito blasted three home runs, including a grand slam, to power Japan to an 8-1 win over Puerto Rico. Although she entered the game with just two runs batted in, Saito's power surge produced seven of Japan's eight runs.

CHRIS J LEZOVICH • MICHAEL LEZOVICH • ALICE S LI • ANDY W LI • B.J. LI • CHARLIE C LI • CHRISTINE T LI • JIANMIN LI • JING LI • LI LI • MING LI • NED C LI • QIAN LI • SUNNY W LI • THEODORE LI • WEIHUA LI • WENKAI LI • YING LI • SIMON X LIAO • INA L LIBERA • DAVID E LIBMAN • ANN C LICHTEFELD • LOUIS J LICHTEFELD • EILEEN M LICHTENFELD • BRENDA K LICHTENSTEIN • WAYNE R LICKER • RONALD J LICUDINE • SANDRO LICURSI • SYLVIE LICURSI • MARCIA H LIDELL • AARON W LIEBERMAN • ADAM K LIEBERMAN • SHELLEY LIEBERMAN • JEFFREY D LIEBERMAN MD • JEFFREY D LIEBERT • BRAD LIEBLEIN •

In the next game, the US dropped a 2-1 decision in 10 innings—only the second international loss for the US in a decade-long 115-game stretch. With two outs in the fifth inning, US hitter Danielle Tyler's home run was disallowed after she failed to touch home plate. Without the run, the game remained tied at 0-0 and was forced into extra innings. During regulation play, US starter Lisa Fernandez pitched a perfect game. After two overtime innings, the International Softball Federation's tiebreak system went into effect (a runner is placed on second base at the start of each half-inning), and the US scored a run at the top of the 10th. Still pitching, Fernandez was only one out from a perfect game when Australia's Joanne Brown hit a game-winning two-run homer at the bottom of the 10th.

A day later, Australia (5-2) clinched one of the spots in the semifinals with a 5-2 win over Canada (3-4). Leading the way again was

Brown, who in her first plate appearance after the dramatic game-winning long ball against the US, hit her second two-run homer in back-to-back plate appearances.

On the heels of its stunning upset loss to Australia, the US rallied to beat the People's Republic of China 3-2 on a sixth inning two-run homer by first baseman Sheila Cornell. The win guaranteed the US (6-1) the no. 1 seed in the semifinals, while the loss dropped the People's Republic of China (5-2) into the no. 2 spot. Japan (5-2) clinched the final remaining spot in the semifinals with a 5-1 win over Chinese Taipei (2-4).

The two teams with the highest batting averages and best pitching staffs from the preliminaries squared off in the opening game of the semifinals. Under the playoff format, the winner of the game between the US and the People's Republic of China (the no. 1 and no. 2 seeds, respectively) drew an automatic bye, thus advancing to the gold-medal game. The losing team faced the winner of the game

left: The Australian team celebrates after Joanne Brown's game-winning two-run homer in an upset victory over the US.

right: This structure, decorated in the Look of the Games motif, welcomed visitors to the softball venue.

facing page: Japan's Chika Kodama is pleased after tagging out a Puerto Rican baserunner in Japan's win in the preliminaries.

ALAN LIECHTY • SHU-CHEN I LIEN • MARY ELLEN LIESKE • CASSANDRA M LIEVSAY • KEVIN C LIEVSAY • KATARINA LIFKOVA • ALLAN J LIGGETT ATC • DIANA R LIGGITT • CLAUDE W LIGHT • DEANNE F LIGHT • JAMES R LIGHT • MARY I LIGHT • ROBERT L LIGHT • WINFIELD S LIGHT • LAURA B LIGHTCAP • THOMAS W LIGHTCAP • NANCY K LIGHTFOOT • ALLEN LAWERENCE LIGHTNER • CONNIE LIGHTNER • CHRISTINE D LIGHTSEY • GREGORY R LIGHTSEY • REBECCA LIGHTSEY • TOM LIGHTSEY • JEFF R LIGHTSEY SR • JULIA G LIGO • VERONICA E LIGON • LESLIE K LIGUORI • KEIJO K LIIMATAINEN • MARK A LILES PM •

top: The People's Republic of China's Xuqing Liu makes a play in the gold-medal game against the US.

bottom: US shortstop Dorothy Richardson raises her arms in victory after a two-run home run.

In a defensive struggle against the People's Republic of China, Cornell broke a scoreless game with a single while the bases were loaded in the top of the 10th to score shortstop Dorothy Richardson and move the US into the gold-medal game. In the other semifinal, Australia eliminated Japan from medal contention with a 3-0 win. Australia's streak of five straight victories ended, however, in the bronze-medal game, when the People's Republic of China's Lihong Wang pitched a two-hitter to lead her team to a 4-2 victory and a berth in the gold-medal game.

For the third time in four days, the US and the People's Republic of China met at Golden Park stadium, only this time the confrontation was for the gold. Controversy erupted in the third inning when the People's Republic of China's centerfielder Chunfang Zhang was thrown out on a close play while trying to steal home on a delayed double-steal. Her team argued the call unsuccessfully. In the bottom of the inning, Richardson gave the US a 2-0 lead after a highly disputed home run call.

between Australia and Japan (no. 3 and no. 4 seeds, respectively) in the bronze-medal game, with the loser taking home the bronze and the winner advancing to the gold-medal game.

The sold-out crowd of 8,500 spectators on hand to watch the two top seeds in the opening game of the medal round included IOC President Juan Antonio Samaranch, who was attending his first softball game.

SONJA K LILIENTHAL • MIKE D LILLARD • MOLLY J LILLARD • JASON P LILLEY • SHANNON M LILLEY • DAVID L LILLIE • RONG L LILLIEROOS • WILLIAM N LILLIOS • CHICK L LILLIS • EDWARD C LILLY III • VLADIMIR N LILOV • ARTHUR R LILYANDER • LAWRENCE Y LIM • PHILIP C LIM • PRESCOTT P LIM • SHARON S LIM • SHIRLEY LIM • IZABEL LIMA • DAVID M. LIMBERGER • LUIS A LIMERES • OLGA LIMON • CHRISTOPHER C LIN • CHUNCHIEH LIN • CHUNCHIEH LIN • CONG LIN • FANG LIN • JEAN H LIN • JUDY W LIN • LILY LIN • PATTY C LIN • SARAH J LIN • SHINEMIN S LIN • WAN-SHAN P LIN • AMY LIN-MEYERSON

Richardson's blast curled around the foul pole, and the umpire immediately signaled the ball was fair after it left the park. However, China's rightfielder Qiang Wei and coach Minkuan Li disagreed, and the ensuing argument lasted nine minutes. The call stood.

With the excited, full-capacity crowd chanting "USA! USA!" Fernandez, in relief of starter Michele Granger, got the final out in the American gold-medal victory. "It took me 44 years," said 72-year-old US head coach Ralph Raymond, who retired after the tournament.

The bronze-medal–winning Australian team comprised Joanne Brown, Kim Cooper, Carolyn Crudgington, Kerry Dienelt, Peta Edebone, Tanya Harding, Jennifer Holliday, Jocelyn Lester, Sally McDermid, Francine McRae, Haylea Petrie, Nicole Richardson, Melanie Roche, Natalie Ward, and Brooke Wilkins.

CONCLUSION

With sold-out sessions each day, more than 120,000 spectators warmly welcomed softball

The People's Republic of China's Zhongxin An tags out the US's Julie Smith at home plate during the US's semifinal win in 10 innings.

"This is the top of the mountain. There's no more to conquer."

The US team members were Laura Berg, Gillian Boxx, Sheila Cornell, Lisa Fernandez, Michele Granger, Lori Harrigan, Dionna Harris, Kim Ly Maher, Leah O'Brien, Dorothy Richardson, Julie Smith, Michele Smith, Shelly Stokes, Danielle Tyler, and Christa Lee Williams.

The People's Republic of China team consisted of Zhongxin An, Hong Chen, Liping He, Li Lei, Xuqing Liu, Yaju Liu, Ying Ma, Jingbai Ou, Hua Tao, Lihong Wang, Ying Wang, Qiang Wei, Jian Xu, Fang Yan, and Chunfang Zhang.

to the programme of the Olympic Games. No one was more pleased to hear the cheers than the gold-medal–winning hosts. For the US team, much of their success could be attributed to the strength of their pitching staff of Lisa Fernandez, Michele Granger, Lori Harrigan, Michele Smith, and Christa Lee Williams. In the nine-game tournament, the US pitched four shutouts and gave up an average of just 0.88 runs per game. In addition, the US outscored its opponents by a combined total of 41-8 en route to compiling an 8-1 tournament record and capturing the first Olympic gold medal in the sport.

Atlanta 1996®

TABLE TENNIS

Venue Used:
Georgia World
Congress Center

Days of Competition: 10

Medals Awarded: 12
Gold 4
Silver 4
Bronze 4

Number of Nations: 51

Number of Officials: 36

Officiating Federation:
International Table Tennis
Federation (ITTF)

DURING THE CENTENNIAL Olympic Games, a total of 170 athletes (87 men and 83 women) representing 51 nations took part in the table tennis competition, the ultimate test of reflexes. The 10-day competition was held 23 July–1 August. Table tennis was one of the more popular sports at the Games. It was one of the first sports to sell out (53,393 tickets were sold), and each session was filled with a vocal and supportive crowd representing many different nationalities.

VENUE

Table tennis was one of seven different competitions housed in the halls of the Georgia World Congress Center, the second-largest convention center in the United States. This facility, along with the Georgia Dome and the Omni Coliseum, comprised the Olympic Center—the most concentrated cluster of competition venues within the Olympic Ring—and was located approximately 1.9 mi (3 km) from the Olympic Village.

Hall D of the Georgia World Congress Center was the site of the table tennis competition. Seating capacity within the hall was 4,100. The spacious 89,000 sq ft (8,277 sq m) competition area contained eight 52.5 x 26.3 ft (16 x 8 m) playing tables lined in a row. On each table,

the small, white celluloid balls were smashed back and forth from a distance of 9–20 ft (2.7–6 m) in rapid-fire sequence at more than 120 mph (193 kph). Adding to the difficulty level was the spin the athletes put on the balls, especially during the serve, in which the ball must be tossed at least 6 in (15.2 cm) high from a flat, open palm.

The playing conditions for the athletes were of the highest standards. Through the use of specially designed air locks on all outside doors, air movement over the field of play was limited to an almost nonexistent level of 10 cm per second. At the same time, temperatures were kept at a level that was comfortable for both athletes and spectators. Lighting in the competition area was of television broadcast quality, and every table featured a computerized statistics system located courtside. This system provided

• CAROL LEE LINDNER • PERRI L LINDNER • CORDES LINDOW • OUTI E LINDQVIST • JARL LINDROOS • DIANE LINDSAY • HERTENCER U LINDSAY • JOHN D LINDSAY • LEA ELLEN LINDSAY • LEONARD C LINDSAY • MICHAEL LINDSAY • ROBERT K LINDSAY • VENORIA LINDSAY • ROBERT T LINDSAY III • ANNE K LINDSEY • CAROLINE T LINDSEY • DANIEL T LINDSEY • DELORES M LINDSEY • GARY S LINDSEY • HAYDEE B LINDSEY • JACQUELINE M LINDSEY • JAMES H LINDSEY • JEAN R LINDSEY • KATRINA D LINDSEY • KIMBERLY W LINDSEY • RICHARD LINDSEY • RICKY E LINDSEY • ROBERT M LINDSEY •

the most detailed point-by-point breakdown ever provided at a table tennis event, making the scoring information immediately available to athletes, broadcasters, coaches, and the press.

COMPETITION

Initially, the athletes were bracketed into 16 groups of four for singles and 8 groups of four for doubles and competed in a round-robin format against competitors within their own group. In this preliminary stage, matches were

best-of-three games. The winners in each group then advanced to the single-elimination playoff stage, which consisted of best-of-five matches.

Singles. In men's individual play, it was one up and one down for Belgium's first family of table tennis, the Saives. Jean-Michel, who was Belgium's flag bearer in the Opening Ceremony, and his brother Philippe were preceded by their parents, Jean-Paul and Geanene, former Belgian national doubles champions. Jean-Michel, the no. 3 ranked player in the world, went undefeated (3-0) in his group to advance

Olympic spectators enjoy women's doubles action at the Georgia World Congress Center.

facing page: Look of the Games banners hung from the ceiling in Hall D of the Georgia World Congress Center during the table tennis competition.

out of the preliminaries. Philippe, the world's no. 32 ranked player, went 1-2 and subsequently failed to advance.

Sweden's King Carl XVI and Queen Silvia Gustaf were on hand to cheer for Swedish countryman Jan-Ove Waldner, the 1992 Olympic champion, in the first round of the single-elimination stage. Canada's Wen Huang ensured that there would be no repeat gold medalist in men's singles, however, by knocking Waldner out of the 1996 Olympic competition (21-15, 17-21, 21-16, and 21-15). In an-

other of the day's notable upsets, Korea's Taek-Soo Kim defeated top seed Linghui Kong of the People's Republic of China, the world's no. 1 ranked player, 21-17, 21-18, 20-22, and 21-12.

In the quarterfinals, Korea's Kim faced Germany's Joerg Rosskopf in a seesaw battle that was 2-2 after the first four games. As the drama unfolded in the decisive fifth game, the German fans were chanting "Rossi! Rossi!" and the Korean contingent was yelling and waving flags in support of Kim. The drama ended when Rosskopf smashed a lightning-quick forehand shot for a 26-24 win, earning himself a spot in the semifinals.

The People's Republic of China's Guoliang Liu defeated Rosskopf in the semifinals, setting up a gold-medal match between Liu and his teammate Tao Wang—a winner over the

left: En route to gold, the People's Republic of China's Guoliang Liu reacts passionately to his semifinal win over Germany's Joerg Rosskopf.

right: Men's singles bronze medalist Joerg Rosskopf smashes a return in his quarterfinal win over Korea's Taek-Soo Kim.

Czech Republic's Petr Korbel. In the final, Liu took command in the fifth and decisive game to capture Olympic gold 21-12, 22-24, 21-19, 15-21, and 21-6, and Wang took home the silver. Meanwhile, Rosskopf defeated Korbel 21-17, 19-21, 21-18, and 21-19 for the bronze.

In the round-robin of the women's singles competition, the biggest upset came off the paddle of the Democratic People's Republic of Korea's Hyon Kim, the no. 42 seed, who stunned no. 9 seed Jie Schopp of Germany in two sets. Kim finished the round-robin unde-

feated (3-0) and advanced to the quarterfinal round before dropping a three-game match to the People's Republic of China's Wei Liu. Also advancing to the semifinals were Liu's teammates Yaping Deng and Hong Qiao, as well as Chinese Taipei's Jing Chen. In the semifinals, Deng defeated Liu, and Chen advanced over Qiao.

Billed as the "showdown of the century" by some, the final pitted the only two Olympic gold medalists in women's singles history—the legendary 1992 gold medalist Deng and her former teammate Chen, who won the 1988

Olympic gold medal. The match drew a boisterous and flag-waving crowd that included IOC President Juan Antonio Samaranch.

The match lived up to its enormous billing. After winning the first two games and dropping the third and fourth, Deng easily won the decisive fifth game in a 21-14, 21-17, 20-22, 17-21, and 21-5 gold-medal victory, with Chen taking the silver medal. Deng's teammates Qiao and Liu squared off in the bronze-medal match, which Qiao won 21-17, 15-21, 21-19, and 21-11.

left: Chinese Taipei's Jing Chen puts paddle to ball in the women's singles final.

right: Repeating as the women's singles gold medalist, the People's Republic of China's Yaping Deng hits a return in her gold-medal win over Chinese Taipei's Jing Chen.

Doubles. At the 1996 Games, the gold medalists in men's doubles changed names but not countries. In the all–People's Republic of China final, Linghui Kong and men's individual gold medalist Guoliang Liu defeated their teammates Tao Wang and Lin Lu, who had won the 1992 Olympic gold. The game scores were 21-8, 18-21, 21-19, and 21-17. In the bronze-medal match, Korea's Chul-Seung Lee and Nam-Kyu Yoo beat Germany's Steffen Fetzner and Joerg Rosskopf in straight games 21-18, 21-13, and 22-20.

terfinals, the duo survived two match points before slipping past Chinese Taipei's Jing Chen and Chiu-Tan Chen 18-21, 21-16, 21-19, 22-24, and 23-21. After a semifinal win over Korea's team of Moo-Kyo Kim and Kyoung-Ae Park, Deng and Qiao faced teammates Wei Liu and Yunping Qiao in an all-Chinese final.

For the showdown, a crowd of more than 5,000—predominantly Chinese supporters clad in red and waving flags—packed the Georgia World Congress Center. The defending world champions struggled early on, but a rally in

left: In an all–People's Republic of China men's doubles final, Tao Wang and Lin Lu face teammates Linghui Kong and Guoliang Liu.

right: Korea's Nam-Kyu Yoo and Chul-Seung Lee serve up bronze in men's doubles play.

The People's Republic of China's women's doubles team of Yaping Deng and Hong Qiao, the defending Olympic champions, had to persevere through tough matches in order to return to the top of the medal stand. In the quar-

the second game propelled the nine-year partners to a 18-21, 25-23, 22-20, and 21-14 gold-medal victory. In the all-Korea bronze-medal game, Hae-Jung Park and Ji-Hae Ryu beat teammates Moo-Kyo Kim and Kyoung-Ae Park 21-16, 21-8, 14-21, and 21-13.

CURTIS R LITTLE • DIANNE E LITTLE • DOLORES E LITTLE • ELLEN Y LITTLE • GEORGE G LITTLE • JAMES L LITTLE • JOSEN LITTLE • LINDA B LITTLE • MARCUS A LITTLE • MARY P LITTLE • MARY V LITTLE • RICK K LITTLE • ROBERT D LITTLE • SHANNON M LITTLE • TANYA H LITTLE • TIMOTHY S LITTLE • TODD A LITTLE • VICKIE C LITTLE • WILLIE F LITTLE • MADELINE D LITTLEFIELD • CHARLES E LITTLEJOHN • ELIZABETH LITTLEJOHN • STACY L LITTLETON • JERI L LITTMAN • PAM A LITTON • KAREN P LITTRELL • LIZA W LITTRELL • JERRY G LITVAK • LAURIE LITWA • BECKY L LITWILER • LEWIS P LITZINGER

top: Yunping Qiao and Wei Liu fight for the gold in an all–People's Republic of China women's doubles final.

bottom: Korea's Hae-Jung Park and Ji-Hae Ryu claim the bronze in women's doubles.

CONCLUSION

In only its third Olympic Games, the table tennis competition proved worthy of its popularity with fans. All four events (men's and women's singles and doubles) featured the return of a previous Olympic gold medalist, and each of the current world champions was also in Atlanta.

Asserting its dominance in the sport, the People's Republic of China won 8 of the 12 medals awarded during the 10-day competition: gold in all four events, silver in three events, and a bronze in one event. Leading the way was Yaping Deng, who proved her outstanding playing abilities by becoming a gold-medal winner for the second straight Olympic Games.

Atlanta 1996

ARTHUR C LIU • CHING-LAN LINDA LIU • ERIC LIU • ESTHER J LIU • FENGMEI LIU • JINGLI LIU • KENT C LIU • LI LIU • NING LIU • YAWEI LIU • ELENA Y LIUTKINA • BRUNHILDE I LIVELY • CAROL J LIVELY • FRANK HARVEY LIVELY • HOYT M LIVELY • KEN W LIVELY • NANCY J LIVELY • ROBERT P LIVELY • WENDY S LIVERANT • CHARLES E LIVERPOOL • JOAN A LIVERPOOL • LUCIAN I LIVESCU • SMARANDA LIVESCU • CHERYL C LIVINGSTON • DON L LIVINGSTON • ELBERT D LIVINGSTON • PATRICIA A LIVINGSTON • BRUCE M LIVINGSTONE • JANIE M LIVSEY • RUTH LIZANA-JACKSON • MIREIA LIZANDRA •

Venue Used:
Stone Mountain Park
Tennis Center

Days of Competition: **12**

Medals Awarded: **12**
Gold 4
Silver 4
Bronze 4

Number of Nations: **62**

Number of Officials: **141**

Officiating Federation:
International Tennis
Federation (ITF)

TENNIS

A **TOTAL OF 185** athletes (96 men and 89 women) representing 62 nations participated in the tennis competition between 23 July and 3 August. Eight of the top 10 (and 16 of the top 20) world-ranked female tennis players and 3 of the top 10 men were on hand to compete in the Games' four medal events: men's and women's singles and men's and women's doubles.

VENUE

Built especially for the Centennial Olympic Games and as a permanent public legacy for the tremendous amateur tennis league in the metropolitan-Atlanta area, the Stone Mountain Park Tennis Center provided a spectacular setting for the tennis competition. Located at scenic Stone Mountain Park, the tennis venue was approximately 16.5 mi (26.6 km) from the Atlanta Olympic Village.

Comprised of 16 courts, the facility featured seating for 10,400 spectators at the main stadium center court, plus seating for 4,900 spectators at court 1 and 500 spectators at court 2. The additional surrounding 13 courts each had a seating capacity of 500. All of the court surfaces were Plexipave, an acrylic cushioned hard surface.

COMPETITION

The tennis competition included some format changes from the 1992 Games. Bronze-medal playoff matches in all four medal events were added to the Olympic programme. The single-elimination tournament format was changed from best-of-five sets to best-of-three sets, with the exception of the men's singles and doubles finals, which remained best-of-five sets. A tiebreaker was used in all sets except the third set and in the finals of men's singles and dou-

DARIO D LIZCANO • PETER LIZON • PASKA LJUCOVIC • MIGUEL A LLAMOZAS • SUSAN L LLEWALLYN • CARL R LLEWELLYN • MICHAEL A LLORCA • FRANK B LLOSA • APRIL T LLOYD • CAROL H LLOYD • FRANK J LLOYD • JAMES L LLOYD • JANICE E LLOYD • JOHN H LLOYD • MARGARET A LLOYD • ROGER J LLOYD • THOMAS C LLOYD • JOAN A LLOYD-BRUCE • MARGARET LO • ANTHONY L LOADHOLT • COURTNEY B LOADHOLT • KAREN A LOADHOLT • RITA W LOADHOLT • BARBARA LOAR • ELENA LOARING • G R JOHN LOARING • SHERI L LOBACH • LOUIS H LOBE • CAREN A LOBEL • JOHN P LOBER • JULIA A LOBER •

bles play, where advantage scoring applied in the fifth set. The final modification involved changing the tournament draw to ensure that players from the same country would not meet before the quarterfinals.

Singles. In the first round of men's singles action, no. 2 seed Goran Ivanisevic of Croatia, the hard-serving left-hander who won bronze medals in both singles and doubles at the 1992 Barcelona Games, was upset by the no. 104 ranked player in the world, South Africa's Marcos Ondruska, 6-2 and 6-4.

Heading into the third round, only 6 of the 16 seeded players were still competing. One of the favorites who was knocked out of the competition was defending men's singles gold medalist Marc Rosset (no. 8 seed) of Switzerland, who withdrew due to illness during a match with Italy's Renzo Furlan (no. 14 seed).

At the end of the quarterfinal round, the US's Andre Agassi was the only remaining seeded competitor. India's Leander Paes—at no. 127, the lowest-ranked player ever to ad-

vance to the Olympic semifinals—Spain's Sergi Bruguera, and Brazil's Fernando Meligeni rounded out the semifinal field. Backed by what he would later say was "the best crowd we've seen in any tennis arena in the United States," Agassi thwarted Paes's upset bid by winning in straight sets 7-6 (7-5) and 6-3. In the other semifinal, Bruguera defeated Meligeni in straight sets, 7-6 and 6-2.

top left: Spirited Sergi Bruguera of Spain hits a return during his semifinal win over Brazil's Fernando Meligeni.

bottom left: In men's singles play, the US's Andre Agassi focuses on winning his first Olympic championship.

right: Columns draped in Look of the Games banners and topped with plants stood at the entrance of the Stone Mountain Park Tennis Center.

facing page: During the first round of men's singles play, South Africa's Marcos Ondruska pulls an upset over no. 2 seed Goran Ivanisevic of Croatia.

NANCY P LOCASCIO • NANCY LOCEY • CLAIRE A LOCH • WENDY S LOCKARD • GREGG G LOCKE • MEGAN L LOCKE • BILLY R LOCKEAR • MARK F LOCKENMEYER • DON B LOCKERBIE • RICHARD M LOCKERT • EDNA LOCKETT • MARCUS LOCKETT • GAIL S LOCKHART • MARGARET H LOCKHART • MICHAEL L LOCKHART • RICH LOCKHART • TONYA L LOCKHART • ROBERT LOCKHART JR • JENNIE L LOCKIN • CHRISTOPHER E LOCKLEAR • ELIZABETH LOCKLEAR • PATRICK D LOCKMAN • ANITA S LOCKRIDGE • STANLEY C LOCKRIDGE • CAROLYN R LOCKWOOD • DIANNE G LOCKWOOD • KATHLEEN M LOCKWOOD •

In the gold-medal match, Agassi needed only 77 minutes to defeat Bruguera, who became the silver medalist, 6-2, 6-3, and 6-1. Afterward, Agassi labeled his Olympic championship as the most prized of his 33 career titles, which include Wimbledon (1992), the US Open (1994), and the Australian Open (1995). "I'll keep this over all of them," he said. "This is the greatest accomplishment I've ever had in this sport."

Meanwhile, in the bronze-medal match, Paes rallied after dropping the first set to take the bronze by defeating Meligeni 3-6, 6-2, and 6-4. "The only thing I've ever wanted to do was emulate my dad's bronze medal," said Paes, whose father won a bronze in hockey. "I used to see that [medal] hanging up in the showcase at home when I was a kid."

Unlike the men's tournament, the women's first two rounds witnessed few surprises as 13 of the 16 seeded players advanced. The first major upset happened in the quarterfinal round as top-seeded Monica Seles of the US fell in three sets (7-5, 3-6, and 8-6) to the Czech

top: **Argentina's Gabriela Sabatini eyes a return in her win over France's Nathalie Tauziat.**

bottom: **Brazil's Fernando Meligeni follows through a return in his quarterfinal match against the Russian Federation's Andrei Olhovskiy.**

THEA MELISSA B LOCSIN • ALYSSA LOCUS • BARBARA A LOCUS-MAFFETT • JAMES A LOCUST • FRED F LODDEN • GUY LODGE • LAURA H LODZINSKI • B D LOEB • KIMBERLY M LOEB • L SAM LOEB • NANCY W LOEB • ALBERT C LOEBE • JESSE S LOEBSACK • LYNN M LOEFFLER • SUSAN E LOEGEL • MOLLY K LOEHLE • ANN V LOESCH • RICHARD W LOEWEN • TERRY L LOEWEN • ROBERT J LOEWENTHAL • CYNTHIA K LOFTIN • FRANCENE H LOFTIN • LARVETTA LOFTIN • REBECCA L LOFTIN • WILL T LOFTIN • SANDRA M LOFTIS • SANDRA T LOFTLEY • BERT A LOFTMAN MD • CAROL A LOFTON • HOLLY F LOFTON •

Republic's Jana Novotna. Also in the quarterfinals, Lindsay Davenport of the US (no. 9) defeated Croatia's Iva Majoli (no. 4), and Spain's Conchita Martinez (no. 2) dropped a three-set decision to the US's Mary Joe Fernandez (no. 7). In the other quarterfinal match, Spain's Arantxa Sanchez Vicario (no. 3) edged Japan's Kimiko Date (no. 8) in three sets.

The semifinals provided a pair of intriguing matches—one game pitted best friends against each other (Davenport and Fernandez), and the other placed Women's Tennis Association doubles partners (Novotna and Sanchez Vicario) on opposite ends of the court. Davenport handed Fernandez a 6-2 and 7-6 (8-6) loss, for which she apologized to Fernandez after the victory. In the other semifinal, Sanchez Vicario prevailed, 6-4, 1-6, and 6-3.

In the finals, Davenport defeated Sanchez Vicario 7-6 (8-6) and 6-2 for the women's singles gold medal. For no. 9 seeded Davenport, the win was her fourth over a higher-ranked opponent. "This means everything to me," Davenport said. "No matter what happens in

left: Olympic rookie Lindsay Davenport of the US powers her way to women's singles gold with a win over Spain's Arantxa Sanchez Vicario.

right: The Czech Republic's Jana Novotna dives to return a bronze-medal victory over the US's Mary Joe Fernandez.

KATHRYN ELIZABETH LOFTON • LUCILE W LOFTON • BRUCE W LOGAN • CHRIS D LOGAN • CLARKSON C LOGAN • DAWN M LOGAN • EVA H LOGAN • KATE LOGAN • LEMUELLA C LOGAN • MARGARET C LOGAN • MARTIN NECA LOGAN • MICHAEL LOGAN • MICHAEL B LOGAN • NECA M LOGAN • NNEKA LOGAN • PATRICIA Y LOGAN • PATRICK H LOGAN • PEARL J LOGAN • ROBERT D LOGAN • WILLIAM G LOGAN • BENJAMIN F LOGAN SR • DAVID T LOGAN JR • ROBERT S LOGAN JR • BEN R LOGGINS • DONALD G. LOGGINS • SHIRLEY R LOGGINS • LYNN L LOGMAN • LAURIE O LOGSDON • PAUL A LOGSDON • BRYAN D LOHEIDE •

my life, I'll always be a gold medalist." In the bronze-medal match, Novotna defeated Fernandez 7-6 (8-6) and 6-4.

Doubles. After the preliminary rounds, men's doubles action heated up in the semifinals as top-seeded Todd Woodbridge and Mark Woodforde of Australia survived the longest final set in Olympic men's doubles history to earn a 6-2, 5-7, and 18-16 win over the Netherlands' Jacco Eltingh and Paul Haarhuis. In the other semifinal, Great Britain's team of Neil Broad and Tim Henman beat Germany's Marc-Kevin Goellner and David Prinosil 4-6, 6-3, and 10-8 to assure Great Britain its first tennis medal since 1924.

Woodbridge and Woodforde, known as "the Woodies," captured the men's doubles gold medal with a straight-set 6-4, 6-4, and 6-2 win over Broad and Henman. Woodbridge and Woodforde's victory earned Australia its first Olympic men's tennis medal since Australia won a bronze in doubles play 100 years ago at the 1896 Olympic Games in Athens. Goellner and Prinosil won the bronze medal

left: Germany's Marc-Kevin Goellner and David Prinosil celebrate the winning point in their bronze-medal match.

right: Australia's "Woodies"—Mark Woodforde and Todd Woodbridge—win men's doubles gold at the Stone Mountain Park Tennis Center.

DEBRA S LOHEIDE • DONALD C LOHEIDE • JULIE K LOHFF • ANDREA B LOHLA • BEN K LOHMAN JR • ERIC J LOHMANN • BRIAN K LOHMULLER • SUSAN B LOHR • DAVID C LOHSE • ANTONELLA LOI • KATHLEEN A LOJAS • LANI J LOKEN-DAHLE • MARKO LOKMER • SOLFRID S LOKSLID • LARRY L LOKUTA • CORTNEY E LOLLAR • ANDREAS LOLLING • AMANDA L LOLLIS • CHERYL F LOMAX • DELPHYNE L LOMAX • ANN V LOMBARDI • JOSEPH L LOMBARDI • RICHARD JOSEPH LOMBARDI • JOSEPH R LOMBARDO • MARY L LOMBARDO • STEPHEN P LOMBARDO • DANA R LOMSKY • PAULA T LONDE • CHARLES LONDON •

for Germany with a 6-2 and 7-5 win over Elt-ingh and Haarhuis.

In the women's doubles competition, all top four seeds advanced to the semifinals, including the no. 1 seeded team of the US's Mary Joe Fernandez and Gigi Fernandez, who won 63 of 101 points in their 6-2 and 6-1 quarterfinal victory over Great Britain's Clare Wood and Valda Lake.

In the semifinals, Jana Novotna and Helena Sukova defeated Spain's Arantxa Sanchez Vicario and Conchita Martinez 6-2 and 7-6 (7-1). In the other semifinal match, Fernandez and Fernandez advanced past the Netherlands' Brenda Schultz-McCarthy and Manon Bollegraf 7-5 and 7-6 (7-3).

In the women's doubles gold-medal match, Fernandez and Fernandez of the US successfully defended their title from the 1992 Barcelona Games by beating the Czech Republic's team of Novotna and Sukova 7-6 (8-6) and 6-4.

Sanchez Vicario and Martinez won the bronze medal in straight sets (6-1 and 6-3) over Schultz-McCarthy and Bollegraf.

CONCLUSION

In the tennis competition at the Centennial Olympic Games, three of the four top seeds took home Olympic gold, including Australia's no. 1 seeded team of Woodbridge and Woodforde, who won the men's doubles competition and brought Australia its first Olympic medal in men's tennis since the first modern Olympic Games in 1896. In addition, the US dominated play as Americans Agassi (men's singles), Davenport (women's singles), and Fernandez and Fernandez (women's doubles) captured gold medals.

top: The US's Mary Joe Fernandez and Gigi Fernandez win their second straight gold medal in women's doubles.

bottom: Several Look of the Games design elements were employed at the entrance to the Stone Mountain Park Tennis Center.

Atlanta 1996.

NATHANIEL L LONDON • RENEE L LONDON • RICHARD L LONDON • SAROLYN LONER • KELLY LONETTI • AMY R LONG • BRIAN J LONG • CAROLINE T LONG • DARRELL L LONG • DEBORAH S LONG • DELL LONG • DEMPSEY R LONG • ELLEN A LONG • GARY S LONG • GEORGE T LONG • GLADYS E LONG • JAMES LONG • JENNIFER G LONG • JESSICA C LONG • JIMMIE F LONG • KIM A LONG • LELA H LONG • LINDA A LONG • LINDA E. LONG • LINDA S LONG • LISA M LONG • MELANIE M LONG • MELISSA B LONG • MELISSA S LONG • MICHAEL E LONG • MYRON E LONG • NOEL D LONG • PAULA D LONG • RANDALL B LONG

Volleyball—Beach

Venue Used:
Atlanta Beach

Days of Competition: 6

Medals Awarded: 6
Gold 2
Silver 2
Bronze 2

Number of Nations: 21

Number of Officials: 38

Officiating Federation:
International Volleyball
Federation (FIVB)

VOLLEYBALL

FOR THE FIRST TIME in Olympic history, two volleyball disciplines were contested at the Olympic Games. In addition to the traditional indoor sport, the Centennial Olympic Games introduced beach volleyball to the Olympic programme. A combined total of 372 athletes representing 30 nations competed in the two disciplines. Three venues—Atlanta Beach, the Omni Coliseum, and the University of Georgia Coliseum—hosted Olympic volleyball action, which drew a combined total of more than 617,000 spectators.

BEACH

Over the past five years, beach volleyball has grown in popularity and claimed its place in the spotlight. A total of 21 nations were represented as 84 athletes (48 men and 36 women) took part in the men's and women's tournaments. More than 108,000 spectators—many of whom were boisterous flag-waving fans dressed in the national colors of their respective countries—attended the competition, which was held for six days, from 23 to 28 July.

VENUE

Atlanta Beach, located approximately 20 mi (32 km) south of the Atlanta Olympic Village, hosted the first-ever Olympic beach volleyball tournament. This spacious facility, which received significant renovations and improvements in order to stage the competition, contained lakes and other recreational facilities, as well as the sandy beaches that hosted the fields of play. Two stadium courts were constructed—a center court (stadium court) with seating for 9,600 and court 2 (grandstand court) with seating for 3,000.

COMPETITION

Although beach and indoor volleyball are played on the same size court, the discipline of beach volleyball involves just four players (two per side), as opposed to six people per side in the indoor game. Other differences concern the playing conditions; unlike indoor volleyball players, beach volleyball players compete on a sand court in outdoor weather conditions.

The men's Olympic tournament consisted of 24 two-person teams, while the women's Olympic event had 18 two-person teams. Both women and men competed in a double-elimination format. Preliminary and semifinal matches were decided in one 15-point game, while the medal-round matches were the best two out of three 12-point games.

Men

Spain made waves in the preliminary round of the men's Olympic beach volleyball tournament. The no. 9 seeded team of Sixto Jimenez Galan and Javier Bosma Minguez of Spain sent both the no. 1 seeded team of Roberto da Costa Lopes and Franco Jos Vieira Neto of Brazil and

• RICHARD G LONG • RICHARD L LONG • RONALD E LONG • SALLIE D LONG • STEPHANIE LONG • SUSAN A LONG • SUZANNE M LONG • TAY LONG • TERESA L LONG • TIMOTHY D LONG • URSULA H LONG •
VICTORIA L LONG • VIRGINIA A LONG • VIRGINIA Y LONG • VIVIAN R LONG • WILLIAM M LONG • XIAOPING LONG • LLOYD E LONG II • JEFFREY U LONGBOTTOM • LOUIS LONGCHAMPS • HEATHER L LONGDON
• DONALD D LONGINO • DULCY L LONGINO • JULIE LONGINO • MARY L LONGINO • WALTER B LONGINO • MARY KAY T LONGLEY • JUANITA M LONGMIRE • SHIRLEY R LONGMIRE • JAN A LONGNECKER •

the no. 8 seeded duo of John Child and Mark Heese of Canada into the losers' bracket.

Impressive play also came from the no. 18 seeded team, Joao Carlos Pereira Brenha Alves and Luis Miguel Barbosa Maia from Portugal. After dropping into the losers' bracket themselves, Alves and Maia earned their way into the semifinals by eliminating Carl Henkel and Christopher St. John Smith (no. 2 seeds) from the United States; José Marco de Melo Ferreira N. and Emanuel Rego (no. 5) of Brazil; Jan Kvalheim and Bjorn Maaseide (no. 6) of Norway; and Martin Alejo Conde and Eduardo Esteban Martinez (no. 7) of Argentina.

Meanwhile, a pair of US teams—no. 3 seeded Karch Kiraly and Kent Steffes and no. 4 seeded Michael Dodd and Mike Whitmarsh—continued undefeated through the preliminary

top: **New Zealand and Italy square off at Atlanta Beach.**

bottom: **Portugal's Luis Miguel Barbosa Maia and Joao Carlos Pereira Brenha Alves celebrate their win.**

Dodd and Whitmarsh finished with the silver. Kiraly and Steffes won in straight games, 12-5 and 12-8. The gold medal in beach volleyball was the third gold medal for Kiraly, who led the US indoor volleyball team to victories in 1984 and 1988.

The bronze-medal contest featured the two teams from the losers' bracket: Canada's Child and Heese versus Portugal's Alves and Maia. In a score identical to that of the gold-medal match —12-5 and 12-8—the Canadians captured the bronze with a strong attack and service game.

left: **In an all-US final, Kent Steffes spikes the ball against fellow countryman Mike Whitmarsh.**

right: **Canada's Mark Heese dives for the ball in the bronze-medal match against Portugal. Canada took the bronze in straight games.**

phase of competition. In one of the tournament's most anticipated matches, Kiraly and Steffes defeated fellow US players Henkel and Smith 17-15.

In the semifinals, Dodd and Whitmarsh held off Alves and Maia 15-13 in a contest that lasted more than one hour. In the other semifinal match, Kiraly and Steffes needed just 37 minutes to defeat Canada's Child and Heese 15-11.

The all-US final matched the tournament's only two undefeated teams against each other. Kiraly and Steffes took the gold medal, while

Women

Although the no. 1 seeded team of Sandra Tavares Pires and Jacqueline Louise Cruz Silva from Brazil and the no. 6 seeds, Australia's Natalie Cook and Kerri Ann Pottharst, progressed through the preliminaries undefeated, other top seeds were not as fortunate. Three pairs from the US—the no. 2 seeded team of Holly McPeak and Nancy Reno, the no. 3 seeded duo of Gail Castro and Debra Richardson, and the no. 4 seeded team of Barbra Fontana Harris and Linda Hanley—were defeated in the preliminaries and forced to compete in the losers'

• IRIS A LOPEZ • JOE R LOPEZ • JOSE E LOPEZ • LOLITA LOPEZ • MARCIANO LOPEZ • MARSHALL LOPEZ • RAMON BENITO LOPEZ • SARA L LOPEZ • YANINA L LOPEZ • LINDA Y LOPEZ-BUTNER • NANCY LOPEZ-MOTA • JUANITA S LOPEZ R.N. • JOHN LOPICCOLO • ADAM M LORBER • ALEXANDER LORCH • BRENDA M LORD • CARLOTTA A LORD • EUNICE S LORD • JAMES L LORD • JOSEPH A LORD • KATHARINE B LORD • LOUIS E LORD • MARIAN G LORD • MICHAEL E LORD • PATRICIA C LORD • PHILIP R LORD • RICHARD D LORD • ROBIN E LORD • SYL A LORD • CAROLYN M LORE • HERMAN E LORENZ • WILLIAM W LORENZ •

bracket. Also in the losers' bracket was the no. 5 seeded team of Mônica Rodrigues and Adriana Ramos Samuel from Brazil.

Rodrigues and Samuel persevered, however, giving South America's largest country two entries in the semifinals. Also advancing out of the losers' bracket and into the semifinals were Fontana Harris and Hanley of the United States.

Both Brazilian teams won their semifinal games, setting up a rematch of their earlier meeting in round four of the preliminaries. Before a crowd of 8,500, undefeated Pires and

Silva moved into the finals with a 15-8 win over the US's Fontana Harris and Hanley. Brazil's other team, Rodrigues and Samuel, needed just 27 minutes to advance over previously undefeated Cook and Pottharst of Australia with a 15-3 win.

The women's gold-medal match featured competing compatriots. In front of 9,800 fans, many dressed in Brazilian colors of green and yellow, the two teams squared off for the second time in tournament play. Although the

scores differed from their first meeting, which Pires and Silva won 15-4, the result did not. Pires and Silva were crowned the first-ever Olympic women's beach volleyball champions after their 12-11 and 12-6 win, and Rodrigues and Samuel took home the silver. These four players became the first Brazilian women in any sport to win Olympic medals.

"I feel it is really an honor," 34-year-old Silva said. "We made history for us."

In a closely contested match that lasted one hour and 51 minutes, Australia's Cook and

Pottharst recovered from their loss in the semifinals to claim the bronze with a win over the US's Fontana Harris and Hanley. In the crucial opening game, the Australian team survived four set points before scoring the final three points to win 12-11. They took the second game 12-7.

CONCLUSION

Amidst an exhilarating atmosphere, spectators at the inaugural Olympic beach volleyball tournament enjoyed the warmth of the sun and plenty of heated competition. The event sold a record number of tickets for beach volleyball, including 11 consecutive sold-out sessions at center court.

top right: Brazil's beach volleyball players celebrate on the medal stand. (from left to right) Mônica Rodrigues and Adriana Ramos Samuel (silver) and Jacqueline Louise Cruz Silva and Sandra Tavares Pires (gold).

left: The US's Linda Hanley reaches for the ball hit by Kerri Ann Pottharst of Australia during the women's bronze-medal match.

bottom right: Look of the Games banners decorated the seating areas of the competition venues.

MARY T LORENZ-HALLING • SAMUEL J LORENZO • MARIA LORET DE MOLA • MARIA LORET DE MOLA • JUDITH C LORIER • VICKI LORING • KAREN S LORITTS • ANGELA B LOSACK • PATRICK F LOSACK • SCOTT C LOSACK • TRENT N LOSEKE • DANIEL LOSIN • JOHN LOSSMAN • CARSTEN LOTH • SUSAN L. LOTH • ADRIENNE R LOTSON • BRIAN W LOTT • DORIS A LOTT • FRANKLIN E LOTT • GENE LOTT • HOMER L LOTT • JACK E LOTT • JEAN P LOTT • JOAN E LOTT • ROBERT L LOTT • ROBIN M LOTT • VICKIE M LOTT • VIRGINIA G LOTT • CHRISTOPHER W LOTTIER • JOHN PAUL LOTZ • THOMAS M LOTZ • PINGPING LOU •

Volleyball—Indoor

Venues Used:
Omni Coliseum

**University of Georgia
Coliseum**

Days of Competition: 16

Medals Awarded: 6
Gold 2
Silver 2
Bronze 2

Number of Nations: 18

Number of Officials: 101

Officiating Federation:
**International Volleyball
Federation (FIVB)**

INDOOR

The sport of volleyball was invented in the United States in 1895. Appropriately, the tournament at the Centennial Olympic Games served as the centennial competition celebrating the sport's 100-year anniversary. More than 508,000 tickets were sold to the sessions, which lasted from 20 July to 4 August.

VENUES

Both the Omni Coliseum and the University of Georgia Coliseum in Athens were venues for the tournament. The Omni—site of preliminary matches, quarterfinals, semifinals, and finals—held approximately 16,500 spectators and was located in the Olympic Ring in downtown Atlanta, approximately 1.9 mi (3 km) from the Atlanta Olympic Village. The University of Georgia Coliseum, located 65 mi (105 km) from the Atlanta Olympic Village, hosted 10,000 fans for 10 preliminary games.

The field of play at both arenas included courts with identical dimensions of 60 x 30 ft (18 x 9 m).

COMPETITION

Eighteen nations were represented by a total of 288 athletes, who took to the courts in the 24-team (12 men's and 12 women's) Centennial Olympic Games volleyball tournament. In the preliminary round-robin, teams were divided into two pools of six teams, and the top four teams in each pool advanced to the single-elimination medal rounds. Matches were best-of-five sets, and a team won a set when it scored 15 points with a minimum 2-point advantage, or reached the 17-point limit.

Two key international rule changes went into effect in Atlanta: the service zone behind the end line was increased from 9 ft 10 in (3 m) to 29 ft 6 in (9 m), and a player's entire

RANDY D LOUCHART • ALLISON M LOUD • DEBORAH M LOUDEN • BENNIE LOUDER • CASON M LOUDERMILK • LEONARD C LOUDERMILK • JULIE A LOUDERMILK ATC • JANET LOUER • PHOEBE L LOUGHREY • SCOTT W LOUGHREY • HARVEY J LOUIE • JOSEPHINE LOUIS • RICHARD LOUIS • ANDY LOUIS-CHARLES • STEPHANIE M LOUSIA • VAN LOUSSARIAN • GAIL L LOUTON • SCOTT LOUX • BO E LOV • MARY E LOVATT • ADAM -JON J LOVE • CARLOS M LOVE • CHARLENE M LOVE • CHARLES E LOVE • CHERYL G LOVE • CONNIE J LOVE • DOMINIQUE V LOVE • JANICE D LOVE • JENNIFER M LOVE • LADON LOVE •

body, not just the part of the anatomy above the knee, could be used to strike the ball.

Men

Leading the way in the men's tournament was Italy, which beat Yugoslavia in the two teams' last game of the preliminaries in three straight sets to finish as the only unbeaten team in pool play. The eight teams that advanced from pool play to the quarterfinals were Italy (5-0), Cuba (4-1), the Netherlands (4-1), Argentina (3-2), Brazil (3-2), Bulgaria

(3-2), Yugoslavia (3-2), and the Russian Federation (2-3).

In one of the most exciting quarterfinal matches, Yugoslavia stunned a large contingent of dancing, singing, and whistling Brazilian fans by winning a five-set thriller (15-6, 15-5, 8-15, 14-16, and 15-10) over Brazil, the defending 1992 gold medalist. All four of the teams from Pool B (Italy, the Netherlands, the Russian Federation, and Yugoslavia) won their quarterfinal matches to advance to the semifinals, where Italy defeated Yugoslavia 3-1 and the Netherlands topped the Russian Federation 3-0.

In the finals, Italy and the Netherlands met for the second time in tournament play, with the Olympic gold medal at stake. In the earlier preliminary-round contest, the Italian team had handed the Netherlands' team its only defeat. In the final, the Netherlands returned the favor by handing Italy its only defeat of the tournament. The Netherlands captured the gold in five tension-filled games: 15-12, 9-15, 16-14, 9-15, and 17-15. Late in the contest, however, things had looked bleak for the Netherlands, when, after forcing a fifth set,

Italy's star Andrea Giani spiked the ball off the arm of the Netherlands' star Bas van de Goor to give Italy match point in the fifth set. Van de Goor, a 6 ft 11 in (2.1 m) middle blocker, responded with a spike down the middle to tie the score 15-15. The Netherlands' Ron Zwerver then struck a kill to give the Netherlands its own match point, which they won. After entering the Games as the world's no. 2 ranked team, the defending silver medalists finally found themselves on top.

The members of the Dutch team were Peter Blange, Guido Görtzen, Rob Grabert, Henk-Jan Held, Misha Latuhihin, Jan Posthuma, Brecht Rodenburg, Richard Schuil, Bas van de Goor, Mike van de Goor, Olof van der Meulen, and Ron Zwerver.

The silver-medal–winning Italian team consisted of Lorenzo Bernardi, Vigor Bovolenta, Marco Bracci, Luca Cantagalli, Andrea Gardini, Andrea Giani, Pasquale Gravina, Marco Meoni, Samuele Papi, Andrea Sartoretti, Paolo Tofoli, and Andrea Zorzi.

facing page: **Dutch players celebrate the Netherlands' gold-medal victory over Italy.**

left: **Argentina's Alejandro Romano hits a return in front of teammate Marcos Milinkovic during Argentina's win over Bulgaria in the preliminaries.**

middle: **The Russian Federation's Dmitri Fomin spikes the ball past Zarko Petrovic and Nikola Grbic of Yugoslavia in the bronze-medal match.**

right: **Look of the Games structures marked the entrance to the Omni Coliseum.**

LEE B LOVE • LOIS A LOVE • PAMELA G LOVE • SUE K LOVE • VERONICA D LOVE • WILLIAM A LOVE • WINIFRED A LOVE • SAMUEL A LOVE JR • HARRY P LOVE MD • DEE G LOVEDAY • ANDREA T LOVEGREN • SVEN O LOVEGREN • ELIZABETH H LOVEJOY • JEFF W LOVEJOY • JENNIFER C LOVEJOY • JULIA R LOVEJOY • AMY R LOVEKIN • ROSEMARY A LOVELACE • EDWIN P LOVELADY • LA MERLE C LOVELAND • KATHY J LOVELESS • ELAINE LOVELY • RITA K LOVENTHAL • DORA R LOVERN • JAMES E LOVERN SR • H M LOVETT • JAMES D LOVETT • JAMES S LOVETT • JAMES SR D LOVETT • JOSHUA D LOVETT • MICHAEL B LOVETT

left: Germany's Christina Schultz and Ines Pianka block the ball past the Netherlands' Henriette Weersing.

right: Ana Beatriz Moser sends the ball past the Russian Federation's Evguenia Artamonova and Natalia Morozova in Brazil's bronze-medal win.

Despite playing without its captain, Dejan Brdjovic, Yugoslavia won its first men's volleyball medal by beating the Russian Federation in four sets—15-8, 7-15, 15-8, and 15-9—to capture the bronze. Absent from the 1992 Games, Yugoslavia made a surprising and highly successful run through the tournament. The team had been together only since 1995, and Brdjovic was the only player with Olympic experience. Three matches into the preliminary round, however, Brdjovic had to return home when his 14-month-old son died of a brain tumor. "We said when he was going home, 'We will bring you a medal,'" said teammate Djula Mester. "We kept our promise."

Yugoslavia's team members who captured the bronze were Vladimir Batez, Dejan Brdjovic, Djorde Djuric, Andrija Geric, Nikola Grbic, Vladimir Grbic, Rajko Jokanovic, Slobodan Kovac, Djula Mester, Zarko Petrovic, Zeljko Tanaskovic, and Goran Vujevic.

Women

In the women's indoor volleyball competition, Brazil and the People's Republic of China were the only two teams that finished preliminary play undefeated (5-0). The Russian Federation and the United States followed with 4-1 records, while Cuba and the Netherlands went 3-2. Germany (2-3) and Korea (2-3) were the other teams to advance. In quarterfinal play, the People's Republic of China defeated Germany 3-0, the Russian Federation beat the Netherlands 3-1, Cuba topped the United States 3-0, and Brazil blanked Korea 3-0.

Although the competition for the Olympic volleyball title was heated from the outset, the intensity peaked with defending champion Cuba's five-set win over previously undefeated Brazil in the semifinals. In the other semifinal match, the People's Republic of China defeated the Russian Federation 3-1.

• RUBY L LOVETT • SHARON L LOVETT • SHIRLEY C LOVETT • TERESA N LOVETT • WALTER M LOVETT • JAMES D LOVETT III • WILLIAM H LOVIN • DONNA L LOVING • JACQUELINE LOVING • ZENA D LOVINGER • STARKE W LOVINGOOD • TONY A LOVITT • ANN H LOW • DEBORAH H LOW • ROBERT L LOW • DAVID C LOWANCE • GARY V LOWDER • CLAYTON LOWDER JR. • ANDRE T LOWE • CAROLYN J LOWE • CONNIE LOWE • DARLA M LOWE • DION A LOWE • EMILY H LOWE • FREDERICK H LOWE • JAMES D LOWE • JAMES H LOWE • JANET S LOWE • JENNIFER L LOWE • KENNETH B LOWE • NINA LOWE • PHYLLIS D LOWE •

For the People's Republic of China, this victory in the semifinals was its first-ever victory over the Russian Federation in international competition. Despite playing against the much taller Russians, 5 ft 10 in (1.8 m) Yongmei Wu hit a team-high 19 kills during the four-set semifinal victory. At the conclusion of the historic win, China's players embraced and cried while the crowd of 14,000 at the Omni erupted with cheers.

With the gold medal at stake before a crowd of 15,300 at the Omni, the Cuban women defeated the team from the People's Republic of China, which came into the finals with a tournament record of 7-0 and captured the silver medal. In the 14-16, 15-12, 17-16, and 15-6 victory, Cuba was led by its powerful hitter Luis Mireya, who hammered 31 kills, and blockers Magalys Carvajal and Ana Ibis Fernandez. Despite dropping two matches in the preliminary rounds, Cuba beat the only two teams in the tournament that had been undefeated after preliminary play. With the final victory, Cuba earned its second straight gold medal, joining the former Soviet Union as the only other country to win back-to-back Olympic volleyball titles.

The members of the gold-medal–winning Cuban team were Taismari Aguero, Regla Bell, Magalys Carvajal, Marleny Costa, Ana Ibis Fernandez, Mirka Francia, Idalmis Gato, Lilia Izquierdo, Luis Mireya, Raiza O'Farrill, Yumilka Ruiz, and Regla Torres.

The members of the People's Republic of China's team were Yongmei Cui, Qi He, Yawen Lai, Yan Li, Xiaoning Liu, Wenli Pan, Yue Sun, Lina Wang, Yi Wang, Ziling Wang, Yongmei Wu, and Yunying Zhu.

Brazil won its first Olympic indoor volleyball medal by outlasting the Russian Federation in five sets (15-13, 4-15, 16-14, 8-15, and 15-13) to take the bronze. The Russian Federation's loss ended the longest and most remarkable winning streak in women's volleyball history, which included four gold and two silver

medals while competing as the Soviet Union between 1964 and 1988, and the silver medal in 1992 as the Unified Team.

Brazil, the third-place finisher, had the following team members: Ana Beatriz Moser, Ana Flávia Chritaro Sanglard, Ana Margarida Vieira Alvares, Ana Paula Rodrigues Connelly, Ericléia Bodzick, Fernanda Porto Venturini, Helia Rogério de Souza, Hilma Aparecida Caldeiras, Leila Gomes de Barros, Marcia Regina Cunha, Sandra Maria Lima Suruagy, and Virna Cristine Dantas Dias.

Cuba's Regla Torres and Raiza O'Farrill block a spike by the People's Republic of China's Yan Li in Cuba's gold-medal victory.

CONCLUSION

During the Centennial Olympic Games indoor volleyball tournament, teams from six different delegations earned Olympic medals, and only two were repeat winners from the Barcelona Games. For the Cuban women's team, the gold-medal triumph was a reaffirmation of their greatness in the sport, while for the men of the Netherlands, receiving Olympic gold was a long-sought confirmation.

Atlanta 1996.

RICHARD H LOWE • WALTER J LOWE • CHRISTOPHER R LOWELL • JAIME I LOWELL • GREGG C LOWEN • CAROL A LOWENBERG • DAVID A LOWENKOPF • SHARON G LOWENSTEIN • KATHLEEN LOWER • DANNY F LOWERY • EMILY L LOWERY • ERICA LOWERY • FRED U LOWERY • JASON LOWERY • JIMECE Q LOWERY • KERMIT NMI LOWERY • LENITHRA LOWERY • LESLEY M LOWERY • LINDA H LOWERY • MATTHEW B LOWERY • RANDI L LOWERY • RICHARD LOWERY • DOUGLAS W LOWERY III • PEGGY LOWMAN • VAUGHN P LOWMAN • JACK P LOWNDES • JOHN P LOWNDES • BRYAN D LOWNEY • ERIKA L LOWRANCE •

WEIGHTLIFTING

Venue Used:
Georgia World
Congress Center

Days of Competition: 10

Medals Awarded: 30
Gold 10
Silver 10
Bronze 10

Number of Nations: 79

Olympic Records: 25

World Records: 19

Number of Officials: 65

Officiating Federation:
International Weightlifting
Federation (IWF)

AMONG THE SPORTS in which the most records were broken at the 1996 Centennial Olympic Games was weightlifting. During the 10 days of competition, weightlifting's titans of strength assaulted the Olympic- and world-record books with remarkable lifts. A total of 25 Olympic and 19 world records were established throughout the preliminaries and the finals.

VENUE

The weightlifting competition took place in Hall E of the Georgia World Congress Center, the second-largest convention center in the United States. Resting within the Olympic Ring, approximately 1.9 mi (3 km) from the Atlanta Olympic Village, the venue provided seating for 5,000.

The athletes entered the arena and moved to a 129 sq ft (12 sq m) stage, which was raised 3.3 ft (1 m) and topped with a 13 x 13 ft (4 x 4 m) solid wood competition platform. A piece of frosted Lexan was placed in the floor where the athletes stood to lift. This translucent material, strong enough to resist breaking and textured to provide good footing, allowed a camera to film from a unique angle beneath the platform.

The athletes were flanked by two stadium-size video screens designed to show replays and take the audience into the warm-up room. The 10 x 25 ft (3 x 7.6 m) scoreboard, one of the largest at the Games, displayed results for up to 16 competitors.

COMPETITION

The competition was held 20–24 and 26–30 July. One weight category was contested each day, beginning with the lowest weight class and ending with the superheavyweights. The weightlifters were split into the following weight classes: 54 kg, 59 kg, 64 kg, 70 kg, 76 kg, 83 kg, 91 kg, 99 kg, 108 kg, and 108+ kg. A total of 253 men representing 79 nations took part in the competition.

Within each weight class, the athletes were separated into groups according to their qualifying totals in pre-Games competitions held worldwide. The athletes with the highest qualifying marks were placed in group A, while the remaining competitors were placed in group B. When necessary, a group C was added to accommodate a greater number of competitors. Competition for group B (and C, when necessary) was held early in the day, while group A athletes lifted later in the afternoon.

The athletes were given three attempts in both lift categories—the snatch and the clean and jerk—and the gold medal was awarded to the athlete who successfully lifted the greatest weight in his weight category.

ROBERT P LOWRANCE • CHRISTINE LOWREY • MARY E LOWREY • TRUDY LOWREY • SUSAN M LOWREY-FLAHERTY • TROY A LOWRIE • BEVERLY F LOWRY • CAROLE A LOWRY • ELIZABETH G LOWRY • JERRY D LOWRY • LINDA I LOWRY • PETER J LOWRY • RILEY LOWRY • LYMAN J LOWRY SR • ADELINE H LOYD • JAMES W LOYD • RILEY E LOYD • DANIEL E LOZANO • THOMAS F LOZICK • ALICE J LU • CHUNG-SHIH P LU • YAFEI LU • JAMES O LUBBOCK • ELEANOR LUBER • JUSTIN LUBER • STEPHEN J LUBER • SAMUEL LUBIN • KATHY S LUBKER • KRISTIN J LUBNIEWSKI • ALECIA R LUCAS • ANN K LUCAS • BEVERLY A LUCAS •

Each day, the weightlifting venue was dotted with fans dressed from head to toe in their country's colors and waving flags to support their nation's competitors. Adding to the festive atmosphere was the rock 'n' roll music broadcast from loudspeakers. Feeding the enthusiasm was the wave of record-smashing results posted daily on the competition scoreboard.

54 kg. On day one, the records rush began as Turkey's Halil Mutlu, whose every lift was cheered by the large contingent of fans from Turkey, established a world record. The 23 year old snatched a world-record 132.5 kg on his final attempt and won the gold in the 54 kg class with an Olympic-record total of 287.5 kg.

top: **Against the backdrop of one of the Games' largest scoreboards, 253 athletes participated in the Olympic weightlifting competition at the Georgia World Congress Center.**

bottom: **Turkey's Halil Mutlu establishes a new snatch world record en route to winning the gold with an Olympic-record total in the 54 kg division.**

BEVERLY B LUCAS • BOB J LUCAS • DAVID D LUCAS • DEWONDA F LUCAS • ED LUCAS • FRANCINE LUCAS • GERALD S LUCAS • JACKIE LUCAS • JIM M LUCAS • JOAN T LUCAS • JOHN M LUCAS • LAMONTE LUCAS • LAYARETTE LUCAS • LOIS A LUCAS • MARY E LUCAS • MAX LUCAS • NANCY LUCAS • PATRICIA A LUCAS • SARA ELIZABETH LUCAS • STEVE LUCCI • BRIAN D LUCE • ADDISON L LUCE JR • ALANA D LUCERO • JOSEPH T LUCERO • JEANNE A LUCEY • KAREN A LUCEY • LINDA L LUCHETTI • DANA H LUCIANI • VINCENT P LUCIANI • DENISE LUCIANO • LISA LUCIANO • SUSAN A LUCIANO •

441

left: Silver medalist Leonidas Sabanis of Greece celebrates after lifting 167.5 kg in the clean and jerk of the 59 kg division.

right: Naim Süleymanoglu, Turkey's "Pocket Hercules," hoists 335.0 kg to become the first Olympic weightlifting three-time gold medalist by capturing the 64 kg title.

In the process, he held off a challenge by the People's Republic of China's Xiangsen Zhang, who won the silver (280.0 kg), and Bulgaria's Sevdalin Minchev, who won the bronze (277.5 kg).

59 kg. Lingsheng Tang of the People's Republic of China stepped up on day two and outlifted Greece's Leonidas Sabanis for the gold in the 59 kg division. It was a perfect day for Tang, as the 25 year old succeeded in each of his three lifts in the snatch and the clean and jerk, finishing with a world-record total of 307.5 kg. Sabanis won the silver (305.0 kg),

DORIS G LUCIER • ROBERT LUCISANO • DAVID J LUCK • MARTA G LUCKER • DOLORES G LUCKETT • TOM LUCKETT • PHILLIP A LUCKEY • RYAN D LUCKEY • JOE R LUCKIE • CHARLES R LUCKMAN • DELICIA D LUCKY • PEGGY L LUDAWAY • BRIAN W LUDEKE • HAYDEE C LUDENA • BRIAN F LUDERS • CAROL A LUDGATE • ROBERT C LUDOWISE • CAROL J LUDT • MICHAEL T LUDT • FLEMMING S LUDVIGSEN • KATHLEEN F LUDVIGSEN RN • COSANDRA L LUDWIG • MARTY P LUDWIG • RICHARD L LUDWIG • RITA J LUDWIG • ROSE LUEBKERT • R JASON LUEDTKE • MELISSA J LUEKEN • JANET R LUEPKES •

and Bulgaria's Nikolai Pechalov (302.5 kg) earned the bronze.

64 kg. The pulse of the competition at the Georgia World Congress Center quickened on day three—a day that made weightlifting history. The Turkish fans, whose numbers grew with each passing day, arrived early and began cheering and singing 35 minutes before the competition began and rarely stopped throughout. The reason: their Olympic hero Naim Süleymanoglu, the man they call "Pocket Hercules," earned an unprecedented third Olympic weightlifting gold medal, which he won in the 64 kg division. Despite his diminutive stature, the 4 ft 11 in (1.5 m) Süleymanoglu captured the top spot with a final clean and jerk lift of 187.5 kg. Süleymanoglu's successful lift forced rival Valerios Leonidis of Greece to attempt 190 kg—more than he had ever attempted, even in practice—on his final lift. Leonidis, however, missed, and the crowd, which included IOC President Juan Antonio Samaranch, erupted as announcer Lyn Jones said, "You have witnessed the greatest weightlifting competition in history." While Süleymanoglu captured the gold (335.0 kg), Leonidis received the silver (332.5 kg), and Jiangang Xiao of the People's Republic of China took the bronze (322.5 kg).

70 kg. Xugang Zhan of the People's Republic of China rewrote the record book on day four with one of the sport's most outstanding performances. In the 70 kg weight class, Zhan took Olympic gold by setting world records in all three categories: snatch (162.5 kg), clean and jerk (195 kg), and total (357.5 kg). Zhan, 22, defeated former world-record holder Myong Nam Kim of the Democratic People's Republic of Korea, who took home the silver medal (345.0 kg), by an amazing 12.5 kg and surpassed bronze medalist Attila Feri of Hungary (340.0 kg) by 17.5 kg.

top: Greece's Pyrros Dimas establishes two world records in the process of winning the 83 kg division.

bottom: World Champion Xugang Zhan of the People's Republic of China sets a world record in the snatch, lifting 162.5 kg.

left: The Russian Federation's Sergey Syrtsov lifts 190.0 kg in the clean and jerk event to earn silver in the 108 kg division.

right: Cuba's Pablo Lara raises 165.0 kg in the snatch to win Olympic gold in the 76 kg division.

76 kg. Cuba joined the medal parade on the fifth day of competition as Pablo Lara seized the gold in the 76 kg classification. In the first day that did not see a world record fall, Lara finished the competition with a total of 367.5 kg, followed by the silver medalist, Bulgaria's Yoto Yotov (360.0 kg), and the bronze medalist, Chol Ho Jon of the Democratic People's Republic of Korea (357.5 kg).

83 kg. From his first lift in the 83 kg competition, there was little doubt that Greece's Pyrros Dimas would soon be wearing Olympic gold. With 172.5 kg resting on the bar, Dimas thrust his first snatch attempt into the air with such ease that he almost seemed capable of twirling the bar on his fingers. Looking right and left, Dimas acknowledged his ecstatic fans from Greece and then peered resolutely at the fans in front of him before dropping the bar. The successful lift, which was more weight than all but two of his competitors even attempted, left Dimas leading his weight class by an overwhelming 10 kg after the snatch category. En route to capturing the gold, Dimas set

a pair of world records: snatch (180.0 kg) and total (392.5 kg). Meanwhile, Marc Huster of Germany set a world record in the clean and jerk with 213.5 kg and earned the silver with a total of 382.5 kg. Poland's Andrzej Cofalik garnered the bronze medal (372.5 kg).

91 kg. Alexei Petrov of the Russian Federation walked away as the 91 kg division Olympic champion. Petrov, who finished with a total of 402.5 kg, established a world-record mark in the snatch at 187.5 kg, which propelled him to victory and the gold medal. Leonidas Kokas of Greece, Germany's Oliver Caruso, and Sunay Bulut of Turkey all finished the contest with identical totals of 390.0 kg, but because of body weight, Kokas (silver) and Caruso (bronze) earned the Olympic medals.

99 kg. On day eight, rallying from his third-place position after the snatch category, Greece's Akakios Kakiasvilis vaulted into gold-medal position in the 99 kg division with a world-record mark in the clean and jerk (235.0 kg). The lift gave Kakiasvilis a world-record total of 420.0 kg,

NATALIA LUNA • SILVIA C LUNA • CHRISTOPHE LUNARDON • JOHN K LUND • KATHY L LUND • ROB LUND • SUSAN LUND • MARIAN G LUNDBERG • JOHN R LUNDE • RONALD V LUNDGREN • CLAUS E LUNDHILD • JOANNE K LUNDHILD • MELANIE D LUNDQUIST • RICHARD B LUNDY • WILLIAM E LUNDY • MARIA O LUNK • CHARLES V LUNSFORD • JOHN LUNSFORD • KAREN J LUNSFORD • KURT E LUNSFORD • MICHAEL E LUNSFORD • WEI LUO • LINDA M LUOMA • SHELLEY A LUPER • KERRIE A LUPICA • JOHN T LUPISELLA • JERRY W LUPO • TERRI A LUPO • JOHN C LUPPENS • NADINE L LUPRYPA • SAADIQ LUQMAN •

making him one of only 14 lifters (including fellow countryman Pyrros Dimas) to seize a pair of Olympic gold medals. Anatoliy Khrapatyy of Kazakhstan captured the silver (410.0 kg), and Denis Gotfrid of Ukraine took the bronze (402.5 kg).

108 kg. Tied with the Russian Federation's Sergey Syrtsov upon entering the clean and jerk phase of the 108 kg competition, Ukraine's Timur Taymazov hoisted a world-record 235.0 kg to move ahead of Syrtsov and win the coveted Olympic gold medal with a total of 430.0 kg. It was another disappointment for the Russian strongman, who finished second for the fourth time since 1991 in both Olympic Games and world championship competition. Syrtsov earned the silver with a total of 420.0 kg. Romania's Nicu Vlad took home the bronze (420.0 kg).

108+ kg. In this event dominated by world records, the superheavyweight division (+108 kg) provided a perfect record-setting ending for the 10-day weightlifting competition. Twenty-six-year-old Ronny Weller of Germany appeared set for his coronation as Olympic champion after raising what was then a world record of 255.0 kg in the clean and jerk to take a 7.5 kg lead in the overall competition. Following his record hoist, Weller hurled his wooden-soled shoes into the crowd in celebration of his achievement. To win the gold, the Russian Federation's Andrey Chemerkin had to lift a remarkable 260.0 kg. Snugly wrapping his fingers around the bar, Chemerkin paused before violently jolting the bar to his shoulders. Then, with the noise of the crowd building, Chemerkin quickly elevated the bar over his head. After Chemerkin's performance, Weller collapsed to the ground in utter disbelief. Chemerkin lifted a total weight of 457.5 kg to capture the gold. Placing behind silver medalist Weller (455.0 kg) was bronze medalist Stefan Botev of Australia (450.0 kg).

CONCLUSION

Record-breaking lifts were familiar during the Centennial Olympic Games. Throughout the weightlifting competition, an astonishing number of world and Olympic records were set. Certainly, this can be attributed in part to the International Weightlifting Federation's shuffling of the weight classes following the Barcelona Games. Passionate fans constituted another intangible factor in the success of these Olympic titans.

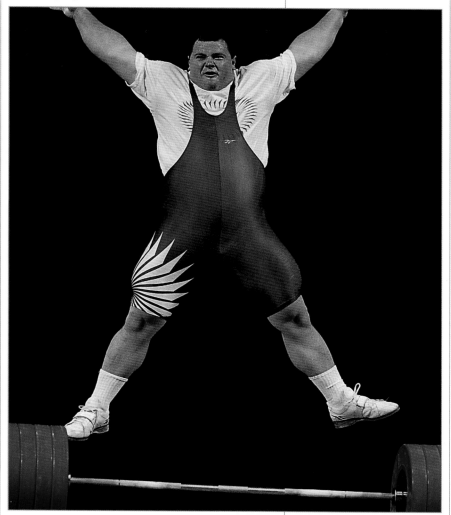

The Russian Federation's Andrey Chemerkin celebrates his gold-medal lift in the 108+ kg classification.

Atlanta 1996.

MARIA I LURE • FRAN T LUREY • JANE A LURWIG • JANA B LUSBY • SHARON R LUSCH • MICHELLE J LUSHBAUGH • ALBERT J LUSSIER • CHARLES J LUSSIER • STEPHEN LUSTER • JANET N LUSZCZKI • ALEXANDER R LUTHER • ANDRYA J LUTHER • BETSY A LUTHER • JOHN D LUTHER • RANDY M LUTHER • DAVID R LUTMAN • COURTNEY R LUTON • FRANK E LUTON • RONALD L LUTRI • JUANITA H LUTTON • JOHN J LUTTRELL • SANDRA K LUTYENS • ADAM LUTZ • ERIC L LUTZ • JANET LUTZ • STEPHEN P LUTZ • VINCENT LUWIZHI • JOSEPH F LUX • KATRIN LUX • RICHARD G LUX • TINA M LUX • RENEE C LUZE • R. DALE LWEIS

WRESTLING

Venue Used:
Georgia World
Congress Center

Days of Competition: 8

Medals Awarded: 60
Gold 20
Silver 20
Bronze 20

Number of Nations: 74

Number of Officials: 122

Officiating Federation:
International Federation of
Associated Wrestling
Styles (FILA)

DURING THE EIGHT DAYS of the Centennial Olympic Games wrestling competition, 74 nations were represented as a total of 406 men competed in 20 medal events. Each athlete took to the mat in the hope of adding his name to the long list of Olympic medal winners headed by wrestler Carl Schumann—the first gold medalist in the inaugural modern Olympic Games in 1896.

VENUE

Along with six other sports, competition in both wrestling disciplines was held in the Georgia World Congress Center, located approximately 1.9 mi (3 km) from the Olympic Village. Greco-Roman competition took place in Hall G, and freestyle occupied Hall H. Both halls had a seating capacity of 7,300. The field of play in each hall was fully carpeted and bounded on four sides by corrals displaying the Look of the Games. Within these field-of-play borders, each hall featured three wrestling mats placed side by side on a fully carpeted podium, which was 132 ft x 52 ft x 32 in (40 m x 16 m x 81 cm).

AMADOU T LY • LINH LY • STEPHANIE SOEGIHARTO LY • ELIZABETH I LYALL • ALISHA N LYAS • LINDA M LYCETT • PAUL W LYCETT • KEVIN W LYDAY • CHRISTINE A LYDEN • BILL R LYDERS • DAVID M LYDON • WILLIAM E LYELL • ROB LYERLA • SHARI L LYFORD • RON LYKINS • SANDRA D LYKINS • BEVERLY J LYLE • JANET M LYLE • LAWRENCE A LYLE • NANCY C LYLE • PAM LYLE • SHIRLEY C LYLE • PENNY LYLE-NORTON • HENRY L LYLES • KATHLEEN M LYLES • BARBARA LYLES-ANDERSON • PANAYOTIS J LYMBEROPOULOS • HEATHER N LYMBURNER • ALANA A LYNCH • ANITA R LYNCH • BAHAMA LYNCH •

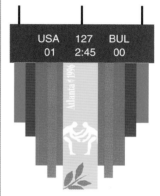

COMPETITION

Wrestling, which has been practiced for centuries and is considered one of the oldest sports in the world, has two disciplines for Olympic competition: freestyle, which relies more on speed and quickness; and Greco-Roman, which relies on upper body strength because only the upper body may be used against an opponent (competitors may neither grasp the legs of their opponents nor use their legs in any aggressive action; touching or using the legs is not allowed).

In Atlanta, the Greco-Roman competition was held from 20 to 23 July, and the freestyle competition was staged from 30 July to 2 August. Both disciplines were divided into 10 weight classifications: 48 kg (105.5 lb), 52 kg (114.5 lb), 57 kg (125.5 lb), 62 kg (136.5 lb), 68 kg (149.5 lb), 74 kg (163 lb), 82 kg (180.5 lb), 90 kg (198 lb), 100 kg (220 lb), and 130 kg (286 lb).

top left: **Andriy Kalashnikov of Ukraine is brought down by the Russian Federation's Samvel Danielyan during Kalashnikov's bronze-medal victory in the 52 kg classification.**

bottom left: **Gold medalist Yuriy Melnichenko of Kazakhstan takes down the US's Dennis Hall in the 57 kg final.**

right: **Look of the Games banners hung from the scoreboard in Hall G of the Georgia World Congress Center.**

facing page: **Greco-Roman wrestlers compete at the Georgia World Congress Center.**

BRENDA L LYNCH • ERIC L LYNCH • FLORENCE L LYNCH • JOAN A LYNCH • JOHN F LYNCH • KARLA D LYNCH • KATHY H LYNCH • MATT LYNCH • MEGAN D LYNCH • MICHAEL A LYNCH • MICHAEL A LYNCH • MICHAEL C LYNCH • NANCY L LYNCH • PEGGIE J LYNCH • ROBERT J LYNCH • TERESA T LYNCH • ZOE-ANN S LYNCH • ELIZABETH LYNCH-HALUSKA • WALT H LYNCH IV • KERRY R LYNE • JENNY R LYNESS • NICOLE M LYNK • GAIL LYNN • GAY S LYNN • JUDY E LYNN • KARL M LYNN • AMMEE R LYON • CAMILLE D LYON • CYNTHIA P LYON • FREDA G LYON • KRISTA K LYON • THOMAS M LYON • THOMAS M LYON •

GRECO-ROMAN

48 kg (105.5 lb). In the lightest Greco-Roman class, the 48 kg, 19 athletes competed. In the medal round, Korea's Kwon-Ho Sim captured the gold medal after defeating Aleksandr Pavlov of Belarus, who won the silver. The Russian Federation's Zafar Gulyov took the bronze.

52 kg (114.5 lb). Twenty wrestlers took part in the 52 kg weight class competition. Armen Nazaryan gave Armenia its first taste of Olympic

glory when he defeated the US's Brandon Paulson for the gold. Paulson, competing in his first senior-level tournament, was also pleased with his showing. "I got a silver medal," he said. "I achieved a lifelong dream for millions and millions of kids from around the world." Receiving the bronze was Ukraine's Andriy Kalashnikov.

57 kg (125.5 lb). The 57 kg weight class included 19 competitors. The medal contention culminated in a rematch of the 1995 World Championship final; however, Kazakhstan's Yuriy Melnichenko reversed the outcome by

top: Turkey's Hamza Yerlikaya flips with excitement after beating Germany's Thomas Zander to win the 82 kg division.

bottom: Gold medalist Wlodzimierz Zawadzki of Poland tangles with Cuba's Juan Luis Maren Delis in the 62 kg championship match.

taking the gold 4-1 over World Champion Dennis Hall of the US, who earned the silver medal. Zetian Sheng of the People's Republic of China took his place on the medal stand to receive the bronze.

62 kg (136.5 lb). Nineteen wrestlers competed to reach the finals in the 62 kg weight class. With Polish President Aleksandr Kwasniewski on hand, Poland's Wlodzimierz

JAMES R LYON CATC • JAMES W LYON IV • JOHN C LYON JR • ANDREW S LYONS • CATHERINE LYONS • CHERYL A LYONS • CYNTHIA L LYONS • DAVID A LYONS • DEREK W LYONS • DOROTHY S LYONS • ELIZABETH L LYONS • JACKIE L LYONS • JOHN B LYONS • JOHN C LYONS • MARK D LYONS • MARY M LYONS • SHEILA J LYONS • TANYA J LYONS • TERESA J LYONS • TERRENCE P LYONS • THOMAS L LYONS • WILLIAM LYONS • JOHN T LYONS III • JOHN T LYONS JR • THOMAS C LYSEN • MICHAEL J LYSTER • RUSLANA LYSYUK • ROBERT G LYTHGOE • FLORENCE J LYTLE • MERRY A LYTLE • SHAWN V LYTLE • ARCHIE K LYTLE III •

Zawadzki conquered Cuba's Juan Luis Maren Delis 3-1 to garner the gold. "I am very happy because the president doesn't attend all the events, just the big ones," Zawadzki said afterward. Turkey's Mehmet Akif Pirim took home the bronze.

68 kg (149.5 lb). Twenty-two athletes wrestled in the 68 kg class. Before a crowd of 6,335, wildcard surprise Ryszard Wolny of Poland won the title with a shutout win over European champion Ghani Yolouz of France, the silver medalist. Aleksandr Tretyakov of the

top: With the 100 kg bronze medal in the balance, the Russian Federation's Teymuraz Edisherashvili tries to take down Sweden's Mikael Ljungberg.

bottom: In head-to-head competition, the Russian Federation's "Siberian Bear," Aleksandr Karelin (right), confronts the US's Matt Ghaffari (left) in the 130 kg gold-medal match.

Russian Federation earned the bronze. After the medal presentations, the Polish Greco-Roman team was literally flipping over its second gold-medal victory of the day. Wolny's teammates celebrated by picking him up and tossing him in the air six times.

74 kg (163 lb). Twenty-two athletes fought to determine the finalists in the 74 kg division. Feliberto Ascuy Aguilera of Cuba won the gold with a victory over Finland's Marko Asell,

who captured the silver. Finishing third and gaining the bronze medal was Poland's Jozef Tracz. Following the formal medal ceremony, Aguilera took a victory lap in the hall waving a Cuban flag.

82 kg (180.5 lb). Nineteen wrestlers started the competition in the 82 kg division. Hamza Yerlikaya earned a gold medal for Turkey by defeating Germany's Thomas Zander in the 82 kg

ROBERT J LYTLE III • MICHAEL CABALLERO • MARY ANN JOHNSON • DIANJUN MA • REX C MA • YUANCHUN MA • SHANE A MAACK • HEIDI C MAASER • SAUNDRA A MAASS-ROBINSON MD • JOAN M MABEE • CARLA A MABIE • MARIE E MABIN • BERNADINE P MABRA • FRANCISCA R MABRY • ROGER A MABRY • TODD C MABRY • DONNA J MAC CONNELL • STEPHEN J MAC DONALD • MICHAEL R MAC EACHERN • MONICA M MACALA • REBECCA MACALLISTER • DAWN M MACALUSO • MARIA T MACARLE • ALLAN B MACARTHUR • DEBORAH B MACARTHUR • HEATHER MACBRIDE • HEATHER C MACBRIDE •

top: **Valentin Dimitrov Jordanov of Bulgaria captures his first Olympic gold medal against Azerbaijan's Namik Abdullayev in the freestyle 52 kg final.**

bottom: **While winning his second straight Olympic championship, Il Kim of the Democratic People's Republic of Korea attempts a leg hold on Armenia's Armen Mkrchyan in the freestyle 48 kg division final.**

1992 Olympic champion Maik Bullmann of Germany captured the bronze.

100 kg (220 lb). Nineteen athletes competed for one of the four spots in the finals of the 100 kg class. Andrzej Wronski of Poland won the gold with a win over Sergey Lishtvan of Belarus. Later, Wronski celebrated his victory by doing a back flip on the mat in front of the crowd of 6,335. Placing behind silver medalist Lishtvan was bronze medalist Mikael Ljungberg of Sweden.

130 kg (286 lb). Eighteen athletes participated in the 130 kg division, and six-time world champion Aleksandr Karelin of the Russian Federation continued his reign. The massive superheavyweight wrestler from Siberia remained undefeated in international competition as he won his third straight Olympic gold medal. The US's Matt Ghaffari, however, came close to pulling off an upset. In the final, Ghaffari pushed the "Siberian Bear" into a classic overtime battle. Karelin, with his 20-year international unbeaten streak and his 3-year streak with no scores against him on the line, held on to beat Ghaffari 1-0 in probably his toughest Olympic championship. Ghaffari earned the silver medal, and the Republic of Moldova's Serguei Moureiko took home the bronze.

"I wanted victory," Karelin said. "I was determined to win." With the victory, Karelin joined Alexander Medved of the former Soviet Union as the only two wrestlers in history to win gold medals at three Olympic Games.

Conclusion

Poland dominated the Greco-Roman wrestling competition at the Centennial Olympic Games by winning medals in 5 of the 10 weight classifications. The Polish medal total included three gold, one silver, and one bronze. The Russian Federation, which had held three straight world titles, captured one gold and two silver medals.

Nearly 46,000 tickets were sold for the events in the Greco-Roman discipline.

final. Zander took home the silver, while Valeriy Tsilent of Belarus seized the bronze medal.

90 kg (198 lb). The 90 kg had the largest number of competitors of all the weight classes, with 23 athletes participating. Ukraine's Vyacheslav Oliynyk overcame Poland's Jacek Fafinski 6-0 to win the gold, while Fafinski took home the silver. Three-time world champion and

JANICE RITA MACCALLON • MILLLICENT C MACCHIONE • AMY MACCONNELL • ALICE W MACDONALD • BEVERLY A MACDONALD • BRUCE A MACDONALD • JASON E MACDONALD • MARTHA L MACDONALD • MARY W MACDONALD • NANCY MACDONALD • SANDRA E MACDONALD • SUZANNE A MACDONALD • WILLIAM A MACDONALD • AL MACDONALD • GEORGIA R MACDOUGAL • HAROLD I MACDOUGAL • JAMES A MACEDON • LISA M MACEY • ANTON F MACFARLANE • KATHLYN G MACFARLANE • FRED J MACFEE • ROBIN J MACGOWAN • KHALED A MACHACA • CARMEN RAE MACHACEK • RAUL R MACHADO •

FREESTYLE

48 kg (105.5 lb). Nineteen athletes took part in the 48 kg class of the freestyle competition. Il Kim of the Democratic People's Republic of Korea successfully defended his gold medal in the division, earning his country a gold medal in wrestling by defeating Armenia's Armen Mkrchyan, who took the silver. Cuba's Alexis Vila Perdomo took home the bronze medal.

52 kg (114.5 lb). Battling in the 52 kg classification were 19 wrestlers. In the finals, seven-

Bruce Baumgartner. Kazakhstan's Maulen Mamyrov won the bronze.

57 kg (125.5 lb). Kendall Cross of the United States defeated Giuvi Sissaouri of Canada 5-3 to win the US's first wrestling gold medal of the Games. Placing behind Cross and Sissaouri, the silver medalist, was Yong Sam Ri of the Democratic People's Republic of Korea, who captured the bronze medal. These medalists emerged from a field of 22 athletes.

62 kg (136.5 lb). Twenty-one wrestlers competed in the 62 kg division. With twin brother

Ukraine's Elbrus Tedeyev puts a move on Italy's Giovanni Schillaci during their match in the 62 kg classification.

time world champion Valentin Dimitrov Jordanov of Bulgaria finally captured his first Olympic gold medal. His victory over Azerbaijan's Namik Abdullayev, the silver medalist, gave Jordanov a total of 12 world and Olympic medals, tying him for second on the all-time list with former Russian great Alexander Medved, just one medal behind American

Terry, the 1995 world champion in the 57 kg class, in his corner, 1993 World Champion Tom Brands of the US controlled his opponents, surrendering just one point in four matches en route to winning the gold. "Terry helped me a lot," Brands said afterward. "He warmed me up for every match. He was there to support me." In the finals, Brands recorded a 7-0 win over Korea's silver medalist Jae-Sung Jang. Taking home the bronze was Ukraine's Elbrus Tedeyev.

SANTIAGO MACHADO • ANNA M MACHAMER • ELISABETH J MACHAMER • MELVIN MACHANIC • PATRICIA L MACHEMER • BROOKE A MACHEN • CRAIG A MACHEN • SAM MACHIDA • ANTONIO E MACIAS • CARLOS V MACIAS JR • PAUL E MACIK • ANTHONY G MACINTYRE • ELISE C MACINTYRE • BRIAN S MACK • DANIEL MACK • DEBORA S MACK • INGEBORG G MACK • KATHY R MACK • KERRI A MACK • LINTON R MACK • PATRICIA A MACK • ROBERTA A MACK • VERA J MACK • CONSTANCE A MACK-ANDREWS • BEVERLY J MACKAY • DOUGLAS J MACKAY • SCOTT A MACKAY • STACY L MACKEL SAT • JACK MACKENROTH •

68 kg (149.5 lb). Nineteen athletes competed in the 68 kg division. In the struggle for the gold and silver medals, the Russian Federation's Vadim Bogiyev defeated Townsend Saunders of the United States. Ukraine's Zaza Zazirov won the bronze.

74 kg (163 lb). Twenty-two wrestlers took part in the 74 kg classification competition. Buvaysa Saytyev of the Russian Federation overcame Jang-Soon Park of Korea to earn the coveted Olympic gold. Park received the silver medal, and Japan's Takuya Ota won the bronze.

took home the silver medal. Winning the bronze medal was the Islamic Republic of Iran's Amir Reza Khadem Azghadi.

90 kg (198 lb). In a field of 21 wrestlers, Amir Azghadi's brother Rasull Khadem Azghadi, also of the Islamic Republic of Iran, captured the gold in the 90 kg category. In the final match, Azghadi—the current world champion—denied five-time world champion Makharbek Khadartsev of the Russian Federation his third consecutive gold medal. Azghadi, who had defeated Khadartsev in the last two world championship finals, won the match 3-0, while Khadartsev took the silver. Earning the bronze was Eldari Kurtanidze of Georgia.

100 kg (220 lb). Nineteen athletes took to the mat in the 100 kg classification. More than 7,000 were in Hall H of the Georgia World Congress Center to see possibly the longest 90 seconds of Kurt Angle's life: the time Angle spent waiting for three officials to confer and break a 1-1 overtime deadlock in the gold-medal final between the US's Angle and the Islamic Republic of Iran's Abbas Jadidi. For Angle, however, it was worth the wait. After hearing his name announced as the winner, Angle fell to his knees and wept. His emotions were echoed on the medal stand as nearly 300 family members and friends stomped their feet and chanted his name.

left: The Russian Federation's Makharbek Khadartsev and the Islamic Republic of Iran's Rasull Khadem Azghadi compete in the 90 kg final.

right: The Russian Federation's Khadzhimurad Magomedov battles Hyun-Mo Yang of Korea in the 82 kg final.

82 kg (180.5 lb). In the 82 kg division, 21 athletes hit the mat. Khadzhimurad Magomedov completed the Russian Federation's sweep of the three middleweight classes, winning the gold by defeating Hyun-Mo Yang of Korea, who

DOUGLAS MACKENZIE • ESTELLE A MACKENZIE • ARRINGTON MACKEY • COLIN C MACKEY • DAN M MACKEY • GERALD F MACKEY • KENDRA S MACKEY • LILY S MACKEY • MARY ANN E MACKEY • SANDRA MACKEY • SANDRA S. MACKEY • THERAL E MACKEY • WENDELL MACKEY • LAURA T MACKEY-VASZARI • LAWRENCE A MACKHOUL • JAMES H MACKIE ATC • THOMAS B MACKIN • DEENA M MACKINNON • BROOKS MACKINTOSH • JUDY G MACKINTOSH • ANDREW M MACKLER • BENJAMIN MACKOWIAK • JEROME MACKOWIAK • MATTHEW D MACKOWSKI • FRANK W MACKZUM • VICTORIA A MACKZUM •

"This is the best thing that's ever happened to me," he said. Angle's victory was especially poignant because he was the only member of the wrestling club named for the late Dave Schultz to make the Olympic team. Jadidi received the silver medal, and the bronze medalist was Germany's Arawat Sabejew.

130 kg (288 lb). Among a group of 18 competitors, Mahmut Demir captured the 130 kg freestyle gold medal for Turkey by downing Belarus's Aleksey Medvedev. Demir retired following the match. Bruce Baumgartner of the United States earned a piece of history by winning the bronze medal. The victory secured Baumgartner's 13th medal in world or Olympic competition, which is the most medals ever won by an individual in international wrestling. In addition, Baumgartner also became only the fifth US athlete to collect medals at four Olympiads.

CONCLUSION

In a tight race for supremacy on the freestyle mat, the United States took medals in 5 of the 10 events, finishing with a total of five medals: three gold, one silver, and one bronze. The Russian Federation was close behind, winning medals in four events: three gold and one silver.

More than 45,000 tickets were sold for the freestyle wrestling events.

The US's Kurt Angle responds emotionally to his gold-medal victory in the 100 kg final.

Atlanta 1996

YACHTING

YACHTING SET SAIL off the Georgia coast near Savannah in Wassaw Sound and the Atlantic Ocean. Some of the nautical routes the Olympic athletes navigated were the same as those followed by James Edward Oglethorpe when he founded Savannah—Georgia's first settlement—on 12 February 1733. Located 250 mi (402 km) southeast of Atlanta, Savannah is one of the most scenic and historic cities in the southern US. Ancient oak trees draped in Spanish moss embellish 24 historic parklike squares (22 of which date from the settlement's original design) and shelter the 18th- and 19th-century homes and buildings that survived the Civil War.

Amid this beautiful downtown setting, Savannah held its own Opening Ceremony. A crowd of 8,000 celebrated the start of the Olympic yachting competition with a parade of the yachting athletes, the lighting of the city's Olympic cauldron, and a fireworks display.

VENUE

In addition to the four racecourses—course A in Wassaw Sound and B, C, and D in the Atlantic Ocean—the yachting venue included a satellite Olympic Village in downtown Savannah, an Olympic marina on Wilmington Island, and a temporary day marina on the northern side of Wassaw Sound. The Riverfront Marriott, located in the historic district, served as the satellite Olympic Village. Sail Harbor Marina on Wilmington Island, located about 15 mi (24 km) southeast of the Village, was the site of the Olympic marina, and the day marina was a 150,000 sq ft (14,000 sq m) barge moored at the mouth of the Wilmington River.

The day marina, the first of its kind to be used at an Olympic Games, enabled athletes to store their boats safely and securely in close proximity to the racecourses, thus eliminating the long sail or tow for all events except the keelboats (Solings and Stars). The National Weather Service provided significant on-site support with excellent, highly detailed forecasting.

COMPETITION

The Olympic yachting competition (22 July– 2 August), consisting of 10 medal events with a total of 459 athletes (359 men and 100 women) representing 78 nations, was the largest Olympic regatta ever. Racing in the board (Mistral, IMCO one-design) events took place on course A in Wassaw Sound, while all other events used courses B, C, and D in the Atlantic Ocean just outside the sound.

For the first time in Olympic history, a trapezoidal course configuration was used in the Laser, Europe, 470, Soling, and Mistral, IMCO one-design events. Also for the first time in Olympic history, a maximum number of

TIM O MACY • JOHN E MADALA • JAMES A MADALENO CATC • JELANI M MADARAKA • BENJAMIN MADDEN • BERT C MADDEN • BRIAN E MADDEN • CHRISTL V MADDEN • DAVID M MADDEN • PATRICK D MADDEN • TRUESDELL G MADDEN • CAROLINE A MADDING • LUCIA G MADDIX • ROXAN MADDIX • JOSEPH G MADDOX • AGNESE E MADDOX • BARBARA A MADDOX • CHRISTY R MADDOX • CLARENCE L MADDOX • DAVID H MADDOX • JEAN M MADDOX • JILL M MADDOX • JOAN M MADDOX • KIM L MADDOX • LARRY A MADDOX • LARRY C MADDOX • LONNIE W MADDOX • MICHAEL D MADDOX • NAN G MADDOX •

On day eight of the yachting competition, Kaklamanakis won the gold by sailing to his fourth victory in the nine-race series. Argentina's Carlos Mauricio Espinola finished second in the final race (his fourth second-place finish) to capture the silver over Israel's Gal Fridman, who won three of the nine races and captured the bronze.

In one victory, Lai Shan Lee earned the distinction of being both the first and last medal winner for Hong Kong in 44 years of Olympic competition (the British colony returned to

athletes for the yachting events was set. The International Yacht Racing Union (IYRU) approved two event modifications in the Olympic programme. In the centerboard dinghy classification, Laser replaced Flying Dutchman; in the board classification, Mistral, IMCO one-design supplanted the Division 2, Lechner sailboard.

ACOG provided all of the single-handed boats—Soling, Star, Tornado, and 470. The boats were not only inspected throughout the building process, but were also all built with materials acquired at the same time to ensure uniformity of construction. Between 12 and 19 July, all athlete-provided boats, as well as the spars and sails of the Europes and Finns, were measured to confirm that they met race specifications. All calibrations were supervised by the class measurers under the direction of the IYRU.

The Olympic yachting events were boards (Mistral, IMCO one-design); single-handed dinghy (Finn), men; single-handed dinghy (Europe), women; double-handed dinghy (470); dinghy (Laser), mixed; two-person keelboat (Star), mixed; multihull (Tornado), mixed; and fleet/match race keelboat (Soling), mixed.

Boards (Mistral, IMCO One-Design). Greece's Nikolaos Kaklamanakis was on top of the leader board at the end of each of the four days of competition in the men's Mistral class.

left: **Greece's Nikolaos Kaklamanakis celebrates after winning men's Mistral gold.**

top right: **Athletes in the women's board Mistral class approach the starting line.**

bottom right: **Hong Kong's Lai Shan Lee captures her country's first and only Olympic medal by winning the women's Mistral class.**

RANDY MADDOX • RONALD MADDOX • ROSA MADDOX • SHARON MADDOX • SHERMAN B MADDOX • YOKO S MADDOX • ESTHER M MADDUX • SPENCER MADDUX • STEVE L MADDUX • ELLA F MADDY • YVETTE R MADEAM • IRIS J MADERE • SAMIRA MADHANY • STEVEN MADHAVAN • ELLEN E MADIGAN • JEANNE M MADIGAN • JANICE A MADINCEA • LINDA L MADISON • KAREN L MADORE • CYNTHIA M MADRID • MARIA D MADSEN • MIKE M MADSEN • SHANNON MADUZIA • ANDREW K MAEBIUS • MIHO MAEDA • EDMOND F MAES • ROSE M MAESTAS • MARYANN S MAESTRETTI • TERESA MAESTRO • MARK C MAESTRONE •

top: Gold medalist Mateusz Kusznierewicz of Poland (right) races in the men's Finn single-handed dinghy.

bottom: The Netherlands' Margriet Matthijsse leads Denmark's Kristine Roug in the Europe class regatta.

some energy for the end," she said. After Lee crossed the finish line with a 10-second victory over 1992 gold medalist Barbara Kendall of New Zealand, her champagne victory celebration was televised live in Hong Kong. Kendall won the silver, and Italy's Alessandra Sensini took the bronze.

Single-Handed Dinghy (Finn). Poland's Mateusz Kusznierewicz best managed the tricky sailing strategies needed to shift between the windswept tides and the local water currents from the converging Savannah and Wilmington Rivers to win the men's Finn class. "People were getting nervous and making big mistakes," Kusznierewicz said after clinching the gold early on day seven of the competition. "I'm glad I wasn't one of them." Placing behind him in the men's Finn class were silver medalist Sebastien Godefroid of Belgium and bronze medalist Roy Heiner of the Netherlands.

Single-Handed Dinghy (Europe). Denmark's Kristine Roug captured the gold in the 11th race of the women's Europe class on day 10, while the Netherlands' Margriet Matthijsse took the

the People's Republic of China's rule on 1 July 1997). She also became the first Asian to win an Olympic yachting medal. Lee, 25, clinched the gold on the seventh day of competition when she won the eighth race of the women's Mistral class. Although the reigning world champion's victory was her first in eight races, she easily captured the gold with four second-place finishes, a third-place finish, and a fourth-place finish.

"Because the regatta is so long, at the beginning you better play conservative and save

SHIRLEY S MAGABO • MARIN G MAGAT • MARIA LEONOR S MAGBAG • FREDERICK A MAGBY • ANN K MAGEE • ANTHONY MAGEE • CAROLYN L MAGEE • CAROLYN Q MAGEE • DAVID P MAGEE • LOVELL MAGEE • MARYBETH MAGEE • KELLY A MAGENNIS • HANSA MAGGAN • DAVE MAGGARD • KRISTEN L MAGGARD • MARISSA MAGGIO • RALPH P MAGGIONI • LESLEY C MAGGIORE • MARIAM N MAGHRIBI • JESSICA MAGLIANO • STEFANO MAGLIULO • ALICIA MAGNANT • LB MAGNUS • MAREDDA L MAGNUS • SANDRA H MAGNUS • MARGARET MAGOVICH • JEAN E MAGRINI • DENISE M MAGTANONG • BARRY E MAGUIRE •

silver. In the battle for the bronze among the 28-boat fleet, Courtenay Becker-Dey—the navigator on the all-female crew aboard *America 3* in the America's Cup—finished ahead of Great Britain's Shirley Robertson to win the United States's first yachting medal of the Games.

Double-Handed Dinghy (470). Though tranquil breezes swept across the courses on day nine, the competition was anything but calm. In the men's 470 class, Yevhen Braslavets and Ihor Matviyenko clinched Ukraine's first gold medal in yachting, but the silver and

final two races in the 11-race series. "I was very relaxed going into the race. I was confident," Zabell said after the final victory. Japan's Yumiko Shige and Alicia Kinoshita won the silver, and Ukraine's Ruslana Taran and Olena Pakholchik took the bronze.

Dinghy (Laser). Despite having been disqualified for starting early in the final race of the mixed Laser class—the largest class, with 56 entries—Brazil's Robert Scheidt maintained a two-point lead to win the gold. Great Britain's Ben Ainslie only needed to compete in the

left: Ireland leads Japan, Norway, Greece, and the US at a turn in the women's 470 competition.

right: Red, gold, and blue banners were used to decorate the yachting competition venue in Savannah, Georgia.

bronze were undecided through 10 races. On day 11, Great Britain's John Merricks and Ian Walker held off Portugal's Hugo Rocha and Nuno Barreto in the decisive 11th race to claim the silver and give Portugal the bronze.

With Theresa Zabell at the helm and Begona Via Dufresne on the trapeze, Spain's duo successfully defended its gold medal by winning the women's 470 class on day 11. They captured the gold going away, winning the

final race to overtake Scheidt for the gold, but he also started prematurely and was disqualified. Placing behind Scheidt and Ainslie, who won the silver, was bronze medalist Peer Moberg of Norway.

Two-Person Keelboat (Star). In the final race of the mixed Star class, Brazil's team of Torben Schmidt Grael and Marcelo Bastos Ferreira captured the gold by finishing third. The Brazilian pair, which had five top-three finishes, was able to move into the top spot when

KELLY K MAGUIRE • KENNETH LOUIS MAGUIRE • MICHAEL D MAGUIRE • PATRICIA A MAGUIRE • SUSAN M MAGUIRE • CYBIL E MAH • NICOLETTE T MAH • ELIZABETH C MAHACH • JEFFREY S MAHACH • LINDA C MAHAFFEY • MCDAVID M MAHAFFEY • VIRGINIA MAHAFFEY • SUMATI M MAHAJAN • KANWAL P MAHAL • SUTHAKAR SAM MAHALINGHAM • MARY JANE MAHAN • MELISSA M MAHAN • GARY W MAHANES • MARK K MAHANES • AQUILA MAHDI • JOSEPH MAHDI • HUMBERTO A MAHECHA • THERESA G MAHECHA • KATHLEEN L MAHER • MICHAEL MAHER • RUTH M MAHER • KAREN A MAHER-CARL • MAXINE MAHER

Australia's team of Colin Beashel and David Giles, winners of 3 of the 10 races, was disqualified for starting prematurely in the final race and subsequently fell from first to third, taking the bronze medal. Winning the 10th race were Sweden's Hans Wallen and Bobbie Lohse, who moved from ninth to second to capture the silver, with five top-four finishes in the final six races.

Multihull (Tornado). In the next-to-last race in the mixed Tornado class, Spain's pair of Fernando Leon and Jose Luis Ballester clinched

top: Skipper Lars Schmidt Grael and crewman Henrique Pellicano of Brazil sail to bronze in the Tornado class regatta.

bottom: Sweden's team of Hans Wallen and Bobbie Lohse wins silver in the Star mixed two-person keelboat classification.

the gold by finishing third. Although they did not win a race, the Spanish team was consistent, registering top-five finishes in 9 of the 10 races in which they competed. Despite winning three races and finishing second twice, Australia's Mitchell Booth and Andrew Landenberger finished second overall to win the silver. Brazil's Lars Schmidt Grael and Henrique Pellicano finished third in the 11th race to capture the bronze.

Fleet/Match Race Keelboat (Soling). In the Soling—the largest Olympic sailboat—mixed class, the showdown for gold and silver came on day 12. Germany's crew of Thomas Flach, Bernd Jaekel, and Jochen Schuemann proved

to be unbeatable for the Russian Federation's team of Dmitriy Shabanov, Georgiy Shayduko, and Igor Skalin, who took the silver. The German team went 3-0 in the match-race final to secure their second gold medal in the last three Olympic Games. "Our crew, boat handling, and teamwork were superior, but I think the Russians had more boat speed," Germany's skipper Schuemann said. In the bronze-medal match, the US team of Jim Barton, Jeff Madrigali, and Kent Massey defeated Great Britain 3-1.

CONCLUSION

The Georgia coast provided a yachting venue of changing wind conditions with constant temperatures in the 90°F (32°C) range and a heat index of approximately 105°F (40°C). These factors produced the most broadly contested yachting competition in the history of the Games. In all, 22 countries won medals in yachting, a significant increase from the 12 nations that won medals at the 1992 Barcelona Games. Leading the way was Brazil, which won two gold medals and a bronze. Additionally, Austria's two-time silver medalist Hubert Raudaschl, 53, established an Olympic record for having made the most Olympic appearances, with 10.

left: The gold-medal team from Germany contests Great Britain in the Soling class semifinals.

right: Banners decorated the entrance to the Olympic marina in Savannah.

Atlanta 1996.

MAHTANI • PAULA S MAIBERGER • DAVID J MAIER • KRISTA R MAIER • PATRICK J MAIER • VALERIE M MAIER SPEREDELOZZI • JANICE M MAIETTA • LAWRENCE A MAIJER • MARIANN M MAIN • ANDREW C MAINS • JOHN W MAINS • DAVENE H MAINWARING • HUGH M MAINZER • RICHARD D MAIORE • ANNE M MAISH • VERONIQUE MAITRE • GAIL F MAJAUCKAS • KRISTEN A MAJCHER • ESTHELLE MAJEKODUNMI • RICHARD A MAJESKA • MARK H MAJESKI • PAMELA B MAJETTE • KSHITIJ V MAJMUNDAR • DEBORAH L MAJOR • FRANCES S MAJOR • JANE MAJOR • PAUL C MAJOR • TONY B MAJOR • VICKIE D MAJOR • JOHN D MAJORS •

459

NURTURING THE MEMORIES

ATLANTA'S QUEST for the 1996 Centennial Olympic Games began in 1987 when one man—William Porter "Billy" Payne—began sharing his dream of bringing the Olympic Games to Atlanta with others. Many were inspired by this idea and passed it on, from person to person, until it gradually became the shared dream of the entire city. This dream was realized on 18 September 1990, when IOC President Juan Antonio Samaranch announced that the Centennial Olympic Games would be held in Atlanta. ACOG and the people of Atlanta devoted the next six years to making preparations for hosting the largest and best-attended Games in history.

For 100 years, the Olympic Family has gathered—summoned by the power of the Olympic Flame and its promise of unparalleled competition, fairness, friendship, and international solidarity. A total of 10,700 men and women assembled on the field of Olympic Stadium during the Opening Ceremony of the Games of the XXVI Olympiad to represent the record number of 197 participating delegations. Culminating a journey throughout Greece, to each previous Olympic host city, and throughout the United States, the Olympic flame—the compelling symbol of the Olympic Spirit—was greeted at Olympic Stadium with thunderous applause. When the final torchbearer, Muhammad Ali, stepped from the shadows to light the Olympic cauldron with the Olympic flame, the Games were declared officially open.

And what memorable Games they were! A total of 7,000 men and 3,700 women competed in a vast array of 26 sports, comprising 271 events in 37 diciplines, in the process setting 28 world and 130 Olympic records. During the 16 days of competition, the Games attracted over 5 million spectators and a broadcast audience of 3.5 billion worldwide. Spectators, volunteers, athletes, and Olympic Family members alike gathered together to witness the events, visit exhibitions, and attend dance, music, and theatrical performances. At the center of this activity, both figuratively and literally, Centennial Olympic Park brought people together to cool off in the Fountain of Rings, enjoy the

KAMALAKAR MAKARLA • DONALD M MAKARUK • PATRICIA P MAKGAMATHE • LANA MAKHANIK • SAMIR B MAKHLOUF • MARK E MAKI • WILLIAM A MAKI • NOEL J MAKIDI • ROBERT J MAKIN • SHARON KAYO MAKITA • MICHELE MAKIYA • ELLEN C MAKNAUSKAS • CAROLINE MAKOKHA • FIONA MAKONI • MOHAMAD MUATAZ MALAK • CHRIS MALARNEY • SUZANNE M MALAVET • LORRAINE M MALAWSKI • JOSEPH W MALBROUGH • YVETTE N MALCIOLN • CAROLYN A MALCOLM • PAUL MALCOLM • WESLEY R MALCOLM • NANCEY K MALCOM • JOHNNY MALCOME • ANTHONY MALDONADO • J. CHUCK MALDONADO •

Centennial Olympic Park continues to inspire community spirit in downtown Atlanta.

Southern Crossroads Festival, and share the Olympic Spirit that prevailed in the park's friendly atmosphere.

When the Olympic flame was extinguished on 4 August 1996, it signified to the world that the first century of the Olympic Movement was over. To the citizens of Atlanta, it also signified the dawn of a new era.

For as long as Atlanta has been a chartered city, its efforts to survive and grow have been best represented by the image of a phoenix rising from the flames. Rising from the Olympic flame that traveled from the very heart of ancient Olympia to burn in the Olympic cauldron for the 16 days of Games competition, as well as the Olympic Spirit it represents, is a city with a refreshed sense of unity, hope, goodwill, and aspiration after excellence. Though the Olympic flame that burned in Atlanta has been extinguished, it will continue to burn in the hearts of the people whose dreams and efforts brought the flame to Atlanta.

We, the people of Atlanta, are proud and thankful to have had the opportunity to host the Centennial Olympic Games. We feel that

MARIA K MALDONADO • MIRNA L MALDONADO • ANDREW J MALEC • PATRICIA E MALEC • KIMBERLEY A MALEK • ROSANNA J MALEK • BEHNAZ C MALEKNA • RONALD J MALESKI • RICHARD A MALETTO • CARLA M MALEY • BERTRAND MALGUID • RAKESH MALHOTRA • RICARDO MALIBRAN • ABUBAKR H MALIK • FATIMA MALIK • RUBINA F MALIK • CAREN B MALIN • PAIGE MALIN ATC • POLLYANNA L MALIONGAS • PRITI R MALKAN • RAJIV R MALKAN • GRIT MALKIN • SCOTT W MALL • BRENDA MALLABURN • IRENE MALLAM • TINA A MALLAM • LEO E MALLARD • SANDRA C MALLARD • STEWART P MALLARD • DENNIS J MALLAST •

left: **Olympic Stadium's new role as a baseball park continues to draw sell-out crowds.**

right: **In addition receiving regular use from the students of Georgia Tech, the Aquatic Center is also being used to host sporting events, such as the State Games competitions.**

see the Atlanta Braves in action. The Aquatic Center, in addition to being used by Georgia Institute of Technology students, recently hosted the State Games competition. Even more recently, the Stone Mountain Park Tennis Center was used to host the US Women's Hard-court Championship competition.

Among many improvements to cultural programs realized through the Games, *From Rearguard to Vanguard: Selections from the Clark Atlanta University Collection of African-American Art*, restored and established as a permanent

we have been more than rewarded for the efforts we contributed to making the Centennial Olympic Games possible. Welcoming the world to Atlanta gave us an enlightening opportunity to be inspired by other nations, cultures, and traditions, both through coordination and exchange prior to the Games and with the influx of visitors during the Games. Celebrating the Games themselves brought much joy and celebration to our city. The Games also encouraged Atlanta to have faith in its people, demonstrating how they can come together to accomplish an enormous task. Atlanta is also proud to have helped the athletes live their dreams of participating in the Games and attaining the magnificent results that were recorded.

The Games have also left us with many new collaborative relationships, facilities, monuments, and exhibitions that will serve both to preserve the memories of the Games and support the realization of future dreams.

In the year since the Centennial Olympic Games, many sports facilities built for the Games have been adapted and opened to serve the community. Olympic Stadium has been converted into a new baseball stadium. Sell-out crowds are already pouring into the facility to

NADIA J MALLEGOL • PAUL G MALLEGOL • CHRISTOPHER R MALLET • JAMES C MALLET • MARC P MALLET • STEVE M MALLEY • ALVIN MALLICOAT • HEIDI ANNE H MALLIN • DIANE J MALLORY • HEIDI A MALLORY • RICHARD P MALLORY • KAREN L MALLOW • PATRICIA A MALLOY • DEE A MALMO • KATHERINE MALMQUIST • KATHERINE E MALMQUIST • ALETHEA R MALONE • CAROL R MALONE • J PATRICK MALONE • JANE A MALONE • JOHN S MALONE • MERRY C MALONE • MICHAEL E MALONE • MICHELLE MALONE • PATRICIA W MALONE • PATRICK J MALONE • PENELOPE J MALONE • RAY L MALONE • SAMUEL MALONE •

The first Olympic Games memorabilia collection, *Let the Memories Begin,* offers the public an opportunity to learn more about and relive many aspects of the Games.

exhibit through ACOG's efforts, is presently being enjoyed by Atlanta residents and visitors. A number of the city's cultural institutions, such as the Atlanta Ballet, Atlanta History Center, Atlanta Symphony Orchestra, and High Museum of Art, are presently enjoying increased national and international recognition. Throughout the city, many of the sculptures and public artworks created for the Games remain to decorate the city and pass on their message.

Even after the Games, Centennial Olympic Park continues to be an epicenter of Olympic Spirit, as people gather to enjoy the Fountain of Rings, find their bricks, and relive memories.

In the words of ACOG President and CEO Billy Payne, "One of the important legacies of the Centennial Olympic Games is the creation of a permanent record that has meaning and value for current and future generations." The Georgia Amateur Athletic Federation (GAAF) has been entrusted with preserving and maintaining the Centennial Games Collection, an assortment of memorabilia and archival records that document the staging of the Games, and making portions of it available to as broad an audience as possible. Through an

agreement between GAAF and the Atlanta History Center, these materials are being organized for presentation to the public and archived for research purposes.

In coordination with this archival project, the first public presentation of the Centennial Olympic Games Collection, *Let the Memories Begin,* opened at the Atlanta History Center on 12 July 1997. At this exhibit, visitors are able to learn about and relive the Olympic Games while enjoying a close look at Opening and Closing ceremonies props and costumes, sports equipment used in the competition, victory medals, pictures and video footage documenting the most memorable moments, and hundreds of Olympic pins. While this exhibit is scheduled to close on 4 January 1998, the GAAF is presently exploring possibilities for a permanent home for the Centennial Olympic Games Collection.

Exactly one year after the Opening Ceremony of the Games, ACOG held a celebration to show its appreciation to the athletes, staff, and volunteers who participated in the

VIRGINIA G MALONE • WILLIE O MALONE • MOLLIE D MALONE ATC • FERDINAND MALONE JR • AMY MALONEY • GLENN E MALONEY • JOHN F MALONEY • JUDY O MALONEY • KENNETH H MALONEY • LISA M MALONEY • MARY K MALONEY • SHERRY A MALONEY • SONYA M MALONEY • TAMI J MALONEY • CAROLINE T MALONEY ATC • PATTI MALOOF • SHARON H MALOOF • SHARON H MALOOF • THOMAS G MALOOF • DEEPA K MALPANI • BECKEY E MALPHUS • ROSANNE B MALTESE • RYAN Z MALTESE • SHARON L MALY • JANET E MALZAHN • NICK D MAMALAKIS • PATRICIA MAMBOLO • YEUNG MAN • WENDY E MANARD •

Games. The festivities renewed the Olympic Spirit in Atlanta and marked the opening of several significant legacies that will also help the memories—and the dream—continue. Festivities included a "Parade of Memories," which people were invited to join, dressed in their Games costumes and uniforms, and a preview of portions of the *Official Film of the 1996 Olympic Games.*

As the focus of the commemorative festivities, a public dedication ceremony was held for the presentation of two monuments. The

nied by a performance of "The Power of the Dream," speeches by ACOG officials, and a fireworks display.

Also on this special day, the Flag of Nations, which had once been the central feature of *Apostasy,* a temporary art installation commissioned by the Cultural Olympiad, was raised at its permanent location, Woodruff Park. One side of the 40 x 60 ft (12 x 18 m) flag is a quilt of flags representing the 197 delegations that participated in the Centennial Olympic Games, while the other side is a solid white

left: A total of 1,738 athlete names are listed by sport on the tribute wall.

right: An athletes tribute wall located near the Olympic cauldron is a permanent reminder of the outstanding performances at the Centennial Olympic Games.

Olympic cauldron and the tower that supports it were presented in a permanent, new location adjacent to Olympic Stadium. This structure was connected by a plaza to a wall bearing the names of all the athletes who won medals at the Centennial Olympic Games. Both monuments will remain on a permanent basis to remind Atlanta residents and visitors of what is most important about the Centennial Games—the athletes who inspired audiences with their achievements, and the Olympic Spirit in which the Games were conceived and accomplished. The dedication was accompa-

field signifying the surrender of these nations to the ideals of the Olympic Movement.

On 30 June 1997, ACOG held the final meeting of its Board of Directors, thus officially beginning the legal process of dissolving the private corporation that—through the work of its more than 132,000 paid staff, volunteers, loaned employees, and contractors—planned, financed, and conducted the Centennial Olympic Games over a period of seven years. ACOG completed its financial operations in a manner reflecting its original mission to stage the Centennial Olympic Games with financial integrity and without cost to taxpayers. Through the revenue of over

FREDDIE MANCE • LARRY DARNELL MANCE • GAIL P MANCEWICZ • LARA A MANCHIK • PHILIP G MANCUSI UNGARO • ELIZABETH M MANCUSO • LOUIS MANCUSO • BARRIE MAND • BARBARA R MANDAL • ROBERT D MANDARINO • JEROME MANDEL • NORMAN A MANDEL • ROSLYNN L MANDEL • HOWARD I MANDELBAUM • LANCE H MANDELL • RITA MANDELL • TREVOR W MANDER • ROBERT M MANDERS • BRUCE MANDERVILLE • ALEKSANDRA D MANDIC • RADWAN MANDILY • MARILYN R MANDISH • ELWIN MANDOWA • SHEILA R MANEAR • MARY ALICE MANELLA • JOY MANER • DEVON MANESS • SHARON C MANESS •

top: The Olympic cauldron stands permanently in a public plaza near the original Olympic Stadium for the enjoyment of all.

bottom: The Flag of Nations, a quilt of all participating delegations' flags, flies in Woodruff Park.

$1.7 billion raised through broadcast rights fees, corporate sponsorships, licensing, and ticket and merchandise sales, ACOG completed financial operations in a break-even position.

In addition to finalizing financial matters, ACOG devoted a large portion of the last year to working with the publisher to create this *Official Report*, in which we have endeavored to convey the concept and spirit of the Centennial Olympic Games.

At the end of July 1997, ACOG officially closed its main offices in the Inforum building. A small number of staff members moved to a nearby location to complete all remaining business.

The Olympic Games have left an indelible mark on the face and character of Atlanta. The Olympic flame and the spirit it represents will live on in the hearts of Atlanta's people, acting as a beacon and inspiring them to believe in and achieve their dreams. It remains with the people of Atlanta to live out the fulfillment of their Olympic dreams in the years to come.

Atlanta 1996.

WARNER L MANEY • RENEE M MANFREDI • DAVID J MANGANELLO • WINSTON A MANGAROO • RAGHBIR S MANGAT • ROBERT E MANGINE CATC • TONI MANGINI-LIPSCOMB • PETER R MANGLER • CURT R MANGOLD • RIGOBERTO MANGUAL • DARBY S MANGUM • PAUL L MANGUM • LYNN S MANGUNO • JAMES MANIGAULT • JOHN E MANIGAULT • OMAROSA ONEE MANIGAULT • TIFFANY MANIGAULT • LINDA S MANION • JEFFREY E MANK • JOANNE MANKA • CHRISTOPHER A MANLEY • DANETTE MANLEY • HARRIETT E MANLEY • JAMES A MANLEY • JULIE M MANLEY • LISA M MANLEY • MARCY E MANLEY •

INDEX

MARY A MANLEY • MARY LYNN MANLEY • ROBERT L MANLEY III • ALLISON C MANN • ANGELA B MANN • ANITA W MANN • BARRY S MANN • CAROLYNN A MANN • CHANREUNN MANN • DORIS M MANN • GLORIA J MANN • HARRIETT M MANN • JENNIFER B MANN • JUNE M MANN • LOIS A. MANN • LORIS A MANN • MARILYN F MANN • MICHAEL C MANN • MICHAEL W MANN • OREON E MANN • RITA C MANN • STEVE J MANN • TONY MANN • ALEX MANNING • CAROLINE C MANNING • DEXTER K MANNING • JOHN F MANNING • JOHN M MANNING • JON ALAN MANNING • JULIA MANNING • KELLY G MANNING • KRISTI L MANNING • MIRANDA E MANNING • OLYMPIA F MANNING • RENNODDIS K MANNING • ROBERT B MANNING • ROBIN I MANNING • ROSEMARY K MANNING • SCOTT F MANNING • V. YVONNE MANNING • VIRGINIA D MANNING • ROBERT H MANNING JR • JEANNE D MAN-

NINGS • STEVEN M MANNINO • JOHN F MANNION • MAUREEN C MANNION • DAN W MANNIX • JOSEPH A MANNO • BEVERLY MANNS • RON D MANNS • THOMAS D MANNS • WILLIAM J MANNS • MURRAY W MANOCHEO • ANGELA I MANOLAKAS • KINA M MANOLIS • VAN P MANOLIS • DENEEN S MANOR • KONSTANTINE K MANOUILOV • LIDIA S MANOUILOVA • KENNETH MANOUS • LLOYD A MANOWN • MARLENE MANOWN • PETER S MANOWN • ABAYOMI MANRIQUE • MELISSA F MANROW • BROOK MANSFIELD • PAMELA J MANSFIELD • SANDY H MANSFIELD • SHIRLEY A MANSFIELD • WHITACRE T MANSFIELD • WILLIAM G MANSFIELD • JERRY C MANSHEIM • BEV-ERLY D MANSON • CATHERINE C MANSON • THEODORE F MANSON • JAMES E MANSOUR • LINA S MANSOUR • NEKO S MANTOOTH • SLOTT G MANTOOTH • DIANNE F MANUEL • MONICA MICHELLE MANUEL • ROBERT L

ACKNOWLEDGMENTS AND CREDITS

The Atlanta Committee for the Olympic Games (ACOG) acknowledges with warmth and admiration the dedicated efforts of the many ACOG staff members of each department, whose insights and experience contributed to the text of this volume. We also acknowledge with equal enthusiasm the talented staff members of Peachtree Publishers, who with the experienced guidance of Margaret Quinlin, assisted in the development of the *Official Report* and creatively enhanced our efforts through their skillful writing, editing, design and typography, and print production.

ACOG STAFF

Editor
Ginger T. Watkins

Managing Editor
Paul F. Acocella
Matthew Alan Mason

Design
Andrea Pavone Said
Sheri E. Thomas
Jewell Johnson Sanders

**Look of the Games
Venue Graphics**
Dennis Hoover

Photography
Shirley Allen
Cheryl E. Cagle
Holly Gardner
Nancy Haselden
J. Ross Henderson
Leslie E. McCoy
Laurie I. Olsen
Terri D. Parnell
Michael L. Pugh
Linda S. Rosenbaum

Editorial and Administrative
Susan M. Boeckman
Nila R. Garcia
Loy A. Hayes
Cindy B. Kaufman
Betty Kinder
Stewart Lathan
Connie R. Siewert
Carol Thompson

VOLUME II WRITERS

*Prologue: Atlanta—Gateway for
Dreams*
Marian K. Gordin

Spreading the Olympic Spirit
Donna G. Jonsson
with contributions by
Rennie J. Truitt

Celebrating the Games
Jeffrey N. Babcock
with contributions by
Paul F. Acocella
Matthew Alan Mason
Laurie I. Olsen

Living the Dream
Matthew Alan Mason
with contributions by
Shirley Allen
Stacy L. Brown
Kellie A. Buckley
Elaine M. Keller
Alan Neely
Robert Stiles
Landon M. Thomas

Epilogue: Nurturing the Memories
Lucinda G. Tinsman

PEACHTREE PUBLISHERS STAFF

Publisher
Margaret M. Quinlin

**Senior Editors and
Contributing Writers**
Lucinda G. Tinsman
Melanie M. McMahon
Sara M. Stefani
Marian K. Gordin

Design and Typography
Loraine M. Balcsik
Nicola Simmonds Carter
Robin Sherman
Matt Karmack

Print Production
Dana L. Laurent
Simone René
Imago, USA, Inc., NY
Dana Celentano
Darren Schillace

Editorial and Administrative
Tiffany Anne Tamaroff
Vicky L. Holifield
Amy R. Sproull

FRENCH EDITION

Editorial
Fabienne Boulongne-Collier
Vicky L. Holifield
Tiffany Anne Tamaroff

Design
Loraine M. Balcsik

Typography
Melanie M. McMahon

MANUS • MANSUKHLAL P MANVAR • CHRISTIANA J MANVILLE • WENDELL R MANWARREN • CATHERINE MANZ • MICHAEL P MANZELLA • JULIAN L MAPP • DONALD V MAPP SR • CARLENE M MAPSON • GLENN A MAR • MARJORIE L MARA • CONSTANCE S MARA RN • KYLLE G MARABLE • MERYL W MARABLE • RICHARD O MARABLE • JOANNE B MARAN • GERALDINE L MARANKIE • KATHLEEN A MARANO • LAURA C MARANO • MARK A MARANO • ALICIA MARANTZ • GAIL MARANTZ • JOAN E MARANTZ • MELISSA B MARANTZ • SID G MARANTZ • CHRISTINE J MARASI • JOHN MARASI • VIRGINIA MARAVILLAS • JOHN H MARBLE JR. • MATT MARCELL • KENNETH L MARCELLA • MICHAEL A MARCH • PETE G MARCH • CAROLINE G MARCH-LONG • ELAINE C MARCHANT • GLADYS H MARCHANT • LARRY W MARCHANT • MARLO L MARCHANT • RAY L MARCHANT • WALTER J MARCHANT •

PHOTO CREDITS

The Atlanta Committee for the Olympic Games extends its heartfelt thanks to Associated Press, AFP, Allsport, Reuters and all their photographers and to the ACOG photography staff and volunteers who graciously provided the images found in this volume. You have helped us create a visual legacy that will nourish our memories and enrich our understanding of the Centennial Olympic Games.

IOPP/Associated Press

—186B, 187T

Vincent Amalvy—293T

Elise Amendola—164T, 429R, 430R

Frank Augstein—138, 215R, 343TR

John Bazemore—146R, 355L, 356R, 357R, 358B, 359L, 360R, 390B, 400T

Al Behrman—91R

Porter Binks/Anne Ryan—279BL

Roberto Borea—153L, 201R, 427BL

Gabriel Bouys—152T

Rick Bowmer—199, 334T, 336R

Joe Cavaretta—90TR, 322R, 370R, 417L

Lionel Cironneau—102R, 200R, 349L

Tim Clary—165L

Doug Collier—323T

Hans Deryk—132L, 277B

Eric Draper—92B, 241TL, 299R, 305R, 306M, 307L

Dieter Endlicher—122BL, 396B

Ruth Fremson—405BR

Bob Galbraith—241B, 434L, 434R, 438R

John Gaps III—110L, 134, 225B, 374BL, 443T

Greg Gibson—93R, 367

Michael S. Green—62T, 292, 293B, 294R, 295R

Mark Humphrey—341

Thomas Kienzle—101L, 176T, 238L, 265B, 451

Karl-Heinz Kreifeltz—391R, 444R

Kevin Lamarque—430L

Marta Lavandier—370L

Michael Leckel—310T

Wilford Lee—58L

Michael Lipchitz—203BR, 384R, 447BL, 448B, 453

David Longstreath—81TL, 213T

Tannen Maury—6T, 343L, 406T, 414R, 441B

Doug Mills—150, 174T, 198L, 299L, 300, 303BL, 309R, 312

Alan Mothner—151

Anja Niedringhaus—152B

Chris O'Meara—92I

Denis Paquin—132R, 279BR, 303TL

David J. Phillip—407TR, 408L

Michael Probst—68R, 69L, 297M, 301, 303TR, 383TR, 424R, 449T

Susan Ragan—331L

Ed Reinke—63, 198R, 211TL, 377L

Eric Risberg—185, 323B, 346, 347BR

Amy Sancetta—146L, 230T, 273T, 274R, 275L, 373BR, 376R

Lynn Sladkey—277T, 282, 431T

Jack Smith—200TL, 457L

Rick Stewart—56

Yoshikazu Tsuno—425B, 425T

Kathy Willens—177R, 250B, 337B, 426

Alexander Zemlianichenko—284R, 401T

IOPP/AFP

Gabriel Bouys—228–29, 379M, 409T

Gero Breloer—243B

Eric Cabanis—455TR, 456T, 458B

Tim Clary—6T, 69R, 81TR, 94B, 273B, 278L

Doug Collier—225T, 321B

Bob Daemmrich—384L, 437L

Don Emmert—82T, 310BR

Eric Feferberg—133, 143, 374R, 375L, 376BL, 385

Michael Gangne—78, 79T, 145L, 411L

Daniel Garcia—211R, 302B, 308TR

Pascal George—253

Georges Gobet—64L, 111BL, 383L, 447TL, 448T, 450T

Pascal Guyot—231T, 315L, 455BR

Jeff Haynes—175B, 189L, 313

Patrick Hertzog—57, 153R, 307R, 308TL

Michael Jung—121T, 347TR, 357L, 359R, 360L, 361R, 361BR, 403R

Menahem Kahana—214B, 229BR, 350B, 365B, 365L

Toshifumi Kitamura—82B, 216L, 280L, 287, 281T, 316L, 316R, 317T, 318, 319

Michael Lipchitz—187B

Philip Littleton—202, 340TL

Dimitri Messinis—93M, 101R, 378, 442L, 443B, 444L

Olivier Morin—244L, 291T, 352R, 427TL

Anja Niedringhaus—145R, 191B, 203TR, 244R, 244R, 342, 343BR, 344B, 345T, 406B

Michael Probst—442R

Joel Robine—188R, 286T, 325T

Roberto Schmidt—93L

Antonio Scorza—122TL, 141B, 228L

Omar Torres—190L, 242B, 332, 333T, 334B, 336L

Yoshikazu Tsuno—103T, 123, 203L, 375R, 422L, 422R, 423R

Pedro Ugarte—135, 428B, 428T

Tao-Chuan Yeh—387B, 393L, 394L, 395BL, 396T

Allsport

Allsport—94T, 240L

Al Bello—329, 113L, 113R, 260T, 276M, 328R

Nathan Bilow—162, 144B, 200BL, 294L, 339R

Marcus Boesch—164B, 435L

Clive Brunskill—369B

Simon Bruty—226R, 445, 452L

David Cannon—278R, 368L, 371, 388

Michael Cooper—27B, 304T

Tony Duffy—188L, 227R, 298R

Stu Forster—11TL, 83B, 111R, 121B, 250T

Mike Hewitt—103B, 156R, 175T, 238R, 322L, 395R

Jeb Jacobsohn—80, 110TR, 226R, 275BR, 276R, 355BR

Rusty Jarrett—112R, 142R, 236R

Ross Kinnaird—62B

David Leah—399

Richard Martin—397TL

Doug Pensinger—81B, 211BL, 373L, 373TR, 424L

Mike Powell—17B, 174B, 176B, 210, 305L, 352L

Gary M. Prior—79B, 166T, 166B, 249R, 306R

Pascal Rondeau—157B, 356L, 377TR, 407L, 449B

Jamie Squire—154B

Rick Stewart—112BL, 189R, 216BR, 217, 241TR, 291B, 415T, 423L

Matthew Stockman—163L

David Taylor—58R

Gerard Vandystadt—446

PHYLLIS M MARCHANTE • JOHN T MARCHBANKS • JOHN J MARCHINO • LEIGH A MARCHINO • MARY L MARCHMAN • MARYKAY MARCHMAN • DAVID F MARCILLE • AL MARCINEK • CRAIG A MARCINIAK • JACQUELINE M MARCINKO • JOAN M MARCINKO • STEVEN S MARCO • ALAN S MARCUS • BRAD MARCUS • CAROL J MARCUS • DEMETRA A MARCUS • GARY W MARCUS • LAWRENCE J MARCUS • MARTHA A MARCUS • ROBERT I MARCUS • JILL L MARDEN • RAYMOND A MARDEN • ALAN M MARDER • GAIL H MARDER • DAVID G MARDIS • LESLIE L MAREK • MARTIN MAREK • RICHARD G MARENCIN • MARK A MARES • STEVEN C MARES • FRANK A MARESCA • CONNIE I MARESCO • MIROSLAV MARGETIC • MELINDA B MARGETSON • MICHELLE MARGOL • AVIVA MARGOLIES • BOB MARGOLIN • REYO MARGOLIN • JON M MARGOLIS • MARY KAY MARGOLIS • GREGG S MARGOLIS PM

IOPP/Reuters

Mark Baker—119, 120L, 142L, 279T, 317B, 387T, 391TL

Yannis Behrakis—154T, 190R, 240R, 252, 281B

Pat Benic—239

Mike Blake—122R, 297B, 374TL, 437M

Jim Bourg—83T, 213B

Gary Cameron—335L, 337T

Gary Caskey—215L, 455L, 456B, 458T

Tami Chappell—416

Andy Clark—452R

Zoraida Diaz—381R

Nick Didlick—368R, 411T

Grigory Dukor—383BR

Gary Hershon—59L

John Kuntz—251BR, 331BR, 333B, 393R, 418B, 419

Kevin Lamarque—347L, 353B, 429L

Jerry Lampen—308B, 391BL

Kimimasa Mayama—102L, 309L, 394BR, 394TR, 397R

Win McNamee—298L

Sergio Moraes—165R, 435TR

Sue Ogrocki—380

Charles Platiau—91L, 112TL, 397BL

Oleg Popov—251T

Wolfgang Rattay—310BL, 376TL

Jason Reed—230B, 285B, 412L, 414L, 415B, 436

John Schults—79M, 407BR

Juergen Schwarz—344T

Mike Segar—157T, 167, 459L

Blake Sell—66–67

Ruben Sprich—214T, 295L

Ray Stubblebine—439, 324T

Eriko Sugita—314

Thomas Szlukovenyi—227L, 311T, 363L, 364B, 365TR, 400B

Rob Taggart—280R

Jeff Vinnick—120R, 144T, 324B, 351R, 412R, 413B

Rick T. Wilking—66L, 155, 408R

Andrew Winning—389TR

ACOG

—31L, 124, 231B, 386, 421

Kelli C. Bail—88TR, 149T

Anthony L. Banks—41L, 43T, 126R, 209B, 196, 237, 390T

Dee Bowers—84L, 84T

Dirk Bulwalda—105T

Roger Cabello—219

Claude Cloete—401B

Tom Croke—25B, 25T

Steve Dinberg—96, 108T, 131B, 139, 171, 181, 206, 246, 288, 289B, 358T

Wingate Downs—212, 339L, 369L, 379T, 381L

Norman Drews—5, 256

Shannon Esquivel—148

Kara Guinn—16T

Ken Hawkins—109, 125L, 125TR, 197L

Lee Heizer—39TR, 85BL, 90L, 97, 106, 179L, 220T, 229TR, 389L

Ross Henderson—8L, 9L, 9R, 10B, 28R, 29T, 33T, 46B, 47T, 51R, 86, 88TL, 88BL, 178, 184T, 197R, 224, 247, 266, 340TL, 340BL, 466L, 466R, 467T

Stephanie Klein-Davis—19B, 39BL, 41R, 74B, 89, 100BL, 127L, 130R, 147B, 147T, 163R, 216TR, 232, 242T, 248, 251BL, 327L, 330, 364T, 450B

Simon Kornblit—29B, 76, 149B, 222, 351L

Richard S. Krauze—15R, 47B, 83TL, 110BR, 137, 141T, 161, 169, 194, 403BL, 403TL, 433B, 433T

Erik S. Lesser—53MR, 68L, 70L, 70R, 72, 98, 118, 172B, 177L, 182, 184B, 193T, 261BL, 261R, 262, 263, 264L, 265B, 265T, 267, 268, 328L, 395TL, 438L, 441T

Frank Borges Llosa—5T, 73, 92T, 183, 195, 259L, 260B, 261TL, 304B, 321T

Matthew Mason—75B, 77R

Laine McCall—19T, 31R, 37T, 53BL, 53TL, 61, 64–65, 156L, 258T, 264R, 269BL

Theresa Montgomery—49R, 53BR, 88BR, 95, 99, 107, 108B, 128, 129, 131T, 136–137, 207, 209T, 218, 234, 236L, 269TL, 302T

Faryl S. Moss—173R

Jeff Najarian—21B, 117, 125BL, 205R, 243T, 245R, 249L, 257, 259R, 348, 402

Rob Nelson—17T, 51L, 51M, 59R, 60R, 126L

Rory O'Connor—22R, 37B, 160, 192

Michael O'Neill—127R

Abraham P. Ordover—75T, 87, 130L, 140, 223, 345B,

Sandy Owens—6R, 11T, 35TL, 43B, 45B, 205L, 418T

Michael Pugh—34, 48, 14L, 14R, 15L, 16B, 18L, 18TR, 20L, 20R, 22L, 26B, 26T, 28L, 30T, 32L, 32R, 36B, 42B, 42T, 44L, 46T, 50L, 50R, 460–61

M. Richardson—168

John W. Rossino—77L, 90BR, 104, 105B, 204, 283, 284L

Terry Schmidt—18BR, 24, 30B, 36T, 38, 40, 51M, 52L

Sheryl Siegel—100TL, 269R, 413T

Kari Stauder—27T, 49L, 74T

Marilyn Suriani—4, 11B, 17B, 21T, 23, 33B, 35B, 35TR, 39R, 44R, 45T, 53TR, 60L, 71, 84BR, 114, 115, 116L, 116R, 159B, 170, 172TL, 172TR, 173L, 208, 233B, 235, 254, 255

Mandi Wright—191T, 353T, 405T

Jennifer Yard—220B, 221

W also wish to thank the following organizations for allowing us the use of their photographs to enhance this volume of the of the *Official Report.*

Alliance Theatre Company (David Zeigler—245L)

ART Station (Jim Cook—180)

Atlanta History Center—6L, 7, 8R, 465; (William Hull—158L, 158R)

Atlanta City Hall (Susan J. Ross—52R)

Atlanta Journal-Constitution (William Berry—464B; Jean Shifrin—467B; David Tulis—464T)

Center for Puppetry Arts (Yang Feng—159T; David Zieger—193B, 233T)

EMI (Christian Steiner—85R)

Georgia World Congress Center—463

Image Bank (Flip Chalfant—2–3, 10T)

Metropolitan Atlanta Rapid Transit Authority (MARTA)—100R

The graphics utilized in this book are owned by the The Atlanta Committee for the Olympic Games.

Note: Multiple photos on a page are identified with the following abbreviations: T, top; B, bottom; L, left; R, right.

• CATHERINE M MARGRAVE • EARLY H MARI • VIORICA MARIAN • STEPHEN A MARIASH • VILA MARIBEL • ROBERT BOBBY M MARIE • ALLEN MARIN • M. KENT MARINKOVIC • BERNIE D MARINO • DENISE M MARINO • JEFFREY A MARINO • JOSEPH MARINO • KERYN L MARINO • M FLORENCE MARINO • MARK T MARINO • MICHAEL A MARINO • DEBORAH E MARINOFF • ANDREW A MARINOS • MARY S MARINOS • DANIEL P MARION • NATHAN J MARION • RALPH MARION • ROSIE M MARION • ANDREW B MARION JR • KAREN R MARK • PAMELA MARK • WILLIAM Y MARK • ANN F MARKEL • WENDY J MARKER • DAVID MARKER MT • DAVID R MARKEY • FAYE J MARKEY • LAURA MARKEY • ROBERT F MARKHAM • ROBERTA A MARKHAM • RUDOLPH F MARKHAM • SHARON F MARKHAM • WILLIA MARKHAM •